Synopsis *of a* Purer Theology

Volume I | *Disputations 1–31*

EDITED BY WILLIAM DEN BOER & RIEMER A. FABER

DAVENANT PRESS

ISBN: 1-949716-15-5

ISBN 13: 978-1-949716-15-3

Cover design by Orange Peal Design

Typeset and proofread by Mikael Good

Indexed by Brian Marr

Printed in China

Praise for *Synopsis of a Purer Theology*

"In the Christian faith, we cannot do without each other, but we need the insights of each. In the *Synopsis of a Purer Theology*, Reformed theology from the best theologians of the time comes together, resulting in a finely crafted rendition of the Christian faith. For the study of Christian faith and Reformed theology, this handbook is indispensable today."

—**Willem van Vlastuin**, Professor of the Theology and the Spirituality of Reformed Protestantism, Vrije Universiteit Amsterdam, Dean of the Hersteld Hervormd Seminary, and Director of the Jonathan Edwards Centre Benelux

"Having taught theology at Leiden University myself for several years, I can only rejoice over this republication and translation of one its most outstanding and influential theological products ever: the so-called *Leiden Synopsis*. It is a great benefit to so many pastors, scholars, and interested lay people alike that this complete survey of solid Reformed Scholastic theology is now becoming widely available and accessible."

—**Gijsbert van den Brink**, Professor of Theology and Science, Vrije Universiteit Amsterdam

"Finally in English in two volumes, the *Leiden Synopsis* can now take its well-deserved place as a standard reference work for a wide readership. Its clear organization, careful distinction-making, transparency to scriptural sources, respectful engagement with the full Christian tradition, and organic coherence as a system make it a tool to be used regularly. The four authors' steady awareness of their location in a particular confessional tradition makes their work eminently useful not only for those who share their full confessional position, but also for those who listen in to overhear Reformed Protestant theology at its best."

—**Fred Sanders**, Torrey Honors College, Biola University

"Through the publication of the *Leiden Synopsis* in English, the essence of Reformed theology is no longer exclusively available to traditional, Western historiography and church history. Its original Latin format limited its impact to professional theologians and specialized philologists focusing on theology, while its religious core remained inaccessible not only to the general public but also to geographical venues beyond the West. Now, however, this treasure of theological insights is no longer the appanage of expert scholars; from lay people to academics with vested interests in religion, the *Synopsis* will become accessible to every person who wishes to know more about Reformed theology regardless of whether one lives in the West, the East, or the Global South. This is an achievement with unprecedented possibilities for Reformed theology and its rich ecclesiastical tradition."

—**Corneliu C. Simuţ**, Aurel Vlaicu University (Romania)

"The Leiden theology faculty was the 'Sorbonne' of Reformed orthodoxy. And the *Leiden Synopsis* represented the consensus after the Synod of Dort. Weaving into its exegetical arguments support from patristic and medieval sources, the authors display the catholic and evangelical spirit of Reformed theology. Avoiding internecine disputes, the *Synopsis* focuses on the doctrines that all Reformed Christians confess. Given its spirit, scope, and learned arguments, it deserves to inform the tradition today as it did so persuasively in the past."

—**Michael Horton**, J. Gresham Machen Professor of Systematic Theology and Apologetics, Westminster Seminary California

"The *Synopsis of a Purer Theology* is a codification of Reformed orthodoxy, concise and precise in its presentation of early modern Reformed theology. The translator, editors, and publisher are commended for making this monumental work available in English. Indispensable for any serious scholar and student in Post-reformation Reformed theology."

—**Adriaan C. Neele**, Vice President, Professor of Historical Theology and Homiletics, Puritan Reformed Theological Seminary

"The *Leiden Synopsis* is among the most important and comprehensive systematic accounts of Reformed theology of the seventeenth century. Its appearance in this English-only edition will doubtless invite a fresh outpouring of scholarly and lay reflection."

—**S. Mark Hamilton**, Senior Managing Editor, Davenant Institute and Research Associate, JESociety.org

"Doctrinal controversy brings strife but it also brings clarity and precision to doctrinal formulation, which is a blessing. This benefit of debate is no less true of the *Leiden Synopsis*, written in the wake of the Arminian controversy. This collection of theological disputations is grounded in Scripture, razor sharp in its distinctions, and conversant with the history of doctrine. No serious student of theology can afford to ignore this theological work."

—**J. V. Fesko**, Harriet Barbour Professor of Systematic and Historical Theology, Reformed Theological Seminary, Jackson, Mississippi

"The *Leiden Synopsis* distills the principles of Reformed theology with clarity and economy. It needs no endorsement, but if it did: Herman Bavinck ranked it alongside giants like Zanchius, Junius, and Voetius. Thanks to the translator and Davenant Press, this indispensable resource is now also accessible and affordable."

—**Tyler R. Wittman**, Assistant Professor of Theology, New Orleans Baptist Theological Seminary

"The *Synopsis of a Purer Theology* is one of the most significant translation projects in recent memory. This set of disputations is already considered essential for work in Reformed theology, and so I am delighted that Davenant is making it available for a wider audience. For Reformed pastors and theologians, the *Leiden Synopsis* proves to be a profoundly useful companion, and I have no doubt that it will be a significant aid in the work to retrieve Reformed Scholastic theology."

—**Kyle Strobel**, Associate Professor of Classical Theology, Talbot School of Theology, Biola University

"The *Leiden Synopsis* has long been a theological treasure. The publication of this edition will bring its rich theological wisdom to pastors, theologians, and theology lovers."

—**Gayle Doornbos**, Associate Professor of Theology Dordt University

"Davenant does theology and church a great service with offering this selection of the *Leiden Synopsis*. That deep and highly relevant source of Reformation theology becomes now available to even a much wider community, what the *Synopsis* deserves and the community needs. I'm also very happy that the great efforts of Riemer A. Faber and William den Boer can be made fruitful for all interested in clear, biblical theology. There is no doubt that this publication will find many readers."

—**Herman Selderhuis**, Theological University Apeldoorn / REFORC

"Set forth in the wake of Dort, the *Leiden Synopsis* has enjoyed critical influence on Reformed thought since the early seventeenth century. This accessible, two-volume edition of Riemer Faber's hailed English translation—with fresh editorial guidance by William den Boer and Faber— is a ready resource for learning today from the Leiden faculty's attempt to read Scripture in conversation with those who came before."

—**Christina Larsen**, Associate Professor of Theology, Grand Canyon Theological Seminary & College of Theology

"The *Leiden Synopsis* is one of the crown jewels of Reformed theology. Profoundly collegial in its origins, it presents a compact yet compelling account of post-Reformation dogmatics that is deeply rooted in Scripture yet acutely aware of tradition. It serves not only as a historical landmark in the development of the Reformed tradition, but also as a contemporary provocation to engage deeply with the wisdom and insight it offers. This elegant translation of the *Synopsis* will thus reward careful reading and re-reading, and comes warmly recommended."

—**Paul T. Nimmo**, King's Chair of Systematic Theology, University of Aberdeen

"Can the past inform the present? Absolutely! Here the seventeenth-century theology, piety, and practice of the *Leiden Synopsis* informs the Reformed church in the twenty-first century. The Davenant Institute is to be commended for publishing this time-honored resource. Scholars, professors, ministers, and even laypersons of Reformed theology will benefit from these excellent volumes."

—**Tyler Taber**, Minister of Word and Sacrament, Redeemer Presbyterian Church, Amarillo, Texas

"Both polemical and pastoral, the *Synopsis* deserves wide and careful attention in the church today. Deeply rooted in careful exegesis of Scripture, this doctrinal and moral theology from the early modern period remains a treasure house for subsequent generations. Contemporary readers will quickly note that the *Synopsis* is a work appropriately shaped by the Spirit's work in the fathers of the church from every generation, because the work of theologians should be done in obedience to the fifth commandment."

—**Rev. Michael McClenahan**, Union Theological College, Belfast, Northern Ireland

Table of Contents

Acknowledgements

Gratitude is expressed to the following former or current members of the research group "Classic Reformed Theology" (in Dutch: 'Werkgezelschap Oude Gereformeerde Theologie'), as this edition would not have been made possible without their prior unstinting efforts. This group was founded in 1982 for the purpose of studying early modern scholastic theology. Throughout the years it has conducted research and organized conferences leading to publications in Dutch and English. Please see the Introduction for a brief account of the project that culminated in the publication of the three-volume academic edition, *Synopsis Purioris Theologiae* / *Synopsis of a Purer Theology* (Leiden: Brill, 2014–20). We are grateful to Brill Academic Publishers for permission to use the English translation of that edition here.

Andreas J. Beck

Simon Burton

Kees de Niet

Rein Ferwerda

Philip J. Fisk

Albert Gootjes

Harm Goris

Jeannette Kreijkes-van Esch

Matthias Mangold

Pieter Rouwendal

Siebold Schipper

Dolf te Velde

Willem J. van Asselt †

Henk van den Belt

Gert van den Brink

Elco van Burg

Jan van Helden

Kees Jan van Linden

Wilco Veltkamp

Antonie Vos

In 2020 the research group commenced a new project: 'Early Modern Reformed Disputations on Divine Providence.' For further details, please see the website: www.classic-reformed-theology.org.

A Brief Introduction to the *Synopsis of a Purer Theology*

WILLIAM DEN BOER & RIEMER A. FABER

This edition of the *Synopsis of a Purer Theology* offers to English readers an important document of Reformed teaching in the seventeenth century.[1] Composed by four professors at Leiden University between 1620 and 1625, it gives a full yet compact summary of theology as it was understood in the years after the Synod of Dort which was held in 1618 and 1619.[2] Occasioned by an ongoing conflict between the Remonstrants and Counter-Remonstrants in the Dutch Republic, the Synod had affirmed the orthodox teaching and summarized it in the Canons of Dort. The Canons contain a response to each doctrine that was expressed in the so-called "Five Articles of the Remonstrants" (1610): divine predestination, the scope of Christ's atonement, human depravity and conversion, the efficacy of grace, and perseverance. The *Synopsis of a Purer Theology*, which was intended to serve as an educational textbook in the decades following the Synod and has become

---

[1] The English translation presented in these volumes is reprinted with permission and only minor alterations from the three-volume edition published by Brill (Leiden), *Synopsis Purioris Theologiae / Synopsis of a Purer Theology*, *Latin Text and English Translation*, of which the general editors are Willem J. van Asselt †, Andreas J. Beck, William den Boer, and Riemer A. Faber. Volume editors are: Dolf te Velde, Volume 1, Disputations 1–23 (2014); Henk van den Belt, Volume 2, Disputations 24–42 (2016); Harm Goris, Volume 3, Disputations 43–52 (2020). The English translation was prepared by Riemer Faber with the assistance of members of the research group "Classic Reformed Theology" (see below and the Acknowledgements).

[2] The material presented in this brief introduction is derived in large part from the introductory essays in *Synopsis Purioris Theologiae / Synopsis of a Purer Theology*, Vol. 1–3 (Leiden: Brill, 2014–2020): D. te Velde, Vol. 1, p. 1–16; H. van den Belt, Vol. 2, p. 1–19; H. Goris, Vol. 3, p. 1–7. It draws also upon A. J. Beck, D. te Velde, "The Synopsis of a Purer Theology in Its Historical and Theological Context," Vol. 3, p. 8–91.

popularly known as "the Leiden Synopsis," includes a fuller discussion of these doctrines and extends them to a wide range of biblical teachings, from the time of creation and the fall into sin to the last judgement and eternal life.

The individual chapters—more accurately, disputations—that make up the *Synopsis of a Purer Theology* began as oral debates organized in the department of theology at Leiden from 1620 to 1624. Such disputations were academic discussions about a particular theoretical or practical topic. The professor who was to preside over a disputation would first introduce the subject and his own understanding of it by means of a number of written statements, or theses, that were circulated beforehand. A graduate student was appointed to defend the theses. He would address also any questions or objections that might be raised by members of the audience. Following the event, the professor would weigh the discussion and present a definitive, fuller disputation in printed form. In the case of the *Synopsis*, some fifty-two disputations were collected into a single volume and published. The printed volume was dedicated to the governing lords of the States of Holland and West Friesland.

The custom of holding academic disputations may be traced back to the early modern period, and towards the end of the sixteenth century the Leiden faculty of theology had started a series of disputations covering the scope of biblical doctrine. After a series was completed, it was usually repeated, sometimes with minor changes in the order or themes covered. After the death of Jacob Arminius in 1609, and the departure of Franciscus Gomarus in 1611, the theological faculty of Leiden, together with ministers and other church leaders throughout the Lowlands, continued to experience doctrinal and ecclesiastical differences that would culminate in convoking the Synod. When Dort rejected the Remonstrant teachings, a Remonstrant spokesman, Simon Episcopius, was removed from his teaching post, and new colleagues were appointed to join Johannes Polyander, at that time the only remaining professor of theology. Thus, towards the end of 1619, Antonius Walaeus and Antonius Thysius delivered their inaugural lectures at Leiden, and in the fall of 1620 Andreas Rivetus was added to the staff. These four professors together agreed to start a new series of disputations and to take turns presiding over them. The plan for the series that later culminated in the publication of the *Synopsis* was born.

The Four Authors of the *Synopsis*

The authors of the *Synopsis* had been trained by some of the leading Reformed theologians of their day, including Theodore Beza, Lambert Daneau, Jerome Zanchi, and Zacharias Ursinus. On several key topics the *Synopsis* reveals the influences of these thinkers, who either were pioneers of Reformed scholasticism or who belonged to the second generation that had developed Reformed theology into a fully academic pursuit.

Antonius Thysius (1565–1640) completed his preparatory studies at the Latin School of Antwerp, the city of his birth. He studied theology in Leiden, and also travelled extensively elsewhere, to Geneva, Strasbourg, and Heidelberg, among other places. During the Synod of Dort, he assisted in drafting the Canons, and a catechetical textbook for use in the local churches. An expert in Hebrew, Thysius was appointed substitute-translator and revisor of the Old Testament for the authorized Dutch translation of the Bible, the *Statenvertaling*. In 1619 he became professor at Leiden, where he taught Old Testament alongside Rivetus.

Johannes Polyander (1568–1646) was born in France, graduated as a student of theology in Heidelberg in 1586, and moved from there to Geneva and Leiden, whereafter he was ordained as pastor to a French-speaking congregation at Dordrecht. In 1611 he was appointed professor of theology in Leiden. Moderate in personality and thought, Polyander promoted harmony within the Church. He was involved actively in the Synod of Dort, and he, too, helped to draft the articles that refute Remonstrant teaching. Following the Synod, Polyander served in translating Scripture into Dutch for the *Statenvertaling*. He was an initiator of the disputations held at Leiden that would culminate in the production of the *Synopsis*.

Andreas Rivetus (1572–1651), also from France, had studied with Daneau in Orthez, and later at La Rochelle, before becoming a Reformed pastor in Thouars. A leading participant in several provincial and national synods, Rivetus also was appointed as one of the delegates of the French churches to the Synod of Dort, but king Louis XIII did not give him permission to travel there. Following the Synod, the curators of Leiden University recruited Rivetus, as a leading French theologian, to strengthen the theological faculty. He joined the faculty in 1620, as professor of Old Testament; besides his contributions to the *Synopsis*, Rivetus was a prolific and wide-ranging scholar.

Antonius Walaeus (1573–1639), born in Ghent, matriculated as student of theology at Leiden University in 1596, whereafter he traveled to Geneva, Lausanne, Bern, and Basel, and then returned to the Netherlands in 1601. He later served as a Reformed pastor in Middelburg. In the years prior to the Synod, Walaeus became involved in the conflict between the Remonstrants and Counter-Remonstrants. He was delegated to Dort by the provincial synod of Zeeland, when he, too, helped draft the Canons; he also was appointed as a translator and revisor for the New Testament portion of the *Statenvertaling*. He became professor of dogmatics at Leiden in 1619.

The Meaning of "Purer" in *Synopsis of a Purer Theology*

The teachings presented in the *Synopsis* reflect the concerns not only of the four authors but also of the Reformed churches that had been established in the Lowlands in the mid-sixteenth century. The word "purer" in the title *Synopsis of a Purer Theology* may be understood as indicating the authors' desire to be perceived as promoting the orthodox Reformed teaching that had been confirmed at the recently held Synod of Dort. Thus whereas disputations that had taken place in the decades before 1618 may have exposed contradictory views on certain teachings, the *Synopsis* was to project unanimity in collaboration. The collection would support the fragile harmony among the churches in the refined doctrines.

At the same time, the *Synopsis* may be understood as an academic textbook. It responds to philosophical, theological, and ecclesiastical trends that had developed in the first decades of the seventeenth century. The teachings and practices of the Roman Catholic church continued to require responses from the growing Reformed communities. Moreover, different beliefs and practices were being promoted by Anabaptists and other groups that could not be ignored by the Reformed theologians in the Netherlands. In addition to these more obvious differences, Reformed theology was faced also by forms of anti-trinitarian thought that had taken root in the preceding decades. Thus a sort of "purification" had occurred in the Dutch Reformed churches on the basis of the theological teachings positively conveyed in the Canons.

Method and Genre of the *Synopsis*

The disputations in their originally oral and later published forms were composed according to the methods of what is called scholastic discourse. The term Scholasticism refers to the manner of instruction that was used in universities during the early modern period. It was marked by a consistent use of definitions, distinctions, and logical reasonings. It involved a brief expression of the topic under discussion, a detailed explanation of terms, and a comprehensive treatment of relevant aspects by means of a topical structure. There were explicit statements of proof, and argumentations that were accompanied by references to texts of Scripture or other authoritative sources. Counter-arguments were anticipated and refuted. The reader will find that traces of this format of oral presentation remain visible in the written, published disputations.

As was noted above, the complete work contains fifty-two disputations. Each consists of a number of theses or concise paragraphs that advance a single step in the argument. In compiling the material, the authors normally followed this pattern of thought: What does the term mean? For example: what is "Justification"? Does the object exist? What is it? What are its component parts? What specific aspects of the object may be identified? What are the causes of the object? What effects or consequences follow from it? To what other entities is it related, and how? What object is the opposite? These questions, sometimes posed implicitly, recur throughout the disputations and lend them their common form.

The Structure and Content of the *Synopsis*

It is not certain whether the authors had contemplated publishing the disputations as a textbook when the series first commenced in February 1620, but it does appear that the structure of the *Synopsis* was agreed upon beforehand by Polyander, Walaeus, and Thysius (Rivetus joined at a later stage). The disputations of the *Synopsis* may be placed into groups arranged according to traditional scholastic Reformed theology, and summarized as follows:

The Foundation of Theology is Scripture (1–5)
The Triune God: Father, Son, and Holy Spirit (6–9)
The Creation of the World (10–12)

The *Synopsis* begins with the biblical foundation of theology and moves on from there to discuss the doctrine of the triune God, the creation of the world and humanity, sin, and the way in which God reaches out to human beings through the Law and the Gospel. The Bible serves as the starting point because it is God's own revealed will for the salvation of humanity, and since its origin is divine, the Bible is the highest authority (1–2). Indeed, it is the only, complete, and perfect source of the knowledge of God; no church tradition or so-called "prophetic" revelation is needed to know God (4). As it is in his Word that the triune God has revealed himself, the authors next focus on the doctrine of the Father, Son, and Holy Spirit (6–9). It is the triune God who created the world out of nothing (10), and he preserves, directs, and guides the world by his providence (11).

The next group of disputations treats the creation of human beings in the image of God (13), the Fall of the first parents Adam and Eve in Paradise (14), and original and actual sin (15–16). All of humanity participated in the fall, and so bears responsibility for it; moreover, original sin means not only the loss of what is good but also a tendency toward evil, and our original and actual sins merit punishment both in this life and in the next. A discussion of the doctrine of free choice (17), both before and after the Fall, logically follows the discourse on the creation of human beings.

Disputations 18–23 take us back to the topic of God's self-revelation in Scripture. It is presented here from the perspective of God's revelation in the Law (18–21) and the Gospel (22–23). While the Law exposes the sinful nature and misery of fallen humanity, the Gospel teaches redemption by Jesus Christ the deliverer. The reader may be surprised to learn that the *Synopsis* does not contain an explicit discussion of the doctrine of the covenant; Disputation 23 does allude to the covenant, however, in its presentation of the Old and New Testaments as two administrations, or economies, of God's covenant of grace.

The next nineteen disputations deal with different aspects of the doctrine of salvation, starting with predestination, election, and reprobation (24). It is perhaps worthy of note that the discussion of predestination in Disputation 24 is premised on infralapsarianism, according to which predestination occurred after the fall into sin. The *Synopsis* then dedicates five disputations to the doctrine of the Son of God, the Lord Jesus Christ: his human and divine nature, his three-fold office as prophet, priest, and king, the states of his humiliation and exaltation, and his work of satisfaction (25–29). Christ's passion and death suffices to redeem all people, but its power to save is manifested only in those who believe (27). The satisfactory work of Christ leads to a treatment of the universal and special calling to fallen humanity, including the outworking of salvation in the response by humans in obedient faith and repentance (30–32). The doctrines of justification and sanctification come thereafter (33–38).

Following a polemical rejection of the Roman Catholic teaching on purgatory (39), the *Synopsis* then draws our attention to the doctrine of the Church (40–42), the gathering of those whom God has called out of their natural state. The sole overseer and head of the Church is the Lord Jesus Christ; the Pope has no authority over it (41). Those who do legitimately minister to the Church have been called to serve as servants of Christ, whose Word explains their calling and duties (42).

Five disputations are dedicated to the biblical teaching on the sacraments, of which there are two, baptism and Lord's Supper. As the nature, function, and purpose of the sacraments had been debated at length in the previous generations, the authors of the *Synopsis* deemed it worthwhile to give ample treatment to the Reformed understanding of them. Disputation 43 deals with the sacraments in general: the meaning of the term "sacraments," the institution of them by Christ, the administration of them, and their cause and effect. The sacrament of regeneration, that is baptism, is treated next (44), while that of the Lord's Supper is given extensive discussion in Disputation 45, which contrasts the Reformed understanding with the tenets of the Roman Catholics, Lutherans, and Zwinglians. Especially the Romanist teaching and practice of the Eucharist is confronted in Disputation 46, which rejects the papal mass as unbiblical. The Roman Catholic sacraments of confirmation, penance, extreme unction, holy orders, and marriage are addressed and refuted in Disputation 47.

As it was treated also at the Synod of Dort, so too does the *Synopsis* address the biblical principles for the internal structures and governance of the relatively young Reformed churches. The "keys of the kingdom" are a distinguishing feature of a faithful church, as they consist in the administration of the Word and the exercise of discipline (48). The Church's authority in spiritual matters derives not from the secular state but from Christ and his Word. The meetings of regional, provincial, and national councils or synods are explained on the basis of their biblical origins (49), and the broad outlines for their structure, purpose, and membership are sketched. The relationship of Church and State is defined, too, and also the distinctions between them, whereupon the *Synopsis* turns to a discussion of the civil magistrate (50).

The final disputations deal with the end of times, the resurrection of the dead, judgment, and life everlasting (51–52). As shown in Scripture, it is by the power of the triune God that all human creatures, both good and evil, will be raised. All will be judged, including the angels. Life eternal, which has commenced already in this age, will bring eternal happiness and unspeakable joy for all who believe. Quoting 2 Peter 3:13, the *Synopsis* ends by looking forward to "the new heavens and a new earth in which righteousness will dwell."

The Sources Used by the Authors of the *Synopsis*

As the summary of the structure and contents shows, the most important source used by the authors of the *Synopsis* is Scripture. References to the Bible abound, and many theses are supported by prooftexts. The reader will note how frequently texts of Scripture are cited as the basis on which the theses are developed. The authors make it clear that the entirety of their scholastic reasoning arises from Scripture itself, beginning with the definition of the theological term or concept treated in each disputation, and including the distinctions, causes, modes, efficiencies, and goals of each. Moreover, refutation of incorrect perceptions or false teachings is also buttressed by quotations from or references to Scripture. While the genre of the disputation did not lend itself to extensive exegetical explication, it is clear that the particular texts of Scripture were included only after careful consideration of them. For the modern reader the inclusion of numerous prooftexts serves as a window to understanding the underlying premises and assumptions in each thesis.

The *Synopsis* refers much less frequently (but not sparingly) to historical and literary texts from classical antiquity, both Greek and Roman. Classical authors are quoted to demonstrate definitions or etymological origins, to illustrate the meaning of particular words, and as avenue to the ideas and practices of the pagan cultures of the past. These include not only philosophical and historical authors but also rhetoricians, grammarians, and poets. Medieval authors are also cited or referenced, and the majority of these worked in the scholastic tradition. These include especially Thomas Aquinas, Peter Lombard, and John Duns Scotus, but we also find some references to spiritual writers such as Bernard of Clairvaux. Authors in the Roman Catholic tradition are quoted often to illustrate their difference from Reformed thought, and also as representative of official teaching or its practice. The most frequently cited authors of this type are Robert Bellarmine and Gregory of Valencia.

Editions of the *Synopsis*

The *Synopsis* was printed first by Elzevier in Leiden, in 1625. It was followed by four editions in the seventeenth century (1632, 1642, 1652, and 1658), which suggests that the work was read widely. In the Netherlands, towards the end of the nineteenth century, there was a revival of interest in Calvinist, classical Reformed theology. A sixth edition of the *Synopsis* was produced by Herman Bavinck in 1881, as part of a new series called *Bibliotheca Theologia Reformata* initiated by Abraham Kuyper and others. More recently, between 2014 and 2020, a three-volume Latin-English edition was published by the research group "Classic Reformed Theology," a group consisting of specialists in scholastic theology, philosophy, and classics. The edition comes complete with introductions that provide theological, historical, and ecclesiastical contexts; critical notes on the Latin text; fulsome annotations explaining scholastic terminology and modes of discourse; a glossary of concepts and terms; and bibliographies and indices.[3] Readers wishing to delve deeper into the texts, their meanings and socio-political contexts, are encouraged to consult the scholarly edition. The English translation in the current volume is reprinted (with minor changes and corrections) from the Brill edition (2014–2020).

Intended for the general reader, this edition intends to make the text of the *Synopsis of a Purer Theology* accessible to a readership that has little or no training in the Latin language. The English translation nevertheless seeks to preserve the flavour of the original language, tone, and sentence structure employed by each of the four authors.

The editors take this opportunity to signal the significant debt that is owed to the colleagues who contributed extensively to the project that resulted in the publication of the academic edition of the *Synopsis of a Purer Theology* on which the current edition is based. We are grateful to Brill Academic Publishers of Leiden for permission to employ the English translation of the *Synopsis* as it appears in the three volumes published between 2014 and 2020. To that text only a very few, minor changes have been made (e.g., the abbreviation of the books of the Bible). For some ten years members of the research group "Classic Reformed Theology"—experts in various disciplines and associated with universities and institutes in Belgium, Canada, Poland, and the Netherlands—collaborated in producing the Brill edition. These scholars determined the accuracy of the Latin source text, produced an English translation that is faithful to the original text and accessible to the modern reader, wrote introductory essays, composed an instructive glossary of technical and scholastic terminology, and compiled useful bibliographies and indices. The following general and volume editors performed an important role in the production of the Brill edition: general editors Willem J. van Asselt †, Andreas J. Beck, William den Boer, and Riemer A. Faber; volume editors Dolf te Velde (Vol. 1, Disputations 1–23), Henk van den Belt (Vol. 2, Disputations 24–42), and Harm Goris (Vol. 3, Disputations 24–52). Important contributions were made also by other current and past members of the research group "Classic Reformed Theology," and the reader is directed to the Acknowledgements where we thank them by name.

As a historical Reformed handbook, the *Synopsis of Purer Theology* opens

---

[3] See footnote 1, above.

up avenues of exploration for anyone wishing to become familiar with the Reformed tradition as it was shaped in the first decades of the seventeenth century. The harmony of theological thought which the four authors of the *Synopsis* sought to express ensured a certain consensus, even in the heady years surrounding the Synod of Dort. Moreover, while comprehensive in the range of doctrinal topics covered, the *Synopsis* employs a conciseness of expression and restrained argumentation that makes the material readily accessible. The constant use of biblical evidence exposes underlying premises and assumptions that invite further exploration and comparison with current exegetical trends. Moreover, as the authors explicitly situated their theses both within the long tradition of theology that begins with the Church Fathers and continued in their own time with Romanist, Lutheran, and Anabaptist thought, the *Synopsis* offers the opportunity to explore the inter-relationships between Reformed orthodoxy and other confessional outlooks. The generally (but not entirely) irenic and positive approach to the theological *loci* lends the *Synopsis* an appeal that suits modern tastes. Thus, the *Synopsis* may be read not only as a document of historical significance but also as a touchstone for the theological questions and issues of the twenty-first century.

Preface Addressed to the Most Honorable and All-powerful Lords of the States of Holland and West-Friesland[1]

Most honorable, all-powerful, highly respected sovereign lords,

The two foundations of the Christian Republic are Truth and Peace. The former provides the basis of our spiritual relationship with God, while the latter is the basis on which we associate with fellow-humans here on earth. The prophet Zechariah, when he exhorts us to "love truth and peace," [Zech 8:19] gives pride of place to the Truth, as she is leader and mistress; and he rightly grants the next place to Peace, as she is her attendant. For by its very nature the Truth is always fair and just, acceptable to God, and salutary to all who profess her. But Peace, if she should deviate from the pathway of Truth, would become unfair, offensive to God, and destructive to everyone who walks in her ways. Hence when the apostle Paul exhorts each and every Christian to dwell in peace with all fellow-humans, he makes only two restrictions: "as much as it lies within you" and "if it is possible" [Rom 12:18]—that is, on the condition that the truth be professed. And because the men who preceded you in this distinguished and noble office have pondered all this carefully, they were eager to foster peace at every turn and in every way, so long as it was grounded in the truth. Or, as the saying goes,

---

[1] The *Synopsis of a Purer Theology* is introduced by a prefatory address to the lords of the States of Holland and West-Friesland, the political body of the Province of Holland which in the decades before and after the turn of the seventeenth century led the Republic of the Seven United Netherlands. In laudatory tones the authors of the *Synopsis* suggest that it was with the support of the lords that the Synod of Dort was held, new professors of theology were appointed at Leiden University, and the Reformed Church was strengthened. Despite the doctrinal issues that had divided the faculty in the recent past, the authors profess a 'total single-mindedness in what we believe and think, and that we share a consensus in all the headings of theology.'

they fostered peace 'right up to the altar'—no rather, as far as our altar, Jesus Christ, who is the very embodiment of Truth, as he himself declared [John 14:6].

Our own history offers a splendid illustration of the loyalty, courage, and constancy with which your predecessors fought in defense of the true teachings of Christ as revealed in his Word, over against the frightful attacks of the Antichrist and his foremost henchmen. For there was a time when it was a capital offense to contend for the freedom of your Republic and its Religion and to defend the cause of those who retracted only so much as the 'width of a finger-tip' from the idolatry and feigned traditions of the Romanist pope. And they applied an equally great amount of courage in vindicating the freedom of our fatherland when they succeeded, fortunately, in resisting the leading armies of the tyrants who oppressed the reformed churches. And it was with the same courage, and success, that they introduced faithful preachers of the Gospel to the churches after they were swept clean of the desecrations done to the divine worship-service, so that they could expose to the light of day, as if in open theatres of wholesome truth, the Holy Scriptures that had been obscured and oppressed by the Antichrist for so many ages, so that they might guide the common folk whom he had wretchedly led astray back along the path of truth to the goal, the harbour of salvation that Christ had obtained.

No, what is more, there was the added benefit that they expended very much effort and support for the restoration of our churches throughout this entire province, in order to expand the boundaries of true religion further. And it was their determination to bestow as much dedication and industry in establishing an academic storehouse for all the sciences in this city, but especially for that of Religion. And you, most honorable and sovereign lords, just as you followed your predecessors in the other heroic and meritorious deeds, so also in this matter did you follow them. For in subsequent years it was you who caused this our Academy to flourish, when you endowed it with the appointments of learned men from every quarter. And when the 'weeds' of heterodox fancies were plucked out—weeds which some in our midst had caused to be spread abroad—you not only granted restoration and complete recovery to orthodox Theology, but you also lent your support when she was being freed from the false accusations of gainsayers at the recently-held Synod of Dordrecht. It was you who additionally increased the number of professors of Theology, thus raising it to the required full complement.

And now it is our resolve to honour, venerate, and publish abroad with praise eternal the care and vigilance with which you have rescued this seminary of our churches from the gravest dangers of bygone tempests and placed it upon a firm and peaceable footing. And to make this testimony public, we announce the following as monument of the gratitude and esteem that we owe you: the *Synopsis*, namely, the *Synopsis of the Purer Theology* of which we are professors in your Academy. And it is in your name that we present it to everyone, to study it and to test it against the touchstone of Holy Scripture. We do so in order that the entire globe may acknowledge that you are its most stalwart and steadfast defenders, but also in order that those candidates of the sacred letters who are entrusted to us may fix their gaze upon this North Star and direct their way by it in the course of their studies. And finally we do this so that it may be clear to anyone and everyone that there is a total single-mindedness in what we believe and think, and that we share a consensus in all the headings of theology. We have no doubt whatsoever that the pastors of our churches, when they behold this work as the longed-for proof of the harmony in our teaching, will join with us in congratulating the Province that you command for the fact that by the special grace of God under your watch the flames of our internal dissentions have been quenched. And what is more, that they may now once again behold that on the lecterns in our Academy and on the pulpits in our church-buildings Truth and Peace "greet and kiss one another" (to use the words of king David the prophet [Ps. 85:10]).

And finally we beseech you in all humility, O most highly respected and sovereign lords of the States, to accept this small token of our deepest devotion and commitment with friendly countenance, and to continue to surround us with your benevolence. And may the most high, almighty God, under whose protection we have undertaken, in this sanctuary, to cultivate the garden-estates of Wisdom herself, protect you under the shadow of his wings and keep you safe for as long as is possible. May he enrich your Republic with an over-abundant increase of every blessing, for the glory of his name and for the increase of his Church.

Presented in Leiden, December 28, 1624 by the most devoted servants of your highly distinguished dominions Doctors and Professors of most holy Theology,

Johannes Polyander   Antonius Walaeus
Andreas Rivetus   Antonius Thysius

VOLUME I

CONCERNING THE
MOST SACRED THEOLOGY

President: Johannes Polyander
Respondent: Johannes Swalmius

Theology is the study of God, and nothing can be known with certainty about God without a special revelation from God Himself. That is why Scripture as God's divinely inspired self-communication is the basis of Theology and that revelation receives full attention in Disputations 2–5. The ultimate source of our knowledge of God lies in the intimate self-knowledge of God as Father, Son, and Holy Spirit. This is called 'archetypal theology' (3), in which 'archetype' denotes an original pattern from which copies derive. Human understanding of God, being finite, is limited to what God wills to make known to us by revelation. The limited 'copy' of the original is called 'ectypal theology' (4–6), or theology of revelation. This revelation can be natural or supernatural (7–8). Next, all elements of the definition of supernatural revelation are discussed (9–21). The goal of Theology is to increase knowledge of the truth that accords with godliness (18–19), that renders us wise unto salvation (20) and leads us to glorify God (21). True Theology (as opposed to false theology, 25–26) is a practical science that stirs the human will and emotions to worship God and to cherish one's neighbor (22–24). Both the Old and the New Testament advance this theology: God's single will to redeem the human race and the promise that salvation must be obtained through Christ (27–28).

We shall commence our disputations with Scripture, since it, being divinely inspired, is the principle for the most sacred Theology, its source of proof, and its means of instruction.

1. According to the derivation of the noun, Theology is according to some 'the word of God'; or rather, as we think, 'the word about God.'

2. This noun was first used by pagan Greeks (witness Lactantius, *On the Wrath of God*, book 1, chapter 11) and thereafter by the Christians themselves, as can be gathered from the title of the book Revelation, in which John the evangelist and apostle is identified by the epithet, "the theologian;" and from the Second Letter of Basil to Gregory of Nazianzus, where he calls the doctrine of Holy Scripture "Theology."

3. Theology is of one kind if we consider the matter in itself; it is multiform if we consider the way in which the matter consists in its various subjects. For with respect to God, insofar as Theology is the knowledge whereby He knows himself and all divine things in his divine way, it is archetypal theology. And hence, as it is the case with the very essence of God, so this knowledge is common to the Son with the Father and the Holy Spirit. And just as the divine essence has three persons most closely joined together in fellowship and communion with one another, so too those persons know one another intimately and as perfectly as possible. With a view to this relationship Christ states in John 7:29: "I know the Father, because I am from Him," and in John 10:15: "Just as the Father knows me so I know the Father."

4. And if Theology is viewed insofar as it is the knowledge that God either has communicated to created beings endowed with understanding in this age, or that He will share in the age to come, it is ectypal theology. And this knowledge communicated by God has been, so to speak, reproduced from the original in various ways and degrees of communication in people living on this earth, obviously through the grace of revelation. It was certainly received in angels and the spirits of the saints in heaven through the grace of vision—through which kindness we, too, shall see God himself face to face after this life, that is, with our own eyes and in person (1 John 3:2).

5. This theology has been communicated by God with Christ the 'God-and-man' in a unique and exceptional manner, that is, by the grace of the union, which produced in Christ's soul as much fullness of wisdom as was necessary for the most complete performance of his calling. Regarding that fullness God is said to have "anointed Him with the oil of gladness beyond his peers" (Ps 45:7[8]) and "has given Him the Spirit without measure" (John 3:34), so that from his fullness all who believe in Him would receive a certain measure of that same Spirit (John 1:16). Therefore, it is said that all the treasures of wisdom and knowledge have been hidden in Him (Col 2:3).

6. In this locus we restrict Theology only to persons who are proceeding in

faith in the current age, and in order to differentiate it, we call it 'the Theology of revelation.'

7. Taken more broadly, revelation can be divided into natural and supernatural revelation.

8. We call natural revelation what is either internal, written upon the hearts of all people through natural truth and natural law (which the apostle explains in Rom 1:19 and 2:15), or external, through the contemplation of the things God has created (which the same apostle discusses in Rom 1:20). We call supernatural revelation what the prophets and apostles have obtained by the direct agency of the Spirit of truth in order to unfold its genuine form to the Church of God, partly through the spoken word and partly through their writings, and to transmit it for safe-keeping. Hence the revelation of sacred theology which God gave the prophets and the apostles was direct and without intervention; however, the revelation that has been disclosed through them to the Church of God was via them as intermediaries.

9. Because in this locus we are discussing supernatural revelation, we define Theology as the knowledge or wisdom of the divine matters that God has revealed to people in this world through ministers of his word inspired by the prophetic Spirit, and that He has adapted to their capability, to lead them to knowledge of the truth which accords with godliness and renders them wise unto their own salvation and God's eternal glory.

10. We classify the genus of Theology as knowledge or wisdom. It is knowledge,

1. Because Holy Scripture ascribes to it the epithets and effects of knowledge: Isa 53:11, Jer 3:15, John 17:2[3], and 2 Cor 8:7.

2. Because it is the knowledge of things that are necessary, either without relation to any other being, as for example of God and his attributes, or of things that are necessary on the presupposition of God's will, such as knowledge of his worship and works.

3. Because it brings forth the knowledge of the truth (Titus 1:1), that is, a definite recognition fixed very deeply within the mind by the clearest shows of proof, either through things that are prior and that are principles of being (as in Matt 11:26, Eph 1:5), or through things that are posterior and that are principles of knowledge (as in Rom 1:20).

11. We classify the genus of Theology also as wisdom, for the following reasons:

1. Because Solomon calls it by this name in Prov 1 (and following); so too the apostle Paul in 1 Cor 1:21, and 12:8.

2. Because it presents to people, by way of teaching, its own most accurate and superior principles, which are loftier by far than the principles of the other sciences, namely, the most holy and majestic mysteries of God himself that cannot be fathomed by the human mind.

3. Because what it contemplates deals especially with subjects that are eternal, infinite, inexpressible, immovable, spiritual, heavenly, and not liable to any change or decay. Augustine writes extensively about this matter in *On the Trinity*, book 12, chapter 14.

4. Because it is, so to speak, like an architectonic standard that guides all the disciplines and as the final judge of all actions and thoughts outshines all other sciences and prescribes for them the standard for living well and happily, and for directing all things back to the glory of God. For whatever a man learns outside of Theology (as Augustine says in *On the Trinity*, book 12, chapter 14), if it is harmful, Holy Scripture discredits it; if it is useful, it is found and commended therein.

12. When we assert that matters pertaining to God are the object of theology, we include in the range of application: 1. God himself; 2. The doctrines and divine benefits required for a saving knowledge of God, for fellowship with and enjoyment of Him. 3. Everything that God has created and ordained in the nature of things as they must be related to God as their origin and goal. Regarding this last point Augustine shows in the *Letter to Volusianus* that within the terms of Theology are contained also Physics, Ethics, Politics, and the other disciplines.

13. God is the chief efficient cause of Theology, regarding three ways in which He brings it about. For 1. his Spirit supplied it to the prophets and apostles by his inspiration, as Paul testifies in 2 Tim 3:16, and Peter in 1 Pet 1:11,12 and 2 Pet 1:21. 2. He has appointed the true standard for treating Theology and placed it over against false standards (1 Tim 1:3, 6:4[3]). And

3. He has bestowed upon it the power to instill his wholesome teachings into our minds (John 6:45, 1 Cor 3:7, 1 Thess 4:9).

14. The instrumental cause of Theology is the Word of God, spoken through the mouth of men divinely inspired and called directly by God, and recorded in the holy books (1 Pet 1:11, 2 Pet 1:21, Acts 20:27, 1 Thess 2:13 and 4:8).

15. The manner God chose to use for disclosing Theology is divided by some into 'the inward manner', solely through inspiration by the Holy Spirit, and 'the outward manner', conferred by God upon men through certain instruments and devices.

16. This manner of revelation formerly flowed forth from God the Father, the Son, and the Holy Spirit in different ways. Sometimes He spoke by using clear speech, sometimes by means of dreams, visions, signs, appearances or likenesses. On other occasions He spoke through angels who had assumed human shape. Sometimes He spoke to our fathers in the Old Testament through human prophets who were driven by the Spirit of Christ (Gen 15:1; Num 12:6,8; Gen 18:13; Exod 23:21; Acts 7:30; 1 Cor 10:9). And at last He spoke most fully through his own Son as He was revealed in the flesh (Heb 1:1).

17. Although these different ways of revelation have been adapted by God to everyone's capacity for receiving them, some people have grasped them more fully and others less so, according to varying measures of faith.

18. The foremost fruit and goal of Theology is knowledge of the truth that accords with godliness (Titus 1:1). By this description supernatural truth is distinguished from natural truth; the latter does not suffice in a man who is not yet reborn, and it does not have the power to infuse his heart with godliness and true service to God, as is evidenced by many proofs in Rom 1 and 2.

19. This truth is the form that pervades Theology in its entirety as well as its individual parts, and therefore the theologian always contemplates it in one and the same way throughout the sacred letters.

20. The second use and goal of Theology is that it renders us wise unto salvation and to every good gift in this present life and the life that is to come (2 Tim 3:15, 1 Tim 4:8).

21. The glory of God is the highest goal of Theology, whereby He has

prepared this glory only for himself, because He is all-sufficient unto himself and is in want of nothing, and because not a thing can be added to Him by our doing.

22. From this the question arises: Is the most holy Theology a theoretical or a practical discipline? The reply of some theologians to this question is 'theoretical,' of others 'practical,' and of others yet again 'a mixture of the two.' We concur with the last reply in that we reckon Theology ought to be called both theoretical and practical both because of the combination of its two-fold goal, that is, the increase of knowledge and of the worship of God in this life, and because of the arrangement of the one below the other. For just as godliness is placed in the service of our blessedness and God's glory, so too knowledge is ranked in service to godliness in sacred literature (1 Tim 4:[7–]8; Col 3:16; Titus 1:1).

23. Therefore in Theology theory and practice are not placed in opposition to one another, but they are conditions associated with each other for the purpose of obtaining everlasting life, and placed in their proper order.

24. And Theology consists not of bare and empty theory but of a practical science that powerfully stirs the human will and all the emotions of the heart to worship God and to cherish one's neighbor. Hence it is said that faith works powerfully through love (Gal 5:6; 1 Thess 1:3). Hence also they are said to deceive themselves by false reasoning who only hear the Word of God but in reality do not put it into practice (Jas 1:22 ff.).

25. The true Theology we have explained to this point is opposed by false theology, which errs in two ways:

1. By utterly departing from the orthodox teaching of the prophets and the apostles, partly regarding the matters themselves, and partly insofar as it concerns the treatment of these matters (1 Tim 1:3 and 4:7[6]; 2 Pet 2:1).

2. By empty chatter and disputes about words, whereby those who rage madly over foolish enquiries stray from the real goal of pure worship (1 Tim 1:6; 6:4).

26. This false Theology can be summarized in three particular types, namely, the Theology:

1. Of the pagans, who do not know Christ as the Savior, which the

Holy Spirit condemns (Acts 17:22, 23, 30, and 19:34; and Rom 1:21).

2.   Of the Jews, who reject Christ (whom Jerome in his commentary on chapter 12 and 13 of Matthew calls the source of Wisdom) and therefore who are not able to understand anything wisely.

3.   Of the pseudo-Christian heretics, who (as the same Jerome states in his commentary on chapter 23 of Jeremiah) steal Christ's words and usurp the speech of the prophets, evangelists, and apostles in order to transmit their own deceptions under the semblance of a spurious truth, either on the foundation of Christian doctrine or in matters concerning its foundation, to those who are rather careless.

27. Even though the Old and the New Testaments differ with respect to some of the tools whereby the teachings are administered (and also their circumstances), yet they agree as far as the substance is concerned. And the same Theology is advanced in both Testaments: God's single will to redeem the human race and the one basic promise that salvation must be obtained through Christ (Gen 3:15 and 22:18; Acts 15:11, and 10:43, etc.).

28. Accordingly we must reject the opinion of those people who make up a three-fold way of obtaining salvation: the first for those who lived before the Law was recorded, by observing the law of nature; the second for those who lived under the written Law, by keeping it; and the third for those who live under the grace of the Gospel, through faith in Christ Jesus.

29. But we must battle especially the opinion of those who are not afraid to claim that anything at all that has been disclosed by God, regardless of the manner and degree it has been made, is even now sufficient for them to obtain salvation.

30. Theology is not only noetic and semantic, but also dianoetic. For often it employs arguments to refute those who oppose it, and it either draws logical conclusions to confirm the truth from its own principles that in and of themselves cannot be demonstrated from foregoing principles, or it produces solutions to refute the harmful objections of the Sophists (Matt 22:32, 33; 1 Cor 15:20, 21, 22).

ON THE NECESSITY AND
AUTHORITY OF SCRIPTURE

President: Antonius Walaeus
Respondent: Johannes Crucius

Holy Scripture is the foremost means by which knowledge about God and salvation is revealed (1–3). While its divine origin guarantees certainty, its written form guarantees a reliable preservation of truth (4–8). Also the Holy Spirit works through Holy Scripture alone (9). From the most elementary to the most advanced knowledge of God, Scripture is absolutely necessary (10). Scripture derives its authority—the conviction that it proceeds from God—ultimately from the internal witness of the Holy Spirit (12). Besides that, many marks reveal the divinity of Scripture (13–27). That holds true for all Scripture and not just for a part (28). The Church has no authority over Scripture, but serves and proclaims it (29–32). Holy Scripture, the supernatural principle of all sacred teaching, and the unmoved rule of faith and moral conduct, can depend on nothing but God who has granted it, and on its own light, which He has put into it (33–34).

1. As the nature of Theology was treated in the preceding disputation, it now follows that we deal with the foremost means whereby it is revealed, namely, Holy Scripture, which is the principle and foundation for all Christian teaching.

2. By Holy Scripture we here mean not the actual characters of the alphabet but the word that is signified and expressed in those characters and letters. For all scripture is a sign and indicator of the word; in fact, the word is a sign and indicator of the thoughts and concepts conceived in the mind.

3. Moreover, we define this Scripture as the divine instrument whereby the doctrine of salvation was handed down by God through the prophets,

apostles, and evangelists as God's secretaries, in the canonical books of the Old and New Testament.

4. Before the exodus of the Israelites from Egypt, God established his Church only through the spoken word, which He imparted to the patriarchs "in many and various ways" [Heb 1:1] and through the tradition of the elders [cf. 1 Pet 1:18 and Matt 15:2]. However, when length of life was shortened and the state of wickedness was increasing daily, and Satan by means of his misleading oracles and apparitions with which he imitated God and his appearance was deluding the human race throughout the world, it pleased God from then until the end of the world to establish his Church also by means of the Scriptures, to preserve the divine truth more reliably, to widen its extent, and to restore it more easily where it had fallen into ruin.

5. For this reason, too, at this point of time God Himself furnished the prophets with a precedent when onto stone tablets He wrote the law which He had announced previously from Mount Sinai in public to the entire people (Exod 24:12, and 34:28). And He commanded Moses and the other prophets and apostles to do the same, partly by means of a direct command (as in Exod 17:14, 34:27; Jer 36:2, and 28; Rev 1:19), and also partly by means of hidden instigation, He instructed them to record in writing what He revealed to the Church. "For all of Scripture is God-breathed" (2 Tim 3:16); and Peter (2 Pet 1), in dealing with the prophetic writings testifies: "No prophecy was ever produced by the will of man, but holy men of God spoke as they were carried along by the Holy Spirit."

6. From this it is clear how false is the claim of papal teachers that the written Word of God is not necessary for the Church, and that it is less crucial to the existence of the Church than to its well-being; that to the contrary, even the Church can do without Holy Scripture, in the same way that it managed without it before the law was given. They likewise foolishly assert that a great portion of the truth that proceeds from God is preserved nowadays in the Church's own unwritten traditions.

7. For we grant that God even today can gather and defend his Church without Scripture just as He did in former times. However, He did determine that his Word be recorded in writing, and Holy Scripture bears witness in Eph 2:20 that "it is the foundation of our faith." And indeed even Christ himself directed his listeners to the Scriptures of the Old Testament in order there to obtain salvation (Luke 16[:16–31], John 5[:39, 45–47]). And the

apostle John in chapter 20:31 states that: "These things are written that we may believe that Jesus is the Christ, and that believing we may have eternal life in his name." On these grounds we steadfastly maintain that even today Holy Scripture is altogether necessary, and that the Church cannot exist without it.

8. From this it becomes clear also what is the godless thinking of contemporary Libertines, who call themselves zealous followers of the Spirit. Some of them claim that the literal and genuine sense of Holy Scripture, like a letter that kills [cf. 2 Cor 3:6], is of no use to the Church of the New Testament, and they try to foist on people some fanatic dreams of their own, figments of the imagination in the name of Spirit. But others of them grant that there surely is some use for Scripture in the Church, but only for the first, initial lessons in the Christian faith. However, as soon as those converts have matured, been regenerated, and have reached perfection, then they should progress beyond the elementary principles solely by the instigation of the Spirit, leaving outward Scripture behind, and they must follow his order only, as much in matters of the faith as in conduct.

9. This thinking is false and harmful. Because if Holy Scripture is neglected, then nothing in the Christian religion can be established with certainty, for from outside of it no criterion or guidance could be given to distinguish the divine truth from false influences and erroneous forces, which God as just judge often sends on those who disdain the Gospel. This opinion is false also because the Holy Spirit works salvation in the hearts of people only through the outward Word and Holy Scripture. Whence also Paul calls his ministry the ministry of the Spirit (2 Cor 3, esp. 3:3).

10. The other opinion is equally wrong, and contrary to Holy Scripture. For not only to those who are untrained in the Christian faith, and beginners, but also to those who are more accomplished and have been regenerated, Holy Scripture everywhere commends its own use and necessity, in the Old and the New Testament. This is clear from many passages and instances in Scripture, but especially from the introductions to almost all the apostolic letters. For Paul declares in Rom 1:7, 8 that he is writing to "all who are at Rome, who are loved by God and called to be Saints, whose faith is renowned throughout the world." In 1 Cor 1:2 he writes: "To the sanctified in Christ Jesus, and to all who call on the name of Christ in every place." In chapter 10:15 he writes "to sensible people;" in Phil 3:15 "to those who are mature."

He sent letters to Timothy and Titus, who had been discharging the office of evangelist for a long time already. Peter, in the Second Epistle chapter 1:1, writes to those who "had received a faith as precious as his own." John in the First Epistle chapter 2:12[–14] writes "to the fathers who have known Him who was from the beginning;" the same: "To the young men who are strong, in whom the word of God dwells, and who have overcome the evil one." In the same way also the apostle Jude addresses his letter "to the called, the ones sanctified by God the Father, and kept by Jesus Christ" (verse 1).

11. And so, now that the necessity of Scripture has been proved over against the Jesuits and Libertines, we must explain next from where its authority derives, or to say it more clearly, from where we get the conviction that it proceeds from God and is *autopistos* [self-convincing]. We must consider this question, then, over against two kinds of people. First, against pagans, who along with Celsus, Porphyry, Julian, and similar enemies of Christ's Church, call into question the divine origins of Scripture. And secondly, against the papal teachers who derive its authority from the affirmation of their Church alone.

12. As far as those are concerned who call into question the divinity of the entire Scripture, since they still are devoid of the Spirit of Christ, they cannot be refuted by the witness of the Holy Spirit, which is more effective than all arguments. For, as Christ testifies in John 14:17: "The world does not know that Spirit, nor can it accept Him." Therefore, we must procure other weapons against them, to restore their spirit little by little to submit to Christ [cf. 2 Cor 10:5] (if perhaps through his Spirit He will enlighten their hearts), or else so that they themselves, convicted in their own stubbornness, may remain self-condemned [cf. Titus 3:11]. We shall summarize those arguments according to the following three kinds.

13. We draw the first kind of argument from those marks and criteria whereby the truth and reliability of any history whatsoever can be and normally is tested. For if the statement holds that sacred history is true and reliable, then by the same token it unavoidably follows that it proceeds from God and is *theopneustos* [God-breathed], because history itself everywhere supplies the fullest evidence of its own divine character.

14. Arrian, in the preface of book 1 about Alexander's expedition, states that in human history reliable criteria exist to establish the truth. First, if the writers are credible persons. Second, if they themselves participated in the

events which they commit to writing. Third, if neither an obligation nor a financial reward was offered them, to cause them to write something different from what had happened. To these Josephus, in *Against Appius* book 1, adds this also: If all writers wrote the same things about the same subjects.

15. These and whatever other criteria can be produced for historical certainty occur more abundantly and convincingly in sacred history than in any human writings. For some of the holy writers were kings and rulers, while others, of more modest wealth and standing, were renowned for surpassing human wisdom. But all were holy and honest men who did not hide their own failings or those of their people—if there were any—and who won a reputation for holiness and equity not only from among all of their own followers but also from foreigners and enemies. In the same way Flavius Josephus in book 1, *Against Apion*, mentions the Egyptians themselves as witnesses for this fact, as they considered Moses "a man worthy of their respect, and godly." And Strabo in book 16 of the *Geography* provides this witness about Moses and the early Israelites: They were "promoters of justice and truly devout." And Josephus himself gives the same testimony about John the Baptist, James the brother of our Lord and Savior. So too Pliny the Younger in the Epistle to the emperor Trajan (*Epistles*, book 10.101) was constrained to testify the same thing about the first Christians who were either contemporaries of the apostles or living shortly thereafter.

16. Also the sacred writers witnessed with their own eyes and ears those things which they preserved in writing; and they recorded them with the awareness of many thousands of people who had seen and heard the same things. Furthermore, through their writings they sought no earthly glory or wealth; to the contrary, they could hope for nothing in this world except suffering, crucifixion, and death. Meanwhile, weapons were not rallied to support but oppose them, and very many of them freely sealed with their own blood the truth they promoted. In fact, all of them with one accord in different places, different times, and different circumstances taught entirely the same things and bequeathed these to those who came after them. Therefore either no human writings at all must be considered as true, or everyone must acknowledge that the sacred accounts are true and reliable— and hence, also divine.

17. This reasoning can convince the mind of an unbeliever; the ones that come next are able even to instill faith, by God's grace. Thus, the second kind

of argument is drawn from the perfect integrity and divine quality of the religion that these books comprise. For no-one has ever stated that true religion did not proceed from God alone, because it constitutes God's covenant with humanity; for that reason, also the authors of false religions have feigned some divine character. Now as to the fact that the Christian religion alone is the true one of all the religions which till now have been commonly accepted in the world is demonstrated in that it alone displays the marks of true religion, and so is the one that proceeds from God.

18. Now the infallible marks of true religion, as the consciences of human beings prescribe, are these: First, that in it the true God, as creator and ruler of everything, is acknowledged and honoured, as is the case in the Christian religion alone. For paganism, which is the oldest religion after Christianity, worships created beings, indeed even evil spirits as though they were gods. In fact, the Turkish, and today the Jewish religion, besides the fact that their beginnings on earth are recent, even though it boasts about the true God, pollute the knowledge of the true God and his deeds with silly stories and inventions.

19. The second mark of true religion is that only it explains the true ground on which sinful man can be restored to God, and that is to be found in the Christian religion alone. For in it alone one finds the only sacrifice fitting for the atonement of sins, and one sufficient to appease God's anger. On the other hand, in pagan religion atonement is sought vainly in abominable rites (such as of Saturn, Venus, Ceres, Bacchus, etc.); and in the Turkish and Jewish religion nowadays it is sought in meaningless and superstitious rituals, which can clean dirt from the skin and body, but not the heart and conscience.

20. The third mark of the true religion is that in it are prescribed the right and complete duties towards God and the neighbor. This, too, occurs in no religion except the Christian one, in which all of man's inner as well as outward deeds are directed to the honour of God, and all matters weighty and holy are taught. In it we are demanded to love God above all things, and our neighbors—no, even our enemies—as ourselves. But the pagans worship their deities with base gladiatorial games and theatrical plays. The Jews give heed to empty ceremonies and the outer shell of the law only and inflict noticeable violence upon the Old Testament of Holy Scripture. But the heathens and the Turks, besides the superstitious forms of worship whereby

they purport to revere God, either teach flawed duties towards other people or they permit horrible misdeeds against them, because their religion allows these, or at least lets these go entirely unpunished.

21. The third and foremost kind of argument is drawn from the specific marks of divinity which God has willed to stand out in Holy Scripture in a special way. For it is true that in every passage Holy Scripture bears witness to its own divinity to those who have their eyes opened by the Spirit of God. Yet, just as some rays coming from the sun are more brilliant and visible than others, so even in the divine light of Holy Scripture certain very bright rays of divinity come out in different passages that display their author most vividly.

22. First among these marks are the miracles that far surpass every created possibility and first sealed the Word of God in the sight of all peoples, even before the very eyes of those who resisted this teaching with all their might. There are also many instances of miracles in the non-biblical historians, of the kind that Justin Martyr, Tertullian, and other ancient Christian writers demonstrate in their own apologetic writings against the gentiles.

23. Secondly, the content of Holy Scripture clearly shows the same mark of its divine origin; for this we give as examples: the time and order of the creation of the world; the increase of human beings and peoples on earth; the teaching about God the three-in-one; Christ the God-and-man; the resurrection of the body; the final judgment; and similar doctrines, which have not ever entered the minds of any wise man of this age, and so could have been disclosed only by God. Likewise the ten words of the Decalogue, which contain all piety and justice; the six petitions in the Lord's Prayer— each of them necessary for salvation, clearly framed in a divine manner. For this we also cite as examples the sacred prophecies and predictions which preceded the actual events by several hundreds—even thousands—of years. Such pronouncements include especially the prophecies about the coming of the Messiah, while the Jewish state still existed; the prophecies about the calling of the gentiles into the fellowship of the Church; the prophecies about the removal of pagan idolatry through the coming of Christ, the release of the Jewish nation from slavery in Egypt and Babylon; about the final destruction of the city [Jerusalem] and of the Jewish people; about the rising of many heresies; about the formation and overturning of the kingdom of the Antichrist, and so on. And finally, we mention the spiritual promises that

have been made to believers in Christ, specifically concerning the forgiveness of sins, the peace of the conscience, the circumcision of the heart, the spirit of prayer and sonship, of endurance in the cross; and the like. The true believers feel their impact; the unbelieving, however, are forced to be astounded by miraculous events of another sort, whether they like it or not, and are forced frequently to undergo the corollary threats of spiritual punishments in their own persons.

24. The form and the goal of Holy Scripture prove the same divine origin. And foremost is the ubiquitous agreement regarding the same divine doctrine, the highest loftiness and effectiveness in the most plain style, the same laws granted to kings and to subjects, the same promises and punishments announced to both groups equally, and that not only by outward deeds, but also by their most private plans and deliberations. And everywhere the goal is the glory of God, the salvation of humanity, mercy towards the meek, and the display of judgments against the obstinate.

25. Add to this the effects that are clearly of divine doing; for wherever the Word of God and Holy Scripture find a place, there the mockeries and spiritual forces of the devil fade away—as we saw happen throughout the known world after Christ's ascension, while the gentiles marveled and wondered why the demonic oracles disappeared. In our times, too, when Holy Scripture is first taken up in the hands of people, the magic tricks of the devil and all the power he had wielded previously in the shadows of ignorance generally disappeared from sight. To this we should add that so many gentiles who were dwelling in darkness turned to Christ without the force of weapons, only through this spiritual sword and the endurance of the saints; the transformation of so many people who previously had been wrapped up in criminal activities and worldly filth, into models of holiness and justice in all ages and places. Not any other religion has produced any results such as these.

26. Finally there is the evidence of certain accompanying attributes in these books. Among these is the fact that they are from antiquity, by far surpassing the age of all writings of human origin; for the oldest religion is from God, as it must be close to its origin in time. So too for the continuous hostility and efforts of Satan against it, the persecutions and vain attempts by tyrants, indeed even the terrible judgments of God against them, such as the whole world witnessed in the case of Antiochus Epiphanes, Julian the Apostate, and the like.

27. These are the marks whereby the divinity of these books is revealed more clearly than the light of day; which anyone whosoever will find out in fact, who with an honest heart and eager for his own salvation prepares to read and meditate upon them earnestly.

28. And here one ought not to pay heed to Socinus and several other Christians who grant that Holy Scripture is divinely originated in issues of special importance, but that its authors in situations and circumstances of lesser importance were abandoned by the Holy Spirit and could have erred. Because this opinion paves the way for contempt, and expressly contradicts Scripture which testifies that "everything that was written was written for our instruction" (Rom 15:4), and "all Scripture is God-breathed" (2 Tim 3:16). Likewise, "no Scripture is of one's own interpretation" (2 Pet 1:20); indeed, "not even one iota will disappear from the Law" (Matt 5:18). "And it is not permitted for any man to add to or remove from it" (Deut 4[:2], Rev 22[:18–19]).

29. From these arguments that we have explained and proved thus far it is now abundantly clear how wrong the contention of many papal teachers is, that greater authority rests with the Church than with Scripture; and that of others, too, who claim that the authority of Scripture derives from the testimony of the Church alone, at least insofar as it pertains to us.

30. For we admit freely that it is the Church's duty to guard Holy Scripture, to preserve its integrity with all reverence and care, to vindicate it from people's corrupting influence, to exhibit and prove its divine quality to others, whence it is called, "the pillar and bulwark of the truth," by Paul in 1 Tim 3 [:15]. Be that as it may, from this no authority over Scripture should be drawn for the Church, but only service and proclamation, just as the edicts of leading civic officials do not get their authority from the heralds and servants, even though by these men they are made known and published.

31. It is made clear to us that the authority of Holy Scripture is much greater than that of the Church by the fact that the Church is capable of erring while Scripture cannot. Moreover, it is clear that the authority of the Church (whatsoever that may be) is derived from Scripture, just as the papal teachers themselves recognize, since they try to prove their own authority from Scripture. And finally, because the testimony of the Holy Spirit, shared by all of Christ's true sheep (John 10), as well as those divine marks that present themselves in Holy Scripture, is of much greater authority and weight—even

16

as far as we are concerned—than the mere testimony of the Church, since this testimony of the Church is nothing but human persuasion. But the Holy Spirit, by means of those divine marks in Scripture instills into our souls the divine faith that brings salvation.

32. To be sure, the testimony of the early Church, which was contemporary with or immediately after the prophets and apostles, is much greater and weightier to us than today's. For that Church of long ago, besides the proofs it shares with the contemporary one, heard and saw also additional and unique wonders of the prophetic and apostolic mission. And those are: answers given by means of the Urim and Thummim, miracles, exceptional gifts of the Holy Spirit, extraordinary prophecy and similar acts. Therefore, also the Church of today is and should be accustomed to use the affirmation of that early Church to acknowledge the authority of the divine books. For every instance of proof whereby anything is proved should be more evident and more accepted as valid to us than the conclusion itself.

33. For believers the authority of the sacred books is so far from depending solely, or even mainly, on the testimony of the Church that it in fact does not depend on it at all. For just as a law given by some magistrate is dependent on no-one except those on whom the magistrate depends, so too the divine law can depend on no-one except God himself, who is dependent on no creature. And just as the first principles and immovable norms do not depend on the authority of those who use them, but only on the one who has established them, and on its own light and evidence, so too Holy Scripture, the supernatural principle of all sacred teaching, and the unmoved rule of faith and moral conduct, can depend on nothing but God who has granted it, and on its own light, which He has put into it.

34. Therefore also the prophets and apostles never subjected the authority of the word they preached and recorded to human, let alone angelic authority, but only to God's authority—as is evident everywhere in the prophetic and apostolic preambles and declarations. And for that reason, lastly, Christ and the apostles never pointed their disciples or listeners to the authority of the Church, but either to the Scripture of the Old Testament, or to those signs and truly divine results which are displayed in the hearts of those people whose minds have not been blinded by the god of this age (Gal 3:1–2; 2 Cor 3:[2,]3, 4; 2 Cor 13:5, 6, etc.).

CONCERNING AND CANONICAL AND APOCRYPHAL BOOKS

President: Antonius Thysius
Respondent: Theodorus Gisberti

In his providence God determined some books to be necessary to everyone as the authoritative, reliable canon or rule and norm for truth and worship. Taken together, these books—the sixty-six books of the Old and the New Testament—are called the canonical books (1, 17). God inspired the authors of these books (2, 6, 9); they were involved in the process with their human intellect, activities, and style, but were kept from every error (7). Not only the writing but also the collection of the sacred books was divinely ordained. First the writing of the individual books is considered (6–11), next the arrangement and distribution of the whole (12–41). Attention is paid as to which edition of Scripture should be considered authentic (10) and to the status of translations of Scripture (11). Scripture alone is the fundamental principle by which, and the material from which, every saving truth must be drawn. It is the rule and standard by which every true and also every false teaching about the things of God must be determined. It is a self-convincing (credible of itself) and irrefutable witness and judge by which every controversy which arises over divine matters must be resolved (18). True doctrine, therefore, is not only the content of Scripture itself but also whatever agrees with it explicitly or by a necessary consequence. Every other teaching is either not necessary for salvation, or false (19). The apocryphal books (36–39), as well as the universal synods of the early church and the symbols which emanated from them, must because of their human and ecclesiastical character be judged and tested against Holy Scripture (41). The Apostolic Creed (Symbol of faith), however, enjoys an almost canonical status: 'if not divine with respect to its authorship, is clearly divine in its substance, and nearly so in words.' (40)

1. Having related the *locus* concerning the authority of Holy Scripture

generally, we add next to it the one about the Canonical books. For from the very many godly sayings and writings (regardless of the opinions of others) which served as a benefit to the Church as it existed at that time (Num 21:14; Josh 1:13; 2 Chron 33:19; 1 Cor 5:9; Augustine, *The City of God*, book 18, chapter 38; Theodoretus [of Cyrus] *On Joshua*), God in his special provision chose and determined to preserve those books which were necessary and useful to the entire Church as a canon or rule for truth and devotion (Luke 1:1, 2, 3; John 20:30, 31). Taken together, these are called Sacred Scripture or the canonical books.

2. Sacred Scripture (or the canonical books) is the arrangement or compendium of sacred books originally composed by God through his divinely inspired servants, with consideration for each era and people, in writing and language best understood by them. They have been entrusted to the entire Church for worldwide and lasting instruction in the truth of salvation—that is, the truth about God and his bountiful and generous good pleasure—and to preserve his Word and truth in a reliable way; further to proclaim them and surely to restore them in case of corruption.

3. These writings are called "the holy Writing of God" (Exod 32:16), "sacred" (Rom 1:2), "sacred writing" (2 Tim 3:15), and simply "writing" (John 10:35) or "writings" (John 5:39). They are called "holy" because they have been set apart from every-day use; "sacred" because they have been dedicated to God. They are called "most holy" because the holy God is their author, because their subject matter is holy and devoted, because the nature of the writing accords with the divine holiness, and because their goal and aim is holiness of life. The Scripture is also called Word, Speech, Utterance, Prophecy of God; also Law, Teaching, Testimony, Covenant and Testament of God, etc. (Ps 19:8, and Ps 119; Isa 2:3; Rom 3:2; 2 Cor 3:14; 2 Pet 3:16). And just as these names generally apply to the Old Testament, so too do they cover the New Testament. And in these names is a declaration of their superiority over all human writings of any quality whatsoever, indeed, of their separation from them.

4. When Sacred Scripture is defined as an arrangement, it means an entire unit, or sort of corpus, that consists of many parts and pieces, or a collection and volume formed by many sacred books (2 Tim 3:16). Moreover, just as an individual book of Scripture is called *biblos* or "book" (Luke 3:4; Acts 1:20), so several books together, and also the book as a whole, are called not only

"Scripture" (with an improper use of the singular), but above all "Scriptures," or "Sacred Books" or simply "Books" (Deut 29:21; Acts 7:42; 1 Cor 15:3, 4).

5. In this arrangement we give consideration to the writing of the individual books [6–11], and, taking them all together, we consider their arrangement and distribution [12–41].

6. God the Father, in the Son and through the Holy Spirit, is the first efficient cause of the writing of these individual books by his order and instigation (Exod 17:14; Jer 36:1[-4]; Rev 1:1, chapter 2, etc.). The ministers or instruments are holy servants of the Lord, 'called by God and breathed upon by Him,' and 'driven' by the Holy Spirit. Hence Scripture is called "God-breathed" (2 Tim 3:16; Rom 16:26; 2 Pet 1:20). But even so, God himself with his own finger inscribed the Ten Commandments, which in that special case are called the "Writing of God" (Exod 32:15; Deut 10:4). And by divine action a hand in human form appeared at the impious banquet of King Balthazar and wrote upon the wall clear words foretelling his demise (Dan 5:5, 24). And it is recorded that Christ with his own hand wrote something upon the ground (John 8:6, 8).

7. The manner of writing was as follows: Sometimes God was the one who inspired and dictated, while the writers, like secretaries, were the ones who wrote according to a fixed formula (Exod 34:27, 28; Rev 2:1). At other times God assisted and directed (Matt 22:43; Heb 1:1), while they had a task as interpreters and authors (Luke 1:1, 3). For they never conducted themselves purely passively, but being involved in the process, as ones who applied their own intellect, mental activities and processes, recollection, order of the arguments, and their own style of writing (from where comes the variety of writing-styles among them) (Amos 7:14, 15; 2 Cor 10:10 and 11:6). But the Holy Spirit was constantly leading them, as He directed and guided them to such an extent that they were kept from every error in thought, memory, word and pen (2 Sam 23:1, 2; 1 Cor 7:25, 40).

8. In fact, even those writers occasionally enjoyed the assistance of other men as their scribes, such as Jeremiah of Baruch (Jer 36:4), Paul of Tertius (Rom 16:22); or they approved one another's writings with their own word of support and authority, such as Peter of the Gospel of Mark, and Paul of the Gospel of Luke, as the early church-fathers argued (Origen in Eusebius, *Ecclesiastical History*, book 6, chapter 19).

9. The subject-matter of the writing is the spoken word whereby something is declared—in this case the intent and thought of God, namely, about his nature and his unmerited and bounteous good will. And this spoken word, or the sort and nature of this word, is derived completely from God (1 Cor 2:13). The form exists in the divine expression, turned into writing, of the divine truth and intent brought forward by speech. And lastly, the goal is instruction in matters pertaining to God of all people, not only those present, but especially those then absent (2 Cor 10:10, 11; John 20:31; Rom 15:4). This instruction is either more specific or more general, whether the initial writing was directed and aimed at fewer or at more numerous people.

10. Furthermore, the edition of Scripture that should be considered authentic is the one that was issued 'originally' and 'directly from its source,' by the authority of God. This is the archetype itself (Deut 31:9, 24, 26; 2 Kgs 22:8, 13; 2 Chron 34:14), or "the copy of it" (Deut 17:18). These certainly include the individual books of the Old Testament in Hebrew (with the exception of a very few words, sentences, and chapters written in Aramaic), and those of the New Testament in Greek, except for a few small insertions in Hebrew and Syrian—nearly all translated into Greek, because that was the most common language of the East as well as the West (Cicero, *In Defense of Archias the Poet*). As far as the style is concerned, it was partly in the common language, partly in the Hebraic-Greek style that the Hellenized Jews used.

11. Another rendering of the authentic version is itself also Sacred Scripture, so long as it has been translated into other languages as devoutly as possible, and corresponds to it precisely and completely—as much, at least, as this can be done. Such translation is not only permitted and useful (contrary to what certain papal teachers have determined), but also entirely necessary (Acts 2:4, 6, 11; Neh 8:8, 9, 14, 18), so that it may be of use to all people (Deut 31:11; Col 3:16), and so that it may be understood, read, and heard by all people and those of any kind—also lay-people. However, it would be foolish (along with those same papal teachers) to declare either the Septuagint, or the Latin translation of either Testament, or any other version, not only the received and commonly employed version, but even the authentic one. (Council of Trent, session 4, chapter 2).

12. Thus far about the writing of the sacred books. The accumulation and collection of them itself was also divinely made, and that was partly non-mediated, and partly mediated. Immediately distributed books are those

which from the start were entrusted and commended by the divine writers to the Church as a whole (Rom 3:2) just as they were written down for the first time. Such is the case for the Old Testament books of Moses (which he himself carried into the sanctuary and which by divine order were placed beside the ark, Deut 31:26) and for the New Testament Gospels, which, as they share the same subject matter, have no individual dedication—with the exception of Luke. And these books comprise the foundation of the truth that brings salvation.

13. Books that were distributed in a mediate way, however, are those that were written by the authors themselves for specific peoples or churches (these being the most venerable and metropolitan ones) or their leaders (and often on a particular occasion, 1 Cor 1:11, and chapters 5, 6, 7, 8, 9) and that first had a specific address. And these books were preserved by them not by chance or some rash decision, but by God's special providence (which looks out for the special needs of the Church), and they were communicated to others (Col 4:16; 2 Thess 3:17; 2 Pet 3:15) and were received by them and indeed by all recipients as sent by God, both by command and by the law of piety and sacred fellowship, through the initiative of God. This happened not by some free act of the Church but as a necessary undertaking. And these books contain a more fulsome exposition of the truth that brings salvation.

14. This communication and reception took place at the time when a sure assessment of these books could be made and upheld (besides their previously mentioned obvious inherent qualities) in the ordinary fashion and by the usual means, either by the testimony of the divinely-inspired writer himself (John 21:24; Luke 1:1,3) or by writing "with his own hand" (Gal 6:11). Or the testimony was in his signature, which was known to the believers at that time (by which test Paul determined that falsely-authored letters, be distinguished from genuine ones, 2 Thess 2:2, and 3:17). Or it was by faithful witnesses of the events, who are named in the opening greetings (Rom 16:21, 22; 1 Cor 1:1 and 16:19), in special fashion by the authority of the prophets (when the gift of prophecy in the Church still flourished, 1 Cor 12:4,7 and 14:29, 32). And this authority was only for the early Church; for the later Church it was proper to acknowledge it and to recommend and transmit to future generations what had been entrusted by God to its safe-keeping (Rom 3:2).

15. Hence it happened that occasionally some people doubted and disclaimed

the authority of certain books, which the succeeding Church later joined to the others when authorization by the prophets and apostles ceased. At any rate, these are all the books written and published after the last prophets, Zechariah and Malachi (after whom the numbering of 'the Wise' by the Jewish Synagogue starts, Josephus, *Against Appian*, in Eusebius, book 3, chapter 9), and also those books written and published after the death of the apostles and the apostolic leaders, when the gift of prophecy, along with the exceptional gifts, came to an end or at least was interrupted (at which time the patristic era of the Church begins). While these books are useful and relevant to the Church, they have not been considered sacred or inspired by God.

16. The goal of the arrangement and combination of sacred books was for this Scripture to be the complete and everlasting Canon for the whole Church, and the rule of heavenly truth, that is, of faith and life (Ps 102:19; Rom 15:4; 2 Tim 3:16[, 17]), and that the Word of God and the truth it contains be preserved, further increased, and, if any corruption should come about, be restored more firmly (Luke 1:4; Matt 22:29).

17. Therefore this Scripture and its books are called 'canonical' by ecclesiastical designation (in the Synod of Laodicea, Eusebius, *passim*; Athanasius in *Synopsis*, drawn from Scripture, 2 Cor 10:[13–]16; Gal 6:16; Phil 3:16). And rightly so, because the individual books have been gathered into the canon and belong to it, and they together comprise the complete canon in every way, that is, not only as the full number and series of sacred books, but also as the rule and norm for every sound and sacred teaching, and of divine worship. And as each book individually is called canonical it must be understood not just for a portion of them but for the whole generally, and equally for the things of which they are the canon.

18. So then this Scripture alone is the fundamental principle by which, and the material from which, every saving truth must be drawn. It is the rule and standard by which every true and also every false teaching about the things of God must be determined (Isa 8:20; Luke 16:29; Acts 17:10,11). In sum, it is a self-convincing and irrefutable witness and Judge, namely by virtue of its own demonstrated proof by which every controversy which arises over divine matters must be judged (John 5:39, 45).

19. Moreover, the criterion or norm for judging is comprised of these axioms: 1. Whatever Scripture contains, or whatever agrees with it either explicitly or

by a necessary consequence from it, is true doctrine. 2. That which disagrees with it must be false. 3. Whatever is not contained in it, although it may not be openly opposed to it, is a teaching not necessary for salvation.

20. The canonical books, and thus the canon, at first comprised the books of Moses (Deut 4:2; Rom 2:17, 18, 19, 20). To these others were added, partly regarding the practice and the history of the Church (such as the subsequent historical books), partly for the interpretation, application, and fuller proclamation about the Messiah (namely the so-called didactic and prophetic ones), and partly to complete and fill out the preaching about the Messiah and his kingdom (namely the New Testament, etc., 2 Pet 1:19). As the Old Testament is the foundation of the New, so the New Testament is the fulfillment of the Old. And so the canon was not made more complete by means of these books insofar as the universal doctrines of salvation are concerned, but insofar as their unique qualities, clarity, and evidence are concerned.

21. The division of the books into the Old and New Testament (2 Cor 3:14) should not be understood merely with respect to Law and Gospel, in that the one contrasts with the other (for the Gospel, which essentially is identical to the promise, is found also in the Old Covenant, and the Law equally in the New, Gal 3:8, Heb 4:2, Rom 10:4), but with respect to the entire dispensation of salvation granted to the people of the Old and the New. And what appears as promise in the Old is a manifestation in the New, or the Gospel in the strict sense (Rom 1:1,2), for the name can come from the predominant part.

22. Even the distinction between prophetic and apostolic (Rom 16:26; 2 Pet 1:19) should not be taken in such a way as though only and specifically the books of the Old Testament are prophetic regarding their stated subject, but with respect to their authors, because they have been written by prophets, or at any rate have been endorsed by them. Nor because they only are prophetic, since also the New Testament books are such (Eph 2:20, and 3:5, and 4:11), but the term 'prophets' is limited to the prophets of the people of old, and to those who foretold the coming of Christ and his kingdom.

23. If you count all the books of the two testaments one by one, there are sixty-six; thirty-nine in the old, and twenty-seven in the new. The names in the list are as follows: the five books of Moses, Joshua, Judges, Ruth, 1 and 2 Samuel, 1 and 2 Kings, 1 and 2 Chronicles, Ezra, Nehemiah, Esther (which Melito and the others following him omit [Eusebius, *Ecclesiastical History*,

book 4, chapter 25]). And some deem the book Esther doubtful, like Nazianzus (in *On Metrics*)—but clearly erroneously, judging the entire work apocryphal on account of the added portions; Job, Psalms, three books by Solomon, namely Proverbs, Ecclesiastes, and the Song of Songs, Isaiah, Jeremiah, Lamentations, Ezekiel, Daniel, Hosea, Joel, Amos, Obadiah, Jonah, Micah, Nahum, Habakkuk, Zephaniah, Haggai, Zechariah, Malachi.

24. The Jews of antiquity reduce the number of books to twenty-two, in keeping with the number of letters in the Hebrew alphabet (Josephus, *Against Apion*), by combining each of the following: Judges and Ruth, 1 and 2 Samuel, Kings, Chronicles, and also Ezra and Nehemiah, the Prophecy of Jeremiah and Lamentations, as well as the twelve Minor Prophets. This arrangement most of the early Christians follow (Jerome, in his *Helmeted Preface*), except that those who leave out Esther, count Ruth apart (Melito in Eusebius, etc.; Origen in Eusebius, *Ecclesiastical History*, book 6, chapter 19 and others). However, in keeping with the number of Hebrew letters of double characters, a good many wish five to be counted together, as Jerome (in the *Preface*) does for the last five, or Epiphanius (*On Measures and Weights*) for the first five. Some count twenty-four, separating the story of Ruth and Lamentations (Jerome, *Helmeted Preface*). Accordingly, the later Jews call the Scripture of the Old Testament 'the Twenty-Four.'

25. To the calculation of the number we add the division into groups. Leaving aside altogether the chronological divisions based on the authors and the time of writing, because it is somewhat unclear and in need of more precise investigation, we divide them into certain groups which are not the same for the Jews, Greeks, and Latins. And they are generally arranged and grouped by them in the sacred books following the order they made up.

26. The oldest division is the one thought to have been made by Ezra, which the early synagogue used, and which Christ and the apostles endorsed, who sort these books either into two groups, the Law of Moses (which simply is called the Law, and Moses) and the prophets (Acts 28:23, Matt 5:17, Luke 16:29), or sometimes into three, namely also the Psalms (Luke 24:44), among which as the foremost book they include the remaining hagiographical ones, which Josephus calls hymns and 'precepts of life' (Josephus, *Against Apion*), and Jerome 'hagiographies' in the *Preface*, applying the particular meaning of the general word.

27. The difference is only in number. Josephus has thirteen in the second

group, as he counts Job and Daniel among the prophets; he makes the remaining four belong to the third group. Jerome, following the thinking of the Jews, says that after the Law, which they call *Torah*, of which they call the individual books by the first word, namely *Bereshit*, that is, 'in the beginning, etc.,' they assign to the second group eight books, which are: Joshua, Judges and Ruth, Samuel, Kings, Isaiah, Jeremiah, Ezekiel, and *Tere'asar* ('twelve'), that is, the twelve prophets, who are also called the book of prophets (Acts 7:42). The remaining books they assign to the Nine Hagiographers: Job, David, whom they include in five sections within one volume of Psalms, and the Proverbs of Solomon, Ecclesiastes, Daniel, the Words of Days, or Chronicles, Ezra, Esther—to which some add Ruth and Lamentations.

28. The division into sections by the Jews of our day is similar, although it appears they make four groups. For after the Law, which they call *Chamisha Chumshei Torah*, that is, 'five fifths' (i.e., parts, or 'the quintet' of the Law)— to the Law they join or append *Sefer*, or *Chamesh megillot*, that is, these five volumes, namely: Song of Songs, Ruth, *'Echa*, that is 'how' (from the opening word [of Lamentations]), Ecclesiastes, Esther. They do this not as the second part of the Bible-books, but on account of its special use for the Synagogue, namely the annual reading at special times, according to their law, separate from the Hagiography. Thus the second group for them is *Nevi'im*, that is, 'of the prophets,' whom they divide into former and latter; those of the first group are counted by Jerome from Joshua up to Isaiah; the rest perhaps received their names from the time in which they wrote and in which their books were placed into the treasury of the Church. Lastly, the third group is, *Ketuvim*, which they call 'the writings,' others 'the sacred writings.'

29. The Greeks, and from them the Latins, keep nearly the same names, number, order, and division. They call the five books of Moses, pronounced by the Chaldean word *Chomas, the Pentateuch*; the individual books are called by the subject-matter: Genesis, Exodus, Leviticus, Numbers, Deuteronomy, as certain Jews call *Mishne thora*, that is 'the repetition of the Law.' In the historical writings they maintain generally a chronological order, and call it 'the Octateuch.' And these are Joshua, Judges, Ruth, the four books of Kings (in which they combine Samuel and Kings), 'the two remaining books' (as they denote the books of Chronicles), Ezra and Nehemiah, Esther, with which they end the History section. Thereupon they add Job, Psalms, Proverbs, of Solomon, Ecclesiastes, Song of Solomon. Lastly, the twelve

prophets, and the four remaining books (among which is also Daniel, who was a foremost prophet; Dan 1:17, Matt 24:15). But the Latins place them at the front of the prophets.

30. As for the divisions of books into groups, some are different from others. Among the Greeks Gregory of Nazianzus in his *Poems* makes twelve historical books: Moses is counted among the historians; five Metrical or Poetic books, reckoning Job among them; and lastly, five of the prophets, by gathering the twelve prophets together into one volume. Not much different is Epiphanius (*Book on Measures and Weights*), whom also John of Damascus follows. He makes four quintets and one book of two's. The first is Law, or Legislation. The second, 'the writings,' or as with others, 'the holy writings,' which are Joshua, Judges with Ruth, 1 and 2 Kingdoms (or rather, Kings), likewise the third and fourth, 1 and 2 Chronicles, which are so named outside the Jewish tradition. The third 'rows,' enumerated previously. The fourth, prophetic, namely the twelve prophets, and the remainders separately. Lastly, the twofold Ezra and Esther.

31. The Scholastics make a similar division into Legal, Historical, Dogmatic or Wisdom Books, as they call them, and the Prophetic Books, which they split into Major and Minor.

32. Now for the New Testament there are twenty-seven books. In their arrangement consideration was given not so much to the time when they were written but to their content and worth.

33. They are commonly divided into four groups. The first is the Gospel, that is, the history of the words and deeds of Christ (Luke 1:1,2; Acts 1:1) by four writers, of whom two were apostles, Matthew and John (John 21:20, 24), and two of apostolic status, Mark and Luke—the former of whom was co-worker of Peter and Paul, and the latter especially of Paul (a description found in 2 Tim 4:11; 1 Pet 5:13). The second group is the Acts of the apostles, which sets forth the beginnings and expansion of the Church through the apostles, and of which Luke is also the author (Acts 1:1,2).

34. The third group includes the Letters of the apostles, written as the need arose, to divulge more fully the Gospel truth. These are the fourteen letters of Paul to the most prominent churches, namely to the Romans, two to the Corinthians, Galatians, Ephesians, Philippians, Colossians, two to the Thessalonians. And he wrote letters to those in charge of governing them,

two were given to Timothy and [one] to Titus; one to Philemon about a domestic matter. And lastly, one letter to an entire race, namely to the Hebrews. Then there are seven from the other apostles, James, two of Peter, three of John, and one of Jude. These letters (with the exception of the two from John, to "the elect lady" and Gaius), because they were written for many people, are called Catholic, and because they were sent under one heading to many people, they are called canonical, as Cassiodorus uses that word (Book 11, Letter 23), which Suetonius (*Life of Domitian*, chapter 13) calls 'formal letters.' And then the last group contains the Revelation to John the apostle, which contains a prophecy about the state of the Church to the end of the world.

35. Of these books some have expressed doubt about the Letter to the Hebrews and its authorship; about James as well as the two last letters of John, Jude; and about Revelation and its author (Eusebius, *Ecclesiastical History*, book 2, chapter 22; book 3, chapter 18 and 19). The reason is that perhaps they were introduced to the canon rather late, or because some of them seemed to contain things that were not consistent enough with the others. But that was more the personal opinion of some individuals, nor has a sufficiently careful and sound assessment of the issues been undertaken. To the contrary, in light of the judgment of the early Church (Origen, on Psalm 1, in Eusebius, *Ecclesiastical History*, book 6), and of the godly worth of their subject matter and the style, it prevails that these books are of divine origin. The reference to Timothy the co-worker of Paul, the usual form of greeting (Heb 13:23, 24), and the authority of Peter, who addressed also his own letter to the Hebrews who were scattered throughout Asia (2 Pet 3:15), support the position that the one to the Hebrews is from Paul. The ancients attribute the difference in style to the translation of Luke, or Clement, or someone else. Tertullian ascribes the work to Barnabas. The manner of expression exonerates the Revelation to John.

36. Well then, these books are divine, authentic, and canonical; besides these the ones either the Greeks or Latins connected to them are called 'non-canonical,' which we consider as human, ecclesiastical, and apocryphal books (Origen, in Eusebius, *Ecclesiastical History*, book 6 chapter 19; Jerome, in the *Preface*). Those of the Old Testament may be additions and appendices to the sacred books, such as: the prayer of Manasseh, published in Latin, added to the book of Chronicles; the appendix to Esther, from chapter 10 to the end of the book; the addition to Job, from chapter 42:56; Psalm 151, added to the

Psalms, which appears in the Greek edition. Also Baruch, and the letter of Jeremiah added to the prophecy of Jeremiah; the Preface to the book of Lamentations; the hymn of the three youths, added to Daniel; the history of the dragon, Habakkuk, and Suzanna. To this group we also assign the omissions and additions by the authors of the Septuagint, beyond the Hebrew text. There may also be entire books, such as book three and also book four of Ezra (which exists only in Latin), Tobias, Judith (Jerome states that he translated both of these books from Chaldean), two books of the Maccabees, and a third in Greek; Wisdom, which is reported to be from Solomon, but is actually Philo's under the name of Solomon, the Ecclesiastic Jesus Sirach, which he claims was written in Hebrew by his grandfather, but which has not survived.

37. Also the papal teachers assign some of these to the apocrypha, namely the prayer of Manasseh, the Appendix to Job, Psalm 151, the Preface to Jeremiah, the two of Ezra, and the last book of the Maccabees; the rest they include among the sacred books (Council of Trent, Session 4). But we consider them all to be of the same rank as far as their authority is concerned, and we affirm that they should not be mixed with the sacred, nor read publicly in church as if they are divine (Synod of Laodicea, chapter 59), although we do not deny that they can be kept and read with benefit privately.

38. The reasons why we should consider none of these writings as sacred are: In the first place, that they were not produced by the Spirit of prophecy, since they were written after the time of Artaxerxes, in which no succession of prophets was found (Rom 16:26, Josephus, *Against Appian*, 2). Second, because they were not placed in the ark, as the tables of the Law were, or beside the ark, as the books of Moses were (Deut 31, Epiphanius, *On Measures and Weights*). Third, because they were not written or preserved in the Hebrew language, nor did the Jewish church, to whom the divine oracles had been entrusted, ever acknowledge them as such (Josephus, *Against Appian* 4). Fourth, because neither Christ, nor the apostles, nor the early Church acknowledges them as such, but they considered them not genuine (Amphilochius and Gregory of Nazianzus, both in *Balsamon*), and were admitted by the later Church with considerable variance and dispute, and then only as ecclesiastical (Synod of Carthage, 3; Augustine, *On Christian Doctrine*; Rufinus, *On the Creeds*, 5). Fifth, and finally, because they contain nonsensical, mainly fictitious things, and things that are not in harmony with the sacred writings—which it would take too long to review here.

39. Furthermore, we rank the books that are introduced under the names of the apostles or their disciples among the apocrypha as pseudonymous, although they are not of the same sort. Many were honoured highly among the ancients, such as the *Book of the Shepherd*, signed by Hermas, formerly of such authority in some churches of the East that it was read publicly in them (Eusebius, *Ecclesiastical History*, book 3, chapter 3, etc., chapter 32, etc.; Jerome in the *Helmeted Preface*). So too the Letter of Barnabas, two of Clement (Irenaeus, book 3, chapter 3) and several other books. The rest were clearly rejected as more deserving of concealment, than of reading as Athanasius says in his *Synopsis*.

40. As far as the Symbol of faith and hope is concerned, the ancients have also called it the Faith, the Catholic Faith, the Explanation, the Confession or Profession, the Rule and Norm, the Articles, and the Headings of Faith and Truth, and the Symbol of the apostles (Synod of Laodicea, chapter 46, and Irenaeus, book 1, chapter 1 and 2, Tertullian, *The Prescription Against the Heretics*, and *Against Praxeas*; Jerome, *To Paumachius*, Augustine, *Sermons on the Liturgical Seasons* 19, *on Time*, and *On Faith and the Creed*, Ambrose in *Letter* 81). Even before the Synod of Nicea, in the churches at various places (especially in response to the rise of heresies) the symbol differed not at all in content but somewhat in wording. In the western churches, however, it was preserved unaltered. It is called a Symbol, that is, summary or sign because with wonderful candor and conciseness it provides a collation and summary of the Christian faith. And [it is called a Symbol] so that it would be a sign, indication, or token, with which they could testify to their unity and distinguish themselves from unbelievers and heretics. [Ps.-]Clement of Rome (*Letter to James*) and Rufinus (*On the Apostolic Symbol*) call it 'Apostolic,' either because it was compiled by the apostles when they went separate ways throughout the whole world, as some writers explain (though not credibly enough). It is not as though each one individually contributed his own article (from where some derive their number of twelve, quite foolishly, except perhaps for the sake of remembering them), but it was compiled by mutual consent (Augustine, *Sermons on the Liturgical Seasons* 115, *on Time*). Or it is called 'Apostolic' because the apostolic fathers or the early Church gathered it from the teaching and writings of the apostles as a summary put together and devised in about so many words, and handed down by word of mouth in the churches (at least in the western ones) to be entrusted by the instructors in the catechism for memorization by the catechumens, and then recited by

those who were baptized as they solemnly renounced the devil and professed God (Augustine, *On the Creed to the Catechumens*, book 1; Synod of Laodicea, chapter 46; Matt 28:19). This summary, I declare, if not divine with respect to its authorship, is clearly divine in its substance, and nearly so in words.

41. And finally, we value highly the writings of the Church, that is, of the synods, and especially on the symbols of the universal synods such as that of Nicea, Constantinople, Ephesus, Chalcedon (to which we join also the Athanasian one)—as much as upon the judgment of the entire Church that is based upon the Word of God; and so too upon the saints and church-fathers, and of their unanimous consent. However, we reckon that all of these must be judged and tested against the foremost truth, namely Holy Scripture, from which, like the moon from the sun, they receive their own light and trustworthiness (Augustine, *Against Maximus*, book 3, chapter 14).

ON THE PERFECTION OF SCRIPTURE, AND THE FUTILITY OF ADDING UNWRITTEN TRADITIONS TO IT

President: Johannes Polyander
Respondent: Abraham Swalmius

The fourth disputation deals with the question whether Holy Scripture is perfect or sufficient for a saving knowledge of God, or if some additional traditions are needed. On this issue, Reformed theology is diametrically opposed to Roman Catholic theology. The starting point for the disputation is therefore the definition of the state of the question by the papal theologian Bellarmine (3–7). Next, the perfection of Scripture is demonstrated by means of twelve reasons, all taken from Scripture itself (8–24). Many Church Fathers affirm these proofs from Scripture (25). A distinction is then made between traditions and rituals that are not explicitly found in Scripture but are in harmony with it and therefore qualify as 'divine' and 'apostolic,' and traditions that are merely human, because they neither occur nor are mentioned in Scriptures (26–39).

1. While in the preceding investigations we explained the necessity and authority of Holy Scripture, and the number of canonical books that we must keep separate from apocryphal ones, in this fourth one we shall investigate its perfection.

2. Some look at the perfection of Holy Scripture in two ways: either with respect to its content (the very things that one simply must know in this life in order to be saved), or with respect to its outward form (the words and phrases that lend clear expression to the true meaning of those things), which by another name we call 'perspicuity.' At this point we shall debate the

perfection of Holy Scripture only in the former sense, both absolutely or in itself and in relation and opposition to the unwritten traditions.

3. Bellarmine, in his treatise, *On the Unwritten Word of God*, depicts the state of the question as follows (Book 4, chapter 3), that our theologians teach "that all things necessary to the faith and moral behavior are contained in the Scriptures, and hence that there is no need for the unwritten Word;" but the papal teachers contend that "the Scriptures do not explicitly contain all the necessary teaching, either about faith or about moral behavior, and therefore that in addition to the recorded Word of God the unwritten Word of God is required, that is, the traditions from God, the apostolic traditions, and the traditions of the church."

4. In this portrayal of the dispute as it stands currently three things are missing that he left out; the first is that all the doctrines about the faith and moral conduct necessarily required for a comprehensive and saving knowledge of God and for the pursuit of supreme blessedness are contained sufficiently in the written Word of God, either explicitly in so many clear wordings, or by analogy in words of equal significance, and deduced from the very source of Holy Scripture through an immediate, necessary, transparent and indubitable logical inference. That is what we affirm.

5. The second is that "those unwritten traditions, as if either proceeding straight from the mouth of Christ or dictated by the Holy Spirit and preserved by an unbroken sequence in the Catholic Church, must be accepted with the same amount of awe and reverence with which we accept all the books of the Old and New Testaments." This the Council of Trent has decided (Decree 1, session 4).

6. The third is that "without the traditions the Holy Scriptures were neither simply necessary nor sufficient." This is what Bellarmine argues about the unwritten Word of God (Book 4, chapter 4, etc.; cf. Stanislaus Hosius, *Against [Johannes] Brenz*, Book 4, *On the Traditions*).

7. Some of the proofs we used to demonstrate the truth of our assertion against the papal theologians in thesis number 4 above have their origins in God, and others in the church. We draw the former kind of proofs from the written Word of God itself, and the latter from the writings of the orthodox church fathers.

8. The first of the former kind of proofs is taken from the passages that heap high praise upon the written Word, and which indicate its surpassing perfection, whether by the author or by the power and efficacy that the author communicates to it to reach the goal which he has planned for it flawlessly. For by its author, namely God, who is the supreme cause of everything and perfect in all his works (Deut 32:4), the written Word is sometimes called "the Word of God" (as in 2 Pet 1:21), sometimes "the Law of God" (Ps 1:2; 19:8; 119), sometimes "Scripture that is God-breathed" (as in 2 Tim 3:16). And by the power and efficacy that God has bestowed on it directly, it is stated that the Word "is able to render a person wise unto salvation" (2 Tim 3:15).

9. The second proof comes from the qualities of perfection and sufficiency that are attributed explicitly to it (Ps 19:8, 9): "the Law (i.e., teaching) of God is whole." For something is whole when it lacks nothing, and when it can receive nothing beyond what it possesses, as Aristotle rightly noted (*On the Heavens*, Book 2, ch. 4). Therefore, nothing that belongs to the Law of God is found over and above the written Law of God.

10. Hence formerly God commanded that nothing be added to his Law or taken away from it (Deut 4:2). We must realize that the prohibition is about the Law as it was recorded by Moses himself, as both Moses's and Paul's explanation shows. For Moses calls God's Law in its entirety the words that have been written in his book (Deut 28:58), and so too Paul (Gal 3:[10–]13). It is for this reason that everything Moses on behalf of God communicated to the Israelites by word of mouth was also delivered in writing, as Moses himself testifies (Exod 24:4; Deut 31:9).

11. From this integrity of the Law a further argument is drawn through comparison: if the Law of the Old Testament is whole and lacked nothing that was necessary for the salvation of the Israelite people, then how much more is the entire doctrine of the Old and New Testaments complete and can lack nothing that is necessary for the salvation of the Christian people. In that same Psalm 19 David proves this to be the case by pointing to the traits and effects of the Law, that it is right, just, more precious than gold and sweeter than honey, making the simple truly wise, and causing all who ponder it sincerely to be blessed.

12. The third proof rests upon the title "Testament," which identifies Holy Scripture (Heb 9:15–17). Now the chief property of a testament is that it

makes known the complete will of the testator and is very well suited to identify for the heir each and every requirement he must meet in order to take possession of the inheritance. The second property is that once a will has been ratified, no-one annuls it or adds anything to it, as the apostle shows with the example of the Gentiles' law (Gal 3:15). Basil also cites this passage when he discusses faith, and so too Augustine on Ps [54:]21.

13. The fourth proof is derived from the fact that it is the "rule" of faith and life, as can be seen in Gal 6:16: "And peace and mercy shall come upon whoever walks by this rule" (and Phil 3:16). For every rule is so complete that it allows nothing to be removed or added to it; otherwise, it would not be a rule. Gerson has applied this proof suitably to the rule of Holy Scripture, in his treatise *On the Examination of Doctrine*, Tome 1, part 2.

14. Therefore the apostle John seals the canon of Holy Scripture with the following word of final warning in such a manner that it should be extended to the whole corpus of Scripture (Rev 22:18, 19): "If anyone adds to these words God will inflict on him the plagues described in this book. And if anyone takes away from the words of the book of this prophecy, God will take away his share from the book of life and from the city of the saints, and from what is described in this book."

15. The fifth proof is derived from the equation that is made between the spoken word and the written one, like two complementary and equally strong supports. For even Scripture is called "the Word of God," and vice versa. For this reason, Christ and the apostles resolved to say nothing beyond the Scriptures of the Old Testament (witness the evangelist, Luke 24:27; Acts 17:2, and 26:22), in order to signal that everything Moses and the prophets long ago had delivered orally is the same as what they had expressed in writing, as far as the main points and the content are concerned. For the same reason also the apostles and the evangelists, inspired by the same Spirit just as much as Moses and the prophets were, and out of the same sense of duty which the Spirit of Christ had laid upon them, entrusted to writing the entire Gospel concerning Christ which they had proclaimed, as one can conclude from various places, and particularly Phil 3:1: "It is not irksome to me to write the same things to you" that is to say, the things you had heard from me. And 2 Thess 2:15: "Hold to the doctrinal tradition you were taught by us, either by preaching or by our letter." 1 John 1:3,4: "That which we have seen and heard we proclaim also to you, so that you may have fellowship with

us; and our fellowship may be with the Father and his Son Jesus Christ. And we are writing this that your joy may be complete." Luke 1:3,4: "It seemed good to me to write all these things to you, so that you may recognize the truth of those things which you have received by hearing." And Acts 1:1: "I have completed a book about all the things which Jesus began to do and teach."

16. The sixth proof derives from an account of the parts that make up the essence, namely matter and form. The matter of Scripture exists in the scope of the things God was pleased to reveal to his elect. The form exists in the unerring certainty of those things and the true representation of them following God's prescription. Of these we draw forth the following two:

17. First, with respect to the matter: everything that is necessary for a person's salvation has the character either of the means or of the goal that corresponds to them. And both are found in the sacred writings. For the means that correspond to the goal are included in the faith in Jesus Christ, and the goal with its corresponding means is included in the name "eternal life". as part for the whole; John 17:3: "And this is eternal life, that they know you the only true God, and Jesus Christ whom you have sent;" John 20:31: "These things are written that believing you may have life through his name."

18. Secondly, concerning the form, which thanks to God's remarkable economy pervades the entire sacred book and each individual page to such an extent that it presents God himself everywhere before our eyes as the archetype of the truth that saves. For that reason, Moses in the presence of all the people calls it above all "wisdom" and the most complete knowledge [Deut 4:6], Christ "the truth itself" (John 17:17), and Paul "the truth that accords with godliness" (Titus 1:1). And also "the faithful, sound, irreproachable word that is worthy to be received in every way."

19. The seventh proof arises from its integral parts, namely the Law and the Gospel, that is, the commands of love and faith that comprise the whole of religion pleasing to God and for us means salvation. For whatever consists of all the parts that combine to make up the whole is whole and entire, and whatever is entire is perfect, and vice versa. For these two things are interchangeable.

20. The eighth reason comes from its perfect results, the fact that it renders a person perfect through its instruction and perfectly equipped for every

good work, and showers him with perfect joy (2 Tim 3:17; 1 John 4). It is necessary that the cause of these perfect effects itself must be perfect also.

21. The ninth reason is sought from the very stern admonition of Isaiah who calls everyone away from human inventions to the only rule of Mosaic and prophetic Scripture (Isaiah 8:20): "To the Law and to the testimony; if they would not speak according to this word, then there is no spark of light for them." Moreover, if the ancient Jewish church is led back by Isaiah to the only Scripture that was recorded in writing under the Law, then by the same reasoning—no, by greater reasoning—is the Christian Church sent back to the single testimony of the Old together with the New Testament.

22. The tenth reason comes from the commonly professed testimony of the Jews, one that was approved even by Christ himself, in John 5:39: "You search the Scriptures, because you think that in them you have life." If this estimation of the Old Testament Scriptures by the Jews is right, as can be taken from Christ's statement, then we more rightfully hold the same with regard to the entire book of the two testaments.

23. The eleventh comes from Abraham's reply, in Luke 16:29, where he testifies that if the brothers of the rich banqueter heed Moses and the prophets, they are able to draw from their writings the only knowledge sufficient to avoid torment in the realm of the dead.

24. The twelfth reason is from the usefulness of Holy Scripture for the "man of God" (that is, to the teacher of the church) and therefore also for the hearer who must be fully instructed according to all the parts of the most holy ministry. For it says that Scripture is "profitable for teaching, for reproof, for correction, and for training in righteousness" (2 Tim 3:16), and "for encouragement" (Rom 15:4).

25. In order to restrain the papal theologians who commonly abuse the authority of the Fathers against us, one can add to these proofs from the divine sources the statements of proof by Irenaeus in book 3, chapter 1; Basil, *Letter* 1 and 80; Chrysostom, *Sermon* 1 on Acts; Tertullian, *Against Hermogenes*; Ambrose, *Hexameron* book 1, chapter 6; Jerome, *To Demetriades on Virginity*; and *Commentary on Micah* book 1, chapter 1; Justin Martyr, *Dialogue with Trypho*; Origen, *Sermon* 1 on Jeremiah; Augustine, *On Christian Doctrine*, book 2, chapter 9, and *Confessions*, book 7, chapter 7; and of other Fathers, who affirm that the Scriptures are the pillar and source of faith, and that their fullness is

so great that in them one will discover sufficiently everything that contains faith and the habits for living a good and blessed life, namely hope and charity. For the sake of brevity, we do not record these testimonies here.

26. Up to this point we have demonstrated that Holy Scripture, examined absolutely and by itself, is perfect; when we examine it in relation and in opposition to the unwritten traditions, we assert that it is perfect in two respects. For some [traditions], taken in a broader and improper sense, are beneficial and necessary for salvation; others, taken in a more specific and proper sense, are not useful or necessary. The former, by virtue of equivalence, being of the same kind, and in harmony with Holy Scripture, are included within the boundaries of Holy Scripture; the latter, by being of a different kind and divergent, are excluded by the boundaries. Concerning the former Gregory of Nazianzus (*Theological Orations*, Book 5) correctly teaches that they do indeed occur, but are not mentioned explicitly in Scriptures; concerning the latter, that they neither occur nor are mentioned in them.

27. Both are either doctrines or rituals. Only the former are divine, prophetic and apostolic; the latter should be called human traditions.

28. For everything that originated with God was recorded by the prophets and the apostles, either tacitly or expressly, either generally or singularly. Therefore, Bellarmine wrongly distinguishes divine from apostolic traditions (*On the Unwritten Word of God*, Book 4, ch. 2). For no traditions should be viewed as divine, except the sacred writings recorded by the hand of the apostles. No traditions should be put in the list of apostolic ones as if coming "from the apostles with the assistance of the Holy Spirit," to quote the words of Bellarmine, of which their main points are found nowhere in Scriptures.

29. In the list of traditions that are found in the sacred writings, or that occur there by having the same force by analogy, we think (contrary to what the papal teachers think) that, besides the articles of the Apostles' Creed, the following axiomatic statements may be assembled: That the children of Christians ought to be baptized; that the Lord's Supper ought to be given also to women; that Jesus Christ is of the same essence with his Father; that there are two sacraments of the new covenant, namely Baptism and the Lord's Supper; that Baptism is not to be repeated; that the apostles, inspired by the Holy Spirit, chose the day of the Lord [Sunday] instead of the Sabbath-day that had been sanctified by the Jews until their times; and similar things which are loosely called apostolic traditions by some of the church-fathers;

namely, by Origen (in the commentary on Rom 6.); Augustine (*On Baptism, Against the Donatists*, ch. 23); by Theodoretus (*History of the Church*, Book 1, ch. 8); Epiphanius (*Against the Arians*, Heresy 69); and by others.

30. In the catalogue of traditions which do not appear at all in Holy Scriptures, or which are incompatible with them, we place the following: the celebration of Easter under the new testament on the Sunday following the fourteenth day of the [new] moon of March; the superstitious keeping of the forty-day fast; the worship of images and relics; the invocation of saints; the worship of the sign of the cross; the offering of the mass; the transubstantiation of the bread in the Lord's Supper; the discontinued use of the cup in the same; the carrying about of the bread through neighborhoods and at crossroads for the purpose of adoration; blessing of lustral water; monastic vows; pilgrimages; the repeated chanting of the angel's greeting to the virgin Mary. So also the *Canons [of the Apostles]*, which like most of the other forementioned traditions the papal teachers wrongly attribute to the apostles.

31. For some of the church-fathers have rejected these *Canons* altogether for being forged, while others have accepted at least a few of them, as can be seen in Zephyrinus, and Gratian (1 Part Decret. Dist. 16). Others have made changes to them, as is clear from Chapter 6 of the Sixth Synod: such as Canon 68, among others, which commands that "the cleric who does not fast for the forty days [of Lent] must be removed from office, while the laic must abstain from communion."

32. The fact that very many of the traditions (as we have indicated above) are diametrically opposed to the apostolic writings proves that also the other traditions listed above are forged and spurious. For all the things that the apostles have handed down, either by word of mouth or in writing, are in harmony with one another from both sides, since they were pronounced by one and the same Spirit of truth, who never contradicts himself and who wanted that no contradiction or any kind of contrariety be found in the teaching of the apostles (2 Cor 1:19).

33. Nor should we overlook the fact that the papal teachers are at odds with each other regarding that list of unwritten traditions. For (leaving aside all the other traditions), Cajetan ascribes the sacrifice of the Mass to the unwritten traditions of the apostles (at 2 Thess 2:2). But Bellarmine spends much effort

to prove from various passages that it is taught in Holy Scripture (*On the Mass*, Book 1, ch. 6 and following).

34. We should observe further that the papal teachers claim the apostles did not share with their listeners everything God had revealed to them, but that they entrusted some things to everyone and publicly and other things to only a few and privately. Tertullian in his book *Against the Heretics*, rightly calls that claim insane.

35. For by that claim the apostles are obviously charged with faithless and unpardonable disobedience, as if in their sermons as well as in their writings they had left out some part of the mysteries that God had revealed to them, for the purpose of making them known to everyone whom they were to instruct, according to the necessity of the task imposed on them (Matt 10:27, and 28:19). The apostle Paul denies this (Acts 20:27), and actually states the opposite (1 Cor 1:5,6, and 15:1,2; 1 Thess 1:5; 2 Thess 2:13, 14, 15).

36. From the same claim it follows that no-one can know for sure what those hidden traditions are, and by what rules and marks the true ones are to be distinguished from the false ones.

37. For the rules and marks Bellarmine puts forward outside Holy Scripture are doubtful, as Scripture alone is the most reliable indicator of right and wrong in all the things one must believe and keep (*On the Unwritten Word of God*, Book 4, ch. 9). His rules are not clearly spelled out, and misleading. For then we must of necessity believe that not all the teachings which the universal church embraces about Scripture (which it preserves from the age immediately following the apostolic one, and which are endorsed by the common consensus of its teachers), proceeded from the apostles; but, to the contrary, on account of the fact that they have been received and retained by the church and its teachers without the sanction of Scripture, they must be deemed as non-apostolic traditions.

38. For everyone who together with the Roman church, which claims for itself an unbroken succession from the apostles, errs in thinking that Holy Scripture does not contain everything that is necessary for salvation, can be deceived easily in the following aspect also: that some other doctrine which actually did not emanate from the apostles is apostolic.

39. A demonstration of this point is the early church, immediately following the apostolic one. For under the guise of apostolic tradition Papias imported

the error of the Chiliasts into the church (witness Eusebius, Book 3, ch. 39); and Irenaeus (Book 2, ch. 39, 40) taught that, according to the tradition of the apostle John, Christ's suffering took place around his fiftieth year of age. Even the papal teachers admit that the church of that time was misled by its own teachers in these matters.

ABOUT THE PERSPICUITY
AND THE INTERPRETATION
OF HOLY SCRIPTURE

President: Antonius Walaeus
Respondent: Rombert Stellingwerf

The ability to understand Scripture is of the greatest importance, because faith, personal edification, and consolation depend on it (18). The Synopsis states that in this respect Scripture is perspicuous. Perspicuity refers to the clarity, lucid quality, and transparency of Scripture. Because of its perspicuity, all believers, when endowed with intelligence and led by the Holy Spirit, are able to understand and interpret Scripture correctly (5–10). This holds for all matters that are indispensable for faith and moral conduct (11–18). From this it does not follow that the explanation of Holy Scripture or the preaching of the Word is superfluous (19). Who is the lawful interpreter of Holy Scripture? (20) No one is dependent upon anyone else, not upon the Church, councils, a pope, or pastors. Papal teachers state that ultimately only the pope has all the infallible power to decide and judge regarding the true interpretation of Scripture (21–22). According to the Synopsis, however, Scripture is its own Interpreter. God speaks in and through the Scriptures (23) and is its highest Judge (24) who himself works with and through his Word (25–26). The power to judge the right or wrong meaning of Holy Scripture in a private capacity in matters indispensable to one's salvation applies to all the true believers (27–31). The authority to expound Scripture in public, and to determine the truth of interpretation, is not for everyone, but only for those who by their gifts and their calling have been trained for this task (32–35). The competency to interpret, however, remains subject to the Word of God, and to the Holy Spirit who is speaking in Scripture. Interpreters develop their own judgment and its underlying support from Holy Scripture, and bring forward those teachings which subsequently the believers through their gift of discernment and testing individually recognize as certain and true. In this way, only the Word of God and the Holy Spirit remain the highest judge of faith (36–39).

1. The matters concerning Holy Scripture that have been debated up to this point aim to confirm its divine majesty and dignity; in what follows we shall commend especially its use and benefit in the Church of Christ. For the recognition of its divinity, authority, and perfection would be of no advantage to us at all, unless we believers can understand Scripture correctly and explain and apply it in the Church of Christ in order to establish the doctrines of faith and moral conduct.

2. Therefore in order for this use and benefit of Holy Scripture to remain intact for the Church of Christ, we must now treat the perspicuity and interpretation of it.

3. The lucid quality or perspicuity of Holy Scripture can be considered in two ways: either absolutely and by itself, or in relation to us and our intellect.

4. Considered apart and by itself, the light of Holy Scripture is recognized by the most sensible papal theologians, along with us. For since Holy Scripture proceeded from the Father of lights [cf. Jas 1:17], it is impossible that it should not possess in itself the truth and the purest light, whereby the minds of those who come to know it are illumined, and are freed from the darkness of error. For this reason, Scripture is also called "Wisdom," and "the storehouse of knowledge," and its purity is affirmed to be like gold seven times refined, and more precious than jewels (Prov 3:13[14–15]), etc.

5. Therefore the entire point of discussion is about the perspicuity of Scripture in its relation to us, for properly speaking in this context 'perspicuous' is said to be what by its clarity is transparent to others and can be learned and understood by those who have been endowed with intelligence.

6. This definition of perspicuity can be related to two kinds of people: Either to the understanding and faculty of natural man, that is (as Chrysostom rightly explains) people "whose intellects have been endowed with no other light than the one God has implanted in the souls of all people through natural reproduction," albeit in various degrees, as Scripture itself also states (John 1:9). Or the definition can be related to the understanding and faculties of the spiritual man, that is, whose mind has been enlightened additionally by

a supernatural light from above (also in varying degrees). The distinction is articulated in this way in 1 Cor 2:14, and elsewhere.

7. As far as the first kind of people is concerned, we acknowledge that the sacred books narrate and teach many things which a person in the natural state understands in a natural manner, if he applies some thoughtful attention, and if he is trained in employing the languages and other useful disciplines, since most of the time God spoke through his Prophets and Apostles in everyday popular language and in modes of speech drawn from the general public—even when He deals with matters that far surpass the human intellect. From here we see also that some pagan philosophers borrow some things from Holy Scripture for their own purposes, whereas others have attempted in their own writings to contradict them, which they could not have done if they had not understood the meaning of the words and the grammatical sense, at least in a natural way.

8. However, we declare that a natural or unspiritual man, whoever he may be, is not able, in the way that is fitting (that is, with spiritual lucidity, acuteness, heartfelt respect and holiness, much less with certainty of thought and agreement), to understand those things, to discern between them, and to apply them to himself for salutary effect, unless he has been enlightened by the Holy Spirit. As for instance Christ says about Peter's confession in Matt 16:17: "Flesh and blood has not revealed these things to you, but my Father who is in heaven." And 1 Cor 1:23[–24]: "We preach Christ crucified, a stumbling block to the Jews and folly to the Greeks, but to those who have been called, we preach Christ, who is the power and wisdom of God." And 1 Cor 2:14: "The natural man does not perceive the things of the Spirit of God, nor is he able to perceive them, because they have been discerned in a spiritual manner."

9. But the difference in understanding between us and the papal teachers concerns especially the man who, in different degrees and to different ends, has been illumined by the Spirit of Christ; and over against them we assert, together with Augustine, that God has so accommodated the style and wording of Holy Scripture, that: "Whatever things contain faith and moral conduct, namely hope and love, are stated plainly in the Scriptures," and in accordance with the calling and the measure of faith, everyone can discern and apply them for their own wellbeing.

10. And yet we do not deny, meanwhile, that in the Scriptures also some matters that are more difficult to understand appear, as the final chapter of the Second Letter of Peter shows. And there are things that have been transmitted in a more abstruse style, sometimes to eliminate contempt and aversion from continually reading it; sometimes to break pride, and to stimulate everyone's attentiveness; and finally, at other times so that we do not undertake reading and searching it except with a sense of awe, with sanctification of ourselves, and with prayer, as in the case of David (Ps 119). Yet, again with the same Augustine (*On Christian Doctrine*, Book 2, ch. 6), we state: "That almost nothing is dug up from those difficult passages, which is not found elsewhere set forth most plainly, precisely so that the Holy Spirit meets our hunger by means of readily-grasped passages, but drives away boredom with the more obscure passages."

11. This perspicuity of Holy Scripture in matters that are indispensable for faith and moral conduct is demonstrated by many irrefutable arguments and eloquent passages of Holy Scripture.

12. First is the argument from the fact that if this were not the case, it would have been in vain that God in the Old Testament commanded, for instruction in the faith and morals of his people, that not only the priests and Levites but also every believer whosoever should read Holy Scripture (or hear it read). Deut 17:19 expressly commands the king: "That he shall read in it all the days of his life, that he may learn to fear the Lord his God, to keep all the words of this Law, and its statutes, by doing them." Deut 31:11–12 teaches that: "This Law shall be read before all Israel in their hearing, etc., so that they may hear it and learn, and may fear the Lord, etc." And in Isa 8:20 the entire people is sent "back to consult the Law and the testimony."

13. So also in the New Testament, in John 5:39, Christ bids: "That they search the Scriptures, because they suppose that they will find eternal life in them." In Luke 16, Abraham sends the brothers of the wealthy man back to "Moses and the Prophets," so as to be able to avoid the punishments of the world below. John 20:31 states: "These are written that you may believe (he is speaking to anyone and everyone) that Jesus is the Christ, and that believing you may have eternal life in his name." 2 Pet 1:19 states: "That they (the believers to whom he is writing) will do well to pay attention to the prophetic Word, that is the Scriptures, until the Morningstar rises in their hearts."

14. Indeed David calls them "blessed" who "day and night meditate on the law of God" (Ps 1:2). And in Acts 17:11 the Jews in Beroea are praised beyond the others "because they were examining the Scriptures daily to see whether these things were true." And in Rev 1:3 they are said to be blessed "who read and hear the words of this prophecy, and keep what is written therein." All of these things in no way could be commanded and entrusted to believers unless Scripture had been adjusted in such a way that they could understand, according to the calling of each, the things which concern their salvation, in matters of both faith and moral conduct.

15. Even the introductory greetings of numerous sacred books demonstrate this point, especially the letters of the Apostles, which are directed "to all who believe and who call upon the name of the Lord." This would make no sense at all, unless people could read and understand them in accordance with their calling, when they come to a reading of them with the appropriate manner and reverence.

16. In fact, in many eloquent passages Holy Scripture bears witness to its own perspicuity and transparency. In Deut 29:29 Moses states: "These things have been revealed to us and our sons, that we may perform all the words of this law." Chapter 30:11 states that: "This commandment is not obscured from us, nor is it far away." In Ps 119:105 it is called a "lamp to our feet and a light to our path." In Prov 6:23 the Law is called light. In 2 Pet 1[:19] it is called a "lamp shining in a dark place." In 2 Cor 3:14 the Apostle testifies that the "veil which had been placed over the hearts of the hardened Jews has been done away with through Christ and would be lifted from their hearts when they should turn to the Lord." In chapter 4:2 he writes that "by the open statement or evidence of the truth, he commends himself to the conscience of all men in the sight of God; but that even if the Gospel is veiled, it is veiled only for those who are perishing, in whom the god of this world has blinded their minds, lest the light of the Gospel should cast its rays on them."

17. The same point is demonstrated by the effects upon all kinds of people, which throughout Scripture are attributed to the written word—indeed even upon unskilled and the unsophisticated people. Ps 19:8: "The Law of Jehovah is whole, reviving the soul; the testimony is sure, bringing wisdom to the ignorant; the precepts of Jehovah are right, rejoicing the heart, the precept of Jehovah is pure, enlightening the eyes." Ps 119:130: "The unfolding of the words gives light, it teaches prudence to the simple." Prov 1:1: "The proverbs

of Solomon, etc., for giving wisdom to the foolish, knowledge and learning to the youth." Rom 15:4: "For whatever was written in former days was written for our instruction, that by steadfastness and encouragement of the Scriptures we might have hope." 2 Tim 3:15: "from your childhood up, you know the sacred writings, which are able to make you wise unto salvation." 1 John 2:13: "I write to you, fathers, because you know Him who is from the beginning; I write to you, young men, because you have overcome the evil one; I write to you, children, because you know the Father, etc."

18. Finally, the very word "Testament" demonstrates this, which is applied everywhere to the sacred writing of the old and new covenant. For what true father has ever intentionally written his own will in such a way that when it was needed, it could not be read nor understood by his heirs, at least in the things that really mattered? Or why is it that Councils, church-fathers, or pastors are used to proving their own teaching to the people from Holy Scripture—and so they ought to do in everything that pertains to the necessary faith and moral conduct—if the faithful could not, according to their calling, understand them? For understanding the words and sentences necessarily comes before faith, which is born of the Word of God, not of men. Nor can any upbuilding or consolation be taken from a word if it has not been understood, as Paul openly demonstrates in 1 Cor 14.

19. However, from this it does not follow that the explanation of Holy Scripture, or the preaching of the Word, is superfluous; because matters that have been subordinated to one another do not conflict, and the preaching of the Word is, among other things, a means ordained in the Church by God, whereby the other believers learn both to understand Holy Scripture more easily and to apply it to themselves more accurately. Therefore both of these must be joined together, not separated, in the true Church of Christ: just as Christ has instituted both of them in his Church. For He warns the Jews to search the Scriptures, which He explained everywhere in their assemblies and applied to the salvation of the elect. So in Acts 8 He sends Philip the evangelist to the eunuch of Queen Candace, to explain to him that text from the prophet Isaiah which he was reading and which he could not understand sufficiently on his own, but which he came to understand when it was explained; and as soon as he understood it, he embraced it in true faith. And in Chapter 17, the people of Beroea are praised because they connected the teaching of Paul with the reading of Holy Scripture.

20. Now that this foundation has been laid as a premise, the second question which we must deal with here over against the papal teachers will be solved more easily, namely: Who is the lawful interpreter of Holy Scripture?

21. The papal teachers maintain that the Church is the highest, infallible interpreter of Holy Scripture; but when asked what they understand by "church," they admit that they do not mean the Church of the sheep, but of the shepherds. When asked again whether they mean any shepherds whatsoever, they usually take recourse in their "representative" Church, that is the bishops and prelates when these meet in council. And finally, when asked what they understand by "councils," they are compelled to reply that all councils are capable of erring, and therefore that they are unreliable interpreters of Scripture, unless they are approved by the pope. They hold the view that the pope passes a judgment in the councils and about the councils, like some king is used to judging in his own senate. Accordingly, all the power of deciding and judging rests with him, as if he alone is not able to make a mistake in the interpretation of Scripture—with the result that the distinguished name of Church, about which they tend to boast so much, in the end comes down to and ends in the name and person of the Roman Pontiff alone.

22. But that the Roman Pontiff is not the lawful and definitive interpreter of Holy Scripture is proved firstly by the fact that many Roman popes—as the canonical law itself and their own historians admit—were heretics; secondly, because many popes have published conflicting decrees, and because some have repealed the Instructions of others; thirdly, because many popes were wicked, unholy, criminal, and devoted to magic arts; and finally, because from among the popes many were patently unfamiliar with Holy Scripture, and in their decrees interpreted it most non-sensically and contrary to the straightforward meaning of Scripture. This is so obvious, that Bellarmine and other papist teachers are forced for that reason to take the position that the Pontiff is able to err in argumentations and presuppositions, but that in the conclusions—even though these are based on false premises!—they nevertheless always draw up true decrees.

23. Therefore in order to explain this question correctly according to the norm of God's Word, we say that Scripture is its own Interpreter, or rather, God, speaking in and through the Scriptures, who openly indicates his own will to the believers in the more transparent and indispensable passages, as

was demonstrated earlier, while in the more obscure passages He increasingly confirms his same will through a comparison of them with the more clear ones.

24. For just as some emperor or king is the judge and interpreter of his own will in civil disputes (not only whenever he is present and speaks to those who are present, but also when he does this through his written decrees or letters), so too God is not only the highest Judge of disputes and the Interpreter of his will, when He spoke with Moses, the Prophets and the Apostles, and through them to the Church, but also when through his written decrees and word entrusted to writings, He expounds his own will to the churches.

25. For Holy Scripture is not a speechless or dead thing, or one which cannot vindicate its meaning from people's spoiling influences, but: "The Word of God is living and effective, sharper than any two-edged sword, piercing to the division of soul and spirit, of joints and marrow, and discerns the thoughts and intentions of the heart" (as Paul testifies, Heb 4:12. And accordingly it is called the ministry of righteousness and of the Spirit (2 Cor 3:8,9), because by means of it the Holy Spirit has the power to effect truth and justice in people's hearts.

26. For this reason in Ps 50:4 "God calls upon the heavens above and the earth, to pronounce judgment upon his people," and in Isa 8[:20] He sends the Israelite people "to the Law and the testimony" to seek counsel of their God. And therefore in Ps 25[:12, 14?] Jehovah discloses "the sacred mystery to those who fear Him, and his covenant, so that he gives witness to them by experience." Therefore all who come to Christ are "taught by God" (John 6:[45]), and "if anyone is minded otherwise, God will reveal that to him also" (Phil 3:13[= 15]). In all these and many other passages it is stated that God himself performs what is brought to pass by the Word; because He, being present always to his churches through the Word and with his Word, works all these things in the hearts and gatherings of believers.

27. But because God, even if the growth comes from Him alone, still uses the ministry of men, and also their power of judgment—and accordingly Paul must plant while Apollos must water—therefore we freely confess that in the true Church of Christ there is also another kind of interpreter, namely "ministerial," and established under God and under his Word; and Holy

Scripture ascribes the power to judge to this kind of interpreter: 2 Chron 19:8; Ezek 44:24; Zech 3:7; 1 Cor 2:15; 1 Cor 10:15; and chapter 14:29, etc.

28. Moreover that power of interpretation or passing judgment is twofold: either public, or private; and both of them rest upon a special calling and gift.

29. The power of judging the right or wrong meaning of Holy Scripture in a private capacity in matters indispensable to one's salvation applies to all the true believers; for the strengthening of their personal faith and the upbuilding of another's, according to the law of love, the measure of the grace received, and the reason for a different calling. John chapter 10:3 and following clearly teaches this: "The sheep hear the voice of the true shepherd, and they follow Him, because they know his voice; but by no means do they follow a stranger, instead they flee from him, because they do not know the voice of strangers." And Matt 7:15: "Guard yourselves from false prophets." Paul speaks in this way in 1 Cor 10:15: "I speak as to sensible people; you yourselves judge what I am saying." 1 John 4:1: "Beloved, do not believe every spirit, but test the spirits, whether they come from God."

30. This type of judging rests on the gift that Paul calls discernment (1 Cor 2:15): "The spiritual man discerns all things," and Heb 5:[13–] 14 says: "Some are children who have need of milk; others are complete or mature, who through practice have their senses exercised for discerning good and evil," and by the same Apostle it is called "the testing of things that differ" (Phil 1:10): "And I pray this, that your love may abound more and more in knowledge and all feeling, that you may approve or distinguish the things that are a matter of dispute."

31. Yet this gift is not imparted to all believers in the same measure, but to some as adults and to others as children, as Paul testifies in Heb 5 (in the passage just quoted); nevertheless it is necessary that we acknowledge that there is at least some measure in all Christ's sheep and in all true believers. For otherwise their faith would not rest upon the Word of God, but on human testimony alone, contrary to the statement in Rom 10:17. And all sheep have some familiarity with the voice of their own shepherd, as Christ testifies in John 10[:4]; and also the children in the Church of Christ are able to discern true and nourishing milk from unhealthy and poisonous milk, at least in doctrines that are absolutely necessary for salvation.

32. The power to expound Scripture in public, and of publicly deciding upon the truth of interpretation, does not apply to everyone, but only to those who by their gifts and their calling have been trained for this task. Paul deals with the varying degrees of calling in Eph 4:11, 12, and 13. "Christ," he says, "has given some as Apostles, some as evangelists, and others as pastors and teachers, for equipping the saints, for the work of ministry, for the edification of the body of Christ, etc., so that we may no longer be children who float away and are carried about by every wind of doctrine, etc.," and in many other places.

33. The Apostle calls the gift that is necessary for this task "the gift of prophesying and instructing." And this gift includes the preceding one, namely, the gift of discerning and testing the spirits.

34. Paul speaks about this in Rom 12:6: "Having gifts that differ according to the grace that has been given to us: if prophecy, let one prophesy in proportion to his faith; if service, in serving; if teaching, in teaching." So too 1 Cor 14:3 and following: "He who prophesies speaks to men for their upbuilding and encouragement and comfort; he who speaks in a tongue edifies himself; he who prophesies, edifies the church, etc." And verse 29: "Let two or three prophets speak, and let the others judge," etc.

35. And yet we should not deny that among other Christians also throughout the ages there were people who through diligent reading and meditation upon the Holy Scripture, received the gift to interpret Holy Scripture for public benefit, and of testing the spirits, in greater measure than some pastors. And yet Holy Scripture in many passages (and also experience itself) witnesses to the fact that this gift must be sought among those especially whom God has called specifically to establish his Church publicly; for: "The lips of the Priest should guard knowledge, and the Law should be sought from his mouth, because he is a messenger of the Lord of hosts," as God himself teaches in Mal 2[:7]. And Titus 1:9 demands from all pastors that they should: "Hold fast to that trustworthy word, which makes for instruction in doctrine, that they will be able both to give instruction in its doctrine, and to confute those who contradict it."

36. However, both these gifts, and the competency to interpret, are subject to the Word of God, and to the Holy Spirit who is speaking in Scripture; for those who have been adorned with the gift of explanation and prophesying in public, develop their own judgment from Holy Scripture, and show to the

other believers its underlying support from Holy Scripture, and bring forward those teachings which subsequently the believers individually recognize as certain and true, through that gift of discernment and testing. Alternatively, if false teachers have not produced these conclusions with enough credibility from Holy Scriptures, or twist them into a strange meaning, then they reject and condemn them, as we have proved in thesis 29.

37. And yet we do not for that reason make anyone's personal thinking the highest judge of the faith of other individuals, much less of the entire Church, but only the Word of God and the Holy Spirit, who from out of Holy Scripture seals the same faith—at least in the necessary doctrines—upon the whole true Church and its individual true members, out of those same fundamental elements.

38. It is not fitting in this chapter to deal with the way in which controversies should be settled that sometimes arise in the Church of Christ about the teachings themselves of the faith from the same Scripture, and through the same guidance of the Holy Spirit. By God's grace this topic will be treated when we reach the chapter on church councils and governance.

39. In lieu of a conclusion we offer the following: That God through the Spirit and his Word is present to help his true Church (which is his house [cf. 1 Tim 3:15 and Titus 1:7]) so constantly that neither it, nor any living members of it should wander to their own destruction in at least the necessary elements of faith and morals. For otherwise the true Church of Christ would cease to be, contrary to Christ's promise in Matt 16:18: "The gates of hell shall not prevail against it," and in John 10:5: "In no way shall Christ's sheep follow another."

Corollary

1. Although Holy Scripture can be applied in many places for the use of the church anagogically, tropologically, analogically, and by similar modes of explanation, yet the only immediate and certain meaning of it is the grammatical or historical sense.

2. We are not permitted to build allegories on Scripture, unless where Scripture itself leads the way, or where a necessary reason taken from Scripture urges us to do so.

3. From the allegories and parables of Scripture no definitive arguments can be taken to confirm faith and morals if one looks at the circumstances of these allegories and parables. Nevertheless, if their primary objective and scope is considered, no less definitive arguments are taken than those from other places. And for this reason we say that this maxim of the Scholastics, "Parabolic theology provides no arguments," should be understood either in view of allegorical interpretations advanced by the human mind, or merely with respect to the circumstances of the allegories and parables.

DISPUTATION 6

ABOUT THE NATURE OF GOD
AND HIS DIVINE ATTRIBUTES

President: Antonius Thysius
Respondent: Ludwig Renesse

After the treatment of Scripture as the divine source of our knowledge of God, Disputations 6–9 treat the Triune God as the primary subject of Theology. As the first thesis of Disputation 6 states, the doctrine of God is a teaching fundamental to the Synopsis, and several other doctrines derive from it. In theses 3–8 the existence of God is demonstrated over against 'certain atheists.' For knowing God's essence we are entirely dependent on what He gives us to know. Therefore, the divine names by which God makes Himself known in the Old and New Testament form the introduction (10–16). Next, the divine essence is expressed in a simple but direct statement about God as Triune: Father, Son, and Holy Spirit (17–18). As a way to expand upon these statements, the Synopsis discusses two groups of divine 'attributes.' These attributes may be perceived as qualified, but should not be deemed separable from the essence of God; they approximate his essence 'relationally' (19–22). Attributes may be called 'incommunicable' insofar as they demonstrate the special character of God only, and his unique essence (23–29). God is different from us in that He is simple, undivided; He does not alter; He is infinite, eternal, and omnipresent. Scriptural proofs underscore God's greatness, patience, and truth. The 'communicable attributes' are properties that demonstrate how God does relate to external reality. These attributes include his life, wisdom, will, and power. There are also God's affections: his 'truth, love, goodness, gentleness, charity, generosity, mercy,' etc. (39). The perfection of God consists in all those divine attributes, as of one in whom there are no shortcomings (30–43). The disputation concludes with the enumeration of some heretical views (44–45).

1. In most-sacred Theology God is treated not only as the principle upon which it is constructed and the source of our knowledge of it but also as the

subject and the foremost, primary locus of theology from which all the others flow forth, by which they are held together, and to which they should be directed. Hence Theology derives its very name from this starting-point.

2. God is not simply the subject of contemplation in the sense that a metaphysical philosopher undertakes to reflect upon God and in the way God truly knows himself, and as we in the next life shall come to know God more fully (1 Cor 13:9, etc.; 2 Cor 12:4); but in the sense that to know Him in this life is what we have to do in order to obtain eternal life by truly knowing Him (John 17:3).

3. Furthermore, in Theology one should not ask "whether God exists," since Theology takes for granted that He does exist (as any science assumes of its subject), and since it is as clear as day that believers have no right to debate that question. Nevertheless, because of the foolish and devil-surpassing blasphemy of certain atheists who deny (although more as an attempt than as a result of experience) the existence of God (Jas 2:19; Ps 10:4; Ps 14:1; and Ps 53:2)—, we shall demonstrate his existence by two kinds of evidence: nature and reason.

4. The first evidence comes from our human nature, because the notion of God has been inscribed on the human soul as a first truth and a first principle (Rom 2:15), and since humanity is thus and so strongly inclined, and so disposed that to have observed this fact is to have proved the point (Rom 1:19; Acts 17:27, 28). And so experience and the common consent of all humanity prove that God exists.

5. In fact, nature and its order, that is, the whole world, display to us the wisest, most generous, and most powerful master-mind and designer, by its craftsmanship, order, disposition, by its adornment and its diverse uses; and especially the human being as a microcosm, who as the image of God displays God very closely (Job 12:7,8,9, etc.; Ps 19; Rom 1:20; Acts 17:26).

6. To this other arguments can be added, weighty and diverse ones. That is to say, one can reason from the movement of the universe (and especially the constant and regulated motion of the heavens) to the prime mover and the author of motion (who exists in actuality) (Aristotle, *Metaphysics*, book 12, chapter 6). One can argue from the sequence of efficient causes to the first efficient cause where the sequence stops, and on which the other causes depend. Or one argues from the goals to the final goal and the force that

determines the goal; from being, from the good, from perfection, up to the prime essence, the highest good and the most perfect nature. Or one can use the argument from the dread of the conscience as it fears the highest judge if sins have been committed, or from the terrible punishments whereby God punishes those scorning Him, and their heinous sins (Cicero, *On the Nature of the Gods*).

7. But this conviction of God's existence is maintained much more firmly by believers through the testimony of God and the light of faith, in keeping with the Apostle's statement: "For whoever draws near to God must believe that He exists" (Heb 11:6).

8. There are, however, also testimonies of God's existence in the manifest oracles, in the various works of creation and in the maintenance and ruling of the universe; the various appearances whereby He has revealed himself so frequently, as in visible shapes and in other modes (Exod 19:16; 20:19, etc.), the well-known miracles (Ps 72:18), prophetic predictions and their outcomes (Isa 41:23)—especially those of the promise of the Messiah and his appearing. And finally, in the inner, vivid and effective revelation of the Holy Spirit by means of these things. This revelation implants and produces a faith in us that responds to the divine testimony.

9. Thus God does exist, and we have knowledge of Him, wherefore the Apostle calls it "what may be known of God" (Rom 1:19). However, revelation can be viewed either as natural (Ps 19:2; Acts 14:15, 17, and 17:24; 1 Cor 1:21), which in the corrupt nature is only a partial, fickle knowledge, ineffective unto salvation (Rom 1:20); or as supernatural, which is unimpaired, reliable, and effective unto salvation in the elect (Ps 19:8; 1 Cor 1:21).

10. Reflecting the variety of different languages, this highest Being is called by different names for the sake of us humans (for otherwise God would be nameless, Gen 32:29)—although they have been drawn in the various languages from his different personal qualities, they conceptually agree. In Hebrew He is called *'Eloah* (rare in sacred Scripture), and from that *'Elohim* in the plural (often with the force of the singular). And that word is not derived from *'Ala*, that is, "He has sworn," but from the unusual root *'Alah* (with *mappiq he*), as it is employed by the Arabians to mean "to worship," as if to say, "to be worshiped," like the Greek *sebasma* [an object of worship] (2 Thess 2:4). From that some want to make the abbreviation, *'El*, that is

frequently used instead of the singular *'Eloah*, although others think that it is derived from the word for might.

11. In Greek He is *theos*, "God," which comes either from *theinai*, "to establish," as in Herodotus (*Histories book 2, Euterpe*), because He ordains all places and things, or from *thein*, "to run," as in Eusebius following Plato (Plato, *Cratylus*, Eusebius, *Preparation for the Gospel*, book 1), not because according to the ancients the gods are stars (as Plato maintains), but, as Eusebius has it, because He imbues everything with his strength and deeds of providence. Or it comes from *theasthai*, "to behold," as Basil has it (*Letter 141, To the Caesareans*), because He beholds and discerns all things; or from *deos*, "fear," not because—as he says irreverently—"Fear was the first to bring about the gods in the world," but because He is worthy of fear. Others add to these Greek terms a Hebrew sense, from *day*, that is, "it is enough," from where comes God's name *Shadday*. The Latins formed the words *deus* from the Greek by turning the aspirate ["th"] into the corresponding medial ["d"].

12. Now this name for God is exercised in two ways in the Scriptures, either essentially in the proper and usual way, or in an improper way. In the proper way, the word "God" is used either of the essence of the Godhead, when the word is taken generally without specifying the divine persons, as in "God is Spirit" (John 4:24), or personally, when the name of God is attributed to a certain person as subject, as of the Father (Rom 7:25, and 8:3), of the Son (1 Tim 3:16, Acts 20:28), and of the Holy Spirit (Acts 5:4). However, it is appropriated to the Father especially (Rom 1:1), both because of the relation between the persons, as well as because of the economy and plan that was established in order to maintain the mystery of our salvation.

13. In the improper and wrong sense the name "God" is bestowed on created beings, either by making it common with angels or people, on account of the surpassing dignity, power and management in which God has placed them, and which they carry out towards others. Or, when misapplied to false gods, out of misconception and error (John 10:34; Exod 22:28; Ps 82:6; 1 Cor 8:4,5); wherefore it happens that the name of God, which is the proper name for signifying his individual essence, has become a common appellative noun.

14. Therefore, in order to set himself apart from all who come by the name "God," He has defined his own name by means of certain personal properties, as when He calls himself "the God of Abraham, Isaac, and Jacob (or Israel)" (Exod 3:6); "the God of hosts" (Isa 1:24); "God of Gods" (Deut

10:17); "the true and living God." So too He calls himself *'El Shadday* (Exod 6), and simply *Shadday*, "all-powerful," from *shadad*, "he has laid waste," in the Chaldean plural form; and *'Adon*, "lord," *'Adonim*, and *'Adonai*, "lords," again in the plural form; and *'Eljon*, "the exalted."

15. God has set himself apart from everything particularly by his special name, that is, the *Tetragrammaton*—as the ancients called it—the word made up of four consonants *YHVH*, and in shortened form *Yah*, because as it is the proper name of God, it is incommunicable (Isa 42:8). And God gave this name to himself and introduced it to the people of God (Exod 3:15); it is well-known and it is to be used with reverence according to God's command (Exod 20:2,7), and once it was uttered both in public and privately, read out loud and so heard, and was familiar even to the neighboring peoples (1 Kgs 17:12; 2 Chron 6:32). At length, after the times of the Prophets, the Jews superstitiously started to reckon that the name belongs to the secret things, and they treated it that way to such an extent that it was mentioned solely on sacred occasions and then only by the priests, and in the end it ceased being spoken altogether. From where it is also called "inexpressible" and it was uttered by means of the substitute words *Adonai* (with *qamets*) and *Elohim* (with their vowel marks placed underneath it), by the Septuagint and the Latin Vulgate (Exod 3:6) where it says *'Adonai*. But if one may express it by analogy with the other names, it would sound *Yeheve* or *Yheve* or *Yave* or *Yihve*. Especially so because *'Ehye* and *Yihye* are one and the same name, with change from the first person (when God is speaking) into the third (as when Moses is commanded by God to speak to the people; Exod 3:14, 15). And yet we do not deny that by analogy his name can be written also *Yehova*; but not so *Yehovi*, because the analogy of the language does not allow that.

16. The name is derived from the word *Haja*, "to be," but the meaning of the name is unique (Exod 3:14). The Septuagint interpret "the one who is" in an absolute sense; John in Revelation more fully: "The one who is, and who was, and who is to come" Rev 1:4,8; and 4:8 and 11:17 and 16:5), so that it conveys the aspect of eternity. For the meaning of the name is that He exists truly and in eternity (so that it is a name for his very essence), and that He grants to every thing its essence. And in particular, its meaning is that He makes his promises to come about, and He reveals himself as faithful and true by fulfilling them. He displayed himself as such to his people when He caused the promise He had made to Abraham about the land of Canaan to be

fulfilled, and about sending the Messiah at last, etc.; while the deliverance from Egypt was a prefigurement of this (Exod 6:3, Maimonides book 1, chapter 60, Jer 16:14).

17. Taking the word in the proper sense of denoting Him, we shall describe God—who cannot be defined, inasmuch as He "surpasses every essence and is incomprehensible"—from the various descriptions of Him apparent throughout Scripture and collected together (Exod 34:6, etc.; Deut 10:17; Rev 4:8; Acts 17:24, etc.; 1 Cor 8:4,5,6; 1 Tim 1:17, and 6:15,16): He is a spiritual essence, entirely simple and infinite, that is eternal and immeasurable, and immutable; living and immortal, understanding, wise and all-knowing. He is goodness itself, love, kindness, mercy, forbearance, righteousness, and holiness, etc. He is one in essence, but three in persons: the Father who has brought forth the Son from eternity; the Son who is born of the Father; the Holy Spirit, who proceeds from the Father and the Son, who even proceeds from the Father through the Son. He is the Creator, the Preserver, and the Ruler of the universe, the Redeemer, Savior and the Glorifier of his elect.

18. This description of God comprises three parts: the revelation of the one Essence by means of various attributes; the enumeration of the divine Persons; and the revelation of his deeds. Leaving aside these latter two, for the present we shall treat the first part.

19. In using the phrase "divine Essence" we mean that what God is; for "to be" is said of Him (Heb 11:6, and "the one is and who was," Rev 4:8). To Him are attributed "nature," (Gal 4:8), and "divine nature" (2 Pet 1:4; although it is restricted to the divine properties), *theotēs*, "deity" (Col 2:9) and *theiotēs*, "divinity" (Rom 1:20), and to *theion*, "the divine" or "the godhead" (Acts 17:29), and *morphē theou*, "the form of God" (Phil 2:6); and He is called *theos*, "God" (Acts 17:24, 29). From and in this divine nature all things are and exist, everything by means of its own way of participation.

20. Moreover, the divine Essence is spiritual. For God is called Spirit in Scripture (John 4:24) in that body and anything corporeal, including its strength and movement is excluded from it (Luke 24:39; Isa 31:3). And moreover, just as He is not a body but a Spirit, so too He has no appearance, form or shape (Deut 4:12); and hence God cannot be perceived by the bodily senses. And indeed He cannot be seen, touched, or imagined, but He is invisible (Rom 1:20, 23; Isa 40:18; John 1:18; Col 1:15; 1 Tim 1:17) and can be grasped only by a pure mind and the soul. Yet according to the degrees of

external glory that are appropriate to Him (Exod 24:16; 33:18, 19, 20, and 23, where this glory is called the hindmost side, the back, and by facial features, Num 12:8, 1 Tim 6:16), He has allowed himself to be seen, but not in his highest glory. However, He is the author of all spiritual nature, wherefore He is called Father and God of the spirits (Num 16:22, and 27:16). And so we know who and what God is.

21. Furthermore, although this essence applies to God in an absolute way so that there is not one thing and another thing in God, but all what He is, is his essence, we nevertheless rightly assign to Him various properties or attributes, which are classified under the title of divinity (Rom 1:20), suggesting that there is a difference between essence and properties and between the properties themselves. Yet this is not a real distinction, but a relational or rational distinction, in so far as they differ in creatures and in our perception. With these properties God himself grants to us the knowledge of who God is and what He is like, and through these attributes we can distinguish the true God from the false ones and from all other things.

22. These attributes, then, are of two sorts: those of the first type are incommunicable, those of the second sort are communicable.

23. Those are called incommunicable which according to the proper and true sense of the words are not really imparted to created beings, but only partially and in a comparative sense—such as true simplicity (on which unity and immutability depend) and infinity, that is, eternity and immeasurability. One may distinguish these features in such a way that some are more general, since they concern more categories (namely, as indicating the negation of them) such as simplicity and immutability. Certain other ones are more specific, such as infinity (pertaining only to quantity) which comprises eternity and immeasurability. And these are infallible marks of the Deity.

24. Simplicity is an attribute of God's essence of the first type, and certainly one of the more general attributes, indicating that the divine essence is altogether without any composition, whether that composition be from material and integral parts, or from the essential parts of matter and form, from genus and difference, subject and accident, act and potency, and finally, essence and existence. Accordingly, it truly is a very simple essence. This is evident from the fact that besides being called Spirit (John 4:24) and Yᵉhova (Exod 3:14), He is called absolutely (without any adjective) "the being" (Isa 43:14[13]), and by the abstract names "life," "light," "love," "truth" (John

14:6; 1 John 1:5; 1 John 4:8; Jas 1:17), etc. From this all the degrees of simplicity in nature flow forth.

25. And again, just as his essence does not allow any composition, so too it does not allow any division in parts, species and number. And thus God is one (Deut 6:4; Mark 12:29, 32)—using the word "one" not in the sense of the first number but as the exact opposite of number. Thus there are not many gods, nor could there be many gods; and there is not any other god, let alone one beside or beyond Him, nor any with or before Him or anywhere else in heaven or on earth. But He alone is God, the one and only (1 Cor 8:4; Deut 4:35; Isa 45:5, 21; Deut 32:39; Exod 20:3; 2 Kgs 19:15; Ps 86:10; John 17:3).

26. The immutability of God is one of the more general attributes of God's essence. It entirely excludes alteration and change (Mal 3:6; Num 23:19), such as begetting or coming into existence, decay and death, growth and decrease, succession and transference (or change of place), alteration or variation, and passions. And it indicates that the essence of God stays the same (Ps 102:13,25, etc.; Heb 1:11). Hence God is called "I shall be," and He is called unchanging, incorruptible, and the same (1 Tim 1:17).

27. The infinity of God is a more particular attribute of God, since it concerns quantity in particular, whereby the divine essence is altogether free from any ending or boundary. That is, the essence is enclosed by no boundaries at all, namely of essence or size, of place, and lastly of time, but it surpasses every one of them. And according to this attribute nothing is equal to or on a par with God (Jer 10:6; Phil 2:6). It is divided into eternity and immensity.

28. Eternity is an attribute of the duration assigned to the essence of the infinite God, whereby his being is exempt from a temporal *terminus a quo*, a beginning, and a *terminus ad quem*, an ending; it is also free of any succession (i.e., former and latter), of bygone and future time. Accordingly the essence of God is now, and has been before now and shall be hereafter, and each of these infinitely, to such an extent that it embraces all parts of time at once, indeed that it surpasses all time—no rather, that it is unaffected by time. Therefore in Scripture He is called "the Ancient of Days" (Dan 7:9, 13); "His years have no end" (Ps 102:13, 27[28]) and "the number of his years is unsearchable" (Job 36:26; Gen 21:33). He has been from eternity, and He is in eternity, even before the ages, and He will remain in eternity. The King of the age and of all ages is from generation to generation; for ages and always

He is and was and will be, from before the world and everything in it. He dwells in eternity, and is simply called "the one who is, who was, and who shall be," "eternal and everlasting". He is called "the first and the last" (Ps 29:10, and 90:2; Rev 4:8; 1 Tim 1:17; Rom 16:26). Therefore He is the first being and is dependent on no-one.

29. Immensity is the attribute of the essence of the infinite God, whereby He surpasses all boundaries of essence. Properly speaking He is devoid of any size, and of measurement, of length, width and depth, and of parts and of a specific position in space—whether below or above, in front or behind. Accordingly his essence is here, and there, and elsewhere, and everywhere, and consequently omnipresent, embracing all places at the same time and surpassing them. In fact it is not spatial, and existing in and of itself, it embraces and contains everything. From this He is called in Scripture "exalted" (Gen 14:19, 20, 22), and He is called so great and so ample (Job 36:26; Deut 10:17[14]) that simultaneously He is in heaven above and on earth below, and in the depth of the sea; that He fills heaven and earth, in fact He is higher than the heavens, lower than the world below, and wider than the earth, broader than the sea. Heaven is his seat and the earth his footstool, and the highest heaven cannot hold Him (Ps 139:7; Jer 23:24; Job 11:8,9; Isa 66:1; 1 Chron 16:18 [more adequately: 1 Chron 16:14, 25 or 2 Chron 6:18]; Acts 19:28).

30. Attributes of the second sort, which pertain to quality, belong to God in such a way that they are communicated also to created beings to some degree, who thus actually participate in them. And therefore, because of the relation creatures have to God, these attributes are predicated of both God and creatures by way of analogy. Foremost of these are life, wisdom, will, and power; and because they are qualified by the attributes of the first sort they belong to God in the proper sense. And so no-one is considered similar to God (1 Chron 17:20; 2 Chron 6:14; Acts 17:29).

31. These attributes can be divided into those which point out God's immanent potency, strength, and activity. Life is immanent; it is an attribute of God's essence, displaying perfection in itself, whereby the essence of God is declared as full of activity in itself, that is, living—and that in the most simple or essential way; and by itself, unchangeably, or constantly and unendingly, that is, from eternity and without increase or decrease, and everywhere. From this it is said that God not only is living and alive (Deut

5:26; Acts 14:15; Num 14:21), but also that He has life in himself, and is life itself, and lives eternally, that He alone has immortality, and is incorruptible or immortal (John 5:26; 1 John 5:20; Deut 32:40), and that He is the author and source of all life in created beings, and life-giving, and that everything lives in Him (Ps 36:10; Acts 17:25, 28).

32. This life of God exists in intellect and will. The intellect, knowing, knowledge, and divine wisdom are a faculty or activity of God's life, and is first in nature and order. By this faculty the living God in his infinite essence understands, perceives and knows all things, namely himself, and all universal and individual things outside himself which can possibly exist and which He wills to exist. And these things which He performs or which He wills or permits to be done by his creatures and which do exist, including their causes, ways and circumstances, present, past and future things, great and small (through which the divine knowledge is not made worthless), and the thoughts of the rational creature, the recesses of the heart, the statements, attempts, deeds, beginnings, advancements, and endings (Ps 139:1, etc.; Job 34:21; Ps 44:22)—all these things He knows with a distinct knowledge, as most intimately familiar with things. Himself He knows directly and through himself; as regards the other things outside of himself, He knows indirectly what is good (since they bear his image) and what is evil He knows by their opposite.

33. Moreover, God exercises knowledge in a simple, single, immutable, infinite and eternal act; that is, He knows all things, always, immediately and at once, and necessarily (Acts 15:18; Heb 4:13). He knows everything in such a way that He is unaware of nothing, has to learn nothing, does not advance in knowing anything; He does not err, He supposes nothing, forgets nothing, and He does not remind himself of anything. Indeed, properly speaking He even does not have foreknowledge (Ps 90:4; 2 Pet 3:8; Isa 40:14), although in respect of future things it is rightly said that He does have foreknowledge, as well as that He remembers bygone events, knows the current ones—not successively (one after the other), or one thing by reasoning it from another, but He understands and sees one thing simultaneously with another. Therefore wisdom and understanding are accorded to Him (Rom 11:33)— and He is called "wise"—but wisdom also is with Him and from Him, and He is called "the only wise one" (1 Tim 1:17), "all-knowing," "knowing the hearts," and the source and fountain of all wisdom (Ps 147:4[-5], etc.; Dan 2:20, 21, 22; Prov 2:6; Acts 15:8).

34. God's will is the other faculty of God's life; it is the act that follows upon God's knowledge, whereby the knowing God wills and approves himself and all good things, as they accord with his nature and the structure of his mind, and whereby He necessarily disapproves of the things that are opposite to them. This is called the "approving will." And from the things He can do outside himself, He freely wills by his prior wisdom certain things, chooses them, decides to do them and actually does them which is called his "efficient will." And the will with which He wills and requires the good things He has commanded to be done by his creatures, is called "the commanding will." But the will according to a particular counsel to permit bad things which He forbids and which are yet done by his creatures, is called "the permitting will."

35. Moreover, what He wills, He freely wills, and He also wills it from eternity and immutably (Isa 46:10; Mal 3:6), and thus whatever He wills is not by compulsion or involuntarily (Matt 20:15); nor does any other initiative or prior cause force or drive God to will, but his will is the prime and highest cause (Eph 1:11). For what He wills He wills from himself and on account of himself; nor does He will contrary or contradictory things; nor does He will and not will the very same thing (Ps 89:35), nor does He now will or not will what He simply did not will (or did will) previously; nor does He will more or less things now than He willed before. And finally, his will cannot be hindered from being performed and completed regarding what He willed absolutely (Isa 14:27; Rom 9:19, and 11:29).

36. Thus far about the attribute that pertains to his immanent faculty and action. What follows explains the emanating potency, that is, the power that concerns and is practiced upon things that are outside of Him—whereby things can happen. Well then, the power of God is the attribute whereby the living, knowing, and willing God through his strength and potency has the power to perform deeds that are external to Him. This potency, when treated simply by itself and separate from the will, is absolute, and relates to all possibilities, and similarly does not relate to all that is simply impossible (Matt 3:9, and 19:26; Luke 1:37). However, when joined to the will it is actual (Ps 115:3; Eph 1:11), and it is exercised either without or with an intervening agent (for which reason He is called Lord Sabaoth, the God of hosts).

37. That power of God, then, resides in God in a simple, unchanging and infinite way, so that it is not on account of some quality that God is powerful, but by himself. He does not obtain his power from another but from himself;

it is not a passive power, but as "working within" (Eph 3:20). He does not start to be capable of something that He had not been capable of previously, but what He is able He has been able from eternity (Rom 1:20). He also could not be capable of more, or less, but He can do all things which He can to do, and He performs his power upon whatever He wills to be, and that without labor or effort. But in this exercise of his power, He can do other things and in another way, more, greater and more excellent things or minor or less things. Therefore Scripture even deprives God of inability, but ascribes to Him power, strength, firmness and efficacy (1 Cor 1:25; Eph 1:19; 1 Tim 6:15,16) and He is called powerful, only-powerful, and 'El Shadday, or all-mighty (Gen 17; Rev 1:8).

38. Closely linked to these two attributes (namely, the life of the knowing and willing God, and his power) is God's dominion: his strength, rule, and authority over everything outside of himself that He is able and willing to do, and does. This dominion, too, is everlasting and unchangeable. Therefore He is called Lord, and Lord of Lords, God of gods, King of kings (1 Tim 6:15), and He is said to have the most free and absolute power towards everything (Rom 9:21; Matt 20:15) which is to be without master and in one's own power. And every dominion issues from Him and is established by Him (Rom 13:1).

39. God's good affections (which in human beings are the passions), and the virtues of his intellect and will (which in mortals are the ethical and moral qualities which designate regulation of the affections), are: truth, love, goodness, gentleness, charity, generosity, mercy, and long-suffering, anger, hatred, justice, and also holiness, etc., and are truly and properly said of God (of course with the removal of every imperfection from them); and they are nothing other than God's ardent will towards us, and its power and effect in creatures. These are classified by different names, according to the variety of things that are their object, and according to the ways in which they are performed, and their various effects.

40. Truth, or veracity, is the virtue whereby God both in words and signs, in works and deeds, loves and exercises the truth—but most of all the virtue whereby He is willing and able to show his trustworthiness in his promises (Ps 145:13[17]; Rom 3:3,4).

Goodness is the virtue whereby He is able, willing and performing unto his creatures, both the acts of willing the good and doing the good (Exod 33:19; Rom 2:4).

Love is whereby He wills and approves the good in created beings and He abides in it; He wills, is able to present, and actually presents himself kind and gracious (though He does not have to do so). When applied to human being it is called philanthropy (Mal 1:2,3; Titus 3:4).

Compassion and mercy are whereby He wills, is able to provide, and actually does provide help to those who are wretched (Ps 136:1, etc.; Exod 34:5,6,7). Justice is the virtue whereby He deals with everything fairly, and whereby He decrees rewards for the upright, and punishment for the unjust, and whereby He wills to work retribution, and He does so powerfully (Ps 11:7, 119:137, and 145:17).

Anger is whereby He is disposed to punish the sinner and wills, is able to avenge and actually does avenge the sin.

Hatred is whereby He abhors the sin as well as the sinner, and whereby He is able and willing consistently to cast the wicked away from himself.

Holiness, finally, is the virtue whereby He, being most pure, approves everything that is pure, and whereby He is repulsed by its opposite. For this reason in Scripture God is called truthful, good, kind, the judge of the whole world, and the just judge, etc.; in fact, the only one who is truthful, good, holy (Rev 4:7; Rom 3:4; Matt 19:17), etc. And so concerning all that remains, He is the source of all truth, good, justice, and holiness.

41. Moreover, just as these qualities rightly are attributed to God, so too the vices opposite to these virtues are far from God: falsehood, injustice, and the rest (Num 23:19; 2 Chron 19:7; Rom 9:14). Therefore He is also called: "The one who does not know how to lie," "He who does not know how to be tempted by evils," and the One "of whom is denied that He is unjust" (Titus 1:2; Jas 1:13; Rom 3:5). Even regret, fear, grief, hope and desperation, and the likes are not found as befitting God's perfect nature (Num 23:19).

42. Finally, there are things predicated of God that actually denote perfection in created beings also (though not absolutely, but in some fashion appropriate to creatures), which do not apply to God properly, but because of some similarity to God they are expressed through figures of speech and metaphorically. Such are the names, parts, limbs, properties and actions of

inanimate and animate things, and especially of man (Ps 94:7[-9]). We may add to them the qualities which God in his dispensation makes his own, like a physical body that He assumes for the occasion, or speech, a voice, a word He formed in the air. All of these are said of God in an anthropopathic way, but they must be understood in a way that is appropriate to God and taken as indicating the properties and workings of God.

43. What is more, the perfection of God consists in all those divine attributes, as of one in whom there are no shortcomings. There is excellence and pre-eminence above all things, for nothing is similar or equal to Him. There is glory or majesty, whether inwardly in his personal properties, whereby He enjoys glory in himself (Isa 48:11), or outwardly, in unapproachable light (Exod 33:18, 22; 1 Tim 6:16). And there is blessedness in which He lacks nothing and enjoys in himself the fullness of all good things and abides in himself (1 Tim 6:15; Acts 17:25). And we must acknowledge only Him, and we must bless, honour, worship, and serve only Him, and adore, praise, invoke, and glorify Him in words and deeds (Rom 1:21; Titus 1:16). This is actually the goal and purpose of knowing God.

44. Opposed to this teaching are the following:

—   Atheism, that is the total denial of God.

—   Polytheism, or the completely fabricated construction of many Gods, as was done by the gentiles, whom Paul calls "without God; godless" (Eph 2:12), or by those who add false gods to the true God, as the Israelites did.

—   The idol-worship of the gentiles, and the Jews, who used to shape idols into gods, or by means of them worshiped gods, or even the true God.

—   Fantasizing about God, that is, although with some knowledge of the true God, yet not such as He really is and has revealed himself in his Word, but as someone imagines Him to be. Such the Samaritans once did (whose understanding is called ignorance of God, John 4:22), and nowadays the Jews and Mohammedans.

—   And finally, Epicureanism, that is, the denial of God's foreknowledge and providence, which essentially is the denial of God.

45. Likewise among Christians in former times there was the Manichaeans' heresy of the two principles: good and bad. The heresy of the Anthropomorphists, who ascribed to God a physical body; the papist *apotheōsis* of the saints. The worship of idols by the making of images and by worshiping God and the saints by means of images. And the heresy of those who make up a god different from the one He has revealed in his Word. Lastly, all blasphemies and false claims about God; and a crooked lifestyle— which itself is also called the denial of God (Titus 1:16).

DISPUTATION 7

ON THE HOLY TRINITY

President: Johannes Polyander
Respondent: Tobias Dammanus

Three disputations (7–9) are devoted to God the Triune God, and deal with the internal relations that constitute God's essence. The confession of the 'Three in One,' of the three persons in one essence, forms a succinct expression of the biblical revelation about God, Jesus Christ, and the Holy Spirit, and the inter-relations and distinctions between them. This seventh disputation offers an exposition of this Trinity of divine persons. Whereas the Synopsis stresses the biblical foundation for the teaching of the Trinity (33–35), it also is wary about conjectures concerning the precise nature of the relationships between the three persons (14, 35). That doesn't mean that technical and theological terms are avoided. Most of them are explained in the text itself; others deserve some elucidation to the modern reader. When speaking of each member in the Trinity, English often uses the word 'Person'; it is a rendering for what in philosophical discourse is called 'Subsistence' (a transliteration of the Greek word, 'hypostasis'), which connotes the singular instantiation of the essence. Each of the divine persons possesses intelligence and volition, and each is in reality distinct from the other persons to whom He relates. At the same time, the disputation states that the subsistence of each person of the Godhead resides in the subsistence of another; hence the term 'enhypostatic,' which means 'having subsistence within' (another). This is usually applied to the union of the dependent human nature with the independent divine nature in the person of Christ. In this disputation, it is applied to Father, Son, and Holy Spirit, subsisting in one another (20). The divine persons are distinguished from each other with internal and external marks (21). Internally, the Father is unbegotten, the Son is begotten, and the Holy Spirit flows forth from the Father and the Son (22–25). Although the outward workings of the three persons in part belong to the one essence which is equally common to the three persons, in part these workings are personal. In this way, for example, Creation is ascribed to the Father, Redemption to the Son, and Sanctification to the Holy Spirit (26). Each one of the divine persons is called the entire, complete God (29). The disputation then explains what it means that the entire divine essence exists in each of the divine persons from eternity (30–32). After the basic theological explanations, biblical material is adduced as evidence for the doctrinal statements (38–49).

1. Just as the Christian faith worships one God in Trinity, so too does it worship the Trinity of Persons in the unity of the divine essence.

2. In setting out to present the argument about this Trinity of divine persons, we shall consider first the words and then the actual subject-matter.

3. In Latin the word "person," like *to prosōpon* in Greek, has a two-fold meaning. For sometimes it stands for facial mask; a person's distinguishing features; or countenance, as in Acts 10:34. At other times it means subsistence endowed with reason, as in 2 Cor 1:11. Adjusting this word by means of analogy to the persons of the Trinity, it is with the latter meaning that we employ it.

4. Although the Greek word *prosōpon*, to which the noun "person" corresponds, when attributed to the divine persons does not occur in the sacred writings in precisely these letters or with as many syllables, there is a word which is equivalent to each in the Epistle to the Hebrews, in chapter 1:3, where Christ is called "the expressed image of the subsistence of the Father."

5. We make the same claim for the term "Trinity." For its synonym, according to the linguistic rule for cognates, is "three." For the number that counts in a concrete sense and the number that is counted as an abstraction are exactly the same in fact and meaning. The apostle John allots that number to the Father, to the Word or the Son, and to the Holy Spirit (1 John 5:7), when he says: "These three bear witness in heaven."

6. For this reason, just as "decade" can be assigned to ten things, so "Trinity" may be assigned to three; and just as the Apostle construes the word "Deity" from "Deus" (Col 2:9), so the orthodox church-fathers rightly construed "Trinity" from the word "three."

7. Although the later Greek church fathers made a careful distinction between essence and person by using the former term for absolute and shared nature, and the latter for a singular and relational nature, the Latins preferred to employ the term "person" on the grounds that—understood in the strict sense—it can be attributed equivocally to the first and to the second

substance (both the rational and the irrational), while "person" can be attributed only to the first and rational substance.

8. In general, "person" is defined as a substance, or individual nature, endowed with intelligence, subsisting by itself, really and truly distinguished from others by its own incommunicable property.

9. This definition, adjusted to any one person of the holy Trinity, is restricted in sense so that it is a divine substance endowed with intelligence, subsisting by itself, in reality distinguished by its own incommunicable property from the others to which it relates, and possessing in itself the same and entire divine essence from eternity.

10. In this definition there are five points which we should ponder. The first of them is that it is an independent substance, distinguished and circumscribed by some peculiar mode of subsisting, which the Greeks call "manner of existence."

11. A divine person or subsistence differs from the essence of God as something narrower and determinate than that which stretches out more broadly and is indeterminate.

12. However, it is not at all our view that a person or subsistence in this mystery amounts to the same as the first substance, or that the essence amounts to the same as the second substance. For the very essence of God is, in the highest possible degree, unique, individual, and singular, and therefore it can in no way be said of the three persons, just as species is not said of individuals.

13. And we think that one cannot state that the essence of God is imparted as something whole to the three divine persons, or that the persons exist in that essence like parts in a whole that they share. For since God's essence is infinite, and utterly incapable of being parted, it cannot be predicated of the divine persons as a whole is of its parts.

14. Therefore, as it cannot be explained by human reason, the mode of this mystery should be adored in humble faith, rather than be defined by risky statements.

15. Next, that subsistence must be ascribed to the Son and to the Holy Spirit as well as to the Father may be gathered from the fact that nouns as well as actions, which belong to self-subsistent individuals, are attributed to them.

16. For by means of the title, "Lord," which is appropriate to a subsistent person, Holy Scripture designates not only the Father and the Son, but also the Holy Spirit; this is evident from the comparison of these two parallel texts: Isa 6:8 and Acts 28:25. But the names of Father, Son, and Holy Spirit are only appropriate to subsistent persons (Matt 28:19).

17. Personal actions are: to appear before someone, to charge a certain duty by one's command, to assume the seed of Abraham, to take on the appearance of a dove. The first of these—depicted in Isaiah 6:8—is assigned both to the Son (John 12:14) and to the Holy Spirit (Acts 28:25); the second is assigned only to the Son (Heb 2:16); the third only to the Holy Spirit (Matt 3:16).

18. The second point we make in a description of the divine person is that it possesses intelligence and, consequently, volition. It is evident that this applies equally to the Father, the Son, and the Holy Spirit from the fact that everywhere in the holy Book the Son and the Holy Spirit are awarded the same descriptions of wisdom, knowledge, truth, counsel and goodwill as the Father is, as in Prov 8; Isa 12:2; John 14:17; 1 Cor 12:11, etc.

19. The third thing that should be noted in the definition of the divine person is that the person is in reality, by his incommunicable property, distinct from the other persons to whom he relates. The relative names "Father," "Son," and "Holy Spirit" affirm that this is correctly said of any person of the Trinity.

20. For although the divine persons differ from human ones in that in the latter sort, one person does not exist within another, the former persons are enhypostatic; that is, they exist mutually in one another, as Christ testifies (John 14:11): "Believe me, that I am in the Father and the Father is in me." They are, however, distinct from each other not only conceptually but also in reality, so that one of them is not the other, nor can he be.

21. The marks whereby these divine persons are distinguished from each other are either internal or external ones. The internal ones are recognized on the basis of three different characteristic properties, which connote their inward workings.

22. The first of these properties is that the unbegotten Father has generated the Son by the imparting of his own essence from eternity. The Greeks call this property of the Father "unbegottenness," and we, less fittingly, "incapable of being born."

23. The second is that the Son, begotten of the Father, participates in the same essence with the Father. The Greeks express this property of the second person with the word "birth," and we with "nativity."

24. The third is that the Holy Spirit flows forth from the Father and the Son. The Greeks call this property of the Holy Spirit "the proceeding," and we "procession."

25. With these three characteristic properties, which connote internal personal actions, the three persons of the Trinity are distinguished from each other not only by an internal distinction, but also by a mutual relation as if they are opposed to one another, namely the Father who generates, over against the Son who is generated, and both of them spirate, as distinct from the one who is spirated, and vice versa.

26. The outward marks whereby the distinction between these persons is noted are their outward workings; in part these workings belong to the essence, insofar as they go out from the principle of the whole essence, which is equally common to the three persons. In part they are personal, either insofar as one considers in them the order of the acting persons—like creation, which, regarding the order, is attributed pre-eminently to the Father (as the first person) or insofar as one sees in them the particular administration or dispensation of divine wisdom, regarding which the sending of the Son for the work of redemption is ascribed in particular to the Father, the redemption to the incarnate Son, and sanctification to the Holy Spirit.

27. The fourth observation we make in delineating the divine person is that He possesses the same and entire essence in himself. This is proper to the divine person in the fourth mode; and hereby He differs from a human person, who possesses the entire human nature with regard to the species, but a separate human nature with regard to the individual.

28. Therefore the essence is not something that in reality is abstracted or separated from the person, but it is distinguished from it only conceptually. For the mode of subsistence does not in reality divide the person from the essence, but it differentiates them only conceptually and notionally.

29. Hence each one of the divine persons is called the entire, complete God, in the Old Testament as well as in the New Testament, in terms of being a subject and its attributes (Gen 1:1; Acts 5:4 and 20:28).

30. The last thing we attribute to the divine persons is that the entire divine essence exists in it from eternity.

31. Therefore, one divine person has not arisen from another person at some specific point in time, as is the case with each and every human person, but He has always been in existence through an eternal sharing of the one and the same eternal essence with the other person.

32. Hence the essence of the one person is the essence of the other, and whatever is said about God collectively is declared also about any person of the Trinity individually, namely that He is most simple, infinite, eternal, immutable, endowed with intelligence, tenderhearted, just, good, holy, omnipotent, etc.

33. This Trinity of divine persons cannot, unlike the unity of the essence of God, be demonstrated from documented proofs in nature, but from what we can learn from Scripture alone.

34. For the book of nature shows to our human reason how the route rises up from created beings to God the Creator, as from effects to the prime and universal cause of beings (Rom 1:19, 20).

35. The book of Scripture, however, by the supernatural revelation of the Holy Spirit alone, conducts the Christian faith to that profound secret of piety about the one God who is threefold in persons—which cannot be comprehended by reasoning, nor be perceived by senses, nor be expressed in words, nor be taught by experience, nor be explained by an example.

36. The things that are said by Hermes Trismegistus in the Fourth Dialogue of the book entitled *Pimander* [iv.10.11], "that a Monad begot a Monad, and reflected his own ardour in himself," are so vague and ambiguous, that they can be dragged into having various meanings. They appear to have to be understood, as being about a production from an only god on account of his love for himself, rather than about what we believe: the production of the one and only Son from the one Father by generation, and of the Holy Spirit by procession from them both.

37. For although it appears that there are a few remnants of the purer Religion (either gathered from the Jewish tradition or from a reading of the Bible-books) in the works of the aforementioned Hermes Trismegistus, and in Plato, and in their followers, it cannot be shown from them that they

acknowledged three distinct persons in one Deity; rather they made up three different essences.

38. This mystery of the Trinity is handed down much more clearly, elegantly, and frequently in the New Testament than in the Old, because surely God was pleased to delay the full and complete revelation of this profound mystery until the coming of the Messiah.

39. Meanwhile we shall bring out several passages of the Old Testament from which the plurality and even the Trinity of persons can be gathered as foreshadowed by a plural number. These passages can be gathered together into six groups.

40. The first group is of those passages in which *'Elohim* is joined with Yehovah. For in them Yehovah stands for a single essence, while *'Elohim* stands for many persons distinguished within the essence, especially because adjectives and verbs in the singular are very often connected to the plural noun *'Elohim*.

41. Yet although *'Elohim* occasionally is expressed for only one person of the Trinity (as in Ps 45:7), nevertheless the title does not function exclusively, but inclusively through a synecdochical expression, whereby the other persons are included within the name of one person by metonymy—sometimes on account of the unity of essence that is common to the three persons, sometimes on account of the mutual interexistence of the persons.

42. The second group is of those passages in which God speaks specifically about himself in the plural number, as in Gen 1:26: "Let us make man in our own image," and Gen 3:22: "Behold, Adam is like one of us," and chapter 11:7: "God said, 'let us go down and confuse their speech'," etc.

43. No example like this can be found in Holy Scripture even for those overly pretentious kings, but to the contrary, it can be shown that they spoke about themselves in the singular number, as is evident in Gen chapter 14, 20, and 41; Dan chapter 2 and following, 2 Chron 36; Ezra chapter 1, 6, and 7.

44. As for the other kings whom the Jews cite in objection to us (2 Sam 16:20, Job 15:3 [Job 15:18?], Dan 2:36, Song 1:4), it can be proven from the circumstances in those passages that these kings were speaking not specifically about themselves only, but also figuratively about other people whose persons they were representing.

45. The third group is of those passages in which the name Yehovah and "God" is repeated on three separate occasions in one sentence, as in Num 6:23, 24, 25, and 26: "Thus you shall bless the sons of Israel: Yehovah bless you, and guard you; Yehovah make his face to shine upon you, and be gracious towards you; Yehovah lift up his countenance upon you, and give you peace."

46. The fourth group is of those in which God is adorned by three invocations appropriate to him, as in Isa 6:3: "And the Serafim were calling to one another: 'holy, holy, holy, the Lord God of hosts.'"

47. The fifth is of those in which the Lord is talking about the Lord, as in Ps 110:1: "The Lord said to my Lord: 'sit at my right hand';" Hos 1:7: "Thus says the Lord: 'I shall pity the house of Judah, and I shall save them by the Lord their God.'"

48. The last group is of those passages in which more persons are addressed separately and by different names, such as Yehovah and the Angel of Yehovah and of the face of Yehovah, Wisdom, the Son, the Word of Yehovah, and the Spirit of Yehovah (Gen 48:16; Exod 14:19, and 23; Ps 2; Prov 8 [:1, 12, 14]; Isa 63:9; Hag 2:6, 8, etc.).

49. The proofs from the New Testament can be read in Matt 3:16, 17, and 28:19; John 14:16, and 15:26; 2 Cor 13:13; 1 John 5:7; Rev 1:4,5, and very many similar passages that are not unfamiliar to the devout Christian reader.

50. From the above-mentioned assertions consistent with the divine Word it follows that the idea of all the Antitrinitarians (both the ancient as well as the more recent ones) is false and blasphemous, along with the opinion of the Socinians nowadays, who hold that there is only one divine person, namely, God the Father of our Lord Jesus Christ. They abuse the testimonies of Holy Scripture (wrongly understood) in order to prove this, such as John 17:3, 1 Cor 8:6, Eph 4:6, and similar ones, wherein the God upon whom Christians call is separated from the false gods whom the gentiles worship by this epithet and expression that is common to the three divine persons: That He alone is true God. And it is for this reason that the Father is placed exclusively over against the idols, and not over against the Son or the Holy Spirit.

CONCERNING THE PERSON
OF THE FATHER AND OF THE SON

President: Antonius Walaeus
Respondent: Antonius Scriverius

The Trinity remains a mystery, but some things can and may be elucidated. In disputation 8 Walaeus explains how the Son was 'generated' by the Father from eternity, and how the individual, personal dimensions are to be distinguished from their essential qualities. Why do we call the Father the 'first person' of the Trinity (2–13)? As He shares the same essence and is equal with the Son and the Holy Spirit (14–31, 34), how can He be 'in reality' distinguished from them through his own characteristic properties at the same time (20–21, 31–34)? Why is it impossible to think of the Father apart from the Son (10)? Arguments from Scripture play an important role in the explanation of the Trinity (e.g., 9–10, 22–23, 27–30, 32). In cases where Scripture is not fully transparent and distinct, the Synopsis 'prefers an honest admission of ignorance to an all too daring assertion' and 'to await eagerly that day when we shall see God face to face, and when we shall know perfectly and fully what we know only in part here.' (17) But over against 'all the recent and the ancient heretics of every kind' the conclusion is maintained 'that Jesus Christ the only-begotten Son of God, is the one and eternal God with the Father, who in the same divine essence exists in a distinct mode of subsistence, to whom with the Father and the Holy Spirit be the honour and glory for ever and ever' (34).

1. As we treated the mystery of the holy Trinity in the preceding disputation, the previously established order requires that we deal now with the person of the Father and the Son, separately.

2. When we call the first person in the most holy Trinity "Father," we do not refer to created beings, which have been produced by God out of nothing. Nor do we use it as referring to believers whom God has adopted as his

children, and whose God the Scriptures sometimes indeed do call "Father." But we use it in relation to the Son who was begotten by Him from eternity, and we employ the term "Father" in a hypostatical or personal way.

3. It is generally acknowledged by all Christians that the person of the Father truly is a person, and that his origin comes from no other person. Therefore, when it is stated that He comes from himself, and He is called "self-grown and self-generated" by some orthodox teachers, it must be taken in a negative sense, and not as a positive affirmation. For without a doubt He comes from no-one, but He is in subsistence from himself and through himself from all eternity.

4. And no Christian has called into question his true and eternal Deity, except that the Marcionites and those like them have sacrilegiously fantasized that one God is the creator, and the author of the Old Testament, but another God is the Father of Jesus Christ and the originator of the New Testament. This is contrary to the consensus of the entire Holy Scripture, which everywhere presents one God the Father to us, and consistently provides evidence that the same person is also the Father of Jesus Christ and author of the New Testament, in particular Christ himself (Matt 11:25; John 8:54) and also the apostles (Acts 8:14; Gal 3:17; Heb 8:8, etc.).

5. Moreover, we say that the Father is the first person; firstly regarding his subsistence, which comes from no other person, and from which the other persons have their own origin. We say this secondly regarding the divine operations that are outwardly directed, and that derive from Him as if from a fountainhead through the Son and the Holy Spirit. And we say this thirdly regarding the order which the Holy Scripture employs it everywhere, most notably in the formula for our baptism (Matt 28:[19]).

6. And the property characteristic and internal to the Father, whereby He is distinguished from the Son and the Holy Spirit hypostatically, is active generation. For though active spiration also applies to the Father, nevertheless that property is not a characteristic of Him, because He shares it with the Son.

7. Well then, this active generation is the internal and personal action of God the Father, whereby in a spiritual and indescribable manner He has, from eternity and from himself, begotten his own Son in the same essence, as his own image, and through that generation He made Him share the same

infinite essence entirely. We should explain and prove the individual elements of this definition more carefully.

8. When we call this internal and personal generation the action of God the Father, we distinguish it from the creation and governance of things that are performed outside of God and his essence. We distinguish it also from the internal and immanent essential actions of God, such as the eternal foreknowledge of all things (Acts 15:18), our election from eternity (Eph 1:4), the eternal pre-ordination of the Lamb that would be slain for us in the fullness of time (1 Pet 1:20, etc.). These actions, while immanent and eternal, belong to the essence and are shared by the persons, because they are carried out upon created beings, or at least with respect to them. Even so, in them one is able to assign a peculiar and proper mode of action.

9. We supply very many proof-texts of this generation from Scripture, such as Ps 2:7: "You are my Son, today I have begotten you." Prov 8:22: "The Lord possessed me at the beginning of his way," and verse 24: "When there were no depths, I was brought forth" or conceived. Mic 5:1 [= 2]: "His origin is from the beginning, from the days of eternity." For that reason, the Son of God is called "only-begotten" and also "only-begotten of the Father" (John 1:14), and likewise "God's own Son" (Rom 8:32) and "begotten before all creation" (Col 1:15) and the Father is called "his own Father" (John 5:18). The same is shown, albeit figuratively—by the names that are given to Him: "Wisdom," "Word," "Image," "character," and "radiance" (Prov 8, John 1, Col 1, and Heb 1). These clearly show his origin and this offspring.

10. The same proof-texts show also the eternal nature of this generation, besides the many others that are produced to support the eternity of its subsistence. In fact, even the very nature of this generation requires it. For since we must posit that this generation, no less than God the Father himself, is necessarily devoid of all change and variation, it follows that it is wholly free from any beginning in time. For it is impossible to think of the Father apart from the Son.

11. But just as this generation lacks any starting point in time, so too we must necessarily grant that it lacks any ending, since the foremost property of eternity is that it is "all at once" and "free from any limit." Therefore, in the act, just as in all spiritual generation, it is continuous and in its outworking, it is always perfect. In a similar fashion the sun produces its light constantly and unfailingly, without any weakening or strengthening. For otherwise there

would be a change in God the Father when He begins to generate, is in the process of generating, and stops generating. Therefore, also the ancients wisely understood the passage, Ps [:7]: "Today I have begotten you," as about this act of generation that is eternal and always the same.

12. When we say that this generation is internal and spiritual, we mean something different than the offspring of corporeal entities in which what is born issues forth outside the body of the one that is giving birth. We also mean something different from the opinions of various heretics who on this point have dreamt up some "flowing forth," "flowing down," or "some partitioning" of divine essence. This point is proved by the identity of the divine essence in the Father and the Son, which we shall provide with irrefutable arguments a little farther below. Similar proof is in the comparisons supplied by Holy Scripture on this subject-matter; these are presented in thesis 9 above. And lastly, the point is proved by clear passages of Holy Scripture, especially the words of Christ in John 10:30, where He asserts that his power is the same as that of the Father. And in verse 38 He testifies that the Father is in Him, and He in the Father; and "that the Father dwelling in Him does these works" (John 14:10), which the Greeks call mutual interexistence, and the Schoolmen, "mutual circumincession" [co-inherence].

13. What has been stated here easily pulls apart the twisted ploy whereby the Arians once tried to entangle the ancient fathers. That is: Whether the Father begot his Son by willing so or by not willing so. And also that it cannot be said that He who did not so will it, begot Him, and not even by so willing it, because the acts of the will are free, and consequently it is possible that they are not. For the true and certain answer is this: That God the Father begot his own Son by nature, even as He is good, just, and wise by his nature. To be sure, his will always accompanied and approved this generation, as it does also his goodness, justice, and wisdom—but it did not precede or produce it. Hence also the Son is called the Son "of his pleasure" and "of his love" (Matt 17:5; Col 1:13).

14. The equality of the Son with the Father proves definitively that the Father shared his entire essence with his Son through this eternal generation. In John 5:18 it says that "He had made himself equal"—that is, by what he himself said—"to God;" and Phil 2:6: "He did not consider being equal or on par with God something to be grasped." John 5:20[–23]: "The Father loves the

Son and shows Him all that He himself is doing, etc., for just as the Father raises the dead and gives them life, so also the Son grants life to whom He wishes, etc., that all may honour the Son, even as they honour the Father." Other clear manners of expression, which Scripture employs elsewhere, prove this too, such as John 5:26: "Even as the Father has life in himself, so also He has granted the Son to have life in himself." And John 10:30: "I and the Father are one," namely, in power, and therefore also in divine essence, since in verse 33 it is rightly inferred by the Jews themselves. And John 16:14: "He himself"—namely the Holy Spirit—"will glorify me, for He will take what is mine, and He will declare it to you. All that the Father has is mine; therefore I said that He will take from what is mine and declare it to you."

15. Concerning the manner or shape of this generation the ancient church-fathers long ago ventured to debate the Arians and Samosatenians, and many among them (whom also the Schoolmen followed), stated that the Father had begotten his Son in the same essence, since He knows and beholds himself fully and perfectly in his eternity and infinity in a way that cannot be explained. And in the same manner as our soul ponders and knows itself through reflection, and fashions in itself some image of itself (even though it is neither complete nor has a distinct existence), so too God the Father, since He knows himself in the most lofty and divine—and thus inexplicable—manner, has eternally produced and produces an image of himself that is most perfect, one that exists distinctly. They [the church-fathers] likewise perceived that the Holy Spirit, through the mutual love of the Father and the Son, proceeds from them both.

16. From there they also noted the two-fold distinction between the generation of the Son and the production of the Holy Spirit. 1) That for a true generation only one active principle is required, but in the production of the Holy Spirit two persons act in unison together. 2) That for a true generation a likeness or image of him who is producing is required in him who is produced. This image, however, is found in the action of the intellect, not in the natural action of the will.

17. They gathered this manner of production from an analogy to the mind of humans, who more so than all other creatures bear the image of God; and from the epithets and names whereby Holy Scripture denotes the Son of God in particular. Namely, when it calls Him the wisdom of God (Prov 8:1; 1 Cor 1:24), the Word, or the Word of God (John 1:1), the brilliance of his glory

and the stamp of his nature (Heb 1:3), the image of the invisible God (Col 1:15). All of these texts seem, so to speak, to lead the believer's mind by the hand to this conclusion. Moreover, the word "power" rather than "love" is used for the Holy Spirit (Luke 1:35). But because Holy Scripture does not make this claim so transparently and distinctly, we judge that an honest admission of ignorance is to be preferred to an all too daring assertion. And we prefer to await eagerly that day when we shall see God face to face, and when we shall know perfectly and fully what we know only in part here.

18. From the fundamental observations that were put forth previously it is clear whether or not the Son of God is rightly called "God of himself." Certain Jesuits, in line with that scurrilous Génébrard, maliciously accused Calvin of holding the latter view, even though Bellarmine pleaded in his defense. For we assert that, if one considers his deity or essence as absolute, the Son of God rightly is and is called *autotheos* [God of himself] as some of the church-fathers also called him in this regard. Yet, if you consider the same essence as existing in the Son under a certain and distinct mode of subsistence, then He is God of God, light of light, as defined in the Nicene Creed.

19. The things said thus far about the person of the Father also make plain to us what is to be known about the Son of God, because it belongs to the nature of related persons that they exist and are known at one and the same time. However, in order that this orthodox doctrine may be established much more firmly against ancient as well as contemporary heretics, we must explain some additional points about Him.

20. Well then, the Son of God is the second person of the Trinity, begotten of the Father from eternity, of the same divinity and essence with the Father, and yet in reality distinguished from the Father and the Holy Spirit through his own characteristic properties. Several elements of this definition are clear enough from what has preceded, but the ones that are in need of further proof will be put forward in what follows.

21. For the sake of good order, we shall summarize these elements under the two following headings. First we shall prove over against the Samosatenians, Arians and Socinians, that the Son of God is truly "of the same substance" [*homoousios*], that is, of the same essence and divinity as the Father. Next, contrary to the Sabellians and Servetians, that He is still a true person, and distinct from the Father.

22. That the Son of God is truly and absolutely of the same substance as God the Father is proved by the following two unshakable fundamental arguments. The first comes from the various places in the Old Testament where the very same things that are known and predicated about the true and eternal God and Father are asserted in the New Testament as known and preached about Jesus Christ the Son of God. This fact could not occur upon any grounds unless both have the same essence and divinity.

23. From the many places of this sort we furnish only these three: Num 14:22, Ps 95:8, Isaiah 63:10; and in many places elsewhere it is stated that the true Yehovah and God of Israel is tested by the Israelites in the desert, but Paul in 1 Cor 10:9 says with clear words that it was Christ whom they had tested in the desert. In Ps 102:26 [25] this is stated about the true Yehovah and God of David: "From the beginning you, Lord, have laid the foundation of the earth, and the heavens are the works of your hands. They will perish, but you remain, etc." These words are spoken about the Son of God, as the same apostle clearly testifies in Heb 1:10. In Isaiah 6 the Lord appears to the prophet seated upon the throne of glory, and surrounded by a throng of Cherubim, and He sends him to the people of Israel to pronounce divine judgments against their hardness of heart. But John in chapter 12:41 states that "Isaiah said these things because he saw his—that is, Christ's—glory and testifies concerning Him."

24. The second foundation is taken from the names, properties, works and divine veneration that are shared in common by the Son and the Father as true and eternal God.

25. For to whomever the names that suit God are attributed absolutely and simply—as well as the essential properties of God, the truly divine works and the veneration that befits God alone—He is true, eternal and coessential God with the Father. And all these are indeed attributed to the Son of God as one, and without reference to another. Therefore, the Son of God is true, eternal, and coessential God with the Father.

26. The major proposition of this syllogism is self-convincing. For since there can be only one God who does not bestow his own glory upon another [Isa 42:8, 48:11], and since through these signs of recognition He sets himself apart everywhere from created beings and from imaginary gods, it follows necessarily and without question that He to whom the same things are attributed as to the Father, is of the same essence and divinity as the Father.

And the minor proposition rests upon the many clear and reliable places in Holy Scripture, from which the following ones are enough.

27. The names which are proper to God, and which are shared with the Son either absolutely or with the sort of epithets that apply to no one else, are, among others, these: The name of Yehovah (Jer 23:6): "and He will be called Yehovah our righteousness." The name of God, either as an attribute, as in John 1:1: "The Word was God," or as a subject, in Acts 20:28: "God redeemed the Church with his own blood." See also Ps 45:7 and 1 Tim 3:16. The name Lord, in Ps 110:1: "The Lord said to my Lord," and in combination: "My God and my Lord" (John 20:28). And He is also called "He who searches the kidneys and hearts" (Rev 2:23). "King of kings and Lord of lords" (Rev 17:14, etc.; 19:6). "The beginning and the end, Alpha and Omega, the first and the last" (Rev 22:13). Likewise, by Paul: "God to be praised above all" (Rom 9:5). "Lord of glory" (1 Cor 2:8); "God the great" (Titus 2:13), and lastly by John he is called: "The true God and life eternal" (1 John 5:20), etc.

28. Throughout the Scriptures the essential properties of God are also shared with the Son; they are of the following sort. Eternity (John 17:5): "Father, glorify me in your own presence with that glory which I had with you before the world existed." And Col 1:17: "He is before all things." (More about this attribute in thesis 9 above). Infinity and omnipresence, Matthew 18:20: "Where two or three are gathered in my name, there I am in their midst," and chapter 28:20: "I am with you every day until the closing of the age." Thus, in John 3:13 He was speaking upon this earth with Nicodemus and yet "He was in heaven." Omniscience, even of a person's thoughts, John 2:24: "Christ did not trust himself to them, because He himself knew them all." And 21:17: "Lord, you know everything; you know that I love you." Omnipotence, John 10:29: "The Father is greater, or more powerful, than all, etc." "I and the Father are one." In Philippians 3:21 capability is attributed to Him, "whereby He is able to subject all things unto himself." Such a property is also his immutability: "You are the same and your years do not fade away" (Heb 1:12). And Heb 13:8: "Christ Jesus is the same yesterday, and today, and forever."

29. The works proper to God are also everywhere attributed to the Son. Such work is the creation of the world, John 1:3: "All things were made through Him." Col 1:16: "Through Him all things were created that are in heaven and

on earth, visible and invisible." The maintenance of all created things, in Col 1:17: "All things hold together in Him." Heb 1:3: "He upholds all things by the word of his power." Such work is the revival of the dead, John 5:21: "For as the Father raises the dead and gives them life, so also the Son grants life to whomever He wills." And John 6:40: "I shall raise him up on the last day." So too the sending of the Spirit, John 16:7, and the performing of many other divine miracles, Mark 16:20, etc. Such works also include our sanctification and glorification, which everywhere in the Scriptures are ascribed to Christ, and yet in other places they are claimed as proper to God.

30. And finally the veneration that is appropriate and peculiar to God, is also conferred upon the Son no less than upon the Father. Such veneration includes adoration and prayer, Acts 7:59: "And they stoned Stephen as he was praying, saying: 'Lord Jesus, receive my spirit.'" And in Acts 9:14, Ananias says about Saul: "He has received the power to bind everyone who calls upon his name." And so Paul everywhere calls upon Him at the beginning and end of his letters, and he gives the same thanks and praise to Him as to the Father, which also the saints in heaven do (Rev 5:9), as well as all the angels of God (Heb 1:6, and Rev 5:12), etc. Thus, we are also "baptized into the name of the Son," just as into the name of the Father and the Holy Spirit (Matt 28). In Him we believe, John 14:1: "You believe in God, believe also in me." In Him we hope, 1 Cor 15:19: "If in this life only we hope in Christ, we are of all men most wretched." No indeed, all are bound "to honour the Son, even as they honour the Father" (John 5:23).

31. What we have brought forward thus far proves irrefutably before the consciences of all people who desire sincerely to subject their own faith to the Word of God that this basic article of our faith is firm and sure. It remains for us now briefly to prove against the Sabellians and the followers of Servetus that the Son of God is a true person and distinct from the Father.

32. The conditions that are required in a real person show that He is a true person. For He is an individual, who exists through himself, "because before Abraham was, I am" (John 8:58). He is alive, "for the Father has granted Him to have life in himself" (John 5:26). He has understanding, "for He knows everything" (John 21:17). He has a will, "for the Son grants life to whomever He wills" (John 5:21). He possesses the power of doing, "for He has the power of laying down his own life and of taking it up again" (John 10:18). He

performs action, "for whatever the Father does, that the Son does likewise" (John 5:19).

33. All of the passages adduced above also prove clearly and without a doubt that He is a person distinct from the Father. And besides these there are the passages which testify that He is in the presence of the Father, in the bosom of the Father, the Son of God, sent by the Father, another witness from the Father, sending the Holy Spirit from the Father, the expressed image of the Father. Likewise, the places in which the Father is said to have created all things through the Son, that in Him and through Him He has chosen us, that He has reconciled us in Him, and similar countless places which occur everywhere to the reader of the Holy Scriptures, and indicate an explicit distinction.

34. Therefore we conclude contrary to both all the recent and the ancient heretics of every kind, who have stumbled over this corner-stone upon which the entire house has been founded and built up, that Jesus Christ the only-begotten Son of God, is the one and eternal God with the Father, who in the same divine essence exists in a distinct mode of subsistence, to whom with the Father and the Holy Spirit be the honour and glory for ever and ever, Amen.

ON THE PERSON
OF THE HOLY SPIRIT

President: Antonius Thysius
Respondent: Franciscus Josius

The Holy Spirit is the third Person of the Trinity. He proceeds by means of spiration from God the Father and the Son from eternity (4); He shares the single and entire divine essence (8, 22–28). The Spirit has his own substance and life, understanding, will, power, actions, and effects, and therefore is a person (or, subsistence): an individual instance of the divine essence, distinct from the Father and the Son (5–7). The disputation then goes into detail about the nature of how the Spirit is distinguished from the Father and the Son, namely by proceeding 'from the Father, through the Son' (8–20). On this issue the Synopsis displays an ecumenical attitude. The debate between the Eastern and Western traditions of the Christian Church regarding the relationship between the Holy Spirit and the two other Persons of the Trinity is presented considerately, with an acknowledgment of the complex manner in which the Holy Spirit proceeds from the Father and the Son (15–20). In the work of redemption, the distinct origin and order of the persons inside the Trinity is reflected toward the outside: the Father assumes and accomplishes the role and office of God who has been angered and who must be appeased and who is the source of our redemption; the Son assumes and accomplishes the role and office of redeemer and mediator; so too the Holy Spirit assumes and accomplishes the role and office of the one who applies the merit and benefits obtained by Christ and who illuminates and sanctifies our life (21). Over against all old and new heretics it must be maintained that the Holy Spirit to such an extent is in God, from God, and of God, that He is God (28–29).

1. Since we have treated the three persons of the Godhead (first jointly and then separately about the Father and the Son), it follows that in this disputation we treat the Holy Spirit in a similar fashion.

2. Although it is obvious that the word "Spirit" must be kept detached from any notion of a created being, nevertheless because some kind of analogy exists between a created being and God it will not be unreasonable to explain them generally. Well then, the proper sense of the word *a, pneuma, spiritus*, is "a blowing," and thus a fine and powerful essence—whether it be the wind (Gen 8:1, John 3:8) or the breath of a living being (Isa 2:22). And from there it comes to mean figuratively the soul of a person (Ecc 12:7; Luke 23:46; 1 Cor 2:11) or of an angel (Heb 1:7, 14); but also the zeal of a creature, a state of mind, and a lively stirring (Hag 1:14).

3. From there transferred via a suitable analogy to God, the word signifies the divine essence taken in an absolute and general way (John 4:24), the characteristic of his essence, the power and strength that resides in God or that is disclosed to creatures. Or, taken in a relative way, it signifies the third person of the divinity: the Spirit of God (Gen 1:2; 1 Cor 2:11) and of the Lord (Isa 61:1), and the breath of the Almighty (Job 33:4)—namely with a relation to the God who breathes, "the Spirit," that is, breathed by God. He is called also Holy Spirit (Isaiah 63:10) and Holy Spirit of God (Eph 4:30) because of his nature, office, and effect. For that reason also the new man who is reborn, and even the renewed and sanctified activities come by the name "spirit" (John 3:6). And it is according to this relative sense in God that we take it here.

4. The Spirit of God, then, or the Holy Spirit, is the third *hypostasis*, that is, person, of the Godhead or the most holy undivided Trinity, who proceeds by means of inexpressible spiration from God the Father and the Son effortlessly and from eternity. And so He is distinct from the particular person of them both, and joined to them through a unity and sharing of essence.

5. The definition of a person, and everything belonging to a person, demonstrate and prove that He is a *hypostasis*, or person, and a divine one at that. Such things include: substance and life, as He is the author of all being and life—"Send forth your Spirit, and they will be created" (Ps 104:30). Understanding: "He searches and knows the deep things of God" (1 Cor 2:10). Will: "He distributes to each one individually as He wills" (1 Cor 12:11). Power, actions, and effects, such as creation, regeneration, sanctification, etc. (1 Cor 12:11). Similarly, that He testifies about Christ, glorifies Christ, teaches the Apostles, and shows the way to all truth, brings consolation, declares to

them the future, convicts the world, etc. (John, chapters 14, 15, 16). And also whatever happens concerning Him, the fact that He appeared in the guise of a dove, of the wind, and of tongues of fire (Matt 3:16, Acts 2:[2–]4), that He is aroused to anger (Isa 63:10), that He is grieved (Eph 4:30), that sin and blasphemy are committed against Him (Matt 12:31–32), and other things which properly belong to a person are applied to Him.

6. In fact He is a person distinct from the Father and the Son. For He is not the Father or the Son, but one other than the Father and the Son, John 14:16: "I shall ask the Father, and He will give you another Paraclete." The Father and the Son send Him; He comes, John 15:26: "But when the Counselor comes, whom I shall send from the Father." Surely the Father and the Son who send and He who comes are different persons. And also, whenever Holy Scripture speaks about the entire Trinity, it presents the Holy Spirit as a person distinct from the Father and the Son (Matt 3:16, and 28:19).

7. Among the divine persons He is the third (Matt 28:19), not by a difference in nature or a disparity in majesty, but by the order of subsistence— wherefore He is also called the third person.

8. The Holy Spirit's mode of existence, held by Him in common with the Son, consists in the communication of the divine essence and in participating in it; not partly, through some division (for the divine nature is not divisible) but through a sharing of the single and entire essence. And that sharing is not time-bound (for the author of time is a-temporal, and outside of time) but from eternity, and accordingly it does not know of periods of time; therefore the person cannot be spoken of as going to be made, or becoming, or having been made. And so, whether explained in the present tense, as when it is said that He is proceeding from the Father, or in the past tense, as when it is said that He was breathed—this act should be understood without reference to periods of time.

9. The particular mode which comprises his subsistence, and whereby He is distinguished from the Father and the Son, is in God's spiration and in the procession that corresponds to it. For as He is brought forth by spiration, so He has subsistence by emanating—which the word "Spirit" bears out, as He is said to go forth in a proper sense, namely from someone who does the breathing.

10. Moreover, the word "procession" should not be taken in the sense of the flowing forth of God's power and efficacy, insofar as the works of God proceed from Him who performs the works; nor in the sense of an interior and immanent act residing within God's essence but aiming at an object outside of God, such as the decrees that are of God and that proceed from Him. But it should be taken according to God's act directed toward the inside (as the schoolmen say), that is, whereby God so acts within his own essence, that the reflection upon himself constitutes a real relationship by a communion of the divine essence.

11. And "procession" also should not be understood in the sense that it can apply commonly to the Son as well, to whom, by reason of his personal existence from the Father, even "exodus"—the going forth from the days of eternity—is attributed, and in reference to his sending and to his coming into the flesh, a "going out," or issuing, from the Father is attributed (Mic 5:1; John 16:27, 28). But rather it should be understood in the way that "the proceeding," or going forth, is ascribed in the sacred writings uniquely to the Holy Spirit, as his personal characteristic property (John 15:26).

12. But all the ancient interpreters understand the well-known passage which states, "The Spirit of truth who proceeds from the Father" (John 15:26), as being about the eternal procession of the Holy Spirit, whereas some of the more recent ones take it to concern what occurs within time—of his activity and operation. We, however, keep the two acts together, though the one is primary, and the other secondary.

13. The distinction between the generation [of the Son] and the spiration [of the Spirit], between being born and proceeding, becomes clear in some way from the terminology and the thing itself, when it is transferred from human reality to the divine things (that is why the terms as well as the concepts fluctuate). The former term applies to a father and to a son, the latter refers to a mouth by which the interior strength of a soul presents itself. Accordingly, He is also called "the Spirit of the mouth and lips of God" (Ps 33:6; Isa 11:4).

14. But since these things, being stated figuratively and in an anthropopathic way, must be understood in a way that befits God, many ancient authors as well as more recent ones have posited that just as the Son was born by means of the intellect (for He is called the Wisdom and Word of God, Prov 8 and John 1), so too the Holy Spirit proceeded by means of the will, of love, nay

rather, of power. For this reason, the terms "Holy Spirit" and "the power of the most high" are rightly used interchangeably (Luke 1:35; Matt 12:28, compared with Luke 11:20). For us it suffices that somehow by means of these different words and concepts the difference is indicated in the production of the divine persons; and we do not presume to give definitions recklessly to matters that cannot be expressed in words.

15. In fact, the Holy Spirit is singly distinguished from the Son, because the Son is only from the Father, but the Holy Spirit is from the Father and the Son jointly. Concerning this point a serious and long-lasting debate arose between the eastern and western Church, the former claiming that He proceeds from the Father only, the later from both, namely, from the Father and the Son.

16. In fact, the unity of essence in these two persons—which should be given prior consideration—demands that He proceeds from them both—or else the unity would be destroyed. For if the spiration of the Father is considered without the spiration of the Son, it will be necessary to place the Son's essence apart from the Father's. Thus also the personal order among the divine persons would be destroyed, and the Holy Spirit would no longer be the third person, but He would be positioned in an order and ranking equal to the Son, and, as it were, placed over against Him. And lastly, because the relation and relatedness demand this, for otherwise there would be no relatedness at all between the Son and the Holy Spirit.

17. And this would be contrary to the definition in Holy Scriptures. For He is called not only of the Father (Matt 10:20), and the Spirit of God the Father, but clearly also of the Son (in Galatians 4:6) and of the Son of God and of Christ (Rom 8:9), and of Jesus Christ and of the Lord (Phil 1:19; 1 Pet 1:11). Indeed, the things He is to teach to others He receives not only from the Father but also from the Son (John 16:14, 15), and that through eternal communication and through temporal manifestation.

18. Thereby the right of sending Him, and the sending, and the giving, and the outpouring, and whatever belongs with it are attributed also to the Son. Indeed, Christ bestowed the Holy Spirit upon the Apostles by the act of breathing (John 20:22). For even the sending of the Holy Spirit within time, although it is not the same as the eternal procession, nevertheless has its groundings in the origin and order of persons. For this reason, the Father is sent by no-one, because He is from no-one except himself; the Son is sent

by the Father, because He is from the Father. And in the same way the Holy Spirit is sent by both of them, because He is from both of them. But as to the fact that it is stated elsewhere that also the Son is sent by the Holy Spirit (Isa 61:1; Luke 4:18), it must be understood not in so far as He is the Son, but with reference to his human nature, like also his anointing.

19. But in order to put the controversy between the Greeks and Latins in its proper place and settle it, some have conveniently said, in keeping with the phraseology of some ancient authors, that the Father spirates the Holy Spirit through the Son, and that the Holy Spirit proceeds from the Father through the Son. For by that manner of speaking it is shown that He comes from both; and the mode of subsistence is shown, too; that is to say, He proceeds in a mediate and subordinate way from the Father through the Son. Thereby the Greeks' position is not destroyed, namely that the one and even personal principle of the spiration and procession of the Holy Spirit is the Father—because the Father precedes in origin and order. To be precise: their position of the personal starting point is the Father on account of the Father's antecedence in origin and rank. And hereby both the relationship and subordination of the Spirit to the Son is established (John 15:16 and 16:14, 15).

20. Moreover, by reason of the origin, the mode of relation, and the order which the Holy Spirit has towards the Father and Son, the following property arises: Just as the Holy Spirit has everything from the Father and the Son (or from the Father through the Son) and therefore acts and operates in a similar way, so too does He render everything to the Father through the Son. And in this regard there is a certain eminence and worthiness from the Father himself and the Son towards the Holy Spirit, which is entirely a matter of origin and order alone.

21. Well then, just as from this point the wonderfully charming economy (or disposition) of that unspoken divine counsel arises, which in the work of redemption is most wise and corresponds very closely to the origin and order of the persons, so too does the work and office of the Holy Spirit. And it does so to such an extent that just as the Father assumes and accomplishes the role and office of God who has been angered and who must be appeased and who is the source of our redemption, and just as the Son assumes and accomplishes the role and office of redeemer and mediator, so too the Holy Spirit assumes and accomplishes the role and office of the one who applies

the merit and benefits obtained by Christ; who illuminates and sanctifies our life. By the offices and that order of working, as well as by his work of saving us, the Holy Spirit is once more distinguished from the Father and the Son.

22. Therefore, as the distinction of the Holy Spirit from the Father and the Son becomes clear from these things—namely their operations directed both toward the inside and toward the outside, which are evident especially in that most gracious work of our redemption—so from these same things is demonstrated his sharing of one essence *homoousios* with the Father and the Son. But for the sake of the pneumatomachians who deny his deity, we undertake the following, more abundant demonstration of it. Someone to whom the name, attributes, works, dominion, worship and honour that are appropriate to God apply, is true God. Surely all these do apply to the Holy Spirit.

23. As for the name of God: it is in this way that "the Spirit of the Lord" who spoke through David is shortly thereafter called, exegetically, "God of Israel" (2 Sam 23:1, 2[2, 3]). The Holy Spirit, to whom Ananias lied, is shortly thereafter called God (Acts 5:3, 4). We are called the temple of God and of the Holy Spirit (1 Cor 3:16, and 6:19, 20). And in fact He is addressed by the proper name of God, which is rendered by the name Lord (Isa 6:9, compared with Acts 28:25, 26). For the "Lord Sabaoth" who is speaking in that passage, is revealed in this passage as the Holy Spirit.

24. And considering his attributes, these are: eternity, as in the text, "He offered himself to God through the eternal Spirit" (Heb 9:14). Omnipresence: "Whither shall I go from your Spirit" (Ps 139:7). And "He dwells within the believers" (1 Cor 3:16; 6:19). Omniscience: "God has revealed to us through his Spirit; for the Spirit searches everything, even the depths of God" (1 Cor 2:10). Wherefore He also announces the future (John 16:13). Through him the prophets spoke (1 Pet 1:11; 2 Pet 1:21).

25. Likewise his most free will and his almighty power. Thus the Apostle, after he recalled the various and splendid gifts of God, which no-one is able to grant except God himself (such as the gift of sound health, prophecy, wisdom, etc.) says: "All these things, the one and same Spirit works, apportioning to each one individually as He wills" (1 Cor 12:8,9,11). For when he sets the Holy Spirit, as the one who bestows, apart from the gifts that are bestowed, he places the bestowal in his completely free will and rule, and he declares that they flow forth from his power.

26. Then the works: such as of creation and its maintenance, according to that text, "The Spirit of God has made me, and the breath of the Almighty has given me life" (Job 33:4). Of redemption, for He brought about the conception of Christ (Luke 1:35; Matt 1:18,20); He anoints Him, He rested above Him, and He sent Him (Isa 61:1,2; Luke 4:18); and Christ performed miracles through Him (Matt 12:28). He enlightens people who are sitting in darkness; He regenerates, renews, recreates, sanctifies, renders spiritual, saves, and revives from the dead (John 3:5,8; Titus 3:5; 2 Cor 3:18; Rom 8:11).

27. And finally there is the worship and honour that is owed to God alone, as when faith and worship in prayer are ascribed to Him (Matt 28:19; 2 Cor 13:13; Rev 1:4). And, on the opposite side, when pronouncement is made concerning sin committed against Him: "Every sin and every blasphemy will be forgiven men, but the blasphemy against the Holy Spirit will not be forgiven, either in this age or in the future one" (Matt 12:32). In this the sin against the Holy Spirit is not so much equated with one perpetrated against the Father and the Son; rather, with a view to us, it is deemed even more serious, and is declared unforgiveable—which is in no way possible unless He is equal with the Father and the Son in his nature and majesty.

28. From all these passages it is obviously clear and we conclude that the Holy Spirit is of the same essence as the Father and the Son. Certainly, He is to such an extent in God, from God, and of God, that He is God.

29. And this is the orthodox doctrine about the Holy Spirit, against which these heresies are opposed: First, those of Macedonius, who held that the Holy Spirit is a creature, and a minister of the Son; and, in this, our own age, those of Campanus and his followers. And so too the heresies of all the Anti-Trinitarians, real opponents of the Spirit, who deny the distinct person of the Holy Spirit in God, and who, therefore, madly assert that it indicates merely the Father or his power, a gift and holy affection, or the capability of a regenerated man. And finally, the godlessness of those who blasphemously state that it denotes a particular way of revelation, as nearly all the Libertines do.

CONCERNING THE
CREATION OF THE WORLD

President: Johannes Polyander
Respondent: Henricus Hamers

Creation means that God almighty produced the world from nothing (3–5), for the purpose of the revelation of the goodness, wisdom, and power of God, and the everlasting praise of these virtues through all creatures, especially those endowed with reason (5, 29). The joint roles of Father, Son, and Holy Spirit in the creation of the world underscores the Trinitarian outlook of the Synopsis (6–13). Creation is a fully and uniquely divine work which He cannot and will not delegate to someone else. God's 'goodness' is the impelling cause for creation (18); in creation God bestows this goodness upon humanity (14–21). It zooms in on the fact that creation is 'from nothing' (22–23), 'in time, not from eternity' (24–27). In the structure of the disputation we recognize the typically scholastic use of the four (Aristotelian) causes: 1. The efficient cause (6–21); 2. The material cause (22–23); 3. The formal cause (28); and 4. The final cause (29–30).

1. Up to this point we have discussed the essence and persons of the greatest and most high God. As for his work, the first one (in order) is the creation of the world.

2. Here we take 'world' in the strict sense of this universal framework, which Holy Scripture portrays by its parts, calling it heaven, earth, sea and all that is in them (Exod 20:11).

3. We understand 'creation of the world' to mean its production from nothing, achieved by the almighty power of God alone. Therefore, also in Holy Scripture and in the Apostles' Creed, the Creator of heaven and earth is designated with the epithet 'God almighty.'

4. God has shown his omnipotence in the things He has created in two respects: Either immediately, since He has produced the nature of many things entirely out of nothing (such as the earth, water, angels, and the souls of our first parents). Or mediately, since He shaped some things from raw, pre-existing matter (such as the plants of the earth, the body of Adam, and non-rational animals).

5. Hence we define the creation of the world as an external action of the almighty God that cannot be shared with human creatures, whereby through himself and by his own most free will (and influenced by no-one else), He founded the heavens and the earth out of nothing, at the beginning of time. And in the space of six days, He arranged in their proper order all the individual things which He willed to mold from that prime matter, in order to reveal the glory of his own immeasurable wisdom, power, and goodness to his creatures—especially to the ones endowed with reason—and to summon them to the praise of his name.

6. With this definition of ours we make the almighty God, who is one in essence but three-fold in persons, the efficient cause of the world, relying as we do on these proof-texts of Holy Scripture: Gen 1, Ps 33:6, Job 33:4, and texts like them.

7. It was on account of this that the Arians and Dulians of former times were deservedly condemned, because they held that the world had been made by Christ as if He were an instrument of the Father. In fact, in the collective working that issues only from God's omnipotence, each person is co-equal to the others.

8. We assign this work of creation jointly to God the Father, the Son, and the Holy Spirit, because all the workings of God that are called 'outward workings' are indivisible—although, as in other works, so too in the work of creation a different mode and order of operation may be noted.

9. For the Father created the world by himself through the Son and the Holy Spirit, the Son created the world by the Father through the Spirit, and the Spirit created the world by the Father and the Son, as is well known from these passages of Holy Scripture: Gen 1, Job 33:4, John 1:2,3, 1 Cor 8:6, Col 1:15, etc.

10. Hence this creation of the world is attributed sometimes separately to God the Father (1 Cor 8:6), to the Son (John 1:3; Col 1:16; Heb 1:2,10), and

to the Holy Spirit (Job 33:4); sometimes jointly, either to the Father and the Son (as 1 Cor 8:6) or to the three persons together (as Gen 1; Ps 33:6).

11. Moreover, as God the Father is said to have manifested himself in a singular way in the creation of the world (Gen 1:26)—evidenced in his speech to the Son and the Holy Spirit: "Let us make man in our own image"—so in many places of Holy Scripture (as well as in the Apostles' Creed), the creation of heaven and earth is pre-eminently and particularly attributed to Him.

12. And yet this does not conflict with the other witnesses in the sacred Book, in which creation is ascribed jointly to the three persons. For nowhere is God the Father alone called the Creator, to the exclusion of the Son and the Holy Spirit. And even though the external actions of God are common to the Trinity, they nevertheless can be referred to one person in particular, either because of the foremost position of the acting cause (like creation to the Father), or on account of the special divine economy or arrangement (like redemption to the Son), or on account of the closest and immediate principle of action in us (like sanctification to the Holy Spirit).

13. We assert that this creation of the world is the work of God alone, because He founded it merely by the word of his power, without assistance from any others, and without applying any model from elsewhere. Witness Moses, in Gen 1:3: "God said, 'let there be light,' and there was light." And David, Ps 33:9: "He spoke, and they came to be; God commanded, and all things were created." With respect to this, Isa 40:13 says: "Who has assisted the Spirit of the Lord? Or who was his counselor?"

14. As to the question: "Whether creating the world can in any way be common with creatures," we reply without hesitation (as many of the Schoolmen do) and emphatically that creating the world cannot be common with creatures. In support of our assertion, we shall produce three major reasons.

15. The first of them is that the creation of the world is an act of infinite power, and consequently could have been communicated to finite creatures no more than the infinite power of God.

16. The second is that in this action no created being was able to collaborate with his Creator, neither as principal cause nor as instrumental cause. Not as principal cause, since no creature is able to work on equal terms with his

Creator. Nor as instrumental cause, since in the creation out of nothing there is nothing in which an instrument is used.

17. The third is that Holy Scripture frequently demonstrates from the creation of the world that the one true God, Father, Son, and Holy Spirit, is set apart from phony gods (Isa 40; Jer 10; John 1; Heb 1:2).

18. The impelling cause of the creation of the world is God's highest goodness, whereby He was moved to communicate and reveal himself as the highest good to the things He would create. In his *Enchiridion*, chapter 9, Augustine speaks about it as follows: "It is enough for the Christian to believe that the only cause for the creation of things is the goodness of the Creator."

19. The Psalmist praises this goodness of God in various Psalms, and especially in Ps 8, 104, and 136, where this phrase is repeated several times: "Praise the Lord, because He is good."

20. The directive cause of this creation is God's wisdom; the executive cause is his infinite power. The latter is seen in the new coming-about of things; the former is seen in the meticulous arrangement and sequence of the various forms.

21. For the variety of created things is so great, their makeup so precise and wonderful, that to every person who beholds them they proclaim their Creator's divine wisdom and power with mouth wide-open, so to speak, and they point to it with outstretched finger (Ps 19:2,3; Rom 1:20).

22. This whole of things was brought forth out of nothing (taken in the negative, not privative sense), and so our minds conceive of what is brought forth by means of the removal and negation of all entity. By some this idea is loosely—and quite inaccurately—called 'the matter from which'; but where nothing exists, there it is incorrect to speak of matter.

23. But as for the matter that was brought forth out of nothing, in the beginning it was without order and unsuitable for all those things which God willed to put in their proper places later, and to be adorned with their own unique forms.

24. We deem the overly-inquisitive question of the Schoolmen, "Whether the world could not have been created from eternity," not worthy of a reply by Christians, who very well know that the sacred writings everywhere teach by the very word 'creation' that the world was established by God within time,

and that only God is without beginning and eternal in himself. Augustine, in applying this to the angels, states in Book 12, chapter 15 of *the City of God*: "How can it be said that angels were created, if it is understood that they have always existed?"

25. But as we assert that God founded this world within time, He did so freely, too, and according to the good pleasure of his own will at a time determined by himself—which He could have created earlier or later in time, whenever it pleased Him to do so.

26. To this question of idle men, "Why did God not establish the world earlier?," we reply that it is not for them to make such meddlesome enquiries about times or opportunities, which only God in his power possesses, and that by his own choice God has created the ages no less than this universal framework (Acts 1:7; Heb 1:2).

27. And as to their question, "Whether God was idle before He created the world," we reply that it is uttermost folly to ask of God whether He was ever idle, who besides himself has carefully contemplated from eternity all the things that would be created by Him. And it is said that He knew and chose us in Christ, his beloved Son, before the foundations of the world were laid (Rom 8:28; Eph 1:4).

28. The form of the world created by God is discerned in the most skillful assembly of all its parts, the very functional arrangement within them, and the greatest harmony among them.

29. The goal is the revelation of the goodness, wisdom, and power of God; and the everlasting praise of these virtues through all creatures, especially those endowed with reason.

30. The men of God, in the Psalms as well as in the other passages of Holy Scripture, have pursued this goal for the glory of God, for the recreation of their own souls, and for the common instruction of all devout people in various ways.

Corollary

1. Since Holy Scripture teaches both that there is only one world and that its only Savior is Jesus Christ, Jerome and the other orthodox church-fathers rightly refuted the opinion of Origen, whereby he posited that while there is only one world at one time, yet before this one there were others, and after

this one there will be another (and thereupon another, and another will always follow); and for that reason Christ, too, will suffer more often, on the ground that what was beneficial once will be beneficial always.

2. Since Holy Scripture declares that "in the beginning God created heaven and earth" (Gen 1; Prov 8:22, ff.; John 17:5; Eph 1:4), the axiomatic statement that "the world was created by God in time" should not be considered among debatable issues, as though one could argue about it in either way.

3. Since the same Scripture testifies that every creature of God is good (Gen 1:31; 1 Tim 4:4), the Manicheans of former times were rightly condemned, who were of the opinion that some natures simply are evil and were created by an evil God.

ON THE PROVIDENCE OF GOD

President: Andreas Rivetus
Respondent: Carolus Becius

Providence is God's continuous preservation, direction, and guidance of all created things to the end He has determined from eternity and for his own glory (1–3). Over against nascent 'Deism' (identified with 'Epicureans' in the Synopsis), and the Remonstrant emphasis on human free will, God's all-encompassing involvement in everything is stressed: only and everything what He decides, comes to pass, and that in the way He wills (4–19). God is the first cause and effector of each and every thing, although He makes use of means and 'secondary causes.' In this respect it is stated that all creaturely freedom of the will arises from sharing in God's uncreated freedom as their first cause. Freedom is not destroyed by providence, but cannot exist without it (10–11). God, deciding not only the goals but also the means to the goals, considers and concurs with the nature of the things (the secondary causes) in question, but never depends on them. He remains the direct provider of all things, even of the actions of the free wills (12–15). This is emphasized because of the effects of Pelagianism (read also: Remonstrantism) on the understanding of faith and good works (16). God directs all things to their goal (17–19). Next, the question regarding providence and sin is addressed: If God is the first cause and effector of everything, isn't He responsible for sin too? God indeed exercises providence concerning sins, but at the same time cannot be held responsible for the evil character of sinful deeds. In this respect an important argument is God's willing permission, and His destination of sins to something good (20–25). Some questions regarding providence may remain hidden from human reason, but one must be humble and content with God's revelation about it (27–28). The goal of providence is clear: the glory of God, and the salvation of the elect (26).

1. An inquiry into divine providence must, in good order, follow the investigation into the creation of all things visible and invisible. For it is not true that in the beginning of creation God established and arranged all this in

such a way that when He had accomplished and finished everything completely, He put away from himself every care for it. Rather, we assert with Salvian "that our God neither withdraws the benefit of his most generous observance nor entirely removes the rule of his providence from everything; He also does not withdraw the favor of his most benevolent faithfulness" (*On the Government of God*, 50.2).

2. And so, as we set out to treat providence, we shall leave aside the definition of the word, which is sufficiently known from other sources, so that we make our way straight to the subject proper. The subject is considered as a two-fold act: The one is eternal, the other is within time. We can combine the two into one definition if we say that it is "the pre-existent structural ordaining, in God's mind, of things towards a goal; that is, the practical knowledge of God whereby He pre-ordained each and every single thing from eternity and directs them in time to their proper goal—for his own glory." From this it is plain that providence pertains partly to the intellect and partly to the will. For as it is situated in the intellect, it presupposes the will of the goal.

3. Since we have two things here, the eternal structural order, which properly speaking is providence and its execution within time (which is called government), and also a kind of maintenance of creation in the present, which we must treat in particular, we shall define it as: "The actual and temporal preservation, direction, and guidance that God has achieved very wisely and justly, according to his eternal unchangeable and entirely free decree, of all individual things which exist and come into being, to the end that He has determined for them, and to the praise of his glory."

4. No-one, unless he is an utter atheist, can deny that providence exists in God, because the reason for its existence is bound up with the divinity to such a degree that it cannot be separated from it in any way. Indeed, so much so that all who otherwise lack true religion are compelled by its power and by a certain necessity to realize that everything depends upon God and is moved and ruled by Him. For they saw that since God is the cause of everything, and since every agent acts for the sake of a goal, it follows thereupon that God, who cannot be God and lack wisdom, ordains everything towards its own goal. And they could not consider that order— that most fitting linkage of everything in the universe, that most apt and suitable arrangement of all the parts, that succession of constant motions and actions by definite laws, even in things that lack feeling and reason—without

coming to the conclusion that there is some wise mind that effects, directs and preserves that order. "For what can be known about God is plain to them, for God has shown it to them" (Rom 1:19,20).

5. For Christians the very clear witnesses of Scripture ought to be enough, which inculcates this divine teaching more frequently and carefully than any other part, since it teaches that God grants life to all, and breath, and everything (Acts 17:25). It teaches that all things are sustained by the Word of God (Heb 1:3); that in Him we live and move and have our being (Acts 17:28); that the sparrow does not fall to the ground without our heavenly Father; that all the hairs on our head are numbered (Matt 10:29, 30); and that God accomplishes everything according to the good pleasure of his will (Eph 1:11).

6. These and similar witnesses prove that the subject-matter of providence is not just the heavenly and incorruptible things—as those people suggested who thought that "thick clouds form a concealing curtain for God" and who reckoned that He did not look down on things below but that "He traversed the pathway of the heavens" (Job 22:14). The witnesses prove that no thing, whether it be of a higher or lower nature, should be excepted; but rather, with an unwavering faith one must hold and maintain the position that in God resides the providence for all things, both singly as well as together; things that are subject to decay and contingent (or fortuitous, as they call them) as well as things incorruptible and necessary; things that are humble and lowly, as well as of those which have received a more lofty nature.

7. Scripture attributes to God the power to effect all things, actions, and movements—such as the fact that He works all things in everyone (1 Cor 12:6); that from Him, through Him, and to Him are all things (Rom 11:36); and that He gives life and breath to all (Acts 17:25). And since the things that exist and the things He has done are considered one and the same, and since God does nothing within time which He had not decreed from eternity, and since He so conducts things as He once had decreed they would be done, it follows clearly that the ground of all the things which are and which come about in the world is in God from eternity, and they are ordained for their own goals in time.

8. Nor is it foreign to the majesty of God, as some think it is, for him to rule and keep account of even the most minute things, since He is the Creator and Lord of everything. It is not a source of shame for Him to have created

them, and much less to govern that which He has made. And He who cares for humble things does not himself become humble; and He who looks down upon the lowliest does not cease dwelling in the highest places (Ps 103:19). Thus, it must be said that the Apostle deprives the oxen of God's care (1 Cor 9:9) not in an absolute sense, but in comparison with people, especially believers, since the former enjoy the benefit of his general providence, and the latter his specific and exalted protection. For in any case our God gives food to the hungry, and to the young ravens that cry (Ps 147:9). Architects state that large stones cannot be laid well without small ones (so says Plato). Therefore, we should guard ourselves from thinking that God is a less worthy craftsman than mortal ones.

9. However, since nothing in the whole world is exempt from the laws of divine providence, we must profess that by how much more God cares for humans than for other things (that lack intellect), by so much more are the actions of humans subjected to the providence of God than the actions or behaviors of things that lack intellect. "From his dwelling-place He looks upon all the inhabitants of the earth; He who formed their hearts observes all their deeds" (Ps 33:14,15). Hence Scripture shows that the hearts, wills and actions of men are in God's hand, power, and control. Accordingly, it accredits all the good works of men to God, and to his governance; and it teaches that the events, good things, and outcomes depend upon Him (Prov 21:1; Gen 45:8; Exod 4:11; Jas 1:17; Phil 2:13; Jer 10:23; Prov 20:24, etc.).

10. For also in actions of the free will a creature endowed with intellect is not exempt from the ordering of the first cause; because it is altogether necessary that every creature and its every action, and even the manner and completion of whatever action it takes are traced back to God, as to the first, most perfect and accordingly most efficient cause. Therefore it follows that in creatures there is no freedom of the will which does not arise from sharing in the highest, uncreated freedom, which is the first, proper and innermost cause of the created freedom, and of all free actions (insofar as they are of that sort).

11. The notion that the functioning of divine providence destroys the freedom of the created will is so far from the truth, that the will cannot exist at all without it. For since not only each and every action of the creature but also the manner of his action depends upon the effective working of the divine will, it follows that the freedom of human actions is established, and not destroyed, through God's providence. This must be said even of the

contingency of things in general. For divine providence does not corrupt nature, but perfects it; it does not take it away, but guards it. And everything which He created He administers in such a way that He allows each one even to carry out and perform its own particular motions (Augustine, *On the City of God*, book 7, chapter 30).

12. Also continuance or maintenance belongs to this government of God, as it too is a work of the divine power of preservation and sustains and upholds all created things so that they survive and continue to exist and remain in the state of their own nature and natural properties. This power also prevents created things from falling back into nothing, which would happen if God were to withdraw his strength. For all the elements of the world do not receive growth generally by secret inspiration merely, but each and every one of them "is terrified as soon as God hides his face; when He takes away his Spirit, they die, and when He sends it forth, they are created, and the face of the earth is renewed" (Ps 104:28, 29, 30).

13. The creatures whose nature and peculiar properties God sustains are moved and driven by Him to conduct themselves according to their own nature; and He gives them his concurrence. And He so concurs with them that through his working He directly influences the action of the created being, so that one and the same action is said to proceed from the first and the second cause, inasmuch as one work, or the completed work, results from this source. If there is anything in it that is not in order, it comes from the action of the creatures and not of the Creator; just as in wood-carving some things happen through the fault of the object or the instrument—things which should not be imputed to the artisan via the axe he wields.

14. From what we have stated it is clear that often God governs the inferior matters through the superior ones not without any means; that He establishes secondary causes which He uses in order to effect ulterior results—not because he lacks the power, but because of the abundance of his goodness, by communicating the worthiness of his own causality to creatures. He does this so that through the secondary causes we may more easily perceive with the senses that God is supplying his aid to us, that we may acknowledge as Lord of all things Him who employs created beings as much as He wills for his own glory and our salvation. Nor do we abuse the means, or neglect what has been ordained by God, since He has decided not only the goals of the

actions but also the means to the goals, subject to and subsumed under his providence.

15. For this reason we must maintain that even when He employs means He nonetheless provides for all things directly, deeply within and without depending on the middle causes through which He operates, since He is directly at work in all of them, is always present to them, and reveals his own special power through them, according to these words: "Man does not live by bread alone, but by every word which proceeds from the mouth of God" (Deut 8:3).

16. One therefore ought not to state that God produced only the secondary causes, and attributed to them the power to act (and that He preserves both the causes and the powers He conferred on them), but that He does not incite them on to motion and action through an inner force. Similarly: One therefore ought not to state that the actions of the free will do proceed from God, in as much as they are indifferent in good and evil. And therefore, that God is not the cause of the free will's actions, except insofar as the free will comes from God and is preserved by Him. From this belief it follows, in addition to other absurd beliefs, that the second cause regarding individual actions will take over the essential role of the first cause and of the first mover, because it moves without having been moved. And so there are many principles, and God—who is the first being—is not properly the universal cause of all beings. We add that, with respect to faith and good works, Pelagianism is introduced by this belief.

17. We place under God's providence also the direction of things to their goal—especially their final goal. Indeed, to his providence belongs not only directing the means towards the goal, but also achieving the goal. When considered in the case of human beings, providence is subject to failure and can be thwarted and it often exists without the pursuit of the goal intended by the one who exercised the foresight. However, the same should not be said concerning God's providence, because what God as the universal supervisor has ordained and proposed to himself to happen always does happen. For what among the created things goes beyond the direction of some particular cause, through some other particular cause meets the direction of the first and universal cause.

18. Therefore we shall say more correctly that the concern of providence is not to direct each and every thing to a particular goal suitable for it; rather, it

is in itself a goal that agrees with the operation as a whole. It is as when someone in the family burns wood and so uses the wood for a goal that is not particularly suited for it, but one does execute responsibility for the family. This is a better way of speaking than if we make the harsh statement made by some (not to say anything more offensive), that the providence of God sometimes is prevented from pursuing its goal (in whatever way that is understood). For the providence whereby God governs things is similar to the providence whereby the head of the household governs the home, and the king his state, for whom the common good takes priority over an individual one. This is the reason why they pay attention more to what is beneficial to the community than to only one individual.

19. Among the things subject to God's government we ought to note also the fact that He exercises his providence over some things for the sake of the things themselves, but that there are other things in which He shows providence for the sake of something else, as in a home those things are provided for in which the very well-being of the home consists—such as the children, possessions and similar things. But other things are provided for the benefit of the prior ones, such as dishes and the like. So too in the universe: For its sake provisions are made of things which pertain essentially to the perfect condition of the universe; on account of that these things are not destroyed. However, for its sake there are also certain particular things which are liable to destruction, and they remain only so long as it is necessary in these matters because of which they are provided for.

20. At this point we should see whether sins, too, fall under divine providence. We assert that it is wrong to say God provides sins in the sense that 'to provide' means 'to attend' and 'to care for.' But we do not doubt that it may, and indeed should be said that God exercises providence concerning sins. For He foresees sins in advance, and wills to permit them; and as they are seen beforehand, He destines them to some universal or particular good, whether for a display of his mercy or justice, or for some other good. And so it is rightly said that He exercises providence regarding them, since He disposes to do well regarding them. But if one considers only that which is real in sin and 'positive,' as they say, what others call 'the matter' of sin, namely, as an entity or as an action, in this sense sins can be said even to be provided by God, but only in a relative sense and not in itself. That is because the formal structure of sin exists in the absence of being and of good, in a

certain deformity and disorderliness, which does not come from God and so cannot have been provided for by Him.

21. Here is a place for a distinction in the ways God handles providence when He implements it—it is either effective, or permitting. The first is the one whereby God works effectually, and in all things generally and individually perfects his work (namely all things both general and specific in nature), not only the essential good—the substances, motions, actions and completions of things—but also the moral good, such as all civic and spiritual virtues. Because, as the highest good, He is also the author and source of all good.

22. The second is attributed to God also in Scripture, in which it is often said that He permits something; not only when He allows us to obtain what we wish in actions and affairs that are good, or middling actions that make no difference, for which the permission is linked to God's approval and effective operation (Heb 6:3 and 1 Cor 16:7). But even when He does not prevent the evils and the sins which He forbids (though He is able to), as He does not have a law about hindering things. For this permission is granted; nevertheless, the things that are permitted by it are not approved continuously. In this way the following texts are interpreted: Isa 2:6, Jer 16:13, Acts 14:16; Rom 1:24 and 28; Ps 81:13.

23. We acknowledge that this permission for all sins belongs to God's providence. For although sins are evil, and accordingly cannot be provided by God, nevertheless the permission of them is good. So then, God both wills and directly decrees the permission, and ordains it for some good purpose that is greater than that of which the absence is the evil that is permitted. For since God is good to the highest degree, He would in no way permit there to be anything evil in his workings, unless He were not so almighty that even concerning evil He would still do good, as Augustine justly states (*Enchiridion* chapter 11).

24. And so we think that God's permission is not idle, or that something happens without the will of God, or without his care, or that He is neglecting anything that happens. And accordingly, his permission should not be understood as opposed to his will and counsel. For it is in accordance with his will and after taking counsel that God grants permission. And He powerfully controls direction over sins, and it is not unusual for Him to apply his permission to carry out his judgements, occasionally even as a recompense for previously committed sins. In this sense the Schoolmen

acknowledge that God "possesses a practical knowledge of sins, insofar as He permits, or prevents, them, or—once committed—appoints a goal for them" (Thomas Aquinas 1.14. art. 16).

25. In addition to this we state that before they occur, and while they are occurring, God in his great and most holy wisdom directs the arguments and opportunities that are like incentives to an act that does not happen without sin on the creatures' part, yet these opportunities are not evil in and of themselves, so that He does not refuse his concurrence to the act as such (though not as sin). We state "that He presides (as Bellarmine himself admits) over wrongful wills, and rules and governs them, is invisibly at work in them, so that from his divine providence, though evil by their own vice, they are led more to the one than to the other." Likewise he adds that God "bends and twists the wills" of the ungodly (*On the Loss of Grace and the State of Sin*, chapter 13), not shunning those types of expressions, instead using even harsher ones than those he adopts from others and distorts into a false accusation.

26. The goal of this teaching is the same as that of teaching that God has created everything: the glory of God, to which is joined the salvation of the elect, who derive manifold benefits from it. By his government of everything the elect come to acknowledge God as most wise, good, and powerful, the Lord of all things, upon whom all creatures depend. They learn to place their trust in Him like a Father who in all things provides for their best interests, as they rest securely in the protection of the one to whose judgement they subject themselves. They are patient in times of adversity, as they raise their eyes up to the prime cause, acknowledging and correcting their own sinful ways. They are grateful in prosperous times, bringing praise to his name; they fear and honour God in whose hand are all creatures, and with the utmost love they follow after Him whom they know exercises his particular care for those who are his own, and who has prepared for them an inheritance in heaven.

27. If anyone desires more and expects answers to all the minor questions arising from human reason, let him listen to the same person whom we praised at the outset of this disputation, Salvian: "I can say with sufficient reason and confidence: I do not know what is hidden, and I am ignorant of the counsel of the divine. In support of this position the revelation of the heavenly statement is sufficient for me: God says that by Him all things are

observed, by Him all things are governed, and by Him all things are judged. If you wish to know what it is you must hold on to, you have the sacred writings. There is a perfect reason to hold on to what you have read. However, I do not wish that you ask me for what reason God so performs the things about which we are speaking. I am only a man; I do not understand the secret things of God. I do not make bold to search into them and therefore I am afraid even to attempt it, because if you desire to know more than is permitted to you, that too is a kind of irreverent impudence. Let it be sufficient for you that God bears witness that all things are performed and managed by Him" (*On God's Government* book 3).

28. Since these things are so, "we recoil in terror from the madness and folly (the words are those of Isidore of Pelusium, book 3 Epistle 154) of those who posit either that there is no God, or that there is one, yet who by no means whatsoever founded the world. Or that if He had founded it, does not govern it at all; or that if He governs it, He takes delight in those who embrace vice. Or that if He does not enjoy it, that He forfeits rule over it to others; or that if He has not forfeited the rule, that it was snatched away from Him against his will. Or that if the rule was not snatched away, that He is unwilling to avenge evil-doers; or that if He did wish to avenge, that He is not able to. Or that if He is able to, He has been idle for a very long time. Or that if He has nothing more valuable to do, that He is being over-ruled by the motion of the stars; or if He is not being over-ruled, that He wishes to be idle and lazy." And if the mouths of the wicked spew forth any other blasphemies like this, they will in the end realize that:

Great in Heaven
Is God who beholds and rules over every thing,
To whom belongs the glory for ever and ever.

CONCERNING THE GOOD
AND BAD ANGELS

President: Antonius Walaeus
Respondent: Adrianus Hasius

Some created beings have a special state; the angels as the foremost of these deserve special attention. Angels are spiritual creatures, subsisting separately and on their own, endowed with intellect, free will, and exceptional power (2, 8, 13). They were created out of nothing in the beginning of time, and all were created good and in God's image (3–7). As mere spirits, they are entirely devoid of all body (although they often appear in human bodies), and immortal (9–11). The Synopsis then goes on to discuss the angels' knowledge (14–24), their (free) will (25–34), and their power (35–47). The wisdom, knowledge, will, and power that angels possess are limited and finite because they are created beings, like humans (21); their abilities, however, do supersede those of any human beings. It is likely that the first sin into which the angels fell consisted of some desire to be like God (28). Like human beings, the eternal state of angels is subject to God's predestination; it is not because of any inherent merit of their own that some angels were preserved in the truth, but because of the grace bestowed on them through the mediating work of Christ (29–33). Although the good angels had no sin from which they needed to be redeemed, nevertheless, for the reward of eternal life even in angels God's justice would find something lacking (33). Evil angels have the power to suggest evil thoughts, but they do not exert direct control over people's practical judgments or over their will (45–46). Bad angels are not able to do anything against people except by God's judgment and permission (47). Lastly, the number, movement, place, rank, and duties of angels are explained (48–52).

1. Since we have treated the creation and the government of all things in the preceding theses, it follows now that we deal next with the special state of

some created beings. Since the angels indeed are the foremost of these, we shall start with them in this disputation.

2. The name 'angels' is peculiar to Holy Scripture (the pagan Greek writers express it roughly by the word *daimones*, and the Latin ones by *genii*) and signifies spiritual creatures which subsist on their own, are equipped with intellect and a free will, and have exceptional power and ability to perform tasks suitable to their nature outside of themselves, being more powerful than other creatures.

3. It is abundantly clear from the service they render to their God and also from the many clear passages of Scripture that angels have been created by God. For besides the fact that "from Him and through Him and to Him are all things" (Rom 11:36), there is also: "By the Word of the Lord the heavens were made, and all their hosts by the breath of his mouth" (Ps 33:6). Indeed, "for in Him all things were created, in heaven and on earth, visible and invisible, whether thrones or dominions or principalities or authorities—all things were created through Him and unto Him. He is before all things and by Him all things consist" (Col 1:16,17).

4. Concerning the time of their creation, however, there was a debate among Christians in the past. Origen, along with many Greek church-fathers and several Latin ones, contended that they were created long before this visible world was established. But they are refuted very strongly by the fact that throughout Scripture the phrases "before this world existed" and "before the foundations of the world were laid" mean eternity itself, as can be seen also from John 17:5, Eph 1:4, 1 Pet 1:20, etc.

5. In fact Moses glorifies the eternity of God on the grounds that "He existed before the mountains came to be, before He formed the earth and the habitable world" (Ps 90:2). And because of this excellence, uncreated wisdom is glorified over and above every created wisdom: "For before the beginning of the earth [divine Wisdom] was anointed, and it was brought forth when there were no depths" (Prov 8:22, etc.). And John the evangelist commences his demonstration of the deity of God's Son with the fact that "in the beginning was the Word." Now all these statements would be entirely devoid of force if the angels or any other creatures existed before this world was founded, or before this beginning of time.

6. Whereas the precise day of their creation should not be debated too fretfully, we nevertheless judge that the opinion coming closest to the truth is of those who posit that they were created on the first day, along with the highest heaven itself. For just as mankind was instantly placed upon this world after it had been completely made, so too is it altogether consistent that once their dwelling-place was constructed, the angels came into existence and were placed in it as residents. Add to this the fact that in this whole work of God there was a progression from the most simple essences to the more composite ones. And God himself (in Job 38:7 and following) states that these sons of God "sang the praises of their creator, when He laid the foundations of the earth, when He determined its measurements, when He established its foundations etc."

7. Therefore contrary to the Manichaeans and the followers of Priscillian we assert that they were created out of nothing at the beginning of time, and also that they all were good and in God's image. "For God saw everything that He had made, and behold it was very good" (Gen 1:31), and therefore in Holy Scripture they are called sons of God, servants of God, angels of God, powers and principalities, indeed, even 'gods.' And it is said of those who have fallen away from them that they did "not stand firm in the truth" (John 8:44) and "did not keep their original state" (Jude 6)—from where it necessarily follows that they had been in the truth and that they had a holy beginning.

8. From this peculiar creation of them we succeed in demonstrating against the Sadducees of long ago (Acts 23:8) and the Libertines of our age that angels are true substances that subsist separately and on their own. For we do not read that God created any accidental properties separately. This is proved also by their actions and works, which are ascribed to them everywhere. Appearances of them, also through the bodies they have assumed, demonstrate this. The rewards that are bestowed on the good angels and the punishments that are kept in store for the bad ones prove this, too; and there are many other proofs, which we shall treat later on.

9. But whereas not a few of the ancient as well as recent writers attribute to angels also their own bodies, whether heavenly, fiery, or airy ones, we firmly assert that they are mere spirits, and that they are entirely devoid of all body in the proper sense of the word. Not only because Scripture clearly calls them spirits (Matt 8:16; Heb 1:14) which do not have flesh and bones, and are not

able to be grasped by the outward senses (Luke 24:39). But also because they penetrate corporeal things without being moved or wounded by them, as is evident from the people whom they affect, as well as from the fact that they ascend and descend through the heavens, and from the manifestation of them in buildings or locked prisons (Matt 2:13, Acts 12:7, etc.). And finally, also because many spirits (Matt 12:45), indeed even an entire legion (Luke 8:30), often enter into one man.

10. Nor is it contrary to this viewpoint that they often appear in human bodies. For also the Son of God before his incarnation, and the Holy Spirit sometimes, appeared in bodily form, yet it is not thereby proved that his essence was corporeal; and Moses (in Matt 17) was seen by the disciples in outward form, and yet it must not be granted therefore that souls are corporeal. Because either those corporeal bodies were able to be such in appearance (as happens in dreams or ecstatic visions), or if they were truly bodies—which in the case of some apparitions must be acknowledged as fact—these bodies were attached temporarily to the spirits by divine power, and thereupon were resolved into their original elements once again, like the clothing they wore during their occasional interaction with human beings.

11. From the fact that their nature is spiritual it follows that they are also immortal. For even if the same power which brought them forth out of nothing is able also to render them into nothing, nevertheless because their essence is not composed of diverse internal elements, they cannot of their own accord ever be resolved into other principal elements, nor will they ever be resolved out of God's will. Wherefore Christ asserts that "those who will be worthy of the future age can no longer die" (Luke 20:36) because they will be on a par with angels. But the wicked angels, although they will be punished with spiritual death, are being kept in eternal chains in darkness until the day of judgment (Jude 6), and an eternal fire has been prepared for them also after the final judgment, as Christ says (Matt 25:41).

12. This much must be said from Holy Scripture, then, about the substance of angels; now a few observations should be made briefly about some of their attributes and qualities.

13. All their actions sufficiently demonstrate that angels are endowed with the gifts of intellect, will and outstanding power; wisdom also is attributed explicitly to them (2 Sam 14:20): "My lord, the king possesses wisdom, like the wisdom of an angel of God." Internal and proper actions of the will are

attributed to them—Dan 4:17: "This word comes from the decision of the angels that keep watch." And 1 Pet 1:12: "Things into which even angels long to look." They possess strength and singular power (Ps 103:20): "Praise the Lord, you his angels, most powerful in strength," and elsewhere in other passages.

14. Concerning the intellect of angels the Scholastics hold many wildly inquisitive debates. As for us, not entering upon what has not been revealed to us, we shall indicate briefly as much as we can gather from Scripture or sound reason.

15. Philosophers are generally agreed that every understanding arises through some coming together of the thing that is known and the faculty that knows. However, this coming together occurs either through the essence of things themselves, or through the ideas or concepts of them. These concepts are innate to the intellect, or are abstracted from things through the senses and logical reasoning, or they are implanted in our souls through divine revelation.

16. As far as the first mode of cognition is concerned, we must hold that God himself is understood by the angels by means of his own very essence in the same way as light is seen by the eye. For Holy Scripture bears witness that "they always behold the face of the Father" (Matt 18:10), and with all the blessed they share the fact that "they see Him as He is" (1 John 3:2), and "they know Him just as they themselves are known" (1 Cor 13:12). And in this same way they know also themselves, for if the spirit of a man which is in him knows what is in a man (1 Cor 2:11), we should all the more view the intellect of angels in this way.

17. It is beyond doubt that they also know very many things through the concepts naturally planted in them when they were first created. For if the first principles are innate in the souls of men at the moment they come into being (as the sounder philosophers have acknowledged), and if so much ability had been produced along with the intellect of the first man as to make him capable of perceiving the natures of all living beings, we must confess all the more that, at the moment angels came into being, God implanted in their intellects at least universal concepts of all created things. And on the basis of the application of these universals to individual things also the knowledge of individual things exists in them, insofar as this knowledge is necessary to carry out the task for which they are summoned.

18. A harder question concerns the knowledge that arises through the senses or logical reasoning. For although 'external senses' or 'logical reasoning' properly speaking does not apply to angels, since they lack internal and external organs, we should not deny that they do receive the concepts of very many things from without. And thus, they obtain knowledge from experience, albeit in a more eminent way, and they gather both the causes (from the signs and their effects) and the effects (from the causes and the signs) that were previously unknown to them. Paul testifies to this effect in Eph 3:10: "Now to the rulers and authorities in the heavenly realms, through the church the manifold wisdom of God should be made known." The same fact is abundantly clear from the conversations and other actions of the angels, which Holy Scripture presents to us.

19. Regarding the final mode of cognition, which occurs through extraordinary revelation, the issue is clear in the sacred prophecies. For "no-one, either in heaven, or on earth, or under the earth, could open the book of God's providence, sealed with seven seals until that very time, except the Lion from the tribe of Judah," from whom the angel thereupon received and revealed it to the servants of God (Rev 1:1; 5:5).

20. However, it is a curious rather than useful question whether everything the angels know is always present to them in actuality or whether their understanding in some instances is also in potency. We ascribe only to God the special right of being 'pure act.' Nevertheless, we do believe that those things in which the angels' blessedness exists as such, or which relate to the nature of the task God has imposed upon them, are always present in actuality to the angels' understanding.

21. From all this it is clear that the angels' wisdom is very great, though not infinite, because finite nature is not capable of infinity; and they also do not have knowledge of all the things and actions which occur in the world, since Scripture declares this as belonging to God alone, "because nothing in creation is hidden from God's sight, but everything is laid bare and revealed before his eyes" (Heb 4:13).

22. Much less do we attribute to them a knowledge of the thoughts of human beings, except when these reveal themselves through signs, "for only God knows the hearts of all the sons of man" (1 Kgs 8:39). Nor do we assign to them a definitive knowledge of future contingencies dependent upon the choice of men or upon God's singular providence, except when these have

been revealed to them by Him. In this way Christ speaks of the day of judgment that is unknown to them (Mark 13:32), and God testifies in general to the prophet Isaiah (44:7): "Who proclaims to be as I am? Then let him declare it. Or let him lay out before me what has happened from the time when I established my ancient people. Or let him reveal what the future is or what is yet to happen."

23. From this it clearly follows that we should not call upon angels, because we should call upon Him only who knows the groanings of the heart and our thoughts (Rom 8:27) and in whom we can fully confide (Rom 10:14), since He knows, and has power over, all things. Not to mention the fact that the worship and adoration of angels is condemned expressly by the apostle Paul (Col 2:18), and also by the angel himself (Rev 19:10, 22:9).

24. Meanwhile, however, for the comfort and preservation of believers we learn that the angels in general do have a knowledge of every individual person. For the bad angels are at work in the sons of disobedience (Eph 2:2), and they surround the pious like roaring lions (1 Pet 5:8). But the good angels, besides the fact that they have been entrusted with guarding all pious believers (Heb 1:14), distinguish the impious from the pious in imposing God's punishments (Ezek 9:4[-6]; Rev 7:3). And on the last day "they will be sent by Christ to gather his elect from the four winds of heaven, from the ends of earth to the ends of heaven" (Mark 13:27), and they "will gather out of his kingdom everything that causes sin and all who do evil, and throw them into the fiery furnace" (Matt 13:41).

25. The will is the second faculty which all intelligent nature, and consequently also the angels, possess. About it the Scholastics debate no less speculatively than they rashly come up with many definitions from outside the Scriptures.

26. But, to stay within the same boundaries which we previously established for ourselves, we acknowledge that angels have been endowed with a free will from the beginning of their creation, no less than men—indeed, a will as much more free as they surpass them in the pre-eminence of intellect and holiness.

27. We confess that this freedom had been bestowed even in this point: That they had the power to persevere in that natural good in which God had first placed them through creation; for instance, this is demonstrated by the fact

that God is said "not to have spared the angels who sinned but handed them over to hell to be kept for judgment" (2 Pet 2:4), and that "the devil is the father of lies, and when he speaks lies he speaks out of himself" (John 8:44). Therefore those who fell did not sin out of some defect or weakness in their nature but out of pure obstinacy.

28. The Scriptures do not so clearly express what the very first sin was into which the angels fell by the free abuse of their will. However, it is very likely that it consisted of some desire to be like God, and in a particular obstinacy against the Son of God. For this can be gathered from the temptation whereby Satan seduced our first parents, and from the constant attempt whereby he strives to draw the glory of God unto himself. This can be gathered especially, however, from the hatred with which he pursues Christ and his church; a vivid picture of this is portrayed to us in Rev 12.

29. But it is a useful and equally difficult question to ask for the reason why some angels stood firm in the truth and kept their origin while other angels abused their own free choice.

30. A majority of the Scholastics argues that the angels' perseverance arose from the fact that [God's] act by which He made the angels beatific, excludes in the creature's will every contrary action, and that they merited this beatific influence upon their will by virtue of the first act of their free choice.

31. This claim, besides the fact that it is rash and beyond Scripture, is refuted also by passages of Holy Scripture. For "who has ever given to God that God should repay him? For from Him and through Him and to Him are all things" (Rom 11:35–36). And what comparison is there, I ask, between one act of obedience which by virtue of creation is owed, and this eternal reward that is not indebted?

32. We therefore make the contrary assertion that even the blessed angels must boast in nothing except in the Lord, since Holy Scripture evidently derives their blessedness from God's individual grace, when it everywhere calls them sons of God and elect angels (1 Tim 5:21). But the inheritance of sons does not come as a result of merit, nor is there any election to this sonship except by grace. Whence also Paul says that "God's purpose according to election stands not by works but by the one who calls" (Rom 9:11).

33. There is a debate among ancient and recent orthodox writers whether the angels were in need of a Mediator for the preservation of their original state. We readily concur with the affirmative position (which has very weighty authors), because, on the one hand, in Scripture Christ alone is called the Son in whom the Father, namely by himself, was well pleased; and because, on the other hand, Christ specifically is called the prince and head of angels. And finally, we concur because although the angels had no sin from which they needed to be redeemed, nevertheless, even in them would God's justice find something lacking for granting the reward of eternal life to them, if He would compare them with himself, and would take notice of them as they are in and of themselves alone, as appears from Job 4:18 and 15:15. To say nothing now about those passages in Eph 1:10 and Col 1:20, which admittedly are explained by others (but without providing a parallel of similar wording elsewhere) as referring only to the souls that were dwelling in heaven at the time of Christ's death.

34. From all these points we firmly conclude that angels are already in the state of blessedness and altogether certain of their own election and perseverance. But the things the Scholastics additionally state about the freedom of exercise and the freedom of specification in the will of angels (in respect of the other acts of obedience that do not pertain to their essential blessedness), we pass over on the grounds that they are debated rashly and defined without argument. For we are certain of this one thing from Scriptures, that they obey the will of God and of his Christ constantly and in everything, and that they do so with utmost dedication and the highest eagerness—as it is for this reason that the Scriptures often present them to us as exemplary.

35. A reasonable creature's intellect and will are necessarily followed by power, whereby the creature is effectual outside itself, and whereby it produces actions befitting its own nature. It is clear from their marvelous deeds that this power is exceedingly strong in angels, wherefore they are said to excel in strength (Ps 103:20) and are called angels of God's power (2 Thess 1:7). But Satan, in Matt 12:29, is called "the strong one," and in 2 Cor 4:4 "the god of this world."

36. This power of the angels will be explained best from the objects around which it operates in this world. And these objects are either souls or bodies,

the former being either alive or dead, and the latter being either elementary or ethereal.

37. As far as the ethereal bodies are concerned, very many philosophers assign to the heavenly spheres powers of intelligence that are to support them and propel them constantly in their orbit, or to conduct individual stars in their circle. We reject this, however, as an invention not based on any solid argument. For Holy Scripture, which everywhere describes the duties of the angels most fully to us, makes no mention of this matter, but to the contrary places the angels' dwelling-place in the highest heaven or Paradise, and asserts that they all are being sent for the salvation of believers (Heb 1:14). And the Bible clearly indicates that the force by which the heavens and the stars are carried in their orbit had been grafted in them by divine providence from the first creation onwards, and is preserved by God's singular providence—as can be seen from Job 38:31, Ps 19:5[-6] and 104:22[19–23], Eccl 1:5, etc.

38. Also false and altogether worthy of being assigned to devilish illusions is what the magicians once claimed that by their chanting they could stop the course of the sun and the moon, or turn back the stars, since Holy Scripture reckons this among the extraordinary miracles that are restricted to God himself in particular (Josh 10:13; Isa 38:7).

39. But Holy Scripture does teach that angels possess a greater power over the elementary bodies, namely to excite them, or change, stop, scatter them, etc. For Sodom and Gomorrah where overturned by the work of holy angels (Gen 19). The force of fire was checked by them (Dan 3); they stopped winds from blowing (Rev 7); and prisons and iron chains were smashed without a sound (Acts 5 and 12). And by Satan fire from heaven and stormy winds were hurled down upon the herds and home of Job's sons (Job 1:16, 19), and similarly upon the earth (Rev 13:13)—from where also the power of the air is assigned to him specifically (Eph 2:2).

40. Upon the bodies of human beings and the other living creatures they exert powers that are equally effective. They very quickly transport them through the air, as is evidenced in the case of the body of Christ himself (Matt 4), and of Philip's (Acts 10[8:39]); they impede their natural movements. They render bodies dumb deaf, and blind, while the organs remain intact, and they use their muscles and tongues at will, as is clear from the instances of the possessed and those healed by Christ in the Gospel. The good angels, no less than the evil ones, have the power to inflict diseases, as is seen from 2 Sam

24:16, Job 2:7, Acts 12:23 and elsewhere. And in one night one of them slew many myriads of human beings (Exod 12:23; 2 Kgs 19 [:35], etc.).

41. A more difficult question is whether they possess the same power to cure the sick. We do not deny that they are able to cure many types of diseases, but they do so through the secondary causes, or by hidden remedies that they apply secretly and cleverly; or they do so by the removal or transference of matter that brings disease. But we flatly deny that they are able to cure diseases that are obviously fatal, or diseases by which some body-part completely loses its form—because this belongs clearly to the jurisdiction of God's power, and is an extraordinary sign of a divine calling or mission.

42. Much less do we ascribe to them the power of restoring dead men to life, or of arousing their souls from the underworld, as the ancient heathens and not a few of the papal teachers believed. We are altogether certain that the case of Samuel summoned by the incantation of the medium (mentioned in 1 Sam 28) was a deception of Satan, who put himself forward in the guise of Samuel.

43. From this we also draw the clear conclusion that angels are not able to perform true miracles. For even the good angels never claim these for themselves, since Scripture counts them among the works that belong to God (Ps 72:18; 136:4), whose glory they never seize for themselves. But the signs which are put forward by the bad angels consist either of tricks and illusions, or of works which surpass human understanding—in such a way though that wiser persons can give some of their causes out of nature itself, whence they are also called "counterfeit signs and wonders" by the Spirit of God (2 Thess 2:9).

44. A much more difficult question, though one which must be answered, is what power they possess over human souls. We hold that both good and bad angels are able to influence the external and internal senses of men in amazing ways, as when they struck the eyes of the men of Sodom with blindness (Gen 19:11). Without needing the outward senses, they habitually portray their own likenesses, or those of other persons and things, to the minds of people when they are awake or asleep, which is evident from the prophetic dreams and visions. Thus, an angel of Satan was a lying spirit among the prophets of Ahab (1 Kgs 22[:21–24]), and people who are possessed experience various apparitions of them, as experience reveals.

45. Moreover, just as good angels have the power to prompt good and holy thoughts, so too on the other hand do the evil ones have the power to suggest evil thoughts (1 Chron 21:1), also in order to confuse and upset people's feelings, as the case of Saul (1 Sam 16:15) shows.

46. However we deny that they exert direct control over people's practical judgments, or over their will, because Scripture ascribes that to God alone, in Prov 21:1 and elsewhere. Therefore the influence which Holy Scripture attributes to bad angels over wicked people is only a moral one; yet by God's just judgment it is so effective that they are able to drive them wherever they wish, like slaves. For when they are abandoned by God, or when He implants a 'strong delusion' in them [2 Thess 2:11] in order to punish them for their lack of gratitude or for prior obstinacy, like dumb animals they are carried away by their passions, and like blind people they get lost even where the way is clear, as can be seen in Rom 1:28, Eph 2:2, 2 Cor 4:4, 2 Thess 2:11, etc.

47. Therefore the devout must guard diligently and pray that they may never be led into temptation, but be delivered from the evil one. And they should be certain always that good angels are not able to do anything for them without God's command, nor are bad angels able to do anything against them except by God's judgment and permission. In fact, people may even beseech God for the support of the holy angels; through their power and help even Satan's power and influence can be hindered, and Satan himself can be bound up, as is attested in Scripture (Rev 12:8, 20[:2], etc.).

48. Now that we have considered the essential characteristics of angels, it remains to explain some attendant circumstances (which we shall note briefly), namely their number, movement, place, rank, and duties.

49. It is clear from many passages in Scripture that the number of the angels is very great; for thousands upon thousands, and ten thousand times ten thousand stand around God's throne (Rev 5:11); and an entire legion of demons possessed one man (Luke 8:30). Their movement is extremely swift, and as fast as lightning (Luke 10:18), for which they are compared to wind and fire (Ps 104[:4]). Though not confined (as bodies are), their place is determined—which is the apposition of a certain 'somewhere' not only in their activity, but also in their essence.

50. We do not deny that a ranking of some sort exists among angels. Concerning bad angels the matter is clear from Matt 25:41 and Rev 12:7. Also

concerning good angels the same may be gathered from some situations, even though Dionysius the Pseudo-Areopagite and following him the Scholastics have rashly determined precisely what that order is.

51. Their offices are set forth for us everywhere in the sacred books. For they stand before the throne of God constantly, they praise Him and his Christ, and they receive orders from Him, not only to teach, comfort, and guard those who are heirs of salvation, but also to carry out his judgments against the ungodly. But God also uses the work of bad angels to test his own people, and to punish and trouble the faithless and unrepentant.

52. It cannot be gathered so clearly from Scriptures whether a single angel is assigned to each individual person. For us it is enough to know that often an entire army of them has been put in charge of guarding one saint, as is clear from the case of the patriarch Jacob, and Elisha. Often many angels are put in charge of a certain type of believers, as in Matt 18:10; and often one is put in charge of an entire region, or people, as appears from Isa 37:36 and the prophecy of Daniel.

ABOUT MAN CREATED
IN THE IMAGE OF GOD

President: Antonius Thysius
Respondent: Johannes Olivarius

Humanity not only is the high point and goal of creation, it also forms the bond that links earthly and heavenly things (2, 6–8). Human beings are created for the knowledge and glory of God (54). The creation of man and woman (4–5, 48–53) is in accordance with this high goal. Human beings consist of a body and an immortal soul, tightly connected. The latter can exist apart from the former, but unlike angels, the human soul is incomplete, 'not entirely blessed,' without body (3, 9–31). The soul possesses awesome gifts and functions, like thinking, reasoning, self-reflection, self-awareness, but above all the knowledge and worship of God, its discernment of true and false, just and unjust, discovery of arts, and so on (28–29, 32–34). In both soul and body, men and women are created in the image of God. They are 'a rather close copy' of God and that shows their enormous dignity (7–8, 12, 35–36). 'Image of God' refers to the goodness of humanity, its uprightness and perfection, surpassing excellence over all other living creatures, and its closer approximation to God. Man and woman represented God's image by his wise, holy, and just dominion over the whole earth (37–47). In their pristine state before the Fall, Adam and Eve enjoyed 'original righteousness': harmony of body and soul, of affections and actions, a will in harmony with the will of God, free from the necessity of sinning, and immortality (38–39). However, the Fall caused a loss of the image of God; original sin replaced original righteousness (42).

1. We have given a general treatment of the work of creation and a particular one of the creatures endowed with reason, the angels—both the ones who keep the state and the truth they had at first, and those who have fallen from it. It follows that we now deal with man as created in the image of God.

2. Man is clearly the high point and goal of nature's lower order, yet he also belongs to a higher order, he is the 'sum' of everything and the bond that links earthly and heavenly things.

3. However, by that we do not mean the body and the soul separately but something that is composed from both, that is from the rational soul and the body which a very tight and close bond binds together into one nature, united in one person.

4. We view the creation of man as two-fold: a first and immediate one (Gen 1:27) and a second, mediated one (Gen 6:7; Ps 102:19). The former is of the first parents, the latter of the other people they brought forth.

5. The first people were made by God without mediation, both with respect to efficiency and with respect to the physical matter. With respect to efficiency, because they were made by God without the collaboration of any angel. With respect to matter, because for fashioning them either no physical matter existed (as in the case of the soul), or there was no physical matter that was proper, suitable, and apt (in the case of the body), if you look at the proximate matter.

6. But God made man last, after everything else, so that there would be a progression from less to more perfected things. And since everything exists for the sake of mankind, all things that are directed to him as their goal had to be in existence beforehand, things that make his condition a good and happy one. This sequence of creation is a unique feat of divine providence, and also an illustration of the dignity of humanity.

7. To enhance the scope and greatness of dignity of mankind further, God saw to it that when He was going to create him, He did not produce man in the same way as the other creatures, by his word alone, but He took council concerning his creation, and made a plan. Better yet, He girded himself for the task, like someone about to fashion a unique and exceptional work with great effort. In fact, in this matter God does not go by his collective name, but the three persons of the Godhead are brought on to act together, since God says, "Let us make man in our own image, according to our likeness." This obviously indicates the plurality of the divine persons (Prov 8:22–30; John 1:3; Job 33:4; Ps 104:30).

8. Indeed, the fact that God "decided to create him in his own image" shows the superior dignity of mankind. For other things created do bear some

vestige, shade, and likeness of God, but only mankind was made "according to the image of God"—which declares that he is a rather close copy.

9. God also created man to consist of two parts, "a body and a soul" (Gen 2:7), although elsewhere Scripture divides it into three parts, body, soul, and spirit (1 Thess 5:23), taking the word soul in a stricter sense. The first distinction is the main one, the second is useful.

10. In the beginning, God created the body of the first man in its essence and with all of its parts; and like a potter He fashioned him "from the dust of the earth" or "the dust from the earth." Yet Scripture does not say whether God fashioned him also from other elements; if that were so (from earth softened with water especially), then we could infer the other elements from that predominant one. But in itself the material was not capable or fit for forming a body (especially such a body), but it received that entire body by God's power.

11. By this 'fashioning,' which also is accorded to the hands of God (John 10:8[28–29?]; Ps 119:73), we do not literally mean a physical, manual action by God after He had assumed bodily form, as some would have it. We mean a careful, unique, and, as far as the unfit material is concerned, a direct creation by Him. The other living creatures He produced through water and earth, all at once and fully formed; but He molded the body of man first and uniquely, as if by his own hand. Hence also Adam derives his name from the Hebrew 'adama, like [the Latin] homo (man) from humus (ground), and so all men after him (Gen 3:19; 5:2).

12. Moreover, just as the earthly material is a reminder of our weakness and proof of our humbler nature (Gen 3:19), so too the immediate and exceptional fashioning is a testimony to our dignity.

13. The body, then, was thus formed by God to be fit for a human soul, and it was made ready so as to be a suitable instrument for such a soul and its actions—and for no other spiritual nature by itself.

14. God added to this sort of body by putting the soul or the breath of life into it, which goes by the general Hebrew word ruah, 'spirit.' More precise is nefesh, 'soul,' which applies only to a living creature; and most precise is neshama, that is 'breath' or 'exhaling,' which is usually applied to mankind. In Latin a similar distinction exists between spirit, soul, and mind [literally: 'wind'], not because the spirit is some sort of blowing, or wind, or an exhaling

or something fleeting, but because the subtlety and the power of its nature is portrayed by its similarity to them, namely its spiritual as opposed to bodily nature.

15. And so the soul is not an accident, or a quality, but a substance. But it is actually not corporeal, subject to the senses of touch and sight; it is completely spiritual. Yet there are some among the ancient Greek church-fathers, and also among the Latin ones (Arnobius, Tertullian, etc.), who seem to hold that it is a very delicate corporeal body. But we separate the soul clearly from the nature of the body.

16. Indeed the soul is a spirit of such kind that it can exist apart from the body, as the following witnesses from Holy Scripture bear out: Gen 2:7, Eccl 12:7, Matt 10:28, Luke 23:43, 46; Acts 7:59, etc.

17. But the nature of the human soul is not like the angels (who are also spirits), because angels are essences that are distinguished from body to such a degree that they do not tend by nature to have a body; but the soul, on the other hand, does have that tendency.

18. Yet the soul does come from God, though not from God's material being or as an offshoot from him, nor as some particle from him. It comes from Him as the efficient cause, and from some very close approximation of its nature to the essence of God, and from its being made similar to the divine properties (Acts 17:28, 29).

19. And the soul also was not created or made from any one essence whatsoever, whether celestial or elementary; but for that first man the soul was blown "out of nothing" into his face, mouth, and especially his nostrils, and it was created by means of the blowing, as Augustine puts it.

20. Some understand 'inblowing' or 'inbreathing' literally (like 'fashioning'), for the physical action of the mouth that was performed after a corporeal body was assumed, and they argue that it was an outward symbol of the created spirit which causes man to live. Others understand it figuratively for God's special and simply direct and powerful action in making the human soul. And we agree with this way of thinking. To be clear, two facts must be observed here: That the soul came from without, and, that it corresponds to the divine essence by analogy.

21. There have been various debates about the seat of the soul, and in particular that of the mind. There are those who consider this question

unanswerable. Some argue that the soul has been spread out evenly throughout the whole body (completely throughout the whole body, and completely in any given part of it), but that it is evidenced more in one specific part because the main instrument of its abilities is there (as the scholastics hold, following Ambrose and Augustine). Others assign a specific seat to the mind: The Academics the head, or the brain; the Peripatetics and Stoics the chest or heart.

22. We embrace this last way of thinking, in line with Sacred Scripture and nearly all the ancient fathers, and we hold that with regard to its essence, the soul has the heart as its central place of retreat (wherefore the heart stands also for all of the soul's faculties, namely, wisdom, the will, and feeling). However, we are of the view that the soul exercises its powers within the body, and in fact by means of its appropriate instruments, just as understanding is conducted through the brain. In essence, then, it is located in this specific part, but its workings are throughout the entire body (Deut 29:4, Rom 1:21, Matt 15:19, and 22:37).

23. As to the fact that other passages state that the soul of all flesh—and so of man, too—is in its blood, indeed, that the blood itself is the soul (Gen 9, Lev 17, which also Empedocles and others asserted), we must understand this not about the soul as it exercises reason, but in its function of sustaining life, and as life itself.

24. The soul has a natural, constant feeling for and leaning towards the body as towards the other half of a composition, and to its aptly suited and proper instrument. And it is the soul that grants feeling, life, and movement to the body. In the body the soul exercises its authority, control, and government. However, the soul does not depend entirely upon the body; nor is it organic, since it can be separated from the body, can subsist by itself, and can attend to its own duties without the support of the body, and since it continues to outlive the body. Nevertheless, without the body the soul is not entirely blessed, but it is fully happy only when it is united with the body. This is proof that the resurrection of the body is necessary for mankind's blessedness.

25. However, the soul is not only separable from the body and outlives it, it is also immortal by nature, as the witnesses of Scripture and evident arguments prove. The witnesses from the Old Testament are Ps 49:16; Eccl

12:7; 1 Sam 28:11; 1 Kgs 17:21. Witnesses from the New Testament are: Matt 10:28; Phil 1:22, 23; 1 Pet 3:19; Rev 6:9 and 7:9, and throughout.

26. The evident arguments are these. The first argument is from the form of its creation, for it was created by the inbreathing of God, not with any precast matter whatsoever, but rather from God himself, through an assimilation to his essence, and thus in the image of God. However, nothing that is mortal can be the image of the immortal God.

27. Secondly, the argument from its own nature, for it is a simple essence that has nothing mingled, added, joined or fastened to it; wherefore it also cannot be separated, divided, or dispersed, and hence it is immune to death. For death is like a separation, breaking-up, or splitting-apart of those parts which before death were held together by some union.

28. And then there is the argument arising from the marvelous gifts, effects, and godlike functions of the soul. For its clever genius is awe-inspiring, as is its swift thinking, its ease of perception, its sharp discernment, its discourse and reasoning about all things, its recollection of past events, its consideration of current events, its ability to foresee future events, and especially its ability to turn towards itself and reflect upon itself, and its self-awareness. All of these abilities come not from a combination of (physical) elements, but from a more divine nature, and they prove that the soul is immortal.

29. The foremost argument comes from the soul's knowledge and worship of God that has been implanted in the soul, by the discernment and perception of true and false, fair and unfair, just and unjust, beautiful and base, honest and dishonest, and by the discovery and knowledge of countless arts. For a strength that passes away would not be able to rise up to the immortal God and the source of life, or to contemplate the heavenly and divine realms with such admirable power of intellect.

30. There is the argument from the witness borne by our conscience, which devises horrible fears from the guilt of our sins. Surely if people's souls did not remain alive after death, the godless would have no reason to fear even the tiniest future punishment.

31. Yet the food for the human soul is also immortal, as that is God and the enjoyment of Him. And if the soul were not immortal, then our faith and hope would be futile along with our whole worship (1 Cor 15:14). And lastly, the consensus [about the soul's immortality] that is common to nearly all

races, even the most uncivilized ones, provides additional support for this fact.

32. As far as the faculties of the soul are concerned, leaving aside the more subtle debates of the Philosophers, we divide them into the intellect (or the mind) and the will; or, with the apostle, into the spirit and the soul. In a more restricted sense we mean by the word 'spirit' the higher faculty, that is the mind; whereas with the word 'soul' we mean the lower one, the one of the senses and of (vegetative) growth. The Latins express these by means of *animus* (spirit) and *anima* (soul).

33. With the intellect we grasp objects and decide whether they should be approved or condemned. And this process is two-fold: Theoretical, whereby true is distinguished from false, and practical, whereby good is distinguished from evil, and fair from unfair. In this process we regard science and conscience, which, when joined together, constitute a practical syllogism.

34. But by the will, whose nature it is not to be forced, and in keeping with the first nature's ability is not restricted by any necessity towards things beyond itself, we choose objects or reject them, as the intellect judges them to be good or evil. Often the choice is between equal and between unequal things; then, in fact, the will halts its own operation.

35. And so man was made into a living soul, personally united in body and spirit together, which constitutes the whole man.

36. Moreover, the whole man in both soul and body "is created in the image of God and according to his likeness," in which the latter phrase serves to expound the former. It even bears the force of an epithet which 'amplifies' the former, as if to say a "similar image" (Gen 1:27, 5:1). This is different from the understanding of some of the church-fathers who take "image" as referring to the nature, and "likeness" as referring to the actions conforming to God.

37. By this expression we mean the goodness of man, his uprightness and perfection (or ideal state), his surpassing excellence over all other living creatures, and his closer approximation to God.

38. An inner integrity is found in the soul, the body, the affections and actions, and in the immortality of the whole man. Regarding intellect, man was of outstanding knowledge (Gen 2:19, etc.). He had such freedom concerning his will that he was not only free from coercion but even from

the necessity of sinning; he was in harmony with the mind, the good reason, and the will of God. The affections (or inclinations and appetites) were so composed that they complied with the intellect and the will. His body and limbs formed a constitution that was holy; upright and wholesome actions were to arise from them all.

39. In addition to these there was "immortality," not only of the soul, but also of the body, or, "of the whole man" (Rom 5:12 and 6:23). And each of these was naturally immortal, because the soul, being non-composite, could die in no way whatsoever. And the body was immortal, because it was not going to die, both because of its good constitution and by being preserved by the soul, which would have nurtured and preserved it constantly and vitally.

40. We attribute this harmony and consensual action of all the parts of the created man to original righteousness, as to a mother or a mistress. This may be called natural, because it was bestowed and man received it, in the sense not of the individual but the whole species, and because its opposite, original sin, is of a corrupt nature. However, this does not therefore preclude every further grace of God, but it includes it, so that in this way grace may foster nature.

41. With the word "dominion" Scripture expresses this surpassing prominence of man over all living things, indeed, over the whole earth (which the other creatures serve), when it says: "That they may have dominion over the fish of the sea, etc.," and "have dominion over," etc.—in which phrase also man's descendants are implied. Furthermore, by means of those words for dominion and majesty, Moses seems to be representing God's own image via its properties and effects. Indeed, for someone to exercise dominion, he must be endowed with the gift of a soul that reasons; but to do so fairly and peaceably, he must certainly be wise, holy, and just. And if he would also put his dominion into practice, he must have a body well-prepared for actions that accord with a soul that is sound. And finally, for the dominion to be perpetual, the man must be immortal.

42. Consistent with this the apostle places the image of God, viewed from its beginning, in wisdom, holiness, and justice; this can be gathered also from its opposite, after the image of God had been lost, and from its restoration (2 Cor 3:18, Eph 4:22–24; Col 3:9,10).

43. And from here comes the closer access to God, since man conforms to God, and is united with and clings to Him. This act, too, is expressed and embraced by the image of God.

44. Therefore the condition of mankind was a very blessed one. And in addition to it there was the external dignity, as he was placed in the garden, or Paradise planted by God, which Moses exquisitely portrays in its location, setting, and environs. Leaving aside the debates about its rivers, the size, and how long Paradise existed, we are of the opinion that it should be placed in or near Mesopotamia, near the Tigris and the Euphrates.

45. Moreover God furnished the garden with every kind of very beautiful plants and trees which would serve for food and enjoyment. Among these trees was the "tree of life and [the tree] of the knowledge of good and evil." The first one is so called not because it possesses life within itself or because it has the power—like some panacea—to grant life to the body or the soul (as the Schoolmen following some church-fathers think), but rather in virtue of the sacraments, since the tree would seal each sacrament—indeed, would foreshadow the spiritual life that is to come (Rev 2:7).

46. The other tree, however, is called the tree "of the knowledge of good and evil" not because it possessed knowledge (that is silly) or that implanted in it was some secret power to bring about knowledge or to sharpen the mind, as Josephus thought. But it is so called because it is a sacramental tree by God's decision, which bids man not to wish to know more than what God wills, or to measure good and evil by his own ways of thinking. And by this tree also God would test man's obedience in the eating of the fruit, so that he was going to sense and experience the good from which he would be deprived and the evil into which he would fall.

47. Into this garden "the Lord put the man" like a master in his kingly court, "to work it and to maintain it" (Gen 2:15). Indeed, "to work it" as a pleasant and sacred task, without tiring or wearying. And "to maintain it" in the condition in which he received it, and to guard it from the incursion and destruction of wild animals. And as our ancestors were placed in Paradise in person, in the same manner would their descendants be included there.

48. And God created humans (using the word 'man' in a general sense) of two sexes, as it says, "male and female He created them," namely, for the propagation of the human race in the world (Gen 1:27). Yet they were

unequal in nature and dignity, as she was more feeble and lower—whence especially the woman is called the image and glory of the man, as man is the image of God (1 Cor 11:7).

49. Nor did God create both of them at the same time or in the same manner. For first He constructed the man, and then the woman, so that the dignity of man would be set above the woman's (1 Cor 11:8). And just as God is the one starting point of creation of things, so the first man was to be the one starting point for the generation of all men, so that while they would know that they are all from one man, they would love one another as one and be united with each other in a common bond of blood (Acts 17:26).

50. And then God also formed man "from dust," but woman from "the rib of the man as he slept," and He clothed her with flesh, and took her from his side and not from his head or his feet. She was made ready not as his sovereign, nor as his handmaid, but as his companion, so he would learn that she, whom he knew was taken from his side, should take her place at his side. And they were made into one flesh, in order that their origin, conjugal relationship, and their common offspring would strengthen the bond of mutual affection in marriage (Eph 5:28).

51. Thus far concerning the first creation of man; what follows next is the second, mediated creation, which is of the human nature that had been made and equipped with organs suitable for reproduction, whereto God through his blessing also granted the power to reproduce. And He made it fruitful in such a way that man may be generated from man (namely male and female) in order to fill the earth with people, according to that word: "He blessed them, and said, 'grow and multiply, and fill the earth.'"

52. On this point there once arose a discussion among the church-fathers, 'whether the souls of people stem as offshoots from their parents, or are in fact created and infused by God.' Some fathers, including Tertullian and others, were of the opinion that the entire man is propagated from the whole man, namely, body from body, soul from soul, in the same way that light is kindled from light, or as others thought, from the power of the reproductive seed.

53. The common consensus, however, counters this view, namely, that it is not from an off-shoot, but from God (not, to be sure, as though already in existence from before the beginning of the world, as Origen thinks), as

created immediately and in bodies—when in the mother's womb a body has been put together and arranged in order to receive such a soul—, infused, or rather, as others prefer, created within the body, from heaven above. Augustine leaves the matter undecided. We think that the conventional thinking accords better with the truth.

54. The goal and profit of creation and of the created man is that he himself, from such a marvelous workmanship that he is, and from such pre-eminent status, should come to know God's exceeding wisdom, power, and benevolence, which He reveals in our origin. And once man has come to discern these things, to worship God inwardly as well as outwardly, for every sort of bliss for himself, and for the glory of God.

ON THE FALL OF ADAM

President: Johannes Polyander
Respondent: Johannes Zelius

In Adam, as the head and universal beginning of the whole human race—the chief parent by virtue of the covenant God established with him—God includes all people (5). In his disobedience to one divine commandment (6), Adam also transgressed the entire moral law (7–8). The sin of Adam can be characterized as unbelief, because its first step was doubting the truth of the threat whereby God had sanctioned his command not to eat from the tree of the knowledge of good and evil. Unbelief opened the door to ambition, and so to ingratitude, impiety towards God, and willful disobedience (9–18). After this brief narrative account of the first sin, which is developed on the first chapters of Genesis, the disputation proceeds according to the scholastic mode of causation: external causes (20–29), internal causes (30–33), formal and final causes (34), and also the effects of sin, of which the foremost is the privation of righteousness (35–40). The first sin was caused neither by God (20–26), nor by the devil, although the latter is the principal external cause (20, 27, 33). Sin is an act of the human free will (30), created good in a way that it was able to sin (31–33). The conception of sin as being volitional (or willed) shows that it is not seen as a weakness of the mind or the emotions, etc.; the act of sinning was intentional, and so we are 'without excuse' (37). This volitional aspect of sin is retained throughout the disputations that follow. All people sinned in Adam and Eve originally, got the same damaged nature and so were counted guilty of the same crime and death (40).

1. Sin is lawlessness or a vice that conflicts with the law of God (1 John 3:4).

2. The subject of sin is the rational creature made in God's image who falls away from the good that the law of God prescribes and who falls into the evil it forbids.

3. Sin may be examined in wicked angels, in our first parents Adam and Eve, or in their descendants.

4. We undertake to give a treatment of the sin of our first parents, which the apostle (as to its generic character) calls disobedience, transgression, or fall (Rom 5:12 ff.).

5. Although this sin was committed by Adam and Eve, the apostle assigns it only to Adam (Rom 5:12) as the head and universal beginning of the whole human race, from whom Eve, too, had been created (1 Cor 11:8). In him God includes all people, as he is the chief parent by virtue of the covenant God established with him.

6. The divine commandment which Adam straight out violated by his disobedience was stated directly by God in Paradise: "You may eat from every tree of the garden that is for eating, but from the tree of the knowledge of good and evil you shall not eat" (Gen 2:16–17). In ignoring that decree, man willed to test whether the tree possessed the power to bestow greater knowledge on him.

7. By the same disobedience he consequently transgressed the moral law, the stated sum of the natural law implanted in him by God.

8. For he violated the first table of the law through his unbelief and his godless behavior; he violated the second table by his ungratefulness toward his heavenly Father, by the murder of himself and his descendants, by his lack of self-control, by the theft and seizure of another's possessions, by complying with a false witness, and by the wrong desire for a higher knowledge and status.

9. The opinions of the scholars are divided about the specific character of this sin.

10. Some of the papal theologians hold that it was pride, others gluttony whereby our parents ate the apple before it was right to do so (as though this was not a permanent prohibition). Others hold that it was lack of self-control whereby they had intercourse while not yet being married.

11. Brenz is of the opinion that it was by a desertion from Christ, the Son of God, that they snubbed his rule.

12. Most of our teachers state that it was unbelief whereby they withheld their faith in that divine threat, "on the day on which you eat from the tree of the knowledge of good and evil, your will die" (Gen 2:17).

13. We can admit this interpretation if we give the right weight to what our parents first did, rather than what they first saw or directed their attention to.

14. For the beginning of that sin, its first move or step, was doubting the truth of the threat whereby God willed to sanction his command; this can be demonstrated clearly from the order in which the devil led Eve into temptation.

15. For he first solicited her to doubt God's word by his doubtful question: "Did God really state, 'you shall not eat of every tree in the garden'?" (Gen 3:1).

16. Then, being more emboldened by the reply of the wavering woman as she added something to God's command, he removed God's sanction through this obvious contradiction: "You will not die, but God knows that on the day you eat of it your eyes will be opened, and you will be like God, knowing good and evil" [Gen 3:5].

17. Eve, placing her trust in the devil's lie rather than in the divine truth, endeavored passionately to have that likeness and divine knowledge by eating of the forbidden fruit.

18. And after that first act of unbelief many inordinate emotions and feelings came rushing along. For as the unbelief of our parents opened the door to ambition, so linked with it were ingratitude, thanklessness, impiety towards God, and willful disobedience (the 'mother' of defection), by which Adam and Eve spurned God and abandoned Him and took refuge in devil's camp.

19. The cause of this sin is either external or internal.

20. The external cause of it was not God's foreknowledge, nor his permission or impulse, but the instigation of the devil.

21. It was not God's foreknowledge, whether that knowledge is seen separately from the act of the deciding will, or jointly with it.

22. For the cause of things that are known beforehand cannot be a theoretical or indeterminate foreknowledge of God, since this knowledge does not act in anything other than itself, nor do events occur because God foreknew

them with a bare cognition. Instead, He foreknew things that were going to happen precisely because He decreed them to happen or to permit them so that they would be done by others.

23. Moreover, practical foreknowledge, which has God's will joined with it, does not act externally from itself, but in its partnership with the act of the will. Nor does it have future events in view only for their existence and truth, but also in the aspect of being good and as the objects of its own very just will.

24. For this reason, since sin is not a good but a turning away from the good (the natural good God effects in all his creatures, the moral good He teaches in the law, and the final good He proposes to himself as He governs and directs everything most wisely), the cause of the sin committed by Adam and Eve in no way whatsoever can be attributed to Him without manifest blasphemy.

25. Nor can God's permission be stated as the cause of that sin, since by its intervention God did not bring about sin, but He let our parents, whose unlawful desire He was not bound to restrain, to commit the sin—in order that He might draw the highest good from it.

26. Nor can an impulse of God be the cause, for God cannot be tempted by any evil, nor can He tempt anyone else to evil [Jas 1:13], as He declares in his explicit law that He hates it and will punish it with the penalty of death.

27. In fact the principal external cause for the sin of our parents is the instigation of the devil. For just as he led Eve astray through the agency of the snake, so he seduced Adam through the prompting of Eve.

28. We should note that in leading them astray the devil took four actions:

1. He appeared to Eve in the form of a serpent to hide his deception more effectively.

2. He took on the body of the animal which surpassed the others in its cunning and in its talent for creeping into the garden.

3. He attacked the woman before the man because her resolve was weaker.

4. He enticed the man through the woman, his life-partner, into a partnership in the same sin.

29. In considering this, the apostle says that the first to be seduced was not the man but the woman, and that she was the cause of his transgression, obviously as the instrumental and supportive cause (1 Tim 2:13, 14).

30. The internal cause of the fall is the free will of both our parents; better yet, it is the bending of the will that listened to Satan instead of God.

31. Both of our parents were created by God in such a way that they were able not to sin if they willed not to sin, and that were able to sin if they willed to.

32. And although God created each of them good in such a way that they could change, nevertheless that changeability in their good state was neither a defect in the nature that was created in God's image, nor was it sin or the cause of sin. It was the condition that suited the creature from whom the Creator is set apart by this incommunicable mark of perfection, that He in himself and by nature is unchangeably good.

33. Yet it does not therefore mean that our parents are to be excused because they over-stepped God's command by the instigation of the devil; for the devil by his external suggestion could not adduce any coercive necessity to their will.

34. One cannot assign a proper form to sin, because sin is a lack of form or a distortion of and departure from the perfect law which God had given to man. Nor does it have an end, because it is a deviation from the law and from the ordering towards the end for which man was created.

35. The effects which followed upon that sin were punishments, either shared by both parents or specific to one or the other.

36. The shared penalties are: 1. the loss of their original righteousness; 2. their awareness of nakedness; 3. the terror of their conscience; 4. the ejection from Paradise; 5. the mound of all kinds of struggles and sufferings; 6. the necessity of dying.

37. Therefore those people err who think that the sin of both parents, but chiefly Adam, was minor and pardonable. For the less burdensome and easier it was to observe God's commandment, so much the more without excuse was each of our parents before God on account of that transgression, and guilty of temporal and eternal death.

38. The punishment specific to the man was a certain singular worry and anxiety for the things that he was to manage throughout the whole course of his life.

39. The punishment specific to the woman was a very great hardship in childbearing and in the upbringing of children.

40. Just as all people sinned in both parents originally and were infected by this common ailment through the proliferation of that same damaged nature, so too were they counted guilty of the same crime and death (Rom 5:12).

41. We do not, in the meantime, hesitate to assert that both parents through faith in Jesus, the promised seed of the woman, have been reconciled to God and have become partakers of eternal salvation.

DISPUTATION 15

ON ORIGINAL SIN

President: Andreas Rivetus
Respondent: Abraham van Eldere

The 'origin' of all sin lies in the sin committed by Adam and Eve; the term 'original' sin, however, indicates primarily the sin that resides in all of their offspring, who participated in the first sin. In this 'inherited lawlessness' all people are corrupt; they not only lack righteousness, but also are inclined to every sort of evil. God transmitted the guilt and depravity of nature, caused by the fall of Adam and Eve, to all posterity (1–10). Justly, because Adam in Paradise not only bore his own personality, but also that of the mass of humanity. 'We all are considered to have committed what Adam did' (17). For this reason, even original sin is in some way voluntary, and that entails the accountability of man for his being sinful from birth. From the will of Adam as a root, the will of every individual is evil, perverse, and hostile to God. This sin is transmitted not by imitation of the devil or Adam, but through propagation (11–21). Next, the matter or subject (22–23), and the form of original sin is explained: this corruption entails not only a destitution of what is good, but also a depraved tendency to evil (24–29). Therefore, this corruption that entered into human nature and infected it completely is rightly called 'concupiscence.' Concupiscence is not a consequence of sin, nor does it lead to sin: it is sin, in and of itself, indwelling both in people who are not reborn and in those reborn and holy. Concupiscence does not rule over the regenerate; the guilt of it has been removed, and it is weakened and diminished as the grace of regeneration increases (30–36). The effect of original sin is guilt, and guilt deserves punishment. By itself original sin earns temporal and eternal punishment for all people, but for those in the covenant the guilt of eternal death has been cancelled (37–39). The doctrine of original sin reveals to us the need for the second Adam, Jesus Christ, as the one who regenerates us (40).

1. At creation God granted man a two-fold life: a natural life, and a spiritual life. The former is situated in the union of soul and body, the latter in the

linking of the soul to God, who is its craftsman. As natural life is lost by the disjunction of that natural union, so spiritual death follows man's alienation from God. If by his rebellion Adam also brought the other creatures down so low that therefore they became subject to a curse, it is entirely plausible that the curse was passed down to his whole offspring. Being made partaker of the sin whereby death entered the world, his offspring remains burdened by the deformity and charge of guilt until someone else relieves it.

2. And so, having treated the first sin of our ancestors, for the sake of proper method we should discuss the sin that has its origin directly in that first transgression, and that was passed on to his descendants. To do so in an orderly fashion we must first enquire whether a sin of this kind exists, and second, what that sin is. At that point we shall have to give separate treatments of its causes, subjects, and effects.

3. We should perform this task all the more meticulously because, with Augustine, we judge "that strictly speaking the Christian belief is founded upon the position of two men, namely Adam and Christ, of whom through the one we were sold under sin, and through the other we are redeemed from sins" (*Concerning Original Sin*, chapter 14). For this is the reason why the Son of God assumed human flesh and willed to suffer in it: To release the human race from slavery to sin, in which it was held prisoner following the transgression of the first parent. As a result, already in former times—but also in this age—the Church has suffered and suffers the same enmity against Christ's grace, which it meets in the opposition against [the doctrine of] original sin.

4. At various times men who knew of nothing beyond what is natural bemoaned the distortion and perverseness of the natural state. Plato observed, "by their very nature men are evil, and cannot be persuaded to cherish justice" (*Republic*, book 2). And Cicero lamented the fact that "man is brought forth to the light of day by his step-mother, nature, with a body that is naked, frail and powerless, with a soul that is anxious over troubles, abject in the face of fears, crippled at the prospect of hard work, inclined towards wanton passion, in whom the divine fire-light, its talent, and character, lie hidden from view." This is quoted from the *Book about the Republic* by Augustine, Book 4, against Julian. But even so they did not acknowledge evil sufficiently, nor could they reach the cause and source of evil, as they lacked spiritual light.

5. The Scripture of the Old and New Testament most clearly shows that it is right to say that from Adam sin is passed down to his descendants. In Scripture God himself asserts that every imagination and the thoughts of the heart of man are only evil all the time (Gen 6:5)—and that from the time of childhood (Gen 8:21). And Job states that what is conceived from an impure seed cannot possibly be born pure (Job 14:4). David confesses that he was conceived in iniquity (Ps 51:7). And Christ asserts that "whatever is born from flesh is flesh" (John 3:6). And Paul: "Through one man sin came into the world, and through sin death, and so death came to all men, in whom all sinned, even those who did not sin in the manner of Adam" (Rom 5:12–14). And, "we all by nature are children of wrath" (Eph 2:3). These few texts (picked from many) sufficiently expose the disease which Satan tries to make incurable by hiding it.

6. Similar proof is found in the very convincing arguments drawn from the analogy of faith. 1. The argument from the circumcision administered to infants in former times, and baptism nowadays: Each is a sign of the righteousness of faith and of the forgiveness of sins. It is not, surely, the forgiveness of actual sins in those children, since they could not have sinned in deed; therefore it is the forgiveness of original sin. 2. The argument based on the fact that death is shared by all people, and from which infants are not exempt. Moreover, "death is the wages of sin" (Rom 6:23), which can be imposed with justice only upon those who have sinned, since every punishment—if the penalty is just—is a punishment for sin, and because one should not be pricked by death who does not feel its sting [cf. 1 Cor 15:55-56]. 3. The argument based on the redemption made through Christ and the generation through the Spirit. For those who are born without sin do not need a redeemer; nor are they in need of spiritual regeneration who have not been affected by carnal generation. But "Christ died on behalf of everyone," and thus on behalf of infants, too. And "unless one is born again from the water and the spirit, he will not enter into the kingdom of heaven" (2 Cor 5:14; John 3:3,4). Add to that the fact that everything that is born is similar to that which brought it forth; "Adam bore a son in his own likeness" (Gen 5:3). Adam's likeness replaced the image of God that sin had wiped out; therefore what was corrupt has produced something corrupt, and the leprous has produced what is leprous.

7. The orthodox consensus of antiquity is in harmony with these arguments, teaching "that we must believe most firmly, and not doubt in any way

whatsoever, that everyone who is conceived through the sexual intercourse of man and woman, is born in original sin, is submersed in unrighteousness, is subject to death, and therefore is a child of wrath." These words of Fulgentius [bishop of Ruspe], in *On Faith to Peter*, express the Church's belief even before the Pelagian heresy arose, as also Augustine demonstrated against Julian with passages quoted from Irenaeus, Cyprian, Hilary, Gregory of Nazianzus, Basil, Ambrose, Jerome, etc. Moreover, at the time of Augustine and in the ages that followed, besides countless other writers, the same belief was expressed by the Councils that were held against the Pelagians and semi-Pelagians held at Palestine, Milevis, Toledo (the sixth), and at Orange.

8. Since by both biblical authority and reason it is agreed that such a sin does exist, we must next see what it is. First, then, about the various names given to it in Scriptures and the works of other writers. For Paul calls it "sin that is sinning," and "indwelling evil" (Rom 5:12, 7:13), "the sin that so easily ensnares" (Heb 12:1), and "desire," "the law of our members," "the body of sin," etc. (Rom 7:7.23). By several church-fathers it is called "the ancient snare of the serpent," "poison," "the burden of the ancient offense," etc. But after Pelagius arose, Augustine, in many places called this sin "original" or "from the origin," so that even by means of the very word he could render useless the adversaries' dodgy tricks, which they had invented when they seized the opportunity to make up other names. From that time on this term was frequently used in the Church, and we retain it too, as it is suitable enough and convenient for explaining the topic.

9. And it is called "original" not to restrict its meaning, as if "sin" is an equivocal term, but to distinguish it from actual sin. Nor is it called "original" because it is the fount and source of all other sins by transference of meaning and by reason of its effect (even though that does also apply to the original sin itself). But it is so called because either it exists in each and everyone from birth, that is, from the very moment of conception, or because it derives from the first origin, that is, from the first parent. Or it is so called because all men sinned already from the beginning in Adam. These three explanations, taken from various previous sources, can be drawn together into this one explanation: It is called "original" because by hereditary propagation it has sullied our birth, and it resides in us straight away, as soon as we are human beings, and it is passed on to us by a law of nature and origin. And so by the very etymology of the word the doctrine of the Pelagians may be opposed,

who state that no sin comes with man's birth, but that in man when he is born one finds only what God has created. The passages of Scripture mentioned above also lend support to this naming: for example, Gen 8, Job 14, Ps 51, and Eph 2.

10. Now concerning the matter proper: We define original sin as inherited lawlessness or vice effected in the loins of that first parent, committed by the rebellion of all men who from Adam have been generated in the natural way. In this all people in existence are corrupt, and so they are hostile to every good thing, and tend or incline to every sort of evil only; they deserve the wrath of God and are worthy of eternal death.

11. The efficient cause of this sin is the fall of the first parents, whereby in God's righteous judgment the guilt and depravity of nature was attracted and transmitted to all posterity. For in Paradise Adam bore a two-fold personality as he carried in him the mass [of humanity] that included all posterity as well as his own. So, his sin, too, had two aspects: One looked to himself, and thus was his own, personal and actual transgression—not original in the proper sense but originating or giving origin to all other sins and to the effects of sin. The other aspect concerns the whole race of posterity which lay concealed in his loins and sinned along with him, in the same way as Levi paid tithes "while he was in the loins of his father Abraham" (Heb 7:8,9). Similarly, also the universal guilt or universal sin of the entire nature or species was to be passed on to all men by generation, to whom in Adam this statement had been directed: "And on whatever day you eat of the fruit, etc. you shall certainly die" (Gen 2:17).

12. For this reason even original sin is in some way voluntary. For although infants do not exercise a will of their own, nevertheless even in them original sin is called voluntary, through the will of the first parent. From that will as the efficient cause, this evil was passed on to posterity, as from a root or source, whereby it happens that the will of an individual, as soon as it comes into existence, is infected with the vice of concupiscence. Hence the will is called evil, perverse, and hostile to God. Augustine summarizes both meanings of being voluntary when he says that it is not inappropriate to call original sin voluntary because it was contracted from the first evil will of man and somehow became hereditary (Book 1, *Retractations* chapter 13), namely taken in the general meaning of voluntary, referring to the will of a first principle of some totality (whether that be individual, or specific).

13. In this sense, it should be said that this sin is not only opposed to the law but was also forbidden by the law. For although infants are of themselves not liable to any command (as Pelagius objected), nevertheless, they were bound by a certain command even before they actually existed—not, to be sure, a command which they ought to have followed by their own will, but one which they ought to have fulfilled (and were able to fulfill) by the common will of the human race, as the will of our nature or species existed in Adam. For to him, as the head of the human race, the command had been given so that by means of an obedience that is both personal and for the entire human race, he would preserve perfection in himself. The sin which we are here treating exists in the loss of that perfection, and in the subsequent contrary corruption.

14. The way of this propagation is therefore clear, because our death in Adam can only be understood if Adam, by committing sin, not only brought ruin and destruction upon himself, but also cast our human nature down to similar ruin. And because the Lord had entrusted him with the gifts He willed to be joined to our nature, for that reason when Adam lost what he had received, he lost them not only for himself but for all of us, who by reason of our shared human nature were all as that one man, as Augustine neatly states in *On the Merits and Forgiveness of Sin*, book 3, chapter 7.

15. However, for this propagation it is not necessary that the soul be transferred from Adam through a physical offshoot, or that it must suffer damage from the spoiled vessel of the body (like a fruit, a flower, or something else of that sort we see spoiled by the foul humors of the organism which contains it), because this infection does not have its cause within the substance of the flesh or the soul. It suffices to say that man—part of whom is his soul—comes from Adam. This holds true even though the soul is not from the substance of the parent. For man is rightly and properly said to generate man, because the generation ends at the production of the thing composed. And although the rational soul is not drawn forth from potency to act by virtue of generation, nevertheless a body suitable for that soul is propagated, and human nature results from the union of the two. Therefore, it is said that human nature is propagated along with the seed not through the effective reproduction of the soul, but through a suitable and proportionate disposition of matter, which the soul infallibly follows once it is so arranged. The ultimate dispositions which the man who generates brings

forth are sufficient reason to consider him as truly generating another human being.

16. From what has been stated it is clear that this sin was not transmitted to other people through imitation, but through propagation. This point is demonstrated also by the argument that, properly speaking, imitation does not follow each and every thing that is similar, but only that which someone has come to know and has chosen to portray and fashion through his own actions. And therefore, since there have been and are very many people from Adam's descendants who have not heard or known anything at all about the first man and his sin, it would follow that although they are most grievous sinners, the sin of the first man did not cross over to them (which is contrary to the apostle's general judgment). However, if imitation is extended to those who have committed comparable sins—even unbeknownst to themselves—the apostle would have said that sin entered into the world through the devil rather than through one man; because imitation implies that wicked people are called sons of the devil and that he was the first one who had sinned.

17. At this point people get all twisted up for nothing as they pryingly dig up and pose these questions: "What would have happened if only the woman, or only the man, had fallen?" For since both did fall into sin, and since one cannot find that Scripture contains anything about what would have happened otherwise (assuming what in fact did not occur), it is best not to think more highly than we ought to think, and not to risk making a decision about some matter of which ignorance is not an offense. But concerning the question whether sin is handed down to their descendants only from Adam, or also from Eve, we are of the opinion that a truthful answer can be that it proceeds chiefly from Adam as the head and active principle of the generation (and so from the head of the human race), not only on the level of our human nature and our political life, but also in those things that look to the supernatural gifts of grace and happiness on the supernatural level—so that we all are considered to have committed what he did. But because in the order of nature generation is not achieved apart from a woman, and because both parents were stained by the fall and corruption, we attribute also to Eve her own role in that propagation of evil, albeit of secondary rank.

18. Moreover, when our Lord Jesus Christ became man, although He received the physical material for his body from the blessed virgin (who was a descendant of Adam), yet He did not assume a body that had been

fashioned by the active power of a man's seed but by the power of the Holy Spirit, who ordered the material and made it holy. Hence it happened that He was not infected by original sin, so that He "should be such a high priest as is fitting for us—holy, without sin, without blemish, set apart from sinners, and exalted above the heavens" (Heb 7:26).

19. Since this miraculous mode of conception is unique to Christ and applies to no-one besides him, we exempt no other person from the stain of original sin, not even the chosen blessed virgin, bearer of God, whom we (with Epiphanius) "do not consider to have been generated outside of human nature, but, like all people, from the seed of a man and the womb of a woman" (Epiphanius, *Collyridean Heresy* 79). Accordingly, she was subject to the law that is common to all, as she was in need of Christ the Redeemer, whom she acknowledged as her Savior (Luke 1:47). She was subject to the hardships of the body and ultimately death, and she is to be found in the company of all who have sinned in Adam, who are all mortal, for all of whom Christ died (Rom 5:12; 2 Cor 5:15).

20. As we intend no affront in forming this judgment about the blessed virgin, far be it from us to bestow on anyone else the special status of being conceived or born without original sin. Nevertheless, the papal theologians and pseudo-Lutherans most slanderously impute to people of our confession as if they taught that no children of believers are infected by this sin, while in fact the ones to whom this is ascribed very often state the opposite. Moreover, the logical consequence which they attach to our teaching that children of believers are counted as in the covenant, and that therefore they are said to be, and in fact are, holy, is pointless and far-fetched. Neither does this entail that such children had not acquired original sin by nature, because the guilt of sin is forgiven them by grace. Add that this outward inclusion in the covenant and sanctification (even though it brings with it a certain tie to the church) bids us to draw good hope also for their inner sanctification from the plausible signs of God's good favor, yet it does not make for a firm faith in true justification and regeneration for each and every person who traces his birth to righteous parents, since we must leave it to God to make his own particular judgments.

21. In other respects, if we consider nature, we believe that even a regenerate man begets offspring, not in keeping with the fact that he is regenerate but according to the flesh, and therefore his offspring is born sinful. In this same

way a son who is uncircumcised can be generated by a father who has been circumcised, and a kernel with a husk can be produced by a kernel that has been purged; because it is not generation, but re-generation that makes Christians, and no-one is cleansed from sins by being born but by being re-born. Add to this the fact that in our judgment sin partly remains in the regenerate, although the guilt has been taken away, as will be said below.

22. Concerning the matter of original sin, this matter, generally taken, has the role of subject of a category and this subject of a category is comprehended in the definition with the following words: "All people who issue from Adam in the natural manner." However, the subject is a subject of inherence, when sin is considered not regarding the species as a whole of which it is predicated, but regarding the individual with whose birth it comes about and to whom it adheres. In this case, the subject is not only the person's body, nor his soul only, but his body and his soul together. And so it is the person and all that he is, along with all the faculties of body and soul, according to his whole being and as a complete person in himself. However, it is so in such a way that the soul is the subject especially, as the principle of action, while the body is the subject insofar as it is the instrument by which the soul acts. Hence in Scripture original sin is described as the blindness of the mind, the wickedness of the heart, the uselessness of the body and all its limbs (1 Cor 2:14; Eph 4:18; Gen 6:5 and 8:21; Jer 17:9; Ps 14:2,3; Rom 3:12 and 6:12, 13, and 19; John 3:5[-6]).

23. However, it does not therefore follow that original sin is a substance, or the substantial image of the devil within mankind or that it is man's very soul or heart. For sin is not a thing of essence that has its own existence, but it is concomitant, dwelling among us, easily ensnaring us (Rom 7:20, 21; Heb 12:1). It is something that inheres in human beings as an accident in the subject. Although these things [essence and sin] cannot be separated within corrupt man, yet we do assert that they should be distinguished. For God is the creator of all substances; yet sin neither was created by God, nor is it a created thing or an essence. Even Adam, after the fall into sin, kept the same essence of his own nature that he had previously, and he remained the same man. Our essence indeed does not change into another essence either by sin or by grace, even though it is spoiled by evil or made perfect by good.

24. The form of original sin exists in that lawlessness and disobedience whereby all have sinned with Adam who were in him by virtue of a 'seminal

relation' (as they call it). God the judge justly imputes this disobedience and offense, along with the attendant charge of guilt, to all of Adam's children, insofar as all were and are one with him. But if one considers what remains in man after the deed and what has the true nature of sin wherefore man properly and formally is called a sinner—it is nothing else than the perversion and deformity of the whole human nature, whereupon, the likeness with God having been lost, the fall and foulest corruption of all the parts of man followed.

25. And so those who locate original sin only in the absence of original righteousness do not express the force of this sin meaningfully enough. For our nature not only is destitute of what is good, but it also is so prolific in all things evil that it cannot be idle. And so along with Scripture we recognize two parts to this corruption: the failure and loss of the good, and a depraved tendency to evil. For in addition to the ignorance of the mind and a turning-away from God in the heart, there clings in all people a propensity for knowing and doing those things which God's law prohibits. Hence some people of our confession have said that the tinder of sin is not without actual sin, but in fact is actual sin. This is a loose statement, yet it should not have been turned into slander by the opponents, since nothing else was intended than that this sin is also real, and that it is active and busy, too, so that it is at rest not even in little children, but it stirs up sinful behavior.

26. It is certain that whenever Scripture implicates us with original sin it usually drives home the point that it is not merely a lack or deficiency, but something that is somehow positive. That is, it is something affirmative, some vice whereby the flesh lusts against the spirit, that is, whereby man becomes prone to evil and is turned against the divine law. Thus Romans 6:12: "Let not sin reign in your mortal body that you should obey its desires." These words show that concupiscence is a kind of habit in man, of which the proper actions are actual desires. This habitual evil is called sin by the apostle: "Sin," he says, "having seized the opportunity by the commandment, works every concupiscence in me," that is, every kind of crooked desires as its own proper actions (Rom 7:8).

27. From these and similar texts it appears that although one cannot deny that original sin is the lack of that righteousness or uprightness which each and every person should possess at birth, yet its nature is more fully expressed by 'an evil tendency,' or 'an inclination toward every wickedness,' rather than

'a lack.' For actions are not a property of a deficiency, while Scripture in fact does attribute actions to original sin.

28. The same conclusion may be reached by means of reason. For no-one turns himself away from anything good unless he is drawn by a longing or desire for something else that seems good, which cannot co-exist with the former good. Well then, we should think that what holds true in actions holds similarly also for the habitual vice incurred at the time of birth. In fact it is for this reason that we are born averse to the unchangeable good, since we are born crooked and inclined to good things that are changeable. Augustine gives to both of these evils (the aversion as well as the inclination) this general definition of sin: the turning away from the superior good, and the unjust turning towards a lesser good. That lesser good, however, is really a moral evil, insofar as man turns himself to it and away from God (Augustine, *On Various Questions, To Simplician*, question 2).

29. Hence it happens that some of the more sound schoolmen recognize that original sin is some disordered disposition and a disruption that results from the break-up of that harmony in which original righteousness consisted. As examples they adduce illness and diseases in which there is something lacking (insofar as the balance of good health is disrupted) and something positive (namely disorderly arranged temperaments). And thus they judge that original sin takes away original righteousness resulting in a disorderly arrangement of the soul's parts. Accordingly, it is not a plain lack but some corrupt habit. Thus Thomas, *Summa theologiae* 1/2.q.82.art.1. And in the commentary on this passage Cajetan asserts that a mere privation only consists in a negation in a subject that was born apt, but that corruption adds some contrary positive thing, on which privation is founded.

30. Those who said that this corrupt habit is concupiscence (taking the word broadly, in a general sense) spoke in line with Scripture. With the words "flesh" and "concupiscence," which are rejected as evil and sinful, Scripture does not mean desire in general (entailing rational as well as sensual desire); it also does not refer to the senses in particular, nor to him who is especially subject to carnal lust; nor again does it refer to some natural capacity or condition of human nature as such. For those qualities existed in Adam at the beginning of creation, and Christ assumed them along with his true human nature. But the corruption which entered into nature through sin also infected nature itself and made it punishable, so to speak.

31. Nevertheless the corrupt habit does involve all the things man can pursue wickedly and illicitly. Thus, when he said "the flesh lusts against the spirit" (Gal 5:17), in order to show how broad the extent of concupiscence is, the apostle appended a list of some of the works of the flesh, among which he mentions not only sexual immorality, filthiness, etc., which are done through the desires of the senses, and which are called sins of the flesh in particular. But he also mentions witchcraft, hatred, discord, murder, factions or heresies and the like, which are usually called sins of the spirit. Therefore, with the words "flesh" and "lust" the apostle means the vice that gives rise to every sin, whence he demonstrates that even the Corinthians are carnal, from the fact that "there are jealousies and quarreling among them" (1 Cor 3:3). And he shows quite clearly that from concupiscence every kind of sin comes forth, when in speaking about that he says: "Through the commandment sin worked every kind of concupiscence in me" (Rom 7:8), to make us understand that in its longing concupiscence reaches as far as the commandment reaches in forbidding it.

32. In many places Augustine acknowledges the general scope of meaning in the word "concupiscence," especially in the *City of God*, book 14, chapter 3, when he sees the apostle attributing the vices that are primarily present in the devil to the flesh—which the devil certainly did not have. But the pride that is the source of all these vices does rule in the devil. Bellarmine himself, in his book *On the Loss of Grace and the State of Sin*, book 5, chapter 15, did not dare to deny that the same vice occurs also in the higher region of the soul— in fact that the power of concupiscence has its abode in the mind. Having proved the meaning of concupiscence in such a way that whatever is in man, from intellect to will, from soul to body, should be understood as being defiled and crammed with it, we affirm that original sin can be called and actually is concupiscence. The desire of this sort should not be guided by reason, but it should be totally eradicated, because we are unable to use it in a right way but we should always resist it. It is not only a punishment inflicted by sin, but it always has the proper character of true guilt. As Augustine says against Julian (Book 4, chapters 1 and 2): "Nothing good comes from it, it does nothing good, nothing good is desired from it, but whatever is desired by it, is evil."

33. Neither should we listen to those who, while condemning Pelagius for saying that such concupiscence was implanted by God as something good by nature, also admit that it leads to sin, not just by prompting something wicked

(in the way that the devil incites it), nor through some chance event or occasion (as wine or a woman's beauty may lead to a lack of self-control in drinking or sexuality), but by itself, by its very nature, and through its own action. Accordingly, they say concupiscence should not be loved but hated as a sin that distracts and diverts us from what we should love most dearly. Nevertheless, they make bold to claim that strictly speaking it is not a sin, not even in those who have not been born again, except by reason of the action or effect of the first sin that was imputed to them, when it bursts forth into actual sin.

34. Once this basis is laid it is no wonder if they deny not only that in those who have been born again "sin" is the right word for concupiscence (insofar as it is taken as a habit), but also make this claim about its action and chief movements, which they call "involuntary"—because the guilt has been removed from them and the dominion of concupiscence has been taken away. Therefore, they claim those people who become aware of concupiscence and those wrong movements deserve neither censure nor punishment; for these are not voluntary in them, and consequently are not sins.

35. But we assert with Scripture that "sin" is the proper name for the perversion of nature and concupiscence, an indwelling sin in people who are not reborn as well as in the reborn and holy for as long as they live in this mortal body. For although concupiscence does not rule over them and the guilt of it has been removed so that God does not impute it to them, and although it is weakened and diminished as the grace of regeneration increases, nevertheless it is properly called sin in them. And it remains not only in the desire of the senses and the soul's lower part, but it also occupies some place in their minds and wills (since the mind is still subject to ignorance, doubts, and mistakes, and the will suffers from self-love), so that even in those who have been born again there is a need for reform "through the regeneration of the mind, the renewal of the spirit of the mind, and of the inner man day in, day out" (Rom 12:2; 2 Cor 4:16; Eph 4:23).

36. To be sure, on more than one occasion in chapter 7 of the Letter to the Romans the apostle clearly labels this wickedness [of concupiscence] "sin," not only because it comes from sin and inclines towards it, but also because it resists the rule of the mind and desires against the spirit, and herein sin's real nature exists. For whatever formally resists God's spirit and law is

properly called sin, since the true nature of sin consists in lawlessness. And our opponents do not deny that the loss of original righteousness lingers in those who have been baptized; which, if it is truly sin, did not change its own nature wherever it is found. For also the remission of guilt does not turn sin into non-sin because man is properly freed from guilt (not sin as viewed in and of itself), and it also does not lose the nature of sin by being diminished (because the species of sin is not altered by a greater or lesser amount, even though they do introduce different degrees). And lastly, if it were only a penalty and did not have the nature of sin, John would not say "that the desire is not of the Father" (1 John 2:16), from whom the punishment comes. And Christ, who took upon himself all the "weaknesses" of our nature, "sin excepted" (Heb 4:15), would also have assumed concupiscence, especially when our opponents are in agreement with Pelagius that desire is the material object of the virtues that are to be cultivated and belongs to the basic structure of human nature. (See Domingo de Soto, Book 1, *On Nature and Grace*, chapter 3; Ruard Tapper, Art. 2, and Bellarmine, book 2, *On the Loss of Grace*, chapter 2.)

37. So much for the form of original sin. Now we should discuss the goal of original sin. But because sin does not have a goal for itself regarding the human being in whom it exists, it is customary to examine its effects and consequences instead of its goal. The first effect is guilt, a word indicating an obligation to punishment, or a link inserted as a means between sin and punishment, whereby the sinner is obliged in the strongest possible terms to undergo the punishment and as long as the guilt remains to undergo the harshness of the penalty.

38. Following this is punishment, of which one is temporal and the other eternal. To temporal punishment belongs bodily death and the other hardships and miseries of this mortality whereby man has a life that is short-lived and "full of trouble; he comes forth like a flower and withers" (Job 14:2). According to the word of the apostle, "death comes through sin. In Adam all die, the body is dead on account of sin" (Rom 5:12; 1 Cor 15:21; Rom 8:10). For death, diseases, and all other hardships flow forth from sin, and those who have been reborn are not in this life liberated from them, not even infants who have just been baptized, and they too suffer the first death "as an indication of the misery deserved." This is a clear sign that sin still lingers in them, although for those in the covenant the guilt of eternal death has been cancelled.

39. By itself original sin earns not just temporal or bodily death, but also eternal punishment, of which all are guilty who depart from this life without forgiveness and with this sin. This eternal punishment is usually called the last or second death, which is not only a punishment of damnation (as they call it) and unhappiness, but also of feeling pain and sorrow, since together with the loss of joy, it introduces grief and shame. For it is impossible that those bereft of eternal happiness do not feel that most serious injury, accompanied by eternal banishment from the kingdom of heaven. And since those who are to be saved (not only the adults but also those who died in infancy) will delight in beholding God with a full sense of joy and happiness, the opposite state cannot exist without grief for body and soul. In this matter we acknowledge that just as there are different degrees of sinners, so too are there greater and lesser degrees of punishments and sufferings—a matter we leave to the decision of the just judge.

40. The benefit of this doctrine is that while acknowledging the misery in which we have been infected by sin and polluted by filth from the moment of our birth, and in which we have been estranged from God, let us, putting aside every pride and presumption, in true humility take refuge in Christ the propitiator, and since our first generation was contaminated with sin, let us gratefully acknowledge the second Adam the producer of our regeneration. The righteousness of faith is bestowed upon us through imputation from him, and through sanctification and renewal a new obedience has begun. Thus what we have lost in the first Adam we shall at long last regain in this second Adam, with interest, and having been freed from the hand of our enemies, let us ourselves serve in his presence in holiness and justice, for all the days of our lives (Luke 1:74, and 75). To him be glory and honour.

SOURCES

Augustine *On Original Sin*, chapter 29
Whoever maintains that human nature at any time did not require the second Adam for its physician because it was not corrupted by the first Adam stands convicted as an enemy to the grace of God—not over some question in which sound faith isn't affected by doubt or error, but over the very rule of faith by which we are Christians.

From A Sermon of Bernard

The blame is another's, because it was unknowingly that we all sinned in Adam; the blame is ours, for although in another we are the ones who sinned, and in God's just but hidden judgment it was imputed to us.

ON ACTUAL SIN

President: Antonius Walaeus
Respondent: Laevinus Coolmanus

Actual sin is an intentional, purposeful act of transgression against the commandment of God. This disputation discusses the nature of actual sin (2–28), the causes of it (29–34), and the kinds of sin (35–54). Actual sin is defined as an 'action against the law of God, that causes offense to God, and makes the sinner guilty of the wrath of God and death, unless forgiveness is granted on account of Christ the mediator' (4–5). Sin consists in the absence of righteousness and holiness (6); it is a loss of good and has no nature of its own; it is privation. Even so, however, it is an active privation (7–11). When something isn't a sin in and of itself, because God's law commands it or allows it, nevertheless it can be a sin when the manner by which it is done is sinful (12–18). The effect of sin is both an immediate liability of guilt, because of the damnability of sin, and a more remote liability of punishment. The latter effect is removed completely through the forgiveness and the imputation of Christ's righteousness for believers. The former effect is only covered and hindered from further producing effects, but it cannot be separated from the sin (19–28). Everything occurs by God's secret will and providence, but God isn't the efficient cause of sin. In one and the same action, God is the cause of the good and the creature is responsible for the wicked deed, which come about by God's permission (29–34). As for the different types of actual sins, a distinction is made between internal sins—which exist in the mind, the will, and the affections—and external sins—which are displayed openly in words and deeds (35–38). A further distinction can be made between reigning sins—sins that are served by the entire will—, and non-reigning sins—sins that are resisted through the grace of the Spirit (39). This and other differences serve as indicators whereby true believers can be certain in their own hearts that sin does not have dominion over them (40–46). The only unforgivable sin is the sin against the Holy Spirit (47–54).

1. Seeing that in the preceding disputations we have treated the initial fall of our first parents, and the original sin that thereupon arose, it now remains for us to treat actual sin. Of this sin we shall consider briefly its nature first, and then its causes and sorts.

2. In Latin "to sin," like the Greek *hamartanein* and the Hebrew *hattah*, literally means to wander from the way or to miss the target; but in this case it means to stray from the precept of God's law.

3. In defining actual sin it is usual to follow Augustine (*Against Faustus*, book 22, chapter 27): "Some deed, word, or desire against the eternal law." We can accept this definition if we complete the list by adding the word "thought," and if we understand the word "desire" to include the concupiscence of both the will and the affections.

4. Our own people have handed down a fuller definition, that sin is an "action against the law of God, that causes offense to God, and makes the sinner guilty of the wrath of God and death, unless forgiveness is granted on account of Christ the mediator."

5. This definition is borrowed from 1 John 3:4, "sin is lawlessness" (or sin is the transgression of the law); and from Paul's wording, "cursed is everyone who does not abide by everything that is written in the book of the law, to do them" (Gal 3:10); and [Gal 3] verse 13: "Christ has redeemed us from the curse of the law, having been made a curse for us."

6. It is clear from this definition that the proper nature and form of this sin consists in the absence of righteousness and holiness (or their form), which according to God's law ought to be present in our outward as well as inward actions. For this reason, Augustine rightly says: "Evil does not have a nature, but the loss of the good has been given the name 'evil'" (*On the City of God*, book 11, chapter 9).

7. Therefore when some writers of the Reformed Church assert that evil is not a mere privation of something, we ought not to understand it as though evil has some truly affirmative or metaphysical nature. For all such being is good and comes from God, who alone is the author of all good, as "in Him we live and move and have our being" (Acts 17:28). But they understand this to mean a privation that is inoperative and idle. Lack or absence of this sort is the kind that removes capabilities altogether, as when blindness removes sight.

8. Yet sin is an active privation, whereby the active principle and the very action that proceeds from it is deprived only of righteousness by the corruption—not the removal—of the principle. It is like the dislocation of one's leg, which does not lose its ability to move, but its control and correct movement. For this reason one finds in the Scriptures that sin is expressed not only in negative terms but also affirmatively, and it is granted an efficacy that is contrary and hostile to holiness and justice (Rom 8:7, Gal 5:7), because the movement and action to which the deficiency clings, by the power of that inherent deficiency withstands the holy and just motion and action, and so it also withstands God's law.

9. However, the nearest subject to the sin we are now treating (which the Schoolmen call the "material" subject) is a thing or an action that is physically good, to which that privation clings as though it is a moral form—or rather moral deformity. As a result, not only the wickedness itself but also the whole action that is joined to the wickedness is called sin and evil in a denominative way, as they say in the Schools.

10. At this point we include in actual sin both the commission of an evil deed and the omission of a good deed. For such an omission concerns the actions themselves and good deeds are seldom omitted except on the basis of a wicked action, whether the will within itself intends that omission or whether it is preoccupied in the meantime with other, wicked actions which cannot co-exist with those actions that have been commanded. For no-one is able to serve two masters, etc., nor God and Mammon at the same time (Matt 6:24).

11. However, there is some difference between the privation that is in the sin of omission and the sin of commission, because in the sin of omission it is an omission of the entire deed that is owed, as Christ would say (Matt 25:42): "I was hungry and you did not feed me; I was thirsty and you did not give me drink." But in sins of commission there is a lack of the order and righteousness that is demanded of such a deed in keeping with God's law.

12. Well then, this privation of righteousness and order occurs either with respect to the substance and material aspect of the deed, or with respect to the manner wherein the performance of that deed is prescribed by the law.

13. With respect to substance (or the material aspect), the lack of righteousness and order occurs when one commits something that is

expressly forbidden by God's law, as when a man worships foreign gods contrary to the first commandment. If adultery is committed, it is against the seventh commandment, etc. With respect to the manner, it is when something happens which God's law commands or does allow, but not in the way in which it is commanded or permitted. Some people call the former "sins in and of themselves," and the latter "sins by accident," albeit not very accurately. For the latter manner is included no less in the judgment of the law (which is spiritual—Rom 7:14) than the commanded thing and action itself.

14. The manners, moreover, can be summed up by the following three sorts: by the principle of the act, by its end, and by other intermediate circumstances.

15. By the principle of the act: When something God has commanded actually happens, but not out of true faith or a pure heart; as Paul says (1 Tim 1:5): "Love is the end of the law, from a pure heart, a clear conscience, and a sincere faith." About deeds which lacked this condition the same apostle says (Rom 2:14): "For the gentiles, who do not have the law, still perform the things of the law."

16. An action which in other respects is commanded becomes sinful because of an end that is not right. For example, when the Pharisees fast, pray, and give alms, in order to obtain glory from men (Matt 6:1). For this reason the apostle Paul warns: "So that whether we eat or whether we drink, or whatever else we do, let us do all things to the glory of God" (1 Cor 10:31).

17. An action that in itself is permitted and good takes on the nature of evil because of sinful circumstances. This happened when the sons of Aaron brought profane fire to the altar of the Lord (Lev 10:1); when Uzzah wished to keep the ark from falling by stretching out his hand (2 Sam 6:6); when the Israelites made offerings to God on the high places (2 Kgs 12:3); when believers use their Christian freedom with offense to those who are weak (Rom 14:20). And there are many similar instances in which careful attention should be given to God's commandments.

18. Therefore just as a good action arises only from the combination of all these conditions, so too on the other hand can a sinful action arise from the failure of even one of them, as is demonstrated by the instances presented in the previous thesis.

19. The knowledge of its proper effects makes for a fuller understanding of the nature of sin.

20. The effect of sin (or, as others prefer, its proper outcome) is two-fold: immediate, and distant. The immediate one is called the liability, and the distant one the punishment for sin.

21. The liability (called by some Schoolmen the formal aspect of sin, though incorrectly, since one matter has only one form) is something relative, located between sin and punishment, namely that aspect whereby the sinner through his sin is turned away from God and is obligated to and destined for punishment; Scripture calls this the wages of sin (Rom 6:23), the sting of death (1 Cor 15:56), and the curse of death (Gal 3:10).

22. Some suitably locate the liability of every sin—thus also of actual sin—in two places: the liability of guilt, and the liability of punishment. The liability of guilt is the inward unworthiness or very damnability of sin, whereby the sinner of his own accord makes himself unworthy of God's love and favor, as can be seen in Ps 5:5, Isa 59:2, and other places of Scripture. The liability of punishment is being actually destined and obligated to this or that degree of punishment.

23. The latter effect is removed completely through the forgiveness of sins and the imputation of Christ's righteousness for those who have been reborn and who believe. But the former effect, which still clings to the remnants of their flesh, is surely covered by Christ's righteousness and holiness, and is hindered from producing its effects further, but it cannot be separated from its own sin unless that sin is removed along with it—no more than heat can be removed from a flame, or the ability to laugh from a human being.

24. For this reason also the apostle Paul asserts in Romans 8:1 that "there is now no condemnation for those who are in Christ Jesus, who do not walk according to the flesh but according to the Spirit." He does not say, however, that there is nothing worthy of condemnation in them. In fact, Holy Scripture testifies the opposite: That believers, if viewed in themselves only and just as they really are, cannot be righteous or even stand before God's presence or judgment (Job 9:2; Ps 130:3; Ps 143:2; Dan 9:7, 9, 10, and to Rom 4:1 and following).

25. The punishment that is owed for sins is twofold, being either the pain of loss, or the pain of sense. The 'pain of loss' (a word some people use with

slightly different meaning) we here call the injury that the sinning soul contracts internally from the act of sinning; namely, a greater or lesser removal of God's grace proportionate to the degree of the sin's meanness. The penalty is also a blemish or stain, as they call it, which clings to the soul by its turning away from God. What Christ says in Matt 15:11 can be applied here: "It is not what goes into the mouth, but what comes out of it, that defiles, that renders the man profane or unclean." So too for the witness borne by the apostle in Rom 1: [23–]24: "Those who have changed the glory of the incorruptible God into the likeness of the image of corruptible man, God gave over to the lusts of their hearts for uncleanness."

26. The 'pain of sense' exists partly in the anxieties of the conscience, partly in the other torments of mind or body that unrepentant people will undergo in this life or in the one that is to come. For there will be "wrath and indignation, tribulation and anguish on every soul of man of who does evil" (Rom 2:8,9).

27. Sin, however, merits both temporal and eternal punishment, as Christ will declare: "Depart, you cursed ones, into the eternal fire" (Matt 25:41). And this is fair, for sins which are committed against the most high majesty of God are also atoned for by the harshest penalties, which our mediator fully endured intensively in our place on the cross once and for all, to set us free from them. But since the other mere creatures cannot endure unending penalties intensively, it is fair that they instead undergo the highest punishments extensively, that is, endless in duration.

28. Add to this the fact that sins which are never broken off through supernatural grace and true remorse also never come to an end; consequently, the punishment for them, too, can never come to an end. And since God has promised everlasting rewards to those who obey the law, the nature of God's justice demands that also the punishment which forms the opposite to the eternal rewards must be everlasting.

29. Having explained the nature of this sin sufficiently enough in this way, it remains that we add some observations about the causes of actual sin, and its sorts.

30. It would not be right to look for the efficient cause of sin in God or in his divine providence, for "everything which God made was very good" (Gen

1:31); and "his work is perfect, and all his ways are just" (Deut 32:4). Indeed, "He cannot be tempted to evil, nor does He tempt anyone" (Jas 1:13).

31. We do grant that everything that occurs in the world (including those things which have the character of the greatest misdeeds) occurs by God's secret will and providence (Acts 2:23, 3:18). However, it doesn't follow from this that God is in any way connected to the guilt for them, as the Libertines slanderously claim. For in any one action one must carefully distinguish God's good work from the evil work of the creature.

32. For whereas God is the cause which effects and ordains all good things, so too He is strictly speaking not the effective cause of all the evils which come about by his permission, but only the cause that ordains and moderates them, as Joseph says in Gen 50:20: "You indeed meant evil against me, but God meant it for good, in order to bring it about as it is today." Isa 10:5–7 is a passage like it, and because of this moderation and direction also these wicked doings in the Scriptures are attributed to God, not as the effecting cause but as the ordaining and moderating one; for as Augustine ingeniously—and rightly—states: "For He knew that to do good from evil redounds more to his own almighty goodness than not to allow evil to exist."

33. And so the efficient cause of this sin, or rather its deficient cause, is the depraved mind and will of men. For just as Christ testifies that "the devil, when he speaks a lie, speaks from his own resources, because he is a liar and the father of lies" (John 8:44), so also the apostle states: "But each one is tempted when he is drawn away by his own evil desires and is enticed" (Jas 1:14); and 1 John 2:16 states: "The lust of the flesh, the lust of the eyes, and the pride of life, are not from the Father, but from the world."

34. But it is possible that various attendant and assistant causes come together from outside of us as well as from within. For one sin is often the cause of another one (Rom 1:24 and following), and then there are the promptings of the devil (1 Chron 21:1) and the turmoils of the world (Matt 18:7). There is also the darkened mind (1 Tim 1:13), the weakness of the flesh (Matt 26:69[-75]), and the habit of sinning (Rom 2:5). Satan and the world constantly furnish very many other pretexts; believers must always pray and guard against all of these with dogged concentration.

35. The types of actual sin can be determined (and usually they are established) from a variety of situations. We shall content ourselves with a

summary of those which are challenging in some way, and which cannot be discerned so clearly on the basis of what we have said up to this point.

36. First we divide actual sin into internal and external.

37. Internal actual sin: It has its existence in the mind, the will, and the unruly affections, such as the errors and doubts of the mind about God and his properties, or about the doctrine of the revealed Gospel. It exists in the will and the affections, the initial stirrings of concupiscence—although the spirit fights and overpowers them. For we assert (together with the apostle in Rom 7:7) that they are in direct conflict with the tenth commandment. We assert, too, that those affections with which the will fully agrees, even if they do not result in the performance of an actual deed, are prohibited by the other commandments, as Matt 5:22 and 28 demonstrates, and also 1 John 3:15: "Whoever hates his own brother, is a murderer, etc."

38. External actual sin displays itself openly in words and deeds, notwithstanding the fact that it does not exist without a prior internal sin, as the apostle James testifies in chapter 1:15: "Evil desire when it has conceived, gives birth to sin, and sin through its actions brings forth death."

39. Both sorts of sins are either 'reigning' or 'non-reigning' sins—a distinction that is drawn from Rom 6:14 and 17. 'Reigning sin' is usually defined as sin which a man does not resist through the grace of the Spirit, but which he gratifies and serves with his entire will. 'Non-reigning sin,' on the other hand, is that which a man does resist through the grace of the Spirit, and which he does not gratify. The former is found in those who have not been reborn; the latter in those who have been reborn. This distinction is evident from Paul's prolonged argument in Romans Chapter Six, Seven, and Eight.

40. At this point a rather difficult question arises that we must answer: How reigning and non-reigning sin are distinguished by this resistance or gratification, since there is also a struggle between reason and affections in the natural man who is established only under the Law, as is attested by all the Philosophers, and by the apostle himself in Rom 2:15.

41. But we reply that there is a big difference between the struggle and resistance of the spirit and the flesh occurring only in regenerate people, and the struggle and resistance that takes place between reason and affections in the natural man, too. We summarize the difference briefly under these four headings.

42. The first distinction is taken from 1 Cor 2:14, and other similar places: "For the natural man does not grasp the things of the Spirit of God, but they are folly to him, as is also the crucified Christ himself." In the sins that are committed by such a man against the things of the Spirit there is no struggle of reason against the affections, but reason itself, supported by the will and the affections, casts them aside with full force. It despises and often persecutes the spiritual things, as the gospel-history, and experience itself, proves time and again.

43. The second distinction is drawn from the way in which the very commands of love towards God and the fellow-man are fulfilled, as was explained in thesis fifteen, sixteen, and seventeen. For "what the law requires is written on the hearts of the gentiles also, and their consciences accuse them of this, or perhaps excuse them" (Rom 2:15). Nevertheless, since the true starting-point and end of God's commandments were unknown to them, it necessarily happens that their reason does not struggle against the affections but rather even conspires with them.

44. The third distinction is placed in the effect and result in either struggle. For although the unregenerate man in some cases struggles against his depraved affections by the guidance of reason, yet because also his reason itself is blind in very many matters and helpless in all of them, and because his affections are volatile and untamed, unless they are reined in by the special help of God, it follows that the affections almost always pursue what is worse (although it does happen that they occasionally sense what is better). The very affections drive their reason into the opposite direction most of the time, as the apostle testifies (Rom 1:32, and Eph 2:2). Contrary to this, in those who have been reborn the Spirit is mightier than the flesh, and most of the time He is victorious over it (Rom 6:22); and consequently "they do not walk according to the flesh, but according to the Spirit" (Rom 8:[4,]14).

45. Next, although in this strife believers are sometimes overpowered in some particular deeds either by their own carelessness or by God's special testing, even so the appeal and triumph of sin is made to waver greatly even in the very act of sinning by the power of the Holy Spirit, whom they grieve. And after the sin has been committed they do not remain defeated, but through true repentance and grief towards God they rise up once again, and thereupon wage war against the world, their own flesh, and Satan more seriously and steadfastly, as is evident from the examples of those saints

whose fall Scripture records for us. People lacking faith, on the other hand, enslave themselves more and more through their own sins (John 8:34), and "boast of the desire of their hearts" (Ps 10:3). If they happen to humble themselves for a while because their consciences are pricked and they fear punishment, once that fear has been pushed aside they return to their usual temper, as is seen in the case of Pharaoh, Saul, Ahab, and others.

46. Now these distinctions form reliable indicators whereby true believers can be certain in their own hearts that sin does not have dominion over them, and consequently they are led by the Spirit of regeneration, and they are not under the law but under grace.

47. The third distinction in sin is between forgivable and unforgivable. Forgivable is the sin that can obtain pardon; all sins are of this kind, except the sin against the Holy Spirit (Matt 12:31). Unforgivable is the sin that cannot receive pardon, because it obstinately rejects all means of the cure whereby pardon is obtained.

48. The papal teachers divide forgivable sin into mortal and venial. They call venial sin that which does not deserve death, but which on account of being minor is worthy of pardon. Mortal sin is what deserves death and cannot co-exist with the grace of God.

49. We do grant, however, that sins are not all equal and that one sin therefore causes greater offense to God's justice than another; consequently it merits more serious punishment and pangs of the conscience. Nevertheless, we state that not any sin is worthy of pardon in and of itself, or that it is not deadly, unless it is forgiven for Christ's sake.

50. This is proved, because 1) Holy Scripture declares about every sin that its wages is death (Rom 6:23), the sting of death is sin (1 Cor 15:56), and its end or fruit is death (Rom 6:16). 2), because every sin is against the law, of which every violation deserves the curse (Gal 3:10). That every sin is against the law is proved from the fact that the law demands love from the whole heart, the whole soul, and the whole mind (Matt 22:37). 3) because every sin is against God (1 Kgs 8:46), and against the law of the mind (Rom 7:23).

51. It is also undeniably proved by the foreshadowing in the forgiveness of sins in the Old Testament. For not only for the more serious, but also for the lighter sins, namely of weakness and ignorance (which the papal teachers argue are venial sins) they were compelled to offer sacrifices, as is seen from

Leviticus chapters 4, 5 and following. But, the sacrifices pointed to the one and only sacrifice of Christ which made expiation for all our sins, since He has become the curse for us, to free us from the curse (Gal 3:13).

52. Unforgivable sin is the sin against the Holy Spirit. For while the final refusal to repent is not forgiven either, this happens indirectly: Not because the other sins of which one does not repent are in themselves unforgiveable, but because their course is not halted by faith and repentance.

53. Well then, we define the sin against the Holy Spirit as the contemptuous and ill-willed resistance to Christ and the evangelical grace that one had come to know outwardly through hearing the Word, and that the Holy Spirit had worked convincingly within one's heart. The contempt arises in those people who have not yet professed the teaching of Christ (such as the Pharisees, Matt 12) or in those who professed and then defected from it (about which Heb 6 and 10 writes).

54. And this is the greatest degree of sin, from which Christ in his own special compassion protects those who genuinely believe and are reborn (1 John 5:18). "For we know that anyone born of God does not sin" (i.e., the sin unto death, for which one should not ask for forgiveness, as the preceding verses declared) but "he who is born of God, saves himself, and the evil one does not touch him."

ON FREE CHOICE

President: Antonius Thysius
Respondent: Jacobus Adrianus Thetrodius

The Synopsis dedicates a separate and entire disputation to a theological topic that was the subject of intense debate during the first decades of the sixteenth century, a debate of which the origins may be traced through the Middle Ages to the time of Augustine and the Church Fathers: free choice. Disputation 17 therefore begins with a careful identification of the topic (in Latin, arbitrium liberum) and an explanation of the relevant technical terms (1–11). A distinguishing feature of our humanity is that we possess a will that acts by means of choices that are not externally necessitated nor forced but voluntary and deliberate (12). The Synopsis identifies four distinct stages or 'states' in the history of humanity when human free choice was carried out differently (13–14): 1. When the human being by his or her free will was able to do what God demanded, but by that same free will could also choose to commit sin (15–17); 2. When humanity exercised the free will to commit sin, and all humanity became subservient to the power of evil; from then until now, 'free choice is drawn only … towards the evil' (18–26). Consequently, while in actual practice humans no longer have the ability to choose the good, the good does belong to their freedom to choose as a possibility. Therefore when they choose to sin, humans do so out of their own free choice. 3. When God's grace is worked in the human heart people are regenerated and renewed through the power of the Holy Spirit, and the human will is 'liberated and truly free'— albeit partly (27–42). In fact, reborn believers experience a conflict between their own sinful nature and the Spirit of God. 4. When, after this life, the human will is in its glorified state, by God's continued and continuing grace the human will is freed from all power of sin and consequently has no option to choose what is evil anymore (43). These four states are summed up in thesis 44, which is followed by some final remarks of rejection of (semi) Pelagian positions and a (rare) reference to the recent Synod of Dort (45–46).

1. Whereas the order in this series of disputations would require us to provide a treatment of man's free choice and its power as seen after the fall, for the sake of a fuller understanding we shall treat free choice in general and as it regards all the states of man.

2. We exclude from this disputation the closely related questions about God's infallible foreknowledge, his governing providence, and his efficacious predestination, and also what depends upon it, the contingency and necessity of things, and the cause of sin. For they are divine acts beyond the purview of human choice. Yet it is appropriate at this point to deal with man's powers, since they were yielded and granted to man by God. The same applies to what and how much the human will can achieve by itself, but not as these achievements are related to God's determination and governance.

3. Well then, the word "free choice," not recorded in Holy Scripture, was used by the Latin church-fathers to express what the philosophers and the Greek theologians who followed them call 'a power which is of itself'—one's own power; or 'free choice'; and 'what lies within us' or is placed within our power. The first of these expressions comes from the Academy, the second from the Peripatetics, and the last one from the [philosophers of the] Stoa.

4. Of these the [Greek] word 'a power which is of itself,' which is 'without a master,' means that one is not subjected to the law, rule, or direction of anybody; or, to be dependent on no-one. Given the nature of man with its fragility and freedom of the will, which is never free from obligation to God and his guidance but is subjected to his providence and governance, this word has a somewhat more presumptuous meaning—this judicial freedom only belongs to God. But Origen, in the *Dialogue with Magetius*, makes a distinction between 'a power which is of itself' and 'all powerful', wherein the former applies to the creature, the latter only to God. The former term, however, can be applied to the creature, but in a metaphorical sense only, and in a certain respect, namely according to participation.

5. A better and more fitting term here is the word 'willful' and 'willing,' which is certainly opposed to 'coerced' and 'unwilling,' but is not simply opposed to 'necessary,' which is related to 'compulsion,' as a kind to its species, for necessity is twofold: the necessity of immutability and the necessity of compulsion. The former can be consistent with willing, the latter cannot. Thus God is necessarily and immutably good as one who cannot be otherwise; still He is not coerced but free [to be good]. Sometimes, indeed,

necessity is opposed to pleasure. Here we have a similar distinction between free and contingent; the latter includes the former and is the genus (or type) of what is free and accidental. And so necessity is perfectly in accordance with the creature's will and free choice together with God's foreknowledge and providence.

6. The subject-matter, however, is transmitted by the Holy Scriptures, and they have their own vocabulary for it. It is called 'the will,' and 'freedom,' and 'the power' of the will (1 Cor 7:36, 37, 39). Indeed, 'voluntary' is used in 1 Cor 9:17, in the letter to Phlm, verse 14, Heb 10:26, and 1 Pet 5:2.

7. Well then, when choice is called free, then freedom is an addition and an affection or property of the will. Strictly speaking it is a word for one's legal right and power, so that it certainly does not properly denote mental judgment or choice, or the will of freedom as Scholastics believe—so that two faculties are indicated at the same time—nor a free power to do any possible good or evil whatsoever. Rather, it is the power of willing and willing not, or of choosing and rejecting; a faculty that is free—without compulsion—and that works by its own movement.

8. Therefore the will is in a proper sense the subject of free choice, although the mind's council and judgement occur first and must of necessity precede, for the will follows the judgement of reason. Following their actions, the faculty of pursuing (and doing) good or evil occurs. If we wished to include all these processes, it would have been better to give this disputation the title, "concerning the powers of the human being."

9. The object or the material of free choice is all that is subject to human deliberation, choice, and action; or, all the good and evil things that concern moral behavior and actions (though not the physical things that our natural desires pursue or shun). Or, to say it more succinctly, in the Church its object is God's law and will as conveyed and commanded in his Word.

10. Arising from this is a distinction between the objects of the will. For some things pertain to this natural or present life, which the apostle calls "matters of everyday life" [1 Cor 6:3], such as eating, drinking, walking, being at rest, etc. Other things pertain to respectable, civic life, or the political and domestic enterprises, such as looking after the family and the common good. And what pertains to them is called civil or philosophical righteousness. And lastly, other things concern the spiritual and religious life, the life of devotion

to God and his law—which operations, in turn, are either external or internal. The former of these are called outward (or bodily) discipline and righteousness; the latter are called spiritual righteousness, such as the motions and actions of one's soul, and the inward worship of God.

11. This distinction here between objects is necessary for an unconfused and clear treatment of the topic. The distinction is made also by the author of the *Calling of the Gentiles*, and the other author, who wrote *Hypognosticon* under the name of Augustine.

12. And so when free choice is treated in the Church the question arises how man's will (both the faculty of the will itself and its act) is related to these objects. Here, we certainly give the general answer that a human wills (and does everything that he wills and chooses to do) not out of natural necessity; nor does he will and do anything coerced by external force or against his will, unwillingly. For nature, violence and the necessity of compulsion are opposed to the will. But it is upon prior deliberation, spontaneously, voluntarily, and freely (so that he is able and suited by a principle within himself to suspend his will and to delay choosing between one object and another, or its opposite, or a different one). That is, man is capable of choosing and willing this or that, and of preferring one thing over another by means of a direct or indirect faculty. And this is the nature and property of the human will, and it is perpetual.

13. Although the will is thus free and always remains so, yet because of the inherent quality of a faculty (whether good or bad), there is a proximate principle and cause of the will and its acts (whether good or bad), by which it happens that with respect to that proximate principle the choice truly is free and is judged to be free or not free.

14. And in this regard, because of the varying condition and status of man, free choice has to be considered variously, whether in the state of creation and integrity, or of the fall and corruption, or of grace and restoration, or lastly, in the state of glory and perfection.

15. Well then, it was in the state of integrity that God created man in his own image and likeness, by which the goodness common to all creatures (Gen 1) was uniquely restricted to humanity in particular (Gen 1:31). Solomon says that God created it good (Eccl 7[:29]); and Paul says: in wisdom, justice, and holiness (Eph 4:24; Col 3:10). Now in this state, I say, there was an integrity

of all the inward and outward capabilities, and just as goodness and righteousness enlightened the mind, so there was also true freedom for mankind—not only that natural freedom whereby he could guide himself into any direction, but there was also a freedom and absence from sin. Or, the will had what was good and there was a faculty, a tendency and facility towards the good, whereby he could will and do what is good, could flee what is evil and pursue the good, or he could render complete obedience unto God so that both by nature and by the goodness of its nature the will was truly free to exercise it in a holy manner.

16. Even so, the disposition towards the good that was implanted in our human nature is of such a sort that man, as he was created by nature to be composite and finite, could for the same reason also change his will. And man's nature was not constituted so specifically that he could not turn himself away from good and towards evil by misusing his free will to determine, to choose, and to do evil. Of his own initiative and motion, under the pretext of doing good, he was able to turn aside to rebellion—which in fact happened, with God's permission. The law of God, the severe warning that accompanied it, and the account of the fall offer proof that the fall of man was self-willed (Gen 2 and 3, Eccl 7:29).

17. Therefore the will had the freedom herein to move in a direction that was either good or evil, on account of the principle and its proximate potency. To be sure, it was free of sin, but not free of changing from the good and of the possibility of sinning, and it could be bent into either direction. Whence both by turning away from what is good and by turning towards what is bad, the will ruined itself as well as its freedom, as Augustine states.

18. Then again, in man's corrupt state, or in man as born only naturally and bound up by original sin, although he had not lost the intellect in his intelligence (despite being corrupted entirely) nor the natural freedom of choice in his will, he retained his natural faculties (along with the physical substance of his soul) which form the principle of his actions, and he retained the remote and passive ability to undertake the opposite. Nevertheless, he lost the righteousness and goodness in both his intellect and his will; indeed, he took on the opposite, sinful inclination.

19. And so by the proximate and active capability, instigated by the devil (who has power and dominion over it) free choice is drawn no longer towards the good that is truly good, but only towards the evil that only appears good

(although a choice remains between the sorts and degrees of evil); with respect to the nearest principle it is necessarily carried off freely, willingly, and of its own accord. For he chooses evil and rejects the good.

20. But to maintain proper distinctions in this treatise: the depraved man's will or choice here does not behave in the same way in all things. For in affairs that concern the natural and civic life, in affairs subject to the senses and reason, and which concern external discipline and corporal justice (defined not only by outward actions but also by internal movement), remnants and tiny sparks [of goodness] survive. They survive so much that man is able to grasp them with his mind, to choose them with his will, to desire them with his emotions, and to pursue and even perform them to some degree (Rom 1:19,32, and 2:14,15, and 9:31, and 10:2; Phil 3:6,7; Gal 1:13).

21. But although man possesses some freedom and faculty to act, nevertheless because of the force of his desires the freedom is very weak; and often his will follows not the prescripts of reason but the worse part of his passions, the movement and lead of his desires. And the devil, who is powerful in unbelievers, does not stop inciting this weak nature and throwing it headlong into various misdeeds. It is for this reason that the massive upheavals in civil justice appear, and that civil justice occurs rarely in society.

22. Well then, since man's ability is so small and righteous only occasionally and by exception, it does not extend beyond the political, respectable, and philosophical spheres; nor does it have the power to reach up to what is truly good and pleasing to God. For with respect to the efficient cause, persons of this sort are by no means pleasing to God. Nor do the actions well up from the pure source: the true knowledge of God, faith in him, and reverence toward him. And such actions are not initiated, performed, and directed by the goal of giving God the glory that is owed to him; and yet it is on these grounds that they should be considered as good works.

23. Hence every action of this sort, even if it does result in good and is good in and of itself (if one considers the action per se), nevertheless, because it is not done rightly, is rendered sinful and is counted as sin (Rom 14:23; Heb 11:6). And so the decision of the will, and the consequent action and result, do in fact constitute sin. However, the person who in and of himself chooses, desires and commits evil is a greater sinner than he who morally and of himself does good deeds wrongly. On these grounds God bestows upon such people a corporal recompense (1 Kgs 21:29; Matt 6:2, 5, 26).

24. In spiritual and inward matters, however, the will of the natural, unregenerate man is free only to do evil. For his intellect is largely ignorant of the substance of God's law, that is, of the true God and what conforms to his will (Eph 2:12, Rom 7:7). His intellect is ignorant especially of the substance of the Gospel, which is supernatural (and thus beyond the intellect and the will); it is ignorant of things that can be understood and grasped with firm conviction only by the supernatural light and the supernatural eye— namely, the eye of faith (as it ought to be). So also the will, bound by depravity, wills, chooses, desires, and accomplishes things opposite to the supernatural ones (1 Cor 2:14, Rom 8:6,7).

25. As a result the natural man, given his innate abilities, and by the free choice of his will, is surely not able to rise up from sin, to cast off his ignorance and his depraved tendencies, to turn himself towards God, and of his own accord to receive, commence, and effect new and spiritual motions—the beginnings of true repentance, faith, reverence and love of God and one's neighbor, and of calling upon him. For Scripture ascribes to the natural man the inability to do these things (John 3:3,5, and 6:44, 8:43; Rom 8:3, 7; 2 Cor 3:5); in fact, opposition to them and disdain are attributed to him.

26. Therefore the will has freedom insofar as it has been restricted to the one side (i.e., the side of wickedness), and it inclines towards sin not by the force of necessity but out of pleasure. But because this is the will of a man who has been sold under sin, who is its slave and dead in it, it should be called bound rather than free. I mean, set free from righteousness and enslaved to sin (John 8:34; Rom 6:16). Augustine, in the *Enchiridion*, says it neatly like this: "What sort of freedom can a bound slave have? None, except when it pleases him to sin, for he serves freely who freely does the will of his master. And in this way the one who is a slave to sin is free to commit sin."

27. However, in the state of grace and restoration in which the natural, carnal man is vindicated from the state of depravity by the grace of God and the efficacious power of the Holy Spirit, and in which he becomes spiritual, advancing in the spiritual life wherein he is preserved and renewed by the new disposition infused into him, his free will (actually, his enslaved will) is liberated and rendered truly free (John 8:36). But that will behaves a little bit differently all the time, in view of its beginning towards goodness, its

progressive advancement, persistent endurance, and its steadfastness in the good.

28. But as far as the start towards goodness is concerned, or the initial act of restoration, the natural man's free choice, in keeping with its nature, is truly corrupt—dead, in fact, regarding its spiritual faculties. It must be restored and brought to life by God; it does not work in cooperation with God but it behaves to some extent passively towards him as the one who acts, according to the degree of its nature and subject.

29. Man does not, however, behave with his free choice like some block of wood; for God works in man as a subject endowed with the faculties of mind and will, and He works through his Word (Rom 10:17; John 17:20; 1 Cor 1:21). Yet it is not as though the natural man himself allows God to be at work in him (for that is an act of good will). For by nature man is stubborn and opposes God when He uses his own Word outwardly, with its promise, its warning, and its other means of persuasion (Matt 23:37; Acts 7:51). But God works in man such as he is, entirely weakened and bound by his evil character and habits (Eph 2:1–3; Titus 3:3).

30. Moreover, God herein works in his divine manner, and in fact with a grace, power, and efficacy of such a sort and degree that He effectively takes the depravity out of the will and implants uprightness in it, so that man is changed from unwilling to willing, and from resisting God to obeying Him. This is obviously an act of the almighty God only, as expressed in Scripture by the words recreation, regeneration, awakening from the dead, and the like (Eph 2:10; John 3:3; Titus 3:5; Eph 1:19, 20 and 2:5; Col 2:12, 13).

31. So then, no-one contributes anything to this grace. In fact, man has no more power to prepare, dispose, and apply himself to that grace than he does to contribute anything to his own conception and birth—neither by the benefit of universal grace and the light of nature, nor by the benefit of particular grace, namely the law (which is imprecisely and loosely included in the word 'grace').

32. We do not deny, however, that herein God makes use of certain prior preparations, such as nature, or the law, whereby the sinner is drawn to despair in himself and led by the hand to take comfort in the Gospel, and to hope in God. But it is by the power of the Spirit through the preaching of

the Word that this work is achieved in us—lest anyone should think that we recommend violent seizures or sudden, spiritualist movements!

33. Furthermore, this regeneration (whereby the ability and principle of willing and doing good is divinely bestowed by God) consists of a total reformation and renewal, both in view of the subject (i.e., the entire man and all his powers) and in view of the object (i.e., God's universal law). However, it is not a total reformation and renewal, according to the intensity of degrees or the highest degree of good quality; but it is partial, according to a lesser degree, in which the contrary can and does exist. That is, remnants of our sinful nature remain in the mind, the will, the feelings, in the capability and power to act, which cause recognition to be more obscured and the will and feelings to be more limited, and the power weakened—so much so that we do not achieve everything we wish to do (1 Cor 13:12; Rom 7:8, 24; Mark 9:24).

34. So then, with respect to the different principles (but the same subject) two opposing parts have been placed opposite each other, so to speak, in one and the same regenerate person, a natural and a spiritual part, flesh and spirit (Matt 26:41; Gal 5:17). Indeed, there are, as it were, two persons, the old and the new (Eph 4:22; Col 3:9), an outer and inner one, a revealed and a hidden one (Rom 7:22; 1 Pet 3:4), and finally a natural (or physical) and a spiritual one (1 Cor 2:[14–]15). Consequently, in the regenerate person a struggle arises between the flesh and the spirit (Rom 7; Gal 5). From the predominant quality of the spirit, however, and following significant progress, the person is simply called spiritual (1 Cor 2:15; Gal 6:1). But according to the shortcomings and weaknesses, or comparatively, he also is called carnal (1 Cor 3:1).

35. And so it happens that when man has been renewed (albeit partly) by the Spirit of God, his free choice relates partly to the good, and partly to the bad. To the good, because following the new powers, inclinations and movements produced and bestowed in his mind and will by God's Spirit, man, by means of this spiritual capability and by the leading and accompaniment of the same Spirit, understands, wills, and achieves spiritual things. That is, man is in harmony with God who calls him and obeys Him in repentance, faith, and true holiness—so much so that he begins, strives, and manages to devote himself to inward and outward obedience, or good works pleasing to God. And this he wills and does in spiritual matters that concern the kingdom of

God (1 Cor 2:14), and in civil matters that pertain to outward self-discipline, which the devout person wills and does out of faith and to God's glory (Rom 14:7,8; 1 Cor 10:31; Jas 4:15). In fact, by the Holy Spirit he also improves and perseveres in these matters.

36. Yet these actions and works, as much as they are in keeping with their own good principle (i.e., the help of regeneration and the Holy Spirit), and because they were brought about by the norm of God's law, they are good. Nevertheless, since in light of the remnants of the flesh humanity is sullied with many blemishes, the works and actions are not good in an absolute sense (Isa 64:6). And yet they are deemed to be of a good sort by virtue of God's acceptance in the Savior Christ (who covers our weaknesses), the working of the Holy Spirit, and the predomination of the spiritual part.

37. In this matter the person who has been renewed by God's grace and the Spirit behaves not only passively but also actively, and he begins to work together with God. That is, as Augustine says in several places, as God's grace leads the way, prepares, and is at work in him, the regenerate man, driven by the same grace that leads, accompanies, assists and collaborates with him, wills and acts and, while that grace supports him, progresses and persists. It is like a young boy who is led by his nurse and steadied by her hand as he begins to walk; and like a boy who learns how to write as his teacher guides his hand, and then writes on his own, because he both is acted upon and acts himself.

38. Therefore the will is not idle here, but when liberated it possesses some freedom and action, as Scripture testifies (Phil 2:13; 2 Cor 3:17; Rom 6:18, etc.). And in the same sense Augustine says very clearly in the book *On Corruption and Grace*: "If they are God's children they understand that they are led by God's Spirit to do what they should do, and when they have done it, they give thanks to the one who has done it. For they are led to do them, and not so that they do not do them."

39. Regrettably, time and time again the conduct of free choice relates to evil. For in fact the remnants of the flesh and sin always remain in those who have been reborn, because the regeneration or renewal of their nature (i.e., of their mind, will, feelings, and power) has only begun and has not been perfected. And there remains a great weakness which is also aroused by the attractions supplied by the world and our flesh, and by the different temptations of the devil. And they are not always governed by the Holy Spirit (or, governed to

the same extent) and by special grace, nor confirmed in the good. But occasionally and for a period of time they are abandoned and left to themselves (by God's certain decree). This happens so that He may chastise and humble them, so that they learn to rely upon him. The pious by their own will, free choice, and work, are led to sin, even serious sin, and they fall into them, as is shown by the examples of these saints: David (2 Sam 11:2; Ps 51:13; 2 Sam 24:1; and 1 Chron 21) and Peter (Luke 22:31, 55, etc.).

40. It is clear from these points that the regenerate man cannot in this life accomplish the perfect obedience to every degree and amount because of the imperfection of the nearest cause. And because his flesh opposes him, he is not able to maintain an uninterrupted and constant course of piety, but he stumbles, fails, and sins—contrary to the Catharist Heretics and the Perfectionists.

41. But even so, in the grace of regeneration they are not abandoned by God their compassionate Father, nor by Christ their Redeemer and Head, nor by the sanctifying Holy Spirit. They are not abandoned, nor do they themselves abandon grace to the point where they acquiesce in evil by their own free choice and work, where sin rules in them, and where they fall into indifference and unrepentance, and into sinning unto death; or where they fall away totally and finally. But by God's grace, Christ's care, and the Spirit's power, and by the strength of that spiritual seed, they are called back to, and through, a genuine change of heart, lest they sin unto the end and so perish (Matt 24:[22–]24; Luke 22:31, 32, 61; John 17:11, 12, 20, and chapter 10:[28]29, 30; 1 John 2:27 and 3:9 and 5:4; 1 Pet 1:4, 5).

42. On this point therefore, in the state of grace and restoration, free choice must be set free and it has been freed. In other words, the will is freed not simply from sin, but from slavery or servitude to sin; it is in the service of righteousness and kept safe by God's grace from the risk of total destruction.

43. Lastly, there is the state of glory and perfection in the next age of eternal life, after the current age, when man will be blessed and glorified. For there, then, and in that man the restoration and regeneration will be perfect and actually match the highest degree in which nothing adverse can or does befall him. Then in the mind of man there will shine forth the most perfect knowledge of God and of his will, an integrity of judgement that has no ignorance or doubts. In the will, the heart, the feelings and in all the powers, being perfect in every way, and without any opposition, there will thrive an

inclination, a tendency, an eagerness, and a desire to obey God. And then that man will be ruled and established by God for evermore and to good effect. His will shall be truly free—indeed, most free, as it shall be invariably good, not absolutely by nature (to be sure) but by grace. A consideration of the quality and amount of this freedom, however, we shall defer to that heavenly school (Rom 8:21, 1 Cor 13:10, 12; and 15:28).

44. Well then, when he was in the first state, man was able with his free choice not to sin but to stand firm in the good. In the second state, having become wicked by the abuse of his free choice, man could do nothing but sin—let alone to ascend to the good by the powers of his will. In the third state, created anew by God's grace and power, and established by it in the good, man is not able with his free choice to sin totally and finally, but he advances and stands firm in what is good. And finally, in the fourth stage, glorified by God, man will no longer be able to sin, as Augustine says, but his free choice forever will remain free of sin and misery, without change.

45. We reject the following contrary theses that oppose the orthodox teaching: the first is of the Pelagians, who held that in everything free choice is undamaged and self-sufficient to obey God if it wishes to. And so, by assigning the power of the will entirely to themselves, they committed sacrilege against God. The second contrary thesis is that of the semi-Pelagians, who assert that whereas free choice is indeed wounded, weakened, and worsened, it is not corrupted, and they attribute conversion partly to grace and partly to the freedom of the will, thus splitting it between God and men. For these were their fundamental propositions: "That there is a point at which the will anticipates the will of God, and another point at which it is anticipated by God's will," as Cassian held. Similarly: "God's grace is what saves us, but it is free choice by which, or in which, we are saved," as Faustus says with deceptive attraction. Against him the orthodox posited: "The ground of salvation is uniform," and "free choice is that which is saved."

46. These errors were renewed in various ways by the Schoolmen and by the fathers of the Council of Trent, and also some of the Evangelicals who refurbished them with a coloring of human co-operation, in particular those whose errors were rejected by the Reformed churches at the Synod of Dordrecht.

CONCERNING THE LAW OF GOD

President: Johannes Polyander
Respondent: Arnoldus Schomantius

In this disputation we return to the topic of God's self-revelation in Scripture, in the Old and the New Testament. God's address to humanity is twofold: in Law (Disp. 18–21) and in Gospel (Disp. 22–23). The first thesis on the law connects the theme to the former disputation on free choice. After elaborating the different meanings of the word 'law' (2–9), the conclusion is drawn that 'law' in Scripture is used for the instruction and rule in history whereby God commands people to do anything that agrees with his judgment and forbids them to do what is contrary to it (10–11). Next, the discussion is arranged in three parts, as introduced in thesis 12: natural law (13–25); human or civil law (26–29); divine law (30–51). Natural law is the light and direction of sound reason that informs man with common notions to distinguish right from wrong. After the fall, human beings because of their corrupted and depraved nature failed in applying these unchanged notions to particular things. Natural law, however, remained sufficient to convict and condemn sin (13–25). This internal, implanted law needs the help of external laws for a better understanding and proper obedience. Hence civil laws were introduced among the nations. These laws bind the conscience only if they conform to God's law, the Decalogue (26–29). The most proper goal of the divine law, summarized in the Decalogue (30–31), is love (32–33). This goal is served by three-fold means: 1. Moral law (34–45); 2. Ceremonial law (46–48); 3. Political law (49–51). Moral law consists of two tables that defines our duties-out-of-love to God and to our neighbor. This moral law is relevant to Christians as well as Jews; Christ gave this law its true interpretation. With respect to the unfolding of the different uses of the moral law, the Synopsis reveals the influence of John Calvin, who distinguishes between pedagogical, civil, and normative uses of the law. The Synopsis prefers a distinction between people—that is, between 'all people who are trapped in their willful disobedience' and 'the elect only' (40, 41–42). Boasting in keeping the works of the law is excluded, because no-one is able to keep the law of works perfectly in this life. No-one can be justified before God by means of his own works, so the law of faith is placed diametrically opposite to the law of works (44). The ceremonial law was once arranged to suit the structure of the Israelite nation until the coming of Christ, who fulfilled this law. When Christ had fulfilled the ceremonial law it became not only dead but also deadly for those who continue to uphold it (46–48). The political law contains the civil regulations for the Israelite nation to promote justice and piety. The universal (not the particular Jewish) precepts of this law are valid to the present day (49–51).

1. It is from the law of God that one can learn how much man, after the fall into sin, suffers from the failure of the powers of his free choice, and how great his misery is.

2. The law, called *lex* by the Latins because it used to be read [*legi*] publicly, is called *nomos* by the Greeks because it renders [*nemein*] to each his due, and *Torah* by the Hebrews, that is, instruction, because it instructs [*yarah*] us about the will of God and our duty towards him and our neighbor.

3. In Holy Scripture "law" is used with different meanings, and firstly for anything that has been instituted by God (Ps 1:2, and 19:8).

4. Hence the word "law" is applied to the teaching of the New as well as the Old Testament (Isa 2:3; Jer 31:33; Rom 3:27).

5. Secondly, the word is used with particular meaning for moral law (as in Luke 10:26), ceremonial law (as in Luke 2:22), or forensic law (as in John 19:7).

6. Thirdly, as a metonym of the subject, it is used for the books of Moses that contain the teaching of the law, as in Luke 24:44.

7. Fourthly, it is used by *synecdoche* for all the books of the Old Testament, as in John 10:34.

8. In the fifth place, as a metonym of the adjunct, it is used for the Levitical ministry, as in Heb 7:12, or for the severity and curse of the law, as in Rom 6:14.

9. In the sixth place it is used figuratively for the natural directive of human reason (Rom 2:14).

10. From these usages it appears that "law" in the sacred writings is not used for the eternal law, or for the essential conceptual content that exists in the divine understanding as in an archetype, but for a legal rule that is drawn

down by God, as the most perfect exemplar, for the human race within time, and communicated and declared to it in various ways.

11. Well then, staying within the boundaries of the sacred books, we employ the word "law" for the instruction and rule in history whereby God commands people created in his image to do anything that agrees with his judgment and forbids them to do what is contrary to it, with the promise of reward and the threat of punishment, so that He may direct them to obey his will.

12. According to the diversity of its closely related principles, this law is divided into natural law, human laws, and divine laws.

13. Natural law is the light and direction of sound reason in the intellect, informing man with common notions to distinguish right from wrong, and honorable from shameful—so that he may understand what he should do or shun.

14. Some of those notions are of a primary sort, and we call them practical principles; others, which are secondary, we call conclusions constructed from those principles with the help of reasoning.

15. Before the fall of man, both sorts of notions were unspoiled and coupled together in delightful harmony, together with the power in the will to make decisions according to their directions, and to carry out the commands of the will properly in the affections.

16. After the fall of man, however, the first, primary notions in his intellect remained unchanged, and they shine forth clearly; but the latter, secondary notions stagger with wretched hesitation whenever one goes from general things to particular ones, and they deviate from the sound rule of equity, as is shown by the examples of the very unfair laws and overly corrupt customs that are found in the histories of gentile peoples.

17. After the transgression of Adam those notions were completely covered up and nearly wiped out, partly because of the corruption of his nature and partly because of the depravity of his behavior and upbringing. And yet the little sparks of these common notions that do remain are sufficient to convict and condemn sin, even in those who have been darkened completely.

18. For this reason Paul says that God's judgment was known to the gentiles who in former times had been given over to godlessness and unrighteousness

(Rom 1:[26–]32) and that the requirement of the law was inscribed upon their hearts (Rom 2:14[15]). He demonstrates this with a twofold testimony, external and internal.

19. The external testimony is the law they themselves set up, and Paul asserts that they were a law unto themselves, namely by commanding or prohibiting the very things that God commands or forbids in the law which He had written (Rom 2:14).

20. The internal testimony is that of the conscience, which by its deliberations confronts their wrong actions and defends the right ones by the authority of the law that has been laid up in their hearts (Rom 2:15).

21. Evident in the nature of mankind are two-fold traces of this law, some of which he appears to share with irrational living beings, while others belong properly to him.

22. The ones mankind seems to share with the other created living beings are those to which all creatures endowed with animate life and perception are inclined by natural instinct, in order to protect themselves and their offspring by innate affection and natural feeling. Traces of this kind are: guarding their own lives, propagating, nurturing, and cherishing their own offspring.

23. For the reason that it has taught all living beings, this law is loosely (and with a rather broader meaning) called "natural law" by the lawyers.

24. Traces of the law that properly concern mankind are the ones to which his affections are directed by the bidding and guidance of reason (which the other creatures lack), in keeping with the norm of good and right that God has granted to him. Traces of this kind are: that God should be worshipped, parents and others who rightly deserve it respected, and agreements kept, and the like.

25. However, since the sacred Book does not consider mankind separately as a living being, but jointly, as a living being endowed with reason—better yet, it offers a treatment of him as a creature made in God's image—therefore our theologians restrict that natural law to mankind as its true and proper subject. This is what Paul does in Rom 1 and 2.

26. Although in the judgment and consensus common to all peoples it is agreed that this law is implanted in the souls of men, nevertheless the wiser

heathens acknowledge that for a better understanding and proper keeping of it, this internal law needs the help of external laws.

27. Hence it came about that thanks to the skills of a few wise individuals and the authority of the magistrates in the commonwealth, as many civil laws as possible were introduced among both gentile and Christian nations.

28. These laws are the pronouncements of what is just, established by the solemn and specific order of a legitimate magistrate, and they issue from commonly-held notions that are like principles and sources. And like little streams, they produce certain conclusions and particular provisions according to the needs of persons, things, times, and places, for the public and private good of citizens; and they establish these by promising reward and by threatening with punishment.

29. If in all their edicts these laws conform entirely to the exemplar of God's law, they bind the consciences of their subjects to keeping them or to suffering punishment; if the laws contradict God's law, then they do not bind their subjects.

30. The exemplar of God's law is the one that God himself, through his heavenly angels and through his servant Moses, directly inspired and recorded with his own finger, and that He himself handed to the people of Israel on Mount Sinai (Exod 19:20, and 20:1 ff.; Acts 7:53; Gal 3:19).

31. This exemplar of God's law describes in a summary fashion and encompassed in ten commandments the way to live well and in blessedness before God and our neighbor. Therefore Moses calls it "The Ten Words," and we call it the Decalogue.

32. The goal that is most appropriate and closest to God's law is a single one, namely, the love ordained according to God's precepts wherein the conscience rests securely. However, the means that serve this goal are three-fold, of which the first exists in statutes that are moral, the second ceremonial, and the third political.

33. Hence the law of God is divided into the moral, the ceremonial, and the political.

34. The moral law is the one which by means of general commands that are perpetually and mutually true (commands that are in harmony with the divine and natural right and that are absolutely necessary and useful for each and

every human being) prescribe the just and precise way of living according to God's will. Added to this moral law are promises for the present and future life if one keeps its precepts; added also are the threats of the first and second death if one breaks them.

35. Therefore it consists of three parts: 1) commandments whereby something is required or forbidden; 2) promises of temporal and eternal blessing; 3) threats of damnation (Exod 19:5; Deut 27:26; Luke 10[26–28]; Rom 10:5; Gal 3:10).

36. The moral law consists of two tables, in the former of which four precepts define the duties of piety that we must present to God in the first place, out of the highest and sincere love that we have for Him. Of the latter table there are six that show the duties of righteousness that we must carry out towards our neighbor in the second place, out of true love towards him (Matt 22:38[39]).

37. Christ calls the summary of the former table "the first and great commandment"; He calls the summary of the latter "the second and like the first," in order to teach us that we are required to keep both of them carefully: 1) So that the pious worship that is owed to God may be in harmony with his supreme will and majesty. 2) So that we first love God directly for who He is, and then everything else for his sake (in particular the devout people for their spiritual and closer connection to God). 3) So that the duties of love we have toward our neighbor may yield to the duties of piety to God, and so that we may endure the unjust hatred of our neighbor and every affliction and injustice with constant steadfastness for the sake of our service to Him.

38. We prove, with the following arguments, that this law is as relevant to Christians in the New Testament as it was to Jews in the Old Testament: 1) It is the outward representation of the internal law of nature that before the fall was impressed upon our first parents as they were created in God's image; this law is grounded in holiness and justice. The Decalogue portrays to people one and all the duties that accompany these virtues, and the Gospel urgently demands these duties from the members of the household of faith, who have been restored to God's image through God's Spirit. 2) This law, which had been revealed to our first parents and was restated and reinforced through Moses, was promoted not only by the prophets but also by Christ and his apostles, who observed them and strongly recommended them to others (Matt 5:17 ff.; Luke 10:27; Rom 6:13 and 7:25, and chapters 12 and 13). 3)

The observance of this law's precepts is like a token or emblem whereby those who keep them are described as sons of God; it is infallible testimony of their genuine union with God (1 John 1:6,7 and 2:3,4,5 and 6). 4) The love that comes from a unfeigned faith and a good conscience (which is the goal of the Decalogue) is put before Timothy as the target to which all his actions should be directed (1 Tim 1:5).

39. This law is so complete that nothing has been added to it in any moral injunctions (either by Christ or by his apostles) to raise it up to a more exacting norm of good works under [the dispensation of] the New Testament. But because it had fallen into disuse and had been cast aside by false interpretations and evil corruption before the coming of Christ, Christ fully restored its pristine lustre by his true interpretation (new and unheard of to the Jews who had been misled) and by the repeated admonitions that its commands be observed universally.

40. The use of this law is general for any and all people who are trapped in their willful disobedience and it is intended specifically for the salvation of the elect.

41. The first use is three-fold:

1. To check all the unbridled passions of people with the reins of its own external control.

2. To reveal in its own reflection (like a mirror) to sinners one and all the loss of the original righteousness of the human race in Adam, and the powerlessness of the corrupted flesh or nature; that is, the inability to perform what it has been commanded, and the crooked tendencies to violate those commands. Therefore, knowledge of sin is said to come about through the law (Rom 3:19, 20; 4:15; 5:20; and 7:7 ff.).

3. To be the herald of God's righteous judgment against those who transgress it. Therefore, it is called the ministry of death, working wrath and striking with fear (2 Cor 3:7; Rom 4:15; and Heb 12:29).

42. The second use, ordained specifically for the salvation of the elect, is fourfold:

1. It is, with the additional help of the ministry of the Gospel, to lead those who have been humbled by their sense of sin and guilt, to

Christ our Savior, who for every believer is the goal of the law unto righteousness (Rom 10:4).

2. It is, for those people who believe in Christ, to be the rule for what must be performed and what must be left aside, and the guide on the road that leads to life. For this use it is called the law of works (Rom 3:27), the way of God (Ps 119:3), the way of truth (Ps 119:30), and a light for our feet (Ps 119:105).

3. So that the holy and honorable behavior according to the precepts of the law may be a witness of the believers' true communion with God (1 John 1:6,7; 2:3; and 3:4,5, and 6).

4. So that the law, by its own stimulus, may drive them on more every day to pursue sincere love towards God and their neighbor (1 Tim 1:5).

43. As far as stubborn reprobates are concerned, these people are not of that law; but, insolently hastening by the sin of their own perverse desire into what is forbidden, they harden themselves against its commands, and so they render themselves more worthy of damnation in God's sight.

44. The apostle places the law of faith diametrically opposite this law of works, so that all boasting in works is excluded (Rom 3:27). From this exclusion of boasting it necessarily follows that no-one (however much regenerated he may be) is able to keep that law of works perfectly in this life, and thus no-one can be justified before God by means of his own works.

45. Meanwhile God rightly demands from us the duty of perfect love that we owe him and our neighbor, since in our first parents He has bestowed upon our nature the ability of performing it.

46. The ceremonial law is the 'shadow painting,' the sketched outline of the divine worship which God demands in the four commandments of the first table. This law was once arranged to suit the structure of the Israelite nation, and it consisted of a variety of figurative foreshadowings, of which the bodily substance is in Christ, who in his own flesh abolished its commandments. He did so in order to take away the dividing wall of hostility between Jews and gentiles, and so that through the cross He might reconcile with God the two parties in one body (Col 2:17; Eph 2:15, 16).

47. Regarding this law that axiomatic statement is true: "The ceremonial law is dead, and if it is returned to its former privileged status, it would be deadly."

48. There were various uses of that ceremonial law during the Old Testament period:

1. So that by observing it the people of Israel might be segregated from the other, pagan peoples as if by the enclosure of a wall that separates them; lest through familiar interaction with them they should fall headfirst and together with them into the same impiety and idol worship.

2. So that they might understand from its outward ceremonies that they must dedicate not only the inward worship of their soul to God, but also the outward worship of their body.

3. So that it might be the nerve and tether of the holy Levitical ministry that was to be preserved in the Jewish church until the coming of Christ.

4. So that it might be a public record of the debts that had been held against them in an invisible way; by this law they seal their guilt against themselves, as well as their obligation to the punishment of eternal death on account of their transgressions of God's law (Col 2:14).

5. So that it might be a tutor to lead them to Christ (Gal 3[:24]).

6. So that its characteristic sacrifices might be symbols of Christ's atoning sacrifice and of our sanctification through the sprinkling of his blood (Heb 9 and 10).

49. The political law is what determines the duties of the governing officials and the subjects of the Israelite nation by means of certain civil regulations. It lends authority to them through the corporal punishment of those who rebel, in keeping with the norm of the Decalogue's two tables, and in particular the second one.

50. The foremost use of this political law is that by the precise keeping of the precepts of the moral and ceremonial laws, justice might thrive in conjunction with piety especially among the Jews.

51. Even to the present-day governing officials and their subjects one and all are obliged to obey those precepts in this political law that belong to the universal law; however, the ones that belong to the particular Jewish [political] law have become obsolete along with the Mosaic system of government.

ON IDOLATRY

President: Andreas Rivetus
Respondent: Samuel Bochartus

The discussions in Disputations 19–21, on idolatry, oaths, and the Sabbath, relate to contemporary debates between defendants of the Reformed, Roman Catholic, and Anabaptist faiths. As for idolatry, the law of God commands us to serve the one true God only, and only in the way He himself has commanded. With regard to both the object of our veneration and adoration (namely, the Creator or something created) and to the manner of worship, things can go wrong, and both deviations can be qualified as 'idolatry' or superstition (1–3). In this disputation the Synopsis has in mind especially the idolatry that can be found in the Roman Church: 'all the papal theologians of our own day are such people,' namely those 'who are in the grip of the error of idolatry' or 'who by their speech and example encourage and establish it' (16). The term 'idolatry' is discussed first (4–6), and then its substance or proper definition (8–9). The Synopsis goes on to deal with the formal subcategories of idolatry (10–14). Thereupon idolatry is seen in light of its origin and history (15), and an injunction to abolish it follows (16). A lengthy discussion of five contemporary practices of Roman Catholic idolatry follows next (17–26), which is contrasted with the identification of the lawful use of images (27–29). The disputation ends with a rejection of Samosatenian idolatry (30) and the punishments that will be imposed for idolatrous worship (31–32). What they say about images applies in an absolute sense only to images of the Trinity. The art of making images from creatures is not condemned and brings about some good. But in churches images are 'dangerous, and for that reason unlawful' (27). Biblically speaking, in addition to religious worship (reserved to God), there is also room for civil worship (aimed at creatures). Both must, of course, be clearly distinguished. Creatures should be worshiped with love, not with servitude; with goodwill and fellowship (29). Idolatry, since it is spiritual adultery and sacrilege, is a very serious sin, that will be punished both in this and the future life (31–32).

1. The Law of God, which was treated in the previous disputation, puts before us that we must worship only that "Lawgiver who has the power to save and to destroy" (Jas 4:12) and that we must do so by the inward and outward worship which He himself has revealed and commanded in his Word. This worship is commonly called *'evada* in Hebrew (Exod 12:26), *thrēskeia* in Greek (Acts 26:5), and *religio* in Latin, a word which Augustine (*On True Religion*), following Lactantius (*Institutes* Book 4, chapter 28) derives from *religare* ['to bind, tie'] because through religion "we bind our souls to the one God," so that 'religion' is the word for the fetter of piety which fastens man to God. And Cicero, in Book 2 of *On Invention*, rightly described it as "that which offers homage and reverence to anything of a higher nature that is called divine."

2. Over against 'religion,' and by way of excess, is placed what the Greeks called 'fear of demons' and the Latins 'superstition'; not because someone can sin in religion by excess according to absolute quantity, but only according to so-called quantity of proportion. In this case the latter requires two things: That no worship is given to what should not be worshiped, and that to him who ought to be worshiped no worship is shown beyond what he wills.

3. Hence two sorts of superstition are distinguished, of which the one establishes the worship of God in an inappropriate manner (which the Scriptures call 'self-willed worship'), and the other occurs when something is worshiped that ought not to be worshiped (which the Scriptures call 'idol-worship,' and which sometimes includes both sorts). We do not deny, however, that the former, strictly speaking, is distinguished from the latter, since not every superstitious person is strictly an idol-worshiper (although every idolater is superstitious). We shall now treat this latter topic of idolatry.

4. Idolatry is called by a name made up of two parts, *eidōlon* and *latreia*, like the worship of, or slavery to an idol. Moreover, the Greek word *eidōlon*, if we consider the word's etymology, comes from *eidesthai*, which in Greek means "to seem; or to represent [as something]." And in general, among respected writers in the Greek language it means some likeness and image, whether conceived in the mind or fashioned by hand; and a likeness of something that does or does not exist. Therefore, the word *eidolon* is not, as our opponents would have it, a diminutive of *eidos* for its lack of representation, as though an idol is representative of something that doesn't exist. Even though this is

what Bellarmine contends, still [Jean] Lorin, himself also a Jesuit, on Acts 17:16 admits that this word can have a range of meaning among the pagan authors equally broad as the Greek word *eikōn*, and if we render both of them in Latin, the meaning of 'idol' and 'icon,' or image, would be the same.

5. But when he adds that in ecclesiastical usage the word is always understood in a negative sense, we agree; and we consider an 'idol' not only an external image that is skillfully made to represent a real or imaginary deity for worship, but also any false deity that has no image or that is the figment of man's imagination (since it is not real). It is an idol also if it is something that exists but is a creature deemed to be a god, or on which divine worship is bestowed. Accordingly, the fathers of the Council of Frankfurt rightly said that "they do not call the images of the saints 'idols,' but that they did not wish to worship and honour them, or to pay homage to them, lest they be called 'idols'" (*Capitularis*, Chapter M, Book 2 heading 18).

6. With the apostle [Paul] (1 Cor 8:4) we state also that an idol "is nothing in the world," though not, as some wrongly explain, because something that does not exist in reality is portrayed by an idol; for demons do exist, yet an idol of them is nothing. But an idol is nothing in the world because it is not at all like the thing for which it is worshiped, that it should earn the recognition or worship as a god, or be of any benefit for salvation. The same apostle, in 1 Cor 10:19, denies that sacrifice to idols is anything, as if to say that the consecration of it is useless. Thus, they are called "nothing" because they lack effectiveness and carry no weight, and should be considered as nothing, in the same manner as he "who considers himself to be something" is "nothing" (Gal 6:3), and in this sense the idols in Scripture are called "vanities," "falsehoods," "a lie." Chrysostom says: "It may exist, but it has no power" (*Homily* 20, on 1 Corinthians).

7. But the word *latreia* ['due service'], even when it occurs by itself, often refers to what is owed to human beings; in fact, as Valla has observed and demonstrated by means of examples, it applied more frequently to human beings. And the distinction between *latreia* and *douleia* ['bondage, servitude'], in the sense that has been thought up by our opponents, is pointless if we consider the actual words. Even so, we grant that in conjunction with the words 'of an idol,' *latreia* is used for religious worship and all that pertains to it (things such as adoration, invocation, the placing of trust, the eucharist, sacrifice, oath, vows, the dedication of temples, altars and feasts, etc.). All this

Augustine summarizes with these words: "Worship that is owed to the divinity, or, to express it more precisely, to the deity, occurs when we render things sacred, make sacrifices, or when we dedicate something that belongs to us, or even ourselves, by means of religious rites" (*On the City of God*, book 10, chapter 1).

8. And so a real definition of idol-worship is "worshiping and paying homage to the created thing while ignoring the Creator" (Rom 1:25). Superstition occurs when any worship that is owed to God only is shown in a religious way to something that ought not to receive it, whether it be a creature or a figment of the human mind. By this definition (and keeping the proper force of the word) 'idolatry' has the extended meaning that it is 'the religious worship of a creature' generally, either in the heart only or in outward, physical worship (with or without an image). For people have bestowed religious worship also upon dragons and snakes, as well as fire, wind, air, sun, moon and stars. Nor are the Roman people absolved from the charge of idolatry for that whole period of time, namely the one hundred and seventy years after the founding of the city, when, Plutarch testifies in the *Life of Numa*, their temples were without images or likenesses, because "at that time the Greeks' and Etruscans' inventions for making likenesses had not yet flooded the city," as Tertullian (*Apology* 25) nicely states.

9. According to this definition the genus is 'superstition,' about which we spoke. The object is anything that is not the true God. The form or the difference exists in the religious worship, however that may be, for it makes little or no difference with what word or phrase it is expressed so long as it is clear from the matter itself that it is religious and divine worship that is owed only to God; for Scripture uses these verbs 'to worship,' 'to adore,' 'to serve,' 'to call upon,' etc., loosely and indiscriminately when dealing with the proper worship of God alone.

10. For a complete definition it is not necessary also to add the phrase 'as to God,' whereby some of the Jesuits try to cover up idolatry, as if idolatry is committed only when someone shows divine worship to a creature with the intent "that such estimation as befits God alone be granted to a creature." The falsehood in this is clear from the fact that the papal teachers themselves admit that many heathens did not worship one spirit in their idols, but several different ones, as if they were distinguished from each other by degrees; thus they did indeed have one supreme God, but below him other, lesser gods

(namely spiritual beings created by that supreme God). In worshiping these gods they did commit idolatry, even though they did not honour them with "the utmost inclination and prostration of the will, and with the intellectual understanding of God as the first principle and the final goal, and so as the highest good"—which things Bellarmine considers essential requirements for divine worship (*On the Blessedness of the Saints*, Book 1, chapter 12). All of this [Gregory of] Nazianzus presents concisely and better as "the transference of worship from the Creator to the creature" (*Oratio* 38). If this were not so, the Lord's response would not have been correct when Satan invited him to religious prostration, that it is written: "You shall worship the Lord your God and him only shall you serve" (Luke 4:8). For Satan had not asked Jesus to acknowledge him as "the first principle," but only as the one "to whom had been given the power and the glory" of the kingdoms of the world.

11. Therefore whoever bestows religious worship on something which he knows is not God is not excused; for whatever contrary thoughts he may be having when he worships, invokes, and kneels, Scripture calls that "to consider as God," despite the fact that in his own opinion he does not consider it as God. This is acknowledged by even the schoolmen, who make a distinction between the "speculative" and the "practical" attribution of divinity to creatures. For people who deny creatures the status of divinity "in a speculative way" as far as their understanding is concerned, nevertheless do bestow it "in practice;" that is, by their action and in reality, they do bestow on them a state of independence from their Creator. Thus Varro was an idolator, as he was worshiping idols outwardly, not from the conviction that they possessed an innate Divinity, but for the purpose of conforming to the common people, as Augustine testifies, in whose judgment "also the conduct of Seneca was all the more damnable because what he did falsely he did in such a way that the people thought that he was doing it truthfully" (*On the City of God*, book 1, chapter 6; and of the same book, chapter 10).

12. Besides idolatry in the form of religious worship shown to a creature after God has been rejected, there is also the worship of a creature who is honoured alongside and with God, whether that creature be a hand-made image or some other thing (either artificial or natural) chosen for worship without God's command. Firstly, because when men make up and establish a new form of worship, they also make up and establish a new God. In this sense the same Augustine says, that the Hebrew tribes refused to honour God, "because if they wanted to honour God in a way different than He had

said he should be honoured, they would not at all be honouring Him but whatever they had invented" (*On the Harmony of the Gospels*, Book 1, chapter 15). This manner of idolatry belongs more to the second kind of superstition (i.e., to the mode of honouring God). Secondly, and more fundamentally, because it is idolatry when something that should not be honoured is worshiped in a religious manner, even though it is made as a representation of God. For then two sins are being committed: 1. Because contrary to the expressed Word of God which prohibits anyone from portraying any likeness of Him, a figure of God is being fashioned that is entirely unworthy of his infinite majesty. 2. Because it introduces a worship in association with the worship of God.

13. For it is a pointless and wrong contention of the papal theologians that no instance is found in the Old Testament where the worship of the true God in an image, or with or through an image, is referred to as idolatry. For Scripture clearly testifies that those who worshiped the calf in the desert had declared a public feast to the Lord (Exod 32:1) and that Micha, after the molten image (which was called *Terafim*, Judg 17:4) was fashioned from the silver [money] that is recorded explicitly as dedicated to the Lord, had said: "Now I know that the Lord will prosper me" (Judg 17:13). And Scripture states that the worship of the calves of Jeroboam was called "the fear of the Lord" (2 Kgs 17:28). Indeed Jehu, who was a defender of worshiping the calves, and "who did not depart from the sins of Jeroboam," nevertheless boasted to Jonadab about his zeal for the Lord (2 Kgs 10:16).

14. The fact that Scripture calls those calves "foreign gods" is not an objection; nor that it states the Jews had made offerings to devils and not to God; that they "had offered sacrifice to an idol," etc. For these passages are not concerned with the thinking and intentions of the people who are worshiping, or with their motivations; but they concern the fact of the matter from the perspective of God's judgment, who testifies in word and deed that this worship, undertaken contrary to the prescript of his Word, was displeasing to Him and that it was the devil who had started it. Even so, this second mode of idolatry differs by degrees from the first, wherein a creature is directly honoured as God. Scripture, too, distinguishes these degrees in the case of Ahab when it says (1 Kgs 16:31): "It was a light thing for him to walk in the sins of Jeroboam; to have gone and served Baal, and to have bowed down before him." This difference in degrees would be out of place if

Jeroboam had established a direct worship of the calves, without any reference to the God of Israel.

15. Concerning the origin of idolatry there is no need for us to pursue a long line of controversy if we take 'origin' to mean the time in which it began. If the question is understood to be about spiritual idolatry (to put it that way) then we do not doubt that devils suggested it to people who first struggled in their ignorance of the true God, and who gave themselves over to false emotions. If the question concerns outward idolatry through "signs and images," then too nothing certain can be said about the time. About the opportunity for idolatry nearly everyone thinks from the book of Wisdom that the first makers of idols were those who bestowed this honour upon the deceased, in order to give superstitious honour to their memory—when "a father mourning with bitter grief, made for himself an image of the child who suddenly had been taken from him" (*Wisdom of Solomon* 14:15). Different people explain this passage in different ways; of them the ones who seem to reach the gist of the matter tell us that the author had meant not the initial starting-point of idolatry but rather the well-worn, common one. On this point it should be noted that the author calls the images which the father made of the son "idols" (*Wisdom of Solomon* 14:15).

16. But seeing that there is certainty about the matter itself, we should work more towards abolishing idolatry than to enter into controversy over its origin. And we should seek to free (or at least convince) both those who are in the grip of the error of idolatry, and those who by their speech and example encourage and establish it. We affirm that all the papal theologians of our own day are such people, both those who are led astray and certainly those who mislead them by means of many names and in different chief points.

17. First and foremost is the worship of the sacramental bread in the Eucharist, which they admit they clearly portray as divine when all the people, after the signal has been given at the elevation of the host, worship the sacrament as if it is their god, and their knees are bent or their entire bodies are stretched out on the ground. They perpetrate a second act of idolatry in the ceremonial procession of the bread, particularly at the feast devoted specifically to it, as they pronounce curses upon everyone "who states that this sacrament should not be adored with the worship of adoration (even outwardly), nor carried around in ceremonial procession, nor displayed in public for adoration" (Council of Trent, session 3, canon 6).

18. For what they suppose is wrong, that by virtue of the transubstantiation there is no other 'supposit' [or 'subsistent individual substance'] except Christ; while, as even they themselves admit, the accidents, which Christ had not taken up into the unity of his person, do remain present, and although they are merely created things, they are worshiped in such a way that adoration and all worship is directed primarily at them. This is the reason for their adoration of the sacrament—but God is not a sacrament! And then there is the fact that they cannot be certain about the true consecration of the bread, which depends on the intention of the one who administers it; but since they cannot have any certainty of faith about the intention, they (along with the Samaritans) "worship what they do not know" (John 4:22).

19. Secondly, they commit idolatry by worshiping saints, both angels and humans, and everyone knows they adore and call upon them, and they present votive offerings to them in religious ceremonies. And they attach the status of deity to these saints, at least as far as the practice is concerned, because they are invoked everywhere as though they are infinite. And as if saints are able to search the hearts, they are vowed promises in the silent prayer of the soul, which befits God alone. Temples, altars, and holy days are consecrated to their honour. By these deeds, they either wish to acquire for them [i.e., the saints] the reputation of deity, or they overturn the principal argument of the orthodox for the divinity of the Son and the Holy Spirit. Indeed, they slip and fall into both of these hazards.

20. They commit twice as much idolatry in worshiping the blessed virgin Mary—so much so that they leave nothing proper to God alone, in word or in deed. In fact, they exalt her beyond the Christ, the God who is blessed unto eternity, as though she rules over him even in this state of glory. For thus they speak: "What does it mean to be the Mother of God? The Mother is the cause of the Son, the Mother is superior to the Son; honour is owed to the Mother by the Son, the Son is bound to comply with the Mother's wishes." [Francis] Coster in the [*Meditations*] *upon the Hymn 'Hail, Star of the Sea'*, ascribes to her also "almighty power in heaven and on earth," and others state that God himself bestowed upon her "the realm of compassion, and the distribution of it" while keeping for himself the realm of justice ([Gabriel] Biel, Lecture 80 of the *Canon of the Mass*). Hence it happened that after Bonaventure, in a psalm composed for this purpose, they assign to her everything that in the Psalms is attributed to God and Christ, through the greatest sacrilege—by changing the word "Lord" to "Lady."

21. Thirdly, they are guilty of that sin when they think of the bodies of saints and especially martyrs (that is, if they even were martyrs, as I would object, with Augustine [*On the Work of Monks*, chapter 28]) that some supernatural power is attached to them, or to their body-parts, or to whatever remains. By this power that acts like a physical cause and not merely, as they say, by moral effectiveness, they claim properly to cure diseases, drive out demons, and by touching them bestow blessings upon one's body and soul. They devotedly worship and adore the limbs, ashes, clothing, etc., of these saints, and they dig them out of their graves to worship them, and preserve them in churches, and lock them up in gold and silver boxes, and carry them around in processions. And because they assign divine powers to them, they place their trust in them, and put them on display in sacred places to worship them; they offer them incense, and fall down before them in order to adore them; they consecrate holy days for worshiping them, swear oaths by touching them, and, to obtain greater reverence for them, they undertake promised pilgrimages. There is no reason for us to doubt that these people commit blatant and repeated idolatry, and in return for this horrible profanity God has already exacted punishment from them. For in their utter blindness, they have been deceived by these false and supposed relics, and it has often happened that "they adore on earth the bodies of those whose souls are being tormented in hell." Besides that, there is the dimwittedness wherein they have lovingly bestowed kisses upon the bones of even dumb animals, thinking that they were human (as happened in Geneva before the light dawned there); so too for a deer-limb mistaken for the arm of Anthony, and a wrinkled pumice-stone for the brain of Peter.

22. Fourthly, convicted of manifold idolatry are those who fashion and worship various images of God and of the saints. For they make so bold as to create images of the most holy Trinity, contrary to the explicit prohibition of God, who earnestly warns us not to make any likeness of him (Deut 4:15). Scripture even testifies that this cannot be done (Isa 40:18; Acts 17:29; Rom 1:23), and all the church-fathers who have written about this matter are in agreement on this, even including John Damascene, who is also known as 'the icon-worshiper' and nevertheless admitted that "it is an act of utmost folly and impiety to make an image of God." And so too those among the papal teachers who followed him: Abulensis, Peresius, Hesselius, and others, as Bellarmine himself acknowledges (*On Images*, book 2 chapter 8). It is true that he tried to disguise that sacrilege by adducing some passages of Scripture

which attribute human limbs to God or portray some appearances wherein God's accomplishments, judgments, or works are represented figuratively (which mankind cannot or should not express); yet finally he takes it to the point where he says that in the church of Rome "whether images of God or the Trinity ought to be made is not as certain as of Christ and the saints, because the latter pertains to faith, and the former is a matter of opinion." If the making of images is only a matter of opinion, then surely the worship of them even more so. But worship that occurs apart from faith cannot be pleasing to God; yet one that is contrary to faith is very displeasing to him— and such is the kind that we are handling here.

23. In worshiping images of men who are saints, which the Synod of Nicaea under [the empress] Irene determined "must be adored in a perfect way," the more recent papal teachers speak about it in different ways, as some make the facile declaration that images of the Trinity and of Christ should be worshiped with the same adoration with which the prototypes are worshiped, and that there are not two adorations but only one and the same, as Thomas taught (Part 3, Question 25, article 3). Others, in particular the more recent Jesuits, think up a variety of distinctions. Nevertheless, they all agree to the following: 1. That they consecrate images for religious worship—but "the consecration of images is idolatry," says Tertullian (*Book on Idol-Worship*, chapter 4). 2. That "the images are conceived jointly with the original model that is being adored; and that they are adored not only accidentally and improperly, but also in and of themselves and properly, so that the images themselves become the object of reverence, as they are considered in themselves." "And [the images are to be worshiped] with a worship which by analogy and reduction belongs to the type of worship that is owed to the original model." "And we should not say that they must be worshiped indirectly, because whatever is said only indirectly simply can be denied." All these words come from Bellarmine (*On Images*, chapter 21 and 25). Therefore, together with Baronius, he accuses the bishops of the French Church of error, who at the synod of Paris that was held during the reign of Louis the Pious decreed that images should not be adored, but should be stored in the churches only for decoration and as an illustration of history for the common people.

24. Well then, since this adoration or veneration of images (regardless of whatever disguise of distinctions one uses to cover it up) is considered religious by its worshipers—those who humbly prostrate themselves before

them, uncover their heads, bend their knees, bedeck them with wreaths, crowns, or precious garments; those who light candles for them, burn incense, and plant kisses or curses on them, and carry them about in procession in order to draw rain down from heaven, and who display other forms of divine worship before them—then we must not so much listen to what they say as observe what they do. For Bellarmine's objection to Cajetan is true of himself and his associates, that "they are forced to use the most subtle distinctions, which they themselves—not to mention the uneducated populace—hardly understand" (*On Images*, chapter 22). But those who do not understand the distinctions copy the deeds scrupulously, and so they are implicated in the same crime of idolatry, especially when they hear that an image is consecrated for "a holy expulsion of demons, a call to angels for assistance, and a defense of believers," which words are used in the consecration of an image of John the Evangelist (Pontif. p. 172, p. 2).

25. Here belong also the various forms of cross-worship by the papal teachers. For they determine that the cross which they think is the true one ought to be adored with the worship of *latria* for two reasons: Because it represents the crucified Christ, and because it came into contact with the limbs of Christ. But they also offer adoration to every other cross for what it represents. They place their hope and trust in the cross, and from the wood of the cross that has received blessing they expect "healthy remedies for the human race, strengthening of the faith, progress in doing good works, and the redemption of souls" (Pontif. Part 2, entitled, *On the Blessing of a New Cross*). And on Good Friday everyone, from the greatest to the least, offers adoration to the cross as it "is their only hope, increases righteousness in the pious, and grants forgiveness to the guilty." "They even offer pleasant fragrances to the cross," as Bellarmine admits (*On the Church Triumphant*, book 1, chapter 13). But, "Helena has found a pretext: She worshiped the King and not the wood; certainly so, because it is a pagan deception and a folly of the impious" (Ambrose, *Funeral Oration on the Death of Theodosius*).

26. In the fifth place, to those various forms of idol-mania of the Roman Church belongs also the power which they ascribe to things they have consecrated: water, salt, oil, palm-tree branches, candles, lambs and similar objects, which they claim "acquire certain spiritual, even divine powers by virtue of their consecration," if Bellarmine is to be trusted (*On the Blessedness of Saints*, Book 3, chapter 7, proposition 3). As a result, they place their trust in those consecrated things and hope that they will grant immunity from the

attacks of the devil, from diseases and other perils. When the 'lambs of God' are consecrated, the pope prays that "the spotless lambs may receive the same power as that of the innocent Lamb, sacrificed on the altar of the cross, power against all the trickeries of the devil and the deceits of the evil spirit, that no storm may prevail over those who piously bear these lambs, and that no adversity may overtake them, nor any noxious airs, or debilitating disease, etc.; that the offspring may be kept from harm" (*The Ceremonies of the Roman Church*, Book 1, chapter 7). The same examples can be produced from numerous other places in the books on rituals; from these it is very obvious that they attribute to creatures what properly belongs to God, and that they do so on the basis of human institutions and without any word from God. And so it should be of little surprise to us if they were to worship the pope himself with divine honours, since he is foremost in consecrating these things and in canonizing people as saints; and that he has degenerated into an accursed idol.

27. What we have said about images should not be taken to mean that we generally consider every use of images to be unlawful; in our view this applies in an absolute sense only to images of the Trinity. As far as creatures are concerned, apart from idolatrous worship that is contrary to the first table of the Law, and apart from indecency, shamefulness or other similar abuse contrary to the second commandment, we do not condemn the art of making images; and we don't deny that it brings about some good for the sake of the illustration of history in public life. But we do think that in the sacred places where God is worshiped images are not necessary, even if they do contain some historical or doctrinal use, or help to commemorate something. What is more, we think that they are dangerous, and for that reason unlawful, and that they should not be brought into Christian churches but removed and banished from them, even if they are not adored, and lest people "who seek Christ and his apostles not in the written books but on the painted walls meet up with error" (Augustine, *On the Harmony of the Gospels*, Book 1, chapter 9).

28. And we do not even reject outright all forms of worship or honorary decorations, although we cannot commend that notorious differentiation between *latreia* and *douleia* in the sense used by the papal party. For if one regards not only the meaning of these words but also the way they are used in Scripture, both words are applied to God and to men. The Septuagint calls all laborious work 'servile labour' (Lev 23:7, 8, 21). It is the opposite of religious service, since it concerns those tasks which ought not to be

performed on the Sabbath-day. And Paul (in Gal 4:8) claims the worship of veneration only for God, since he finds fault with the Galatians because they bestowed it upon those who by nature are not gods. One finds nothing about high veneration in Scripture, nor in any of the ancient writers. Therefore, we can render *latreia* and *dulia* to creatures. And to the Creator we must offer both *latreia* and *dulia*; that is, we ought to serve the Creator and the creature.

29. But in order for that service to happen by a different sort of worship (one which is not against the law of God), different parts must be distinguished of religious and civil worship, or of goodwill and fellowship. This distinction was very strongly commended by Augustine, who saw adequately that it is not enough to distinguish simply between *latreia* and *douleia*, because, as he himself says (*On Exodus*, question 94), "*douleia* is owed to God because He is Lord." And that this should not be owed to deceased saints, Augustine also teaches when he says (*On True Religion*, chapter 1) that these saints should be "honoured through our love, not our service." And Martin Perez d'Ayala, a papal writer, admits (*On Tradition*, part 3, *On the Worship of Saints*) that he does not know "whether this duty ought to have been called *douleia*, because the veneration that is commonly owed to saints is least of all an indication of servitude. For we all are servants of God, although unequal in our merits and holiness." Therefore, we should worship only God in a religious manner, but believers and saints "with love, not with servitude; with goodwill and fellowship." All these latter things we render to holy angels and men in a befitting manner, to those who do not keep our company in a familiar way— at least in a visible way (I am speaking about angels)—and who are not infinite. And we do so by piously keeping them in our memory, and by recognizing and declaring their surpassing worth. And lastly, we render civil service and honour to those people with whom we dwell in human fellowship, according to the degree and rank of each. In this way a clear distinction is made between what is owed to God and what is owed to men.

30. But when we ascribe to our Lord Jesus Christ, the eternal Son of God, all manner of religious worship in a measure equal to that of the Father and the Holy Spirit, we thereby proclaim that we acknowledge him as the God who is praised for ever and ever. And accordingly, we loathe the idolatry of the new Samosatenians who have made for themselves an idol of Christ, because after depriving him of his divinity and lowering his status to that of a creature they nevertheless bestow divine honours upon him. They form the front line of an accursed sect, although they are but common foot soldiers, who admit

to this necessary consequence drawn by [Gregory of] Nazianzus: "If He is to be adored, how can He not be worshiped? And if He is to be worshiped, how can He not be God?" Hence the church-fathers and the councils condemned Arius and Nestorius for their idolatry, because they gave adoration to Christ. The former considered him a created God, the latter a man separated from the person of the Word. In fact, the second Synod of Nicaea, and the seventh [ecumenical council] in the *Letter of the Synod to Constantine* [the sixth] *and Irene* strikes "Nestorius' idolatry of a man" with the curse of anathema, and declares that the Arians who worshiped God as created being were rightly called idolaters by Basil. "Whoever worships a creature, even though he does so in the name of Christ, is an idolater, for he imposes the name of Christ upon his idol" (see Athanasius, *Against the Arians*, Oration 1; Nyssen, *In Praise of Basil*; the same, *Funeral Oration for Placilla*, Nazianzus, *Oration* 40).

31. But all the Scriptures, and the nature of the matter itself, testify that the sin of idolatry is a very serious one, since it is spiritual adultery and sacrilege, whereby the love, reverence, and honour that is due to God alone is wrongly shifted to idols as his rivals (Hos 1:2–3), to whom God is unwilling to grant his own glory (Isa 42:8). It is a very grave offense of a wife to break the sacred trust of marriage; so too for a subject who transfers to another the honour that is owed to his king. Therefore, God deservedly added to the commandment about avoiding idolatry that He "is jealous, visiting the sins of the fathers upon the children to the third and fourth generation of those who hate" him, etc.

32. The burden of punishment rightly follows upon the gravity of this sin, both in this and the future life. In this life it is the darkening of the soul, the filthiness of the body, and other temporal punishments that are sent by God's permission. A long list of these punishments is provided in Deut 28:16 to the end. But what we must especially fear is that "outside will be all those who serve idols" (Rev 22:15); that is, they will be barred from the kingdom of heaven (1 Cor 6:9), and "their lot will be in the lake burning with fire and sulphur, which is the second death" (Rev 21:8). Therefore, "little children, keep yourselves from idols, Amen." (1 John 5:21).

Corollary

Since there is no harmony between the temple of God and idols, the orthodox rightly separated themselves from the Roman church, in obedience to the Father's command: "'Therefore come out from their midst and be separate,' says the Lord, 'and touch nothing unclean; and I shall receive you'" (2 Cor 6:16, 17).

CONCERNING THE OATH

President: Antonius Walaeus
Respondent: Petrus Laovicus

This disputation treats the lawful and the unlawful use of the oath (3). First it is argued why it is permissible for Christians to take an oath, as commanded in God's Word (4– 12). Then the nature and the conditions of lawful oaths are treated (13–51). A lawful oath is described as 'a religious act whereby we call on God to be witness of the things we say or promise, in order to render others confident in the truth and certainty of these things, whenever God's glory demands it from us, or the upbuilding of the church, the safety of the fatherland, or the love of our neighbour' (14). In this context, extensive attention is paid to the vow as a 'promissory kind of oath' (26–51). It should be noted that besides the treatment of vows here, Disputation 38 focuses solely and entirely on the topic of vows, which was of contemporary importance; the reader may wish to compare the treatments by Walaeus and Polyander. The disputation ends with ten theses (52–61) on questions concerning the practice of making oaths.

1. It is clear that *iuramentum*, 'oath' (which the Greeks call *horkos*, from *herkos*, because it is the mainstay of the truth), derives from *ius*, 'law,' because that which is sworn should be just as valid as a law. This is even more clear from the word *ius-iurandum*, which has the same meaning as *iuramentum*. Yet there are some who think that the former differs from the latter on the grounds that *iusiurandum* is introduced in the context of a matter that is disputed, whereas *iuramentum* is used more generally, also in undisputed matters.

2. Well then, 'oath' as Cicero avers (*On Moral Duties*, book 3), means "a religious confirmation of truth"; wherefore in Latin it is also called a 'sacrament' because the assertion of the truth is rendered sacred and binding by the intervention of an oath.

3. It is our task now to treat the lawful and the unlawful use of the oath. So that this may be done in an orderly and profitable manner, we shall first demonstrate that the oath is permissible for Christians; then we shall see from Holy Scripture what an oath is and what its qualities are; and lastly we shall investigate some questions that arise concerning the use and abuse of the oath.

4. Among the ancient Jews it was the Essenes who were foremost in condemning every true and false oath equally, as Josephus reports (*On the Jewish War*, book 2 chapter 7). Their followers in former days were certain monks called the Humble Ones, and today it is the Anabaptists. The truth is that many papal teachers also reckon refraining from oaths among their counsels and they place a greater perfection in refraining.

5. As for us, just as we affirm that very many oaths are clearly made in a way that is not permissible, so also do we affirm over against all of them that the oath itself is a permissible thing, and accordingly it is not only lawful for us but even commanded in God's Word, in the New Testament no less than the Old.

6. The first clear demonstration is drawn from the fact that the oath belongs to the law of nature, as is evident from the use that all peoples make of it, whence also Aristotle (in the *Rhetorica ad Alexandrum* Chapter 18) defines it as "an affirmation without proof accompanied by an invocation of the gods," and Cicero as "a religious confirmation to which God is summoned as witness." For although they went wrong in calling on false deities as their witnesses, they all agreed that in serious matters, and in claims of great consequence, what they worshiped as God should be called upon as witness.

7. This argument is much more solidly grounded by the fact that it rests upon the moral, divine, and eternal law. For while God forbids that his name be used in vain, he does, on the other hand, allow his name to be used—with the appropriate awe and respect—in oaths. Moses and the prophets drive this point home quite frequently, as in Deut 6:13 and 10:20: "You shall fear the Lord your God, him you shall serve and you shall cling to him, and you shall swear by his name, for he is your praise," etc. And Ps 63:12: "The king himself shall rejoice in the Lord, whoever swears by him shall glory, because the mouth of those who speak lies shall be stopped," and in very many other places.

8. It should be generally acknowledged by all Christians that the use of the natural and moral law pertains to Christians living in the New Testament state, for Christ in Matt 5, in order to uphold also this commandment of the law in the face of the Pharisees' false interpretations, bears witness that "he has not come to abolish the law but to fulfill it" (5:17). In fact, "he who relaxes even one of the least of these commandments and teaches other men so, will become least in the kingdom of heaven" (5:19).

9. The second clear demonstration is taken from the predictions of the prophets, which foretell that by a unique act of God's kindness it would happen among those people who have turned to Christ under the New Testament that oaths will be made only in the name of the true God. A prophecy of this sort is Isa 45:22: "Turn to me and be saved, all the ends of the earth, etc.; I have sworn by myself, the word has gone forth from my mouth, which will not be recalled, that every knee shall bow to me, and every tongue shall swear." And Isa 65:16, dealing with the time of the New Testament: "He who blesses himself in the land shall bless himself by the God of truth, and he who takes an oath on the land shall swear by the God of truth." A prophecy of this sort occurs also in Jer 5:2 and 12:16. Well then, would anyone be so bold as to claim that the very thing which God promises He will provide as a special benefit to them is forbidden to believers in the New Testament?

10. In the third place, the same thing is demonstrated irrefutably by the instances that occur in the Old Testament as well as in the New. God himself has furnished or approved instances in the Old Testament, and these are obvious everywhere and beyond debate. The examples on record in the New Testament are no less evident and clear. In Rom 14:11 the apostle draws attention to the fact that we shall all appear before the judgement-seat of Christ, because it is written: "As I live, says the Lord, every knee shall bow before me," and in the Letter to the Hebrews chapter 7:20[-21] the apostle comes to the conclusion that the priesthood of Christ is more excellent than the Levitical one because "by the insertion of an oath by God, he was made priest of the New Testament" [Ps 110:4]. Although these words are quoted from the Old Testament, nevertheless, since the force and effect of them would be made fully manifest only in the New Testament, that oath looks entirely to the time of the New Testament. Moreover, since it is through the taking of an oath that God the Father appointed Christ as priest of the New Testament, and since Christ himself in the New Testament clearly stated by

an oath that all would be subjected to him, it evidently follows that both God the Father and Christ by their own example affirm the use of the oath.

11. Other examples in the New Testament confirm the same point. For, leaving aside for now that solemn assertion by Christ, "truly, truly," the apostle Paul in Rom 9:1 expresses the oath in its full form, when he says: "I am speaking the truth in Christ, I am not lying, my conscience bears me witness in the Holy Spirit," and, in 2 Cor 1:23: "I call upon God as witness to my spirit." In a similar fashion also in Rom 1:9 and Phil 1:8: "God is my witness, whom I serve." So too, finally, the Angel "swears by him who lives for ever and ever" (Rev 10:6).

12. And lastly, the same point is brought out by the nature and intended goal of the legitimate oath. For since a true oath is a certain calling upon God's name whereby those who swear acknowledge God as the one who knows the hearts and upholds the truth (as the instances and passages presented above show), and since the goal of a lawful oath is praised by the apostle in Heb 6:16 because "in every dispute an oath is final for confirmation" for people, it must be concluded that the use of it by human beings is commendable and approved by God.

13. Now that the first element of our disputation has been shown, we must next conduct a careful investigation into the nature and conditions of lawful oaths, in order to be able, by God's Word, to distinguish between ones that are permissible and ones that are not permissible.

14. We affirm, therefore, that a lawful oath is a religious act whereby we call on God to be witness of the things we say or promise, in order to render others confident in the truth and certainty of these things, whenever God's glory demands it from us, or the upbuilding of the church, the safety of the fatherland, or the love of our neighbor.

15. The invocation of God's name reveals that it is a religious act; therefore, people of all times have been accustomed to follow some religious rituals in taking solemn oaths. However, in observing them one must be careful to guard against superstition and idolatry.

16. This invocation takes one of two possible forms: Either God is called upon simply as witness to the truth, as was observed earlier from Rom 1:9 and Phil 1:8, or a curse is added to that simple invocation, whereby we call down on our heads the punishment by God if we lie, or his support and

blessing if we swear the truth. Various formulae of this kind of oath occur in the Scriptures: see Ruth 1:17, 1 Kgs 1:29 and 2:23, 24. Similarly, 2 Cor 1:23, etc.

17. In either of these forms of swearing (whether the simple one or the one accompanied by a curse) we affirm that one should call upon the name of God only, since He is the only one who knows the heart and supremely upholds the hidden truth; and in all the passages dealing with the true oath, the sacred writings mention only the name of the true and living God.

18. From this it is clear that some statements of affirmation which even saintly people sometimes used (like Joseph in Gen 42:15, "as Pharaoh lives;" and like Hannah, Samuel's mother, in 1 Sam 1:26, "as your soul lives, my lord," etc.) are not strictly speaking oaths, because no invocation was attached to them. A statement of this sort only draws a comparison with things of which their wellbeing and worth were dear to their hearts, or the truth of which they all agreed upon.

19. Therefore it is impious of some sacrificers (and others too) to imitate the threats that heathens make, in order to reinforce the truth of their seeming piety or their claim in the presence of the people they have shocked. They call on Satan or hellish threats to witness against them, even though the holy writings present to us God as the only judge and upholder of hidden truth. In their oaths the papal teachers also impiously add the invocation of deceased saints to their calling on God's name, contrary to God's explicit command in Deut 6:13, and 10:20; likewise, Isa 45:22 and 65:16, which we cited in theses seven and nine.

20. Lawful oaths have as their subject the things we say or promise. For through the oath we assert the truth of things in the past and promise the certainty of future things, and from this arises the division of oaths into one of assertion and one of promise.

21. Both oaths ought to be by means of words understood according to the common usage of people, without deceit and trickery—contrary to the 'mental reservations' of the Jesuits and the Anabaptists' deceitful ambiguities. For if in all our speech our "'yes' should be 'yes' and our 'no' 'no,'" as Christ teaches in Matt 5:37 and the apostle Paul repeats in 2 Cor 1:18, how much more must we keep this command in the swearing of oaths.

22. When it comes to the specific things about which the truth is asserted by means of the oath, they surely must be well-understood, and transparent. For it is rash to call God as the witness and upholder of a truth about which we are unsure as if it is certain. The true usage of oath-swearing shows this too, for "it is final in every dispute," as we have heard from the apostle in Heb 6:16.

23. As far as the promise of future things is concerned we must swear in accordance with the precept God gives in Jer 4:2: in truth, in uprightness, and in justice.

24. In truth: Because the promise must be made not only with our tongue and our words, but also from the heart and with genuine intent—quite unlike that unreliable type of people who swear with their tongue only but not in their heart. In uprightness: Because we should promise nothing lightly and too hastily, or promise what is not in any way under our control; for otherwise the Lord's name is used in vain. Lastly, in justice: Because nothing should be promised in an oath unless it is honest and just. For it is bad to swear things that are not permissible, and even worse to keep them.

25. From these things it is clear that oaths which proceed from a hot temper or a similar emotion are not lawful. Of such a sort was David's oath when in anger he swore total destruction on the household of Nabal (1 Sam 25:22). Nor should one swear about matters that are uncertain, such as Herod did when he swore to give to his dancing daughter whatever she asked (Matt 14:7). Nor about wicked things, such as those Jews did who swore that they would not eat food unless Paul was killed (Acts 23:13).

26. The conditions that are requisite in every lawful oath pertain to the right use of the vows that belong to this promissory kind of oath.

27. From this it is clear that we must condemn all vows that are made to creatures, or that are spoken rashly or about things that are forbidden or not within our control. Among these we place those vows that the papal teachers make to saints; so too the three that are common to the state of being a monk, namely the vows of voluntary poverty, celibacy, and the obedience which befits regular clergy (as they call it).

28. Lawful vows, however, are those that properly concern matters that look to the worship of God, whether of themselves and directly, or by accident and indirectly.

29. The ones which of themselves look directly to the worship of God are either universal or particular.

30. Again, the universal ones are either ordinary and continuous in the church of God, or they are extraordinary and renewed only in certain cases.

31. Ordinary vows are ones through which individual believers obligate themselves or their parents to keep the whole worship that God has ordained. In the New Testament this obligation begins at Baptism and is renewed and confirmed at Holy Supper. For this reason, the early church called the signs of that obligation 'sacraments.'

32. I give the name 'extraordinary vows' to those which the entire church (or the better part of it) sometimes renews in certain cases or situations over against others who have defected from the true worship of God, or out of a fear of imminent decay, such as the public vows pledged in the midst of God's people by Joshua (Josh 24:25), Josia (2 Kgs 23:3), Ezra (Ezra 10:5), and some others.

33. I give the name 'particular vows' to those which are made by individual members of the church, and which happen either in matters that are urgent or sacred in themselves, or in matters that are intermediate and indifferent in themselves.

34. In sacred and noble matters the pious sometimes subject themselves to the obligation of a new vow in order to give themselves an incentive to keep some precept of God, or to find stronger remedies against some vices that are harassing them greatly. They do so not because through this kind of vow they might make their obedience more pleasing to God, and, as some papal teachers would have it, more meritorious, or to obtain a greater degree of perfection. Rather, deeply aware of their own weakness, by these additional supports they seek to strengthen themselves against the onslaught of Satan and their own flesh.

35. In this way Job testifies that "he made a covenant with his eyes not to look lustfully at a girl" (Job 31:1); and Nehemiah and the leaders of the people bound themselves with an oath that from that time onward they "would not give their daughters into marriage to the neighboring peoples" and that "on the Sabbath-day they would not purchase goods that they have brought to sell" [Neh 10:30–31].

36. A special difficulty exists, however, in those vows that are uttered about intermediate matters, or matters of indifference.

37. And these matters are of two kinds, for either the Word of God commands that the matters themselves are subject to vows insofar as the nature of the work is concerned (while only their circumstances are unrestricted and voluntary), or the matters as well as their circumstances are left to be used according to human freedom.

38. Examples of the first kind are: vows of fasting and self-affliction (Num 30:13), vows of giving alms to the poor, or of other expenses that must be assumed when the Church has need of them (Gen 18:20[–22]), vows of dedicating oneself or one's loved ones to the service of the Church; such was Hannah's vow, in 1 Sam 1:11.

39. Examples of the second kind are found in vows of the Old Testament that are obviously voluntary, like the vows of the Rechabites to abstain from wine, grapes, etc.; and like the vows of not sowing fields and vineyards, of not building houses, and of dwelling in tents, etc. These were mentioned in Jer 35[:1–11], and God commends adherence to them—although some people explain these as being about obedience of a political nature.

40. We deem that it is allowed to place restrictions on one's freedom by means of the first kind of vow. This is so because those matters are for perpetual use in the Church and were not abolished with Christ's coming, and also because the patriarchs, too, had used vows of this sort before the Law was introduced, and hence it appears that all peoples also make use of them by the law of nature.

41. This can be shown convincingly also from the fact that, in a general way at least, the apostles established those vows in some form or other by their own example and instruction. Accordingly, the apostle often fasted (1 Cor 7:5; 2 Cor 11:27), and he gives instruction about our generosity towards fellow believers, according to the measure of God's blessings to us (1 Cor 16:2). And it is testified of Stephanas's family that they committed themselves to service [1 Cor 16:15]; that is, that they devoted themselves entirely to serving the saints. For although no mention is made here of vows, nevertheless since the firm resolve of their hearts is commended, it will be allowed to confirm this heart's resolve also with a vow, to spur us on in our slothfulness.

42. A more difficult question, however, is whether vows of the latter sort are permitted in the New Testament; that is to say, those vows whereby the use of things that of themselves are indifferent is continuously restricted to one party. Nor is there any agreement among the orthodox writers about these vows, as some of them assert that they are not permitted, and others that they are, provided that not any notion of worship accompanies them and that they serve a good goal.

43. And so, without slighting the opinion of others, it is our view that no one is permitted by means of a vow to forbid himself or others completely from using those things which Christ has willed to be unrestricted. For this is in conflict with the teaching of Paul in Gal 5:1: "Stand fast in that freedom in which Christ has set you free, and do not return to being tied up with a yoke of slavery." Likewise, in Col 2:20: "If you have died with Christ from the elements of the universe, why as though living in the world do you submit yourselves to regulations—do not eat, do not taste, do not touch, etc.?" In fact, to abstain from foods which God has created is condemned as the devils' own teaching (1 Tim 4[:1–3]). Well then, if we cannot foist that distinction upon others, then we cannot foist it upon ourselves either.

44. However, in a relative sense, and in some respects we deem that it is permitted to forbid oneself. That is to say, when it is done in a way and for a purpose which sacred Scripture itself prescribes for us: Namely, if their use were to become a stumbling-block for others, or if it were to end up as a license for the flesh for ourselves. For these are the two conditions that Scripture puts forward in Rom 14:20 and Gal 5:13.

45. And in this manner of making vows no prejudice is intended against Christian liberty, because sacred Scripture itself limits that freedom in this way. But daring to do this in a different way or for a different purpose is a superstition that Christians ought to shun.

46. Hence it follows also that when the fear of stumbling-blocks or of licenses of the flesh from the use of those intermediate things ceases, then the force of this vow also comes to an end. For then it does not have the purpose that was prescribed by God, and consequently it becomes a self-willed religion that is forbidden by the Word of God.

47. And so let these comments be sufficient about the objects of the oath in matters that are holy or that look to the worship of God. It still remains to

make some observations about the substance of the oath in political and non-religious affairs.

48. It is required therefore that those things which are to be confirmed or promised by means of an oath be not trivial or mundane. Things of this sort occur every day in the common course of human life, in which our speech should be "yes and no," as is the bidding of Jesus in Matt 5:37. Instead they should be serious and demanding matters, and matters in which there is a special concern for the wellbeing of the nation or love for the neighbor, as is shown by all the Scriptural examples and the purpose for oaths stated in Heb 6.

49. Well then, these matters are either public or private in nature. The public ones are: treaties among rulers or nations, such as between Abraham and Abimelech (Gen 21:31), between Isaac and Abimelech (Gen 26:28), and between Nebuchadnezzar and Zedekiah (2 Chron 36:13), etc. In this category we also place oaths of fidelity between rulers and their subjects, as well as military oaths; an example of each occurs in 2 Kgs 11:4. In this place we also put oaths of a judicial sort (Exod 22:11 and elsewhere), likewise vows of marriage (Mal 2:14).

50. We give the name 'private' to those vows that are made between individuals privately. The spies of the land of Canaan offered such a vow to Rahab the harlot, to save her and her family from slaughter (Josh 2:12). Jacob and Laban promised each other that they would cause no injury or harm to each other (Gen 31:53). David and Jonathan made a vow of friendship and mutual care (1 Sam 20:12).

51. Moreover, here we see that there is a difference: The taking of oaths between persons who are of equal status and not yet subject to each other should occur only when it is by mutual consent. However, between persons of which one is subject to another, the oath may even be demanded and required, as the examples that were adduced above prove.

52. Having briefly explained these matters to this extent, we shall now add a few questions which are brought to bear in the practice of making oaths and which are debated by theologians; the solutions to other questions (which we are not bringing to mind here) are generally derived from these.

53. And in the first place the question is asked whether the making of oaths can be entrusted to those who swear by false gods or by creatures, since we seem to be providing opportunities to sin by offering an oath of this kind.

54. Our answer to this is that when it cannot be avoided by another means, the taking of such oaths can be permitted between people who are not subject to one another. This is illustrated by the example of Jacob, who swore by the true God, and Laban, who swore by the gods of Nahor (Gen 31:53). For it is not so that hereby the fault accompanying the oath is being confirmed, although the truth of the vow and its dependability is being confirmed.

55. Secondly, the question is posed whether oaths made in the name of false gods or creatures must be kept by those people who, when they are better informed at a later point in time, realize that an error was inserted in the oath. We respond that in our judgment such an oath should be kept in its entirety, if the things promised by swearing are good and just, on analogy of Matt 23:16f.

56. In the third place the question is asked whether all the oaths that are devised or uttered about future events must be kept. My answer is that all those oaths and vows must be kept which have the conditions we introduced earlier, even though they may be harmful or detrimental to us, just as David testifies (Ps 15:4), as well as the example found in Josh 9 about the Gibeonites, and Judg 21:1 about the Benjamites, etc.

57. However, if in making oaths promises are made which conflict with the word of God, then that well-known saying applies: 'In a shameful vow alter your decision; in evil promises break your trust.' This is what the example of David (1 Sam 25:33) and the reprimand by Christ (Mark 7:11) demonstrate. For no oath, however sacred and forceful it may be, has the power to free a man from the obedience that is owed to God, nor can any oath bind us to sin.

58. Fourthly it is asked whether one must keep the promise of trust that has been given to a robber or pirate. I answer that one must keep the trust promised to a robber or pirate in those vows which bring in their wake damage only for the individual person, in keeping with David's statement in Ps 15. However, if anything is promised by oath that is contrary to the common good or an upright citizen's duties, then it cannot be kept, because it is in conflict with the law of God.

59. In the fifth place the question is asked whether the trust that is sworn to heretics must be kept. The followers of Rome state that it should not be kept, on the grounds that God's law bids heretics be punished. But I reply that God does not order the punishment of all heretics, and if he does demand their punishment, he does not demand punishment of those who were granted the public promise to the contrary. It is in this way that those who maligned a ruler were punished by God's law; nevertheless David did not want Shimei to be punished for this crime with a just penalty, since that would violate the promise given to him.

60. It is asked in the sixth place whether we should break the trust that is placed in someone who breaks his trust. My answer: It is obvious that in mutual or conditional oaths, when one party breaks the condition, the other party is no longer bound. But if someone has made an unconditional oath to another, and if the other does not make good on his trust, then that is not a reason for the other party to act in faithlessness.

61. And finally the question is posed whether one can be released by someone else from a given oath. I respond that God has given a law concerning minors or those under the control of others in Num 30; however, Holy Scripture does not know of other ways to resolve or discharge legitimate oaths.

ON THE SABBATH
AND THE LORD'S DAY

President: Antonius Thysius
Respondent: Samuel Dambrinus

After discussing the origin, meaning, and use of the Hebrew word 'Sabbath' (1–7), Thysius provides a definition (8–9) and examines the beginnings, divine institution, and cause (10–16) of the seventh day from creation as a solemn and regular feast day that is characterized by rest and divine worship. Subsequently, some goals of the Sabbath are treated, such as the world-wide remembrance that God completed creation and took his rest from it, and to acknowledge and confess God as creator. A civic goal is to reinvigorate and refresh the body after its labours. The commemoration of the deliverance from Egypt, and the sanctification of Israel is a goal special to the Jews. In this, the Sabbath is a symbol of Christ and his benefits: it points to the eternal and spiritual Sabbath day and the heavenly perfection that is to come (17–21). What follows next is a fulsome explanation of the fourth commandment: its observance (23–40), duration (41–49), and the extent to which it relates to the 'Lord's Day' (or Sunday) in the second dispensation (50–58). Thysius thereupon rejects Sabbatarianism (that is, Sabbath-keeping by Christians, 59–60), and ends with a statement about the value of keeping certain feast days, 'to the remembrance of Christ and his special deeds for our redemption' (61).

1. Now that in explaining the first table of the Decalogue we have treated Idolatry and the Oath, it follows that we similarly hold a disputation on the Sabbath and the Lord's Day.

2. In the first place, as far as the verb *Shabbat* is concerned, it has the same force of meaning as 'to cease,' 'to be at rest,' 'to stop.' Whence *Shabbat* (in contracted form), like *Shabbatat* (as Kimchi would have it), and *Shabbaton*, means any form of 'cessation,' that is, from work; and it means 'rest,' namely

rest from movement and work. With reference to God it means in particular God's being at rest, namely from the work of creation on the seventh day. Similarly with reference to man, it means the repeated weekly stoppage on the same day, a day which has been blessed and hallowed for this very purpose. From there both the stoppage itself and the particular day go by the name, 'Sabbath.' And so, this day is called 'the Sabbath day' or 'the day of rest,' and *Shabbat, Shabbaton*, the *Sabbath of rest* (Exod 31:14[15]), and simply *Sabbath*. In fact, 'the seventh day' and 'Sabbath' are taken to mean the same thing.

3. Moreover, the words 'Sabbath' and 'Sabbaths' are given to the entire week (2 Kgs 11:7, Luke 18:12); this means that the other days of the week are counted from the Sabbath. Individual days, too, receive their name from the Sabbath: the first, the second day of the Sabbath etc., which means [the first, the second day] after the Sabbath. By some Gentile people these days are indicated by the names of planets and idols, such as Saturn, Sun, Moon, etc. But the early church, perhaps to distinguish itself from both the Gentiles and the Jews, gave the name 'holidays' to the individual days of the week— although Scaliger in book 1 of his *On the Correction of Chronologies* is of the view that the early church did this as a special token of the first week of the Passover (of which every day was a holiday in antiquity, according to Jerome).

4. Moreover, besides the common one of '[the Sabbath] of weeks' or '[the Sabbath] of days' (which is properly what 'Sabbath' is), 'Sabbath' includes in its range of meanings also '[the Sabbath] of years.' That is to say, it means also the Sabbath of the recurring seventh year, which is called 'the Sabbath of the land' (Exod 23:11), because in that year the land was left to rest uncultivated; and whatever did grow upon it was left for the poor. From this the word is also transferred to the devastation of the land (Jer 25:11). It is used also of the completion of seven times seven years, that is, the fiftieth year, which is called the year of Jubilee, the year of freedom and of release because of the restoration of freedom and property (Lev 25:8, 10) They too stem from the same principle, namely the divine rest, and are included in it through synecdoche. As for the Talmud's 'Sabbath of the seven millennia,' which they call the 'Sabbath of the universe,' we do not trouble ourselves with that here.

5. Additionally, all sacred days and holidays, even when they do not occur on the seventh day, are called Sabbath in a general sense and are included by it

through synecdoche (Ezek 20, 22, and 23). These include the monthly (as in the 'Neomenia' or 'the New Moon') (Num 28:11) as well as the yearly feasts, namely the three most solemn feast days. One of these is Passover, which was held in the first month of the year and by seven days of unleavened bread (whence it is called the Feast of Unleavened Bread) to commemorate the passing-over by the Angel and the deliverance from Egypt, and also to testify to their thankfulness for the new harvest. Another is Pentecost, which falls after the completion of seven weeks from Passover (whence it is called also the Feast of Weeks) and which was held to celebrate the giving of the Law, and of the harvest of the first fruits (from which it also gets its name). And lastly there is the Feast of Booths (to which also the feast of trumpets and the feast of atonement are connected), which happened in the seventh month after Passover and lasted for eight days. It was celebrated as a testimony to their dwelling in tents in the wilderness, and for receiving the left-over harvest (whence it is also called the Feast of Ingathering). Of these both the first and the last days were, and were called, Sabbath-days (Exod 23:14[15], Lev 23, Deut 16).

6. Moreover, if these solemn feast days should fall on the Sabbath, they were called the "great Sabbath-day" (John 19:31) because of the double celebration. But Scaliger simply applies the term to the feast day itself, because the translators of the Septuagint render *mo'ed*, or *hag* (that is, the appointed or solemn feast day) as great day (Isa 2). But if there was more than one sabbath day, such as the last of the Passover or of the Feast of Booths, namely the seventh day of the Feast of Unleavened bread, or the eighth day of the Feast of Booths, then it was called the second-first Sabbath (Luke 6:1), as though the first was repeated on the second, that is, the second equal to and the same as the first. But Scaliger thinks that it is after the second day of Passover, from which point in time one started counting the days to Pentecost (in *On the Correction of Chronology*, the Prolegomena I, and 1.6).

7. In fact, 'Sabbath' throughout entails and assumes the entire outward religious worship, or the public practice of it; that is, the holy things, holy places, holy times, and holy people that have been consecrated and dedicated to God, along with worship of him, by divine decree.

8. But what we are discussing here is the commandment peculiar to the weekly Sabbath, since it is older and more special than the other Sabbaths

and is the basis for them. For this reason, it receives its own commandment here, and that is what will be considered by us in what follows.

9. Well then, the Sabbath is a solemn, regular—namely, weekly—feast day established by God, or the seventh day from creation, which, in imitation of God who on that day ceased his work of creation, the Jews were commanded by God to observe similarly by ceasing and resting externally from their servile and everyday work in order to be occupied with the sacred activities of divine worship.

10. Moreover, this precept for the Sabbath does not arise from a natural necessity, unlike the other commandments which are implanted in the heart and are known through themselves; it exists by design, by the willful institution of God, or the positive law, as it is called. It is natural that certain set times must be assigned for worshipping God, and that whatever comes from a commandment of God must be kept unchanged. However, it is by decree and not by nature that this day in particular was established for this purpose of worshiping God: in order to remember the creation, and for the fact that God ceased from his work at that time; and for observing and celebrating it in precisely the same way—that is, by resting and not working. For it could have been possible for this [resting and not working] to be assigned for commemoration not specifically on this day of the week, whereas the remembrance of creation could have been assigned to either the start or finish, that is, on the first or last day of the week.

11. Hence one sees also that this commandment is presented not negatively (as are the three that come before it) but positively and in a special way, with this formula: "Remember to keep the Sabbath-day holy." And the reason for it follows: "Because God rested from his work on the seventh day;" this is different from what we see happening in the other commandments, which are implanted in the heart and are known through themselves.

12. This day also was not founded by humans or from self-willed service, nor undertaken as an unprompted worship, but it was commanded and ordered by God's Law. Thus, it derives all its necessity from the authority of God.

13. But it is not entirely clear when that day was established, or to whom it was commanded; that is, whether it was presented to mankind as a whole already from the very beginning, even before the fall into sin (i.e., when the world was created), or whether in fact it was ordained later for the Jewish

people, at the time when the Law was given through Moses. It states in Gen 2:2,3 that after he had completed his work on the sixth day of creation, God rested from his works on the seventh day and blessed it, and hallowed it. That is to say, he considered the day not just worthy of honour, but he set it apart from the group of other days and determined that for mankind it be devoted to worship. However it is not altogether certain from this whether the use of that day was designed from the very beginning, or whether it was rather an idea awaiting realization.

14. At any rate, before the Law of Moses no mention is made of the Sabbath-day anywhere, nor is any of the saints referred to as being a keeper of it, as Tertullian observes in his book *Against the Jews*; except that before the Decalogue was provided the name, reason, and use of the Sabbath were manifested (Exod 16:5, etc.). Perhaps this is so because the Sabbath was established at that time; or else it is so because Moses revived and augmented many features of its outward worship rather than establishing it for the first time then—like the offering of sacrifices before the flood (Gen 4[:3–5]), the distinction between clean and unclean animals after the flood (Gen 7[:2]), the prohibition against eating flesh with its blood (Gen 9[:4]), circumcision (Gen 17; John 7:22), and also other things. It is likely that this also applies in the present case.

15. But Ezek 20:12 states specifically that God gave the Sabbath to the Israelites, and Neh 9:14 that he made it known to them, evidently as something of which there was no prior knowledge or use, nor as something that he had recalled and restored to its former use after it had been interrupted and disappeared. But as far as its institution is concerned, it makes little difference what the circumstances of the time or the people were—although the former interpretation seems more likely.

16. At the same time, a cause for the institution of the Sabbath that is reasonable and in harmony with divine wisdom is indicated by the authority of him who commands it and by conforming to the precedent for it, namely God, thus binding us to obedience in two ways. For it was fitting that just as he himself ceased his first work (that is, creation) on the seventh day and rested, so also mankind should rest from his works on that same day, whenever it recurs, in order to celebrate the remembrance of creation and God's resting from it. He chose not the first day, on which creation started; nor did he choose the last, sixth day, on which it was completed. But he chose

the seventh day when he surveyed his labours and ceased from them, so that the seventh day is counted among those included in the days of creation. Some of the heathens similarly honoured the seventh day, either from age-old practice or from imitating the Jews. Or, as reported by Hesiod (*Works and Days*), Linus, and Josephus (*Against Apion* 2), Clement of Alexandria (*Stromata* 5), Eusebius (*Preparation for the Gospel*), and Lampridius in *The Life of Alexander Severus*, they honoured the seventh day for another reason, perhaps such as the rotation of the seven planets. Some, however, consider the ninth day sacred, and others the tenth.

17. And as for the goals of the Sabbath-day, these are many, and can be divided into two groups, of which one is world-wide in scope and the other specific. The world-wide goal concerns the whole human race together, and it is the primary one, namely that this day was appointed by God for the Jews to remember that God completed his handiwork and took his rest from it, or to acknowledge and confess God as creator (Gen 2:2; Exod 20:10)—wherein the exercise of faith consists, according to Heb 11:3. And mankind ceases from his own works so that he can be freed so much the better for the works of God.

18. A civic goal is indicated also: to reinvigorate and refresh the body after its labours. This includes those whose bodies are owned by another, slave and handmaid, even the beasts of burden. Exod 23:12 states: "And the son of your handmaid shall have respite;" Deuteronomy 5:14: "So that your slave and your handmaid may rest as well as you. You shall remember that you were a servant in the land of Egypt." In other words, in order that they not be worn out and destroyed by constant hard work, but rather by relaxing from it, they lift their drooping limbs and regain their strength. For God is not only the one who has made his creatures, he also preserves them (Ps 36:7). And this secondary world-wide goal, too, although it is different from the first, is subordinate and responds to it, as an act of love, so that in its own way this recovery also looks to the worship of God.

19. The special goal of the Sabbath is one that pertains to the Jews in particular, that is, through an additional application or as an adjunct goal that happens outwardly, and it is two-fold. The first is to commemorate the deliverance from Egypt; Deut 5:15 [states]: "You shall remember that you were a servant in the land of Egypt, and that your God led you out from there with a mighty hand and an outstretched arm. Therefore, the Lord your God

commanded you to keep the Sabbath day." And so, the Sabbath is a symbol of the rest in the land of Canaan into which Joshua led them (Heb 4:8).

20. The second specific goal is a loftier one, namely a spiritual one that looks to the eternal well-being of man: the sanctification of the people of Israel. This goal is ceremonial and sacramental, and typical, too. For by this sign of physical rest and relaxation God wanted to testify to them that he is their God and the one who sanctifies them. He did so by separating them outwardly from the other nations and inwardly from all their sins. Exod 31:13, 17: "You shall keep my Sabbaths, because it is a sign between me and you throughout your generations, that you may know that I the Lord sanctify you. And you shall keep the Sabbath, because it is holy for you." And in verse 16 it is called also "a perpetual covenant." There are similar words in Ezek 20:12, 20: "That you may know that I am the Lord your God;" and so keeping the Sabbath was to them the public profession of their entire religion. The Sabbath is even a symbol of Christ and his benefits, in such a way that it points to the eternal and spiritual Sabbath-day and the heavenly perfection that is to come, because the believers rest from their own evil works, allow God on this earth to perform his work in them—work that will be accomplished fully in the next life (Isa 66:[22–]23; Heb 4:3,9).

21. A consideration of these goals makes it plain how important and significant this Sabbath is: The fact that it is hallowed and sacred not just in practice (insofar as it makes for an outward exercise), but also by virtue of being a sacrament whereby it held out and conveyed to believers the additional promise and effect of sanctification. Hence, we also observe in sacred Scripture that the Sabbath comprises the whole worship of God. Therefore, this law is repeated in the Scriptures time and again, it is driven home with great care, it is impressed on us with serious urgency, and for obeying it praise is given frequently, while neglecting or breaking it is punished severely (Isa 56:2 etc).

22. So much for the institution of the seventh day (or the Sabbath) and what its efficient cause and goals are. What comes next is the keeping of the seventh day, which exists in hallowing the Sabbath itself, Deut 5[:12]: "Observe the Sabbath-day, to keep it holy." For the divine sanctification whereby God, by his own doing, deemed it holy when he rested from his work and wanted it to be held holy (that is, by separating it from the other days and setting it apart), and blessed it, corresponds to the sanctification of

it by man, which is called the "keeping and making of the Sabbath-day" (Deut 5:15), "Sabbath-keeping" or "Sabbath-observance" (Lev 25:2) and "honouring the Sabbath-day" (Isa 58:13).

23. The wording for this commandment is unique. For one is not given a simple command, "Hallow the Sabbath" (as in the others), but the following warning precedes it: "Remember the Sabbath-day, that you keep it holy." This shows that the matter is of a sort that can fade easily into oblivion (because it is not engraved into our nature); therefore, we must cultivate it constantly in our memories, and we should not make light of it but guard it very carefully. Moreover, the Sabbath is hallowed so long as on that day we do things similar to those God did on that day and which he commands men to do. On the other hand, the Sabbath-day is lost, polluted, and desecrated when our eyes are distracted from the Sabbath (Ezek 22:26) and we do things on that day which we are forbidden, and we omit what we ought to do (Matt 12:2[, 11, 12]).

24. The Parasceve or getting ready for the Sabbath refers to the trappings required for the Sabbath as well as the actual day that precedes the Sabbath. It is also called the "day-before-the-Sabbath" (Mark 15:42), when on the sixth day of the week one performs and sets in order those things that are not permitted to be done on the Sabbath, and everything necessary for its observance and worship is arranged (1 Chr 9:32, Luke 23:54). In fact, just as the Jews consider a small portion of the preceding day as the Sabbath, so too do they add a small part of the following day to the conclusion of the Sabbath: for the sake of keeping the Sabbath day in its entirety and as religiously as possible. But this practice arose from Jewish superstition.

25. Keeping the Sabbath begins and ends with the setting of the sun. For as at the first creation of the universe the appearance of the created world was covered in darkness, whereupon light was then brought to it, and just as day was established by the length of darkness and light, so in this case too does this matter come by the establishment of God (Lev 23:32).

26. In general Sabbath-keeping rests in the fact that on that day one does not perform any work, servile work, that is, laborious work (Lev 23:8). He says: "Six days you shall labour and do all your work, but the seventh day is the Sabbath of your God; then you shall not do any work, neither you, your wife, son, daughter, nor your man-servant and handmaid, nor the lodger or foreigner who is within your gates." This means that work is prohibited for

your entire household, which includes also all your domestic animals—like the ox and donkey—that are mostly beasts of burden (not because the hallowing of the day applies to animals, but lest they become a hindrance to man's rest by being put to work) and even the strangers and foreigners in your towns, lest by their example they cause a disruption to the public rest (Exod 20, Deut 5). And so by prohibiting work in this manner we are instructed to keep the outward rest as a religious duty; and in this way even such rest is considered as part of the divine worship.

27. And so what is forbidden is any work or business that we undertake: work that is servile, that involves machinery, that is laborious, brings in a profit, work that is daily and ordinary. Both private and public work are included, that is, what we are used to perform either on our own or in public (Isa 58:3[, 13]). Since these have been prohibited for other solemn feast-days (Lev 23:7, 8, 25, 32, 36; Num 28:25), so much the more are they prohibited for the Sabbath-day. Thus it was forbidden for the Israelites on the Sabbath-day to leave their homes to gather Manna (Exod 16:22), or wood (Num 15:32), or even to kindle a fire (Exod 35:3), to cook or bake (Exod 16:14[23–25]). And as a result, they were permitted to eat and drink only what had been laid up the day before, as Ignatius says (in his *Letter to the Magnesians*), and as the uninterrupted practice confirms. They were forbidden to plough and to sow (Exod 34:21), to tread the winepress (Neh 13:15), to bear or carry out burdens (Jer 17:21, 22), to import goods for sale (Neh 13[:15–16]), to sell or buy (Neh 10:31), to go out to battle (1 Macc 2:[34–35]36), to bury the dead (2 Macc 12:30[38, 39]), and similar activities.

28. To these prohibitions are added the ones listed in the New Testament, such as the ones with which the Jews upbraided Christ out of their own conviction that it was a desecration of the Sabbath: As when his disciplines were going through the grain fields on a Sabbath-day and they plucked heads of grain and rubbed them in their hands (Matt 12:2)—as if doing this was preparing a meal. Or when he himself healed and cured the sick (Matt 12:10); when he commanded the man who was healed to "take up your mat and walk" (John 5:8); when he made an ointment from his spittle and earth and anointed the eyes of the blind man; and when he commanded the blind man to "go and wash himself" (John 9[:7]). And there are other prohibitions: To make a journey and to walk distances that are beyond what is prescribed (it is from this that the saying comes, "a Sabbath-day's journey" (Acts 1:12), which was about two thousand feet, according to the calculation of the Jews);

to take to flight on the Sabbath (Matt 24[:20]); to leave the bodies of those who have died hanging on a cross (John 19:31); or to bury the dead and embalm them with spices (Luke 23:56).

29. Here we leave aside the Pharisees' many and superstitious detailed little observances whereby they have further curtailed God's commandment; even the Jews of today have very many of this sort. They include: roasting apples, husking garlic, killing flees, etc. They are mere human perversions of the observance God commanded.

30. Yet that general injunction about not performing any work did have its own interpretation, exceptions, and economy or dispensation. Therefore, excluded entirely from this listing of doing work are the deeds of God and his wonders, as well as the works ordered to display them, since these are of God (in fact, they are his work) although they are performed by men and give the outward impression of being somewhat laborious. Such as when the priests carried the ark and blew the trumpets on the seventh day when Jericho fell, and the people razed everything; and when, on the Sabbath, Christ healed the man with the withered hand (Matt 12:9[-13]); the woman suffering from the disease of infirmity that Satan had inflicted (Luke 13:11); the man afflicted with dropsy (Luke 14[:2–4]); the man smitten with a long-lasting disease and lying by the pool, whom Christ ordered to take up his mat and walk (John 5[:8]); the blind man whose eyes he opened with the ointment he had prepared, and whom he ordered to go and wash himself (John 9:14).

31. Therefore Christ responded to the Jews, when they seized upon these actions to slander him on the pretext of the Sabbath-day, by saying, "My father is working still, and I too am working" (John 5[:17])—thereby implying that his own work, proceeding as it is from God, should never be deemed a violation of the Sabbath, since it is accomplished by the Father's authority, force, and effective power. And then he added this: "Moreover I say to you: one greater than the temple is here; and the Son of Man is also Lord of the Sabbath (Matt 12:6, 8)." That is, he holds the Sabbath in his power to such a degree that he can rule over it as much as he pleases; hereby Christ separates himself from the common lot of men, because he says that he is greater than the temple and Lord of the Sabbath, and he distinguishes his own works from those of the common kind.

32. Moreover, exception is made for the works that pertain to life and to the worship of God and his glory. Such works are all the humble, menial tasks

which the priests carry out on the Sabbath-day apart from the worship, in the temple. About these priests Christ says that "they desecrate the Sabbath without penalty" (Matt 12:5). These include sacrifices and other duties, in particular circumcision, about which Christ says: "You circumcise a man on the Sabbath-day so that the law of Moses still is not broken" (John 7:22, 23). It is from this that Christ derives his defense of his divine works.

33. In fact exception is made for all activities that concern the immediate needs common to living creatures and their well-being; and in particular, first, the care of animals that are dumb, like freeing the ox and donkey from their stalls and leading them to water (Luke 13:11[15]), or pulling up a sheep, donkey, or ox that has fallen into a pit (Matt 12[:11]; Luke 13:15, 14:5). (Unlike former times, nowadays the Jews consider these actions illegal.) Thus, it was permitted to preserve animals from death—to do anything that promoted the necessary preservation of everyone of God's creatures.

34. And then there is the well-being of mankind; for "the Sabbath," as Christ says, "is made for man, not man for the Sabbath" (Mark 2:27). Hence man is not commanded outright to rest or cease from work if doing so harms his prosperity or health, like plucking heads of grain and eating them (Luke 6:1), conducting warfare, or defending against the enemy when they attack (1 Kgs 20:29; 1 Macc 2:40, 41), although they did then refrain from pursuing the enemy and sharing the spoils (2 Macc 8:27). Christ teaches and approves of this by means of a similar case of need, namely the example of David, because when he was hungry "he and his comrades ate of the bread of the presentation, which it was not lawful for him to eat, but only for the priests" (Lev 24[:9]; Matt 12:3,4).

35. Nor does this keeping of the Sabbath put a stop to performing duties that are needed or required out of charity and compassion; such as acts of kindness to someone on the Sabbath, healing and similar deeds that Christ performed and of which he asked the Jews: "Is it lawful on the Sabbath to do good or to do evil, to save a man or to destroy and slaughter him?" (Luke 6:9). And he concludes that it is lawful to do good on the Sabbath (Matt 12:12). For the law of the Sabbath, like the other ceremonies, yields to charity for the neighbor; and in keeping with that, Christ refers to that statement from Hosea: "I desire compassion and not sacrifice," obviously in the comparative sense of "rather than sacrifice."

36. And finally, activities aimed at modest bodily invigoration and relaxation are not prohibited, since they belong to the purposes of the Sabbath-day, provided they do not hinder the chief function and worship of the Sabbath. Thus, besides resting from our labours (Exod 23:12), there is going to a dinner (Luke 14:1,7), going for a walk (Luke 24:13), and similar activities. To be sure, when there was a feast-day of Sabbaths, the Jews were accustomed to make merry something that they eventually ended up abusing with wild dances and clapping, as attested by Ignatius (*Letter to the Magnesians*) and Augustine (*On the Gospel of John*).

37. In fact, on the actual day of the Sabbath what is commanded by the stoppage and freedom from all labour is not merely the physical rest in and of itself; but beyond it and on account of it, religious activity is commanded, that is to say, the religious business, the sacred exercises and duties. For this reason it is called "the Sabbath of the Lord" (Exod 20), or "unto the Lord" (Lev 23), and the "Sabbath of holiness" and "the holiness of the Lord" (Isa 28:12), because it is not only of the holy God, but is itself holy; it is dedicated publicly and privately for the things of the Lord, sacred things, and is to be spent to these things and directed to the sanctification of his name.

38. In the temple, activities of this sort included setting out the bread of presentation on each Sabbath-day (Lev 24:8), the Sabbath-day's double sacrifice, that is, of the two one-year old lambs, and of the two-tenths of fine flour mixed with oil, and the double outpouring of it (Num 28:9, 10; Ezek 26), the sacred assembly, that is the solemn gathering of the entire people in the temple or synagogue (Lev 23:13; Matt 12[:5]; Luke 4:16 and 13:10). The psalms special to the Sabbath-day were to be sung (such as Ps 92, etc.); there was the reading from the Word of God, that is from Moses and the Prophets (Neh 8; Acts 13:14), and the preaching of it (Mark 1:21; Acts 15:21), the exhortation to the people (Luke 4:16; Acts 13:14), the exposition of the ways of God (Acts 17:2), and other pious tasks that must be performed especially on the Sabbath.

39. But the hallowing of the Sabbath would not be complete by resting and keeping these outward practices alone, unless the Sabbath was spent for the purpose for which it was instituted, and unless these practices were undertaken with inner piety and reverence. Without that, God testifies, all the outward things, assemblies, sacrifices, incense-burning, even the Sabbath-day and the New Moons and festivals are abhorrent, hateful, tiresome, and a

source of grief for him. And for this he demands washing, cleansing, the removal of evil thoughts, and resting from doing evil, and doing good (Isa 1:11, etc.; Amos 5:21); that is, "if anyone does not do his own will, nor go his own way, nor speak his own words" (Isa 58:13). That was internal Sabbath-keeping, without which it would not of itself be a sacred event. Therefore, the entire day was to be observed, as much as human condition and weakness allowed, entirely from the heart and with due custom and devotion, to God.

40. For this hallowing of the Sabbath-day the Jews are promised blessings, private as well as public ones, and he is declared "blessed, who observes it" (Isa 56:2, and 58). On the other hand, God threatens a curse for desecrating and polluting it (Exod 31:14; Lev 26:14[15, 16]; Jer 17:26, 27; Neh 13:15, etc.), and he punishes it with the gravest penalties, and death (Num 15:32, etc.), since profaning the Sabbath-day was despising the whole law of God and divine worship.

41. Thus far about the institution and observance of the seventh day after creation, or the Sabbath, that is of the rest commanded by God according to the pattern he set. Next comes its duration, which, like its institution, depends upon God. God has certainly declared that he has confirmed this law for the Sabbath "throughout your generations as an everlasting treaty or covenant, and that it should be a sign forever" (Exod 31:16, 17). It is how this command should be interpreted that we shall consider next.

42. Well then, let us gather together what we have said in diverse places: The Sabbath in the restricted sense of considering what caused it, was established by God's ordinance, and rests on his voluntary will. So too, if you look to the matter and substance of it: God's stopping and resting from creation and the works of creation, and the unique celebration of God as creator. And, if you regard the circumstance of time, it was to be celebrated on the recurring seventh day after creation; to be precise, from the setting of the sun until it sets again. And as to the manner of it, by resting, and also by its exact observance (with the prohibition of starting a fire or cooking, etc.), so much so that even the rest itself is pious. Regarding the goal for it, the Sabbath has received and taken on a special goal, namely of the rest for the Israelite people coming out of Egypt, or the rest following that state of slavery and what it represents. Finally, regarding its genus, the Sabbath is everywhere linked to the other Jewish festivals and ceremonies which this commandment encompasses and which all belong to the positive law (for which reason a

warning and a cause are added to the commandment). For these reasons, the Sabbath belongs entirely to the category of things that are subject to change and abolition.

43. Yes indeed, the duration of the Sabbath itself is like that of the other ceremonies of the Old Testament, which were "types and examples of good gifts to come" (Heb 9:9 and 10:1), or of Christ or his benefits; and they were "shadows whose substance is Christ" (Col 2:17), and "guardians leading the way to Christ" (Gal 4:2). It should be taken to mean that it endures until the time 'pre-ordained,' 'for the right order' (Gal 4[:5–7]; Heb 9:10), and that it, along with the other rituals and shadows of the Old Testament, was abolished at the coming of Christ the Lord.

44. Accordingly, what is stated about its duration 'unto the age,' must be understood not in the strict sense of 'eternal,' but 'lasting a long time' and 'continuously' (in which way that word is frequently used in Scripture: Gen 17:7,8; Exod 21:6 and 29:9), until the time determined by God, namely the time of the Messiah, a time when (it is promised) there will be "New Moon following upon New Moon, and Sabbath following upon Sabbath" (Isa 66[:23])—which means the spiritual and everlasting Sabbath-keeping that remains for the people of God (according to Heb chapters 3 and 4).

45. Surely, when Christ says that he is a greater one than the temple and thus also "Lord of the Sabbath" (Mark 2:28), he means that the Sabbath is so within his power that not only is he able to have control over it but even to do away with it altogether. In fact, the apostle points out that it is abolished, in the general sense of names that are assigned to days, months, seasons, and years. Thus Rom 14:5: "One man considers a day as more important than another, and another man considers them alike;" and Gal 4:10: "You are observing the days, months, seasons, and years. I fear that I have laboured in vain among you;" and, most to the point and expressly, Col 2:16: "Let no-one," he says, "condemn you on account of food and drink, or regarding a religious festival, a New Moon or Sabbath-days, which are shadows of things to come, of which their substance is Christ." And so, in reality as well as in name, in its special meaning the Sabbath is annulled in the kingdom of Christ, to the extent that when the Law is recalled in the New Testament, no mention at all is made of the Sabbath in the sense of being a commandment for Christians.

46. However, it does not follow from the repealing of this Sabbath-day that the fourth commandment (which is a moral one, in a way) was entirely done away with. For there are two aspects to it, a general and special one. The general one is that, like the other moral commandments, it has been implanted in nature, namely

1. That although we must strive for piety the entire time of our lives, yet because our lives are subject to the busy activities of this current age, some time should be set aside from the daily labours and allocated specifically to the worship of God and the public administration of the Word, to the ceremonies and the sacred things that God has granted us, and to develop and foster a pious life.

2. That there be a specific day which God has either determined or allowed to the freedom of the church for an orderly and befitting time which the entire church is bound to observe.

3. That there be a suitable day, that is, after a recurring number of days have rolled around, when our fragile human nature (being proportionate to the recurrence) and the need for worshiping God require it. For this worship God has, from the time of creation, ordained the seventh day for the Jewish people (which is the number of completeness, and which corresponds almost to all of nature and was kept also by other peoples). The apostles, too, kept to this recurring seventh day analogously in ordaining the Day of the Lord.

4. That the cause for this day be reasonable, and that it should be dedicated publicly to the purpose of recalling both the general and the particular deeds and benefits of God.

5. That in its use and observance this day be sacred, and be deemed sacred.

6. And that also the entire soul be diverted from its other cares and that the whole day be spent in the duties of piety and charity—and to do so as much as our human weakness and our present need of life can bear.

7. That no tasks which hinder the sanctification of that day be performed without cause or in defiance of it.

8. And finally, that here we practice our duty to be humane and

charitable towards those placed under us, including even the dumb animals. The law of nature has passed on these duties to such an extent that races all around the world have set holidays shared by all their folk, as well as days that are dedicated to attending to their religious affairs.

47. The special aspect of the Sabbath, insofar as God's ordinance has reduced the general aspect to this special one, is "the seventh day after creation" or the Sabbath, and even the one "commanded to the Jews." It is by means of this specific aspect that the general one is explained and the Sabbath-rest strictly demanded.

48. And so in this way all the commandments of the Decalogue that are common to everyone are applied in a particular way to the Jews. For God's first words are: "Hear, o Israel, I the Lord am your God, who led you out of the land of Egypt, out of the house of slavery." In so doing, however, he foretells that their commemoration of this benefit will change when they receive the new covenant, so that it will no more be said: "The Living one who led Israel from the land of Egypt, but from the land of the North, etc." (Jer 16:14). Similarly, when the reasons for the Sabbath are given, a special statement is added: "You shall remember that you were a slave in the land of Egypt, and the Lord your God brought you out from there with a mighty hand and an outstretched arm. Therefore, the Lord your God commanded you to keep the Sabbath day." Also, in the promise of the fifth commandment: "That you may live long upon the land, which the Lord your God will give to you." Here it means the land of Canaan, promised to the people of Israel, so that the genus here is applied to the species.

49. And so just as the particular aspect assumes the general one that is reduced to the species, so too when God annuls the particular, the general aspect remains unaltered and unchangeable, although it must be specified according to the ground that is unique to the newly established one.

50. Therefore in the New Testament, although the Jewish Sabbath along with the law of other commandments comprising rituals was abolished in the body of Christ and his crucifixion (Ephesians 2; Colossians 2), and although believers were freed from their bondage to them (Galatians 5), nevertheless the apostles, in conversing with the Jews, for a period of time maintained "the Sabbath-day," along with the other elements of the Law—not out of necessity, but out of Christian liberty, economy, and a steadfast resolution

not to be a cause for scandal among those who were weak. They practiced it with the Jews, but not in a Jewish manner, and they conducted solemn assemblies (Acts 13:14, 44; 16:13; 17:2; 18:4), obviously so that, as the ancients say, "the synagogue might be buried with due respect."

51. The apostles, however, after they separated themselves from the Jews and went over to the gentiles (Acts 18:6, 19:8[9]), and when some brothers from the Jews pressed upon them the need for keeping the Sabbath and considered the observance a matter of salvation (Gal 2:4,5), began to have different times for their assemblies for the sake of declaring and confirming Christian freedom, in the same way as they had abandoned the meeting-places of the Jews (Acts 18:7, 19:8[9]).

52. And in fact, in order to celebrate solemnly the benefit of Christ's new work of recreation and restoration, the apostles left aside the Sabbath's function of commemorating creation (although for that entire day the Lord had rested in the grave, which could correspond to the Sabbath-rest following creation), the apostles chose for their public assemblies (Acts 20:7) the day of the resurrection of the Lord (when our redemption was completed which happened on the eighth day following creation, or on day one, i.e., the "first day of the Sabbaths" or first day of the week [John 20:1, Matt 28:1, Mark 16:1,2,9, Luke 24:1,2] and on which day he openly showed himself alive to the women, the disciples, and the apostles [Luke 24:34, John 20:19, 26]), and ordained it to be the one customarily observed. See 1 Cor 16:1,2, where "on the first of the sabbaths," is taken in a distributive sense: "the first day of each week." Hereby is meant the observance by the early Church that became ordinary, continuous, and occurring repeatedly.

53. For this reason people began to call this day not only "of the Lord" (in a relative sense), but also "the Lord's day" (denominatively, with the definite article; Rev 1:10). The reason, surely, is not only because on that day the Lord arose from the dead and showed himself alive, but also because that day was hallowed and consecrated to that very fact; indeed, it was sacred entirely to the Lord and by the Lord. In the same manner also the supper of the Lord is called "the Lord's Supper" (1 Cor 11:20), and the place for assembly is called "the Lord's," and that solemn prayer is called "the Lord's prayer," as Augustine neatly explains (Sermon 15, *On the Words of the Apostle*). What is more, while the day has been instituted by the apostles, it was also authorized by God.

54. What also lends credence to this day of the week is the perpetual attestation, practice, and use of it already from the very beginning of God's church of the early fathers, as witnessed by Eusebius (*Ecclesiastical History* Book 3 chapter 21), Ignatius (*Epistles to the Magnesians, Epistle to the Trallians,* which are judged to be genuinely his by Eusebius and Jerome), Justin (*Apology* 2), Dionysius bishop of Corinth (in Eusebius Book 4 chapter 22), Theophilus of Antioch (*On Allegory in Matthew* Book 1), Melito [of Sardes] (in Eusebius Book 4 chapter 25), Irenaeus (in Eusebius Book 5 chapter 24), Clement of Alexandria (*Stromata* Book 7), Origen (*Homily* 7, on Exodus chapter 15; and in *Against Celsus*, Book 8), Tertullian (in *Of the Soldier's Garland*), Cyprian (Letter 33 and 59), and others. In addition, there is the law concerning it introduced by the emperor Constantine (in Eusebius Book 4 of *Life of Constantine*), and by Sozomen (Book 1 chapter 8), and the laws of the other emperors who succeeded him, as can be seen in the *Codex on Holidays.*

55. Well then, this day, although it was instituted and employed by the apostles, nevertheless is not "holy in and of itself," as though it forms some sacred mystery, figure, or symbol; or as if it is per se a part of or means of piety (as nominally the Sabbath-day in the Old Testament). Rather, according to Christian freedom this day was fixed upon and ordained wisely by the apostles, for the sake of discipline, order, and polity. And it was intended that the day be of service to piety and holiness. Understood in this way, then, there can be an equality in the week-days (Rom 14:5, Gal 4:10, Col 2:16).

56. And consequently the day ought not to be observed in the manner of the Sabbath-day of the people of old, "for its own sake and in utter rest and quiet" (something that was considered part of the piety), but "in the manner of Christian freedom" on account of another reason: That we should be able much more readily to make room for the public and private worship of God. Hence, we should celebrate the Sabbath not in such a manner (nor with such a strict and exact observance) as was required by Judaism or as superstition had imposed, but with a moderate, reverent rest of the sort that is needed for the worship of God.

57. And in an analogous way we should also recall the duties of piety and charity that were common to Jews and Christians: The Jews had to perform them on the Sabbath, and those Christians who still interacted with the Jews performed them, too. Such duties were the public and solemn assembly, and during it the reading and preaching of the sacred Scriptures, and prayers (Acts

13:15, 16, 17, and chapter 18[:19, 20, 26]). And later, when the Sabbath-keeping declined, the following duties were undertaken on the Day of the Lord: in the public assembly the apostolic teaching, sharing with the poor, the breaking of the bread (i.e., the mystical bread) or the administration of the Lord's Supper, and the solemn and public prayers. The worship of God is summed up by these four duties together (Acts 2:42). These are the solemnities of the apostolic church which took place on this day (Acts 20:7, 1 Cor 16[:2]); they are also vividly depicted on that day by Justin (*Apology* 2).

58. We deem, however, that the Lord's Day should be spent in the holy duties of piety not only in public but also privately. Such duties are the reading and contemplation of sacred Scripture at home, conversations about sacred matters etc., and acts of charity, just as Clement says: "On the Lord's Days, which are days of joy, we permit nothing to be said or done that is not holy." Even so, not all bodily recreation is entirely prohibited, as this also belongs to the goals of the Sabbath. Thus, activities may be done that pose no hindrance to the worship of God; activities following the completion of the sacred rites, honourable, decent, moderate things that cause no offense or scandal.

59. Therefore, being in the Christian era, we reject the idea of an "original Jewish Sabbath," and Sabbatarians or Sabbath-keeping Christians. Some of these joined the Sabbath to the Day of the Lord, to celebrate it with equal observance; such were the Ebionites (Eusebius Book 3 chapter 21) and some others mentioned by Gregory (Book 11 letter 3). Others kept the feast in a fashion similar to the Jews, yet without observing rest in the Jewish manner, as can be seen in Clement bishop of Rome (*Apostolic Constitutions* book 2, chapter 63, and book 7, chapter 24). He says: "We keep the Sabbath and the Day of the Lord as a feast-day, because the former is a remembrance of the creation of the world, and the latter of the resurrection." Contrary to this statement is Canon 29 of the Synod of Laodicea.

60. But we reject entirely those who overturn the Lord's Day under the pretext of Christian liberty, such as the Anabaptists of today. We also reject those who hold that the Sabbath-day of old is not so much abolished as merely transferred and altered into the Day of the Lord, and that it is actually a holy day not because of the ordinance and use of it, but because of its significance and effect; such are some of the Scholastics and papal theologians. And finally, we seriously reproach those who profane the Lord's

Day, those who violate it not just by performing unnecessary or irrelevant activities (such as entertainments, games, and plays) but also by their licentiousness, extravagance and every sort of disgrace, with the consequence of irreparable scandals to those who are weak, and horrendous infamy to the Christian reputation.

61. As far as the other feast-days are concerned, which the later Church devoted not superstitiously to the saints but to the remembrance of Christ and his special deeds for our redemption, they are the following annual feasts: the Birth of the Lord, wherein lies the starting-point of our renewed salvation; the Resurrection, or Passover, in which our salvation was made complete and confirmed; and lastly the Sending of the Holy Spirit, or Pentecost, wherein lies the basis of the kingdom and Christian church. These feasts we do not hold in the same regard. Nevertheless, as long as it is understood that they are human institutions, and that any notion of divinely prescribed worship—or superstition—is absent from them; and so long as Christian freedom is not suppressed by the necessity of having them, and the great number of them is not a burden to the church, but that they are held for the good order and the distinguished use of the Church we do think that they may be put to good use. A feast of this sort was Purim, ordained and observed at the time of Mordecai (Esth 9:19), and the Feast of the Dedication of the temple in Maccabeus's day (1 Macc 4:59), as we read in John 10:22.

ON THE GOSPEL

President: Johannes Polyander
Respondent: Petrus Doornyck

The Gospel, as 'the very blessed and highly welcome message about the salvific coming of our Redeemer Jesus Christ' (3, cf. the broader definition in thesis 6) teaches us about the remedy for sin. The cause that moved God to declare the Gospel is utterly internal, namely his 'unrestricted mercy and goodwill with which he purposed to embrace the wretched human race that had fallen into sin by the guilt of Adam' (12). The proper subject of the Gospel is the incarnate Christ, his redeeming work, his satisfaction for our sins, and his other benefits (19). The indefinite object of the Gospel is sinful people (20); the definite object is God's children, as his elect and as believers in Christ (21). Goals of the Gospel are God's glory and the salvation for those who believe (23–24). It is explicitly denied that the destruction of the unbeliever is a goal of the Gospel (25), nor are evil consequences from the preaching of the Gospel its effects (31). Much attention is given to the refutation of the Socinian view that Christ himself and through the apostles added new commandments to the Decalogue (37–52). The Gospel contains two commands: repentance and faith. The promises of the Gospel are especially about justification and eternal life (53). Law and Gospel are in agreement on both what they command and what they promise. But there are important differences, too: 'the Law stirs up the man guilty of sin to despise it, but the Gospel, with its encouragements to faith and repentance, leads the same man to Christ his Redeemer' (52); and 'while the Law promises eternal life to each and every man on the condition of one's own perfect righteousness, the Gospel does so on the condition of an alien righteousness, namely of Christ, and applied through faith' (54). So, the foremost use of the Gospel is to show that 'Christ is the goal of the Law' (55).

1. While it is from the Law (about which we disputed above) that we come to know the contagion and defect of our spiritual illness, that is, of sin, it is from the Gospel that we learn of the remedy for it.

2. Among the pagan classical authors the word *evangelion* means 1) any good and happy news about some pleasant and longed-for matter (Aristophanes, *Plutus*; Augustine, *Against Faustus* Book 2, and 18 *The City of God chapter* 35); 2) the reward that used to be given to those who brought news of this good sort (Homer, *Odyssey* 14; Cicero, *Letters to Atticus*, Book 2, Letter 12); 3) the sacrifices and prayers that were decreed for some happy outcome (Plutarch in the *Life of Phocion*, Xenophon, Book 2, Isocrates in *Areopagiticus*).

3. In the sacred writings the most prominent meaning of the word "Gospel" is: the very blessed and highly welcome message about the salvific coming of our Redeemer Jesus Christ. They sometimes use the word in a general sense, and other times with specific meaning.

4. When taken in a general sense, the word includes in its scope of meaning the evangelical promise itself about Christ, and the fulfillment of it, as in Gal 3:6 [more correctly: Gal 3:8 or 3:16].

5. When taken in a specific way, limited to presenting Christ, it means firstly the account of Christ manifested in the flesh, as in Mark 12 [the reference is probably to Mark 1:1].

6. Secondly, the word is used for the joyful teaching and preaching of the reconciliation of sinful people with God through the free remission of sins obtained for them by the expiatory death of Christ. It is offered to one and all without restriction; it is revealed to the poor in spirit and to little children, and actually applied individually to those who believe, for their salvation and the revelation of God's mercy and accompanying justice, and for his eternal praise (1 Cor 9:14, 15, etc.).

7. The principal efficient cause of the Gospel is God, the Father, Son, and Holy Spirit, with respect to both the divine decree of declaring it to mankind and the declaration itself.

8. Regarding the decree God is the efficient cause, because this mystery of the Gospel was hidden with God before all ages according to the eternal purpose which he accomplished in Christ Jesus our Lord, as the apostle teaches in Eph 3:9,10, and 11. Whence also the Gospel itself is called eternal (Rev 14:6).

9. Regarding the declaration of the Gospel God is the efficient cause, because this action by God, since it occurs toward the outside, is an action that is not divided among the Trinity. And so the Gospel is sometimes called "the word

and power of God" in an absolute sense, as in Romans 1:16 and 1 Pet 1:23. Sometimes it is used in a relative sense for the first person of the Godhead, "the Gospel of God," namely of the Father (Rom 1:1), or for the second person, "the Gospel of Christ" (as in 2 Cor 9:13), or for the third person, the "administration of the Spirit" (as in 2 Cor 3:6).

10. But with regard to the order in which the divine persons come together for that action in the different ways that they cooperate, the declaration of the Gospel is ascribed in different respects to the Father, the Son, and the Holy Spirit.

11. For it is ascribed to the Father as the foremost author of the Gospel, since it is from his bosom that it is said to have proceeded (John 1:18). It is ascribed to the Son as the most trustworthy ambassador of the Father, who earnestly declares that the words he brings forward are not his own but those of his Father (John 14:10, 24). And it is ascribed to the Holy Spirit as the most closely related interpreter of the Son's words, since Christ says that the Spirit would declare nothing new to the apostles, but that he would announce the same things that they had heard from himself (John 16:13, 14).

12. The impelling cause whereby God within himself moves to declare the Gospel is God's unrestricted mercy and goodwill with which he purposed to embrace the wretched human race that had fallen into sin by the guilt of Adam.

13. The object to which God reveals his unrestricted mercy and goodwill in his Gospel is the wretched human race that had fallen headlong into deadly sin by the Devil's deception, and to which God announced the grace of his redemption, sometimes directly and sometimes indirectly.

14. Under the old covenant God the Father declared his grace directly to the families of Adam and Abraham (Gen 3:15, 12:7, and 15:5); under the new covenant he did so to the Jews (Matt 3:16 and 17:5).

15. God declared the same grace indirectly through the prophets and the apostles, of whom the former announced beforehand that our Redeemer Jesus Christ was going to come, while the latter bore witness that he had come.

16. Therefore the apostle Paul, in order to avert from the Gospel any suspicion of novelty, states that "already beforehand God had promised it through the prophets in the sacred Scriptures" (Rom 1:2). To add credence

to this matter he brings forward testimonials from the Old Testament against the Jews who despised the Gospel (Acts 13). In the same way Christ is "servant to the circumcision" and "the apostle of our confession" (Rom 15:8, Heb 3:1).

17. In the meantime, the difference in equality between Christ, who is "God and man," and the other heralds of the Gospel (among whom are reckoned John the Baptist and the heavenly angels themselves) is as vast as it is between a most high Master and the servants sent forth to administer the Gospel in their Master's name for the sake of those who will be heirs of the salvation, obtained through the Master himself.

18. Nevertheless, the Gospel does, on occasion, take its name from these heralds because of the authority and exceptional ability whereby God has divinely taught them, as in Rom 2:16 and 2 Cor 4:3, where God's Gospel is called even the Gospel of Paul and his co-apostles.

19. The proper substance or subject of the Gospel is Christ 'in the flesh,' or the incarnate Christ. For the Gospel is entirely occupied with telling about his redeeming work, his satisfaction for our sins, and his other benefits. In this sense it is called "the Gospel of Jesus Christ the Son of God," i.e., the gospel about Jesus Christ, God's Son (Mark 1:1; Rom 1:3, 16; Rom 15:19; 1 Cor 9:12; 2 Cor 9:13; Gal 1[:7, 11, 12]). In similar fashion it is called "the Word of Christ" (Col 3:16) and "his testimony" (2 Tim 1:8).

20. The indefinite object of the Gospel is sinful people of every kind, whether they are men or women, masters or slaves, Jews or Greeks.

21. The definite object of the Gospel are God's children who have been ordained unto eternal life, who beforehand are called God's elect and afterward are called sometimes the faithful or the believers in Christ, and at other times little children and poor in spirit, weighed down as they are by the burden of their sin.

22. The form of the Gospel is the full and very clearly evident revelation and proclamation of the saving grace promised in Christ through the prophets, which in every way (in its entirety and in all its parts) is in harmony with God's ordained purpose.

23. The ultimate goal of the Gospel is the glory of God, to whom praise of his highest mercy and justice is ascribed in this Gospel's testimony, because he did not spare his own Son, our surety, but gave him up to an accursed

death on the cross for us, in order that he might reconcile us to himself for ever, freed from the curse of the law.

24. The nearest goal of the Gospel is salvation and eternal life for those who believe, and so it is defined as "the power of God unto salvation for all who believe" (Rom 1:16) and the "aroma of life unto life" (2 Cor 2:16).

25. The destruction of unbelievers, however, is not a goal of the Gospel; that is an unconnected outcome from elsewhere, from their sins. For in his Gospel God declares that he takes no delight in the destruction of any sinner, but he delights in transferring everyone to salvation through repentance and faith from the power of darkness into the kingdom of his beloved Son, Jesus Christ.

26. Therefore this saving transfer to the kingdom of God's Son is the proper effect of the Gospel, and therefore it is called the "Gospel of the Kingdom" (Mark 1:14).

27. There are two stages to this transfer; in the first one we are led, in this age, into the kingdom of grace, and in the second we are carried up into the kingdom of glory in the age that is to come.

28. The former kind of transfer happens by God's ordained purpose and through the gift of being called to faith, of being justified through faith, and of being made holy by faith that gives evidence of itself through good works.

29. The latter kind of transfer will take place by the gift of being glorified, whereby we shall be taken up to meet our Lord Jesus and we shall ascend with him far above all the heavens, so that in his Father's house we shall have the joy of beholding him close and in full, and we shall have blessed communion in eternity.

30. When considered separately in light of this effect, the Gospel acquires a variety of names in Sacred Scripture; to be precise, that it is the word "of truth" (Col 1:5), "of faith" (Rom 10:8), "of reconciliation" (2 Cor 5:19), "of peace" (Eph 6:15), "of justice" (Heb 5:13), "of the grace of God" (Acts 14:3 and 20:32); the "regenerating Word" (1 Pet 1:23); the Gospel "of salvation" (Eph 1:13), and "of life" (Phil 2:15[16]).

31. The evil consequences that come about by the guilt of depraved people from the preaching of the Gospel should not be numbered among its effects. Evils of this sort are the offense caused to unbelievers (1 Cor 1:23; 1 Pet 2:8),

the sword-wielding by enemies (Matt 10:31), the complete blindness of those who are hard-hearted (2 Cor 4:4), and a harsher judgment (Matt 11:21[-24]; 2 Thess 1:7, 8).

32. And furthermore, the Gospel sometimes receives the distinguishing title of Law, because it also contains its own commands, promises, and warnings.

33. There are two commands in the Gospel; one is the command of repentance, the other of faith in Jesus Christ; Mark 1:15: "Repent and believe the Gospel."

34. To the former demand belong the New Testament appeals, both legal and evangelical. To the latter demand the evangelical appeals are applied above all.

35. But those that are found in Matt 5, John 13, and elsewhere, are not new commandments of the Gospel in the proper sense of the word Gospel, as if added to the precepts of the moral law and more precise than these. Rather, they are the same commandments which Moses had delivered to God's people, and which Christ repeated and cleansed of the Pharisees' corrupting influences, and which were restored to their former splendor by authentic interpretation.

36. Therefore the Scholastics and the Jesuits go astray when they claim that Christ gave a new law, and that his commandments are by far more perfect, surpassing, and severe than those of Moses (Lombard, *Sentences* Book 3, dist. 40; Thomas Aquinas on Matt chapter 5, and *Summa theologiae* 1/2, question 91, art. 5; Duns Scotus, *Sentences* Book 3, dist. 40; Biel, *Sentences* Book 3, dist. 40; Bellarmine, *On Justification* Book 4, chapters 3 and 4).

37. Going astray also are the Socinians, who think that the commandments of Christ are two-fold: They claim that Christ added some of these commandments to the individual precepts of the Decalogue and handed down others separately to the apostles.

38. There are two commandments that they claim Christ added to the first precept of the moral law: 1) the one whereby Christ directs us to pray in a certain manner; 2) the other whereby he orders us to acknowledge, worship, and call upon him as true God, that is (according to their faulty interpretation) as such a one who wields his divine supreme power over us. Both of these should be referred to the first precept of the law.

39. For by that prayer-formula Christ did not establish some new manner of calling upon God, but one that conforms to the one used in the Old Testament, one that actually had been ordered by God in a general way in the first precept of the law, and that God adapted specifically for use by his people through the composition of diverse prayers by David and other godly men.

40. And Christ, when He willed to be acknowledged and called upon as true God, did not prescribe a new worship of God, but the one expressed in the first commandment. For in it God the Father, when He prohibits us from having any strange gods before Him, wills Him to be worshiped who is one and the same with God himself. And all Scripture bears witness that such a one is Christ—not only regarding his authority (as the Socinians would have it) but also regarding his divine nature.

41. We should make the same assessment of the other additions to the subsequent commandments that they wrongly claim as Christ's. For it is not only the apostles who taught from the second commandment that we must flee from idols (1 Cor 10:14, and 1 John 5:21) but Moses, too, when he interprets this commandment in Deut 7:5, where he orders the Israelite people to demolish the altars of the heathens and to smash their images into pieces.

42. Next, the fact that we are not permitted to swear falsely, nor even to swear in true matters unless the reasons for so doing are very serious and advance God's glory, is something that was taught not only by Christ (Matt 5:34) but also by Hosea (chapter 4:15), according to this prohibition in the third commandment: "You shall not take the name of your God in vain."

43. The same goes for the precepts they think were added in the New Testament to the fifth commandment about the duties of subjects towards the civil magistracy, for these orders are found also in the Old Testament (Lev 19:32; Prov 14:11[21, 35]; Eccl 33:25).

44. Nor is the prohibition against wrath and revenge to be found only in the Gospel, as they suppose; it is given also by Moses (Lev 19:17,18) and Solomon (Prov 24:24) [rather: Prov 24:1, 8, 19, 29].

45. Furthermore, before the coming of Christ the Jews understood from the admonitions of the prophets that the seventh commandment forbids gazing lustfully, indecent gestures and foul-mouthed speech; that the eighth forbids

greed, the ninth deceit of any kind (even that which comes from frivolity), and, finally, that the tenth commandment forbids even the unwilled emotions that arise from our corrupt desires. These are found in Prov 6:25, 23:31, 5:20, 7:13–14, Ps 63:11, Prov 15:27, Isa 56:11 and 57:17, Prov 6:18–19 and 19:5, Ps 10:8.

46. The commandments which the Socinians say Christ delivered separately refer to moral matters (as they call them) or outward religious actions, commonly called ceremonies.

47. By moral commandments they mean: self-denial, bearing the cross or endurance, and the imitation of Christ.

48. The first of these, according to the Socinians' own explication, must be in reference to the seventh and eighth commandments, and mainly to the tenth, since by the self-denial they understand putting aside the lusts of our flesh and eyes, and the haughtiness of the present life, from 1 John 2:15, 16.

49. The second of these is included under the first precept of the law; for in order to keep it, too, endurance and bearing the cross are required.

50. The imitation of Christ (according to their definition of it) is nothing other than structuring our lives by the rule of the life led by Jesus Christ, who fulfilled the law's commandments with his own perfect love towards God and the neighbor. Accordingly, the imitation of Christ consists in the keeping of no law other than the moral one.

51. The Supper of the Lord is not just a ceremonial demand of the Gospel, as the Socinians think, but it is also a eucharistic sacrament that has been ordained as a celebration of the saving grace obtained for us by Christ's death and declared in the Gospel. This can be deduced from Christ's admonition in Luke 22:19: "Do this in remembrance of me;" and Paul's, in 1 Cor 11:26: "Whenever you eat this bread and drink of this cup, you proclaim the Lord's death until he comes."

52. To be sure, the things that are commanded in the Gospel and the Law are in agreement as they prescribe for us the same rule of life, namely, that we live soberly, as befits us, in pious devotion towards God and justly towards our neighbor (Titus 2:12). Nevertheless, they differ from each other in this, that the Law stirs up the man guilty of sin to despise it, but the Gospel, with its encouragements to faith and repentance, leads the same man to Christ his Redeemer.

53. The promises of the Gospel are especially about these two things: 1) the justification in the presence of God through faith; 2) the inheritance of eternal life (Rom 1:17; 1 John 2:25).

54. Although the Law holds forth the promise of eternal life to those who obey God no less than the Gospel does (Matt 19:16), the latter differs from the former in that while the Law promises eternal life to each and every man on the condition of one's own perfect righteousness, the Gospel does so on the condition of an alien righteousness, namely of Christ, and applied through faith.

55. The threats of the Gospel concern the condemnation of unbelievers who do not obey Christ in the presence of God, and the punishment of eternal death (John 3:18, 36; Heb 2:2,3).

56. The foremost use of the Gospel is to show that Christ is the goal of the Law unto the righteousness of everyone who believes (Rom 10:4). The other uses of the law can be learned from the goals and effects that we have pointed out above.

ON THE OLD AND
THE NEW TESTAMENT

President: Andreas Rivetus
Respondent: Daniel Pain

With a reference to Hebrews 9:15–22, this disputation states early on that the terms 'Old and New Testament' are preferred over 'covenant,' as 'it concerns a treaty that was undertaken between God and man and was to be put into effect by the death of Christ, having been foreshadowed first by the blood of slaughtered animals and actually executed by his death.' (3) Reference is made to the 'wondrous way' in which 'the same mediator who was the victim was also the testator who put the testament into effect for his heirs by means of his own death,' whereby 'everlasting reconciliation and peace' was achieved (4). The administration of God's covenant of grace in the Old and the New Testament is depicted in somewhat contrasting ways. One is that of sharp distinction between the two: while the demands of the law of the Old Testament cannot be kept obediently by anyone and so lead to death, the New Testament and its Gospel lead to eternal life through faith in Christ Jesus. Another way is to perceive the differences in aspects of the testaments that are not essential: the difference in time and circumstance, or the material and spiritual character of God's salvation in each (14–21). As the Person of Christ is the substance of God's covenant in both the Old and the New Testaments, it is He and his work of salvation that underscores the underlying unity of the two dispensations, for 'there always was but one way to salvation, and "through the grace of our Lord Jesus Christ we believe that we are saved in the same way as our fathers were" (Acts 15:11)' (21). The disputation concludes with a rejection of various 'false teachings' (22–32).

1. Now that we have given individual treatments of the Law and the Gospel (and their natures) in the preceding disputations, it follows that we should compare them regarding their similarities and dissimilarities, or differences.

And because people use different names to speak about the same matters (among them being the terms "Old" and "New Testament," which are used most commonly when Law and Gospel are compared), we should speak about their meaning. If the meaning is not made clear definitively in advance, nothing is easier than to force things by indicating similarities and noting differences, as one person understands one thing, and another something else, and, depending on the assumptions that each clings to, they differ in wording rather than in content.

2. Some people wish to derive the Hebrew word *bᵉrit* ['covenant'] from a verb that means 'to cleanse' or 'to make clean,' because in a covenant or treaty both parties reveal and endorse their trust without any filthy sophistry, with an added ritual open to the public. The Greek translators of the Old Testament rendered this word with *diathēkē* ['covenant, testament'], the only exception being in Deut 9:15, where they translated it as *marturion*, 'testimony.' In the Greek writers, then, *diathēkē* is used mostly with that singular meaning for which the Latin writers use the word 'testament.' This Latin word, however, has a specific denotation that differs from the Hebrew and Greek words, which mean disposition or arrangement generally. Yet a promise is implied in disposition, whether it be a treaty between two parties that are alive (they call it *sunthēkē*), or a 'testament' in the proper sense of the word, that is, the final arrangement a dying man makes for the things that he will leave behind. This kind of arrangement is made legal by the spoken word or by recorded documents.

3. In Heb 9:15–22 the apostle employs this word with this proper meaning for the subject of the old or New Testament that we are treating here, to denote a testament that came to pass by the death of the testator. For this reason he observes that "the former testament was put into effect not without blood." Following his authority, when dealing with the same subject-matter, we prefer the specific terms 'Old and New Testament' to the general word 'covenant,' as it concerns a treaty that was undertaken between God and man and was to be put into effect by the death of Christ, having been foreshadowed first by the blood of slaughtered animals and actually executed by his death.

4. And yet we do not therefore reject the name 'covenant' if we look at it in the way an agreement or treaty is reached in human affairs: Parties that differ with each other make an agreement on the basis of certain conditions that

each side must meet, and they make these conditions binding by slaughtering animals according to the custom of their ancestors (whence comes the saying, in Latin, 'to strike' or 'slay' a covenant, as well as the Hebrew *karat brit*, 'to cut' or 'smite' a covenant, Gen 15:18), or by exchanging hostages in addition to sealed documents. In the same manner an agreement is made between God and man about the everlasting reconciliation and peace that was achieved for them by the mediator who became the victim on man's behalf. Records of their covenant were drawn up to confirm it, along with additional sacramental signs. But we employ especially this word 'testament' so that it signifies this treaty with its full meaning, because in a wondrous way it happened that the same mediator who was the victim was also the testator who put the testament into effect for his heirs by means of his own death.

5. Moreover, they may be called the "old" and "new" testaments in a literal sense or a figurative one. And the words may be used with wide or narrow meaning. When the sense is literal, the word "Old Testament" stands for the Law, insofar as it was given to the Jewish people through Moses. It promised life to them on condition of perfect obedience, with the provision of a curse upon the transgressors, and it brought with it an unbearable burden of legal rituals and the yoke of a highly restrictive political order. For this reason it is called "the letter that kills," "the dispensation of death and condemnation," "bearing children for slavery, like Hagar" (2 Cor 3:6,7; Gal 4:23, 24). Placed opposite to this is the "New Testament" (in the strict sense), the teaching of spiritual grace and salvation fully revealed by the Son of God himself from the bosom of the Father and spread abroad by the apostles' preaching. It promises righteousness without price, and life everlasting through and for the sake of Christ the testator unto all who believe in him through the grace that he will lavish on them abundantly.

6. In this sense the Old and New Testaments are different not only in some circumstantial qualities and contingencies, but also in essence, and (to use the words of Paul) "there are two testaments" (Gal 4:24). For each one established an entirely different ground for salvation, as the former holds forth the promise of life on the condition of works, while the latter promises the forgiveness of sins and life everlasting to everyone who relies on Christ through faith. Therefore, those people are said "to have fallen away from grace, who wish to be justified through the Law" (Gal 5:4). And the Law is placed over against the promise in such a way that if the inheritance comes by the former, then it cannot come by the latter (Gal 3:18). The same reason

exists for the contrast between the Law of works and the Law of faith (Rom 3:27). The first of these is understood as teaching salvation that is promised on the condition "that you do all these things," while the second teaches that the same salvation is offered on the condition "that you believe." God freely grants that condition so that whoever is justified fulfills it.

7. In this sense, therefore, the Old Testament receives the names "administration of death, the letter that kills" (2 Cor 3:6), "the unbearable yoke" that oppressed its supporters with slavery (Acts 15:10), "a mere shadow of so many good things yet to come" (Heb 10:1), lacking in perfection, intended for abolition, etc. The New Testament is placed opposite it in this strict sense (as we called it). It is the "ministry of the life-giving Spirit," "the easy yoke of Christ," bestowing on us the spirit of adoption and the freedom of being God's children (Matt 11:29, Rom 8:[15–]17), having "the true image of things," perfect and eternal.

8. Figuratively and as metonyms the names "Old and New Testaments" are given to the books that make up the codex of the Old Testament and the writings of the apostles and evangelists, in the same way as in our human affairs the sealed records of our last wills are called "testaments." For this reason also the signs of the sacraments receive the same name of "testaments." In this sense, in 2 Cor 3:14 the apostle speaks of a "veil that remains over the reading of the Old Testament." And by the analogy of this statement the reading of the Gospel can be called the reading of the New Testament; in this sense the word "New Testament" is employed generally for the Gospel-books. But what is said in verse six of the same chapter about "ministers of the New Testament" does not concern the sacred book. As far as the signs of the sacrament are concerned, Christ himself calls the cup of blessing by the metonym "New Testament in his blood" (Luke 22:20), and the apostle speaks of a testament or covenant of circumcision (Acts 7:8).

9. The similarities and differences between these books and the representation of them depends on the subject-matter and the ways in which it has been made known. And when these will be employed in a different sense, anyone who knows the nature of each topic treated (and their differences or similarities) will decide with little trouble what to think of it.

10. When the word "testament" is used with wider meaning and accompanied by the word "old" it embraces the Law given through Moses (about which we spoke) and the promise made to Adam about the seed of the woman, and

the same promise made again to Abraham about his own offspring, in whom all the nations were to be blessed. The apostle expressly calls this promise a "testament considered to have been ratified or confirmed previously" (Gal 3:17), and at Eph 2:12 "the covenants of promise." But "the Law given through Moses" is joined to that same promise insofar as they are understood in a broad sense under the Old Testament. But only to the extent that the Law is "our custodian unto Christ" (Gal 3:24), because the ceremonial law cried out that what the moral law most urgently demanded from the human race was achieved only by Christ and his sacrifice. And the law of the political order provided support to each of the other laws, and attended to them with an outward arrangement that each could use.

11. In this way also "New Testament" is taken in a broader sense for the teaching of grace and faith, as well as repentance and thankfulness, or the new obedience. For the call of the Gospel is: "Repent and believe in the Gospel," and so it demands faith in the Gospel and repentance—two things that are necessarily accompanied by the new obedience whereby one lives a life worthy to God. This is the sense of the word "Gospel" when the apostle says that he "was set apart to preach the Gospel of God" (Rom 1:1), and "God is going to judge according to his Gospel" (Rom 2:16), and similar texts.

12. Both "Old" and "New Testament" are, however, used with strict and literal meaning (as we called it) and then they are opposed to each other so diametrically that they cannot be reconciled. Thus there is no need for us to undertake a lengthy comparison of them. They are similar from the general perspective of their single authorship, namely God. As lawmaker it was he who gave the law, while as merciful Father it was he who gave the Gospel. They are similar also from the general perspective of content, for the teaching in both testaments consists in the command to obedience and the promise of rewards. They agree in the general intent of their goals, namely the glory of God's wisdom and goodness. So too when we consider the subject that they share: the human race. On the other hand, however, a very large difference occurs when one considers each of all these things in particular— we spoke about this particular aspect above, in thesis six. We do admit, however, that the word "Old Testament," in the sense that it is understood here, is never used in Holy Scripture for the covenant of grace.

13. But there is nothing that prevents the covenant of grace or the promise made to the patriarchs (when dressed in the circumstantial qualities of its role as custodian) from going by the name "old testament," because it contained something that had to be renewed and was to become obsolete. For when Paul says "the first testament which God has made obsolete" (Heb 8:13 and 9:1), he takes it to mean the entire religious worship of the old tabernacle—which surely contained the promise, and confirmed it. And although strictly speaking, as we have said, "testament" means simply the covenant of works, nevertheless by adding the name "new" it means only the covenant of grace. But in order to remove any doubt as to its meaning, we ought to undertake a comparison of the Old Testament with the new. As far as the Old Testament is concerned, it is taken for the covenant of grace insofar as immediately after the fall it began with our first parents and was made with Abraham; and to support it there was the law given through Moses. And as for the New Testament, it is taken for the covenant of grace insofar as Christ renewed and confirmed it.

14. Having made these points, we state that these two testaments are one and the same as far as their substance is concerned, as is evident when we consider all their causes. For if we look at the efficient cause for each (which some call 'impelling cause'), then it was brought about by God only because of his mercy and not because he was moved by any human merits. He ordained Christ alone as the mediator, "in whom he was reconciling the world unto himself" (2 Cor 5:19). If we look at the material cause of each, it is one and the same, for both of them demand the same faith and obedience; both promise the same inheritance of eternal life through the imputation of the righteousness of faith, and the same gracious adoption in Christ. If we look at their form, then in both of them an agreement between two differing parties is established by the blood of the mediator, as one who is coming or as one who has been revealed. If we look at their nearest goal, then neither of them was calling people to fleshly or earthly happiness or especially to the good things of this current life, but instead much more to the hope of everlasting happiness. If we consider the ultimate goal: For each it was the praise of God's glorious grace in Christ.

15. And nevertheless they are called two testaments, not by dividing their kind into species but according to the accidental qualities of their subject-matter. For the same thing that remains in their species and substance varies according to the different grounds for their arrangement and the way each is

administered (from both the side of God and of man). God, in administering the testaments inwardly, imparts to the elect (for one and the same sonship) the one and the same Spirit who pours forth as much light of knowledge as is needed for salvation. Nevertheless it is quite obvious that in the new testament the Holy Spirit shines forth with greater efficacy, and the diversity and abundance of gifts shines more brilliantly, if we consider the body of the Church as a community. For then "he poured out upon all flesh his Holy Spirit" who before was imparted more sparingly (Joel 2:28).

16. A consideration of their outward administration, too, produces no small difference. For if we look at the quality in which the testaments are revealed, it is less transparent in the old, since Christ is proffered as yet to come, while in the new he is preached as already revealed. In the former, the heavenly inheritance is put forth as something to be viewed in terms of earthly benefits, and displayed as something whereof the patriarchs were to have a foretaste. And contrary to that, the old testament gives much more obvious demonstrations of the judgment of the ungodly, in the form of bodily punishments. This was the reason why they considered those temporary blessings more valuable than would be fitting today. But as it is now, our hearts are aimed straight and directly at the heavenly heritage, as the grace of the life to come is more clearly and transparently revealed through the Gospel, and as the inferior way of exercising it was abandoned.

17. A third difference is added in this, that when the Old Testament was handed down it was wrapped up in a shadowy keeping of ceremonies that possessed no efficacy of itself; and the various rites and figures in it were a means of foreshadowing Christ as yet to come. But in the New Testament we are offered to behold him with his face uncovered, and the truth of the things themselves and his body are displayed in the here and now. And the signs that were instituted in the New Testament no longer promise some future thing, but they bear witness to one that had been promised earlier and was fulfilled in due time. They form signs and seals of its greater efficacy. And these signs are not bloody, nor so great in number, nor so burdensome or difficult to perceive. In fact, these signs are bloodless, fewer in number, easier to discern, and of greater clarity. In the former testament "there was a shadow of good things that were going to come, while in the latter there is a true, living form of real things" (Heb 10:1).

18. A fourth difference is seen in the quantity of people and the universal scope of those who are received into the covenant. For whereas under the Old Testament the promise was limited in scope to Abraham and his descendants to the exclusion of other peoples—or with the inclusion of a very few who were somehow engrafted into Abraham's family through some extraordinary grace. But now, in the New Testament, when the wall that divided them has been broken down—the wall that for so long a time kept God's mercy confined within the boundaries of Israel—peace has been proclaimed for those who were far off, that they might join with those who were close by into the one people of God. Hence the calling of the gentiles, that most precious gift of the New Testament, is called "the mystery hidden for ages and generations," and the angels themselves marvel at it (Col 1:26).

19. The fifth difference exists in the changed ways in which they are administered on the part of man. For in the Old Testament, it was required not only to keep the moral law, but even "the heir, as long as he is a little boy, being no different from a slave" is kept in practical slavery to the ceremonial law (Gal 4:2,3,4). Hence, even though the heir, as heir, was granted the "spirit of adoption," and so "of freedom," nevertheless, as a "little child" he could not yet actually enjoy complete freedom; the freedom he possessed was moderated even by a spirit of slavery. But in the New Testament, those who believe are no longer subject to these chains and burdens of observances; "they did not receive the spirit of slavery again unto fear, but the spirit of adoption through which they cry out, 'Abba, Father'" (Rom 8:13[15]).

20. The final difference lies in the length of time taken for the administration of each. For the first testament had to cease after the fullness of time had come; therefore, it was subject to change. For it says "the Law and the prophets until the time of John" (Luke 16:16); "for when there is a change in the priesthood, there must be a change also in the law" (Heb 7:12). And, "the law was added because of sin, until the seed should come" (Heb 7:18 [Gal 3:19]). But now that this seed has been revealed, we should no longer expect a change in the priesthood, since Christ remains as "priest forever," Ps 110:4.

21. From these words we gather that the benefit of grace is not to be segregated from the Old Testament, if it is considered in this way, since the announcement of grace concerning the remission of sins through Christ the mediator was heard in it, and all believers were no less justified and saved than in the time of the New Testament. For there always was but one way to

salvation, and "through the grace of our Lord Jesus Christ we believe that we are saved in the same way as our fathers were" (Acts 15:11). "And it was not through the law that the promise was made to Abraham and his seed that he should inherit the world, but through the righteousness of faith" (Rom 4:13). For "Jesus Christ is the same yesterday, and today, and even to the end of the age" (Heb 13:8). And thus Paul, in Rom 4:1 and 6, brings forward the examples of Abraham and David in his dealing with justification so attentively that he succeeds in proving that from the beginning of the world no-one has been justified in any other way than by faith in Christ.

22. Therefore we must detest the presumption of those who together with the vile Servetus felt no differently about the Israelite people than about the swine of Epicurus's herd who have lived beyond any hope for heavenly immortality, being fattened up by God for this earth. We should equally reject the error of others who take away the real difference between the old and the new testaments, and who make keeping the precepts handed down by Moses and Christ into the cause for salvation. They confuse faith with performing the commandments of the Old Testament Law and the new testament Gospel. In their imagination these commandments are more perfect because if you look at their number, more have been added, and because if you look at the excellence of any of them, they have been intensified. And they introduce into both testaments the righteousness by works, a righteousness placed under our control and supplied by our human strength.

23. For it is false to state that Christ added anything to the law of Moses in order to render the imperfect perfect, because the Law, when God first gave it, always has been the most perfect rule for good works, since nothing can be required that is more perfect than to love God entirely from the heart. This love demands the integrity of our entire nature and a conformity of all our thoughts, words, and actions, to the Law of righteousness. Hence it happens that Christ sends those who seek their life from works back to the Law (Matt 19:17; Luke 10:28). Because if a fulfilled Law has any power to bestow eternal life, then nothing can be added to its perfect quality. Even Bellarmine, forgetting his own position, rightly points out that Christ, in Matt 5[:20], "did not say: 'Unless your righteousness exceeds that of the prophets,' but he said: 'that of the scribes, etc.'; hereby he meant that he wished not so much to increase the burdens of the Law's precepts, as to deprive the Scribes and Pharisees of their wrong teaching" (*On Justification*, Book 4, chapter 4).

24. The modern Photinians have adopted these false notions from the Pelagians, differing with the papal teachers only in that they do not acknowledge that grace is necessary for them to be able to fulfill both those old precepts that have been refurbished as well as the ones that have been newly made known. For these people [= the papal teachers], although they make both the old and the new law (which they designate as commandments) into the rule of righteousness, nevertheless they do admit that not only is the grace of outward revelation that comes by the preaching necessary, but also of its inward working—although they make its actions dependent on the human will or determined by it.

25. They go wrong in this matter not only because they ascribe too much to the human will, but because they do not understand the grace of justification. They confuse the two mothers, "free and slave," and they consider flesh and promise to be one and the same thing; they join the Law of works with the Gospel, as though these are similar things in substance, being different only in quantity, clarity, completion, or assistance by the Spirit. In actual fact, they are two different matters in nature and in kind, matters that cannot be joined together in the working of justification. For "those who are under the Law are not under grace" (Rom 6:14). Therefore, Christ who brought grace did not found a new law, as though he ordained that righteousness comes by keeping it.

26. However we do not say, as they falsely claim, that through the Gospel Christ has done away with the moral law. Nor do we deny that Christ has made perfect the same law, by fulfilling it with his perfect obedience, and also by restoring it to its original perfection. He did so by liberating it from the corrupting influences of the elders, but not by adding other precepts of the law to it or by extending those that already had been given. The papal teachers and the Socinians strive in vain to prove that Christ had done this from Matthew chapters five, six, and seven.

27. We also do not deny that the doctrine of works and a variety of commands are contained in the New Testament; in fact, all the commands of the moral law are impressed upon us as needful for the new obedience and the exercise of sanctification. But we do deny this, which they hold, that the new testament strictly speaking, insofar as it is the teaching of the promise of grace given in Christ, demands "the condition of fulfilling the entire law," as Bellarmine would have it (*On Justification* Book 4 chapter 2); or that the

righteous are not free from observing the divine law insofar as it demands complete obedience, whereby someone is declared righteous as he deserves.

28. For the conditions raised by the papal teachers in objection to us as required in the New Testament for eternal life—such as, "unless your righteousness exceeds that of the Scribes and Pharisees" (Matt 5:20), and, "if you would enter life, keep my commandments" (Matt 19:17)—these are threatening warnings or promises of the Law and not of the Gospel. They are not relevant or proper to the New Testament but to the covenant of works and the old testament (strictly understood). And they are put forward in the Gospel in order to demonstrate the hypocrisy of those who would be righteous in themselves. And when the incapability of the Law has been demonstrated, they pave the way for the promise of grace appropriate to the New Testament. And in this way our Lord determined first to teach the young man who sought righteousness from works that no-one is deemed righteous before God unless he has met the requirements of the Law (which is impossible), so that, being convinced that he is not capable in himself, he would turn to faith for his reliance.

29. Furthermore, we do not say that the Gospel and the New Testament demand no condition at all, for the condition of faith and new obedience (which is everywhere impressed on us) is demanded. But God provides these conditions freely, and their imperfect quality forms no hindrance to salvation (which flows from another source), so long as they are genuine. But this is not how we should view the condition of fulfilling the entire Law, which they make into a cause of salvation. God does not bestow it in this life on anyone in such a way that they can bear God's judgment. For "we all err in many ways" and "he who fails in one commandment is guilty of them all" (Jas 3:2 and 2:10). For although Christ has brought also regenerating grace whereby he "writes the law upon the hearts of those who belong to him," nevertheless the cause for salvation does not reside therein, nor does the reason proper for the new testament. But the cause for salvation resides in the following promise: "I shall forgive their iniquity and I shall no more remember their sin" (Jer 31:34).

30. This being the case, we should not tolerate the pride of the papal teachers, who presume that they are able to fulfill that more perfect law which they fancy for themselves, beyond the moral law God handed down through Moses, and to keep it with little trouble, as they confuse it with the "easy

yoke" of Christ. But they also make the additional claim that Christ added certain "matters of advice," which they describe as "belonging to the gospel" and whereby they insist upon being able to achieve a more abundant righteousness of works than the one contained in the prescribed law. They claim that from them they can merit higher steps in heaven beyond the essential blessedness, in such a way that if they don't keep them they will not incur punishment, but if they do keep them they will earn a greater reward. There are three such matters of advice, which they call the three essential [vows] of [the state of] perfection: abstinence, poverty, and obedience. And there are many others also, such as not taking revenge for one's self, bearing injury with patience, etc.

31. This teaching does harm to God's law, as it places perfection in the traditions of man rather than in the precepts of God, by implying that one can keep or transgress freely what in fact was handed down by God in the two testaments and is binding for everyone. Such precepts include: withholding from taking personal revenge, loving one's enemies, recanting oaths that were taken rashly. We must also perform other similar, individual precepts, according to God's gifts and calling. For whatever good a man possesses, since he has received it from God, he is a debtor to the one from whom he has it, and he must confess that he is "an unworthy servant, who has done what was his duty" (Luke 17:10).

32. Having rejected these false teachings, we take our repose in this dispensation of God, whereby God has arranged the law and the promise in such a way that we regard the former as one that condemns and we seek the latter for the comfort it brings. The former demands while the latter forgives, the former finds blame while the latter embraces in love. Nevertheless, in both the old and the new testaments he has offered the same, the only way to salvation through his grace in the mediator Christ, having changed only their circumstantial qualities and the ways in which he dispensed them. But there was not any change in the one who dispenses them, "with whom there is no variation or shadow due to change" (Jas 1:17). It is the same Christ who in different ages and in different ways by his own great wisdom provided for those who were his (according to their own individual conditions), and now "through the church has made known to the powers and principalities in the heavenly places that manifold wisdom of God" (Eph 3:10). To him alone be the glory.

Corollary

The ministry of John the Baptist came between the dispensation of the old and the new testaments; as in merits it yielded to the apostolic ministry, so too did it surpass that of the prophets. We posit that his baptism, being ordained by God, signed and sealed the remission of sins, and was the same in substance and meaning as the baptism that is now received in the Church.

ON DIVINE PREDESTINATION

President: Antonius Walaeus
Respondent: Isaac Biscopius

While complex and hard to explain, the doctrine of predestination should not be ignored, for it is Scriptural and comforting. Reprobation is as much part of predestination as election is, but they are not entirely similar, 'only analogous' (6). Election is explained in thesis 9– 43; the 'difficult question of reprobation,' which 'seems completely opposed to human understanding' (44) in thesis 44–61. Theses 12–14 treat the nature of election, 15–20 the circumstance of it, 21–40 the causes of election, and theses 41–43 its advantages. One of the issues leading to the Synod of Dort (1618–19) was that of the object of predestination. There was a difference of opinion about this also among the opponents of the Remonstrants: Gomarus was an important representative of the supralapsarians. They stated that the object of God's predestination was 'possible human beings,' without taking into account the Fall, or faith. The infralapsarians, who argued that fallen humanity was the object of God's predestination, were in the majority during the synod. Three Synopsis authors, Walaeus, Polyander and Thysius, defended this infralapsarian position at the synod. This view is also held in the Synopsis (22). The Remonstrants opposed to both views that God in his predestination sees man as created, fallen and as a believer. In this disputation, election is defined as 'the eternal and immutable decree of God whereby He chooses from the whole human race that had fallen by its own fault from pristine integrity into sin and destruction a specific number of individual people (neither better nor more worthy than others) solely out of his own good pleasure, unto salvation in Christ Jesus' (14). When Walaeus defines election, he employs diction similar to that used in the Canons of Dort. Referring to the Remonstrants, thesis 34 states that some 'who want to be members of the Reformed church' hold that God elected only those people whose faith and perseverance He had foreseen (34). This view would be acceptable if they would acknowledge that faith and perseverance are gifts of God, granted on the basis of grace to those who are to be saved. Long ago, and also more recently, the Church had refuted Pelagianism; the Remonstrants had similarly attributed faith and perseverance to human free will as well as to the gift of God (35). To explain that election and reprobation—the latter being characterized as a 'passing over,' 'leaving aside,' as the negative implication of election—are dissimilar, the scholastic tradition had distinguished between reprobation that is negative and reprobation that is affirmative, or positive. 'Negative' in this context means that God 'did not resolve to have mercy on those whom He did not elect' and 'affirmative' means that He 'resolved to impose the punishments finally deserved upon those same people who had been left' (50). Interestingly, while the Synopsis focuses on an intellectual explanation of predestination, it explicitly applies the doctrine in the spiritual life of the believer: election 'teaches humility.' Moreover, it is accompanied by many blessings: 'it is the basis of solid trust in God, the source of spiritual joy and Christian hope, the true ground for consolation in adversities, for forbearance in suffering, for steadfastness in the face of the apostasy of others, a spur for gratitude towards God, for love towards the neighbor' (41).

1. Although the doctrine of God's eternal predestination is a difficult one and full of challenges, that is not a reason for us to be silent about it in the Church of Christ, as some backwardly cautious people think. For neither are we able to be more prudent than the Holy Spirit, nor should we wish to be. It is the Holy Spirit who sets forth this doctrine consistently, both in the prophecies and in the preaching, and also in the Epistles that were written to all the churches. And [we also should not be silent about it] because it contains material that is full of consolation and other fruits that serve the upbuilding of the Church, as we shall later demonstrate.

2. We do grant, however, that we should treat it with all spiritual modesty and prudence and that we should be careful above all else that our own knowledge in this matter does not go beyond what is written; but we should follow the lead only of God's Word. True disciples of Christ willingly make themselves captives in order to obey it, and "although they cannot possibly fathom the reason for God's acts and the depth of his judgments, they know perfectly well that what He says is true and that what He does is just," as Prosper correctly states in his *Defense of Augustine against Select Passages of the Genovese Priests*, response 8.

3. And so, to begin with the word 'to predestine,' that is, 'to determine beforehand,' its meaning generally entails these two elements: first, it means to decide something specific in one's mind about a thing that should be done. Secondly, it means to appoint that thing for a specific outcome and end. Hence Augustine, in his *The Good of Perseverance*, 2,17, says: "To arrange his

future works in his foreknowledge which cannot fail or be changed, that—and nothing else—certainly is to predestine." And Fulgentius, in *To Monimus*, book 1, says: "Predestination is nothing other than the preparation of the works of God, who in his eternal arrangement has foreseen that He will act either in mercy or justice."

4. This word 'predestination' is taken either in a more general sense as referring to the deeds of divine providence (both in good and in bad things, as can be seen in Acts 4:28 and 1 Cor 2:7), or as referring to the ordination of persons for a specific supernatural goal.

5. Taken in the latter sense (as we also do here), in Holy Scripture of the New Testament it is used exclusively as referring to the free decree of election, for this entire decree as great as it is (whether we are considering its means or its goal) depends on the merciful arrangement and efficacy of God alone.

6. At the same time we confess that, according to its common usage by Augustine and other ancient writers and according to Acts 4:28, the word 'predestination' is used correctly to refer to both reprobation and election, not as indicating categories that are synonymous in every respect, but only as analogous. For although the act of reprobation itself comes from God, yet not everything pertaining to reprobation stems from reprobation, as we shall see more clearly in what follows.

7. This divine predestination pertains also to angels, some of whom are called elect (1 Tim 5:21) while it says that others are "to be kept in darkness, bound with everlasting chains for judgment on the great day" (Jude 6). However, here we shall deal only with the predestination of human beings, since this concerns the Church of Christ in particular, and because Holy Scripture deals with it more frequently and fully.

8. So that we may discuss this whole doctrine to a point we deem sufficient, we shall—in due order—explain first the matter of election, and then also the difficult question of reprobation.

On Election
9. Taken in its original sense and by its common usage, the word 'election' (in Greek, *eklogē*) denotes choosing some people above others and out of others. Hence, they are also called elect who have been chosen for a certain political or ecclesiastical office (1 Sam 10:24, Luke 6:13); it also denotes a

certain people separated above other nations by God into the outward Church (Deut 4:37, 1 Cor 1:27). Therefore, also that election whereby some, above others, are said to have been chosen unto eternal salvation, should not be understood in some other way, as Christ himself testifies in Matt 20,16: "Many are called but few are chosen (KJV)." Likewise, the apostle says in Rom 11:7: "The elect obtained it, but the rest were hardened." In Holy Scripture, the word 'election' is used only in such a relation to others.

10. This election unto salvation is considered in two ways: first, insofar as it has been established from eternity in the decree of God who elects; secondly, insofar as, in time, the elect of God are actually called forth and taken from the world and engrafted into Christ through faith. About the latter Christ says in John 15:19: "You are not of the world but I have chosen you out of the world." Augustine elegantly combines those two elections in his *On the Predestination of the Saints*, chapter 17, by saying: "We have been chosen before the creation of the world by that predestination whereby God has foreseen his future acts; however, we are chosen out of the world by that calling whereby God has fulfilled what he has predestined."

11. Although these two elections originate from the same source and the latter is properly an effect of the former, this disputation of ours provides instruction especially concerning the first. Accordingly, in what follows we shall explain, one by one, its nature, its circumstances, its causes and its advantages.

12. For an understanding of its nature we must briefly point out several words that Scripture sometimes uses synonymously. The first of these is the term 'foreknowledge,' which the apostles use in Rom 8:29 and 1 Pet 1:2. It always occupies the top-most step on this ladder of election. This term is not used in the sense of God's simple knowledge by which He also knows the rejected, but in the sense of his approving knowledge and most wise counsel by which He knows those who are his. In this manner Christ says about his sheep: "I know my sheep and they know me" (John 10:14). A second term is 'predestination,' which the apostle uses in Rom 8:30 and Eph 1:4, etc. It denotes the actual determination of both the means and the goal, in those persons who already are foreknown. This is clear from Rom 8:29: "Those whom he foreknew he also predestined to be conformed to the image of his Son," etc. Then there is the word 'purpose,' which is used frequently in this subject-matter; it indicates the firm immutability of this divine counsel and,

at the same time, it points to the source of free grace from which this counsel flows. This becomes clear from the combination of two texts, first Rom 9:11: "In order that God's purpose according to election might continue, not because of works but because of Him who calls." And, secondly: "He saved us and called us with a holy calling, not according to our works but according to his own purpose, and grace, which is given to us in Christ Jesus before the world began" (2 Tim 1:9).

13. In order to explain the nature of this decree and divine counsel more fully, we shall present a fuller definition of it and, after that, examine the most important components of it.

14. And so we define election as the eternal and immutable decree of God whereby He chooses from the whole human race that had fallen by its own fault from pristine integrity into sin and destruction a specific number of individual people (neither better nor more worthy than others) solely out of his own good pleasure, unto salvation in Christ Jesus. He decided to give them to his Son in order to redeem them and lead them by a special and efficacious way of working to a living faith in him and to a sure perseverance in that same living faith. He did so in order to demonstrate his gracious mercy, and, to the praise of his glorious grace.

15. That this decree is eternal is shown in that the kingdom which will be possessed by those who are blessed of the Father has been prepared for them from the foundation of the world (Matt 25:34). This appears most clearly in the Epistle to the Eph 1:4: "He has chosen us in Him before the foundation of the world, that we should be holy and blameless before him in love."

16. The immutability of this decree is sufficiently shown by the very nature of God. Someone who changes his plan usually changes it either for a lack of wisdom when he was considering it, or because of a failure of power in carrying it out—neither of these defects can be attributed to God without blasphemy. Hence David exclaims: "The counsel of Jehovah stands firm for ever, his thoughts to all generations" (Ps 33:11).

17. Therefore the distinction that some people make between a complete and an incomplete election, and between a revocable and an irrevocable one, is utterly foreign to the truth. For Holy Scripture knows only one eternal election. It is always connected with a certain and infallible outcome, as is proven by Matt 24:24: "If it were possible, that the elect would be led astray"

and [verse] 22: "For the sake of the elect those days will be shortened." Consider also the 'ladder' of the apostle Paul in Rom 8:29: "For those whom He foreknew he also predestined etc." and "He called and justified and glorified them." And see also the affirmation of the same point by the apostle in Rom 11:2: "God has not rejected his people whom he foreknew," and verse 7: "The elect obtained it, but the rest were hardened," and many similar texts.

18. Although we willingly admit that the election unto salvation and the means of salvation can be considered separately, just as Scripture sometimes also presents them separately, yet we do deny that for this reason these acts are truly separate in God's decree. For He has determined all these things by one simple act, in the same way as He has known all things from eternity by one single act. But these things are said thus according to our way of thinking, because of the multitude of objects that this one act of electing includes, and we acknowledge that a certain order must have been assigned to these objects in eternity. It can be compared with someone who sees many things at once—sees them all at a glance—even though some order can and usually is arranged for those many things.

19. Hence, when the objection is raised that an orderly ranking of means is superfluous since the elect already are absolutely destined to salvation by a certain preceding act, this objection arises from a complete lack of understanding the orthodox point of view: God never elects someone unto salvation absolutely, if 'absolutely' excludes the means which God has appointed to attain that salvation. But such appointment to salvation in God's plan occurs from eternity, and in that same act it is always connected to a consideration of the means that are necessary for salvation. Therefore, Paul says in 2 Thess 2:13: "God chose us from the beginning to be saved through the sanctification of the Spirit and faith in the truth," and Peter writes "to those who have been elected according to the foreknowledge of God the Father and through the sanctification of the Spirit, unto obedience and the sprinkling of the blood of Jesus Christ" (1 Pet 1:1–2).

20. When a human being already has proposed for himself a certain goal and thereupon thinks about the means, or when he chooses beforehand one of many means above others, it implies deliberation on his part. This happens because his intellect is imperfect. For his intellect can only contemplate and choose these things in a successive order. But in the infinite act of divine

wisdom there is no place for such a successive act. But just as both the best goal and the most appropriate means to achieve it have, from eternity, been present simultaneously to God's mere understanding, also before any decree, so also the divine wisdom and will simultaneously have chosen and ordained this goal and the means that are best suited to his mercy and justice, within that same eternity, without any deliberative or consultative process.

21. The material from which God in his grace has chosen some people is the human race, fallen from its original integrity into sin by its own fault, and so liable to condemnation before him. For God established this election from no other human race than the one that would multiply in that state. In 1 John 5:19 Scripture indeed bears witness that "the whole world is subject to evil" and, in Rom 3:9[–10] that "all men, both Jews and Greeks, are under the power of sin and none is righteous, no, not one." And in verse 19: "Every mouth will be stopped and the whole world held accountable to condemnation by God. The conclusion from this is obvious: it is from this same human race that God has decided to choose his people from eternity.

22. And also, nearly all the texts that deal with this eternal election prove the point. "For we have been chosen in Christ that we should be holy" (Eph 1:4) and "He predestined us for adoption as children" (verse 5). Therefore, previously we were outside Christ, and unrighteous, and not fit for adoption as children. "We were chosen to salvation through the sanctification of the Spirit and in belief in the truth" (2 Thess 2:13). Therefore, previously, we were devoid of the sanctification of the Spirit and belief in the truth. "Those whom He foreknew He predestined, to be conformed to the image of Christ" and therefore the image of God was not in them (Rom 8:29). The elect are "vessels of mercy," just as the reprobate are "vessels of wrath" (Rom 9[:21–22]). In a proper sense, God is merciful to the miserable, just as He demonstrates his wrath and hate only towards sinners (Rom 1:18), not to mention the fact that Holy Scripture always passes from election to redemption or calling but never from election to creation in the image of God or to the fall and permission and ordering of sin, as those who 'ascend higher' are forced to state.

23. At the same time we confess that man had been created not with a changeable goal, and also that the fall of man did not occur without God's special providence. For if not even a sparrow falls to the ground without our Father, how much less the whole human race. "But, first of all, it was God's

will to demonstrate what a human being's free choice was able to achieve, and, next, what the benefit of his grace could do." Since God, in the infinite light of his wisdom, foresaw that man, created after his image, was going to abuse his free choice, together with his entire posterity, whereby the way would be revealed to the admiration of his justice and mercy, "He deemed it to be more fitting to his most almighty goodness to do well out of evil than not to permit evil to exist," as Augustine rightly observes.

24. Together with all the ancient authors and many great authors of the Reformed Church, in this decree of election we assign the foremost place to Christ as Head and Redeemer of the Church, just as He is called the "chosen servant of God whom his soul willingly accepts" or that "servant in whom his soul delights" (Isa 42:1, as quoted by Matt 12:18), and who in 1 Pet 1:20 is called "the lamb, known before the foundation of the world."

25. The fact that Christ was chosen for the purpose of redeeming the Church does not conflict with this. For even if we admit that God the Father—"from whom are all things, and who has reconciled us with himself through Christ" (2 Cor 5:18)—had the will or the disposition to bestow mercy upon some people as from that same time eternal He established Christ as Redeemer (and one cannot think of a redeemer apart from the persons who are going to be redeemed), nevertheless, the Scriptures do not call this will or disposition by itself 'election,' because this mercy was hindered by justice from destining salvation for sinners by a complete act unless satisfaction intervened, and because election not only includes the goal but also the means necessary for salvation, just as we have demonstrated in thesis 19.

26. But it goes by the name of election—and indeed is election—only then when Christ has been established as the Head and Mediator of those who are going to be elected, and when they themselves have been destined as his members. And in this respect, we are called "the elect in Jesus Christ" (Eph 1:4) and "those who have been predestined by Him unto adoption as his children" (verse 5); and "we were predestined to be conformed to his image so that He might be the First-born among many brothers" (Rom 8:29).

27. By this arrangement, even before they are fully united with Christ through faith, there is some specific connection and mutual relationship between him, as the head, and the elect, as the members destined for and given to him— and he received them in order to make them alive and gather them into one body. But while they of themselves are his enemies until that time, the

relationship is like that of a bridegroom with his bride whom he had to redeem for himself by his own blood; and it is like the relationship of a king and his subjects who were going to be restored to obedience through him.

28. And so it is that in the Scriptures the elect are called "the people of Christ" even before he had saved them from their sins (Matt 1:21) and they had not yet turned to him (Acts 18:10). They are also called "his sheep" for whom he lays down his life, although they were not yet brought to Him (John 10:26). Hence, they are called "the Church of Christ which he loved, and for which he gave himself up that he might sanctify her" (Eph 5:25[–26]). This means: even before he gave himself up for her and before he sanctified her. For "[God] has saved us and called us with a holy calling, not according to our works but according to his own purpose and grace which He gave us in Christ Jesus before the beginning of the world" (2 Tim 1:9). If the grace of this calling has been given to us in Christ, then it must have been given to us in him before we were considered to be believers, since faith arises from this calling and grace.

29. Consequently, although Christ's merit is not the cause of our election (because Christ's merit itself also derives from election), our election was not completed without a relationship to Christ's future merit, because Christ's future merit and his whole work of mediation take place among the objects of this election and are simultaneously the foundation of all those benefits that have been appointed for us by election.

30. The number of elect is known to God, but to us in this life it is unknown. And admittedly, that number is sometimes called the "little flock" (in contrast to the reprobate) and "the few who have been elected from the many who have been called" (Matt 20[:16]); and, "few are those who strive for salvation through the narrow gate and along the straight path," compared to the multitude that rushes to its destruction along the broad way and through the wide gate (Matt 7:13–14). However, when the number is considered by itself, it is such a multitude that all will be amazed, as we can see in Isaiah 49 (and likewise in chapters 60 and 66). In fact, it is a number beyond the one hundred and forty-four thousand who from among the Jews have been sealed. And so great was the number of those who out of every nation, people and tongue had appeared to John that no-one could count their number (Rev 7:9).

31. Now that we have explained most parts of our definition, the task remains for us to investigate the cause of this election which moved God to elect certain persons. For it is well-known that some people state that the impelling cause for election lies in the future good works which God foresaw that those to be elected either would do or would have done if they were to stay alive.

33. But this Pelagian theory was rightly rejected as heresy by the ancient Church, because it clearly contradicts what the apostle Paul says in Rom 9:11: "For before the children were born, before they had done anything good or bad, in order that God's purpose according to election might remain, not because of works but because of Him who calls, it was said: 'the elder shall serve the younger.'" And again, from Rom 11:5: "So too at the present time also there is a remnant according to the election of grace. And if by grace, then it is no more by works; otherwise grace would no longer be grace." And if neither calling nor justification is based on works—as Scripture everywhere testifies—then indeed also election itself, which pertains to all these things, cannot be based on works. But because this opinion has had few followers in the Reformed churches until this day, we shall not insist on continuing to refute it any further.

34. Another opinion, one that finds more supporters from among those who want to be members of the Reformed church, is of those people who deem that God decisively elected only those whose faith and perseverance He foresaw, at least as a prerequisite quality, and as a cause *sine qua non*. Hence, this election is nothing else than the allotment of the ultimate reward based on the fact that all required conditions had first been fulfilled.

35. If this point of view were to acknowledge that faith and perseverance in faith are merely gifts of God that are granted on the basis of a special grace to the persons to be saved, then it would differ from ours only in the order of the decree and in the way one speaks about it, while there would be agreement regarding its actual substance and basis. But because they evidently require beforehand such a faith and perseverance in it which partly have their origin in the gift of God but partly also in the free will of man, it can in no way be exonerated from the teaching of Pelagianism. And it conflicts with what the apostle says: "His praise is not from men but from God" (Rom 2:29), and that "it does not depend upon man's will or effort but upon God's mercy" (Rom 9:16). And: "Or who has first given a gift to God that he might be repaid? For from Him and through Him and to Him are all things" (Rom

11:35–36). See also 1 Cor 3:6[–7]: "Paul plants, Apollos waters, but God gives the growth. So, neither he who plants nor he who waters is anything, but God who gives the growth"—and a great many similar texts in which Scripture removes everything from man in order to ascribe everything to God, so that he who boasts, does not boast in himself but in God.

36. This point of view falls in line with the opinion that we refuted in thesis 33 and which they themselves sometimes condemn in their own writings, namely that election also occurs according to foreseen works on the pretext that no faith is saving faith except that which works through love (Gal 5:6), that moreover no faith perseveres unto salvation, except that which is adorned with its fruits (Matt 13) and accompanied by good works (Jas 2), and that, according to 2 Cor 5:10, on that great day the ultimate reward will also be given "according to what each person has done in the body, be it good or evil." Consequently, it is evident that if election occurs according to foreseen faith and perseverance, it is also according to the foreseen works that each person was going to do—partly by grace, partly by his own will and freedom (as they think).

37. Add to this the fact that this election of theirs is clearly redundant and that it bears no fruit for an elected person, neither in this life nor in the future life. Not in this life, because all the benefits that are required for believing and persevering must of necessity come before the ultimate perseverance in faith and in the obedience of faith. And not in the future life, because eternal life is due to those who persevere in faith by virtue of the general decree that "whoever believes and perseveres to the end shall be saved" [Matt 24:13]. They themselves acknowledge that the general decree comes before this decisive election of certain persons. One may compare it to this: if some supreme magistrate had composed a general decree whereby pardon would be granted to all pirates who return to the fatherland within a certain time, other decrees granting forgiveness a second time to every individual whom they knew were going to come home would be redundant and also foreign to every reasonable basis of wise action.

38. We shall not now present the individual cases from obvious texts of Holy Scripture that declare faith, holiness, and persevering in them as clearly stemming from election, such as Matt 24:24: "It is not possible that the elect are led astray." See also Acts 13:48: "And as many as were ordained to eternal life believed;" and Rom 8:29: "Those whom he foreknew he predestined,"

etc.; "and those whom he predestined he called." Also, Rom 9:11: "For while the boys were not yet born, and before they had done anything good or evil," etc., and similarly in Rom 11:4: "I have kept for myself seven thousand men," and "so too at the present time there is a remnant, chosen by grace" (verse 5), etc. And Eph 1:4: "For we were chosen in Christ before the foundation of the world that we should be holy." See also a great many other texts which can be found everywhere in the writings of the prophets and apostles. Thus far it has been impossible to overturn these texts by means of any restriction or contrary explanation, as we could easily demonstrate if we were not constrained to keep ourselves within the confines of these theses.

39. Consequently, on the basis of a great number of obvious texts of Holy Scripture we state that the cause which moved God to elect us above others is solely his good pleasure and undue grace. "For He has mercy on whom He has mercy and he has compassion upon whom He has compassion" (Rom 9:15); and "it does not depend upon man's will or effort, but upon God's mercy" (Rom 9:16); and again: "He has mercy upon whomever He wills" (Rom 9:18). Hence, he also said that "this purpose of election continues" (Rom 9:11), not because of works but because of the one who calls; that is, solely through the good pleasure of the one who is calling, as is required by the usage of this word everywhere. That is why this election is also called an election of grace in Rom 11:5. And therefore it says that "the God and Father of our Lord Jesus Christ has destined us to be his sons through Jesus Christ, according to the good pleasure of his will" (Eph 1:5).

40. But the consequence is not that this 'good pleasure' of God is ordained either by fate or at random (i.e., brought about with no specific reason), because God's will is never separated from his wisdom and so not from sound reasoning, but is always in accordance with it, even though it is only in God's kindly will towards us that we should take our repose. This is rightly pointed out by Augustine in his Epistle 105: "Because that whole lump of clay is justly condemned, justice renders the vessel of dishonor what it deserves, while grace bestows an honor undeserved, not for any privilege of merit, not by the inevitability of fate, not by some random fortune, but through the 'depth of the riches of the wisdom and the knowledge of God,' which the apostle does not reveal but admires as hidden. [In Rom 11:33–34,] he exclaims: 'O the depth of the riches of the wisdom and the knowledge of God, how inscrutable are his judgments and how unsearchable are his ways! For who knows the mind of the Lord or who has been his counselor?'" etc.

41. This doctrine provides many significant advantages to Christ's Church; for it teaches humility, it is the basis of solid trust in God, the source of spiritual joy and Christian hope, the true ground for consolation in adversities, for forbearance in suffering, for steadfastness in the face of the apostasy of others, a spur for gratitude towards God, for love towards the neighbor, and a great many other things. We could produce very clear instances of them from the sacred writings, if we were not striving after brevity.

42. But these advantages have their full impact only then when the elect are made more certain of their election. This does not depend on some spiritual enthusiasm or mindless investigation into divine judgments; it happens on the basis of its sure effects and signs, which profane people do not know—and despise—but which pious people discover in themselves with joy, following serious self-examination. Or, if these advantages perhaps fade away in them in times of temptation or through the believers' own negligence, believers make every effort to revive them in themselves by prayer, by listening to the Word, by using the sacraments, by conversations with fellow-believers and by works of charity, etc. Pious men have written ample treatises about these effects and signs, and they can all be included under calling according to the [divine] purpose, justification through faith, sanctification through the Spirit, and the seal of that same Holy Spirit as guarantee of our inheritance, as the apostle Paul says in a set order in his letter to the Rom 8:14 and following.

43. The ultimate goal of all these things is the demonstration of God's gracious mercy and the display of the riches of his glory towards the vessels of mercy which He has prepared for glory (Rom 9:23 and Eph 1:6). And with this goal we too happily reach our goal.

On Reprobation

44. Now that we have explained the first component of this predestination in this way, it remains for us to discuss the second element, too. For whereas the doctrine of reprobation has for a large part become clear from the preceding (because it is hardly possible to know and explain its nature without it), yet lest we leave anything out, and because this part seems completely opposed to human understanding, we shall put forth in a few words what we ought to think about this component, too, based on Scripture.

45. The word 'reprobate' refers in its proper sense to what is disapproved of and rejected, as in Jer 6:30, where God declares that the majority of the people "will be called rejected silver, because Jehovah has rejected and disapproved of them." The apostle uses this word in the same sense in 2 Tim 3:8 and Heb 6:8, and elsewhere.

46. Eternal reprobation, to which temporal reprobation corresponds because "God knows all his works from eternity" (Acts 15:18) is referred to in God's Word in two ways. The first way is negative, the second affirmative. Both provide convincing evidence for the fact that reprobation exists and both are sometimes used by way of synecdoche for reprobation as a whole.

47. First, the very word 'election' implies something negative, as we have pointed out previously. For the one who is choosing only some people, passes over and leaves aside others. Hence the apostle places the elect over against those who are left aside, when he says that "the elect have obtained [grace] and the rest were hardened" (Rom 11:7). Likewise, Christ addresses the workers of iniquity by saying, "I never knew you" (Matt 7:23), whereas the elect are called "those whom God knew beforehand" (Rom 8[:29], and elsewhere). He thus addresses the same [workers of iniquity] by saying: "But you do not believe because you are not of my sheep, as I said to you. My sheep hear my voice and I know them, etc." (John 10:26). So too in John 15:19: "I have chosen you out of the world, because the world hates you," and in John 17:9: "I do not pray for the world, but for those You have given me, for they are yours." In the same way, Rev 13:8 and 20:15 place "those who are written in the book of life" over against "those whose names are not written in the book of life of the Lamb."

48. Other ways of speaking include something affirmative as well as something of a more punitive nature, and they occur frequently. Such are: "The elder shall serve the younger" and "Esau I hated" (Rom 9:12–13). And "He hardens whomever He will" (Rom 9:18); there are "vessels made for honorable use" and "vessels of wrath made for destruction" (Rom 9:21, 22). Likewise, Peter declares that "they stumbled upon the rock of offense whereto they also were appointed" (1 Pet 2:8). And Jude calls them "people who long ago were marked out for this destruction" (Jude 4).

49. On the basis of the twofold way of speaking in this matter, leading theologians have made a distinction between negative and affirmative reprobation, which others respectively call 'a passing over' and 'pre-

damnation.' The nature of this dogmatic point will become clear when we explain the terms.

50. Negative reprobation refers to an eternal act of divine power and judgment whereby, in keeping with the counsel of his will, God did not resolve to have mercy on those whom He did not elect (to the extent that He would grant them that special and undue grace of election). Affirmative reprobation, however, is the act whereby He resolved to impose the punishments finally deserved upon those same people who had been left, justly, in the lump of perdition, or who abuse the light of nature and of the Gospel in various ways by their own free choice.

51. Both acts have sinful man as their object, sinful man liable to condemnation, as all the ancient authors rightly have observed, and which we have demonstrated above regarding election, just as the apostle also testifies: "Does not the potter have power to make from the same lump one vessel made for honorable use, and another for dishonorable?" (Rom 9:21). From this it becomes clear that God hates only sin, and in his certain judgment hardens only sinners, and that his wrath concerns sinners only, and that He makes fit for destruction or proscribes for judgment only those who rightly deserve it.

52. However, we should not take this to mean that these two acts were really different; for from eternity God within himself has determined everything in one single act, as we have pointed out above. We employ this distinction because various things are contained in the same divine decree, and because it has different aspects (i.e., the 'point from which' and the 'point to which'). For the point from which reprobation arises is the leaving-behind in the common corruption and liability. But the point to which reprobation leads is not only common damnation, but also the specific degree of damnation. Therefore, it is necessarily concluded that, as 'passing over' presupposes common sin, so also 'pre-damnation' in God's foreknowledge presupposes all the other particular sins that will be committed against the Law and against the Gospel—sins that would be deserving of such punishment.

53. Therefore it cannot be argued here that either act is an unjust one, for to not grant undue grace to someone who deserves rejection is not an act of injustice but of free judgment, as the apostle indicates when he says: "Does the potter not have the power to make from the same lump one vessel for honorable use and another dishonorable?" (Rom 9:21), and: "Who has ever

given a gift to him that he might be repaid?" (Rom 11:35). And again, to destine anyone to a specific degree of punishment proportionate to the particular and foreseen sin, is an act of vindictive justice, not an act of injustice, as the apostle declares: "What if God, willing to show his wrath and to make known his power, has endured with much patience the vessels of wrath made for destruction?" (Rom 9:22). If He has endured with much patience, therefore even in his foreknowledge He has endured those who abused this divine patience, and so, ultimately, it was to a just destruction that he ordained them.

54. In order to understand this correctly, it should be noted carefully that this 'passing over' does not remove or deny all grace from those who have been passed over, but only the grace that is peculiar to the elect. But the grace that is distributed to mankind in various amounts through the administration of general providence (whether under the law of nature or under gospel-grace) is not taken away by this act of 'passing over,' but rather is presupposed by it, since the non-elect remain under the general government of divine providence and under the exercise of their own free choice.

55. This administration of general providence, however, is always accompanied by that communication of external and internal benefits which in the state of integrity certainly was sufficient unto salvation. This is evident in the case of the rejected angels and the whole human race (as considered in its first parents before the fall). But in the state of corruption, so much of that communication remained (or was given additionally to nature under the Gospel), that when they appear before the divine judgment they are stripped and deprived of every pretext for an excuse, as the apostle testifies in Acts 14:27, Rom 1:20 and 2:1. Likewise, John 15:22, 1 Cor 4:3, and elsewhere.

56. And therefore the Synod of Orange (canon 25) rightly made the following distinction: "Not only do we not believe that by God's power some have been predestined to evil, but also that if anyone wants to believe such evil then we declare them 'anathema' with all detestation." For in those people God did not make the common sins but found them there, as we have noted before. And although God, in his just but to us hidden judgment, does abandon and harden them more and more (Rom 9:18), yet it is they who by their own free choice first become hardened (Rom 11:7) and abandon the benefits of general providence; they abuse God's longsuffering, as Paul testifies in Rom 1:18, 26, and 28. Likewise Rom 9:22, 2 Thess 2:11, and

elsewhere. But although the apostle Peter too, in chapter two of his first letter, says that "they were set to stumble on the rock of offense" [1 Pet 2:8], yet they are set to do this only because they deserve it by some antecedent ingratitude. And it happens in such a way and manner, that all praise of justice is for God, while for them there remains only all the blame. We shall deal with this way of hardening another time, God willing. But as to the fact that God either prevents the elect from abusing their free choice in the same way, or, if they have abused it, that they arise and repent, that has its origin in God's singular grace and mercy—which is owed to nobody—and not in their own choice.

57. From this it is clear that although sin is a condition that is presupposed in those who are going to be rejected (a cause that can be called a condition *sine qua non*)—yet the highest and adequate cause of reprobation is God's free power and his just will that is owed to no-one, since those on whom God had mercy were also sinners, who have abused or would abuse their free choice no less than the others do, if the grace of election had not prevented it. This is what the apostle says in Rom 9:18: "He has mercy upon whomever He wills, and hardens [the heart] of whomever He wills." See also verse 21: "Has the potter no right [over the clay]?" etc., and verse 22: "What if God, willing to show his wrath and to make known his power," etc.

58. And this will, however, is not absolute, as if it lacked a reason, nor is it a tyrannical will (even to use this word is blasphemy). Some interpret the term 'absolute' in this manner, thereby trying to arouse hatred towards us. But this will is very wise, most carefully arranged, and very holy. For, first of all, it is not possible to accuse someone of being a tyrant for claiming from a single offender or guilty person what is his right, even though he does not claim this from other persons who are equally guilty. This holds even more for the One who does so for good and holy purposes. "For if both were to be set free, it would remain unclear what was due to sin because of justice; and if nobody were to be set free it would remain unclear what grace would bountifully bestow" as Augustine (Epistle 105) asserts correctly and in accordance with the apostle in Rom 9:22 and 23.

59. Indeed, what is more, this will is not even absolute in the sense that there is no reason why in God's wisdom He would have rejected this person rather than another one (even if this reason should not be looked for in the diversity of merits), as Augustine correctly observes in his *The Good of Perseverance*,

chapter 11: "All the Lord's ways are mercy and truth; therefore, his mercy is beyond finding out, by which He has mercy upon whomever He wills, without any preceding merits. And the truth is beyond finding out, because He hardens whomever He wills, even if with preceding merits—but merits that for the most part are in common with the one upon whom He has mercy." And Prosper, writing to Rufinus on free choice says: "Since all have been laid low by Adam's transgression, there would have remained upon all of them a blameless justice unless a merciful grace selected some people. Therefore, to inquire into the cause or reason in God's counsel for this division is to go beyond human capability and it will not be known without destroying faith. Let us confess only that nobody perishes undeservedly and that nobody is saved deservedly."

60. Even Calvin himself and Beza have sometimes forcefully impressed this upon those who invented some such absolute will in God, as some Scholastics have done. Immediately at the outset, Calvin speaks about God's hidden providence in this way: "Though in my view God's will is the highest cause, I always taught that when there appears to be no cause in God's counsels and works, this cause lay hidden with Him, so that He decreed everything in a just and wise manner. Therefore, I not only reject but also detest the triflings of the Scholastics about absolute power, because they separate God's justice from his power." Likewise, Beza, in the *Colloquy of Montbéliard*, page 162: "Yet we never separate God's will or decree from justice and true and sound reason, and we believe that this will, though unfathomable even by angels, is very well arranged and for that reason we admire and adore it, but we do not acknowledge that there exists some other absolute will in God."

61. Therefore, all the malicious charges with which some people burden this doctrine will fall apart on their own. And accordingly, we assert that sometimes in Christ's Church this doctrine should be treated, and then with all modesty and on the basis of Scripture. From the present comparison God's favor towards us will shine all the more (as Paul points out in Rom 11:22)—so that because of this we humble ourselves so much more before God's judgments in order to honor and adore his (albeit sometimes hidden to us) justice and wisdom, as the apostle gives us an example in Rom 9:20 and 11:33, and following.

ON THE INCARNATION OF THE SON OF GOD AND THE PERSONAL UNION OF THE TWO NATURES IN CHRIST

President: Antonius Thysius
Respondent: Nicolaus Balbianus

This disputation is part of a group of disputations on Christology (25–29). In the first thesis Christ—or the incarnation of the Son of God, and the personal union of the two natures of Christ—is called the 'object of the Gospel and the basis for the new covenant' (1). In his incarnation, God's eternal Son humbled himself and assumed our flesh and blood from the virgin Mary by the working of the Holy Spirit. The Person of Christ, true God-and-man, was thus constituted in order to reconcile unto God those whom He had elected (4). The involvement of all three divine persons in the incarnation (6–8) is emphasized, as is the true deity (9–10) and true humanity of Christ (11–15). In thesis 18–20 the relationship of Christ's human nature to the Fall and to sin is explained. Because of the supernatural mode of his conception, Jesus Christ was a unique man (21), but otherwise he was like all other human beings, subject to the same natural processes (22) and historical determination (23) of time and place. The manner whereby the only-begotten Son of God became flesh is through the direct union of the person of God's Son with human nature, or through the assumption of human nature in one and the same person. In this context the Synopsis uses the Greek word 'anhypostasis' (24). Whereas 'hypostasis' means that which subsists, 'an-hypostasis' denotes that which does not subsist on its own; the human nature of the Son of God did not constitute a person. In other words, apart from the incarnation, or earlier time, there was no human person that existed independently. The person of the Christ is dependent on the union, hypostatically, of the humanity and the divinity of Christ; this is unique insofar as in beings who are mortal the human nature consists of a hypostasis that is independent. It is this hypostasis or personal union of the divine and human natures that is called Christ, Emmanuel, the God-and-man (26). The mutual relationship of both natures in the one person is discussed (27–38). This all points to the purpose and goal of the Son's incarnation: to fulfill the office that the Father had placed on Him, to obtain our salvation, and to glorify God (40–42). The disputation closes with five 'antitheses' in which the opinions of Jewish thinkers, pseudo-Christians like the Arians, and those who attack the classical understanding of the hypostatic union, such as the Ubiquitarians, are rejected.

1. We have now treated Law and Gospel (including the Old and New Testaments that are bound up with them) and their similarities and differences. So too for Predestination, first, regarding Christ, and thereafter his members, who are in him. It follows that we should next give separate treatments of what is the object of the Gospel and the basis for the new covenant, namely, the person of Christ, or the incarnation of the Son of God, and the personal union of the two natures of Christ.

2. Second to the mystery of the Holy Trinity—namely of three persons in one essence, whereby the three persons, though really distinct from each other, have one and the same essence and are united in an essence that is numerically one—the highest mystery is the one whereby two complete natures are joined together into the one person of the Son of God. Therefore, the apostle calls the mystery that "God was made manifest in the flesh, the great mystery of godliness" (1 Tim 3:16).

3. For this reason also it cannot be taught, or grasped, by human reasoning, because in the entire realm of nature no example for it can be found that matches it perfectly and completely—although it does not conflict with sound reasoning. But it must be taught and shown in a divine manner from Scripture, and it must be grasped with the eyes of faith. And herein lies the evidence that the teaching of God's Word is exalted and obviously divine, and since it reveals and unfolds to us things about God and his economies that surpass human reasoning, we must accept them with great confidence through faith in the testimony of the God who bears the most truthful witness about himself.

4. Well then, the incarnation is a work of God whereby the Son of God—according to the economy of the divine counsel of the Father, himself, and the Holy Spirit—humbled himself, and took upon himself in the unity of his person true, whole, complete and sacred flesh from the virgin Mary, through the Holy Spirit's efficacious activity. He did so in such a way that the flesh

does not exist on its own or apart from the Son of God, but it is maintained and borne by and in him. The two natures, each in its entirety, were united with each other unaltered, unmixed, undivided and inseparate. Out of these the person of Christ, the God-and-man, is constituted, and for this purpose: that he could fully perform the tasks of the mediator before God, that he would reconcile men to God and unite them to him, and that he would reconcile the elect and unite them to God and would bestow on them righteousness, holiness, and eternal life, for the demonstration of God's justice and for the praise of his mercy.

5. In setting forth and defining this thesis, the first term is 'incarnation,' which comes from John 1:14: "The word was made flesh." The Greeks also use the term 'taking on the nature of man,' from the Letter to the Philippians 2:7, "made in the likeness of man." And according to this wording, the Father is said "to have sent his Son in the flesh" (Rom 8:3), and he himself "was sent and came in the flesh," or "by the flesh" (1 John 4:2). "He received the form of a slave" (Phil 2:7), "he took upon himself the offspring of Abraham" (Heb 2:16), and "he was made partaker of our flesh and blood." In the same way it says: "In Christ the full Godhead dwelled in bodily form" (Col 2[:9]), "manifested in the flesh" (1 Tim 3:16), "being found in human form as a man" (Phil 2:8).

6. Well then, if we take the word 'incarnation' in an active sense, it is the work of God. In fact, like every work and activity that God performs, as they say, 'outside of himself' (i.e., what has a relationship external to God), it is common to the whole Trinity. However, the order and the rank [within the Trinity] is kept in the case of the actions, as it is in the case of the divine persons. It happens in such a way that the source of the action comes from the Father, and consequently relates to him. the means of the action lies in the Son, who is the "wisdom of the Father," while the outcome is with the Holy Spirit, inasmuch as he is the strength and power of God most high, through whom the action is carried out. And we should understand it in this way both regarding the decree and the work itself. And as far as the outcome of the incarnation is concerned, the word is used especially of the Holy Spirit (Matt 1:18, 20; Luke 1:35); therefore, in the Creed it says, "conceived by the Holy Spirit."

7. Moreover, the incarnation is a work of God's economy of salvation. That is to say, it is a gracious act of the divine will, following the sure and wise

counsel befitting the order and action that is to be performed, namely for the restoration of our salvation begun and performed through a suitable arrangement (or dispensation) made between the divine persons. It is fitting that the Father takes on the specific roles of the one who sends, the Son of the one who is sent and who comes in the flesh and into the world, while the Holy Spirit takes on the tasks specific to the one who executes the action and prepares a body fit for the Son.

8. When this economy (the name which the early church fathers, following the apostle in Ephesians 1, gave to the incarnation) is in relation to the Son or when incarnation is taken in a passive and subjective sense, then it is not the Father or the Holy Spirit, but only the Son of God who became incarnate or was made man, as Scripture everywhere testifies (Luke 1:35; John 1:14; Rom 1:3; Gal 4:4; Phil 2[:7 and 8]). Nevertheless, it was by the will and good pleasure of the Holy Trinity that he became incarnate.

9. Accordingly, it is the person of the Son of God, and not his nature (which is common to the three persons), that strictly speaking became incarnate (John 1:14)—unless we consider the nature by which the Son is, as distinct by the unique manner of [his nature's] existence. Not because it is different from the deity of the Father or the Holy Spirit, but because it is considered as different in the way in which it is possessed [by the Son]: "God was manifested in the flesh" (1 Tim 3:16); and "in him the whole fullness of the Godhead dwells bodily" (Col 2:9).

10. Therefore the Son of God, who has been in existence from eternity (Prov 8:22, 23, etc.)—"the word which was from the beginning, which was with God, and which was God" (John 1:1), "who was there before Abraham" (John 8:58), "existing in the form of God" (Phil 2:6)—that Son, I say, though he is of the same substance, equal and co-eternal, in time was made flesh (John 1:14).

11. When it says that he was made flesh, it does not mean a phantom of him, but a real body, existing of flesh, bones, and blood (Matt 14:26; Luke 24:39; Heb 2:14). By synecdoche this means that he was a whole man, made up of a physical body and a rational soul, the essential parts of human nature.

12. Indeed, he was a complete man, endowed with the natural and also essential properties, which are part of man in a necessary and inseparable way. Such properties belong to the whole human nature, namely that it is

created and finite; or the properties belong to one part of [human nature,] i.e., the soul, namely that it is incorporeal, invisible, not capable of suffering physically, possessing intelligence and a will, etc. Or [the properties belong] to the other part [of human nature], i.e., the body, namely that it exists regarding quantity and by certain delineations; it has separate body-parts, is defined by a certain size, and regarding quality; it has a shape, can be seen and touched (Luke 24:39; John 20:27; 1 John 1:2).

13. And the parts of human nature happen to have accidental properties which can be separated from it and which can be altered or even removed altogether. In the soul such qualities include: a measure of wisdom (Isa 7:16; Luke 2:40); its emotions, such as being sorrowful unto death (Matt 26[:38], etc.). In the body: a measure of stature (Luke 2:40), hunger, thirst, eating, drinking, tiredness, sleep, bodily pain, tears, sweating blood, etc. (Matt 4:2; John 4:6; Matt 11:19; Matt 8:24; Luke 19:41; Luke 22:44).

14. In short, the name 'flesh' not only means a true, entire, and complete man, of the same substance as we are, but it also entails the humble, wretched, and weak human condition (which nevertheless was so in him [i.e., Christ] only for a time, because of his first state). For this reason, it is said that he took on "the form of a servant" (Phil 2:7), that "from being Lord he was made servant" (John 13:13–17), that "though rich he became poor" (2 Cor 8:9), "having similar feelings" and "like us in every respect" (Heb 2:17, and 4:15). All of these things he underwent readily and willingly.

15. It was such a man that the Son of God became; a man indeed, inasmuch as he was born of man, that he might be a brother to us. That is to say, he was not created directly by God, as the first man was, from the earth. Nor did he descend from heaven in his own essence, but he was brought forth from the self-same blood of Adam (Acts 17:26), while his soul was fashioned in his body in the normal manner, and joined and united with it. For this reason, he traces also his genealogy from Adam (Luke 3:38). He is called "the Son of Man" (Matt 8:20, and 10:23), and "our brother" (Heb 2:17).

16. From the perspective of the promise, however, he is separately called "seed and son of the woman" (Gen 3:15), "of Abraham, in whose offspring all the nations receive the promise of future blessing" (Gen 12:3; 22:18; Gal 3:18), "of Isaac" (Gen 26:3 and 4), "of Jacob" (Gen 28:14). And then "of Judah," and "from his tribe" (Gen 49:10; Heb 7:14), "of David" (2 Sam 7), and so "shoot and flower of Jesse" (Isa 11:1), and "sprung from the loins of

David" (Acts 2:30), and even simply "David" since he was descended from him and prefigured by him.

17. But his descent is traced particularly to Abraham and David as his ancestors, since the promise had been made especially to them (Matt 1:1). And his descent is traced from Abraham to David through Solomon according to the law, and through Nathan by nature (Matt 1[:1–17]; Luke 3[:23–38]), so that in this way the divine promise might reach its fulfillment.

18. But the word 'flesh' does not mean 'flesh that has been corrupted,' in the sense that one normally understands it to be the opposite of the Spirit (John 3:6), but it does not share in the universal fall into sin (Luke 1:35; Heb 4:15). For it was not fitting that the human nature that is subject to sin be united with the Son of God. And yet "he came in the likeness of sinful flesh," or [of flesh] subject to sin (Rom 8:3), as he bore the traces of it in his weakness.

19. For this reason it is proclaimed that he would be born "not of blood, nor of the will of the flesh or of man" [John 1:13] (that is, by way of a man's semen), but without a man's intercourse, by the power of the Holy Spirit, "from a woman" ("whose seed" he is called, Gen 3[:15]) and "from a virgin" (Isa 7[:14]). And expressly from a woman, the blessed virgin Mary, who was engaged to be married to a certain Joseph for her good reputation, her wellbeing, and her care (Matt 1:19–20)—a man who had no carnal knowledge of her (Matt 1:25). It says that he was born of her substance (Gal 4:4; Matt 1:18 and 20), he is the "fruit of her womb" (Luke 1:42); she is "his mother" while he is "her son," even "her first-born son." And just as he was 'without mother,' according to his divine nature, it is declared that he was 'without father,' according to his human nature (Heb 7:3).

20. And so it was beyond the natural way of things that "he was conceived," i.e., "from the Holy Spirit," by the direct working of his power, as he made fruitful the blood and seed that was gathered in and of the virgin Mary and conceived in her womb, in order to turn seed that was otherwise ill-suited into seed suitable for generation. In this regard, therefore, it is particularly said not that he was begotten, but made (Rom 1:3; Gal 4:4). And moreover [the Spirit] took what was conceived and cleansed it from every blemish and uncleanness that was in Mary as it is in all people, and he made it holy, and further kept it holy (Job 14:4, Ps 51:7). And so, "that which is conceived in her is called holy" (Luke 1:35).

21. And as far as the supernatural mode of this conception is concerned, and the Holy Spirit's efficacy in it, the "first Adam" is compared and contrasted in some way to the "second Adam" (or "second man") insofar as he is a unique man. For the former is said to have been made from the earth, while the latter descended from heaven. In other words, [the comparison is] not in the substance of body but in the way in which they are conceived (Rom 5:14; 1 Cor 15:45, 47; John 3:13 and 6:41, etc.).

22. But as for the other aspects of his incarnation, he was formed in a natural way, or according to the usual order of nature, in the womb of the virgin Mary, nurtured, nourished, and carried for nine months. And when the right time came for birth, and nature's restraints were set free and the womb was opened, then he was born and brought forth; and thereupon he was nursed and reared (Isa 7:14, 15; Luke 1:56 and 2:6, 23, 40, 42 and 11:27).

23. And so he was born man, at a time and place chosen by God, and when the time was right, i.e., "at the very last time of the world" (Isa 2[:2]), "when the fullness of time had come" (Gal 4:4), "when the scepter had departed from Judah"—that is, when Augustus was ruler over the Jews (Gen 49:10; Luke 2[:1])—towards the end of the seventy weeks that Daniel had foretold (Dan 9), and "in Judea, in the city of David, Bethlehem" (Mic 5:1; Matt 2:1, 5; Luke 2:4).

24. The manner whereby the only-begotten Son of God became flesh is through the direct union of the person of God's Son with human nature, or through the assumption of human nature in one and the same person (Phil 2:7; Heb 2:16). It so happened that the Son of God, as the second eternal person of the Holy Trinity, did not take on himself a pre-existing person, but from the moment of conception he assumed something 'an-hypostatic,' that is, something without a proper hypostasis or subsistence. He assumed it [i.e., human nature or flesh] into the union of his person, and caused it to be his own; so that flesh has no subsistence apart from the Son of God, but it exists and subsists in him, and by him it is borne and sustained.

25. And thus the Son of God commenced to be the Son of Man, remaining what he was and undertaking to be what he was not—but not that anything had to be added to make him complete. Meanwhile, the Son of Man became the Son of God; i.e., what the Son of God was by nature that is what the Son of Man became, by the grace of union. And for this reason, Mary is called the

"mother of the Lord," Luke 1:35, while the ancients called her bearer-of-God.

26. The mutual union (or unity) of the natures is closely linked to this direct union of the person who assumes and the nature that is assumed, as a property that belongs to it [i.e., to this latter union]. Hereby two entire natures, the divine and the human one, are mutually united, but not naturally in one nature, that is not in one essence and its essential properties. This union occurs into one person hypostatically, i.e., through the mediating action of the hypostasis of the Son of God. This hypostasis, thus having been constituted (but not compounded) of the divine and the human nature, is called the Christ, Emmanuel, or the God-and-man.

27. This is a personal union (though not a union of persons), a union of two natures (though not a natural union), and it came about 'without confusion and without change.' It was made in such a way that the two natures, along with their essential properties and actions, were not mutually confused, nor was the one mixed in with the other, nor was the one turned into the other, nor were they somehow destroyed. That is, God was not changed into man, nor was man changed into God; and man was not swallowed up in God, nor was a third person made up from man and God. But each remained whole and unchanged, so much so that there is a two-fold nature in Christ, and divine as well as human faculties, wisdom and knowledge, will, power, action and activity (John 2:24–25; Mark 13:32; Luke 2:52; John 10:30; Luke 22:42). For in Christ there exists one thing as well as another.

28. The personal union also occurred 'without division and without separation,' in such a way that the one nature is not actually divided or segregated from the other (for at no time or place, not even in death, does he lose what once he had taken up and joined to himself). But both natures forever remain so united in the person that there is no formation of two Christs, of which the one is the Son of God and the other Mary's son, but there is one Son of God manifested in the flesh. For in Christ there does not exist one person as well as another.

29. From this union there arises a communion of natures, so that the disposition of one nature depends on and corresponds to the other. For just as the two natures and their properties are truly and really united with each other through the person who mediates them, so also does the one nature have communion and fellowship with the other, so that the communion is

real also, like the union. To be sure, these are so closely connected that the ancients, following the Letter to the Hebrews 2:14, frequently put 'communion' for 'union.'

30. Therefore, for the sake of the union, "the Word," the assuming person, freely granted the assumed human nature to exist in it, by the grace of union. But also, to carry out such a great task, by the efficacy of its power, the Word truly shared with it the Spirit, and the spiritual and excellent gifts, without measure (Isa 11:1–3; John 3:34; Luke 2:52). As a result, in the man Christ these things reside subjectively and habitually (so to speak). Therefore, this grace is also called 'habitual.' These gifts, however, as they are natural and supernatural, by which nature is perfected are not contrary to nature, in which case it would be destroyed.

31. In performing the duties of his office and all the things that go with it (the things that apply to Christ with respect to both natures) the one nature shares and behaves in consort with the other nature (except that each nature's special properties and order of conduct are unaffected). Thus while each nature has its own operations, the work that is completed by them is a work of the one 'God-and-man.' Thus it is according to both natures that he is the Savior, Mediator, Head of the Church, etc.

32. And the phraseology that arises in relation to this subject-matter is either 'proper' or 'improper.' Proper phraseology is when that which belongs only to one of the two natures is attributed to that nature by different words (used for signifying each nature on its own). Proper phraseology occurs also when to the person, or to what is denominated from either nature, is attributed a property or action of that same nature by a concrete term (which connotes the nature together with the person). Such as: "The Word was in the beginning, it was with the Father, it was God, through whom all things were made" (John 1[:1–3]); "unto us a child is born" (Isa 9[:5]); "the Son of Man is handed over to the hands of sinners, he is crucified and he is raised" (Matt 17:12; 20:19, and 26:2).

33. The phraseology is similarly 'proper' when that which belongs to both natures (or is shared by them) is attributed to the person as denominated from both natures, so that the predicate is equal to the subject. Such words are those that indicate the office or status of the person, such as, Christ is the Savior, Prophet, Priest, King of his Church, etc. All such predications are made in the strict and proper sense.

34. On the other hand, 'improper phraseology' occurs when a property that is common to both natures is attributed to the person denominated from [only] one of the two natures; or, on the other hand, when the property or action of [only] one of the two natures (even the opposite property or action) is attributed concretely to a person denominated from both natures. This improper phraseology is a synecdochical manner of speaking; and that is why, by means of some distinguishing particle that has been expressly added or implied, an attribution is indicated that is not equal, such as: "Christ is from the Israelites," "according to the flesh" (Rom 9[:3]), "from the loins of David," "as far as the flesh is concerned" (Acts 2[:30]), "he suffered, was put to death in the body, made alive in the Spirit" (1 Pet 3[:18], and 4[:2]; 2 Cor 13[:4], etc.). Likewise, "Christ is the Son of David, Christ is David's Lord" (Matt 22:42, etc.). For this reason, theologians make the common distinction between 'the whole Christ' and 'the whole of Christ,' or Christ 'whole' and 'wholly.'

35. Improper phraseology occurs also when a predicate of one nature is concretely said of the person named from the other nature, by reason of the unity of the person, as when all human things are said of the person named from the divine nature. Such as: "The Son of God was made from the blood of David according to the flesh" (Rom 1[:3]); "the God of glory was crucified" (1 Cor 2[:2]); "God redeemed the Church with his own blood" (Acts 20[:28]), etc. The same happens when all the divine things are said [of the person named] from the human nature, such as "the Son of Man descending from the heaven is in heaven" (John 3:13 and 6:62); "The Lord is from heaven" (1 Cor 15[:47]; Ps 47). All these things should be understood according to one or the other nature.

36. The ancients have given different names to this manner of speaking. The terms are as follows: 'interchange', 'alteration', 'conjunction', 'association', and 'mutual placing of a word' or 'the device of putting one instead of the other'. Cassian calls it synecdoche and also a double synecdoche—first in the subject and then in the predicate. The Scholastics call it 'a communication of idioms or properties.'

37. To be sure, this kind of speech is real in the person and proper to him, in order to indicate the closest connection of the two natures in the one Christ; but in the separately considered nature it isn't even a verbal kind of speech. And yet concerning the person, with respect to nature, the verbal kind of

speech (the kind that pertains to an explanation of the wording) is improper, or as some prefer to call it, unusual.

38. Something close to this occurs when an attribute is bestowed on the person that in itself does not match him according to either of the two natures, but only with relation to the other nature. In this way it says: "The Son of God," or "the Son of Man descended from heaven" (John 3[:13] and 6[:33, 38, 41, 42, 50, 51, and 58]), and "the Lord from heaven" (1 Cor 15[:47]). This must first and foremost be understood with respect to the hypostatic union, "having emptied himself, and having been exalted, all power in heaven and on earth was given to Christ" (Matt 28[:18]). That which the Son of God possesses from eternity was given to and accepted by the Son of Man in time.

39. And so from these things, namely, the assumption of human nature by the Son of God, the union and communion of the two natures, and finally, the corresponding phraseology, it is clear what distinguishes the man Christ from other men, even the most holy men. For in him "all the fullness of the Godhead dwells bodily" (Col 2[:9]). For the Son of Man is the Son of God, and whatever is the Son of Man's is of the Son of God.

40. And finally, the goal of his incarnation is to accomplish the office that the Father had placed on him, and to obtain our salvation (Isa 9:6; Luke 2:7). He had to be a man, a true man in fact, so that true salvation for the man who had sinned might be obtained through a man. A complete and whole man, consisting of a soul and a body, and of their essential properties, so that the entire man might be restored, in body and especially in soul. He was lowly, weak, and mortal, so that he could suffer, pour out his blood, and die (for there is no redemption without death, and death is the price of redemption). "Man of man," or Son of Man, so that he should not make atonement by means of another nature. He was made "from a virgin" in a supernatural way by the power of the Holy Spirit, and having been sanctified by him, so that he as unique and set apart from sin, would be able to take sin away and save us (Isa 53; Matt 1:21, 23; Heb 2:9, 14, 16, and 7:26, etc.).

41. He had to be the "Son of God," or, the Son of God had to assume human nature in the unity of person, and to unite the two natures with each other, and to have one nature in communion with the other, so that from the Godhead the worthiness and merit of what he did and what he underwent would be eternal, and the work of redemption would be entirely perfect, and the application of it in the elect would be effective. And to the end that men,

who were separated from God through sin, by the intervention of the Mediator, and by his justice and holiness might be made one with God, might receive the right of sonship and obtain the inheritance of eternal life (John 6:35, 51; Acts 2:28; Heb 9:14, etc.).

42. The more removed, or distant, goal is the most excellent display of the wisdom, justice, and mercy of God, and his love for mankind, to the praise of him and his eternal glory.

Antitheses

Ant. 1. In the first place we reject the Jews who say that the Messiah has not come in the flesh, and who place the goal of his coming in benefits that are temporal.

Ant. 2. Thereafter we reject pseudo-Christians, of which there are several kinds. First are those who refuse to acknowledge the eternal Son of God and who deny his true deity. Such are:

1. Arius, and Ochinus (who has revived Arianism in our time), because he held the view that the *Logos* [Word] was made before all times, was joined to the body and poured into it instead of a soul.

2. Paul of Samosata, and Photinus, along with Servetus and Socinus who in our time have put his ungodly belief forward again. They claim that Christ was god-bearer while being a mere man, and so deny the hypostatic union.

3. Sabellius and Praxeas, the Libertines and some Anabaptists of our day, who construct God as having three distinct names, erase the real distinction of the persons, bring forward only a different way in which God reveals himself, and think that it was actually the Father who became incarnate and suffered.

4. Lastly, the Tritheists of former times, and Valentinus Gentilis, who has brought back their heresy. By splitting up the essence of God, they hold the view that just as the person became incarnate, so too the essence in an absolute way.

Ant. 3. The second kind [of pseudo-Christians] are those who erase Christ's human nature. Such are:

1. Marcion and those like him, who taught that the man Christ was only

a phantom and an apparition.

2. Valentinus and Manes, who hold the view that a body from heaven, a heavenly body, or a body of rudimentary elements was put into Mary. Their error has been brought back by some of the Anabaptists.

3. Apollinaris, who denied that Christ had a rational soul, and who substituted the soul with the Son of God.

Ant. 4. And then there are those who attack his hypostatic union. Such as:

1. Nestorius, who held that as in Christ there are two natures there are also two persons, and that the act of uniting happened not according to person but according presence, indwelling, and relation.

2. Eutyches, who taught the opposite: that just as there is one person so the natures are one in Christ, by confusing and intermingling the two natures. So too for that whole breed of Eutyches, the Monophysites, Monothelites, and Acephalites.

3. And next, those who today are allied with them, namely the Anabaptists, Mennonites, followers of Schwenckfeld, and the Ubiquitarians, who define the hypostatic union of the divine properties (omnipotence, omniscience, and omnipresence) as a real outpouring and sharing in the flesh.

Ant. 5. And then finally, those who destroy the goals of his incarnation, like that faulty Faustus Socinus, and others who have made void the merits of the life and suffering of Christ.

SOURCES

Ambrose, *On the Orthodox Faith, Against the Arians*, chapter 8

He emptied himself by taking the form of a servant, not to become something other than what he was (that is, not to be changed from what he was), but so that by putting aside the honor of his majesty for a period of time, he might take for himself a human body, that by taking it up he might become salvation unto the gentiles. For it is like the sun when it is hidden by a cloud that conceals but does not cut off its brightness, and like the light, scattered all around the world and filling everything with its bright splendor, that is obstructed by the little hindrance of a cloud. In the same way that man, whom God took upon himself, did not in the man remove God, but merely hid him from view.

ON THE OFFICE OF CHRIST

President: Johannes Polyander
Respondent: Nicolaus Reusius

The one office of Christ as Mediator has three aspects: prophetic, priestly, and royal. As prophet, priest, and king Christ made atonement for our sins through his mediatorial sacrifice. Several important terms and concepts in the Reformed understanding of the doctrine of salvation are covered in thesis 3. The Lord Jesus Christ became our 'sponsor'; He took upon Himself the debt we owe; the payment for that debt is expressed by 'expiation' or 'propitiation.' The phrase 'altar of the cross' makes it clear that these terms should be seen in the context of sacrifice: the guilt that arises from transgression has been removed, and the debt that is owed has been paid. The Latin theological phrase 'pactum salutis' that is employed to express the eternal covenant that exists between the three persons of the Trinity arose from the understanding of Christ's own offering of himself to the Father. The notion that satisfaction for sins through Christ's death is not necessary for salvation, as the Socinians taught, is rejected (12, 20–22). In this context, attention is paid to the fact that Christ underwent the death on the cross for which He had been pre-ordained both out of necessity and of his own accord (12–15). The relation of Christ's office as Mediator to the Trinity and his divine and his human nature is treated and defended against several false teachings (16–31), with some axiomatic statements on the topic in thesis 25. Thereafter, the question is raised whether Christ should be called the Mediator also of the good angels (34–36). The three parts and functions Christ performed in his mediatorial office—that of prophet (39–41), priest (42–50), and king (51–54)—and which can be discerned together only in Christ, are treated in the remainder of the disputation (37–54, summary in thesis 38). The discussion of the royal aspect of Christ's office ends in an eschatological perspective: Christ will hand over all the elect together with his mediatorial scepter to his Father (53).

1. The entire disputation about Jesus Christ is arranged into two main questions, of which we very recently have treated the first, about the person of Christ. Now we shall answer the second question, the one about his office.

2. We should consider Christ's office in two ways: either generally, universally, according to the sense of it as a whole, or piece by piece, according to the arrangement of its parts. If it is considered universally, the office consists of one role, namely that of Mediator. If it is examined piecemeal and by its parts, the office is three-fold: prophetic, priestly, and kingly.

3. Christ's office as Mediator is the one whereby, following the decree of the most holy Trinity, Christ freely offered himself to his Father—as it was He whom we had offended by our guilt of treason—as our sponsor and the propitiator for our sins, so that by expiating for them through his own obedience accomplished in our place on the altar of the cross he might bestow eternal righteousness on us who believe in him. By this righteousness he would restore us completely into the grace of his Father, and into the inheritance of life eternal, from which we had fallen through the fall of Adam (1 John 2:2; Col 1:20).

4. The most holy Trinity deemed it suitable to place this office not upon angels, nor on men, but on Christ the Emmanuel alone. It was not placed upon angels, for, since their own power is limited and dependent solely on God's grace to preserve it, they themselves were not able to bear the massive burden of his boundless wrath, nor themselves able to produce from their own, changeable righteousness, that eternal righteousness which could appease God completely, in the name of sinners. He did not place it upon men, for since the guilt of sin has implicated them all, they could not have presented from their own blood anyone who was without guilt, as he could not pay the penalty for even his own sins, let alone those of others. It was placed only on Christ the Emmanuel, because by his own human nature he alone was able to undergo the punishments we deserved; and by his divine nature he alone could overcome them and turn them to our salvation.

5. Having pity on our condition, Christ accepted the office that was placed on him, in order to make us from being sons of Adam and hell into sons and heirs of God, by making peace with the Father through the blood of the cross, and by obtaining the grace of adoption for us (Col 1:20; John 1:12 and 20:17).

6. And so it follows that the efficient or constitutive cause of the mediating work of Christ is God's eternal decree. The impelling cause, the one that drove God in himself to demand the mediating work of Christ, was his favorable will and good pleasure toward us, his love (Luke 2:14; John 3:16; 1 John 4:9,10).

7. Moreover, God deemed that the most fitting display of his own great love towards us would be to not spare his own and only-begotten Son, but to hand him over to punishment for the sake of us all. Thus, he would be the propitiation for our sins, and, having reconciled us unto him through atonement in his blood, to sanctify us and take us as adopted children into eternal glory with him (John 3:16; Rom 8:32; 1 John 4:9; Rom 3:25; Heb 2:10).

8. He also deemed that it would be a very fitting declaration to us of his wisdom, truth, righteousness, mercy, and power jointly together if in his own Son, sent to us in the likeness of the flesh that is under the rule of sin, he should smite our sins that by the Law's warnings deserved horrible death. In this way he would condemn and even abolish the sins in his flesh, while delivering us and also accomplishing his justice (Gen 2:17; Gal 3:10; Rom 3:25 and 8:3,4).

9. Augustine thinks that we should give the following answer to the question whether God lacked another means of delivering us from the misery of this death. No other means more befitting God's worthiness existed or should have existed, for curing us of our misery than through Jesus Christ as the Mediator between God and men. Nevertheless [says Augustine], if we consider his infinite and for us inexplicable wisdom, and his absolute power (to which everything is equally subject), another possible means was available to him (*On the Trinity*, book 13, chapter 10).

10. Even though Augustine's answer is an upright and prudent one (and consequently is approved by some orthodox theologians), nevertheless I see no reason why we should worry and weary ourselves with untangling that question, since the sacred writings everywhere testify that God's eternal and fixed decree had determined only that special way to redeem us through Christ.

11. Even so, to touch on that question briefly, our answer is that one would be foolhardy to investigate (let alone contrive) any method of obtaining salvation for us other than the one we pointed out above from the Word of

God. It is a question we would do better to pass over in silence than to broach so inopportunely. One can judge for oneself how risky it is to wrangle in either direction over the question that Augustine had put forward so long ago. One can judge this also from the latest example of the Schoolmen, who debated the question amongst themselves like Peripatetics, and gave to some people a reason to call into question the truth and need of assigning the work of mediation to Christ, and to others a reason to deny it altogether.

12. The leading member of this group is that godless miscreant, Socinus, who in our current age did not hesitate to maintain that God not only is able but even ought to grant us remission of sins without such manner of satisfaction that sacred Scripture ascribes to our Mediator, Jesus Christ. For he denies that [God] placed on Christ the two-fold hypothetical necessity of reconciling the human race in that way and manner defined from sacred Scripture in thesis three (above), of which the first necessity depends on God's immutable decree and the second on the infallible truth of God's predictions. For this reason, we call the first necessity that of immutability, and the second one the necessity of infallibility.

13. In Luke 24:25 Christ speaks in this way about the second necessity, while he has also the first necessity in view, when he addresses his disciples with these words: "O [are] you foolish and slow of heart to believe everything which the prophets have spoken? Was it not necessary for Christ to suffer these things and [then] to enter into his own glory?"

14. However, it was not any necessity that forced him, but moved by his own free and favorable goodwill for our salvation he embraced that difficult task, and he performed it in his flesh with prompt obedience towards God. Thus, Isaiah testifies about him in chapter 53:10: "The Lord," he says, "was pleased to bruise him, since he has made himself to be the offering for sin." And the apostle says in Phil 2:6[-8]: "Though he was in the form of God he did not consider being equal to God something to be grasped but he emptied himself, taking the form of a servant, and he became obedient unto God even to the death of the cross."

15. Therefore since it was both out of necessity and of his own accord that Christ underwent the death on the cross for which he had been pre-ordained, the opinion that some people hold is wrong, namely that pre-ordained necessity and freedom of will cannot come together in the same subject for

one single task, but that when one of them has been introduced, the other is entirely driven out.

16. Whereas it was by the decree common to the entire Trinity that Jesus Christ was established as our Mediator, nevertheless the consecration of him being given and sent to us to carry out his task is attributed particularly and especially to God the Father in light of the rank that belongs to him (Luke 2:49; John 5:36; 6:27; 8:42, and 10:25). It was God's will to sanction this consecration by means of his own testimony as well as that of those He sent, in both testaments. For his own testimony see Psalm 110:4; for the testimony of those He sent, namely the Prophets, see Isaiah 53 and Zech 12, the angels, see Luke 1:31–32 and 2:10–11, John the Baptist and the apostles, see Acts 10:38–39.

17. We may ponder this consecration of Christ with a view to his divine and his human nature. Regarding the former, inasmuch as he is the Word that is co-eternal with the Father from before all ages, he was appointed to the task of Mediator. Regarding the latter, inasmuch as he was made man (like us in every respect), he was sanctified for that very task by the anointing of the Holy Spirit in the fullness of time as determined beforehand by God.

18. Each nature of Christ performs its own role in the work required to fulfill that task, and it does so jointly, not separately, and yet not jumbled together but distinctly. For in order to perform the work common to the divine and human natures, the divine nature enters upon a partnership with the human nature in a way like the soul of a mere human being behaves as the principle while the body acts as its instrument. So too in the action of Christ the God-and-man the divine nature performs the role of the principal cause while the human nature performs the role of helper, and less that of principle.

19. And so it is that sacred Scripture assigns to the whole Christ the same work for which the two natures of Christ come together, in such a way that it attributes the infinite worthiness and efficacy of the mediatorial office entirely to the power of the Godhead that is dwelling bodily in him [Col 2:9] (which it calls the Spirit), as when it says in Rom 1:3 and 4 that Christ, "according to the Spirit of sanctification was declared with power to be the Son of God through the resurrection from the dead." And 1 Pet 3:18: "He was made alive by the Spirit, and through the Spirit he once went to preach to the disobedient spirits." Similarly, in Mark 2:8 it says that "he knew in his Spirit what the scribes were thinking in their hearts." And Heb 9:14:

"Through the eternal Spirit he offered himself unblemished to God, that he might cleanse our conscience to serve the living God."

20. Therefore the Jews and the Socinians err when they do not acknowledge the divine nature in Christ the Mediator. We have refuted their error elsewhere, in the disputation on the Trinity and the Son of God.

21. And this is also the reason why the Jews and Socinians attack our doctrine about Christ's mediation no less than the one about his divinity. For the Jews deny that Christ is the Messiah who was once promised to the fathers under the Old Testament. The Socinians certainly speak less openly than the Jews against the orthodox understanding of Christ's mediatorial office, but they do try to undermine it indirectly by creating pitfalls, when they claim that Christ had offered himself to God not in the literal sense but metaphorically.

22. If this claim of the Socinians is true, then also the prefigurative sacrifices under the Old Testament were called sacrifices not in the strict sense but metaphorically; and the spiritual sacrifices that we are prescribed in the New Testament, said thus to be metaphorical, are in this aspect on a par with the sacrifice made by Christ. As both of these conclusions are drawn correctly from the claim of the Socinians, they conflict with the very clear testimonies of sacred Scripture.

23. Also the followers of Andreas Osiander err, when they ascribe the mediatorial office only to Christ's divine nature. For according to the command of God revealed to us in his Word, Christ should not only rule his Church inwardly by his Spirit, and powerfully defend it against all enemies, but also instruct and comfort it by the outward preaching of his Gospel; and he not only should have put a stop to God's eternal wrath through his eternal Spirit, but also have atoned for us by the shedding of his blood.

24. Also the papal theologians go wrong, as is evidenced in the writings of Bellarmine, when the discussion is not about the actual subject, Jesus Christ, but about the formal principle of his deeds: that this principle is Christ's human nature and not his divine one (Bellarmine, *On Christ as Mediator*, book 5, chapter 1 and 3). To refute them, one can take the chief, most cogent arguments from thesis nineteen above.

25. For we offer to posit the following axiomatic statements: 1. that Christ is the subject and common principle of the mediatorial work, not in that he is God nor in that he is man only, but in that he is simultaneously God and

man. 2. That Christ's human nature is coming together with the divine nature for that work, as serving the divine, which is the higher cause that acts as the principal one. 3. That the sacred books of the Bible ascribe the infinite worthiness and efficacy of Christ's mediation to his divinity, and from them necessarily come the following points: 1) Christ's mediatorial work proceeds not by the strength of one nature only but by the power of both as each acts following its own property. 2) Christ's human nature serves the divine nature in the work of the God-and-man, and one cannot simply call it the starting-point for the mediatorial action, nor just the strictly formal starting-point, but rather the material or instrumental one. 3) Without the protection and support of his divinity, the man Christ was not able to extend the mysteries of divine wisdom from the bosom of his Father, nor to pay him a ransom sufficient for our sins, nor in time past to rend asunder the gates of hell by his death on this earth. And even now he would not be able to hear in heaven the prayers of his chosen ones dwelling over all the earth and likewise to commend them to his Father or grant them their request to shield them from all evil.

26. While we do maintain that Christ is our Mediator according to his divine nature, yet it is not right for that reason to conclude against us that we must moreover admit that the entire Trinity undertook the mediatorial office. For putting his divine nature over against his human one should not be taken generally for the essence that is common to the three persons, but separately, only for the second person of the Trinity who assumed our flesh.

27. Therefore on this point we mean by the divine nature of Christ not the nature of the Godhead in an indefinite sense, but in the definite sense of one person of the Godhead as distinguished from the others by his own mode of subsistence, namely, the Son of God the Father. Similarly, with the opposite name 'flesh' we designate not the person of a man but the human nature that is joined indissolubly to the Son of God in the unity of person.

28. And while the mediation is related to the works of God that are directed outwardly (and these cannot be divided), it is not for that reason entirely common to the three persons, since it is partly essential (insofar as the starting-point from which it flows is the entire essence) and partly personal (insofar as the dispensation or arrangement concerns the person who is second in order—as in the end-term of the divine essence). For the mediation is here attributed to the Son of God rather than to the Father or the Holy

Spirit with respect to the same thing whereby the incarnation and the redemption of the human race is attributed separately to him.

29. Although the Son of God is less than the Father because of that mediation, he is not therefore less than him in his deity. For he accepted his mediatorial task from the Father by a dispensation that was shared and willed by the Trinity as a whole—and that included himself. But the divinity itself was communicated to him by the Father alone through natural generation. In the age that is to come he will lay aside his office of Mediator when he will hand over his scepter to the Father; yet he will hold on to his divinity with the Father unchanged for ever and ever (1 Cor 15:27, 28).

30. By the same dispensation of grace whereby the Son of God, together with the Father and the Holy Spirit, determined from eternity to accept the mediation for himself, he willed also to discharge it with himself in his flesh at the appointed time. He did so in an analogical and self-reductive sense; that is to say, [he did so] by referring also to himself the divinity he shares with the Father and the Holy Spirit, by the right of the fellowship he has with them.

31. Just as Christ is, therefore, also Mediator for himself by the nature shared by the three persons of the Godhead (whereby he is of one essence with the Father and the Holy Spirit), so by the unique personality proper to himself and the dispensation of grace whereby he was made God-and-man he also performs the office of Mediator before the Father and the Holy Spirit. Nevertheless, in the sacred writings his office is expressly related only to the Father because of the order in the dispensation. In being not only ambassador and go-between but also the surety that atones for our guilt by his death, he executed his office in such a way that on the very cross he clearly triumphed over death and his other defeated enemies (Col 2:15).

32. The examples of other go-betweens and sureties that people adduce from various historical accounts to illustrate this one instance are more than entirely different from it, since either the innocent did not undergo the penalty of death for the sake of the others who were guilty, or if they did undergo it for the wicked deeds of others, they did not come away victorious from that test.

33. We have sufficiently treated the subject of the mediation, Jesus Christ, and its efficient or moving cause. The objects of the mediation are God, the

offended party, and mankind, the party guilty of the offense. The apostle testifies to this very clearly when he says: "There is one Mediator between God and men, the man Christ Jesus" (1 Tim 2:5).

34. At this point a question arises about the good angels: whether Christ should be called also their Mediator. We are in agreement with those who state that Christ is in fact the medial, or mediating, cause for the preservation of the good angels, yet who go on to state that Christ should not therefore be called their Mediator.

35. For in Holy Scripture Christ is never called the Mediator of his elect when it concerns their preservation; but he is always called their Mediator when it concerns their reconciliation with the God whom they offended. For there neither was, nor will be, any dissension between God and the good angels. It was not the angels whom Christ took upon himself, but the seed of Abraham, so that like a propitiator interceding between two differing parties—between God his Father according to his divine nature and us his brothers according to the flesh he had assumed from the seed of Abraham—he might in himself restore us into his Father's grace (Heb 2:16).

36. Therefore, when the sacred letters sometimes call the blessed angels God's sons or chosen ones, we should take it to mean that they, having been chosen by the almighty hand of Christ their head and ruler according to the abiding grace of divine election, are preserved in the original state and truth which they received through him. And so, remaining in that state unaltered, they may have the blessing of seeing God face to face forever (Job 1:6, and 2:1; 1 Tim 5:21; Col 2:10; Heb 12:22; John 8:44; Jude 6).

37. The form of the mediatorial office is clearly evident from the three parts and functions he alone performed by himself: prophet, priest, and king.

38. Because those three functions can be discerned together only in Christ, it says that it was he whom God made to be our wisdom, justice, sanctification and redemption (1 Cor 1:30). He was made our wisdom in order to turn us by his prophetic instruction from being foolish at heart into wise unto salvation. He was made our righteousness and sanctification, so that by the two-fold nature of his priestly office he first might render satisfaction to the aggrieved divine majesty through his atoning sacrifice for our sins, and next to intercede with this majesty on our behalf. He was made redemption for us so that by his kingly power he might keep us (who have been released from

our slavery to sin) within the boundaries of our calling by the restraining reins of his control; and so that by his protection he might keep us safe from all harm done by the enemy.

39. Prophecy is the function whereby Christ establishes his people in the right doctrines of the Law and the Gospel; sealed by his wonders, each of these doctrines is cleansed from the corruptions of the false teachers. Sometimes he does this by himself directly, at other times indirectly, through other servants of his Word who have been endowed with gifts needed for that purpose. Of these the former are included by synecdoche under the name 'prophets' and the latter 'apostles' (Matt 5:2 ff., John 17:8).

40. We should consider the people of God, whom we regard as the object of Christ's prophetic work, under the Old and the New Testament. Under the former nearly all were Jews, while under the latter they were partly Jews and partly Gentiles. The former had been preferred to the latter in the teaching of divine wisdom, so that the promises made to Abraham and the other patriarchs might in the first place be fulfilled in their circumcised sons. For this reason also Christ as the minister of circumcision called to himself especially the lost sheep of the house of Israel (Matt 15:24, Rom 15:8). It was after Christ's ascension into heaven that the apostles declared the Gospel of Christ equally to Jews and Gentiles, so that Christ might be not only the glory of the people of Israel, but also the light to the Gentiles, according to the prophecies in Isa 49:6 and Luke 2:32.

41. In our opinion the prophetic teaching uses two means, immediate and mediate. For the most part Christ made use of the former means, either by only his divine nature for the prophets in the old covenant, or by both natures for the apostles. For he, the Sun of righteousness, with the rays of prophetic light that it possesses, shone powerfully upon both [prophets and apostles]. He made use of the latter means when he commanded his prophets and apostles in their speaking and writing to unfold to his people all the secrets of his wisdom that they must know for salvation. With this in mind, the Church of God was moved to reject every tradition that is not contained in the holy book. In the former [immediate] mode of teaching, the minds of men can be thoroughly enlightened without the help of the latter means, and their hearts could be bent to the obedience of faith. In the latter [mediate] mode, neither of these results can be effected without the help of the former means.

42. Christ's priesthood is the function wherein he appears before God's presence in order to keep the Law (that he had received from him) in our name, to present himself to him as the victim of reconciliation for our sins, and by his intercession with him to obtain for us his constant help and the gift of the Holy Spirit, and to apply them to us effectively (Heb 10:7 ff.).

43. This three-fold way of coming into God's presence was foreshadowed in former times by the Levitic high priest, who by God's command watched over the tables of the Law that had been placed in the ark of the covenant, and who stood before God on behalf of the people like a mediator accompanied by the offerings of sacrifices and prayers.

44. The same priesthood of Christ was formerly prefigured also by the priesthood of Melchizedek, albeit for a different goal, i.e., to demonstrate that its excellence surpassed the Levitic priesthood by these three advantages: 1) its eternal duration, since, like Melchizedek figuratively, Christ in true reality is called a priest to God who is without father and mother, and without beginning and end; 2) its double office, since both are distinguished by the titles of 'King' and 'Priest;' 3) its preeminence over the Levitic order, since it is said that Levi himself, while he was yet in the loins of Abraham, gave tithes to Melchizedek (Heb 7:3, 9).

45. Christ fulfilled the Law of God in two ways: by generally observing all of God's commandments, and by voluntarily discharging the penalties we wretched sinners were liable to undergo as the Law had warned. We shall give more copious explanations of both fulfillments of the Law in the subsequent disputations about Christ's satisfaction and our justification.

46. In the letter to the Hebrews the apostle distinguishes the sacrifice of Christ (who is the Word that offers the sacrificial victim, and the flesh or victim that is offered) from the Levitic priests and their sacrifices with the following points: 1) Because the person who is making the offer is a special priest in the order of Melchizedek who remains forever and so permits no-one else to share his office with him nor to succeed him (Heb 7:3). 2) Because this priest is blameless in himself and set apart from all sinners (Heb 7:26). 3) Because the offering of himself that was made once is sufficient in every way to preserve us perfectly, and so it is never to be repeated (Heb 7:24, 25). 4) Because the flesh or sacrificial victim that was offered is united in person to the Word that offers it (Heb 9:12). 5) Because for God the value and force of this sacrificial victim is everlasting (Heb 7:24, 25, and 10:14).

47. The apostle's five-part distinction completely overturns the traditions of the papal theologians about the primacy of their pope as the vicar of Jesus Christ, and about the sacrifice of the mass that is to be offered to God still today by the secondary priests of the New Testament. The following statements of principle are entirely inconsistent and contradict one another: that Christ is our only High priest, but meanwhile the Roman pope is his vicar. That the bloody sacrifice which Christ offered in his own flesh once and for all to God through his eternal Spirit is the only one that makes atonement, but meanwhile the bloodless sacrifice of the mass, which by their own human spirit the sacrificers offer in the flesh of another (namely Christ's flesh, as they think) is also an atoning sacrifice. Moreover, that in former times men who were mortal and subject to sin could not have offered the atoning sacrifice (in the strict sense of the word) to God in the Old Testament, and that therefore only the Son of God should have offered it, as he is equal with the Father in his essential immortality and holiness; but [they say] nowadays men of the sort that the priests were in the Old Testament should and are able to offer a truly atoning sacrifice. And similar statements, which will be examined more fully afterwards.

48. The intercession by Christ is the function whereby Christ takes his place in the heavenly sanctuary and pleads earnestly on our behalf with God the Father for his mercy and the forgiveness of sins that he obtained by the merit of his atoning sacrifice. He also pleads for his help and the gifts of the Holy Spirit, whereby daily we are rendered better equipped for all the duties of obedience and gratitude.

49. The Son of God brings this intercession about by a voluntarily administered grace and in a manner that befits his mediatorial work, not because he now, after having put off his state of self-renunciation, falls upon bended knees before his Father in heaven, but because like a priest or advocate he takes his place and face to face with him earnestly requests that he continue to grant his grace and the help we need, no less ardently in his human nature than effectively in his divine nature.

50. It is no more possible for Christ's intercession to be communicated to the holy angels or the souls of people in heaven than his sacrificial offer can be communicated to the Roman sacrificers. For he is the sole Mediator of the redemption as well as the intercession, and so the papal theologians who link the holy angels and men departed from this life to Christ as his secondary

intercessors, do him no small harm—as will be made clear in a later [disputation, viz 36.9–20], if God shall grant it.

51. In his office as king, Christ, as its only Head, governs the Church that was purchased with his own blood [Acts 20:28], and he powerfully guards her against every enemy within and without. By his guidance he equips her with suitable weapons as she battles in the 'arena' of this world, so that when at long last she is made partaker of the victory he promised, she celebrates in heaven with him an eternal triumph over her defeated enemies, and without stopping praises God for the victory obtained. For only Christ stands out far above all the members of his mystic body in this unique and boundless way; he does so by the worthiness of his rank and his power to rule, enliven, and preserve her, and also by the amount of perfect spiritual gifts (Rom 8:29, Col 1:18, John 3:34). And in Disputation 41, "On Christ the Only Head of the Church," we shall demonstrate this explicitly over against the papal theologians, who make the false claim that Christ bestowed the world-wide government over his Church to Peter as his vicar alone, and that Peter in turn handed that same government over to the one Roman pope as his lawful successor.

52. But as Christ's Church has a twofold state, the one of grace in this age and the other of glory in the future, we should distinguish the current government of the Church from the one that is to come. For in this life Christ rules his Church through the intervening agencies of ecclesiastical administration by faithful pastors, and he protects it by the administration of devout political magistrates. In the life that is to come he will rule it directly, without the external supports of that kind and by the divinity he shares with the Father and the Holy Spirit, so that together with them he may be all things to every member of the household of faith, whom he shall cause to rejoice in beholding him and communicating with him most closely and happily (1 Cor 15:28; Rev 21, 22 and 23).

53. Hence it says that when Christ will hand over to God all the elect who clung to him in the unity of perfected faith and who have been freed completely from their fear of the enemy, he will also hand over to him his mediatorial (or dispensational) scepter so that he may forever conduct his purely divine reign over his elect with the same glory and majesty that he shared with the Father from eternity (1 Cor 15:24, 26).

54. Handing over that mediatorial scepter will happen on the day of the last judgment, after Christ, by the personal power of judging which the Father has granted him, and by an act of grace undeserved, will bestow on his friends the reward of life, while with vengeance deserved, he will give to his enemies the punishment of eternal death.

ON CHRIST IN HIS
STATE OF HUMILIATION

President: Andreas Rivetus
Respondent: Samuel Rivetus

Christ executes his mediatorial office (Disputation 26) in the two states of humiliation (Disputation 27) and exaltation (Disputation 28). The present disputation posits that 'the entire dispensation for our salvation and the execution of Christ's three-fold office' resides in this arrangement (2). Christ's humiliation is handled according to his suffering, crucifixion and death; his burial; and his descent into hell. His exaltation consists of his resurrection, ascension, and being seated at God's right hand. Salvation is declared without discrimination to all people, but the efficacy of Christ's atoning sacrifice operates only in those who believe in Him. To be sure, Christ's suffering and death suffice to redeem all humanity (22–23), yet 'the life-giving and saving efficacy of Christ's suffering and death manifests itself only in those who believe, to bestow upon them justifying faith and by means of it to lead them on to their salvation with certainty' (23). Interestingly, the discourse on the profession that Christ descended into hell (24–32) concludes that the phrase refers to the state of death rather than the hellish agony of the crucifixion (32). The disputation ends (33–34) with a hymn upon the benefits that come from Christ's humiliation.

1. From what we have said thus far about the fall of our first parent, the propagation of sin, and the demands of God's Law, we have demonstrated that the need for our redemption is so obvious that no-one can question it unless he remains unaffected by every feeling of guilt and eternal damnation. Yet this [realization] would have no benefit, were it not for the fact that we also have come to know him in whom all who are cursed, dead, and lost in themselves should seek their righteousness, freedom, life, and salvation. And therefore, up to this point we also have provided disputations about Christ

the eternal Son of God, who in time was made man—the proximate efficient cause of our redemption—as regards his person in whom the two natures come together, and as regards his mediatorial office (viewed generally or in its parts).

2. What remains for us is to treat the way or manner whereby Christ removed the division between God and us by completely taking away our sins and obtained the righteousness which renders God favorable and well-disposed towards us, so that he might apply it to us effectively every day, and thus might bear the name 'Savior' bestowed on him by God through the angel in Matt 1:21 and in actual fact perform what that name implies. One can examine this way (or manner) in our Mediator's two states—the state of humiliation and of exaltation—wherein the entire dispensation for our salvation and the execution of Christ's three-fold office reside.

3. Logical order demands that we now speak about this state of humiliation. In general, this word ['humiliation'] means the entire economy with which Christ, "by taking on the form of a servant, was obedient to the Father unto death, even death on the cross" (Phil 2:7[–8]). And in an extended sense it means the entire humility of the Son in all its degrees; but in the proper sense it means that final act of subjection, that last deed of life to the point of death, which commonly is referred to specifically as his 'passion,' with a meaning that is found commonly also in the Scriptures.

4. In the disputation that we must set forth about this last point, the passion of Christ, we consider three steps: 1) what preceded the crucifixion, along with the crucifixion itself and the death that followed it; 2) the burial; 3) the descent into hell. We take the starting point of this passion in its proper sense from the time of his capture, although the things that happened to him earlier (and which others call 'pre-passions') could and should be included in it, since they make up a portion of that obedience when taken as a whole. It is for this reason that the Apostles' Creed moves from the birth of Christ to his death because the latter entails the other acts of obedience.

5. [The sufferings] that preceded Christ's crucifixion were: the betrayal of Judas; his capture; handing him over to the meeting of the priests; the different acts of derision; delivering him into the hands of heathens (particularly Pilate); his interrogation, flogging, and lastly condemnation under Pilate, followed by the most shameful punishment of the cross which was the means of his violent death, so that he would become "the accursed

and the curse," not just in the opinion of humans only but by order of the Law of God, which declares: "Accursed is everyone who hangs on a tree" (Deut 21:23; Gal 3:13). Moreover, it was a most horrible form of punishment, one that was accompanied by very great pain because he was pierced in those limbs that are particularly sensitive and endowed with exceptional feeling—his hands and feet—and in this manner he hung there entirely in constant pain for some time.

6. In addition to those very grievous torments of the body Christ suffered also the deepest anguish of the soul, as even the Roman Catechism states (Article 4, on the Symbols). Aquinas grants that Christ's soul experienced everything that causes grief ([*Summa theologiae*], part 3, question 46, article 5 and 6), and he took upon himself every sorrow, the greatest grief in absolute quantity, and all the way to the point of death he not only bore in himself the slanderings, tauntings, scourgings, and shameful humiliations, but with patience, humility, and while enduring his harshest chastisement, he also appeased the wrath and anger of God that burned against mankind. These sufferings were so terribly bitter that when he weighed and turned them over in his mind, he was overcome by the greatest fear and sorrow in the garden; he prayed that conditioned prayer to take away 'the cup,' perspired sweat like drops of blood, did not shy away from using an angel to comfort him, and declared on the cross that he had been forsaken by the Father (Matt 26:37 and 38; Mark 14:33, 34; Matt 26:39, 42, 44; Mark 14:36, 39; Luke 22:42, 43, and 44; Matt 27:46).

7. For because he had offered himself as surety and pledge in the place of sinners, he had to pay in full and clear away all the penalties that they should have borne, and so he had to wrestle (as in a hand-to-hand combat) with the forces of hell and with the horror of everlasting death; and he had to give not only his own body as a ransom for deliverance, but he even suffered dreadful torments in his soul, since he knew that he was standing before the judgment seat of God on our behalf.

8. With these sorrows he died not only a natural death, but in some sense also a supernatural death. He was separated from God in terms of willing what is pleasant, though not in terms of willing what is righteous. To be sure, he was not separated from his Godhead as far as the union in Person is concerned, but the divine power in him hid itself for the time being, so that in his great need there was no display of divine power, and there was no

manifestation of majesty. This abandonment of Christ to hellish punishments should be associated with the punishments that were due to us sinners. Therefore, those places [in Scripture] should be taken as referring to Christ, where the prophet as a type [of Christ] complains that "he was surrounded by the sorrows of hell," "his soul was overcome with troubles," and that "his life had come to the brink of death." And in the end, he acknowledges that "God has redeemed his soul from the depths of hell" (Ps 18:5; 116:3; 83:3; 86:16).

9. Moreover, we state that while he did suffer punishment to the extreme degree, he did not suffer punishment for eternity, and in that suffering of the soul deep within Christ (what the Scholastics call 'intrinsically') there was nothing inordinate, while he was being assailed outwardly ([what they call] 'extrinsically'). From this it follows that he was not affected by that complete damnation wherein those people will abide who because of their own sins will be bound with punishments for ever; death of that kind is accompanied by the loss of all hope. Far be it from us to ascribe that kind of death to Christ, even if we should suffer from the insults of our opponents on account of it.

10. In fact, along with John of Damascus, we refer everything that Christ suffered (whether in body or in soul) to what he called his appropriation. This appropriation is not the natural or essential one (whereby he assumed our nature and all things natural), but it is personal and relative, whereby he immediately after that appropriated our person to himself, in which he made our curse and forsakenness his own—"receiving our person" (as the same John of Damascus puts it, *An Exact Exposition of the Orthodox Faith*, book 3 chapter 25). And we are not inclined to think that God was ever an enemy to the Son, or angry with him. For how could he have been angry with his beloved Son in whom his soul delighted? Or how could Christ have reconciled the Father to others through his intercession if he were hostile to him? (This was Calvin's clever retort to the slander he suffered for this teaching concerning redemption.)

11. From these words it follows that people slander God for being unjust and Christ for being unwise when they dare to make the claim that the smallest droplet of Christ's blood, the tiniest teardrop, and the slightest groaning of the heart could have been enough to redeem the human race. By this backwards preaching about his worthiness, these people make every action

superfluous that Christ performed over and above these, and they intimate that his death was not necessary, even though it did follow upon all of those sorrows of his heart and soul. It was in death that the real (and not just apparent) separation of the body from the soul of Christ occurred, a separation in the natural union, in its effects, and in space. Nevertheless, the hypostatic union of the two natures (which maintains the body and the soul) remained. For since we confess in the Creed that "the Son of God died and was buried"—and these words cannot be said about him except concerning his human nature (although what belongs to human nature or its parts is said about the Son of God only because of this union)—it follows that even in death the Word remained joined to the parts that were separated.

12. We deny, however, that at the time of his death Christ was a man in the restricted sense of the word, as the 'Master of the Sentences' claimed ([Peter Lombard,] *Sententiae*, book 3, distinction 22), and we deny it because Christ truly did die, and it belongs to a man's death that upon dying he ceases to be a man (or a living being) because the soul that completed the existence of both [man and living being] has departed. For this reason, a man who has died is not simply called a 'man' but 'a dead man,' with a qualification that brings in a new element while putting an end to what it defines. For we would not wish to concur with Apollinaris, who thought that the Word was united with the body like form and substance, which would ruin the essence of a real man.

13. The true burial of Christ is premised upon his true death, as it was the self-same body of the one person; in the grave this body was not destroyed by being burned or resolved into its component elements, which John of Damascus calls dissolution and extermination (*An Exact Exposition of the Orthodox Faith*, book 3, chapter 28), although it did cease to be a living body by the removal of the living form (Ps 16:10, Acts 2:27, 13:35). Real death surely is the reason for burial, and that burial happened in a new grave, lest afterwards the story should be fabricated that someone else had arisen. Moreover, as God so provided it, a seal and guards were placed over it, whereby the enemy foolishly and without any consideration sealed the veracity of his resurrection by rolling a large stone before the mouth of the cave, thus also putting a seal over any slanderous tongue.

14. Of relevance here is the fact that the burial happened with the knowledge and permission of Pilate, for after the centurion had made an enquiry into it,

the judge guaranteed the certainty of Christ's death by means of his public statement—so there can be no doubt about the fact that he had died. And it was for this reason also that, according to the dispensation of God's providence, men were used in this affair who were not just from the common folk but would perform this task for the most holy body not in secret but openly, so that everyone might know that no fraud was committed therein.

15. The burial was followed by the confinement of Christ's body in the grave until the third day, during which time the Son of God lay there as though held fast by the mighty chains of death, defeated and lifeless, even though he would conquer death and break its chains asunder. Moreover, this three-day confinement should be understood to mean that he had stayed in the grave not for three whole days and an equal number of whole nights, but for two whole nights (i.e., the nights of the sixth and seventh days of that week) and one whole day, namely the Sabbath-day. And therefore, we should understand what Matt 12:40 writes about the sign of Jonah in a figurative sense: "The Son of Man was in death's embrace for three days and three nights, like Jonah in the belly of the sea-monster." For we call the final part of a natural day a whole day (which consists of day-time and night-time), and in this way the Lord lingered in the grave only for one entire day-and-night, while parts are merely borrowed from the two other days.

16. Having treated the passion, death, and burial of Christ, it follows that we should now investigate their causes. Of Christ's passion there are remote and proximate efficient causes. And the proximate causes, in turn, are direct and indirect. The remote cause is God's eternal decree (or divine ordination), which was from eternity arranging and guiding this matter (because it was not by chance or a fatalistic necessity but by the decree of God the Father, and through a means that God's wisdom found to be very fitting) in a way for Christ to endure those passions to redeem the human race (Acts 4:28).

17. The proximate direct efficient cause consisted of all Christ's enemies: Satan, who pursued the seed of the woman with inimical hatred, and all the people who were instruments in Satan's hands—Judas, the priests, Annas, Caiaphas, Pilate, and the commoners. All these people committed grievous sins, although not equally, but in varying degrees, depending on the greater or lesser extent of their knowledge and evil intent. By this way of reckoning the sin of the leaders who out of envy handed Christ over to be crucified was the most serious of all. The sin of Judas was less serious, if one considers the

fact that he sold his master out of greed; but it was made worse by accompanying factors such as his prior status as an apostle, his keeping company with Christ, and the like. For the same reason the sin of the common Jews was less serious, as well as that of the gentiles who crucified Christ by the order of Pilate.

18. The proximate indirect efficient cause was the eternal Father, who "did not spare his own Son, but gave him up for [us] all" (Rom 8:32). He was the cause: 1) by not hindering his suffering, but by exposing him to the forces of his persecutors and by forsaking him (as was set out by us above); 2) by ordering Christ himself to undergo that suffering on behalf of men, and by imputing to him the guilt of our sins; 3) by instilling in him the intention and willingness to suffer.

19. What also belongs to the indirect efficient cause is the will of Christ himself, who accepted and patiently endured the suffering, in obedience to the Father's commands, whereby he willingly suffered death, which he could have avoided otherwise (if regarded absolutely, though not if regarded hypothetically from the Father's prior command). "No-one takes my life away from me" (John 10:18); similarly, "So that the world may know that I love the Father, and so I do what the Father has commanded me; let us rise and go hence" (John 14:31). It is for this reason that Christ's passion was an offering of a very pleasant fragrance; insofar as it was his enemies who brought the offering, it was a very grievous sin.

20. The material of the passion (or 'what is its subject,' as some call it) is Christ the Son of God in his human nature; and that is the only nature in which he could suffer, in both body and in soul (as we have pointed out). And yet he suffered in a way that one can truly say that the 'whole Christ' (not 'the whole of Christ') suffered; and through the communication of his proper qualities "the Lord of glory was crucified" (1 Cor 2:8), and "through his blood God obtained his Church" (Acts 20:28). And what they call the objective material are all the punishments that were placed on Christ's shoulders, which we treated when we described his suffering.

21. As to the outward form, it consists of Christ's actual suffering and endurance of very grievous punishments. The internal form consists of the obedience that he showed to his Father, to the point of his death on the cross, whereby he made the sacrifice offered on the altar of the cross very commendable. Herein he was at the same time both the priest and the unique

victim suitable for sins, and so he offered and sacrificed his own whole being to the Father (Heb 9:14, John 17:19).

22. From this it is easy to determine the goal or purpose of Christ's death. It consists of two things: 1) the atonement for our sins through a satisfaction that is of infinite worth and value; 2) the mortification and abolition of the body of sin, which his burial signified and in which believers are made partakers when they die to sin and are buried with Christ to rise up to a new life (Rom 6:4 and Col 2:12).

23. However, only those who believe in Christ become partakers of the goal or purpose that has been declared and presented to everyone to whom God sends his Gospel out of the good pleasure of his own will. And even though the value of Christ's suffering and death was indeed all-sufficient for the redemption of all people, nevertheless by God's council (which is entirely free), and by his most gracious will and purpose, the life-giving and saving efficacy of Christ's suffering and death manifests itself only in those who believe, to bestow upon them justifying faith and by means of it to lead them on to their salvation with certainty. For he is the Savior "of his people, his body" (Matt 1:21, Eph 5:23). "He laid down his life for the sheep" (John 10:15), and "of the sons whom he brought to grace he was consecrated as the chief of their salvation through his sufferings" (Heb 2:10).

24. What also pertains to Christ's humiliation is what is added in the symbol of the faith, that Christ descended into hell. This article was not a reading in the past, for it was left out of the symbols of the Roman Church, the Eastern Church, and also by some of the earliest church fathers when they gave summaries of the Christian faith or explained the symbol of the Apostles' Creed. And it cannot be determined for certain at what point in time it was inserted into the symbol. Even so, however, it has some value when the analogy of faith is applied in interpreting it.

25. The word *sheol* to which the Greek word *hades* and the Latin word *infernus* correspond, has a proper and a figurative meaning. The proper meaning is used in Scripture for all that lies below the earth's surface, with the connotation that it consumes and absorbs everything that previously was living. And so because it concerns destruction, insofar as it respects the proper meaning, the sacred letters happen to give the name 'hell' to that entire state of all who have departed this mortal life. Metaphorically, however, the word is used for all the pains and distresses felt by those who have been

condemned. Hence some think that Christ's descent was a real one, while others think it was a figurative one that only was so called.

26. Those who hold that the descent was real in the sense of place have different views, too, depending on whether the place is real or imaginary. Some, who relate the descent to that of Christ's physical body, understand by it nothing other than the burial of Christ's body, or the time that it stayed in the grave; others take it to mean his soul, in one way or another. For some think that Christ's soul descended to the place of the condemned for the purpose of increasing their punishment by being present there, and for commencing his triumph from that descended place. Others relate the descent to some place in the underworld that they have made up, a place where they imagine the souls of the fathers were detained before the death of Christ, and they give it the name 'Limbo.' Yet others again hold that Christ did descend to the place of the condemned, and to the Limbo of the fathers (as they call it), but not in the real presence of his soul, but only by the efficacious power of his divinity.

27. Of these explanations the first one lets in a pointless repetition in this short symbol, and it entails an interpretation that casts obscuring shadows rather than light on the preceding article [in the Creed]. The second explanation is no less absurd, because it offered no support for its primary purpose: Christ's victory could have been made known to the damned by a way other than the presence of his soul, and as it was then separated from his body, his soul would have demonstrated instead that he was still in death's power. And for this reason, the second purpose is refuted as absurd, because the triumph could not have started as long as the separation [of soul from body] lasted.

28. The third explanation is purely an invention of man's imagination, because nowhere in Scripture can such a passage be found. And one cannot prove from any place in Scripture that the fathers who had died in the faith are being kept in prisons of subterranean hells. For those who were in Abraham's bosom were received "in heaven," where Abraham, Isaac and Jacob were, as Christ testifies (Matt 8:11). Augustine says that this place is "the rest of the blessed poor for whom the kingdom of heaven is, where they are taken up after this life" (*Evangelical Questions*, book 2, chapter 38). And the Jesuit Maldonado does not deny that some of the "posterior theologians were of the opinion that under the earth there was a place set apart from the other

places of punishments" (*Commentary* on Luke 16:22). No doubt these theologians borrowed it from Marcion, "because it is in the underworld that they locate the place of reward for those who kept the law and the prophets, a place that awards them torment or consolation" (Tertullian, *Against Marcion* 4.34).

29. Both of these [last two] views are refuted by what Christ says: "Today you will be with me in Paradise" (Luke 23:43). For unless they locate Paradise in hell (which is a terrible thing to say), their Limbo must be broken up, especially as Maldonado admits [in his *Commentary*] on Matt 27:44 that "Christ was speaking about a Paradise he was not in at that time," unless they understand the statement as coming not from Christ as God, and as not being about the state of blessedness. And as for Durand's opinion that [the symbol] concerns "the descent of [Christ's] efficacy," even the papal teachers themselves refute it; and if the statement is about Limbo, since Durand is positing an effect of something that doesn't exist anywhere, then it is as ridiculous as the aforementioned view. Moreover, Scripture nowhere mentions that Christ's 'efficacy' descended into hell; for this descent pertains to the humiliation and rejection of the Christ. Throughout [Scripture] the descent is ascribed to a person, not to an efficacy.

30. There remain some differing explanations of the article that are true in substance and beyond controversy among all orthodox teachers regarding the doctrine as such—though not when it concerns the article taken in its proper sense. For some think that one sense is more fitting, and others another sense—a difference of opinion that is of little import since they all substantially agree. And, as has been noted already, this article did not occur in the symbol of all the churches in early days. Therefore, some are of the opinion that this article contains a recapitulation of everything that was said about that outward humiliation of Christ. Like a brief conclusion, it draws together what had been stated earlier article by article; thus it stands for the whole state of humiliation, from the first step down to the last one. That same interpretation is embraced by those who take 'hell' to mean death, and 'the descent into hell' to mean his going down to death.

31. Others take 'hell' to mean the state of death and take the article to refer to that descent whereby Christ experienced the state of death. For this reason, they point out that Scripture nowhere makes the claim that Christ arose from the grave but 'from the dead'—which indicates that he who previously had

been among the dead did not remain forever in the state of the dead but at a certain point stopped being dead. Not far away from their understanding are those who relate the article to Christ's tarrying for three days, which they consider to be different from his burial and to bring with it a separate benefit. Therefore, they think, it deserved a separate article in the symbol, having the sense that Christ tasted the dishonor that comes to our bodies, which Paul calls "the sowing" (1 Cor 15:43). [This interpretation does not hold] unless we make the distinction that the state of the dead refers to the body and the soul only to the extent that the soul is separated from the body, and moreover that Christ's tarrying in the grave refers only to his body.

32. These latter meanings are the most likely ones if we follow the logical progression of the articles and the order of the events that occurred, as told in the gospel-history; especially because the meaning, 'the state of death,' is among the primary and proper ones in this phrase, as was stated at the outset. And yet the interpretation that is commonly found in the public Catechisms is equally true and no less fitting: the descent into hell means hellish agonies, the weight of God's anger like the forsakenness that Christ experienced in his soul, as we have explained above. Joining these two descents [the spiritual and the physical one] would make for a good fit, as indeed some explainers do. For both pertain to Christ's final humiliation and they are grounded in the phrase; what is more, both of them are true and necessary doctrines, as is abundantly clear from what we have stated.

33. This will suffice for our undertaking to treat the humiliation of Christ. And we should reap the following benefits from it: that in Christ we possess the fullest satisfaction and expiation for all our sins; that the victory has been snatched away from death and the sting of death has been removed; that through Christ's shame we are to be raised up to the highest glory; that the dwelling-place of hell which we deserved has been exchanged for a home in heaven, which Christ the Lord has prepared and made ready for those who are his.

34. Besides these countless benefits, we have obtained also that greatest one of all, namely that in this one act of suffering we possess the most illustrious examples of all virtues: patience, humility, love, gentleness, obedience, etc., so that we can truly state that on that one great day of suffering our Savior manifested in himself all the precepts of life that he had taught us in words throughout the time of his ministry. To him be the glory forever.

SOURCES

Tertullian *On the Body of Christ*, chapter 5

The Son of God was born: this is no shame because it is shameful. The Son of God died: this is entirely worthy of faith because it is foolish. And after he was buried he arose: this is certain because it is impossible. But how shall these things be true in him if he himself was not real, if he did not really have in himself that which was crucified, which died, was buried and rose again, that is to say: this human flesh suffused with blood, supported by bones, interwoven with sinews, entwined with veins, whereby he knew what it was to be born and to die—without a doubt was human flesh born of man.

Ambrose, *On the Incarnation of the Lord*, chapter 6

He offered himself according to our nature, so that he might perform his work beyond our nature. The sacrifice belongs to us, the reward to him.

ON JESUS CHRIST IN
HIS STATE OF EXALTATION

President: Antonius Walaeus
Respondent: Daniel Swavius

The three states of Christ's exaltation—resurrection, ascension, and sitting down at the Father's right hand—counter-balance the three states of his humiliation. First, the physical reality of his resurrection from a real death is emphasized (3). With his resurrection He laid aside all kinds of infirmity, but not the essence of human nature (4–6). The causes, and goals or effects, of the resurrection are explained (7–9). As for Christ's ascension into heaven (10–20) three things receive special attention: 1) the place to which He ascended (12–13); 2) the form or manner in which He ascended (14–19); 3) the goals or fruits of his ascension (20). Christ's 'sitting at God's right hand,' the final step of his exaltation (21–36), is a metaphor for the highest step of glorification to which the Father raised Christ after his passion and ascension into heaven (22). It encompasses glory, power and rule over all creatures, with which He effectively gathers and keeps the Church (25–26, 31). Every day the Church experiences the fruits and effects of Christ's sitting down at the Father's right hand (31), which rest upon Christ's priestly intercession before the Father (32–35). His final deed as reigning priest will be the last Judgement. 'And then at last, when He lays aside his reign as formed by this economy, like a victor of all things and a conqueror He will first hand himself, and then his reign, over to God and the Father, so that God may be all in all' (36).

1. Since Scripture defines the whole office of Christ our Savior by his states of humiliation and exaltation, and since the previous disputation treated the first of these, it now remains for us to offer a successive treatment of the second state, namely his exaltation.

2. In fact, just as the preceding disputation distinctly observed three different steps in Christ's first state (namely his death on the cross, his burial, and his descent into hell), so too in his second state we should set forth the three distinct steps that counter-balance them: Christ's resurrection from the dead, his ascension into heaven, and his sitting down at the Father's right hand.

3. Contrary to the Marcionites, Libertines, and men of similar ilk who dared to attribute to Christ a phantom body and phantom actions, we define Christ's resurrection from the dead as his true and actual resuscitation to life, whereby his body, which really had been separated from his soul and had been kept for a three-day period in the grave with no natural decay, was truly and naturally reunited with his soul which had spent the entire time of his death in Paradise, and was brought back to this same life (in the proper sense of the word), although it had obviously put aside mortality and the other weaknesses of this life.

4. Those infirmities which Christ laid aside with his resurrection are of two kinds: to some of them the human nature is subject by virtue of the first creation into this life as a living being (and the Apostle deals with them in 1 Cor 15:44, and elsewhere in Scripture). Other infirmities are the particular ones to which Christ on account of our sins subjected himself as our surety, "having been tempted like us in everything, sin excepted" (Heb 4:15).

5. However, we state that Christ did not therefore lay aside the essence (or the essential properties) of human nature by his resurrection—no more than we shall lay them aside after this life. For our bodies will be conformed unto his glorious body (Phil 3:21), just as after his resurrection Christ himself bore witness to his disciples that his body consisted of flesh and bones, and accordingly it was exposed to sight and touch (Luke 24:39).

6. Hence we see how badly they err who hold that Christ after his resurrection received a body of the sort that lacked any size or measurable shape, but like a ghost entered into any other bodies whatsoever without them giving way or opening up [for him]. And we see how even more badly they err who imagine that his body is present in many places at once in the same moment of time (something that is granted not even to ghosts) through 'reproduction' (as contemporary Jesuits call it). For "take away their space from bodies and there will be no place where they exist, and because they'll not exist anywhere, they will not exist at all. Take away the bodies from the qualities of the bodies and there will not be anything where [the qualities] are—and so it must be

that they do not exist," as Augustine says, in accordance with nature and with Scripture (Epistle 57, to Dardanus).

7. The principal efficient cause [of Christ's resurrection] is God the Father through his Spirit (Rom 8:11), who for a display of his truth and righteousness made Christ to be alive from the dead, which was not able to keep its hold on him (Acts 2:24). The Son himself is also the principal efficient cause, so that he powerfully declares himself to be the Son of God according to the Spirit of sanctification (Rom 1:4), and so that he might show that he had laid down his life for us by his own will (in keeping with the Father's command), he now as victor over Satan and sin through death (Heb 2:14) called himself back to life by his own, divine power, as he himself testifies (John 2:19 and 10:18).

8. In Christ's resurrection there are several diverse goals, which may also be called its effects or fruits: 1) to testify by this victory over his death that the fullest satisfaction has been made for our sins and that eternal righteousness has been restored (Rom 4:25; 1 Cor 15:17 and 57); 2) so that just as by the power of his death our old man was put to death, so too by the power of his resurrection is the new man brought to life in us, thus restoring God's image (Rom 6:4); 3) so that his resurrection might be a very sure pledge and cause for our future resurrection (1 Cor 15:22); and finally 4) that through his resurrection he might open the way for himself to the other offices that he was going to execute for us, whereby as our Prophet, Intermediary, and King he might apply the power of his death and sacrifice to us for eternity (Rom 14:9).

9. From this it obviously follows that Christ arose in his own body, the body still marked with traces of the wounds he had received on the cross as proof that it was his real body. In the same way our very same bodies, too, will be restored to life before the final judgment, just as they are, contrary to what the Marcionites, some Anabaptists, and like-minded heretics think. "For Christ has indeed been raised up from the dead, and has become the first fruits of those who have fallen asleep" (1 Cor 15:20).

10. Christ's resurrection is followed by his ascension into heaven. For after his resurrection our Savior spent forty days continuously with his disciples. He explained to them more fully the things that pertain to setting up his spiritual kingdom (Acts 1:3), and instructed them with renewed authority to extend it among all peoples throughout the whole world (Mark 16:15). And

then, when leaving this world behind at last, as his disciples were looking on and angels were bearing witness, he conveyed his human nature into the heavenly sanctuary (Acts 1:9).

11. In this ascension of Christ three things should receive special consideration for a good understanding of this article: 1) the place to which he ascended; 2) the form or manner in which he ascended; and 3) the goals or fruits of this ascension.

12. By the consensus of all the Gospel-writers, the place to which Christ ascended is heaven. By this we do not mean the air or these visible skies, for Heb 4:14 states that he traveled through them. Nor do we mean only a glorious and celestial state, which the Ubiquitarians have dreamt up, contrary to the unanimous consent of all antiquity. But he went to the actual heavenly and glorious dwelling-place of the blessed spirits, which Scripture locates above and beyond all the visible heavens. It is to this place that Enoch and Elijah went on ahead by the power of the ascension of the coming Christ (Heb 11:5; 2 Kgs 2:1), and the place where our own bodies will be received after they will be united again with their souls by the power of that same ascension of Christ (John 14:2; Phil 3:21).

13. Besides the literal, genuine meaning of the gospel-history, the names whereby the Scriptures designate this heaven into which Christ ascended demonstrate this. John 6:58 calls it "the heaven from which Christ came down," and "the place where Christ was before" (i.e., before he came into this world, John 6:62). John 14:2 calls it "the Father's house, where Christ went in order to prepare a place for us." Eph 4:10 says that "he ascended higher than all the heavens." The ending of Phil 3[:20] calls it "heaven, where our citizenship is." Heb 11:16 calls it "a supercelestial fatherland," and 12:22, "the heavenly Jerusalem." 2 Cor 12:4 calls it "Paradise," and verse 2 "the third heaven," whereto Paul was caught up and where he beheld and heard Christ. All these and similar passages in the Scriptures are usually understood to concern no other heaven than that eternal seat and dwelling-place of the blessed.

14. The manner of Christ's ascension was real, bodily, as the whole gospel-history testifies; it was not only some 'disappearance' into thin air before the eyes of the disciples, as the Ubiquitarians imagine. For that is how Christ would have ascended before he actually did ascend, since he was miraculously removed from the disciples' sight on several occasions even before he truly

ascended into heaven, as can be seen from Luke 24:31. Nor is it the glorification of Christ's body itself, because even before his suffering Christ was transfigured for a time (Matt 17:2). If so, it would follow from this that he had ascended into heaven for a period of time and then came down again, before his actual ascension. All of this is nonsense and obviously foreign to the manner in which Scripture speaks.

15. Also the kinds of expressions that Scripture everywhere employs for this ascension of Christ into heaven prove that this ascension was true and real. Mark 16:19 has "he was taken up into heaven;" Luke 24:51: "He was carried up into heaven;" Acts 1:9: "He was taken up on high," and verse 11: "This same Jesus who was taken up from you into heaven, will come back in the same way you have seen him go into heaven." And so also the apostle says in Heb 9:12 that our high priest "entered into the most holy place once and for all." But according to [the Ubiquitarians] he would have entered heaven more often, in fact whenever he (in their opinion) appeared on the earth and then disappeared again. And verse 24 states: "For Christ did not enter a sanctuary that was made with hands, which was only a copy of the true one, but he entered into heaven itself now to appear before his Father's face on our behalf." Indeed, in John 16:28 Christ testifies that he is not only "going to the Father, but that he is also leaving this world"—which can only be taken to mean a real change of place.

16. However, it does not therefore follow that if this ascension were a real change of place Christ required a vast amount of time to complete this journey to heaven (as one of them has foolishly concluded). For if even the highest of stars, and whatever parts of the highest moving heaven, in their natural movement can cover as much distance as there is between the highest heaven and the earth in the space of only four hours (as we know from the proportion of the radius and circumference of a circle), how much less a span of time did the now immortal and glorified body of Christ require to be drawn by his divine power from earth up to heaven, which is what Scripture testifies occurred as the apostles were looking on (Acts 1:10).

17. Some debate whether Christ ascended into heaven all by himself or actually with a retinue in attendance, and in triumph. Acts 1 makes no mention of that retinue; but there are some theologians of great renown who conclude this from a comparison of some other places. They are of the opinion that those saints who arose from the dead along with Christ (in Matt

27:53) also ascended into heaven with him, like witnesses and partakers of his life-giving resurrection. For this some others even refer to the place in Eph 4:8: "While ascending into heaven he led captivity captive," that is, leading a multitude of captives from death. But as this place permits also other orthodox explanations, we prefer to reserve judgment on this point. Yet we do not doubt that Christ's entry into heaven, as in what happened at his birth, was filled with glory and congratulation of the celestial spirits, as is clearly described—albeit allegorically—in Ps 68:18, Dan 7:13 and elsewhere.

18. However, over against the papal theologians we deny that the souls of all the fathers who had died before Christ's ascension had been kept in some underworldly Limbo until this time and only then did Christ himself set them free and bring them over to heaven. For there is not any reason and also no place in Holy Scripture that gives proof for this. We have shown the contrary, that Enoch and Elijah were transported to heaven, as 2 Kgs 2:1 and 11 assert with so many words. And Christ, long before his death, promised that there would be "a reward in heaven" (Matt 3:10 and 12) for all who suffer persecution for the sake of righteousness; and to the robber who was hanging on the cross, he promised that "on this same day he would be with him in Paradise" (Luke 23:43).

19. And even though it states in the Acts of the apostles that even after his ascension into heaven Christ sometimes appeared to his disciples, and particularly to the apostle Paul, we nevertheless deny that his body was therefore actually outside heaven, because those appearances were either in a trance, or in dreams, or as the heavens were opened. But Scripture expressly testifies that Christ himself will remain in heaven until he will come to judge the living and the dead (Acts 3:21, and the ending of Phil 3, and elsewhere).

20. There are many, great fruits of Christ's ascension. For with his entry he opened the heavenly sanctuary for us (John 14:2; Heb 9:8); he ensured the hope of our future inheritance in our head [Christ], and our being seated with him in the heavenly places (Eph 2:6). He obtained for us the outpouring of the Holy Spirit (John 16:7); and lastly, by his power our hearts and desires are lifted up into heaven, so that we no longer seek the things that are on earth but the things which are in heaven (Col 3:1–3).

21. The final step of Christ's exaltation is his sitting down at God's right hand, and we shall deal with it in what follows.

22. On this point "the right hand of God" cannot be taken in its literal sense, because God is Spirit and so he lacks flesh and bones; rather, it is taken metaphorically, to stand for that highest step of glorification to which the Father raised Christ up after his passion and ascension into heaven.

23. Moreover, this metaphor is derived from the practice of kings and rulers whose custom it is, when they take their seat upon the throne and administer justice before their court of law, to give a place at their right hand to people on whom they bestow the highest honor (next to their own), or whom they make partakers of their kingly rule, as this is the convention in all dominions. And so when king Solomon sat on his throne he placed his mother at his right hand (1 Kgs 2:19). Similarly, in Ps 45:10 the queen is placed at the right hand of her king. In this way also the mother of the sons of Zebedee in Matt 20:21 desired of Christ that in his kingdom the one might sit at his right hand and the other at his left.

24. And so this sitting down of Christ at the right hand of his Father does not strictly mean that glory and natural kingdom which the Son of God shares with the Father from eternity, for if that were the case then also the Holy Spirit should have his seat at the right hand of God. But it means the economic and voluntary kingdom in which Christ was established as the God-and-man and our Mediator, for the gathering and defense of his Church. Therefore, the apostle Paul asserts that "the Father has put all things under his feet, except him who has made all things subject to him" (1 Cor 15:27).

25. And so the sitting down by Christ at the Father's right hand encompasses these two things: first, that glory and supreme honor whereby he has received the name that surpasses every name, and whereby he was raised up far above the angels and all other creatures and became their heir and head, as the apostle clearly explains (Eph 1:20–22; Phil 2:9–11; Heb 2:7–8 and elsewhere). For this reason, also Heb 1:3 speaks of the "right hand of the majesty," and Heb 8:1, "the right hand of the majesty of the throne," and Heb 12:2, "the right hand of the throne of God."

26. This glory of Christ as Head is not merely in name only, but it is also accompanied by power and rule over all creatures. With this, as the King and Ruler over all things, he effectively gathers the Church out of the world by his Word and Spirit, and by his power he keeps it safe and guards it against

the world and against Satan, and he does so until he will triumph completely over all his enemies.

27. In addition to the places cited above this actual power and rule is demonstrated by a comparison of Ps 110:1 and 1 Cor 15:25. For the words that are expressed as follows in Psalm 110:1: "Sit at my right hand until I shall make your enemies a footstool for your feet," are given by the apostle thus as an equivalent substitute: "For he must reign until he has put all his enemies under his feet" (1 Cor 15:25). Therefore, also Matt 26:64 and Mark 14:62 call it "the right hand of God's power" and Matt 28:18, "all power in heaven and on earth."

28. At this point the question arises: in which nature did Christ, strictly speaking, sit down at the right hand of God? And the correct answer is: in both natures. For just as Christ was established as Mediator in both natures (as each nature, the divine and the human, performed what belonged to it), so he was established as our King in both natures, albeit with the difference that his divine nature received no new gifts here, other than a renewed use and manifestation of the glory and power which he had from eternity, according to the Father's will and the economy of our salvation, as Christ himself asks in John 17:5: "Father, glorify me in your presence with the glory I had with you before the world began." Yet it was his human nature that received both from the Father, the glory and the power (as well as the use of them), as can be gleaned from Matt 28, Phil 2, Heb 2 and other places.

29. The question also arises, whether it was strictly speaking through his passion and death that Christ merited this glory for his human nature. And whereas we really do not wish to enter into a dispute with those who make this claim, since Christ certainly did obtain it for us by the worthiness of what he merited, yet we are of the opinion that the opposite point of view, which is shared by many Reformed writers, rests upon arguments that are stronger. The chief one of these is that this glory was owed to Christ by the right of his hypostatic union, and as the Son's rightful inheritance (Ps 2:7,8; Heb 1:2). And so, by the consensus of all theologians, that hypostatic union does not follow upon any merit, nor the things which necessarily and by God's decree followed it—which is why the apostle Paul also uses the word "to bestow as gift" in this context (Phil 2:9).

30. But as to the fact that some of the Ubiquitarians maintain that by this sitting down at God's right hand Christ's body became present in all places

in heaven and on earth, besides the fact that it fundamentally overturns other Ubiquitarians who derive this imaginary omnipresence from the hypostatic union, they are in disagreement with various obvious places in Holy Scripture, as these mention only one return of Christ into this world, i.e., when he will appear in glory at the end of the age.

31. Every day the Church experiences the fruits and effects of Christ's sitting down at the Father's right hand; and the enemies of Christ, including even Satan himself, whether they like it or not, marvel at it, and tremble. For Christ gathers his Church by his Word and Spirit, while they vainly resist; he preserves it against the tyranny of the whole world and the gates of hell, and he destroys the Antichrist by the spirit of his mouth. And just as he daily more and more unfolds his kindness and the riches of his grace to those who are true members of the Church (both in their consciences and in their outward status), so he also daily manifests the clear signs that the judgment is coming against a great many of [the enemies].

32. What is more, all these fruits rest upon that intercession whereby Christ intercedes before the Father not just in his state of humility but especially in that state of his glorification (Rom 8:34, Heb 7:25, 1 John 2:1, etc.).

33. And this intercession by Christ in heaven at God's right hand is not the only, single action of Christ as priest, as the godless Socinus imagines, but it is one of his [many] priestly actions. By this, after he offered himself on earth outside the heavenly sanctuary as the atoning sacrificial victim for our sins, he also appeals in the presence of the Father's countenance in heaven. And he does so against Satan and all his instruments, and on behalf of the Church and its members, in the manner of which Zech 3:2 ff. presents us with an outstanding example for each.

34. And this intercession, or appeal, by Christ consists of these three features: 1) that Christ brought his atoning sacrifice into the very sanctuary of heaven to sanctify it for us, and there to appear before the face of God on our behalf (Heb 9:23–24). 2) that by his will and burning desire, just as he had done earlier while on earth (John 17:11, 15, 24, etc.) so also in heaven with the Father he asks earnestly that the power and efficacy of his death be applied to us for our salvation, as can be seen from Zech 1:12 and John 14:16 as well as Acts 2:33. Finally, 3) that by what he has merited and his own desire, he causes the prayers that we pour out in his name to be pleasing and acceptable to God the Father (John 14:6 and 13, likewise 1 John 2:1,2).

35. The entry by the great high priest into the holy of holies on that day of atonement formed a representation of all these features, as the apostle Paul himself points out in Hebrews 7 and 9. For 1) the atoning sacrifice was offered outside the sanctuary and then his blood was taken from there into the sanctuary by the same person. 2) the incense was joined to his blood, as it was a symbol of the offerings and prayers, as Rev 8:3 explains. And he also bore upon his shoulders and breast the names of the tribes of Israel, for whom the foreshadowing atonement was obtained.

36. The final deed of his reign as priest will be the last judgment, when he will come again from heaven to judge the living and the dead, and all people, good as well as evil, shall be gathered together to appear before his judgment seat, for everyone to give an account of what he has done in the body, whether good or evil (2 Cor 5:10). And then at last, when he lays aside his reign as formed by this economy, like a victor of all things and a conqueror he will first hand himself, and then his reign, over to God and the Father, so that God may be all in all (1 Cor 15:24, 28).

ON THE SATISFACTION
OF JESUS CHRIST

President: Antonius Thysius
Respondent: Isaac Plancius

After providing an extensive definition (4), the Synopsis treats the different causes of the satisfaction by Jesus Christ. The different causes are God, Christ as the God-and-man, God's love and justice, Christ's love to 'those who belong to Him,' and our sins (5–12). The 'material cause' of satisfaction, or the price, is expounded (13–21): 'all the miseries and torments that Christ bore from the moment of his birth up until that last act of his priestly office, that is, his passion.' Christ's sufferings were bodily and spiritual (15, see also 27.6), the last being the most grievous because it was God who poured them out upon his soul. Christ's greatest anguish arose from the terrible judgment and wrath of God the Father (17). Christ, being at once true God and true man, possessed the power and strength to endure God's eternal wrath and punishments in time. The formal aspect (or cause) of satisfaction means the full payment Christ made to God in our place and for all our sins (22–28). Despite its sufficiency for all people, the object of the satisfaction are 'only the elect and true believers' (29). The highest goal of the satisfaction is the proof of God's divine justice and mercy (30). Other goals mentioned are the revelation of Christ's great love (31) and peace and wellbeing for humankind (32–33). Together the causes of satisfaction as discussed thus far (5–33) illustrate how necessary this work of satisfaction was (34). Yet it is not only the full payment Christ made for the penalty of sins (his 'passive' obedience) that forms the satisfaction and righteousness that are imputed to believers, but also the holiness and righteousness that Christ possessed and accomplished throughout his life (his 'active' obedience) (35). What is required to receive this satisfaction is faith (36). This closing statement foreshadows the discussion of faith and justification in Disputations 30–33.

1. Until now we have treated the incarnation of the person of God's Son, and the goal for it—i.e., his office and its parts and deeds, and also the different states for carrying it out (the humiliated and the glorified one). It follows that we now undertake to study the satisfaction that depends on his person and office, in particular his priestly office.

2. In Holy Scripture the word 'satisfaction' rarely occurs when it refers to people, so too the expression 'to make satisfaction' (Mark 15:15). It means: to do as much as is enough in the eyes of the person who requests it, or enough for the one who demands it after he has been offended or angered. It can also mean to fulfill someone's wish, and that is generally done in words or in deeds. When it refers to a debt, it means to pay for it, and this payment takes one of two forms. Taken loosely (by catachresis) as 'acceptilation,' satisfaction is a fictitious, nominal payment that one has accepted and deems to be paid, while in fact it has not been paid. Or, taken in the genuine, strict sense, the word means a full and adequate payment. It is in this sense that we take the word here.

3. Well then, the word does not occur in Scripture as referring to the debt we owe to God, by which we are bound to perform the required righteousness or obedience to God, or are bound to bear the required punishment—if it were possible, until it is completely removed—whether by ourselves or through someone else. But other words of equal force appear readily, such as 'redemption,' 'full payment,' and the like, and these are attributed to Christ as our surety and bondsman.

4. 'Satisfaction,' then, is a deed of Christ the God-and-man (i.e., a deed of God and man), whereby he according to the divine, favorable, and just decree, and out of his own obedience to the Father and love towards mankind, willingly and freely made himself to stand as the surety and bondsman on our behalf (that is, in our place and for our good). On our behalf he paid all the penalties that were owed for our sins, and by bearing and removing them he made full satisfaction to God's justice, and by his own merits he set us free from God's wrath and curse, and from eternal death. He obtained righteousness and eternal life for the proclamation of God's righteousness and mercy, as well as for our salvation.

5. The primary efficient cause of this [satisfaction] is God, through his will, his good pleasure, and his just and favorable decree. It is just, because it was his will that satisfaction be made; it was merciful, because it was made in such

a way that while by rights he could have made the requirement from us, he destined and gave his Son for that task. Isa 53:10: "It was God's will to strike him, and he fastened the sins of us all upon him." And verse 14: "He is called afflicted and smitten by God." John 3:16 and Rom 8:32: "God did not spare his own Son, but gave him up for us all." 2 Cor 5[:19]: "God was reconciling the world to himself in Christ" and "He made him to be sin for us."

6. The proximate efficient cause is Christ himself, the God-and-man, Son of God and of man, and so both God and man, the intermediary of the salvation-economy. He alone, in this constitution of person, was prepared and well-suited to perform this office; Gal 2:20: "Christ gave himself for us." He gave himself in both natures, with each here doing its own work—the human what belongs to mankind, and the divine what is of God—and the one in communion with the other, so that (with the exception of each nature's own properties) the one nature came together with the other nature for the same result to accomplish the obedience, merit, and satisfaction—the work of the God-and-man. For just as he became incarnate in order to become our Redeemer, so also the property of each nature served this task: from his human nature came the payment, while from his divine nature came the quantity and quality—obviously the infinitude—and the value or dignity of the paid price. Therefore it says that it was through the eternal Spirit that he offered himself to God (Heb 9:14), and "the Lord of glory was crucified" (1 Cor 2:8).

7. Moreover, he performed this "willingly and of his own accord," without any compulsion. Isa 53:7: "He was offered up because it was his will to do so." And verse 10 and 12: "He laid down his life for sin and handed his soul over to death." John 10:15: "I lay down my life for my sheep;" verse 18: "No-one takes it from me, but I lay it down of my own accord. I have the authority to lay it down and to take it up again." And, [he was] obedient to God with a very prompt obedience; Luke 22[:42]: "Father, if it is possible, remove this cup from me. Yet not my will, but your will be done." John 18[:11]: "Shall I not drink the cup the Father has given me?" Phil 2:8: "He became obedient even unto death." Ps 40[:6 and 8] and Heb 10:[5 and] 7: "You have prepared a body for me; then I said, 'behold I have come to do your will, O God'."

8. And as for the internal cause that moved God, on the one hand it was the loving-kindness, grace, mercy, philanthropy, and the exceeding love of God towards mankind. John 3:16: "For God so loved the world, that he gave his

own Son." Rom 5:8: "God commends his love towards us in that while we were sinners, Christ died for us." However, on the other hand there is [the internal cause of] God's justice, which needed to be satisfied so that his mercy could be exercised and its effect achieved. For here we have to do with a good mix of both [mercy and justice] (Rom 3:25–26).

9. And as for the true internal cause that moved God's Son Jesus Christ, it, similarly, is his inexpressible love towards those who belong to him, and whom the Father has given to him: "I have loved you; greater love has no-one than this: to lay down one's life for one's friends" (John 15:13). Eph 5:2: "Christ loved us, and he gave himself up for us as an offering and sacrifice to God." And verse 25: "Christ loved the Church and he gave himself for her." Gal 2:20: "The Son of God loved me, and he gave himself for me," etc.

10. The outward cause for the satisfaction as determined by the Father and taken up by the Son is our wretchedness, that is, our sins, which deserved and required everlasting punishment. For this God was moved to pity and for this the Son of God underwent all the punishment that was owed to us, so that through him we might be restored to our former happiness; Isa 53:5: "And he was wounded, or affected by grief, because of our transgressions, and he was smitten by our iniquities," and verse 8: "He was struck by the transgressions of my people." In this place the Septuagint translates the Hebrew word *min*, 'by'—a peculiarity of the Hebrew language—as 'because of' our sins, and 'because of' our transgressions. Thus, in Rom 4:25: "He (i.e., Christ) was delivered into the hands of sinners and to death" *dia ta paraptōmata*, "because of our offenses," where *dia* with the accusative case means the prior, driving cause. And it is used this way in many places, especially whenever it occurs in conjunction with sufferings.

11. On this point Holy Scripture similarly uses *huper* and *peri* in the same sense of 'over,' 'for,' 'because of.' 1 Cor 15:3: "Christ died for our sins." Gal 1:4: "He gave himself for (or because of) our sins." Heb 10:12: "Christ offered the sacrifice for sins." And 1 Pet 3:18: "Christ suffered once and for all (*peri hamartiōn*), for sins, the just for (*huper*) the unjust." Here *huper* and *peri* especially when they refer to this case, mean no less the impelling cause than the final cause which includes the sense of the impelling one.

12. And so with those ways of expressing it we should understand 'by' and 'for' sins, 'because of' and 'on account of' sins, as the impelling cause as well as the meritorious cause, i.e., the cause which keeps the punishment owed

for our sins in view, and not only an occasion of whatever kind, as that miscreant Socinus nonsensically says. However, if [an occasion] does belong among the causes, then it would have to be related to the impelling cause. But neither Scripture nor the common way of speaking permits such an explanation.

13. The matter, or the price, of the satisfaction are all the miseries and torments that Christ bore from the moment of his birth up until that last act of his priestly office, that is, his passion. And it was especially that unique death which he suffered on the cross, and the collection of accumulated sufferings, which Isa 53 calls griefs, illness, beating, wounds, bruises, and even death. He says: "Indeed, he took our illnesses on himself and he carried our griefs, etc." 1 Pet 2:24: "You were cleansed by his bruises, or stripes." Col 1:20: "In order to reconcile all things to himself through him, by making peace through his blood on the cross;" and shortly thereafter: "In the body of flesh through death."

14. Moreover in the holy Scriptures this death, together with these qualities, is presented as 'savage and bloody' as well as 'shameful and cursed.' And each of these is known by the words 'punishment,' 'blood,' and 'death on the cross,' as in Phil 2[:8]: "He was obedient unto death, even death on a cross." In Col 1:[20–]22 the violent and bloody death is conveyed by a single expression in the word 'blood'; Acts 20:28: "God bought the Church with his blood;" Rom 3:25: "[God] presented him as an appeasement in his blood;" Eph [1:7 and] 2:13: "We have redemption through his blood." And as for 'shameful and accursed,' it is denoted by the word 'despised' (Isa 53:3; Ps 22:7) and by 'the cross,' which occurs together with 'shame' (Heb 12:2) and with 'stumbling-block' (Gal 5:11) and 'accursedness' (Gal 3:13). For "cursed is everyone who hangs upon a cross."

15. Nevertheless, we should take the word 'sufferings' to mean not only the bodily griefs (which arise from the torments and death in the body) but also the griefs of the soul, as "when his soul suffered" (Isa 53[:11]). And these spiritual ones were by far most grievous, not just because they arose from the very special griefs themselves, or from the fear of death due to his suffering [both the physical and spiritual death], not even from a consideration of what their cause was (since the just underwent those sufferings for the unjust). But they were most grievous because it was God who poured them out upon his soul; that is to say, it was the terrible wrath of God provoked over the sins

committed against him that was kindled and poured out upon [Christ], and whereby God punished him most severely.

16. The prophet David (Ps 16:10) and the Acts of the Apostles (2:27) call these spiritual griefs the "sorrows of death and hell:" "You will not abandon my soul in hell;" and the Apostles' Creed summarizes them as "the descent into hell"—not because Christ experienced the punishments of hell in particular (i.e., the burning flames), but because he bore them in a general sense as punishments that were as powerful as those of hell itself, and everything that is bound up with them.

17. And the gospel writers express it by the feelings and sufferings of the soul—as grief and sorrow: "My soul is sorrowful even unto death." And they express the activities of the soul as "being saddened and grievously anxious" (Matt 26:37), "being deeply distressed" (Mark 14:33), so much so that three times Christ prayed that the cup be passed. Indeed, at that moment of his greatest anguish Christ needed strengthening from an angel, and while he struggled Christ's agony or distress was so great that he perspired beyond what was natural, "letting sweat like drops of blood fall to the ground" (Luke 22:43–44). Obviously, this should not only be taken as arising from a great fear of death (for if so, then many martyrs can appear to be stronger and more steadfast than Christ); no, this arises from the terrible judgment and wrath of God the Father, since one can think of nothing more fearful than this. The outworking of God's wrath reached to the point where "he called out that he had been forsaken by the Father" (Matt 27:46). In short: "He became the curse, that in him we might be a blessing to God" (Gal 3:13).

18. It was not necessary, however, that he should despair. For despair is a punishment of such a kind that it is also a sin. But in order to be the avenger of sin the Son of God had to be without sin. For he bore everything that he was able to bear without sin.

19. Nor was it necessary or possible for him to be kept in eternal punishments—as far as its length of time was concerned—that is, in bodily as well as spiritual death. Because Christ did in fact experience the full extent of the hellish agonies and torments, along with God's abandonment and rejection of him (something that of itself always accompanies eternal death), having been forsaken and rejected by him even unto hell, which otherwise it would have been necessary for us to experience. But Christ did not experience them for an unbroken extent of time, which happens when there

is no release. On the other hand, those who have been condemned shall experience both of them.

20. And the reason for this is the fact that the sinners who are guilty of the damnation could not, being mere mortals, have had the strength to bear the infinite wrath of God, nor could they bear all his wrath poured out at once in its fullness (for otherwise the created being would have been swallowed up and destroyed immediately). No, they would have had to bear it only partially and to a limited degree (to the extent that a created being would be able to bear it), and accordingly they would have to endure it successively and continuously. But Christ, in his single *hypostasis* of being entirely true God and man as befits his infinite power and strength, at one and the same time endured [the wrath] completely. So much so that this suffering in time really was equivalent to eternal punishments (Heb 9:14; John 2:19 and 10:18; Acts 2:24, 25 and 3:15).

21. And all these bodily and spiritual punishments for sins, that in God's strict judgment were owed for sins, also come by the name of 'sin.' Hence it says that "He bore our sins," that is, the punishment for sins. "He was made to be sin," that is, he was a substitute for sin. And he was 'a curse,' that is, accursed and liable to the punishment of the Law. In fact, Christ himself is called "the payment by which we have been bought" (1 Cor 6:20 and 7:23) and the "ransom for redemption" (Matt 20:28; 1 Tim 2:6) that is paid as a substitute for something else and that has a value equal to it. Therefore also "we have been redeemed with his precious blood, namely a lamb without blemish or defect" (1 Pet 1:18–19), in such a way that the equivalence of the payment depends on the person and on what is at stake.

22. The form of Christ's satisfaction is most perfect in mode and act, that is: in every way, by the full payment made to God for us all (i.e., in our place) and for all our sins, to purge them and wash them away. For as the matter of satisfaction rests on a punishment equivalent to what is owed for the sins (in which the satisfaction exists), so also its form. First, because the Son of God, in keeping with the will of the Father, being both God and man whose power and strength to bear the punishment came from his deity, has experienced, borne, suffered, and put a complete end to sins. Secondly, because it was on our behalf that he accomplished it, since it was as our guarantor, surety and bondsman that he assumed our person and place. And lastly, because it was to God (since we were obliged to him) as our God, creator, Lord, lawgiver,

and judge that this satisfaction had to be paid. It is in these things that the full form of the satisfaction as such exists.

23. There are three acts in the satisfaction (or in the performance of satisfaction) by Christ. For just as the priests' offering was slaughtered and presented in the fore-court, and its blood was carried into God's presence in the sanctuary, and the people in the fore-court were sprinkled by its blood (Exod 20[:24] and 24[:8]), so too Christ, in his most excellent and final act, as Priest upon the cross, offered himself on our behalf. And, as the Intermediary, he had previously presented himself as the offering in the heavenly sanctuary, and even now makes intercession through the everlasting power of his sacrifice. And as King from heaven he applies his satisfaction to us on earth (Heb 9:12, 13:10–11).

24. For further demonstration and proof of the form of Christ's satisfaction it is relevant to note that in the sacrifices of atonement or expiation the animal was put in the place of the one who had sinned, who by laying-on his hands and confessing his sins over it transferred (as it were) his sins onto it, and the animal was slain in his stead and offered to God (Lev 1:4; 16:21). And so the sacrificial animal was not rarely given the name 'sin,' 'the misdeed'—i.e., the sacrificial offering or offering for sin, and to it was attributed also the atonement for the sins (Num 28:22; Exod 2812). And so, as a type it had a reasonable connection to that truly atoning and expiatory sacrifice of Christ.

25. It is with this in view that the prophet speaks about the Messiah, in Isa 53:4: "Truly, he took up our infirmities, and he carried (conveyed, or bore)— our griefs." Here the latter word is a restriction of the former's generalization, which is used also to mean "take away." And so verse 11: "Knowledge of my righteous servant will justify many, and (i.e., for) he himself carried their iniquities." And obviously "iniquity" does not mean guilt but the punishment for iniquity, when the word "to carry" in Hebrew is juxtaposed with "to carry the punishments," and that is the sense in which we must understand what soon follows it: "And he himself bore the sin (i.e., the punishment for sin) of many."

26. Here it matters also what it says in verse 5: "The chastisement (or affliction, which soon thereafter is called hardship) for peacemaking (or for our peace) was on him," i.e., was placed upon him. And verse 6: "The Lord caused to come upon him the iniquity of us all;" that is, He cast or turned onto him the punishment for our iniquities. The translators into Greek [the

Septuagint] render it as "He handed him over to our sins." And it states emphatically in verse 10: "He will make his soul into a misdeed," that is, an offering for misdeed. In these places it means the imputation of blame and the vicarious bearing and full endurance of punishment, and that he took the place of our person, and in our place underwent and paid for our punishments.

27. And this type and its prophecy is most clearly explained in the New Testament. John has this in mind when he says: "Behold the Lamb of God who takes (i.e., takes upon himself, or bears, and so bears it that he removes it) the sin of the world" (John 1:29). Hence for this reason he is called 'lamb' everywhere in the book of Revelation, and also "the lamb that was slain" (Rev 13:8 and 1 Pet 2:24). "Christ bore our sins" (Heb 9:28)—it does not say 'to take away'—he bore our sins upon his body on the tree, i.e., the tree of the cross, in the sense of [bore] in his body and on the cross, for shortly thereafter it says that we have been cleansed by his wounds. There the joint mention of suffering and our deliverance implies the taking on of another's punishment.

28. In fact it is clear also in those places where he is declared to have borne all these things 'for us,' that is, 'in our place.' Matt 20:28: "The Son of Man came to serve and to give his life as a ransom in the place of (*anti*) many." Romans 5:6,8: "Christ died above (*huper*), i.e., for the ungodly," and for us, as the following verse convincingly shows. 2 Corinthians 5[:21]: "He made him who knew no sin to be sin on our behalf," i.e., in our person, by imputing to him the guilt of our sins, and because he was made an offering for sin that "we might become the righteousness of God in him," i.e., in his person. Similarly, Galatians 3:13: "Christ has redeemed us from the curse of the law, having been made the curse for us," which by the apostle's explanation (verse 10) means 'accursed', and 'subject to the curse'. In these places the words *anti* and *huper* mean primarily on our behalf, in our stead and place, and in our person. Hence comes also the usefulness of the satisfaction for us.

29. So then, the goal of the satisfaction, for whose benefit it is (or who is its object), are only the elect and true believers of the Old and the New Testament. For although the satisfaction, as far as it concerns the magnitude, worth, and sufficiency of the payment (taken by itself), could be offered to all people, nevertheless it was given out only to those whom the Father has chosen and given to the Son, and who by God's free gift were going to believe

in God and his Son. Hence it says throughout Scripture that he gave himself 'for his own' and 'for us,' 'for the sheep,' and 'the Church' (Matt 20:28; 26:28; 1 John 3:16; Acts 20:28).

30. And as for the goal for the sake of which [the satisfaction was made], or the use of the matter, which can be called its effect (when considered as an act), and which—regarding God—even may be called the highest effect, is the proof of his divine justice and mercy. Of justice, because he punished our sins most severely; of mercy, because he did not punish them in us (in whom he could deservedly have done so) but in another, namely his very own Son (Rom 3:25–26): "God presented him as an atoning sacrifice through faith in his blood, to demonstrate his justice; [God did so] out of forbearance by leaving unpunished the sins committed beforehand, in order to display his justice in the present time, so that he Himself might be just and the justifier of the one who has faith in Jesus." Here the words 'justice' and 'just' are taken closely together, since hereby God is the avenger and the punisher of sins, as the words 'appeasement' and 'justification' clearly show; and he is also merciful, truthful, and faithful, as the phrase "appeasement through his blood" declares. And so here the severity of the one who punishes and the grace and goodness of the one who saves are united.

31. However, with respect to Christ or the 'intermediate goal,' it is the revelation of his great love, as he was the one who died for his enemies (Rom 5:6).

32. And lastly, insofar as it concerns us and the lowest or 'proximate goal,' it is to provide peace and wellbeing to us, as in Isa 53:5: "The chastisement for our peace was on him, and his wounds are healing for us." So too for justification: "Through the knowledge of him my just servant will justify many [Isa 53:11]," etc. This goal is explained more fully in the New Testament, with the words "remission of sins" (Matt 26:28), the "doing away with, or taking away of, sin" (Heb 9:26, 28), the "loosening or transference" [of sin] (Rom 3[:25]). It is the justification and preservation from wrath (Rom 5:9), God's justice (2 Cor 5:21), his blessing (Gal 3:13 [and 14]), realized redemption and so salvation (Eph 1:7; Col 1:14), the reconciliation with God (Col 1:20, Eph 2). All these clearly show the deliverance or freedom from punishment.

33. Moreover, this goal contains also the righteousness and holiness that goes with it, especially in those places where Scripture uses those words more

common; as when Christ and his blood (i.e., his blood poured out) purges (1 Pet 1:2), cleanses (1 John 1:7), and washes us from sins (Rev 1:5). These expressions signify chiefly and primarily the deliverance from sin, and then also the amendment and sanctification of the soul. In fact, the two separate notions are joined together in Titus 2:14: "He gave himself for us in order to redeem us from all iniquity, and he purified for himself a special people, zealous for good works."

34. So much, then, for the causes of Christ's satisfaction. The consideration of the causes also makes clear the necessity of his work of satisfaction, and it is two-fold. In one sense it is absolute, as far as it concerns God's nature, whereby he greatly detests and hates sin (as it is contrary to him), but also punishes it most severely—for which reason there could be no forgiveness of guilt and punishment without satisfaction. Yet in another sense the necessity is hypothetical, because as he had decreed to punish the sinner with death, according to the statement "by death you shall die," so he had also decreed that in the very same way satisfaction would be made to him through the death of his own Son, and it was his will that the satisfaction would be granted to this person and that one. This was the manner of the divine decree, and in fact it was in an exceptional accordance with the wisdom and justice of the one who so acted. In this way it was such that God conducted himself not only as Ruler but also as the most just Judge of all people (Gen 18:25; Rom 1:32 and 3:5–6; 2 Thess 1:5–6).

35. Whereas we have given a treatment here of satisfaction insofar as it consists of the full payment made for the penalty of sins, we also include a second part of it—as is the way of Scripture, in fact—because of the relationship which necessarily accompanies it. For by [that part] Christ both possessed and accomplished, throughout the course of his entire life, the holiness and righteousness that we were required and bound to accomplish, so that in him we might be conformed to the Law of God in everything; and so that he might obtain for us the right to life eternal. For that is demanded by the entire account of the one indebted according to the Law, and also by Christ's obedience and righteousness, and by the faith that takes hold of the whole Christ (Gen 15:6; Isa 53:9; Jer 23:5–6 and 33:16; Dan 9:24; Luke 1:35; Matt 3:15; John 17:19; Rom 3:22 and 5:18, 19, and 21; Rom 8:3–4 and 10:3–4; 1 Cor 1:30; Gal 3:14, 18, and 4:4–5; Phil 2:8 and 3:8–9; Heb 10:7 and 10). And this holiness and righteousness concern also Christ's office as priest. For

according to the Law, the priest had to be holy and just, and the sacrificial animal had to be whole and without blemish.

36. Moreover, although Christ presented this satisfaction for us (i.e., on our behalf and for our benefit), nevertheless, for it to be ours, faith is required in addition to it. Hence Scripture links God's giving up of the Son and his blood with faith. John 3[:16]: "For God so loved the world that he gave his Son, that whoever believes in him should not perish but have eternal life." Rom 3[:25]: "God presented him as an atoning sacrifice through faith in his blood."

Antitheses

Ant. 1. And so we reject in the first place the godless notion which holds that satisfaction is impossible to the point that there could not have been (nor ought there to have been) any satisfaction to God. It holds that Christ's sufferings and death are only deeds of martyrdom, a confirmation and seal of God's liberality in forgiving sins, and an example whereby Christ opened the way to salvation with his most holy and blameless life and death, and thus obtained the remission of sins for those who believe (i.e., those who obey).

Ant. 2. In the second place we reject that injustice done to the person and merit of Christ, which replaces Christ's satisfaction with an 'acceptilation,' or with a partial satisfaction as efficient as the complete one.

Ant. 3. And lastly, we also reject the following position (though it is very close to the truth), which turns the necessity of the satisfaction into a hypothetical one only, namely making it only dependent on God's decree, and not also an absolute necessity similarly dependent on the divine nature and the essential justice of God.

SOURCES

Origen, *Sermon 3 on Leviticus*

If one recalls accurately what we've stated, he could well tell us that our position is that the sacrifice we said was offered by the priest for sin contained a figure of Christ, but that this does not match the true Christ (for he knew no sin), namely that he is said to have brought the offering for sin—granted that is was done through a mystery and that the one who is the priest is at the same time also the sacrificial offering. Consider then, whether we can agree on this point as follows. Christ indeed committed no sin, yet he was made to be sin for us, because he who was in the form of God deigned to take on the form of a servant; because he who is immortal actually dies, because he who cannot suffer actually suffers, and because he who cannot be seen is in fact seen. And also since for us mortals death and all the other weaknesses of the flesh were brought on because of our sinful state, so too he himself was made into the likeness of man, and in appearance became known as a man, then it is without a doubt that he, for the sin which he had taken upon himself from us (because he carried our sins), presented to God a calf without spot, that is, his own undefiled flesh, as an offering.

Origen, *Sermon 24 on Numbers*

For as long as sins exist, sacrifices for sins are necessarily required. For suppose (for the sake of the argument) that sin did not exist. If sin did not exist, it would not have been necessary for the Son of God to become the lamb, nor would there have been need for him to be slain when he was in the flesh, but he would have remained what he was in the beginning: God the Word. But since "sin entered into this world" [Rom 5:12], and the necessity of sin demands atonement, and atonement is not possible without a sacrifice, it was necessary that a sacrifice for sin be provided.

Ambrose, *On Joseph the Patriarch*, chapter 4

Joseph was sold in Egypt, because Christ was going to come to those who had been told: "You were sold on account of your sins." And accordingly, it was by his own blood that he redeemed those whose own sins had sold them. But Christ was sold because he took their condition upon himself, and not because of guilt. And he is not detained by the payment for sin, because he himself did not commit sin. Therefore, he assumed the debt in order to pay for us and not for anything that he owed: he took over the promissory note, he removed the lender, and he set the debtor aside. It was one person who discharged the debt that all people owed. It was not lawful for us to escape slavery. It was he who undertook it for our sake, in order to drive out the slavery to the world, to restore the freedom of Paradise and to bestow new grace through the honor of his fellowship.

Augustine, *On the Trinity*, book 13 chapters 10–15

There was no other, more suitable way to cleanse us of our wretchedness, nor was there a need to find one. For what was so necessary for raising our hopes and to set the minds of mortals, cast down by their mortality, free from despairing of immortality, than that we be shown how much God valued us and how much he loved us, etc. What, then, was the righteousness whereby the devil was conquered? What, except the righteousness of Christ? And in what way was he conquered? Because when [God] found in him nothing deserving death and nevertheless slew him, by this work of redemption the blood of Christ was given as a payment for us, and, as it was accepted, the devil was not enriched by it, but bound up, so that we might be loosed from his chains, etc.

DISPUTATION 30

ON THE CALLING OF
PEOPLE TO SALVATION

President: Johannes Polyander
Respondent: Henricus Geldorpius

The Synopsis now turns our attention to the operation of the Holy Spirit in those whom God in his infinite wisdom has chosen to eternal salvation. It therefore focuses first on the call to salvation. It mentions the universal calling with which each and every human being is summoned to know and worship God the Creator (2–4). In his special calling, God calls some people to a supernatural knowledge of Christ away from the corruptions of this world through the Gospel and the power of the Holy Spirit (5). While human beings, since they are endowed with intellect and will, have the ability (in principle) to answer God's call, yet because of the fall into sin and its consequences they actually cannot respond (18–19). God's gracious calling does not extend to each and every human being. That would mix God's love towards humanity with his electing love in Christ and to rob God from his freedom (25–31). By means of the outward or external administration of Word and sacrament, and by the inward operation of the Holy Spirit in the human heart, the special call to salvation takes place (32), even though God may call certain people without the use of the outward Word (33). The conjunction of the inward and outward calling is what makes it effective. Even so, that effectiveness occurs only those persons 'in whom the Holy Spirit implants the full assurance or confidence of a living faith that is rooted in Christ' (34–38, cf. 48). The ineffective ways in which the two sides of the calling can concur lead to the phenomenon of hypocrites mingled among the true believers in the visible church (39–41). The effective calling turns the depraved human will from being unwilling to willing, it is not 'impetuous, but sweet and suitably applied' (42). The disputation closes with the highest goal of both callings—God's glory—and an enumeration of the effects of the calling, which will be treated in later disputations.

1. The election unto salvation (which was treated above) is carried out through certain steps and means whereby God has determined that those whom He has chosen for himself should be blessed with his saving grace in this age and with his eternal glory in the age that is to come.

2. We should make a distinction between this special calling of men to Jesus Christ the Redeemer of the world and the universal calling of them to God its Creator.

3. By the universal calling each and every human being is summoned, by means of patterns occurring generally in the natural world, that he should know and worship God the Creator (Acts 17:27; Rom 1:20). For this reason, it may be named 'the natural calling.'

4. As for the generally occurring patterns of nature, they are partly internal— recorded on the hearts of all people—and partly external, engraved by God in the created things. The former kind is known by the name 'Law' (Rom 2:14), the latter by 'words that declare the glory of God' (Ps 19:4).

5. By the special calling God calls some people out of the whole human race to a supernatural knowledge of Jesus Christ our Redeemer, to share in his life-giving benefits, and [to a departure] from the corruptions of this world; and God does so through the ministry of the Gospel and the power of the Holy Spirit. Therefore, this calling may also go by the name of supernatural and the Gospel-call.

6. The knowledge of God that comes by the first calling is theoretical rather than practical. By the latter calling the knowledge of God is practical as well as theoretical, and in that way justifying faith is ingenerated in the hearts of certain people who have been called.

7. Hence those of this world who are wise, even though they have been summoned to search for God by fumbling about for him (so to speak) with the aid of the first kind of calling, in their stubbornness of heart they in unrighteousness suppress the truth that their minds had received (Rom 1:18). But the sons of light, heeding the second kind of calling "to partake of the lot of the saints who are of the light," "are rendered wise unto salvation through faith in Jesus Christ" (Col 1:12–13; 2 Tim 3:15).

8. Therefore, just as justifying faith is the only instrument to partake in the lot of the saints in the light, so the Gospel-call is the first avenue to faith.

9. And so those people err who make not only the Gospel-call but also the natural calling into an entrance-way to salvation. By the aid of the Gospel-call some people come to a knowledge of our Savior Jesus Christ (which is the only way to eternal life); but no-one comes to it with the aid of the natural calling (John 14:6 and 17:3).

10. The primary efficient cause of the Gospel-call is God the Father, in the Son and through the Holy Spirit (1 Thess 2:12; Eph 1:17 and 4:11–12; Rev 3:20).

11. For the Son, as the Mediator between God and men, and as Head of the Church, calls these people to himself through the Holy Spirit and the Word of truth (Matt 11:28). The Holy Spirit equips the preachers of the Word with gifts that are needed to draw those people—to whom the Father sends them in the name of the Son—into communion with Christ by His summons (1 Cor 12:4; Heb 2:4).

12. The impelling cause, whereby God is moved internally by Himself, is God's grace, his good pleasure and favorably-inclined will to offer, in Christ, his salvation to wretched sinners.

13. God's thoughtful, provident wisdom accompanied his grace, and with it God ordered the saving call of some people from the host of sinful people worldwide in such a way that he could display to them his own mercy, without disadvantaging his own justice or freedom.

14. The initiating cause, or the external compelling one, is Christ's atoning sacrifice for the sins of those people whom God will call.

15. The ordinary instrumental cause is the ministry of the divine Word through the preachers of the Gospel (2 Thess 2:14). And as far as an extra-ordinary instrumental cause is concerned, nothing certain can be determined about it from Scripture.

16. And as for the subject-matter of which the calling is concerned, or the object of the calling, it is the human race that deserves everlasting death on account of sin; in this instance 'human race' is used not in a universal sense, but in a general and distributive sense (Matt 9:13).

17. Accordingly, when we look to the corrupt nature that people have in common, they are all equally unworthy to be called by God to salvation and unsuited for responding [to him]; they are all equally dead in sins and children

of wrath, alienated from the life to God and hostile to him (Eph 2:1–3, and 4:18; Col 1:21)—although outwardly some expose their own depravity less than others.

18. Those who in contradiction ascribe to corrupt human nature some aptitude for responding to God and his calling, confuse things that must be kept apart, namely the human subject of the aptitude and the mode of the aptitude. Regarding the former, human beings, endowed with reason and logically classified as opposite to dumb animals, are rightly said to be capable of listening to God when he calls them. However, regarding the latter, we affirm that the same people are entirely unsuited to listening to God as He calls.

19. For the mode of the aptitude or the ability that sinners have to listen to God when He calls does not come from the blinded eyes of their own minds, nor from the crooked desires of their wills, nor from the blunted feelings of their flesh; but God here bestows it on those people to whom He gives ears to hear, eyes to see, and feet to follow those things that are revealed to us in Christ for the salvation of the soul. With a view to this Bernard says that God works it in us to do three things: "To consider what is good, to will what is good, and to accomplish what is good" (*On Grace and Free Choice*).

20. The 'good' [of which Bernard speaks] is either the good of salvation and eternal blessedness prepared in heaven for us, or the good of righteousness which, as it is pleasing to God, leads us to that blessedness. Both of these good things are not known to the natural man, as the Apostle testifies (1 Cor 2:14; 2 Cor 3:5), and consequently the natural man is incapable of rightly discerning both of these good things and of duly choosing either of them for himself, nor can he attain them.

21. And just as each of these good things is offered to us through the preaching of the Gospel, so too does the Holy Spirit kindle solemn thinking in our hearts about both of them and an earnest longing for them.

22. This longing for the good is different from the desire that the Philosophers in their ethical treatises define by means of the word 'happiness.' For this latter notion comes by natural instinct, while the former comes by supernatural assent, i.e., by faith in Jesus Christ. And the latter is shared by all those who are born of Adam, while the former belongs only to those who are born again in Christ.

23. The people who contend on the grounds of the supernatural assent of faith which the Holy Spirit kindled in our hearts, that the natural longing for true blessedness as revealed in the Gospel had been lying dormant in them long beforehand, argue no less foolishly than if they held that water, which in and of itself is cold, possesses an innate power to heat before it obtains that power when being heated by fire.

24. The evangelist Luke shows clearly that in all those who are called this assent of faith does not arise from some innate longing for blessedness as if for their perfection, but it is God who inspires it in the people whom he calls in his own good pleasure. For example, in Acts 13[: 48] and 16[:14] he says about some of the gentiles, that they believed the Gospel (which was a stumbling-block to the Jews) because they had been ordained to eternal life; and about Lydia that she believed because God had opened her heart.

25. It can be demonstrated with clear witnesses and examples from Holy Scripture that the preaching of the Gospel does not call each and every person to the assent of faith. For just as in the Old Testament the mystery of Christ was kept hidden from the gentiles and revealed through the prophets only to the Jewish people, so too in the New Testament it was not declared to everyone indiscriminately through the apostles, but only to whichever Jews and gentiles happened to be in that place and at that time God had ordained for making it known.

26. Paul and Timothy experienced this on their mission journey: while they had prepared to go into Asia and Bithynia in order to preach the Gospel in those places, God through his own Spirit hindered their plans and sent them into Macedonia (Acts 16:6–7, 10).

27. Therefore they are idle dreamers who extend God's gracious calling to each and every human being. For they mix up God's love towards humanity (whereby God embraces all people as his own creatures) with the love whereby He has ordained to take into his grace a select number of people from the common crowd of sinners who are perishing for their own wickedness, and to guide them in Jesus Christ, the Son in whom He delights. And in so doing, they also rob God, who is beholden to no-one, of all his freedom to set apart some whom He chooses from all those enemies of his who are equally undeserving of his mercy in order to transform them from their condition of guilt into the condition of his grace.

28. However, this notion about God's universal grace is so appealing to some people that they actually think they can prove it very convincingly with three arguments from the sacred writings.

29. Their first argument rests on those witnesses in the holy books which affirm that Christ assumed his flesh from the nature that is common to all human beings. But the pronouncement by Christ himself, who declares that his own flesh by itself and apart from the Spirit and the truth can benefit no-one unto salvation (John 6:63), makes it clear how foolish it is to make a link from this common nature in the flesh to a spiritual communion of those same human beings with Christ. This is clear also from the apostle's restriction, as he limits all people who with Christ are of the same family, to them who are his brothers in the midst of the congregation, and who are the children given to him by God the Father (Heb 2:11–13).

30. Their second argument is taken from a similarity that they draw between Adam and Christ (Rom 5:12), a similarity incorrectly understood, as can be shown from the portrayal there of the two Adams. For the apostle defines the first Adam as a type of Christ, as the head and chief of all people who are conceived in sin, but the second Adam, namely Christ as the head of people who have been justified by faith, in order to intimate that while the sin of the former flows forth to all his descendants through their common nature, the benefit of the latter on the other hand is shared only with believers who have been removed from that common lot through a particular grace.

31. For the third argument they look to the promises of the calling unto the saving knowledge of God, which as far as their wording goes are universal, like: "They all shall be taught by God" (John 6:45), "I shall pour out my Spirit upon all flesh" (Acts 2:17), and similar texts. But regarding the universal application in the wording, surely "all" stands not for particular elements within classes of kinds, but for classes of particular elements, as is obvious from thesis 25 and 26. This is obvious also from everyday experience, and those places in Holy Scripture where the word 'all' refers in the distributive sense to all sorts of people who, without any discrimination in race, age, or gender are being called to that saving knowledge of God through the ministry of the Gospel (as in Rom 1:14; Eph 2:17; 1 Tim 2:1, 3–4; Titus 2:2–3, 6, 9, 11, etc.).

32. The way of calling, when we examine it from opposing perspectives, is divided into external and internal. The former is achieved outwardly through

the administration of Word and sacraments, the latter inwardly through the working of the Holy Spirit.

33. God does not always apply both ways of calling that are possible for him to convert people [together], but He calls some people to himself only by the internal light and divine power of the Holy Spirit apart from the outward ministry of his Word. Whereas this way of calling is sufficient to salvation by itself, it is very rare, extraordinary, and to us unknown.

34. Nor does God always link the two ways of calling equally or in the same way, but the concurrence of both of them is effective in some people and ineffective in others.

35. The ineffective concurrence of the two ways is observed in three kinds of people. For some people are not moved to embrace it, even though the light of the evangelical truth has shone fully upon them. These are the people who receive the seed of the Gospel that is sown along the trodden path (Matt 13:19).

36. Other people allow the light of the truth that they have taken up in their hearts to be choked by the cares and pleasures of this world. These receive the Gospel like seed sown among the thorns (Matt 13:22).

37. To other people the Holy Spirit offers a little taste of his grace so that their hearts are touched by a momentary feeling of happiness. These receive the Gospel like seed on rocky soil (Matt 13:20).

38. The effective concurrence of both ways is perceived by those people in whom the Holy Spirit ingenerates the full assurance or confidence of a living faith that is rooted in Christ, whereby they steadfastly and with perseverance apply to themselves the promise of grace that was sealed with his own inner testimony. These people receive the Gospel like seed sown in good soil (Matt 13:23).

39. Because of the variety in the concurrence of the internal call with the outward one, hypocrites mingle among the true people of Israel within the visible Church (which is the gathering of those who have been called). It is with regard to this mixture that both the good and the evil are said to be invited to the wedding banquet of the Son, the Lamb of God (Matt 22:4), and that many are called, but few are chosen (Matt 20:16).

40. Although some gifts flow forth from the concurrence of the two callings and are shared by hypocrites along with the elect (i.e., the gift of knowing and tasting God's good Word, and the virtues of the coming age [Heb 6:6]), they are not sufficient for the salvation of the hypocrites. But in the elect, they prepare the way for their salvation and—by God's good pleasure towards them—these gifts do lead the way to more abundant grace, of which others are rightly, deservedly deprived because they do not employ those first gifts in the right way.

41. Hence by their abuse of those first gifts the hypocrites are rendered without excuse before God, since from the ingratitude of their evil hearts they once again entangle themselves in the corruptions of the world from which they had escaped through knowing Jesus Christ (2 Pet 2:20).

42. None of the ways and movements of the calling is forced or impetuous, but sweet and suitably applied to turning the crooked will of the one who is moved for the better, so that from unwilling he becomes willing.

43. Christ uses the word 'draw' for this way and movement of calling (John 6:44) so that no-one should think that he himself had undertaken it, but only God. For whoever is drawn into communion with Christ from elsewhere is not brought to desire it by his own decision but is turned to it by the strength of the one who draws him.

44. God, with the same authoritative will whereby He invites those whom he wants to the wedding banquet of his Lamb, also calls some of them into his vineyard in the first hour, others in the third, yet again others in the sixth or the ninth, and lastly others in the eleventh hour.

45. The form of the effective calling by which it is distinguished from the ineffective one, consists in the saving application of this benefit which takes some sinners from their natural communion to that particular grace, from the company of faithless ones into communion with those who are faithful, and from the kingdom of darkness into the kingdom of everlasting light.

46. The highest goal of both callings (shared by both the ineffective and the effective one) is the manifestation of God's mercy towards those whom He calls. The subordinate goal of the effective calling, and [the goal] proper to it, is the saving imparting of God's grace; but the accidental goal of the ineffective calling is the conviction of stubborn disobedience and complete inexcusableness in the hearts of those who impudently withstand and

interrupt the Holy Spirit as He speaks through the mouths of the preachers. From this distinction 2 Cor 2:15–16 calls the Gospel the aroma of life unto life for some, and for others the aroma of death to death.

47. The effects of the calling are faith, justification, sanctification, and glorification. These will be treated in later disputations.

48. The fact that these effects are not received by everyone but only by some of the people who have been called does not happen due to some shortcoming of God's omnipotent power, but happens only by his choosing. For by his infinite power God could (if He willed so) emend the vice of human weakness no less in the former people than in the latter, since He always accomplishes everything that He wills to accomplish (Ps 115:3).

ON FAITH AND THE
PERSEVERANCE OF THE SAINTS

President: Andreas Rivetus
Respondent: Paulus Testardus

This disputation is arranged in two sections, of which the first deals with Faith (1–29), the second with Perseverance (30–42). The different meanings of faith are explained (2– 8) and saving faith is defined (6). Saving faith is 'a firm assent—based on the certain knowledge of divine revelation—implanted in our minds by the Holy Spirit through the Word of the Gospel' (6, see also 20). Then the efficient and instrumental causes of faith are discussed (9–12). As for the 'matter of faith,' it is treated according to its subjects and objects (13–18 and 19–25). The 'form' of faith is located in the correspondence of every believer's faith in the revealed truth and the application of the promise of grace in his or her heart (26–27). Next is a discussion of the goal and effects of faith (28–29). Distinctions are made in faith: faith is justifying, or historical, or temporary, or it is a faith in miracles. Concerning the assurance of salvation in the heart of the believer, we are informed that believers should 'be certain that their own sins have been forgiven and that they have been reconciled through Christ' (20). Based on the Gospel promise and the believer's self-awareness of personal faith, one may conclude that the promise holds true. The second section draws attention to Perseverance, beginning with the meanings of the term and its proper definition (31–33). Just as for faith, so too for perseverance the author treats the efficient cause (34–35), the matter (36–38), the objects (39–40), and the goals and effects (41– 42). Defined as 'the continuous, perpetual progress and successful endurance of true believers, through the grace and justifying faith once received' (33), perseverance is bestowed by the Holy Spirit working through the Word.

1. Whereas the salvation of the elect and the glory of God is the removed, ultimate end in the divine calling unto salvation, the proximate end is that

people respond by faith when God and Christ call them. For after the Father in his compassion appointed Christ as our Redeemer, it was his will to come to our aid through Christ by this rule: that we embrace his mercy by a sure faith. Therefore, after having given a treatment of Christ, his offices, benefits, and his call to share in them, now is a suitable time for us to treat what this faith ought to be like, whereby all those who have been called to the adoption as sons come to possess the heavenly kingdom.

2. And since different meanings are accepted for the word 'faith,' we should set to one side those meanings that are not relevant to our undertaking, and then proceed to explain its nature. And first of all, since we shall be treating godly faith and not the humankind, we leave aside the commonly accepted meaning of faith, that it is the assent whereby people extend their faith or trust to each other. Secondly, we are not speaking about the faith that we give when we affirm or promise something to someone. We do ascribe faith in this sense to God himself, that is, the steadfast truth of his words and deeds. Thirdly, we are not dealing with faith insofar as the word is used for the content of faith, or the material object of faith (as it is called), that is: the things that are to believed, the things that in Scripture are sometimes also meant by the word 'faith.' Fourth, we are not using it for faith insofar as the sign and sacrament of faith are meant by it through metonymy.

3. The entire question is about the faith that we exercise when we believe God, who reveals to us the truth of something, when we give strong assent to him on account of his assurance. It is common to propose four 'species' of faith, and although they are all included in the one general word 'faith,' they do not have one and the same meaning. For we make distinctions between them by adding epithets: historical, temporary, in miracles, and justifying. But we do not distinguish the temporary from the historical faith to such an extent that each forms a different species in a proper sense, but we make two steps (as it were), or stages, or acts of faith. For that historical faith, which some call 'dogmatic,' is the disposition whereby someone believes that everything God has revealed is true or it exists in the fact that the believer is persuaded about the truth of something, apart from having any inner feeling, either toward the one who reveals it or to the thing that is revealed. And this is the first stage, which is entirely theoretical. Or this theory is linked to some feeling, or tasting, or joy, and to outward indications of it. This is the second stage, and it concerns the faith that is called temporary. These two stages are related to each other in such a way that the second stage

assumes the presence of the first one, but not the other way around. But we do not give the first one the name 'historical faith' as though narrative accounts are its only subject-matter. For it entails also the promises, at least to the extent that their veracity as such is believed; and so too is believed the capability of him who makes the promise. But someone who believes the promises only in a historical way, does not apply them to himself steadfastly nor is he convinced that the divine will is directed at him.

4. [And there is] faith in miracles, which others prefer to use in a broader sense and to call 'faith in particular promises,' since with that faith, too, we believe particular promises of some temporal or spiritual good that not all of the elect share, or that is bestowed on some people who are not elect. With this faith we steadfastly determine that what God either has foretold or has willed to happen is in fact going to come about through the power of God either by us or by other people, for our good. Like the previous one, this kind of faith does not extend to the entire Word of God, but only to some special revelation. Those who divide this kind of faith into active and passive want to say the same thing as we said: that God willed it to happen either by us or by others for our good. They have given the name 'active' to that special gift of God whereby someone believes that he himself is about to perform something miraculous (or in some other way bring it about) through the power of God. [They call it] 'passive' faith when someone determines that he will partake of singular benefits that come about by God's special promise through miracles or some other means. An example of the former is in 1 Cor 13:2, and of the latter in Acts 14:9.

5. And Augustine rightly [states] that Paul did not define faith as any kind of faith whereby one believes in God, but he defined it as 'life-giving faith' and 'gospel faith' from which come forth works of love (*On Faith and Works*, chapter 14). It is the same faith that we call 'justifying and saving faith.' And, to make a comment in passing, we do not approve the opinion of those who want justifying faith to be different from saving faith, as though there are people who have been granted justifying faith but in the end were withheld saving faith. For Scripture takes them as one and the same: "To be saved by grace through faith and not because of works" (Eph 2:8). And: "To be justified through by faith" or "to be justified by grace" (Gal 2:16; Titus 3:7).

6. And that saving faith is a firm assent—based on the certain knowledge of divine revelation—ingenerated in our minds by the Holy Spirit through the

word of the Gospel, an assent to everything that God has revealed to us in his Word, and especially to the promises of life that were made in Christ; hereby each and every believer, relying with constant confidence in God, steadfastly determines that forgiveness of sins was promised not only to believers generally but also granted to him in particular, and that he himself has received eternal righteousness and from it, life, out of God's mercy because of the merit of Jesus Christ alone.

7. These words make it clear that there are differences among those kinds or concepts of faith and that historical faith, faith in miracles, and faith in the promises are not identical, as Bellarmine would have it (*On Justification*, book 1, chapter 4). For the first stage, that of historical or dogmatic faith, while it is the same as justifying faith in knowledge and assent, yet because it lacks tasting and effect, and is also shared by the demons, who believe and tremble in fear (Jas 2:19), therefore it cannot belong to saving faith. As for the second stage, [that of faith in miracles], although there is some effect that accompanies the knowledge and intellectual assent, yet because it is flighty and momentary it is like those people who are in love but capable of hate at any moment, and this faith was grounded in motives that are fleeting, like the pleasure of knowledge, or the goodwill of people, or the hope for earthly goods, etc. These people, though they seem to love Christ, within their hearts they love something else, and they lack what is really characteristic of justifying faith—which, if it doesn't have sincere and steadfast love, is null. And the following succeeds in proving that faith in miracles or special promises is not the same as justifying faith: 1) The fact that faith in miracles was granted to those whom Christ "has not known" (Matt 7:22), that is, whom he did not commend—even to Judas, "the son of perdition" (Matt 10:1). 2) The fact that there are many who have had justifying faith, yet have not been granted the gift of miracles or special promises. Therefore, since these two things can be, and in fact are, separate, they cannot be one and the same thing.

8. And yet we do agree that whenever those three kinds of faith flow together in one and the same subject, as happened in the case of the apostles and some of the other servants of Christ, they do not form numerous dispositions of faith but they actually add up to one and the same disposition—so that there is almost an exact analogy between these kinds or modes of faith as there is between souls: a vegetative, sensitive, and rational soul, which although they constitute diverse species of living things, they do flow together occasionally

to compose one soul. Like the vegetative and sensitive soul in a human being, in the person who has been justified historical faith and faith in miracles constitute a particular arrangement, because they are reckoned by justifying faith and are fulfilled by it. The difference lies in the fact that the rational soul necessarily depends upon the vegetative and sensitive soul. But justifying faith, although it is always connected to the historical one, can still be separated from the faith in miracles.

9. The main efficient cause of this faith is God the Father in the Son through the Holy Spirit who enlightens the mind and moves or bends the will which otherwise is turned away from God. God moves the mind not only in some metaphorical way of causation, or by an action that the Scholastics call 'moral,' 'by way of an end' (as they call it), when the good and suitable quality of an object is presented and when the enlightened intellect advances its own final judgment, which the will necessarily follows. But God does so also through his own action that immediately affects the will and influences it into its movement and action, while—to use the words of Augustine in chapter 24 of his book on the grace of Christ—[the Holy Spirit] "by his internal, secret, wondrous and inexpressible power effects in people's hearts not only true revelations but also good actions of the will." These words certainly show a real, proper efficiency. Hence, in a special way, faith is called a gift of God, and the author, the Holy Spirit, is called "the Spirit of faith" (1 Cor 12:9 and 2 Cor 4:13; Acts 16:14; Phil 1:29; Col 2:12; Heb 12:2).

10. This account of the way it works exposes the ingratitude and godlessness of those who share the opinion of Socinus, namely, that the efficient cause of justifying faith is man himself, man who of his own natural power and free choice either accepts or rejects the word of God that is declared to him. And they are of the opinion also that faith is a gift of God no differently than any good thing whatsoever can be called a gift of God in that general way. They have refurbished and patched up a recycled idea of Pelagius; and yet this same inconvenience remains: though they attribute some small amount to grace and divine enlightenment when faith is bestowed (even through the Spirit working inwardly), yet they concur [with Pelagius] that after everything has been provided that is required on God's part for ingenerating and eliciting faith, whether or not the working of God is efficient still remains within the power of man, because while man is moved by God he also is able to not be moved (according to their way of thinking), and after all the necessary things have been put in place, man is able to act or not to act. And so according to

them God is not the proper and immediate cause of faith, because otherwise, God's effect would always follow (or better, would always come about at the same time) if all his acts were performed. Phil 1:29 and 2:13, Eph 1:18– 19, Col 2:13, 2 Thess 1:11, and 2 Pet 1:3 prove the error of those who think in this way.

11. A less principal cause, or the ordinary instrumental cause of faith is "the word of faith that is preached, the word that is nearby, in our mouth and in our hearts" (Rom 10:8). For faith comes about from "hearing the word of God" (Rom 10:17), and especially from hearing the word of the Gospel, since the word of the Law only prepares the way for justifying faith. Moreover, "the Gospel is the power of God unto salvation for all who believe" (Rom 1:16). And to this word certain signs are added, signs that are either ordinary or extraordinary. Extraordinary signs, like miracles, and ordinary signs like the sacraments contribute to the implanting of faith and to nurturing, fostering, and increasing it once it has been brought forth. But the word must always precede the signs, and we should also not doubt that it is the divine truth. And in this [our] era we do not accept as valid any word other than the divinely inspired Scriptures; accordingly, we reject as sacrilegious those people who profess to apply an equal amount of faith in the unwritten traditions (the papal decrees, the sanctions of the councils, and the indwelling forces of reasoning) as in the written Word of God, and who demand "the same attitude of piety" towards them both.

12. Along with Scripture itself we willingly grant that when one hears the Word of God it is "the power of God for those who are being saved" (1 Cor 1:18), that it "is the seed that has been sown in our hearts" (Luke 8:11), and that it "is a two-edged sword piercing the soul" (Heb 4:12). Nevertheless, we disagree with those who ascribe a power of the following sort to the outward preaching of the Gospel as it strikes the ears: that ingenerating faith is a property inherent in the preaching, as though the very performance of that action achieves it, and as though the operation of the Holy Spirit is bound up in it. Even though by [God's] command the outward preaching is a necessary prerequisite of faith for adults, nevertheless the outward act of the preaching is not sufficient for faith if it is not accompanied by the efficacy of the Holy Spirit as he reveals the meaning of the Gospel inwardly and as he presents and seals it upon the 'ears' of the heart. For "neither he who plants is anything, nor is he who waters, but he who grants the increase—God" (1 Cor 3:7). We must therefore see to it here that we not go head over heels to

the extremes and pull apart what belongs together, or mix up what should be kept apart, by attributing to the instrument what belongs properly to the primary cause, and with the same sense. Nor should we do so by looking for the Spirit apart from the Word, or by looking for an understanding of the Word apart from the internal revelation by the Spirit; or, once the Word is understood, by looking for the assent and true confidence from the Word itself (or from the one who administers it) apart from the internal revelation by the Spirit, and to do so by the light of our understanding.

13. One considers the matter of faith in its subjects or its objects. The general subject of faith is the soul of man, as only it is a subject capable of receiving something so worthy. And insofar as faith comes by hearing the Word and insofar as the soul actually believes it, the subjects of faith are only the souls of the elect who are adults. But insofar as faith is taken to mean the beginning of the disposition of faith or as the 'seed' of faith, it has as its subject also the souls of those infant members of the covenant who have a share in the divine election. For just as "the kingdom of heaven" belongs to them, so too does the spirit of faith (Matt 19:14). And so even though they do not actually believe, we say that infants believe by being so inclined through grace, just as they are inclined by nature to sin.

14. However, the proper and special subject of justifying faith in a person, is not only the intellect, but also the will. For while knowledge and assent belong to the intellect, confidence belongs to the will. Nor is it enough for justification that the intellect grasps the things that are of God, but also that the will takes hold of them and embraces them, not only in *thesis* [that is, in theory] but also in *hypothesis* [or actually]. Moreover, Scripture sometimes speaks about faith in such a way that it is more related to knowledge and assent at one time, and to confidence at another time. But just as in Hebrew the words for knowledge often denote the feelings of the heart, so too it shouldn't amaze us if by synecdoche the knowledge and assent of faith connote also the confidence that is adjacent to it. And whenever confidence is expressed by itself, assent and knowledge are also assumed, because there is no such thing as a longing for what is not known.

15. The fact that a quality which is one and the same in number exists in different subjects is not an obstacle, nor the fact that one and the same virtue exists in two different kinds of powers, though some people do consider it impossible and raise it as an objection. For besides the fact that the

Schoolmen are not agreed that the intellect and the will are different kind of powers (Durand and his followers deny it, *Commentary on the Sentences*, book 1, distinction 3, chapter 4), people who maintain that they are in fact distinct admit that "the act of believing arises from the will as well as the intellect, both of which are designed to be completed by a disposition, and so there must be some disposition in the will as well as in the intellect, for the act of faith to be complete" (Thomas Aquinas [*Summa theologiae*] 2/2, question 4, article 2).

16. But we do state that certainly faith, insofar as it is justifying faith, is not one single and absolutely simple disposition, but it is an aggregate (or combined) disposition that somehow is composed of two dispositions that form only one when they are coordinated. That is to say, faith is composite because it involves a disposition that is present simultaneously in the will [besides the intellect]—a disposition whereby the will is made ready to believe and to have confidence in God in the same way that two dispositions can form one virtue and two things can combine into one act. So also many sciences are called a disposition that is only one by coordination, even though each is not a simple disposition or a single quality, but many, because of the diverse powers. Suárez himself admits as much (*On Dispositions*, disputation 44, section 55 and 57), namely that besides the indivisible unity that some dispositions possess because they have a simple quality, a composite unity is granted for other dispositions by the fact that qualities are gathered together in a relative arrangement—otherwise one cannot maintain the way we speak about the unity of the sciences. For, to use an example, geometry is a single science not only as *genus* but also as *species*. The arrangements in the human body show that this holds true also for the category of quality, because in the usual manner of speaking health and physical beauty are considered to be single qualities, notwithstanding the fact that each of them is the result of the inter-relationships of many qualities. In the same way [we state] that the one generosity is a combination of a disposition of the will and a disposition of the sensory appetite or that this "one virtue of faith coming from a disposition of the intellect and a disposition of the devout inclination of the will" nevertheless is not called with the name 'disposition' in a simple way; [and we say] that the one [virtue] exists in both powers, but that a specific name (e.g., 'faith') allows and denotes that composition more often than a generic name does.

17. And so those people who grant such composition in saving faith and who from the one faith make up as it were three parts through aggregation (namely knowledge and assent in the intellect, and confidence in the will) are not letting in a triple-bodied Chimaera, as some of their opponents would have it. For in Scripture nothing is more obvious than that knowledge is a part of faith, as it is called "the knowledge of salvation" (Luke 1:77), and "the knowledge whereby the Messiah will justify many" (Isa 53:11); "life eternal resides in the knowledge of God and of the Christ whom He has sent" (John 17:3). And elsewhere it is called "the knowledge of the will of God in all spiritual wisdom and understanding" (Col 1:9). Therefore, it is wrong of Bellarmine to claim "that faith is so distinct from science that one should define it in terms of ignorance rather than knowledge" (*On Justification*, book 1, chapter 7). We would certainly not say that faith is a science which arrives at all the causes and properties of its object by the light of reason and which follows upon the object's manifest evidence. But what we mean is that understanding is necessary for faith, and by it we come to know that which is proposed for us to believe, in the form of knowing 'that it is so.' And we mean also that this understanding relies on the firm foundation of the divine Word (even though it surpasses our grasp), and that its certainty is by itself greater than the other intellectual virtues that rely on human reason.

18. I shall refrain from proving by means of arguments that assent is necessary for faith, because this is not considered a matter of debate. But because our opponents deny that faith, besides assent, includes confidence, we show it from Scripture in many ways. Not only by etymology—i.e., because 'faith' (*pistis*) and 'confidence' (*pepoithēsis*) have one and the same root, and because the etymologically related words *pisteuein* and *pistos* mean 'to have faith' and 'trustworthy'—used of the one in whom someone else has faith (Matt 24:23 [and 26], Luke 16:11). But also, in Scripture faith is mentioned with those words that necessarily imply confidence: 'full assurance' (Rom 4.21), 'grasping' (Phil 3:12), 'receiving Christ' (John 1:12), 'courage' (John 16:33, Matt 9:22), 'frankness' (Eph 3:12, Heb 3:6), 'boasting' (Rom 5:2, etc.), 'the firm foundation' (Heb 3:14). But what is more, it is because in the Old as well as in the New Testament the verbs 'to have confidence' and 'to believe' are used interchangeably, just as with 'faith' and 'confidence.' For what is expressed by "to have confidence" in Ps 2[:12]—"blessed are all who have confidence in him"—is rendered in Mark 16:16 by "to believe"— "whoever believes will be saved." And the statement "have confidence in the

Lord in your heart" in Prov 3:5 is explained by Paul in Rom 10:10 as "with the heart one believes unto righteousness." In Ps 78:22, [where it says] "they did not believe in him, nor did they have confidence in his salvation," 'faith' is expressed exegetically by 'confidence.' And the matter becomes clear also from what is its opposite etymologically, for placed over against confidence is fear, or doubt; but fear is placed also over against the act of believing, as in Mark 5:36: "Do not fear, only believe;" and in Luke 8:50: "Do not be afraid, but only believe." Therefore, since faith and confidence share a single opposite, it must be that they are one and the same. "Therefore, in the Gospels the word 'faith,' when salvation or the pursuit of everything that we desire, is attributed to it, is used for both, namely that firm assent in the things that we must believe about God and Christ, and also the confidence that is received out of God's almighty goodness" (the words are taken from Jansen, *The Harmony of the Gospels*, chapter 32).

19. Faith has two objects, a material and a formal one. The material object is the name given to whatever faith is concerned about, whatever is being believed. And the formal object is the one which brings it about that the material object is indeed actually made available to the power [of the soul], in the same way that light is the formal object in seeing, and in the sciences the formal object is the medium. The material object of faith is everything that God presents to mankind as needing to be believed—God himself and all that pertains to God. That is to say, God insofar as He comes to us in Christ "who is the image of the invisible God" (Col 1:15), because there is no other way whereby God could become known to us for our salvation. And all faith would have disappeared little by little, had not Christ intervened as Mediator, for he keeps faith firmly grounded in the truth, because otherwise it would be far beyond the reach of mortals to enter upon the majesty of God. Therefore, although faith, taken in the broad sense of including supernatural knowledge, assent and confidence, embraces whatever is revealed in God's Word as conducive to our salvation, yet there is a certain special object of faith insofar as it justifies us. In general, we do not consider everything that Scripture contains as being equally relevant to that special object of faith, but we distinguish between things that are inherently and directly relevant to faith, and things that with a view to faith are accidental to it and are at some remove from it, things that occupy indirectly a secondary place in relation to the object of faith. Things of this sort include some of the narrative descriptions of particular matters, matters that of themselves do not

constitute articles of the faith. They are things in which what some call 'implicit faith' is said to have a place—albeit not in the articles that of themselves are explicitly, unambiguously necessary for salvation. Thus, the fact that Paul had a cloak [2 Tim 4:13], and other similar facts, is only of relevance to the kind of faith that prepares the soul or makes it ready to believe the truth of anything contained in Holy Scripture.

20. To the extent that it justifies, faith has a special object, one that gives it a proper distinction from the other meanings of faith. And that special object is the gospel-promise of Christ as the Mediator, for that [faith] strictly speaking is what justifies and saves, because it takes hold of and embraces Christ's merit as having been revealed to it in the word of the Gospel. For it is not enough for someone to know the history of what took place (i.e., the fact that Christ suffered); nor is it even enough if someone agrees with and believes that Christ suffered for the sins of all mankind. But over and above these things it is necessary that there be full assurance and confidence wherein the sinner believes most steadfastly that the forgiveness of sins which Christ has merited has been granted not only to other believers but also to himself in particular, and that he has been received into grace through the satisfaction obtained by Christ, and so he moreover applies it to himself with confidence. This is what John 1:12 expresses with the word "to receive," an expression that is not suitable to mere knowledge and assent. For "all the prophets testify about Christ that all who believe in him will receive forgiveness of sins through his name" (Acts 10:43). Therefore, those who believe, unless they wish to reject God's testimony, must be certain that their own sins have been forgiven and that they have been reconciled through Christ.

21. And the certainty of this special faith does not suffer from any doubt, even though in the Word of God it does not happen that salvation is declared to me personally (or to anyone else in particular). It is similar to the certainty of being convicted by the moral Law that makes each and every human being guilty of the curse: there is no doubt in that certainty. For, although it names no-one in particular, yet everyone draws the necessary conclusion from his own sense of sin. And the same happens to those who have been granted faith: from the general assertion made in Scripture that "everyone who believes in the Son shall have eternal life" (John 3:16) and that "forgiveness of sins will be granted to all who believe in him" they draw the conclusion that because they believe, they have received forgiveness of sins. Nor is it

true what the papal teachers put forward, namely that when the believers affirm "I believe," it is not the Word or testimony of God, since all believers possess the Holy Spirit, "who bears witness to their spirit that they are children of God" (Rom 8:16); "he is the pledge placed within their hearts" (2 Cor 1:22) and "the deposit of our inheritance" (Eph 1:14). For those who have been chosen are able to know with certainty that they are of the faith: "Examine yourselves to see whether you are in the faith; examine yourselves to see whether or not you know that Christ Jesus is in you—unless, of course, you are reprobates" (2 Cor 13:5). Augustine chimes in with these texts when he writes "that every believer sees faith in his own heart, and holds on to it with the surest knowledge and declares it in his conscience" (*On the Trinity*, book 13, chapter 1). For this reason, believers profess without any doubt: "We believe and know" (John 6:69), "I believe, Lord" (Mark 9:24), and "I know in whom I have believed" (2 Tim 1:12).

22. Of relevance here is the fact that whenever one reads that Christ has forgiven sins it is also reported that he said: "Have confidence, your sins are forgiven;" clearly, he does not want to provide an opportunity for arrogant pride. There is also the fact that we are obliged by Scripture to render thanks to God for our justification, for unless we are sure that we have received [justification] in faith, it would not be possible for us to acknowledge that it was received, since it would be absurd to acknowledge a benefit if one doesn't know for sure whether or not he has received it. Moreover, it would be an enormously shameful thing to charge those people with arrogance who believe that it was the Holy Spirit who summoned them. And finally, how can grace possibly be received willingly (as our opponents claim) by someone if the one who has received it does not really know whether or not he has it? For it must be the case that for something to be received by a willful movement of the mind that the one who receives it of his own accord not only knows that the thing has been given to him, but also that he really does receive it and that he is taking possession of what he has received.

23. For this conviction it is not simply enough, however, for there to be—as they say—a 'likelihood' or a merely human and experiential assurance, as some would like to have it. For that would be like someone who is convinced that he is warm simply because he feels with his senses that he is warm. But the sense of one's soul is different from physical sense, and we should not break the link between that internal sense and God's revelation. And while it is the testimony of the Holy Spirit which furnishes that faith, and while

everyone is bound to believe the divine revelations, we hold the view that that faith should not be given any other name than divine faith. And even though that faith does not have the general doctrines directly as its object (although it surely does suppose them) but a personal conviction of one's own grace, it should nonetheless be free of all doubt; and while it does include in its scope the articles of the faith (which do exceed that special object of the faith by their generality), it still is not inferior to them in certainty and lack of doubt.

24. The formal object of faith, i.e., the thing into which faith ultimately resolves itself, is the revealed first truth, insofar as one considers it as immediately moving to and even leading to believe that object which we called the 'material' object. For when someone believes someone else not on account of an authority or reasoned arguments but simply because he is the one who says so, his veracity takes the place of the formal reason for which one agrees with his statements. So too in matters of the faith we believe God's Word as it reveals something to us not because of someone else's authority, arguments, or the evident proof of the thing revealed, but because it is God who says it. And so it is his veracity and infallible authority in all that he says that is the formal reason for our faith. Thus, Paul says in 1 Thess 2:13: "You have received the word that was heard, not as the word of men, but as it really is, the word of God." 1 John 5:10: "Anyone who believes in the Son, has the testimony of God in his heart." Matt 16:17: "Flesh and blood did not reveal this to you, but my Father who is in heaven." Thus, the principle wherein true faith is resolved is: 'the first truth cannot fail.'

25. And so those people make a very serious mistake when they contend that our faith should be resolved into the authority of the Church, and they put the Church in the place of God. For they either ascribe the first truth to the Church and so turn it into God, or they replace true faith with merely human credulity. As for us, though we do concede that the Church's testimony is one of the foremost extrinsic motives that cause people to be disposed to believe, we can never be led to believe that it has infallible authority in putting forward propositions and passing judgment on them. But as to the possible question, how for us the assertion is certain that faith is resolved into the first truth, we reply that the authority of God as he speaks is made known to us in two ways, an external and an internal one (without which the external one would not suffice). God speaks to us in his written Word, and also as it is proclaimed through the Church's ministry according to what is written.

Besides that external presentation it is God who supplies the supernatural light when He speaks internally directly to the heart of each and every believer, and as his speech is piercing the heart deeply within, true faith is ingenerated, which would have the character only of human credulity and gullibility were it not enlightened by that supernatural light.

26. From what we've said it isn't difficult to determine the form of faith (especially of true, justifying faith). For it exists and is situated in that relationship and correspondence whereby each and every believer not only believes that general word of the revealed truth, but applies to himself especially the special promises of God's grace that are in it, particularly in the word of the Gospel; and with solid conviction he makes his own in *hypothesis* those promises that are promised generally in *thesis*, so that he possesses undoubted assurance about our reconciliation through Christ (John 17:15; Matt 9:2; Gal 2:20; John 1:12).

27. And so they err who claim that the form of faith is love, although (as they themselves admit) it is an external and not internal form, and although love causes faith not so much to come into existence "as to be moved, like a body that is moved and driven by a spirit." If these words of Bellarmine are taken as concerning the spirit of a human being, then they contain a contradiction in terms because the [human] spirit is the internal form of the body. But if the words about the spirit are taken to be about breathing [something] out, then love would be an effect or outcome of faith, as we would have it. He is also wrong in that while he admits that faith has its own internal form that is not love, he wants faith to be 'unformed' when it is deprived of love, since in his view the matter should take its name from the internal and not the external form. But if, as they would have it, love is the form of all virtues by its effectiveness insofar as it moves them to perform their actions, then surely it is faith, rather, that would be the form of all the other virtues, because "whatever is not from faith is sin" (Rom 14:23). And lastly, by nature faith comes before love, and love proceeds from it. And "the purpose of the commandment is love from a pure heart, a good conscience, and a sincere faith" (1 Tim 1:5). Therefore, it is sufficient for us to say that love is the actuality or outcome of justifying faith and it is joined by a permanent perpetual and unbreakable pact with it, though we do not say that it is its form, whether internal or external.

28. Saving faith has two goals. In an architectonic sense, it is the glory of the grace of God our Savior in his beloved Son (Rom 4:20; Rom 11:36; 1 Thess 1:10 and 12). The proximate and subordinate goal is the salvation of our souls which Peter calls the "the reward of faith" (1 Pet 1:9). This faith, however, is one in sort and object in everyone, although it varies in its subjects in number and degree.

29. The effects of faith are almost numberless, both inwardly in us and outwardly outside of us. The primary effects are: 1) justification, which certainly is an effect of faith, not insofar as [faith] is a disposition or act or some deed, but because of the object that it has, that is, because of Christ, who is appropriated through it. Because whatever the primary cause produces is attributed by metonymy to the instrumental cause, in this sense justification is also attributed to faith. 2) Sanctification and the cleansing of our hearts, briefly, everything good whereby God affects us. And in the matter of justification we should be particularly watchful of the followers of Socinus, who would want the form of justification to be something that is inherent within us, our righteousness before God. And by a generous interpretation of 'our righteousness' (for in the strict legal sense our righteousness is not perfect) they take this instead of justification, and thereby twist the meaning of the word 'imputation.'

On the Perseverance of the Saints

30. Saving faith, about which we have spoken thus far, must be accompanied by perseverance to the very end. Now the object of true faith contains also the certainty of this perseverance, and so it must be present in the subject who has been endowed with true faith. If not, faith would not be saving faith or justifying faith, for no-one except "he who believes" (Mark 16:16) and no-one except "he who endures to the end" (Matt 24:13) "will be saved".

31. In dealing with the question of perseverance, we take the word not in the moral sense for a part of human fortitude, that is, as a virtue which perfects the mind, in that, notwithstanding the hardship that comes with the long length of time that is required to finish some good work, the mind keeps doing what it has to do right until the final completion of the work. Augustine, following Cicero (*Book of 83 Questions*, question 31), defines it as 'steady, ongoing continuation in a matter that is well-planned.' But we take the word to mean the continuous safe-keeping of faith, hope, and love, the deeds of which ought to last throughout one's entire life. Thus, it is not

necessary to persevere in them only until the end of some work or other, but all the way to the end of one's lifetime.

32. And the word [perseverance] is used also for an act that is not ever interrupted at all but carries on, maintaining the same course. The word is used also for an act that in some respect was interrupted, but eventually was carried through to the end. These kinds of act do have their place in the perseverance of the saints, but for a different reason, because the dispositions of faith, hope, and love that were once bestowed belong to the first kind of act, since they remain permanently without interruption, and they are never removed. But the individual actions, profession, and sense of them belong to the second mode; we would allow some interruption to befall these actions, although such interruption in no way prevents the existence and identification of perseverance, for we still say that someone who on occasion falls still perseveres until the end, because the disposition always remained and often also the second act in some way, though it is weak. And by these, the person always remains tied to God, as if by a chain, while the perseverance, though interrupted in amount or degree, does not cease to be perseverance in its disposition or quality.

33. Therefore we define perseverance as the continuous, perpetual progress and successful endurance of true believers, through the grace and justifying faith once received, right unto the end of life, thanks to the gracious will according to God's eternal plan of election, bestowed without any merit of the believers, by the efficacious power of the Holy Spirit who works through the administration of the Gospel and who signs and seals the promises of grace, so that believers may abide in them forever and never entirely fall away from them, for the glory of God who bestows it, and for the salvation of the persevering believers (Rom 11:29; Matt 24:24; 2 Cor 1:8; Phil 1:6 and 2:13; 1 Pet 5:10; 1 John 3:9).

34. The primary and secondary efficient causes are the same as the ones for faith, which He who at one time gave it also preserves forever. For this He employs also the same ordinary means and instrumental causes, that is, the preaching of the Word of God and the administration of the sacraments. And since this gift is entirely unmerited, we should not look for a cause for it beyond God and Christ, whether that be an impelling cause (one that moves within), or an external initiating cause (one that stimulates from without). For God bestows it out of mere grace and love towards those whom He has

decreed from eternity to endow with faith; and it was for this that Christ's merit was ordained, and by it he has obtained for us this perseverance in the faith. Hence it is that from our justification and reconciliation obtained by Christ's death Paul gathers the future fulfillment of our salvation, which cannot happen without perseverance (Rom 5:9 and 10). And Christ himself, after he said that he "laid down his life for his sheep" (John 10:15), added "and they shall never perish, nor shall anyone be able to snatch them from my hand" (John 10:28).

35. For this reason any notion of fully merited reward is excluded from the preservation of the saints; the papal teachers also admit this to some extent, although what they grant with the one hand they take away with the other when they make the claim that "the sufficient, actual means of assistance, which they state the just man must have so that, when the more serious temptations that one meets in life are overcome, he may be able to persevere until the end. These means fall in this [category] of merit" with only the first grace being excluded from merit. Concerning the merit of congruity, as they call it, they make the hesitant claim that "it is probable that the just man earns final preservation by his prayers and other pursuits of piety;" but this kind of reward is not always obtained "since it does not rely on a definite promise or rule" (Gregory of Valencia, [*Theological commentary on*] *Thomas Aquinas's* [*Summa theologiae*], volume 2, disputation 8, question 6, paragraph 4). "They do not understand what they are speaking about, nor what they are affirming" (1 Tim 1:7). But people make a ruinous mistake when they put forward the claim that perseverance of the true believers is not an effect of the election, but instead that election was produced from [God's] foresight of perseverance. And they are of the opinion that the effective use (in the same manner as the abuse or neglect) of everything God has worked in the believer to cause him to persevere until the end depends on man's free choice. With this notion they renew Pelagianism and supply material for praising man, and they remove the need to even pray for the gift of perseverance. For, according to them, it is a universal gift prepared for everyone, with a condition that does not depend on God but on our choice.

36. The material in which [perseverance occurs], or its fitting subject, are all those people—and only those people—who have been regenerated and who have been endowed with justifying faith; this was our assumption when we provided the definition [of perseverance]. For everyone who has been elected is in due time endowed with faith, and whoever truly believes perseveres until

the end. Otherwise, faith that does not persevere is not true, justifying faith. Admittedly, whatever is true as far as its essence is concerned is not always true as far as its durability or strength is concerned; and the nature of what is true does not depend on its durability and strength. Yet it is certain that there are some things that possess durability and permanence by virtue of their true nature and essence. We have shown earlier from Scripture that justifying faith is of this sort; the perseverance of its truth is a necessary effect on the basis of which we can afterwards judge about the truth of the faith. Therefore, they are led astray and they lead others astray who posit that there are two species of truly justified people: the one, of the elect who do persevere, and the other, of those who are not elect, who although they were granted true faith at some point in time and were justified, still die in apostasy without repenting. And they even make a distinction between the elect so that they would have it that in many of the elect faith is for a time lost altogether, and that they completely fall from grace, although later, when they are offered repentance that leads to salvation, they accept it of their own choosing. But [we say] the elect are like "trees whose leaves do not fall, and they bear fruit in season" and so always possess the sap of life (Ps 1:3). And "when they fall they do not lose hope, but they are upheld by God's hand" (Ps 37:24). They are like "a mountain that is not moved, but that abides forever" (Ps 125:1). God's Spirit stays with them forever (John 14:17; 1 John 2:27). See, furthermore, these places: Matt 7:24–25; Matt 24:24; Eph 1:13 and 14, and 4:30, etc.

37. It is clear enough from what Paul states in Rom 8:30 that reprobates are never justified; God "has glorified those whom He has justified," but He has not glorified the reprobates. If someone wishes us to prove it, he is more in need of hellebore than arguments! And although there are some among the reprobates who are reported somehow to belong to Christ because they confessed their faith, shared in the sacraments, and used the name of the Church and associated with it—they were not, in actual fact, in Christ. They appeared to be within the boundaries of faith, but they were believers in appearance only, "adhering only to professing Christ, but not binding themselves with cords of love" (Cyril, *On John*, book 10, chapter 24). They are the sort who believe "so that they cherish the glory of men more than the glory of God" (John 12:43) and so they are not truly believing. "For how are they able to believe who receive glory from one another and do not seek the glory that comes from God alone?" (John 5:44). If there are some, then, who by the privilege of an external calling but not the gift of election seem to

belong to the "kingdom of the Son" for some time, who turn aside from the truth and return to their own vomit, that is not a reason to bring forward [the argument of] "the apostasy of the saints"—unless they are the saints "who have gone the way of Cain, and have rushed for profit into Balaam's error" (Jude 11). How filthy is he who was the first to try in vain to foist this rather profane expression on the Church.

38. However, though we are accused of it, we do not deny the fact that saints are able to fall from time to time, and through the weakness of their flesh they can fall seriously into trivial and even very grievous sins. Or, we state positively that in an absolute sense it is impossible for saints to lose their faith; but it is possible in a limited way, only as much as is allowed within the gracious promises of Christ, the faithful safekeeping of the Holy Spirit, and God's unchangeable decree concerning their salvation. For we openly admit that, considering Satan's powers and the infirmities of believers, if they should be left to themselves then they could fall away and perish at any moment. But we deny that believers also lose their faith, or fall away from grace to the point that they actually become unbelievers and enemies of God, like sinners who have not been born again. For God does not treat them strictly according to the Law, even though they incur his fatherly displeasure, and they bring upon themselves a liability to damnation and lose their present aptitude for entering the kingdom of heaven if they are considered only in and of themselves. And we grant that in that interval, before the act of faith and repentance is renewed, such a sinner, although he is elect, does go about deserving damnation, even though by God's firm decree in Christ he will be declared innocent. But after, by God's decree and grace, he will have returned to the right way, through a renewed, second act of faith and obedience—the first act of which is the seed of regeneration—, he is preserved fully restored with those fundamental gifts without which the spiritual life does not exist. And this renewal comes not by the decision or will of believers but by the special love of God and the divine operation and the intercession and safe-keeping of Christ.

39. So much, then, for the material of perseverance, which has the role of being its subject. But the object of perseverance are the promises of divine grace. The certainty of these promises rests not only in the one who makes the promises, and in the promises themselves, but they are also certain to the persevering person. Included in these promises there is also the one about perseverance; since this promise is certain in itself and not only by some

special privilege for certain believers, we do not doubt to state that each and every believer both should and is able to be convinced about his own election and perseverance, and we rely on the same arguments with which earlier we have proved the certainty of faith about our reconciliation, in thesis 30 and following. For the certainty of perseverance flows forth from the very nature of the special faith that is not only related to the thing promised by a direct act but also by a reflexive act is directed to consciousness of itself. Therefore, each and every believer who is certain of the inward act of his faith is able to believe steadfastly in the surest preservation of his own faith.

40. Although each and every believer always has this basis within himself, we still admit that this assurance of the faith does not always actually come out. And even when it does, it does not have that degree of certainty which uninterruptedly excludes all dread of the opposite; but sometimes faith is alive and well, at other times it is feeble, and sometimes it does not show its full actuality in the face of very serious temptations, temptations wherein believers do not always feel the full assurance and certainty of persevering. And yet in the end God, the father of all consolation, "does not permit them to be tempted beyond their strength, but with the temptation He provides a way of escape" (1 Cor 10:13), and through his Spirit He sees to it that they surmount the hardship. And in the midst of those temptations that act of faith, as though dead, is revived, and it does not consist of an uncertain opinion or some speculative hope, but of true, living faith that is aroused and sealed by the Spirit of adoption in one's heart.

41. The proximate goal of perseverance is the salvation of the believers, salvation wherein they conduct a continuous triumph for the victory that has been obtained over the enemy. The ultimate goal is the glory of God's grace and power, the grace to which all true believers humbly attribute whatever present good they observe in themselves and whatever future good they look forward to. And from this one can understand how wrong it is that some people falsely make up the story that this holy teaching by its very nature is harmful to genuine piety and deadly for the whole of religion—as if those people "who presume not upon their own works but upon the grace of Christ" could mount any threat at all against religion. As for us, we prefer to listen to Augustine, when he says: "To declare publicly what you have received is not arrogance, but faith; it isn't haughtiness, but devotion" (*On the Words of the Lord according to Luke*, Sermon 28).

42. In this life, the effects or consequences of the certainty of perseverance are the constant endurance of our hope, the confirmation of our bond with Christ, and a stronger, tighter fastening of the bond of love and peace that binds saints together. And in the future life the effects will be the full possession of salvation and perfect happiness, and a perpetual triumph of the saints together with Christ their head. In both lives it is the everlasting duration of God's love towards us, and an unbroken perpetuity of our love towards God. And, the manifestation of God's glory in those of us who are saved, and our never-ending praise of him who has saved us and glorified us forever.

Synopsis *of a* Purer Theology

Volume II | *Disputations 32–52*

EDITED BY WILLIAM DEN BOER & RIEMER A. FABER

DAVENANT PRESS

ISBN: 1-949716-15-5

ISBN 13: 978-1-949716-15-3

Cover design by Orange Peal Design

Typeset and proofread by Mikael Good

Indexed by Brian Marr

Printed in China

Praise for *Synopsis of a Purer Theology*

"In the Christian faith, we cannot do without each other, but we need the insights of each. In the *Synopsis of a Purer Theology*, Reformed theology from the best theologians of the time comes together, resulting in a finely crafted rendition of the Christian faith. For the study of Christian faith and Reformed theology, this handbook is indispensable today."

—**Willem van Vlastuin**, Professor of the Theology and the Spirituality of Reformed Protestantism, Vrije Universiteit Amsterdam, Dean of the Hersteld Hervormd Seminary, and Director of the Jonathan Edwards Centre Benelux

"Having taught theology at Leiden University myself for several years, I can only rejoice over this republication and translation of one its most outstanding and influential theological products ever: the so-called *Leiden Synopsis*. It is a great benefit to so many pastors, scholars, and interested lay people alike that this complete survey of solid Reformed Scholastic theology is now becoming widely available and accessible."

—**Gijsbert van den Brink**, Professor of Theology and Science, Vrije Universiteit Amsterdam

"Finally in English in two volumes, the *Leiden Synopsis* can now take its well-deserved place as a standard reference work for a wide readership. Its clear organization, careful distinction-making, transparency to scriptural sources, respectful engagement with the full Christian tradition, and organic coherence as a system make it a tool to be used regularly. The four authors' steady awareness of their location in a particular confessional tradition makes their work eminently useful not only for those who share their full confessional position, but also for those who listen in to overhear Reformed Protestant theology at its best."

—**Fred Sanders**, Torrey Honors College, Biola University

"Through the publication of the *Leiden Synopsis* in English, the essence of Reformed theology is no longer exclusively available to traditional, Western historiography and church history. Its original Latin format limited its impact to professional theologians and specialized philologists focusing on theology, while its religious core remained inaccessible not only to the general public but also to geographical venues beyond the West. Now, however, this treasure of theological insights is no longer the appanage of expert scholars; from lay people to academics with vested interests in religion, the *Synopsis* will become accessible to every person who wishes to know more about Reformed theology regardless of whether one lives in the West, the East, or the Global South. This is an achievement with unprecedented possibilities for Reformed theology and its rich ecclesiastical tradition."

—**Corneliu C. Simuţ**, Aurel Vlaicu University (Romania)

"The Leiden theology faculty was the 'Sorbonne' of Reformed orthodoxy. And the *Leiden Synopsis* represented the consensus after the Synod of Dort. Weaving into its exegetical arguments support from patristic and medieval sources, the authors display the catholic and evangelical spirit of Reformed theology. Avoiding internecine disputes, the *Synopsis* focuses on the doctrines that all Reformed Christians confess. Given its spirit, scope, and learned arguments, it deserves to inform the tradition today as it did so persuasively in the past."

—**Michael Horton**, J. Gresham Machen Professor of Systematic Theology and Apologetics, Westminster Seminary California

"The *Synopsis of a Purer Theology* is a codification of Reformed orthodoxy, concise and precise in its presentation of early modern Reformed theology. The translator, editors, and publisher are commended for making this monumental work available in English. Indispensable for any serious scholar and student in Post-reformation Reformed theology."

—**Adriaan C. Neele**, Vice President, Professor of Historical Theology and Homiletics, Puritan Reformed Theological Seminary

"The *Leiden Synopsis* is among the most important and comprehensive systematic accounts of Reformed theology of the seventeenth century. Its appearance in this English-only edition will doubtless invite a fresh outpouring of scholarly and lay reflection."

—**S. Mark Hamilton**, Senior Managing Editor, Davenant Institute and Research Associate, JESociety.org

"Doctrinal controversy brings strife but it also brings clarity and precision to doctrinal formulation, which is a blessing. This benefit of debate is no less true of the *Leiden Synopsis*, written in the wake of the Arminian controversy. This collection of theological disputations is grounded in Scripture, razor sharp in its distinctions, and conversant with the history of doctrine. No serious student of theology can afford to ignore this theological work."

—**J. V. Fesko**, Harriet Barbour Professor of Systematic and Historical Theology, Reformed Theological Seminary, Jackson, Mississippi

"The *Leiden Synopsis* distills the principles of Reformed theology with clarity and economy. It needs no endorsement, but if it did: Herman Bavinck ranked it alongside giants like Zanchius, Junius, and Voetius. Thanks to the translator and Davenant Press, this indispensable resource is now also accessible and affordable."

—**Tyler R. Wittman**, Assistant Professor of Theology, New Orleans Baptist Theological Seminary

"The *Synopsis of a Purer Theology* is one of the most significant translation projects in recent memory. This set of disputations is already considered essential for work in Reformed theology, and so I am delighted that Davenant is making it available for a wider audience. For Reformed pastors and theologians, the *Leiden Synopsis* proves to be a profoundly useful companion, and I have no doubt that it will be a significant aid in the work to retrieve Reformed Scholastic theology."

—**Kyle Strobel**, Associate Professor of Classical Theology, Talbot School of Theology, Biola University

"The *Leiden Synopsis* has long been a theological treasure. The publication of this edition will bring its rich theological wisdom to pastors, theologians, and theology lovers."

—**Gayle Doornbos**, Associate Professor of Theology Dordt University

"Davenant does theology and church a great service with offering this selection of the *Leiden Synopsis*. That deep and highly relevant source of Reformation theology becomes now available to even a much wider community, what the *Synopsis* deserves and the community needs. I'm also very happy that the great efforts of Riemer A. Faber and William den Boer can be made fruitful for all interested in clear, biblical theology. There is no doubt that this publication will find many readers."

—**Herman Selderhuis**, Theological University Apeldoorn / REFORC

"Set forth in the wake of Dort, the *Leiden Synopsis* has enjoyed critical influence on Reformed thought since the early seventeenth century. This accessible, two-volume edition of Riemer Faber's hailed English translation—with fresh editorial guidance by William den Boer and Faber— is a ready resource for learning today from the Leiden faculty's attempt to read Scripture in conversation with those who came before."

—**Christina Larsen**, Associate Professor of Theology, Grand Canyon Theological Seminary & College of Theology

"The *Leiden Synopsis* is one of the crown jewels of Reformed theology. Profoundly collegial in its origins, it presents a compact yet compelling account of post-Reformation dogmatics that is deeply rooted in Scripture yet acutely aware of tradition. It serves not only as a historical landmark in the development of the Reformed tradition, but also as a contemporary provocation to engage deeply with the wisdom and insight it offers. This elegant translation of the *Synopsis* will thus reward careful reading and re-reading, and comes warmly recommended."

—**Paul T. Nimmo**, King's Chair of Systematic Theology, University of Aberdeen

"Can the past inform the present? Absolutely! Here the seventeenth-century theology, piety, and practice of the *Leiden Synopsis* informs the Reformed church in the twenty-first century. The Davenant Institute is to be commended for publishing this time-honored resource. Scholars, professors, ministers, and even laypersons of Reformed theology will benefit from these excellent volumes."

—**Tyler Taber**, Minister of Word and Sacrament, Redeemer Presbyterian Church, Amarillo, Texas

"Both polemical and pastoral, the *Synopsis* deserves wide and careful attention in the church today. Deeply rooted in careful exegesis of Scripture, this doctrinal and moral theology from the early modern period remains a treasure house for subsequent generations. Contemporary readers will quickly note that the *Synopsis* is a work appropriately shaped by the Spirit's work in the fathers of the church from every generation, because the work of theologians should be done in obedience to the fifth commandment."

—**Rev. Michael McClenahan**, Union Theological College, Belfast, Northern Ireland

Table of Contents

Acknowledgements

Gratitude is expressed to the following former or current members of the research group 'Classic Reformed Theology' (in Dutch: 'Werkgezelschap Oude Gereformeerde Theologie'), as this edition would not have been made possible without their prior unstinting efforts. This group was founded in 1982 for the purpose of studying early modern scholastic theology. Throughout the years it has conducted research and organized conferences leading to publications in Dutch and English. Please see the Introduction for a brief account of the project that culminated in the publication of the three-volume academic edition, *Synopsis Purioris Theologiae / Synopsis of a Purer Theology* (Leiden: Brill, 2014–20). We are grateful to Brill Academic Publishers for permission to use the English translation of that edition here.

Andreas J. Beck

Simon Burton

Kees de Niet

Rein Ferwerda

Philip J. Fisk

Albert Gootjes

Harm Goris

Jeannette Kreijkes-van Esch

Matthias Mangold

Pieter Rouwendal

Siebold Schipper

Dolf te Velde

Willem J. van Asselt †

Henk van den Belt

Gert van den Brink

Elco van Burg

Jan van Helden

Kees Jan van Linden

Wilco Veltkamp

Antonie Vos

In 2020 the research group commenced a new project: 'Early Modern Reformed Disputations on Divine Providence.' For further details, please see the website: www.classic-reformed-theology.org.

VOLUME II

ON REPENTANCE

President: Antonius Walaeus
Respondent: Adrianus Jansonius

Regarding repentance, the Synopsis distinguishes between repentance in a general or broad sense that includes regeneration (as a disposition the Holy Spirit works in one's heart) and repentance in a restricted sense (or penitence) that comes from the disposition and consists in grieving for sin. Regeneration (4–26) is a renewal of the whole human soul 'with all its faculties, including intellect, will and affections' (18). Special attention is paid to the question of whether 'the grace of regeneration' also affects the will (19–23), and it is emphasized that all actions produced by regeneration are effects of grace, not of the human will (24–26). Penitence, or active repentance, is treated in thesis 27–53. Persons who are genuinely penitent turn from evil towards the good, and change their minds for the better (31). So true repentance consists of a 'life-saving transformation' (32) from evil to good, from sin and Satan to Christ and righteousness (33). True repentance is characterized by contrition of the heart and hope for forgiveness (34–35, 39, 42); it is accompanied by a hatred of sin itself and a delight in observing God's Law (38–39, 42). In order to possess all this 'it is altogether necessary that in faith we first apply Christ to ourselves, and in him to regard God as a kindly father' (42). In a more general sense repentance includes faith insofar as it may denote the conversion from all sin and a turning towards God; in a stricter sense faith may be described as the cause while repentance is an effect of it (40–41). The disputation goes on to caution against the wrong Romanist perception of repentance as acts of penitence (43–47), and against Anabaptist ecclesiastical discipline whereby sinners in the process of repentance are withheld from the communion of saints (52).

1. Since the main point in the preaching of the Gospel consists of faith and repentance, and as we have dealt with faith in the previous disputation, it follows now that we should treat the second element, namely, repentance.

2. It is customary to consider this repentance in two ways: either as a spiritual disposition poured into our hearts by the Holy Spirit, or as an action from us that proceeds from that disposition. In the first way, it is properly speaking and in its strict sense called regeneration; in the second way, it is called repentance, taken in a more restricted sense, or penitence. And when the two are taken together it is called the circumcision of the heart, the conversion to God, the renewal of the Spirit, the sanctification of man, the new creation, and the first resurrection.

3. First we shall offer some explanations of the two [regeneration and repentance] considered jointly, and then we shall deal in particular with penitence (in the strict sense) and its properties.

4. The principal, effective cause is God through his Spirit, for "unless one is born again of the water and the Spirit he cannot enter into the kingdom of God" (John 3:5), and just as God raised "the author and preserver of life" to his right hand "in order to give repentance to Israel" (Acts 5:31), so too did the Israelite church glorify God "because God has given also to the gentiles repentance unto life" (Acts 11:18).

5. The meritorious cause of this gift is not any prior disposition of our own, or preparation we have done, or some superior exercise of our natural ability to judge (as some people wrongly think); for "when the kindness of God our Savior and his love for mankind appeared, he saved us, not because of works done by us in righteousness, but according to his own mercy, by the washing of regeneration and renewal of the Holy Spirit, whom he poured out upon us richly through Jesus Christ our Savior," as the apostle says in Titus 3:4–6.

6. We do not deny, however, that before He makes people partakers of this benefit, God himself ordinarily uses various ways to prepare them for it, a little at a time, whether through proofs evident in the natural world (Rom 2:4) or through the word of the Law and the Gospel, as we shall explain below. But we do deny that God is bound to behave in this ordinary way; this is clear from the case of the robber who was crucified with Christ [Luke 23:40–43], and of Paul when he was persecuting the Church [Acts 9:1–19]. And we also deny that there is some sort of preparation or disposition that earns this kind of gift on the basis of congruity, for that is shown in Titus 3:5, a passage we have cited earlier. And lastly, we deny that any sort of disposition or preparation that precedes faith is a precursor to which God has attached a sure promise for this gift, for "whatever is not from faith is sin" (Rom

14:23) and "without faith it is impossible to please God," that is, to please him to one's own salvation (Heb 11:6).

7. And we even state that this grace is undeserved for any man, regardless of the extent he has been predisposed; because whatever his disposition, man is guilty of condemnation. For no-one is released from this condemnation "except only those who are in Christ, and who do not walk according to the flesh but according to the Spirit" (Rom 8:1, 4).

8. At the same time we state also that those who refuse to accept the proofs evident in the natural world or in the Law and the Gospel that call them to repentance, or who suppress them by their wickedness, by so doing bring yet another guilt upon themselves and a new degree of condemnation, and so they are more and more without excuse in the judgment of God, as the same apostle teaches us (Rom 1:20, 2:1; John 15:22).

9. The initiating cause of the double benefit of regeneration and repentance is the death and resurrection of Christ, as the apostle teaches clearly in Rom 6:3, Heb 9:14, 1 Pet 1:18–19, etc. For since through his death Christ has saved us from our sins that we might be servants not of sin but of Christ, it was necessary also that his death and resurrection could effectively put the old man to death and cause the new one to live. And the main point of the apostle's prayers (and, following his example, the main point of all believers' prayers) is not merely that "they may be found in Christ, not having a righteousness of their own that comes from the law, but one that is through faith in Christ, the righteousness which comes from God by faith." But above and beyond that the prayer is "that they might know Christ and the power of his resurrection and the fellowship of his sufferings, and be conformed to his death" (Phil 3:9–10).

10. The instrumental cause of this benefit is the Word of God, both that of the Law and that of the Gospel.

11. For it is by the Law, as recorded in nature (Rom 1) and as renewed on the stone tablets (2 Cor 3) that man is led to truly realize his own condemnation and wretched state, as was explained elsewhere [Disputation 23.5–7]. If he does not realize this, man cannot possibly grasp the regeneration and repentance that bring salvation, since Christ himself bears witness "that he has not come to call the righteous, but sinners to repentance" (Matt 9:13 [KJV]).

12. But it is through the Gospel and its promises that man conceives a godly sorrow, lifts up his downcast conscience to hope for forgiveness, and then makes Christ his own. He does so not only for the forgiveness of prior sins, but also for doing away with the old man and bringing to life the new one. For this reason, the Gospel is called "the ministry of the Spirit and of life" (2 Cor 3[:8–10]) and "the immortal seed of God that remains forever, through which we are born again" (1 Pet 1:23; Jas 1:18).

13. The form of regeneration and repentance consists of the dying of the old man, or the abolition of his innate corrupt nature; it also consists of the restoration of the new man who is created in true righteousness and holiness after God (Eph 4[:22–24], Col 3[:8–12]). And this form not only keeps the nature of the old man in check (as some wrongly think), but it even does away with it entirely, and puts in its place true holiness and righteousness which also shines forth in the very fruits of repentance.

14. If one considers this form from the perspective of its ultimate, completed state, it is not brought about all at once, but rather by degrees, and for this reason some who have been born again are likened to children, while others are likened to fully grown adults (Heb 5[:13–14]; Eph 4[:13–16]).

15. But just as children do possess the whole form of a human being and all the parts that comprise it, and although they display it in a somewhat imperfect way, so too do we consider no-one to be truly repentant or born again unless he has the whole form of regeneration, in the perfection of parts (as the expression has it), although he must make daily progress in the perfection of degrees.

16. This essential perfection consists firstly in the renewal of all the faculties of the human soul, the intellect, the will, and the affections, according to all of God's precepts. Secondly it consists in their renewal to the point that "sin no longer reigns in them" (Rom 6[:12]) and that they "do not walk according to the flesh but according to the Spirit" (Rom 8:1).

17. For even though the rule of the Spirit is weaker and less visible in some people while more established and evident in others, we deny that any regenerate person has reached the point in this life where no remnants of the old man still live in him any longer. For this reason those who are born again must pray every day "forgive us our sins," and daily they must produce new deeds of repentance by their true faith in Christ.

18. The subject of this regeneration is the entire man who has been (or is to be) planted in Christ through faith, for "it is by faith that our hearts are cleansed" (Acts 15:9). And just as the principal subject of sin is the soul of man, fitted out with all its natural faculties (while the body is a less principal subject, as the seat or instrument of the soul), so too that same soul, with all its faculties, including intellect, will and affections, is the proper seat and principal subject of regeneration. And in the true regeneration and repentance that lead to salvation all these faculties are more and more affected by the supernatural and inherent grace that comes from God through the Spirit, an action that is direct and immediate.

19. As far as the intellect is concerned, this process is obvious, because by this benefit [of regeneration and repentance] it is enlightened unto the knowledge of God and our Savior Jesus Christ [Eph 1:17–18]. And concerning the affections, no further proof is required, because everyone acknowledges that the same gift stirs the affections to hate sin and Satan, to love God and righteousness, and to hope for eternal life and the inheritance. Regarding the will, however, since there are some who dare to say that the inherent grace of regeneration does not affect the will, we shall have to establish the proof of it briefly with a few arguments.

20. I show this first from the prior corruption of the will, for this spiritual generation renews and corrects everything that has been corrupted on the spiritual level. And Scripture states in many places that the natural man's will was corrupted entirely in and of itself; see Eph 2:3, and 1 Pet 4:3. For this reason also the apostle says "that he does not do the good that he wants, but the evil that he does not want to do" (Rom 7:19), and "I find this law, that when I want to do good evil lies close at hand" (Rom 7:21). He shows that it is by his will, insofar as it was regenerated, that he even seeks after the spiritual good, but that on account of the remnants of the flesh that still cling to him he does not will it so effectively and fully that he always achieves the result that he wishes and wills.

21. In the second place it is demonstrated by the very spiritual quality that is brought on by regeneration. For not only do love and trust in God have their proper place in the will, but so too the holiness and righteousness of the new man (Eph 4:24) is a proper affection of the will, as all the ethical philosophers admit. It is for this reason that the lawyers define righteousness as "the constant willingness to grant to everyone his due."

22. Thirdly, it is proved effectively by the ways in which the Scriptures everywhere speak about this matter. For when it says that God places a new Spirit within us [Ezek 36:26], or that He circumcises the heart [Deut 30:6; Rom 2:29], creates in us a new heart [Ps 51:10], turns our hard hearts of stone into hearts of flesh [Ezek 36:26], removes the foreskin of our hearts [Deut 10:16], and many similar things, no-one has ever explained them as concerning only the baser appetites that we have in common with animals. Nor can these be taken directly to mean the intellect, since no place will be found in Scripture where it is the intellect that is called hard or stony, or where it says that it is the intellect that is circumcised, or that its foreskin is removed, or that it is being created anew in us. To the contrary, when the intellect is treated in Scripture, it is usually called blind or darkened; and the renewal of the intellect is called the enlightening of the eyes of the mind, the writing of the Law upon the hearts, the removal of the veil from our hearts, and the gift of a new mind.

23. And finally, it is proved by the vows and prayers of the saints. For "since it is God who works in us both to will and to act according to his own good will" (Phil 2:13), who would dare to think that apart from the illumination of the mind and the amendment of our affections it is not necessary to ask for the renewal of the will and an inclination towards the spiritual good? Take David, for example, in Ps 119:36. Especially because it is not possible that the will, equipped with only natural powers, of its own accord follows the intellect that has already been affected by the supernatural gift, or that the intellect impresses the will with some inherent supernatural quality. For Scripture everywhere states clearly that this comes only from the Spirit of God, and that the intellect is no more capable of impressing such power upon the will than it can produce the will itself on its own. But just as it is God who has created in man the faculty of the intellect and the faculty of the will, so also is it upon the one as well as the other faculty that he grants the additional supernatural gifts through that new creation.

24. And in order to produce spiritual actions from this spiritual condition it is not sufficient to have only the initial conferment or habitual possession of this gift. But just as preceding and operating grace first produces this gift in our hearts, so too is it necessary that the accompanying, co-operating grace similarly stir up that gift for actions that are worthy of repentance and make the will more and more perfect every day. For "He who goes before the

unwilling so that he wills, follows him when he is willing, so that he does not will in vain." (Augustine, *Enchiridion* 32).

25. For this reason Christ says to his disciples that "they can do nothing without him, and that he prunes every branch in him that bears fruit that it may bear even more fruit" (John 15:2). And hence it says also that "the Spirit helps our infirmities, so that we know what we should pray for as we ought" (Rom 8:26). And the apostle prays in Heb 13:21 and elsewhere that "God equip them with every good thing, working in them what is pleasing in his sight through Jesus Christ."

26. We should not make curious enquiries about the way in which God performs this action in us; but at the same time we should be careful to avoid the errors of the Pelagians, semi-Pelagians, and certain Sophists. They stated that this grace is given on the grounds of our merits, or the good movements of our will, or, in their words, through moral counsels alone and not real works—in short, that the efficacy of the working of God depends on the natural choice of man. All these and similar errors of the Pelagians and semi-Pelagians were condemned long ago, and we, too, condemn them, because they do injustice to the grace of God, and for the man who distinguishes himself they leave some opportunity for boasting. But we, following Augustine, state that "grace would not be grace at all if it were not entirely freely given." And the certain effect of grace that is operating and co-operating in us comes not by the choice of our will but by what the merciful God has purposed [Rom 9:16].

27. Now that we have, in our view, explained the doctrine of regeneration sufficiently, it remains for us to append a few things about penitence, or rather and especially the so-called active repentance.

28. It is obvious that the word 'penitence' derives from 'penalty,' for as A[ulus] Gellius rightly observes, "whatever is cause for trouble and shame has the force of punishment." Therefore, whoever is really driven by penitence over some deed or other within his own heart exacts from himself what amounts to punishment, to the point that the affection of his heart bears the name 'penitence.' For this reason, also the apostle himself, in 2 Cor 7:11, lists among the true properties of repentance "indignation and vengeance" which the sinner demands of himself for that inner feeling of regret which usually comes on the heels of wrongdoings.

29. And in this regard we may allow the word 'penitence' (even though it does not entail the entire form of true repentance) to be kept in usage in Christ's Church as an expression of the part for the whole, provided that we do not think that grief of this sort is able to make satisfaction for sins, as happens among the papal teachers.

30. The word *metameleia*, which properly means the anxious worry of the heart after some punishable deed, corresponds fairly well to the word 'penitence' and is used frequently for the kind of trouble and grief that are not followed by a change in lifestyle; yet it is employed sometimes in order to mean true repentance, as in Matt 21:29 and elsewhere.

31. The Hebrew word *teshuva*, 'return,' or conversion, and also the Greek word *metanoia*, that is, the change of heart for the better after a deed, or 'repentance' as Lactantius translates the Hebrew word (in book 6, chapter 24), are better suited to denote the sense of what we are treating. For someone who is genuinely penitent turns himself from evil towards the good, and he changes his mind for the better, although one finds the word *metanoia* used for a merely legal conversion, for instance Wis 5:3.

32. From what we have said already about the terms one can gather easily what true penitence, or rather repentance, is. For since every change has both a point from which it starts and a point where it ends, so for the life-saving transformation of one's heart we should pay attention to both points.

33. The point from which conversion starts is the evil, or the reign of sin and Satan; the point where it ends is its opposite: the good, or the reign of Christ and righteousness. Regarding the former point, conversion is called "a turning away from sins and evil ways" (1 Kgs 8:35, Isa 59:20). Regarding the latter point, it is called the "turning toward the God of Israel" (Jer 16:19). The two points occur together in Acts 26:18, as people "turn from darkness to light, and from the power of Satan to God." These two aspects of repentance are what is sometimes understood in the New Testament by 'the putting to death of the old man' and 'the coming to life of the new.'

34. And although the whole nature of conversion is expressed in these two aspects or points, certain properties are associated with each of them, and without these it is no repentance.

35. Connected to this turning away from evil is a grief within the soul that is called by some 'contrition' or 'attrition.' And connected to turning towards

the good is a hope for forgiveness and a delight of the soul, because when the wrong way is left behind a shift has been made towards the right way. For "the truly penitent man grieves over his sins, and he is pleased with his grieving."

36. In 2 Cor 7:10 the apostle Paul states that this grief is twofold: it is "a worldly grief that brings death and a godly grief that leads to repentance unto salvation."

37. Worldly grief comes about when the sinner does indeed grieve over a sin he has committed, but then he does so for the same reasons as the people of this world are accustomed to doing. Such grief arises from a verdict of disgrace in the eyes of the Law, either in punishment or in the conscience, a verdict that proceeds from the threats of the Law and from taking them seriously (Rom 2:5, 4:15). If the sinner does not proceed to go beyond this grief, or if he is obsessed by it, then he also falls headlong into despair, as we see in the case of Judas who betrayed Christ. Or, if the sinner does succeed in overcoming his grief, then he reverts to his characteristic ways, as is evidenced in the case of Ahab.

38. But godly grief is distinguished from worldly grief not just in its effect (as the apostle points out in the previously mentioned place) but also in its own nature, because it not only arises from self-love and fear of punishment, but also is accompanied by a hatred and displeasure of sin itself (Rom 7:15, etc.) and a shame for having offended God, whom he now, in faith, begins to regard as a kindly father, as is clear from Rom 6:21, and from the examples of David, Peter, and the parable of the prodigal son.

39. Linked to the turning to God is an approval of God's Law (Rom 7:16) and a delight in observing it (Ps 1[:1] and 119[:18]), a hope for forgiveness drawn from the Gospel promises that have been received in faith (Ps 130:4), and even a sense of comfort and spiritual joy because "God's love is poured into our hearts through the Holy Spirit whom He gave to us" (Rom 5:2, 5; similarly verse 13 and 17).

40. From what we have said thus far there is an obvious answer to the fairly difficult question whether faith is part of repentance, a question over which some of the foremost authors of the Reformed Church seem to disagree. For if we take the word repentance in the wider sense of the whole work of our conversion, as it is used in some places in Scripture (Acts 3:19 and 11:18),

then indeed faith also is included in it, in the same way as the apostle understands faithlessness—the opposite of faith—to reside in the heart that is unrepentant (Rom 2:5).

41. But if we take the word repentance in the stricter sense as we defined it earlier, then it is usually kept distinct from faith, as a cause and the proper effect and result of that cause; it is in this way that Scripture itself in various places distinguishes repentance (Mark 1:15, Acts 20:21, etc.).

42. In order for us to have a true hatred of our sins, genuinely grieve for the offenses we have committed against God as against our kindly father, to cherish righteousness, and in our souls to begin fostering the hope for forgiveness and spiritual joy from him, it is altogether necessary that in faith we first apply Christ to ourselves, and in him to regard God as a kindly father. But we also grant freely that the inner sense of saving faith is strengthened and displayed more and more in us through the corresponding sense of true repentance.

43. From the explanations given thus far we see what we ought to think about that doctrine of the papal teachers who create three parts for penitence (and who also wrongly make it into a sacrament), namely: the contrition of the heart, the confession of the mouth, and the satisfaction in works.

44. As far as contrition is concerned, we deem that it is an element necessary for true penitence in the sense we explained above, provided that we understand the grief for our sins to be a godly grief and also not count it as sufficient satisfaction for our sins. For we must ascribe the forgiveness of sins to the grace of God and not to our own contrition, as it is rightly explained in the note *On Penitence*, distinction 2, chapter 1 (contrary to the definition of the Council of Trent, session 14, chapter 4).

45. And we also approve two kinds of confession as something that belongs to true penitence. Hereby the sinner acknowledges his own sins before God, privately (Ps 32) or publicly as part of the entire church (Neh 9), or in the presence of the church in the case of public scandals (2 Cor 2). Or the confession is made before individual people, the brothers who have been offended, in order to reconcile with them (Luke 17:9).

46. We do not deny that when there is serious mental anguish it is prudent for the sinner, in order to obtain consolation, sometimes to confess his own sins before other, upright men, especially ministers of the Word (for which

one could refer also to Jas 5:16). And yet it does not follow from this that the papist practice of auricular confession should be introduced into the Church, since that is a most cruel torture of the soul, something contrived apart from God's Word, and also impossible for the Christian. "For who discerns his own sins?" (Ps 19:12).

47. And lastly, for the satisfaction of sins in the presence of God we recognize nothing other than the precious blood of Jesus Christ our Savior, "which alone cleanses us from all our sins" (1 John 1:7); and "by his one offering he has for ever made perfect those who are sanctified" (Heb 10:14). And there is no instrument whereby we make the satisfaction by Christ our own except by faith in him, "because God has presented him as the atoning sacrifice for us, through faith in his blood" (Rom 3:25). The fruit and inseparable companion of that faith is the true repentance that we have thus far described.

48. True Gospel-based repentance consists of two types. Universal repentance occurs whenever someone crosses over from a state of sin to a state of righteousness and is converted to God for the first time. And particular repentance occurs when someone who has already been converted and believes is overtaken by sin and then grieves over it and repents from it.

49. And this particular repentance, in turn, is twofold, either ordinary or extraordinary. Ordinary repentance is the one which true believers and saints throughout the course of their entire lives are bound to exercise out of awareness of their weaknesses and daily shortcomings (Rom 7:24). Extraordinary repentance occurs when the faithful fall into some serious sin that hurts their conscience deeply, such as we see in the case of David or Peter after they fell.

50. Then again, this [extraordinary] repentance may be that of a single believer or of the entire congregation and church; and in Scripture one comes across many examples of this type of penitence intended to assuage God's anger or to forestall what he intends to do. And, whether public or private, this penitence is always accompanied by extraordinary signs of grief and humility, such as fasting, weeping, wearing a shirt of goat's hair, tearing one's clothes, etc.

51. For this reason the Novatians make a serious mistake when they think that it is useless to do penitence for back-sliding after one has been baptized,

and when they state that those who have fallen back into sin should not be admitted into the communion of the Church. For, to use the words of Tertullian, "if someone needs to repent a second time, his soul should not immediately be plunged into or be overwhelmed by despair. Let him be ashamed for having put himself at risk a second time, but not for being delivered again. No-one should be ashamed when it is necessary to repeat a cure for a recurring illness."

52. On this point some of the Anabaptists are equally mistaken when they think that sinners should be removed from the communion of the Church and handed over to Satan [1 Cor 5:5] so that they can do penance outside rather than within the Church—even though the sinners have repented. For while we admit that those who have fallen into serious sins can be withheld from the signs of grace for a period of time so that meanwhile the scandal can be removed from the Church and the genuineness of the repentance may be tested by its fruits, yet it is contrary to the clearly-spoken words of Christ (in Matt 18:17) and the practice of the whole apostolic church that the very same church before which a sinner has publicly declared his repentance should treat him as a heathen and a tax-collector.

53. It is this life that we currently lead which forms the goal, or end, of repentance, and for that reason we should not put off repentance any longer but we should attend to it today, while it is yet called 'today' (Heb 3:13). For, as Augustine puts it, it is only here and now that repentance bears fruit; repentance that is to be done in the future is of no benefit, as Christ taught in the parable of the wise and foolish maidens (Matt 25:11 ff.).

ON THE JUSTIFICATION OF MAN IN THE SIGHT OF GOD

President: Antonius Thysius
Respondent: Jacobus Dissius

Justification is 'the foremost locus in theology, and for us the most salutary'; without a sound doctrine of justification, other doctrines cannot be sound either, nor will it be possible to maintain a true Church (1). Justification is defined as 'the judgment of God whereby He pronounces righteous the person who is unholy and of himself a sinner subject to God's wrath' (7). The two parts of justification are distinguished as God's pardon of the sinner and his imputation of Christ's righteousness (8); thereupon the Synopsis treats the different causes of justification (9–32). God is identified as the efficient cause of justification (9), while the proclamation of the Gospel is the attendant, assisting cause (10), and God's peculiar grace is the internally impelling cause (11). Christ the Mediator is the meritorious, or externally initiating cause (13), while righteousness freely bestowed upon us is the material cause (18). Justification takes form in its application and declaration (21, 24), and the goal of it is the glorification of God and salvation of mortals (32). Christ's righteousness plays a crucial role in our justification, since it is because *of his righteousness, by* his righteousness, *and* through *his righteousness that we are justified (23). For man's part, we are made righteous by an appropriating faith in Christ, including trust, as the instrument by which we are made partakers of Christ and his righteousness (25–28). While our justification comes by a faith that is not apart from works, yet it is apart from works that we are justified (29). The justification that arises from these causes produces various fruits, like peace with God, perseverance and hope (33), and sanctification or 'works of righteousness' (35). Thesis 37 sums up: we are justified by the Father as judge seated on a throne of grace, and in Christ who has made satisfaction and acts as our advocate; and we are justified through the Holy Spirit who grants faith and seals grace in our hearts by the preaching of the Gospel. The disputation also includes several antitheses aimed especially at those Roman Catholic teachers who understand justification as referring to the in-pouring of the quality of righteousness, rather than a forensic act of God. Unlike the Romanist perception of justification as a 'habit' of love that is instilled in human beings, the Synopsis views it as the imputation of Christ's satisfaction and his merits which cause the believer to partake of Christ's righteousness in faith.*

1. Now that we have treated the calling [of man] and the obedience—both of faith and of repentance—that answers to it, it follows that we deal with man's justification and sanctification (or sacred works) by faith. And we shall deal first with the justification of the sinner in the sight of God, as this is easily the foremost locus in theology, and for us the one most salutary. And if this locus is suppressed, falsified, or overturned, it would not be possible to keep the purity of the teaching in other loci or to maintain a true Church. Now the main point and basis of this locus is the fact that a merciful and just God pardons the sins of believers through the righteousness of his Son and causes them to be saved.

2. The word 'to justify,' and thence 'justification,' which renders the Hebrew word *hitzdiq* according to its proper usage in the Hebrew language, is strictly speaking nearly always a forensic term denoting a forensic act of judgment by a judge, that is, of setting a guilty party free instead of condemning him (Deut 25:1; Prov 17:15). But it may also denote the actions that precede, accompany, or follow it (even actions undertaken privately), whereby someone is declared, confirmed, commended, or deemed to be righteous.

3. But the word is used with that specialized meaning when it concerns the judgment of God as He absolves the sinner who stands before his judgment seat (Ps 143:2; Rom 5:16 and 8:33–34). And so this entire act of justification is depicted as a forensic process. Yet we still grant that justification sometimes appears also to include sanctification as its consequence because of the very strong, close connection between the two (Rom 8:30; Titus 3:7, etc.).

4. Synonyms and similar words are "to be righteous before God" (Rom 2:13), "to make righteous" (Rom 5:19), "to impute righteousness" (Rom 4:3), "to bless" and "blessedness" (Rom 4:6).

5. And as for justification, insofar as it is "righteousness regarding the person" (whereby a person is justified generally—not with respect to a particular cause, usually called "the righteousness regarding the cause"—and

which is nothing other than the conformity of the entire man and his actions to God's Law), it is twofold: legal justification and Gospel-justification; the former justification is out of the Law and its works, while the latter is out of faith (Acts 13:38–39; Rom 3:20–21, 28; Gal 3:11–12). The former is inherent, the latter is by the imputation of alien righteousness (Rom 4:4–6, and 10:3–5, 6). After the fall no-one is justified by the former, but by the latter everyone is justified who has been granted true faith in Christ (Rom 3:20, 26, 30).

6. This latter one also goes by the name of "reconciliation," "blessing," and "salvation" (Rom 5:10–11; Gal 3:8, 14; Titus 3:4,5), although reconciliation is more a consequence and effect of justification, while salvation often has a broader range of meaning.

7. In the law-court of God, then, the justification of man as sinner is the judgment of God whereby, He pronounces righteous the person who is unholy and of himself a sinner subject to God's wrath. He does so out of his own mere grace and mercy, for the sake of the perfect obedience and righteousness of Christ that was offered on our behalf and that is received by faith. That is, He pardons the sinner from sin and the curse, and imputes to him the righteousness of his Son and so awards to him life eternal, for the salvation of the believing person and the glory of the merciful and just God. Nearly every part of this definition is included by the apostle in Rom 3:24–26.

8. There are two parts to justification: the imputation of passive righteousness (or the absolution of sins), and the imputation of active righteousness. By the former we are set free from guilt and condemnation and delivered from eternal death; by the latter we are deemed worthy even of a reward, and we receive the right to life eternal, which is awarded to us (Rom 5:17–18, 8:3–4). And because of the very close relationship between them, the one entails the other, as a part entails the whole (Rom 4:22), although justification taken in its most specific sense is often considered to consist in the remission of sins (Ps 32:1; Rom 4:7).

9. The efficient cause for justification, i.e., the one by whom we are justified, is God (Rom 3:26, 30 and 8:33; Gal 3:8). For He is the only one, as God and Lord, and so also as the lawgiver and judge, against whom sins are committed and by whom they therefore can be forgiven (Isa 43:25; Luke 5:21; Jas 4:12). It is even by the Trinity as a whole: the Father (Rom 8:33), the Son (Isa 53:11 and Matt 9:2,6), who himself will be the judge of the living and the dead, and

the Holy Spirit (1 Cor 6:11; John 16:8,11), while an order and distinction in persons is retained, so that it is the Father who justifies in the Son through the Spirit. As for the principle of acting and the certain, specific economy, the act of justification belongs to the Father, just as the merit for it is attributed to the Son and the application of that merit is attributed to the Spirit.

10. The assisting cause is the preaching of the word of promise or the Gospel. In this sense the Gospel itself is "the power of God unto salvation" and in it "the righteousness of God is revealed" (Rom 1:17); and it is "the word of reconciliation" (2 Cor 5:19). And it says that the preachers themselves "justify" (Dan 12:3), "bind and loosen" (Matt 18:18), "save" (1 Tim 4:16; Jas 5:20).

11. The internal impelling cause whereby God the Father was moved by himself to justify us is the peculiar grace of God, his mercy, philanthropy, love, and affection, whereby He not only granted a Redeemer (John 3:16; Rom 5:8–9; Titus 2:11 and 3:4) and handed him over to death for our righteousness and justification (Rom 4:25), but also deemed valid and pleasing the obedience that his own Son presented apart from us but on our behalf (Eph 5:2). With respect to both of them together, 2 Cor 5:18 states that He has reconciled us to himself in Christ. And finally, hereby He destined it according to his eternal decree and applied it to his elect by faith through the Spirit (Rom 8:30).

12. And so Rom 3:24 states that we are justified "freely, by his grace," and Isa 43:25 that "he for his own sake blots out our iniquities." It says in Ps 130:4 that "with him there is forgiveness," that our justification itself is "grace" of God, his "freely given favor," a "gift and donation," and it is given "by grace" or by his liberality (Rom 5:15–16). And as far as it concerns us, justification is clearly the opposite of what our works merit (2 Tim 1:9; Rom 4:4 and 11).

13. The initiating external cause, which is also the meritorious cause, is Christ the Mediator and Redeemer, the God-and-man; that is, the Son of God who in one person is true God and true Man (John 6:51; Acts 20:28; Gal 4:4; 1 John 1:7). And he is the cause insofar as he is the Mediator and Redeemer, or, it is his obedience, righteousness, and satisfaction (Isaiah 53). And this satisfaction is expressed synecdochically by the word 'blood' or 'death'

wherein the 'ransom' lies and 'the ransom-price' or 'redemption,' the 'atonement and propitiation' (Matt 20:28; Rom 3:24 and 25; 1 Tim 2:6).

14. And as far as God's part is concerned, this verdict of God did not at all come for free, but only upon the payment of a most costly price (1 Pet 1[:19]). And this had to take place because while God is merciful, He is also just (Rom 3:25), and also because that warning of his truly remains forever and cannot be altered: "On the day that you eat of the forbidden tree, you shall surely die" (Gen 2:17 and 3:3). For this reason, "there could be no remission of sins without the shedding of blood" (Heb 9:22). Hence it says that we are justified "through" and "for the sake of Christ" (Rom 3:24). And this satisfaction is put directly opposite our works and their merits.

15. Regarding the material cause of justification we deny (to put it negatively) that it consists of our works. For we are not justified "by the law, in the law, out of the law, or through the law" (Gal 3:11 and 2:21); and we are justified "not by the law of Moses" (Acts 13:39), "not by works" (Rom 4:2; Eph 2:9), "not by works of the law" (Rom 3:20 and 9:32; Gal 2:16), and "not by the law of righteousness" (Rom 9:31); and there is "not a righteousness of our own that comes from the law" (Phil 3:9), it is "not our own righteousness" (Rom 10:3), and "it is not from works that we have done in righteousness" (Titus 3:5).

16. And in this manner "no-one is justified" (Rom 3:20; Gal 2:16), not Abraham the father of all believers (Rom 4:2), nor David, the man after God's heart (Rom 4:6), nor Paul that chosen vessel—even though in everything his conscience was clear (1 Cor 4:4; Phil 3:8–9)—nor any of the saints (Ps 143:2). But finally, there are those who justify themselves, but who do so wrongly (Luke 10:29 and 16:15). Expressed by its opposite, righteousness comes "apart from works" (Rom 4:6) and "apart from works of the law" (Rom 3:28). Justification excludes every righteousness that is according to the Law, whatever sort it might be and to whomever it might belong; and so it also excludes any boasting (Rom 3:27; 1 Cor 1:31).

17. And we assert (to put it positively) that as far as we are concerned we are justified "freely" and "by the grace of God" (Rom 3:24); to some extent this makes up the material cause of justification, which is put directly over against what our works have deserved or merited (Rom 4:4–5 and 11:6). And so it is granted to us not just apart from any merits but even despite our demerits (Rom 3:23 and 4:5–6; Eph 2:8).

18. And indeed [the material cause] is the "righteousness that belongs to God" (Rom 1:17; 3:24–25; 2 Cor 5:21), "that is apart from the law" (Rom 3:21), and "that is by God" (1 Cor 1:30) and "from God" (Phil 3:9). That is to say, it is not the righteousness whereby God is righteous in himself, but the righteousness that He has prepared and gives or imputes to us (Rom 5:15). It is directly opposite the righteousness of the Law, or our own proper righteousness (Jer 23:6; Rom 3:21–22 and 10:3; 2 Cor 5:21; Phil 3:9).

19. And this is the righteousness of Christ, who is "our righteousness" (Jer 23:6 and 33:16), whom "God has made righteousness for us" (1 Cor 1:30). It is the "righteousness of God in Christ" (2 Cor 5:21) in "whom we are made righteous" (Gal 2:17). And it comes "in the name of the Lord Jesus" (1 Cor 6:11), "through Christ" (Rom 5:11), "through the grace of Jesus Christ" (Acts 15:11), "through the redemption made in Christ" (Rom 3:24) and "in the blood of Christ" (Rom 5:9). It is that very righteousness which comes by the satisfactory work of the Son of God—seen in all its fullness (both active and passive) as obedience placed over against disobedience—by which we are justified. It is placed opposite to a righteousness from the Law, and to our own, inherent righteousness (Phil 3:9).

20. And yet the Law, or the righteousness of the Law and of works, is not placed over against the righteousness of God in Christ, or over against Christ's righteousness simply as its opposite. For we are not justified contrary to the Law, for Christ has fulfilled it both by suffering the punishments owed for our sins, whereby he put an end to our guilt, and by presenting all righteousness and obedience to the Law, whereby he fulfilled what is required for eternal life. But the Law is opposed to righteousness in a certain respect, to the extent that the full payment for it was made by the Son of God for us and not by us ourselves, which was an additional requirement of the Law (Rom 8:3–4; Gal 3:13 and 4:4–5).

21. The form of justification is in its application from the side of God towards us, or in the bestowal and placement [upon us] of God's gratuitous righteousness in Christ, or in the *logismos*, that is, the imputing of righteousness (Rom 4:11), since "God does not impute to the sinners the sins that they have" (Ps 32:1; Rom 4:8; 2 Cor 5:19) but "He forgives them their sins and remits them through Christ" (Acts 10:43 and 13:38–39), and He "imputes [to them] the righteousness they do not have" (Rom 4:3; 1 Cor 1:30; 2 Cor 5:21). This alien righteousness of Christ becomes our own, and so we

are made righteous in the presence of God (Rom 5:19). The form of justification is also in the declaration and pronouncement by God himself, whereby He considers, deems, and judges someone righteous in his sight as well as in his own conscience, where God establishes his judgment-seat (Rom 4:2 and 8:33–34).

22. And this imputation is not some imaginary invention, but it has its proper place in the concept of equity and in legal right which has established that a creditor has the same right towards the one who guarantees the surety as he does to the debtor. Since imputation is a relational term, it has as its basis something that is not inherent in the person to whom it happens (i.e., some deed); as end-point a reward; and as relation imputation according to what is owed—as if there is something within us that by virtue of its own full or partial worth is imputed for righteousness—as the word appears to be used in Rom 4:4 (unless we want to understand the word in a different sense that would fit and match the topic). But the basis is situated in the judgment and will of the God who imputes or ascribes [the righteousness], and not in us (for in us, on the contrary, the foundation evokes wrath instead of righteousness, if God should enter into judgment with us); the end-point is the righteousness of faith or the merit of Christ; and the relation is an imputation which comes not by what is owed but by grace, in such a way that it is equal to being fully paid. Rom 4 uses it ten times in this way, and there the former meaning of imputation is explicitly removed from the matter of justification.

23. And by this point it should not seem strange that the righteousness of Christ has the character not only of a meritorious cause but also a material and even formal one, since it works in different ways, namely as that cause because of which, in which or by which, and also through which we are justified.

24. And as to the application, it is by the Holy Spirit that it comes about (1 Cor 6:11), namely as a gift of faith. For it is the Spirit himself who ingenerates it through the ministry of the Gospel (called "the ministry of the Spirit" in 2 Cor 3:8), and he confirms and increases it through his Word and sacraments (Phil 1:26; Gal 5:5). For this reason, he is called also "the Spirit of faith" (2 Cor 4:13), by which faith we appropriate God as gracious, Christ as Redeemer, and we appropriate his righteousness, and from it life eternal (John 1:12, Rom 9:30)

25. And for our part, we are made righteous, and God makes us righteous "by faith" (Rom 5:2; Acts 26:18), "from faith," and "through faith" (Rom 3:30). I say "by faith in God" and "by faith in Jesus Christ the Lord" (Acts 26:18), "out of faith to faith" (Rom 1:17), and even by way of exclusion, "by faith without works," or by way of its opposite: "By faith and not by works of the law." And "by nothing except by faith" and "only by faith," that is, by faith alone (Rom 3:28 and 30; Gal 2:16; Luke 8:5). Therefore, this righteousness is even called "the righteousness of faith" (Rom 4:11–13), the "righteousness of God by and through faith in Jesus Christ" (Rom 3:22 and 9:30), the "righteousness that comes from God in faith" (Phil 3:9). And that faith and the righteousness from faith similarly is placed opposite the Law, works, and also merits.

26. So then 'faith' does not merely denote the doctrine of the Gospel, the habit and action of the mind (that is, a bare rational knowledge of God, Christ, and the Holy Spirit), but bound up with it is the act of the will (Eph 3:12, 17), namely trust in God and Christ and the promises about the forgiveness of sins, righteousness, and life eternal. And faith appropriates these real, good, and life-giving things not just in general but in a particular way, to oneself individually, and even though they are external objects faith makes them one's own (Matt 9:2, Rom 4:20–21). That kind of faith is commonly called "faith that justifies." But whenever 'justification' is assigned to knowledge (Isa 53[:11], John 17:3), then as an expression of a part for the whole and by a common Hebrew manner of speaking it includes also trust.

27. Therefore our justification is "by this faith, out of faith, and through faith." The apostle even states that "faith is imputed for righteousness" (Rom 4:3, 5, 6, 9, 11, 22, 23 and 24). But faith does not act from its own initiative and by itself, like some quality in the proper sense, or motion (whether active or passive). Nor does it act as some work that is good and of exceptional value, as though faith itself were righteousness or a part of it—or even, by the appraisal and evaluation of God, in the place of righteousness. But faith acts in a secondary place and following something else, so that it is really the mode, means, and instrument, or 'the eye and hand' whereby we are made partakers of Christ and his righteousness. Indeed, faith justifies in relation to its object, Jesus, his righteousness and his promises of grace (Phil 3:9).

28. And we are justified by faith "alone," for it is not possible in any other way to appropriate God's promises, the forgiveness of sins, the alien

righteousness, and thence eternal life. Nor can one point to any other instrument, either from all of Scripture or the whole of the natural world. For these things are received not by love or good works, but for them God has appointed only faith.

29. But true and living faith is not something all on its own, unaccompanied by obedience or good works or love (Gal 5:6); for faith comes about by regeneration, which entails repentance together with faith. And faith coexists alongside repentance, and Acts 15:9 states that "our hearts are cleansed" by faith. And so while our justification comes by a faith that is not apart from works, yet it is apart from works that we are justified.

30. And so all of the following [statements] are connected closely with each other in a most excellent way: "It is God who justifies," "by his grace," "freely," "graciously," and "on account of and through Christ" and his "obedience," "righteousness," "by the imputation of righteousness" and "by faith." The one posits the other, or advances it, or infers it. At the same time, placed opposite to them and yet in their own order, are [the statements that] we are saved or justified "by ourselves, out of the law, and through the law, our works and our own proper righteousness," "by what is owed to us and what we have earned." Indeed, God's gracious justification does not conflict with the merit of Christ and its imputation by God; nor does faith conflict with these. For they are subalterns and that is why the justification of man by God's mere mercy is not prevented from being gracious and Christ's intervention from being meritorious. And through it [i.e., God's free justification] nothing is excluded except our own works, not those of Christ. Nor is God's gracious imputation something absolute, but it is the imputation of righteousness, namely the righteousness of Christ. And faith is judged not by its own worthiness but by the worthiness of its object. Or if the word 'faith' says something other than Christ's merit, it only points to the manner in which the merit of Christ is perceived.

31. Therefore the judgment and justification of God differs so much from that of men. It is abominable in the sight of God that the wicked is justified by the judgment of men (Exod 23:1; Deut 25:1; Prov 17:15), because it happens contrary to the Law. In the case that God justifies the ungodly, the judgment is in harmony with righteousness, because it happens according to the Law while Christ intervenes with a righteousness whereby, he makes satisfaction to the Law, and that righteousness becomes our own by

imputation and faith. Therefore, the apostle says "by faith," or "by the righteousness of faith, the law is not overturned but established" (Rom 3:31).

32. As to the goal of our justification by God in Christ through the Spirit and in faith, it is, with respect to God, the glory of God, so that God in justifying us may show himself to be merciful in Christ and powerful in the Spirit. For an amazing combination of mercy and justice is conspicuous here (Rom 3:26), as is God's extraordinary power (Rom 1:16; 2 Thess 1:11). With respect to us, however, the goal is our very salvation and eternal life (Rom 1:17 and 8:30; Titus 3:7).

33. The justification that arises from these causes, as it is an existing effect, likewise produces various fruits and [other] effects, and these include pacification both with God and in the conscience, and access to this grace, perseverance in the same, a hope that exults in life eternal, a boasting in the midst of hardships, and a boasting in God, etc. (Rom 5:1–2, 11, and 3:27; 1 Cor 1:31).

34. The subject or the object of justification is the sinner and the ungodly (Rom 4:5), that is, the sinner in and of himself, in his own nature, yet one who lives "out of faith" or "a believer" (Rom 3:22, 26; Acts 13:39); indeed, one who is elect and called according to God's decree (Rom 8:28,30).

35. The proper adjunct of justification, its proper affection, or, as others put it, the proper and necessary effect of justification, is sanctification (Acts 15:9) and the good works that flow forth from it, and the love of God and one's neighbor (Gal 5:6; 1 Tim 1:5; Titus 3:8). Although these good works are imperfect, yet because they are undertaken by the norm of the Law and because by that faith they are pleasing to God in Christ, they go by the name of 'righteousness.' And thereby we, too, are called 'the righteous' (Acts 16:35; 1 John 2:29 and 3:7, 10) even in the sight of God, on account of our sincerity and integrity. And we are called 'perfect,' each according to his measure and manner (Luke 1:6). And the righteousness is even called 'our righteousness,' as a righteousness that inheres in us, having been effected in us by the Spirit of God. But it is not identical to the righteousness of Christ, which is imputed to us by faith, nor is it a part of it, since it is distinguished from it (Eph 2:9–10). For in the believers there exists no righteousness of works (Rom 3:20; Gal 2:16). And yet there are works of righteousness in them (Titus 3:5).

36. In fact, justification, salvation, and occasionally even life eternal are attributed to the works, although it is not attributed in the proper sense (Jas 2:21, 23; Matt 12:37). It is attributed because there must be a coherence between justification and the works, and because of the testimony and declaration of faith, that is to say, whereby justification means the manifest proof and declaration (Jas 2:18), also to the external human judgment (Rom 4:2; 1 Cor 4:3–4).

37. In sum, God the Father justifies us as judge (to be sure), but He is seated on a throne of grace, and He does so by remitting sins and imputing righteousness. It is in Christ that we are justified, as he performs the satisfaction on our behalf and acts as our advocate. We are justified through the Holy Spirit, in that he is the one who grants faith and seals this grace in our hearts; and he does so by the preaching of the Gospel as the means of God's power. We are justified by faith, which appropriates the righteousness of God himself and of his Son and makes it her own. And lastly, it is by good works, as they display and declare the righteousness of our faith.

Antitheses of the Papal Teachers and the Socinians, Which We Reject as Contrary to the Truth

Ant. 1. The papal theologians, on the other hand, do not take the word 'justification' as a forensic term for the action of God as judge that relates to an object in the absolution of his guilt. But they understand the term in its grammatical sense and as a proper Latin compound word for the motion towards righteousness or a super-physical action of God whereby He works upon the subject by infusing and imparting the quality of righteousness, or whereby He makes and establishes the just out of the unjust. And so, by mixing up justification with regeneration and sanctification, they hold the view that God justifies effectively (contrary to the use of the word in this matter, at least in sacred Scripture)—and that is 'the first lie.'

Ant. 2. However, we do not think that they are excluding altogether that first [forensic] meaning of justification here, but they consider it too as the second, subsequent one, namely that the one who has already been made righteous and lives justly is also justified by God; that is, God absolves him. But there are some who limit this to the final act of the final judgment, although it is also and especially taken in this sense of justification in this life.

Ant. 3. They state that some kind of preparation must precede that justification, a preparation made partly by God and partly by us, that is, by the powers of human choice whereby man both wills and does what is within himself. And they say that these preparatory works deserve justification by the merit of congruity (although they say that this is not properly merit, and some even disapprove of the term, while like the others they do retain the substance of it). For it is congruous with God's kindness that He lends support to the one who does what he has within himself. But that is so far from being any reason for merit that the apostle declares: "Whatever is done without faith is sin" (Rom 14:23) and "no-one is able without faith to please God" (Heb 11:6).

Ant. 4. They think that justification itself follows upon this ordinary preparation, and they divide it into primary and secondary justification, or unfinished and finished, incomplete and complete justification. But justification is one single act that occurs in an instant, although it has its own application, continuation, and feeling, which come about by degrees and repeatedly (Rom 8:30). For this reason we daily pray "forgive us our sins" and we confess "I believe in the forgiveness of sins."

Ant. 5. They call it the primary justification whereby God makes an unrighteous person into a righteous one by infusing a new habit, and He turns the wicked into good by driving out the iniquity of his guilt and bestowing the uprightness of righteousness. But this is an act of regeneration, not justification.

Ant. 6. They posit that this [primary] justification entails two things. Firstly, the forgiveness of sins, as an act that precedes. And thereupon it entails the infusion of the habit of righteousness, whereby a man is formally rendered righteous, while he obtains the ability of doing works well and he becomes inclined to love and to other good works. However, the act of justification is not an internal act but a truly external one, and its form is in the forgiveness of sins.

Ant. 7. But the justification that they call secondary is the one whereby a man, having been equipped with those qualities, actually does become a righteous man by the acquisition of righteousness. That is to say, by performing works that are just man becomes increasingly righteous; that is to say, hereby his justification grows by his good works and finds its completion and fulfillment in him. And so he merits a greater righteousness and life eternal, and he does so through the merit of condignity because Scripture calls life eternal a reward. But in fact Scripture everywhere rejects justification by works. And the word 'merit' is also foreign to Scripture, and life eternal is received as a gift and by the right of inheritance (Rom 6:23 and 8:17–18); it is for this reason that life eternal is called a reward, though not in its proper sense.

Ant. 8. And they place [secondary] justification first and primarily in love, and thereafter among the other works. Love, however, is an effect of faith and consequently it is an effect of justification (1 Tim 1:5).

Ant. 9. They also want to think that God has established a twofold order or degree for righteousness, and so also for justification. The first one is "necessary, in the observance of God's precepts," in keeping with that statement: "If you would enter life, keep the commandments." And the second order, which is not so much necessary but "advantageous and useful" for a higher degree of blessedness, is "observance of the evangelical counsels," in keeping with that saying (as they would have it): "If you would be perfect, go and sell all that you have and give it to the poor, etc." And it is especially among these things that they place the 'merit of supererogation.' However, the one is to deform the Gospel into Law, while the other is to invent a more perfect righteousness over and above the Law.

Ant. 10. Thus, they think the apostle's statement that "God justifies the sinner and the ungodly" does not mean forgiving a guilty person his sins or being clothed in an alien righteousness (the righteousness of Christ), but from a sinner being made righteous as a disposition and personally. They do admit that no-one can be justified without the forgiveness of sins that is done for the sake of Christ's merit, however they do not consider that to be justification in the proper sense but as a prior justification, or as some put it, 'conjoined justification,' and others, 'subsequent justification.' But this is contrary to the apostle's clear statement, "but to the one who does not perform works but trusts in God who justifies the ungodly, faith is counted as his own righteousness" (Rom 4:5).

Ant. 11. They think that the apostle's statement [in Gal 2:16 and Rom 3:28], "we are not justified by works of the law but apart from works," is about the works of the ceremonial law, or even the moral law (performed, however, before conversion), and that are not yet works of the Gospel. But that is contrary to the examples of Abraham and David (Romans 4).

Ant. 12. They do admit that we are justified "by grace" and "by the grace of God," but they understand the word grace to mean an undeserved act of God whereby he forgives us our sins and infuses the habit of love; or they take it to mean the gifts that are infused through God's grace and mercy; they call this grace habitual and inherent. And by that they mean the theological virtues of faith, hope, and love. But in so doing they confuse grace with its effect, since grace means God's mercy (Eph 2:4) and is opposed to what is owed or merited (Rom 4 and 11; Gal 5:4).

Ant. 13. They do not understand the term "righteousness of God" to be the righteousness that Christ himself has presented and God bestows on us, but a righteousness that God infuses in us and that is inherent in us. But to the contrary, Phil 3:9 places the righteousness of God over against our righteousness.

Ant. 14. They do admit that we are justified "through and on account of Christ, by the merit of Christ and his righteousness," such that the righteousness whereby we are justified emanates from Christ and that the satisfaction is indeed applied to us, but that his merit and its application are not the proximate, full, and non-mediated cause, but a more removed one whereby God is moved to infuse the habit of love and of the other virtues in us, whereby, as the proximate and non-mediated cause, we are justified. Or they say that by his death Christ has obtained that we should be clothed with inherent righteousness and love, by the merit of which we obtain life and salvation. But in so doing, with their own satisfaction and their own merit they actually make Christ powerless.

Ant. 15. They do not take the "imputation of righteousness" or "of faith unto righteousness" to mean a reckoning by God whereby instead of the righteousness of the Law which we should have within us, He imputes Christ's obedience and the righteousness that Christ offered on our behalf, and so reckons us as just (which imputed righteousness they clearly deny), but they want that the inner renewal, faith, and works, or the inherent righteousness, although it is not perfect in itself nor of itself meritorious of life eternal, to be considered as such. To do so is to overturn Paul's entire teaching about the righteousness of God, Christ, and faith, and to put in its place the works and merits of men.

Ant. 16. When Scripture says that it is "by faith that man is justified," they take it to mean that it is some unfurnished, general, and implicit understanding whereby man is persuaded that the Christian religion as a whole and the articles of the faith are all true. And consequently, they exclude from faith trust and the special certainty of salvation, which they understand to be no more than moral and to come from a particular revelation alone. And to do so is to overturn the idea of faith as Scripture takes it, as well as its nature and strength.

Ant. 17. And next, they do not take our justification by faith as such (because faith resides in the intellect and is common even to many wicked people, while righteousness is in the will), but they take it in the sense of a part representing the whole and as a metonym (i.e., initially, partially, principally), and insofar as that act of justification is formed by love and made alive by the other virtues and good works. And consequently, they do not locate the mode whereby justification is applied in faith only, but also in works. But in fact faith is not formed from love. For the one quality is not the form of another. Nor do faith and works concur together for this act.

Ant. 18. And so they make the first justification gratuitous while the second is meritorious of salvation, although it is by the strength of Christ's suffering, or (as some Jesuits say) insofar as our works have been washed by the blood of Christ.

Ant. 19. In sum, they want "God to justify effectively" by acting in the subject; they want the "free choice" to act as a co-cause, the "suffering of Christ" as the meritorious cause, namely so that we are able to merit. They take the "habitual grace of God" in the sense of a formal cause, the "sacraments" as instrumental and as effective by the work performed, the "priest" as ministering and even acting in a judicial sense. They want "faith" to be a beginning cause, and lastly, "good works" to be a cause that perfects and makes complete. And on this point they make up a three-fold righteousness: inborn, infused, and acquired, and to each of them they attribute its own proper parts.

Ant. 20. Therefore, the foremost point of debate between the papal teachers and us is: "What is the principal, proximate, and complete cause of our justification?" Or better: "On account of what thing, and by what thing is it that we, as we stand before God's most irreproachable and perfect tribunal, are considered and judged to be perfectly righteous?" Is it an infused habit of love and the exercise of the other virtues? Or is it actually the imputation, that is, the participation, of the merit and satisfaction that Christ has given, so that Christ's righteousness is ours through faith? The former is their claim, while we steadfastly affirm the latter.

Ant. 21. The ungodly teaching of the Socinians is no different from these, insofar as it concerns the thing whereby we are justified; for like them they hold that it was our own obedience—except that they deny that the meritorious cause of justification (on which nearly all Christians agree) is the satisfaction made by Christ, which they claim is not necessary or likely, and even impossible, and they make up a metaphorical redemption, one that has no price.

Ant. 22. In fact they wrongly define faith not merely as trust but also as obedience to Christ's precepts.

SOURCES

Augustine on *Psalm 130*

"If you should mark transgressions, O Lord, who would stand?" [Ps 130:3]. He did not say "I shall not stand" but "who will stand?" For he observed that nearly all of our human existence is dogged by our own hounding sins, that our consciences are being accused by our thoughts, and that a clean heart which trusts in its own righteousness cannot be found. And so if a chaste heart that relies upon its own righteousness is not to be found, then the hearts of everyone must place their trust in the mercy of God and must say to God: "If you should mark transgressions, O Lord, who would stand?" What hope, then, can there be? "But with you there is forgiveness" [Ps 130:4]. And what is that forgiveness, except that of a sacrifice? And what sacrifice is there except one that is offered on our behalf? It was the outpouring of innocent blood that blotted out the sins of all who were guilty, and the payment of so great a price delivered all the captives from the hand of the enemy who held them fast. "Therefore, with you there is forgiveness." For if there were no forgiveness with you, if you should choose to be only a judge and not wish to be merciful, and if you should mark and search out all our iniquities, who could stand? Who could stand before you and say "I am innocent?" Who could stand in your judgment? Therefore, there is only one hope, because forgiveness is only with you.

Bernard of Clairvaux, *Sermon 23* on the *Song of Songs*

Man's righteousness is forgiveness by God. And while the righteousness of God consists in not sinning, the righteousness of man is that sin is not imputed to him.

Bernard, *Epistle 190*
The alien righteousness was allotted to man because he lacked his own.

ON GOOD WORKS

President: Johannes Polyander
Respondent: Johannes Backerius

Good works are 'the actions of regenerate people that come about according to the precept of God's Law, out of faith that works through love, for the confirmation of our election and calling, for the upbuilding of our neighbor, and to the glory of God.' Following a typically scholastic structure, the disputation moves from this definition (1–3) to the efficient and instrumental causes of good works (4–10), and then to the subject-matter (11–14), form, (15) and goals (16–18) of good works. So-called good works of the gentiles are contrasted with true good works (19–22) and the properties of good works that are non-essential are explained (23–31). Romanist teachings of good works are refuted at some length (32–50). Whereas the primary efficient cause of good works is God himself, the secondary cause may be those whom the Holy Spirit has regenerated (6–8). Only the works which God himself has commanded can be considered 'good' (11–12); and these works in all of their parts must agree exactly the rule of God's Law (15). However, good works cannot be meritorious because of their own inner worthiness, for even the very best works are imperfect. But God deigns to accepts these works for the sake of Christ, whose perfect righteousness covers our weaknesses, and who presents these works to the Father as fruits of the Spirit (36). Therefore, the disputation concludes that our merit is the compassion of God (50).

1. The fruits of faith that befit repentance are the holy, good works that are born from the seed of regeneration and grow from the root of justifying faith, which was explained very recently.

2. Good works are the actions of regenerate people that come about according to the precept of God's Law, out of faith that works through love, for the confirmation of our election and calling, for the upbuilding of our neighbor, and to the glory of God.

3. We should not apply this definition of good works to our first parents in their state of innocence nor to their offspring—Jews as well as gentiles—while they are in the state of corruption. We should not apply it to our first parents, because their works before the fall into sin proceeded not from justifying faith but from the original righteousness with which they had been created. And we should not apply it to their offspring, for since they were deprived of that original justice through Adam's fall into sin and they lack the faith that is rooted in Christ, they are not capable in themselves of producing fruits that are truly good.

4. The efficient cause of works of this sort is either primary or secondary. The primary or principal cause is God alone. For as He alone is God, so it is from him alone that every good gift first comes down (Jas 1:17). And He may be considered as the cause either absolutely or relatively. We may consider him as the relative cause in as much as the three divine persons are connected in essence and coordinated on equal terms for producing these [inner] works as well as the other ones that we call outward.

5. And so although it is God the Father who with the Son softens the natural man's heart hardened in wickedness, and bends it towards a new obedience that conforms to his Law, yet the Holy Spirit is in no way subservient to the Father and the Son in this action as an instrumental cause to a principal cause or as an inferior cause to a higher one; but he concurs with both of them for this action by a power that is co-equal to theirs. At the same time, because the Holy Spirit is the last person in this action according to the order of the divine persons and the one closest to us, for that reason the apostle calls our good works his fruits especially (Gal 5:22; Eph 5:9).

6. The secondary cause is the person who has been renewed by the Holy Spirit, who brings forth good works from his own heart as from the proper principle or starting-point, and he does so from his own personal store-house [Matt 12:35]. Hence those who are reborn are called God's work created in Jesus Christ for the good works which God had prepared beforehand, that they should walk in them (Eph 2:10).

7. This cause depends so much on the first one that no good work can be started or completed without it. To be sure, the good works God begins in us He also completes, and just as the Holy Spirit by his preceding grace bestows new strengths on us so that we become willing and able to do good works, so by his subsequent grace He brings it about that we do in fact work

well. Augustine skillfully describes the two graces with these words: "It is certain that we who have been reborn will what we will, but He who works the will sees to it that we do will. It is certain that we do what we do, but He who works to bring it about is the one who sees to it that we work" (Augustine, *On Grace and Free Choice*, chapter 16).

8. And so we should attribute good works only to the Holy Spirit, insofar as the Spirit of God works them in us not by our power but by his own. But insofar as he works them so that we, too, perform them, then we should call them also our works, as Augustine rightly points out (Augustine, Sermon 93, *On the Liturgical Season*). On the other hand, since the wicked deeds that are mixed in with our own works are not brought about by the Holy Spirit but flow forth from the carnal vices clinging to us in this life, we should not attribute them to the Holy Spirit but only to ourselves, as Augustine points out in the same passage.

9. The instrumental cause is either internal or external. The internal instrumental cause is faith, through which God cleanses our hearts and engrafts us into Christ like branches onto the vine, so that rooted in him we should bring forth much fruit (Acts 15:9; John 15:5; Col 2:7). Therefore Jas 2:22 says that Abraham's faith was the 'handmaid' to his works; persevering in the faith in Jesus Christ is linked with the keeping of God's commands (Rev 14:12).

10. The external instrumental cause is the preaching of the Word, and by administering it God exhorts and drives us on towards the newness of life that befits our faith. Thus Christ compares the preaching of his Gospel with a seed, and those who have been reborn with good and fertile soil, in Luke 8:15, where he affirms that they keep the word that they have heard in hearts that are good and honest, and by perseverance bring forth fruit.

11. The subject-matter, which at the same time is the rule for determining works that are good, is whatever God our lawgiver prescribes for us in his Word, of which the moral Law is a summary, the indicator of the good that God commands and finds pleasing, and of the evil that He forbids and finds displeasing. In the Old Testament God explained it clearly through the prophets, and in the New Testament He did so through Christ and his apostles, and He adapted it perfectly because of varying circumstances to the general instruction of his church as a whole and to the specific instruction of certain people.

12. And just as God is the one and only lawgiver who is able to save and to destroy (Jas 4:12), so too does He demand for himself every right to put before us, his creatures, the rule for piety, honesty, and righteousness (Deut 12:32): "Be careful to observe everything that I command you, and you shall neither add nor subtract from it." And Ezek 20:18–19: "You shall not walk in the statutes of your parents, nor keep their laws. I am the Lord your God; you shall walk in my statutes and keep my laws." From these it is clear that we must perform only those works which God himself has commanded, and we must consider only them as good.

13. Therefore it is right not to reckon among the number of good works those that according to the traditions of papal teachers are done from good intentions, or from self-willed worship [Col 2:23], even though they possess some wisdom or humility of heart and are crowned with the impressive title of apostolic and ecclesiastical instruction (Isa 29:13; Matt 15:9; Col 2:22–23). Works of this sort are the monastic vows and fasting, adoration of saints or pilgrimages to their shrines, and similar works; these have no real connection at all to works of piety.

14. For all the works of piety that God's Law has prescribed lead to the adoration only of God, but worshipping and calling upon saints leads also to a superstitious veneration of creatures. Added to that is the fact that everyone, all individuals included, is required to present all the works of piety commanded by God's Law; they are absolutely good and necessary. But the vows of monks (as the papal teachers themselves admit) are arbitrary and preeminent only for a few people who voluntarily bind themselves to doing them, notwithstanding the fact that it is with the promise of greater merit and reward that they are commanded to do them.

15. The form of good works is their integral conformity, or their exact harmony and congruence, with the rule of God's Law in all of their parts, insofar as their inner soundness and also their outward appearance is concerned. For since God knows the hearts and judges according to the truth, and since his Law is a spiritual one—not just pertaining to words and deeds but also to thoughts and desires—our actions should conform to the Law of God (Rom 2:2, 7, 14; Phil 1:10).

16. Good works have three goals. The first of these concerns us, namely, the testimony of our thankfulness towards God, whereby both our election and calling are confirmed in us (Rom 12:1–2; 1 Cor 6:19–20; 2 Pet 1:5, 9 and 10).

For it is by our good works that we are rendered more certain of our election and calling unto salvation, as the works are like sacrifices acceptable to God, and like undoubted marks of justifying faith, as Peter's word of encouragement makes clear: "Therefore, brothers, be eager to make your calling and election firm, for if you do this, you will never stumble" (2 Pet 1:10). And there is also Christ's promise in John 15:8, where the hearers of the Gospel are assured that by the fruits of good works they will know more certainly that they are his genuine disciples, vine-branches forever engrafted into Christ.

17. The second goal of good works is the upbuilding of our neighbor, whether he is a believer or unbeliever. For when in doing good we cause no offense to others, that is, when we lead the way for others without being a stumbling-block and we show openly that our faith is sincere, then the believer is confirmed in the same faith as we are. The unbeliever, however, is either won over to it or he is put to shame by it, if he nonetheless reproves our good walk in Christ (1 Cor 10:32[, 1 Pet 3:16]). Lactantius sums it up elegantly when he says: "When unbelievers see that they and their people do those things which we have said, but that ours practice only that which is just and good, if they had any sense they might have perceived from this that those who do what is good are pious, and moreover that they themselves, who commit wicked actions, are impious. For it is impossible that they who do not err in every action of their lives, should err in the main point, that is, in religion, which is the chief of everything" (*Divine Institutes*, book 5, chapter 9).

18. The third and final goal of good works, and the one to which the other two are subordinate, is the glory of God. For God has placed the regenerate in this world and in the midst of a crooked generation, not only so that they themselves might be blameless and sincere when they bring glory to God with their works and with their speech, but also so that like shining lights they might by the light of their good works incite all others to bring glory to God (Matt 5:16; Phil 2:15; John 15:1[–8]). An unbreakable bond unites this goal to the preceding ones, and together with them it comes in due order in the wake of good works; for this reason it is called by the same name as they are, sometimes their fruit, or their use, or their effect.

19. When the moral and civil virtues of the gentiles are put to the test in light of the definition of good works as we have fully explained it, then there is no

way whatsoever that we can applaud them as works that are good in God's sight—nor should we, because no part of that definition applies to them. For their virtues do not proceed from the Spirit of regeneration, since they are carnal, nor do they proceed from justifying faith (without which it is impossible to please God), since they either ignore or reject the righteousness of Christ. Nor do those virtues proceed from true love, since love is the 'hand of faith' whereby faith does what God demands in his Law. And the gentiles do not perform these works for the sake of God, who is the general goal that also is connected to the eternal well-being of those who do the works. Instead, they do them for some specific goal that ceases along with their life in this age, that is, for personal gain, to win popular acclaim, or to obtain civic honors for themselves.

20. And yet the virtues of unbelievers are not absolutely wicked, or wicked in and of themselves; they are wicked in a certain respect, and by accident. For they are good in a material way and when they are considered simply in themselves. But it is from the root on up that they are wicked, and so too in their form. From their root, because they emanate from a heart that is wicked and impure; in their form, because they are performed differently than they should be.

21. It is for this reason that Cyprian calls the virtues of pagan unbelievers false virtues, and Jerome calls them corrupt, while Augustine, with an eye to Paul's statement in Romans 14:23, calls them "sin itself," when he says: "Regardless of how much we predicate about the works of unbelievers, we know that the Apostle's saying is true, that whatever does not come from faith, i.e., from God's command and resting upon Christ's righteousness, is sin. If a gentile should provide clothing for the naked, is it then sin because it was not done out of faith? Yes indeed, to the extent that it was not done out of faith it is sin. It is sin not because the very act of clothing the naked is a sin, but because in work of this kind the boasting is not in the Lord; it is only the impious who denies that it is sin" (Cyprian, *On the Virtue of Suffering*; Jerome, *Commentary on Galatians*, chapter 3; Augustine, *On the Palestinian Proceedings*, chapter 14, and *Against Julian*, book 4, chapter 3.)

22. To be sure, in other respects those deeds are partly good and partly wicked. Good, because by the power of the Spirit who restrains the corruption within them they are useful for the respectability of the present life, for obtaining temporal happiness, and for the mitigation of everlasting

punishment. But they are evil because they are of no use for obtaining everlasting life. Augustine illustrates this with the example of the Romans, in his *Letter to Marcellinus*, where he says: "The early Romans established the Republic and advanced it with virtues, even though they possessed no true piety towards the true God. And in this very opulent and illustrious Roman empire God shows that even without true religion civic virtues are capable of so much that one would understand that when the true religion is added people would become citizens of another state where truth is king, love is the law, and eternity is the way of life." And in *Against Julian* book 4 chapter 3 he writes: "Fabricius will receive a lesser punishment than Catiline, not because the former was good, but because the latter was more evil; and Fabricius was less wicked than Catiline, not for having real virtues but for not deviating as much from real virtues."

23. Good works possess three adjunct properties: necessity, integrity, and dignity.

24. Necessity is considered an attribute of good works in many ways. Good works are called 'necessary': 1) by the necessity of the divine command; 2) by the necessity of the means ordained for God's glory and our salvation; 3) by the necessity of the worship and obedience we owe to God out of our natural obligation; 4) by the necessity of a good and tranquil conscience that is rightly conscious of its own salvation and calling unto salvation; 5) by the necessity of the duty to show love to our neighbor.

25. The papal teachers add the necessity of efficiency to the preceding ones, but we repudiate it as false because good works are necessary neither for the beginning of salvation (which consists in the forgiveness of sins and our reconciliation with God) nor for its consummation, which finds its place in eternal glorification and the full fruition of the future immortality, as if they were efficient causes. For they follow our justification in the sight of God through faith and they precede the inheritance that has been prepared in heaven for us only as a way and a required condition in the inheritors.

26. And it is not possible to prove the opposite from those very places in sacred Scripture which the papal teachers misuse to spread abroad their own fabricated opinion. Some of the passages show the quality or condition required of those who are promised eternal life (Heb 10:36, etc.). Other passages show the mark and way of faith whereby one reaches eternal life (as in Matt 25:35; Jas 1:25 and 2:14). And other places point out the fruit and

effect of the salvation that has begun and that consists in the forgiveness of sins (as in Luke 7:47, etc.).

27. The integrity of good works is that by which we, from an entirely pure heart and with all our strength, present everything God demands from us in his Law. By another name this is called the perfection of the integrity and the parts.

28. Neither sacred Scripture nor experience recognizes any other perfection, such as the perfection of degrees. For both of them testify that the good works of even the most holy men in this life are found to be imperfect, spotted with a variety of blemishes if they are examined in light of the perfection which the Law of God demands from us.

29. Scripture declares that the works of holy, believing people are not perfect for three reasons especially. 1) On account of the state and the mode of their regeneration in this age, which is such that it grows in small increments daily, and the works do not reach the final degree of perfection until after the last breath of life has been taken. 2) On account of the remnants of depraved concupiscence that continually clings to them by the vices of the flesh. 3) On account of the constant struggle between flesh and spirit, which is like that of enemies fighting with each other on the same battlefield; from their mutual conflict mixed actions arise, which are called either works of the spirit or of the flesh, because of the quality at which these works aim.

30. For these reasons the prophets and apostles testify everywhere that no entirely pure man is to be found who fulfills the precepts of the Law to the level that it requires (Ps 143:2; Rom 7:7–8; Rom 8:3; Jas 3:2).

31. But those who support perfectionism [in the degrees of good works], in particular the papal teachers, maintain the opposite view when they assign so much power to the regenerate that they are equal to fulfilling the Law of God, yet also are capable of achieving even more works, ones much more arduous than the Law's demands—that is to say, works of supererogation.

32. In order not to appear to be speaking without Scriptural support, they bring forward very many prooftexts from it, which they wrongly draw up into these three conclusions: 1) It is possible for saints in the 'arena' of this life to keep the Law. 2) The works of the flesh, which are mingled with the righteous works of the saints, are not deadly sins incompatible with the Law, but they are pardonable sins committed outside the Law, and therefore they do not

impede the compatibility of their righteousness with the Law. 3) The saints are capable of performing even more and greater works than they are bound to do by the precepts of the Law.

33. With the following arguments we shall demonstrate that they incorrectly are citing those prooftexts with which they struggle to prove their first conclusion. The first is that not one of the places they adduce deals with keeping God's commandments, or the general righteousness of the saints that corresponds to God's Law precisely according to the perfection of the degrees. Instead, some places testify to the zeal and effort of obedience in general, or of righteousness that has been undertaken yet is incomplete in degrees, but which conform to the Law insofar as sincerity of heart and all the elements of obedience are present (Josh 11:15; 1 Kgs 14:8; 2 Kgs 23:25; 2 Chron 15:12; Ps 119:11; Luke 1:6; Acts 13:22). Other places deal with the specific righteousness of the saints, or causes (Ps 7, 27, and 119), or deeds of righteousness (Ps 106:30). The second argument is that some places deal with the duty of those people who are held to aspire to the perfection of universal righteousness (as in John 14:21; Rom 13:8; Gal 5:14; Col 4:12). And other places deal with the greater progress of those who have surpassed others either in knowledge of the faith (1 Cor 2:6; Heb 5:14) or in the exercise of it (Phil 3:15; Jas 3:2). And the third argument is that they encourage us promptly to endure the cross and to carry out God's commandments eagerly (Matt 11:30; 1 John 5:3).

34. A comparison of the testimony of the apostle John (1 John 3:9) with the one which follows (1 John 5:8) shows how wrong the papal teachers are in drawing their second consequence from it. For in the latter passage, wherein he interprets his own statement, the apostle indicates that the earlier passage should not be understood as concerning any sin whatsoever, but the sin unto death in particular, for he asserts that those who have been reborn are immune to that sin, otherwise the apostle's earlier pronouncement (in 1 John 3:9) would be contradictory with the previously made statement in 1 John 1:8 which asserts that no-one is without sin.

35. The third consequence they draw also rests upon a false foundation. For in no place does Scripture call Christ's specific commands (which are prescribed only for certain particular individuals because of their function or a special gift) 'counsels' that are more perfect than the commandments of the moral Law, nor does it anywhere apply the name 'works of supererogation'

to those works of piety, abstinence, or love that must be presented only by those people who have received them. It calls them 'duties' that are owed either to God (according to the first table of the Law) or to our neighbor (according to the second table of the Law), as we shall show in a later disputation, the one on vows.

36. We should assess the dignity of good works not by their merits (as the papal teachers would have it) but only by God's grace, as the Gospel teaches. For if God were to test them against the rigor of his Law, then because of their own imperfection they would be worthy of censure rather than his favor and beneficence. God, seated on his throne of fatherly grace, deigns to accept these works and to crown them with eternal glory for the sake of Christ his beloved Son, who covers all our weaknesses with his own perfect righteousness, and who on our behalf presents our works to the Father as fruits of the Spirit who is working in us through faith.

37. Besides the fact that their own imperfection clearly reveals that our works cannot merit anything in God's sight by their own inner worthiness, there are the four following arguments that can prove the same. The first of these is the fact that for the promised reward of the future life the proportion of those works is not at all equal, since they are finite and temporary while the reward is infinite and eternal.

38. If the apostle Paul asserts concerning this that the brief sufferings which the saintly martyrs endure for the sake of the name of Christ are outweighed in countless ways by the reward of heavenly glory (Rom 8:18), then we should make the same assertion even more about the same reward that is promised for our actions, which we must perform and which are less than the sufferings of the holy martyrs. And the claim by the papal teachers that the distinction between merit of congruity and condign merit can be rightly drawn up from this statement by the apostle is so far from the truth that it would be best for us to reject it altogether. For if there is no equal proportion between works and the reward of the heavenly kingdom, then good works have no merit, nor is the reward a compensation that is to be provided based on an assessment of a proportionate righteousness.

39. The second reason is that good works, to the extent that they are good, proceed from the Holy Spirit (as we have declared earlier in thesis 7) and therefore they are not properly our works but gracious gifts of God that were brought forward by us. They are acceptable to God because we have them

not from ourselves but from him, and we, as instruments of his Spirit, present them to God, as Augustine has rightly noted (Sermon 39, *On the Liturgical Season*).

40. The third reason is that our works are owed, and it is by right that God requires them of us, as He is the supreme and only Lord to whom we owe ourselves and all that we have. If our works are owed to God as our Lord, then surely we can earn nothing from God by them; but if on the contrary they are meritorious, then they are not owed to him by his right of lordship. But in fact they are owed to God by his right of lordship, and Christ shows this by the parable of the slave: "Will the master thank his servant because he did what he was told to do? I think not. So you also when you have done everything you were told to do, should say 'we are unworthy servants, we have only done what we ought to have done'" (Luke 17:9–10).

41. The fourth reason is that with our works we do not bestow on the Lord God anything that by its priority lessens his goodwill in such a way that He gains some benefit for which He should consider himself under obligation to us. Christ links this reason to the immediately preceding one (Luke 17:10) when he says that it is in this regard that we are God's unworthy servants. And Job 35:7 presents the same thought for us to read: "If you are righteous, what do you give to God? Or what does He receive from your hand?" And Job 41:2: "Who has come before me, says the Lord, that I should repay him? Whatever is under the whole heaven is mine." And similarly Rom 11:35: "Who has ever given to God that God should repay him? For from him and through him and to him are all things."

42. To these reasons we may add that the very word 'merit' itself is just as strange as 'doctrine about merits,' and it is used nowhere by God's inspired scribes. And although Jesus Sirach is not counted as one of them and therefore in our view not a self-authenticating witness, yet we shall point out that the [Greek] word *erga*, which he uses in Chapter 16:13, means 'works' and not merits, as the papal teachers think, who prefer to follow the bad rendering of the Latin translator than to cling to the authentic meaning of the text taught by us. This is clear also from the passage in Heb 13:16, where, for the sake of constructing their 'merit of condignity' they would rather, in line with the ancient translator, explain the verb [in the second clause of Heb 13:16] as 'to earn,' than—as we do—'to be cherished,' even though this latter

410

word expresses the meaning of the apostle better than the former. No-one who is skilled in the Greek language—and also orthodox—would deny it.

43. It is no less absurd to adduce the word 'wages' (which occurs very frequently in the sacred writings) in order to lend support to that same merit [of condignity] since the Gospel nowhere promises the salvation of our souls, or eternal life, as wages owed for our good works but as an undeserved and gracious reward. And for that reason, it is sometimes called the "goal of faith" (1 Pet 1:9), the "gift of God" (Rom 6:23), and again, "the inheritance that is kept in heaven for us who are co-heirs with Christ by the grace of adoption" (1 Pet 1:4).

44. Moses looked forward to that reward with the eyes of faith whereby he relied upon the expiatory reproach that Christ bore, in keeping with God's gracious promise made to Abraham and his seed, and he considered the riches of that reproach of greater value than the treasures of the Egyptians (Heb 11:26).

45. As we journey in the rugged desert of this life we may cast our eyes upon the same reward, so long as we look upon it not as a payment in the way that hirelings do, but as an inheritance that will be assigned to us for free by our Lord and heavenly Father, as befits slaves who have been adopted as sons, and who temper the troubles of this present life by the sweet solace of this expectation.

46. In 1 Cor 9:24 the apostle presents that same reward to us as the prize of an imperishable crown, so that, by looking at it we should be driven more eagerly to run our race until the end. And Phil 3:14 shows what kind of prize it is: it is the prize of the heavenly calling of God who supplies us with the strength in Christ Jesus for the valiant and steadfast completion of our race-course. Since God's calling is free, then its effect and its scope must also be free—that is, the prize of the eternal crown.

47. And this does not conflict with the fact that the same apostle defines that imperishable crown as the crown of righteousness that has been laid up for him in the heavens and that Christ the righteous Judge will bestow on the day of his glorious coming (2 Tim 4:8). For Paul does not mean that Christ must give that crown to him following a rigorous appraisal of his works, for he flatly denies that he was justified by that (1 Cor 4:4), even though he was not aware of having committed any misdeed. Rather, he means that—

according to the analogous rule of truth—[the crown] corresponds to the quality of any work whatsoever (good or bad), which in other, parallel passages is explained distinctly and antithetically (or, in comparison with what is opposite to it). This occurs in Rom 2:[6]–8: "God will repay each person according to his works. To those who are persistent: the glory of good work. But for those who are contentious and do not obey the truth but unrighteousness there will be fury and wrath, etc." And: "It is just in the eyes of God to repay with affliction those who afflict you, and to give relief, together with us, to you who are being troubled, when the Lord Jesus will be revealed from heaven" (2 Thess 1:6–7).

48. And from this sort of relation to the works of believers as well as unbelievers it is not right to conclude that the works of either are meritorious, since Christ repays the works of unbelievers with the punishment for unrighteousness by the law of the highest right, but the works of believers with the crown of righteousness according to the Gospel of his covenant of grace, so that he might reveal his righteousness by the trustworthy payment of the promised blessedness no less than his mercy by the favorable declaration of it (Heb 6:10 and 10:23; 1 John 1:9).

49. When the orthodox fathers employ the words 'merit' and 'to earn' 1) they understand the word 'merit' in both ways, as merit for a good work or merit for a bad work. This is seen in *Epistle* 40 of Augustine, where he makes a distinction between the evil merit of the impious and the good merit of the pious. 2) They understand the word 'to earn' as 'to obtain' or 'to acquire,' as in the *Proceedings of the Council of Carthage*, cognition 3, article 258: "let us leave aside how much shedding of Christian blood was done by Leontius, Ursatius, Macarius, and the other executioners whom they *obtained* from the rulers of the world to slaughter the saints." And from the *First Sunday of Advent*: "O Lord, we beseech you to summon forth your power and come, so that by your protection we may obtain escape from the dangers that threaten us sinners and salvation by your deliverance." 3) So that no-one should misuse those words and devise for good works an innate meritorious worthiness, they sometimes state that good works are worthy more of God's sympathy than of a payment of life eternal. See Augustine on Ps 49 and 61, and Bernard, Sermon 67 on the Song of Songs.

50. For this reason the papal teachers deserve to be judged more severely, because by badly twisting the words not only of sacred Scripture but also

those of the ancient church fathers, they feel no shame in conjuring up their doctrine of the merits of good works. And as for us, we bid them farewell, and in keeping with the arguments made earlier, we conclude with Bernard that our merit is the compassion of God.

ON CHRISTIAN FREEDOM

President: Andreas Rivetus
Respondent: Jacobus Henricus

Christian liberty is treated in the Synopsis from the perspective of the saving work of Christ that was delineated in earlier disputations. The satisfaction for sins that Christ has obtained for us and our consequent justification are the basis on which Christian freedom from slavery to sin arises. Locating Christian liberty within the process of sanctification by the Spirit, the disputation rejects the idea that any lawlessness is permissible (1, cf. 47). This subject is important, for without Christian freedom 'we will not be able to rightly know Christ, the true Gospel, nor inward peace' (2). The freedom in question is, like its opposite, slavery, spiritual in nature (4). It is the condition of those set free by the grace of Christ whereby their consciences are no longer enslaved to sin, the power of the devil, and the curse of the law (7). Thus all who believe are free from sin and guilt (11–12), free from the demands of the moral law (13–16), and free from any human traditions that seek to restrain believers' consciences (17–19). Theses 20–23 articulate the nature of the freedom that believers enjoy in light of the Christ who has been revealed in the Gospel. Believers have been set free from Old Testament ceremonial laws (28), forensic laws (29), and political laws (30–31). What follows is a treatment of the so-called adiaphora, or 'indifferent things' that are judged to be good or bad not in or of themselves but from the circumstances of their use (33); they are restricted by the law of faith and love (33–36). The form that Christian freedom takes is the 'undoubted conviction and full assurance in the hearts of believers about their sonship' produced by the Holy Spirit (41). Goals are a good conscience, joy, and the praise of God's grace (42). Those enjoying the freedom of grace look forward to the freedom of glory in the life to come, to which belongs the soul's immortality and the resurrection and the glorified state of our bodies (43–44). There are many benefits of this doctrine, in keeping with the various degrees of freedom (45–46).

1. In the preceding disputations we treated the redemption that is obtained through Christ, and its application by saving faith for all who through Christ's merit have been redeemed from slavery to sin and death; and also the sanctification of those who have been justified and their thankfulness in the exercise of good works. In fitting order, therefore, it follows that we now undertake an investigation into the true Christian, or evangelical, freedom that is shared by all to whom the fruits of Christ's suffering belong.

2. We acknowledge that the need for having this doctrine is such that if we do not keep it then we will not be able to rightly know Christ, the true Gospel, nor inward peace in our souls, nor to perceive these things with earnest awareness in our hearts. Nor could our conscience undertake anything without hesitation, nor could the power of justification be sufficiently understood. Therefore, we must make every effort not to suppress a part of doctrine that is so necessary; and we should also make every effort to explain it so as to cut short any opportunity for criticism or arrogance for those who misuse the name of freedom in order to hurl themselves into unsound activities of lust and unbridled abandon.

3. In terms of kind, the nature of freedom should be distinguished from its opposite, namely slavery, which means a certain state of vile and wretched subjection, whether that subjection is voluntary or forced. It is hence that men are divided into 'slaves' and 'freemen,' the former of which had come under the power of another person according to the rule of law either by the right of war, by birth, by just sentence of condemnation, or by purchase. But the latter were born free and never had served as slaves. The Jewish people proclaimed themselves to be of this sort: "we are the seed of Abraham and we have never served anyone; how can you say: 'you will be set free'?" (John 8:33). Occupying a middle position between these two were the 'freedmen,' who had ceased to be slaves, and whom their masters had set free from their rightful servitude.

4. We are not dealing here with the question of that civic and corporal slavery, nor with its opposite, civic and corporal freedom. But we do use some terms and expressions from those realms in order to explain the slavery and freedom that are spiritual. Concerning that spiritual slavery and freedom Christ says: "If the Son shall set you free, you will indeed be free" (John 8:36). Since this spiritual freedom has its origins in manumission and liberation, it

follows that no-one is born free but becomes it, and that no-one is spiritually a pure freeman but all people who enjoy that freedom are freedmen.

5. This manifold spiritual slavery came about after the first man abused his natural freedom and so lost it for himself and his posterity, and became a slave to what he obeyed by abandoning God, namely sin, to which everyone is kept enslaved by both the guilt of condemnation and by dominion. As a consequence, Satan's sovereignty and domination came over the sons of rebellion (Eph 2:2), a sovereignty that would not exist if it had not arisen from sin. This slavery was followed (so to speak) by its declaration or manifestation (itself also called slavery) when God renewed the force of the moral law and demanded that it be kept carefully—the law which had been nearly obliterated (or at least mainly hidden) from the hearts of men. God did so in order that man might recognize the tyranny of ruling sin from the fact that he would have to abandon all hope of fulfilling the requirements of that law. The ceremonial law was added to it, and by it the condemnation that man deserved was sealed with various types whereby he, convicted of his guilt, would await the ultimate accursedness unless he should be redeemed by being set free.

6. The servitude to empty pride and wretchedness in this and the future life was added to this slavery of sin to which the law bore witness. And opposite to this manifold slavery is placed a triple freedom, namely 1) The freedom of our nature, or innocence, such as Adam had; 2) The freedom of grace, which believers receive in this life as participants in the heavenly calling; 3) The freedom of glory, whereby they will, after this life, be set free from every [form of] slavery to corruption and wretchedness.

7. We ascribe the name 'Christian freedom' especially to that intermediate freedom, which is the freedom of grace granted in Christ to all "who throughout their whole lives were held in slavery by their fear of death" (Heb 2:15). And we describe [that Christian freedom] as the condition of people who have been set free by the grace of Christ, a condition whereby their consciences have been released from slavery to sin, the tyranny of the devil, and from the precise demands and curse of the moral law, and from observing the ceremonial law; and after shaking off the yoke of human traditions, they conduct 'intermediate things' safely without reproach by applying knowledge of faith and practical judgment of love, so that they who have not received "a spirit of slavery unto fear" but a spirit of sonship (Rom

8:15) may serve God willingly and eagerly in soul and in body, "for the praise of his glorious grace" (Eph 1:6) and their own eternal salvation.

8. The chief efficient cause of this freedom is God the Father "who has made us to share in the inheritance of the saints in light" (Col 1:12). It is also the Son, the Mediator between God and man "who has set us free" (Gal 5:1); and the Holy Spirit, 'fellow-worker' with the Father and the Son, who brings freedom with him wherever he dwells (2 Cor 3:17). The principal impelling cause is God's grace and love for mankind in Christ (Luke 1:72 and 74). The initiating cause is the merit and satisfaction of Christ in whom we have "freedom from sin" (Rom 6:22) and a "ransom from the empty way of life inherited from our fathers," a ransom "which was not made with silver or gold but with his precious blood" (1 Pet 1:18[–19]), which excludes the merit of any human work.

9. There are two aspects to the efficient instrumental cause: from the side of God it is the true Gospel whereby freedom is offered through the preaching (Jer 34:15), and John 8:32 ascribes liberation to it. Accordingly the preaching of the Gospel is called "the ministry of reconciliation" (2 Cor 5:[18–]19). For man, however, the necessary instrument, which is ingenerated by the Spirit and the Word, is a living faith, "whereby we have access into this grace in which we stand" (Rom 5:2).

10. The matter in which, or the subject [of Christian freedom], is everyone who believes in Christ and who takes refuge in him as his liberator, whether Greek or Jew, male or female, etc. (that is, of whichever gender, state, nation, etc.) in the church of the New Testament. For it is to the members of the church that 'Christian freedom' in all of its degrees properly belongs. And if all of the degrees are to be grasped fully, then before Christ was revealed no-one could be a member. But if we consider the primary, foremost degrees, the ones that are altogether necessary for salvation, and the very substance of freedom, then we do not deny that freedom had been communicated to believers under the Old Testament, albeit not to the extent that was revealed with Christ's appearance. And that freedom in its own way could even be called 'Christian' freedom, for those who were at that time bearing "the reproach of Christ" (Heb 11:26) realized that Christ was the author of spiritual freedom too; and because they were participants in it with us, some not inappropriately have called this freedom 'shared' in order to distinguish

it from the freedom that concerns the fullness of grace, which is called Christian freedom in particular.

11. The matter concerning which, or the object of the two freedoms (the one that is shared and less complete, and this more complete one), is manifold, and from its variety also diverse degrees (or parts, as others prefer to call them) have been arranged. For 1) it has sin as its object, and the guilt thereof, that is, the dominion of the devil and so his tyranny. [All believers] acquire that degree of freedom from the primary slavery, since through the remission of sin it is not imputed to them, and through the mortification of the flesh it no longer reigns over them. And they acquire it also through the immunity from the second death, because "the law of the Spirit of life through Jesus Christ has set us free from the law of sin and death" (Rom 8:2), and so "there is no condemnation for those who are in Christ Jesus" (Rom 8:1).

12. The fact that sin still dwells in those who believe and remains active in them (1 John 1:8) is not a hindrance to this freedom because the guilt for it has been removed and its powers have been diminished, in order to do away with its kingdom (Rom 6:12). For through the granting of the Holy Spirit the consciences of the pious are set free from sin to the extent that they are no longer slaves to it, but they are soldiers and servants of righteousness (Rom 6:14[,18] and 7:22). Therefore, though the war is not yet over, it is enough that the victory has been obtained from the enemy. And since we have dealt with this matter in the doctrines of repentance and justification, we do not need to pursue it further.

13. 2) The same freedom has a function concerning the moral law, insofar as "by it the feelings of sin are at work in our members to bring forth fruits unto death" (Rom 7:5), since it presents no hope at all of salvation for the sinful man other than in a very precise observance of the commandment "do this and live" (Luke 10:28). This very harsh requirement of fulfilling the entire law was linked to the same law's curse if we did not keep it perfectly (Deut 27:26; Gal 3:10). This yoke was very heavy and unbearable, and Christ broke it, having transferred both obligations to his own person: the curse that came for not fulfilling the law as well as the requirement of fulfilling it. And by the transference he both fulfilled the law perfectly and was made a curse for us (Gal 3:13). "And by sending his Son God condemned sin in the flesh so that the righteousness of the law might be fulfilled in us" (Rom 8:3–4).

14. Accordingly we teach that the law is not superfluous, but we rather state that what it teaches remains unaffected, and that all should obey it; and we know what freedom really is only when we serve God according to the prescript of his law. Therefore, in Scripture 'to be free' and 'to serve God' are in fact the same thing, although they are worded differently (1 Pet 2:16). And Paul, in Rom 6:18, locates Christian freedom in the 'servitude to righteousness.' Therefore, part of the freedom is the fact that in us it is brought about that we, gifted with the Holy Spirit, fulfill the law for a large part, although not in its entirety. And because through the weakness of our flesh we either omit [to keep it], or on the other hand commit [sin against it] it is not considered as an omission or a commission, because the perfect fulfillment of the law—which is in Christ alone—has been imputed to us.

15. Therefore even if those who have been born again are free from the law insofar as it is a means for obtaining justification by it, or insofar as it condemns, [the law] is nonetheless of use to them since it teaches what those good works are wherein they ought to walk. And it guides them to stay within the boundaries of the right way, while it denounces the old remains of the flesh, chides them for the imperfection of the obedience that was begun in them, and provides convincing reasons for being humble, so they are not swept along to a persuasion of their own righteousness.

16. Therefore just as we reject the ravings of the Antinomians, who are of the opinion that the moral law ought to be proscribed and eliminated from the Church (we say that if the teaching [of the moral law] is not preserved undiminished in the Church, then its purity and integrity cannot stand firm, nor the articles about justification, the doctrine of good works, original sin, or free choice), so too do we have the right to complain about Bellarmine's dreadful slandering, which falsely alleges that we situate Christian freedom in the fact that the man who has been justified by faith is in his conscience not subject to any law at all, but is free from the requirement to fulfill the law and he considers everything as indifferent, as neither prescribed nor prohibited (Book 4 *On Justification*, chapter 1 and 5).

17. 3) It has also been a part of the freedom common to all believers, and it will be so until the end of the age, that they have consciences that are free of every yoke of human traditions in matters pertaining to the worship of God and in matters which involve religious actions (which are called 'elicited acts'). For it belongs only to God to prescribe matters that pertain to religion, and

it is for this reason that in matters of worship we should pay attention only to his Word and not to human traditions. For to no-one has God granted authority (whether it be autocratic or legally bestowed authority) over the consciences of other people, when it concerns worship in which God alone binds the conscience in a non-mediated way, as He "alone is the lawgiver who is able to save and to destroy" (Jas 4:12).

18. But since we are speaking about the strictly spiritual government, which we claim belongs entirely to God alone (since it pertains to the spiritual kingdom in which God does not allow a vice-regent), we do not want what we say about spiritual freedom to be wrongly drawn into the realm of politics, as if Christians who are free according to the spirit are therefore exempt from every kind of service to the flesh. For we reject the fanatics who under the pretext of Christian freedom cast off every form of civil obedience, because God through Paul teaches us to obey the magistrate, "not only from fear of punishment, but for the sake of conscience" (Rom 13:1 and 5).

19. However, it does not therefore follow that the consciences are bound in a direct, non-mediated way by political laws that are strictly human laws and not found among the laws of God (which the papal teachers contend), because it is what we must do by God's command that strictly and of itself binds the consciences non-mediatedly, although no command or consideration of any creature is added to it. The subject-matter proper to human laws is not of that sort—human laws which we nevertheless admit do bind the consciences in a mediated way, by force of God's general command, which bids obedience towards the magistrate. For since human laws are not binding in principle and of themselves, but secondarily and through accident, the teaching that Bellarmine defends is false, that "the civil law is no less binding than the divine law, and that all laws that have been made by any one at all (whether God, an angel, or a human being) are binding in the same manner" (*On the Members of the Church Militant*, book 3, chapter 2).

20. So much for now about the degrees and elements of the freedom of God's children that all believers in every age share (whether they believed in Christ yet to come or now believe in Christ as having been revealed), although these stages and elements have been communicated to a greater or lesser extent. Particular to the freedom that befits the times of the New Testament is the release from the dispensationary slavery to the ceremonial law, and in keeping with the law's diverse aspects it has many facets. For in the first place,

the law consisted of the fact that it was a sign of the sinner's verdict and a written record of our indebtedness (Gal 3:21), laid upon us "until the time of restoration" (Heb 9:10), the time that was fulfilled when "Christ blotted out the written record of ordinances against us and took it away" (Col 2:14). For when the verdict was taken away by him, it was no longer necessary that the sign of our verdict stay.

21. Moreover, since the ceremonial precepts are concerned especially with the worship appropriate to the Israelite nation for an outward sign of the mysteries of the coming Christ (Col 1:27; Heb 8:4 and 10:1)—for which reason Moses had been ordered to make everything "according to the likeness and pattern shown on the mountain" (Exod 25:40)—when he did come in the body, the shadow disappeared, and when the prototype came, the type yielded its place, and it now is no longer possible for the mystery of redemption to be truly signified as something yet to come either in word or in deed, for in the outward sign of the deed there would be the same lie as if someone were to say "Christ is still going to come and to die, etc."

22. Indeed, if we take a look at the same rites, because the church of the Jewish people in the time of its infancy (which needed a tutor and pedagogue) was kept in custody under the elements of the universe (Gal 4:3) in hope of the coming Messiah, so that it might be led to believe in him and be led to him, [we see that] the same Apostle who taught this use of the ceremonial law also pointed out that "in the fullness of time his Son was sent forth, etc., to redeem those who were under the law" (Gal 4:1 and following), "so that you are no longer slaves, but sons and heirs through Christ" (Gal 4:7).

23. And lastly, if we consider the other use of the ceremonial law, namely that its rites were the marks of what it professed, the signs and tokens that set the Israelite people and its ecclesiastical form of government apart from all the other peoples, which like an enclosure or a dividing wall distinguished the Israelite nation from the idolatrous forms of worship of the other peoples (Gen 17:13 and 14; Deut 4:8; Eph 2:14), there was no longer any place for this aspect of the law after "the people who once were far off were brought near by the blood of Christ, who is our peace, who has made both one, and has broken down the middle wall of partition" (Eph 2:13 and following).

24. Therefore in former times the ancient heretics were rightly condemned who thought that this law has not ceased but ought to be preserved in perpetuity along with the Gospel: Cerinthus (as witnessed in Epiphanius

Against Heresies 28 and Augustine *Against Heresies* 8), Ebion (as witnessed by Irenaeus book 1 chapter 28) along with the Ebionites and those who were called the Nazarenes (in Epiphanius *Against Heresies* 18 and Augustine *Heretics* 9). The fact that after Christ's resurrection Paul circumcised Timothy (Acts 16:3) does not help their view, nor the fact that on the advice of James he, together with others, purified himself according to Jewish ceremony (Acts 21:26)—an affair wherein Paul showed no prejudice against Christian freedom, as he showed himself to be a forceful defender of it elsewhere, over against the unwise behavior of Peter (Gal 2:14).

25. At this point we must therefore apply the distinction that the 'School of Theology' derived from Augustine, namely that after Christ the ceremonial things could have been observed until such time as the Gospel was sufficiently spread among the Jews—not, of course, as outward signs that foretold that Christ was yet to come, or from the notion that it was necessary for salvation, but as commands proceeding from a good source that by Christ's suffering were put to death and emptied of meaning, but which are to be carried to their graves and buried with due respect. But after that time it was no longer permitted to observe them, nor should anyone observe them now unless he wishes to be seen as a 'violator of the tomb.' But at that time they were dead indeed, but only in the sense that we stated, although they were not yet deadly, so that the two nations might grow together. (But later they would be both dead and deadly.)

26. Nor should anyone state that he is removing the signification and abandoning all necessity, and so (as Cajetan does) excuse the superstition of the Ethiopians who maintain circumcision for the sake of imitating Christ, and not for what it signifies. For even other people of that same school rightly sense that this cannot be right, not only because of the stumbling block but also because that religious observance (both as an outward sign of the coming Christ and as a means) flies in the face of the truth and perfection of the Gospel whereby it was Christ's will that this religious practice should be made obsolete. Not only because it functioned as an outward sign of the things that were to come, but also because it belonged to the manner of worshiping God that was but a shadow and not perfect. If one were to examine the majority of the papal ceremonies by this standard, they would be no less deadly at this (current) time, and all the more so because they were brought in by men for worship and from the notion that they are necessary.

27. Yet we do grant that there is great value in knowing the ceremonial laws, even though Christians are free from them. For just as the things that the prophets foretold about the coming of Christ may have been fulfilled, yet are read in the church with great benefit, so too the Levitical ceremonies are examined and explained no less usefully, so that from an understanding of how Christ and all his benefits had been prefigured in them we derive the strengthening of our faith. What Christ said to the Jews in John 5:46 is relevant here: "If you believed Moses you would believe me, for he wrote about me." By this he meant not just the explicit words of the prophecies but also the ceremonial rites and figures that foreshadowed Christ. In this manner it is from the rite of sacrifices for sin that we today defend the doctrine of Christ's perfect satisfaction, over against the modern-day antichrists.

28. From the things that have been stated about the ceremonial law given to the Israelites we should judge Christian freedom concerning the judicial laws of Moses, which, because they were given by Moses and to such a nation, they neither affect nor bind Christians. And yet we should note that mixed in with those laws were some ceremonial elements, and these are entirely out of date for our time, either because of what they are, or by analogy. A commandment of this sort is the one about the corpse of someone who has been hanged, that it must be buried on the same day lest the land should be polluted which Jehovah our Lord had granted to the Jews as a possession (Deut 21:22 [and 23]). We should place this commandment in the company of those with similar ceremonial admixtures that pointed to Christ and were intended as proper types of him; consequently, these are, in our time, deadly.

29. As far as it concerns laws that are in no way ceremonial, we need to make yet another distinction. For firstly in forensic law there are some commandments that are not at all subject to change. For whatever has been sanctioned for the common good according to universal principles of nature and common sense in moral law (whether by command or prohibition, reward or penalty), that of itself remains permanently, and even though it is not by the force of Moses's government that we should keep it; yet to the extent that it is marked by law and common reason and pertains to the law of nature, no occasion or condition can come about to loosen it, nor could anyone have reason to speak against it or resist it successfully. Consequently Christian freedom does not extend to this point.

30. Other laws are purely and absolutely political, and thus common; and though these do not change in nature or substance, they do sometimes exist in themselves for themselves, and at other times by analogy (by which a judgment can be made about the most similar cases). But depending on the circumstances, they undergo very many changes and they vary according to the time, place, persons, deeds, means, causes and the things that support them (whether in the past, present, or future; public or private). Many laws of this sort that in such circumstances have the character of a private right had been set up by Moses, which had been determined by a particular right (in the manner of the Jewish republic), that is, of persons, actions and a specific goal; and it is certain that Christians are free from them.

31. But if there are laws of the mixed kind, being both moral and political— and there are a few—then we must distinguish between the ethical and the political as follows: we consider anything that is moral to be permanent, but whatever is political is not binding as far as its specific decisions are concerned. But if we ponder these things carefully, then the arguments spontaneously collapse which the Anabaptists and some other fanatics have constructed to eliminate Roman laws or any other laws whatsoever from Christian states, in order to foist upon judges the requirement of passing judgment in civil cases according to the forensic laws of Moses. The experts rightly consider this idea not only dangerous and confusing but also wrong and foolish.

32. It remains for us to treat the other degree, or part, of freedom that is properly Christian, the part which deals with the exercise and use of things that are indifferent, or 'middle matters.' These are things which by their own nature are neither good nor bad in a moral sense, and which neither have been prohibited nor commanded by any law, and so they are things that anyone could use in the right way, or the wrong way, or plainly not at all. It is very important to understand this part in order to remove any feeling of despair or superstition about them. For whenever people's hearts are tied up with doubt, controversy arises over whether it is the will of God (and his will should show us the way in all our actions) to use these or those things. Unless help is offered, it is easy to fall into all manner of superstitious ideas. In this way, once a scruple has befallen someone in the use of wool or linen, he will thereafter not be entirely sure about hemp, either. Or if someone should lack the light of God's Word and still not be affected by any scruple, he may out

of profane carelessness cast off his reverence for God and will cause the way that he otherwise will not see as unencumbered to become his own ruin.

33. Therefore since indifferent things are judged to be good or bad not in or of themselves but from the circumstances of their use, we must ponder carefully what in matters of this sort should be left to our freedom. For although it seems that Paul subjected everything of this outward kind to our freedom (Rom 14:14), it was still God's will to restrict this freedom with a double law: the law of faith and love. The first of these is required for the fact that the reason for the freedom in our hearts is with God, so that we are rightly taught and sufficiently established in the lawful use of things that are indifferent, and so that we do them, or dare to do them with a conscience that doubts nothing. For that which of itself is not common or unclean, to him who considers that unclean it does become unclean (Rom 14:14).

34. And so those who are not yet certain about the freedom they have, and so hesitate or doubt in using it, or are laboring under some superstitious idea, for them the use of things that otherwise are indifferent is not indifferent or allowable because what they are doing is done by them not out of faith (Rom 14:5, 14, 22 and 23), and since their hearts are wavering and their consciences doubting [cf. Jas 1:6–8, 17], they are unable to receive God's good gifts with a giving of thanks that comes from the heart that acknowledges God's beneficence and goodness in his gifts—which is still the only way whereby the things God created are made holy for our use (1 Tim 4:[4 and] 5).

35. The lantern of this faith which lights the way not only investigates the nature of the thing that is called 'the middle thing' and reveals whether or not it is middling in and of itself. But also, while it cleanses their hearts (Acts 15:9) it guards the mind and conscience against uncleanliness and sees to it that such things are not wantonly longed-for, conducted in pride, or extravagantly poured out, and that these vices do not befoul whatever in itself is permissible. And it sees to it that they who are clean make pure use of God's gifts with a pure conscience, "for whom all things are pure" (Titus 1:15), who "whether they eat or whether they drink, or whatever they do, they do everything to the glory of God" (1 Cor 10:31).

36. Freedom in matters of this sort is moreover kept in check by the law of love, which demands that we take into account our weaker brothers who have not yet been instructed sufficiently about the privilege of their own freedom, in order to guide their comprehension (and to do that for as long

as they can be taught) and to attend to their upbuilding. For not always do "all the things that are allowed also build up" (1 Cor 10:23). For this reason, the same apostle said: "If what I eat is a stumbling-block for my brother, I shall never eat meat again, lest I cause my brother to stumble" (Rom 14:22; 1 Cor 8:13). But in this matter, it is the responsibility of the weaker and uninformed brothers to leave untouched the rights and freedoms of those who are stronger, and not to condemn him who, knowing his own freedom, does eat (Rom 14:15).

37. But while we should yield to the weak for the purpose of edifying them, to those who are stubbornly superstitious or who are lying in ambush with evil intent we must give up nothing that might lead them to prejudge our freedom, so that we do not by our abstinence confirm them in their evil superstition, nor should we otherwise prejudge those who are strong and well-taught in their own freedom. Accordingly, Paul chided Peter very severely because, when he withdrew himself from the gentiles in order not to offend the Jews, he confirmed the Jews in their stubbornness and offended the gentiles by his hypocrisy (Gal 2:11). But in these two cases Paul displayed an illustration of Christian wisdom: when he circumcised Timothy out of consideration for the weakness of the Jews (Acts 16:3), and when he did not wish to circumcise Titus after he saw that he had to defend Christian freedom over against those who were stubborn and lying in ambush (Gal 2:3–4).

38. But at the same time that faith determines what is allowed in these things it also teaches that our freedom always remains undiminished, even though we accommodate ourselves to our weak brothers. For faith makes a distinction between freedom itself and the use of freedom, and since the freedom is in our conscience and looks to God, while the use of it is concerned with external things in which the handling of it is not with God only but with people, it judges that among people "not all things are expedient, though all things are allowed" (1 Cor 6:12) and that we must not use our freedom "except for building up" (Rom 14:19).

39. In this way we acknowledge that even the freedom of our consciences is not hindered, because when some political law or ecclesiastical regulation restricts the use of the middle things it is not the freedom itself but only the outward deed that is bound. For strictly speaking it is only God who binds the consciences, as we have said. And yet on occasion a magistrate can, for the good of the nation, order or forbid something to be done that of itself is

an intermediate thing. And the church may decide something of a similar substance for the sake of good order—in such a way, however, that it does not assume for itself any power over the conscience. This case excluded, no one would resist such regulations out of a desire for rebellion without sinning or rightly oppose them—who, whereas he would prefer to guard his conscience, would rather endanger it since it would suffer harm on account of the rebelliousness.

40. But while the magistrate or the church prescribes those actions (if, at least, they are not abusing their rights or transgressing the boundaries of their jurisdiction) and have as their intention not to make the middle matters simply necessary but only because it is on the supposition of the circumstances that they are being commanded or forbidden, then the person will not be committing a sin who, when those circumstances cease to exist, while avoiding an instance of being condemned or scandalized, reverts to using his own freedom, especially if the sword of necessity threatens. For we do not think that regulations of such a sort then retain the power of binding or obligating. But if people extend their own rules to include things that of themselves are good or evil, we don't hesitate to affirm that we should consider this action to be over and above [their right], because there does not exist any cause of danger or offense that we should neglect what God commands or with impunity do what God prohibits us to do, and for this reason we should not, for the sake of our neighbor, offend God (Matt 5:29–30 and 10:37). Nor should we obey the magistrate who makes some rule contrary to God's Word or who does violence to our consciences (Acts 4:19, 24 and 5:29).

41. Until now we have spoken about the objects and degrees, or parts, of Christian freedom, wherein we considered the things that were needed to explain its subject-matter. From these it is easy to see what we should think about the form of Christian freedom. This form exists in having and enjoying those good things by the witness of the Holy Spirit with which He seals that undoubted conviction and full assurance in the hearts of believers about their sonship whereby they have been turned from slaves of the devil into sons of God, and are protected against all the temptations and attacks of sin, the law, and condemnation, and are made certain about their exemption from every bygone slavery (Rom 8:14–15 and following; 2 Cor 1:22; Gal 4:6–7; Eph 4:30).

42. The proximate goal is the tranquility of the consciences of Christians (Luke 1:74; Rom 14:5), who "having been released from sin and become servants of God, have their reward unto holiness, while the goal is life eternal" (Rom 6:22). Therefore, for those who have been granted freedom there follows, as virtues that necessarily accompany them: peace, righteousness, a good conscience, and the joy of the Spirit (Rom 14:17). But the highest goal is the same as the one for God's other benefits: "the praise of his glorious grace" (Eph 1:14).

43. But because that freedom of grace is distinguished from the freedom of glory, those who in this life enjoy the first kind do not yet actually possess the second one; but as children of God they do have the right to it, as they have become his heirs, and are co-heirs with Christ (Rom 8:17). For they are children of the resurrection and sons of God through the Spirit, who is "the pledge, the seal and first-fruits of that inheritance" (Luke 20:36; Gal 4:6; 2 Cor 1:22). In Eph 1:14 the seal of the Spirit "who is the pledge of our inheritance" is said explicitly to have been made "until we acquire possession of it."

44. To this inheritance belongs also the blessed immortality of our souls, as well as the resurrection and the glorified state of our bodies. Although the slavery to corruption and even death itself still keep our bodies bound up in chains, believers do look forward, along with their souls, to the "freedom of glory" and "the redemption of our bodies" on the day when Christ with open hand will declare that they have been redeemed by him. Meanwhile they rest secure in the hope of this freedom "until they, whose lives for a time have been kept safe with Christ in God, when Christ appears will also appear in glory with him" (Rom 8:21 and 23; Gal 5:17; John 6:44; Col 3:3 and 4).

45. From what has been said it can be determined what is the manifold use of this doctrine, following the various degrees of freedom. From the first [two degrees] those who believe possess the fact that their consciences have been put at ease, and they are no longer terrified by the threats of the law, and without compulsion they take delight in the obedience of sonship by the guidance of the law (Ps 1:2). And they are also confident that their acts of obedience, although they are immature and still not perfect, do not displease their benevolent Father, but are acceptable to him in his love.

46. From the two last degrees they reap the benefit that they know their consciences have been released from the power of all people (1 Cor 3:21 and

7:23); and that with true worship (namely, spiritual) they learn to serve God instead of creatures, so that they do not give in to themselves or other people for evil. And that harmony in the church is maintained, while Christian freedom is preserved in indifferent things. And that they are employing God's gifts out of faith for the use to which God had given them, and to guide that use in love for the upbuilding of the neighbor and the general wellbeing.

47. It is also clear that this freedom does not constitute exemption from all laws (both divine and human ones) and that it is not a license for living by the feelings of one's heart and of indulging the sinful desires of the flesh, nor a release from civic responsibility, duties, and payments. For there is nothing to prevent those who are free spiritually from serving with their bodies (1 Cor 7:21); "servants obey your earthly masters, as to the Lord" (Eph 6:5). Therefore, Christians are subject to their kings and magistrates, as before (Rom 13:1), and they seriously condemn all those who under the pretext of Christian freedom attempt to shake off the yoke of magistrates and who enslave themselves to the devil by "turning their freedom into an opportunity for the flesh" (Gal 5:13).

48. The things that the Jews have dreamed up about the temporal kingdom of the Messiah are also in conflict with Christian freedom; nor is the freedom affected by the magnificent arrogance of the Stoics, who paradoxically and illogically make only their own wise men to be free, even though they are possessed by vanity and presumption. Augustine gave this paradox a special status in the church with the following words: "The good man, although he is a slave, is free; but the bad man, even if he reigns, is a slave, and he is a slave not of one man but, what is far more grievous, of as many masters as he has vices" (*City of God*, book 4 chapter 3).

49. But of all people it is the papal teachers who most dangerously affect this very gratifying doctrine, and also the Socinians who are of like mind with the papal teachers, as well as the others who refurbish their teachings; because, not being content with the uses of the law as we described them earlier, they turn the Gospel into a demanding law for us and they present Christ as a second Lawgiver who does not so much fulfill the law of Moses by his own obedience as to perfect it by means of adding new precepts, in order that believers should seek righteousness in the keeping of the law and hope to gain eternal life through it. But Christianity is overturned by this teaching

since it hides from view the office of Christ, and especially takes away his benefits, and completely overturns the foundation of our salvation and the comfort of our consciences.

SOURCES

[Pseudo-Augustine] *Question 61 on the Old and New Testament*

It has been commanded that these things which are not dangerous should be observed in such a way that they would not be harmful if they are admitted out of necessity, because they have been commanded not for salvation but for their reverence. But that which is entirely unallowed and also not mitigated by any kind of necessity that would not make its admission a hindrance, that is never permissible.

Bernard, *Treatise on Grace and Free Choice*

Since a three-fold freedom is set before us, freedom from sin, from misery, and from necessity. The last one of these is bestowed on us in the state of nature; by the first freedom [from sin] we are restored by grace, while the second one is kept for us in the fatherland [Heb 11:14–16]. The first is called the freedom of nature, the second one is called freedom of grace, and the third, the freedom of glory. The first possesses great honor, the second great virtue, and the third, last virtue, possesses the pinnacle of delight.

ON THE RELIGIOUS
PRACTICE OF INVOCATION

President: Antonius Walaeus
Respondent: Antonius Delienus

Invocation, or prayer, is a human duty through which God communicates his benefits to his church and by which at the same time we repay our gratitude for these benefits (1–2). Only God should be invoked, as He is the greatest giver of all good things and averts evil (4); only He examines the heart, and only He is trustworthy as the almighty Lord who knows all our needs (5). In disobedience to the command of God, Roman Catholics pray to angels and deceased saints (6–11). We should call upon God alone, not just in his essence, but also according to the divine persons individually (12–14). Weak and sinful people need a mediator to get access to the holy God: Christ, through the merit and efficacy of his death, is the only one who is able to intercede for us (15–19). Repentance, humility, filial fear of God, true faith, and a true desire are necessary aspects of prayer (21–28). Prayers that are offered in public should be heard and not silent, as is the practice among some Anabaptists; they should be understood by all, and not spoken in a foreign or ancient tongue (31). The words of prayer should not be repeated needlessly (32). So-called 'form prayers' are lawful and very useful (33) but praying freely is fostered (34). Attention is paid to the variety of physical bearing during prayer, and to gestures, location, and time (35–43). Our prayers should focus on people of all kinds and on God's (already received or future) benefits (44–52).

1. Since up to this point, we have given a treatment of God's benefits to the Church, it now follows that we should treat next our own remaining duties, and the means through which these benefits are communicated to us.

2. Among the foremost of our duties and the means of this communication is the true invocation, or adoration, of the true God. This invocation is like a

key whereby we unlock the treasuries of divine benefits, and repay to God the debt of gratitude from our faithful hearts, in the same way that David links the two together: "Offer sacrifices of thanksgiving to God and render your vows to the Most High and call upon him in the time of trouble and I shall deliver you, that you may glorify me" (Ps 50:14 [and 15]).

3. For a succinct treatment of this doctrine of invocation that is so necessary we should explain: 1) who is to be invoked; 2) through whom he should be invoked; 3) how he should be invoked; 4) what should be the object with which true invocation deals.

4. All the rules of invocation taught in various places of Scripture instruct us that, as the greatest giver of all good things and who averts evil, we should call upon God alone, namely the Father, Son, and Holy Spirit. These rules are summarized in Christ's words: "You shall worship the Lord your God and him only you shall serve" (Matt 4:10). The same is taught by all God's promises, the summation of which occurs in the Apostle's saying (Rom 10:13): "Whoever calls upon the name of the Lord shall be saved." And lastly, the same is taught in the Old and New Testaments by all the examples of the saints, none of whom ever directed his prayer to anyone other than the true God. In the same manner Christ himself instructed his disciples to direct their prayers to none other than "our Father who is in heaven" (Matt 6:9).

5. The same is shown also by the requirements that must be met in the one who is going to be invoked. For he should be someone who examines the hearts, so that he can tell apart the ones who worship in Spirit and truth from those who are hypocrites. Solomon (1 Kgs 8:39) and Paul (Rom 8:27) bear witness that it is only God who meets this requirement. Secondly, he should be the kind of person in whom we can place our trust, not just as a bountiful and kind-hearted father, but also as an almighty Lord. The prophet Jeremiah (17:7) and also the apostle Paul (Rom 10:14) teach that we should place this trust in God alone. And lastly, he should be someone who knows the general and specific needs (both internal and external ones) of all those people throughout the whole world who call upon him. And this requirement is met only by the omniscient and omnipresent God, as seen in Ps 139:2, Matt 6:32, Heb 4:13, etc.

6. There is clearly nothing that can be brought in to contradict the first two requirements. And what the papal teachers put over against the third requirement is foolish and beside the point: the 'mirror of the Trinity'

wherein all these earthly things shine forth. This is foolish because their claim is made apart from Scripture (and therefore as easily rejected as it is stated), and because it is by an act that is voluntary and of free choice and not by a natural and necessary act whereby the objects of divine knowledge are communicated to the blessed ones. For even the "angels who always behold the Father's face" (Matt 18:10) still "do not know the day of judgment" (Mark 13:32); "and to the principalities and powers in the heavenly places the manifold wisdom of God is made known through the church" (Eph 3:10), and "no-one in heaven or on earth or under the earth was able to open the book (that is, the book of God's providence concerning the church) nor to look into it, except the victorious Lion of the tribe of Judah and the root of David" (Rev 5:5).

7. The argument that others bring forward, that these things are revealed through angels or through believers who have departed from this world into heaven, does not match their hypothesis. For they confine deceased believers to the fires of Purgatory for a period of time, away from the sight of God. Secondly, neither angels nor dying believers know our inward needs, since they are not 'knowers of the heart' [Acts 1:24, 15:8]; nor are we always in the presence of the angels or the departing saints, nor they with us. For following their death, these saints are occupied with their own salvation, while the angels for the most part spend their time in their own abode, that is, heaven (Gen 28:12; Luke 1:19, etc.).

8. Nor are they helped any further by this last thing that they fabricate: that God reveals and commends the needs and prayers of believers to the saints in heaven so that they in turn reveal and commend them to God. For there is no need whatsoever for this detour circumventing Scripture; for the access to God in Christ that lies open for us is the same as the one that was always available to believers before any saints were received into heaven. And this is invincibly refuted by those places in Holy Scripture wherein the ones who have died are deprived of this knowledge of particular things of this life, as can be seen from Job 14:21, Eccl 9:2, 2 Kgs 22:20, Isa 64:2 [probably Isa 63:16 or 64:6], etc.

9. This being the case, it follows that when they call upon angels or the deceased, the papal teachers not only contradict the commandments of God and the examples of all the saints, but also they commit blatant idolatry when

in their prayers they ascribe to them things that God willed to keep for himself alone.

10. And also the little difference in meaning between *latreia* ('due service') and *douleia* ('bondage') does not excuse them from the charge of idolatry, because Holy Scripture conveys the idolatry of the gentile and Jewish peoples no less with the word *douleia* than *latreia*, as can be seen in Gal 4:8.8 Indeed, if we must make a distinction between those two terms, then it would be one of increased submission in *douleuein* compared to *latreuein*, since the latter term is used for any and all who provide a service, while the first is properly used of slaves.

11. This difference in the words' meaning introduces a much smaller distinction in the actual matter. For besides the fact that it is obvious (however much they explain it away) how in this invocation of theirs they ascribe divine properties to created beings, there is the additional element that very many of their prayers to the saints are conceived and pronounced with the same words (and the same sentiments) that Holy Scripture teaches should be used in our prayers when we beseech God. This is clear from the expressions in, among others, their 'Little Garden of the Soul' and the 'Marian Psalter' that are taken nearly verbatim from the Psalter of David.

12. When we state on this point that we should call upon God alone, then we are thinking of God not just in a general sense and in his essence, but also according to the [divine] persons. And although Holy Scripture more frequently puts forward the name of the Father in invocations, because the other persons owe their origins to him, and because in the work of our redemption he occupies the primary position, even so there are passages and examples from Scripture that demonstrate that it is possible to call upon the other persons individually, too.

13. For when the Father brings his only-begotten Son into the world, He proclaims this order about him: "And let all the angels of God worship him," as the apostle in Heb 1:6 testifies from Ps 65:6 [apparently Ps 97:7]. Indeed, "therefore he has received the name above every name (even as the Mediator) that at the name of Jesus every knee should bow" (Phil 2:10). And for this reason also Christ's Church throughout the world, and the individual apostles, very often call upon his name in particular, as can be seen from Acts 9:14, 1 Cor 1:2, Rom 1:7, 2 Cor 1:2, Gal 1:3 (etc.), 2 John 1:3, Rev 1:5, etc.

14. All the properties that we stated above as required for genuine invocation show that also the Holy Spirit can be called upon individually. This is shown moreover by the example of the apostles and the first church, as in 2 Cor 13:13, Rev 1:4, and likewise in Acts 4:24 when compared with Heb 3:7 and Acts 28:25 in comparison with Isa 6:3, etc.

15. The second question that we undertook at the beginning to answer is: by whom ought this prayer to be made. For since God is a consuming fire and his eyes are so pure that they cannot stand to look upon iniquity (Hab 1:13), it follows that weak and sinful people must seek a mediator through whom the access to the throne of grace is opened (Heb 4:14, etc.).

16. We think that this mediator should not be sought among angels (as the Platonists once contended) or among deceased saints (as formerly the Antidicomarianites thought, and now the papal teachers who follow them think), because the sort of properties that are required in this mediation do not belong to any one of the angels or the saints who have been received into heaven.

17. For neither angels nor deceased saints were chosen by God for this part of the priestly office, "since no-one takes this honor upon himself, but only he who is called by God, as was Aaron" (Heb 5:4). Nor are they able to appease God's wrath by their own merits and death, or to open for us the access to the throne of grace, as they owe their salvation to nothing other than God's mercy and Christ's mediation (Col 1:20). And not being in all things of like nature with us [Acts 14:15 and Jas 5:17], they cannot know all our needs, or be touched by them in their feelings, as they are not affected by the circumstances of even their own surviving children (Job 14:21), nor do they see the evils that befall their subjects, or their own household (2 Kgs 22:20).

18. But it is only of Christ that the Father swore: "You are a priest forever after the order of Melchizedek, etc.," and therefore He is able to the utmost "to save perfectly those who draw near to God through him" (Heb 7:25). And it is He who through the merit and efficacy of his death "has opened for us a new and living way, and freedom to enter into the heavenly sanctuary" (Heb 10:19). Lastly, it is He who in every respect has been tempted as we are, yet without sin, who can sufficiently be touched with the feelings of our weaknesses (Heb 4:15).

19. Therefore Holy Scripture testifies about no-one else but Christ that he is interceding on our behalf at the right hand of the Father (Rom 8:34), and because "as our high priest he has entered into heaven itself now to appear in the presence of God on our behalf" (Heb 9:24) and because "in him we have a just advocate with the Father" (1 John 2:1). Even Christ himself asserts about himself alone that "I am the way, the truth, and the life, no-one comes to the Father but through me" (John 14:6); and again: "whatever you ask of the Father in my name I shall do it, so that the Father may be glorified in the Son" (John 14:13, etc.), and: "Truly, truly I say to you, whatever you ask from my Father in my name, he will give it to you" (John 16:23).

20. All these things do not, however, prevent the souls of the blessed who are in heaven in the company of the angels themselves from yearning for the coming of the kingdom of Jesus Christ with constant prayer, and from seeking the deliverance of the militant church here on earth, as is seen from the illustration of it in Rev 5:8 and 6:10. And like the believers living on the earth, they solicit God with one accord through the only Mediator Jesus Christ not only for themselves but also for their brothers and their needs, because they are fellow-servants of one and the same master, and members of the same body under the same head. In their eagerness for God's glory and the law of common love, they have been restricted by God, in keeping with their state and knowledge, to fulfilling these reciprocal duties, as is shown by the very many instances and commandments of it that one meets in Scripture.

21. After this explanation of the first two elements, the third one now follows: in what way this invocation should be made so that our prayer may be pleasing to God and salutary and fruitful for us.

22. To this mode we relate the legitimate inward form and disposition of the prayers and the people praying, and also their outward form and disposition.

23. A true and genuine sense of repentance in the one who is going to pray is required before all else for the internal disposition of the prayers and the one praying. And this is not just that general and first repentance, but that particular repentance from sins that have been committed. And it is just as Scripture testifies: "God does not heed sinners" (John 9:31), and many "ask but do not receive because they ask wrongly, so that they may spend it on their own pleasures" [Jas 4:3]. And so [God] warns his people to "put away the evil of their own doings," if it wishes its prayer to be heard (Isa 1:16), and

the apostle John asserts: "If our heart does not condemn us, we have confidence toward God, and whatsoever we ask, we receive of him because we keep his commandments and do what is pleasing to him" (1 John 3:21 [and 22]).

24. On this point Holy Scripture advises us especially to be reconciled with our brothers, and to forgive from the heart those wrongdoings which have been committed against us, as Christ instructed both generally (Matt 5:23) and specifically in the prayer for the forgiveness of sins (Matt 6:12), and most broadly in the parable of two debtors (Matt 18:23 and following).

25. The second element necessary in prayer is "true humility accompanied by child-like reverence" in the one who is praying, in view of both our own state and the majesty and kindness of the one we are beseeching in our prayers, as is clear from the examples of the saints Abraham (Gen 18), David (2 Sam 7), Daniel (Dan 9), etc. It is clear also from what Christ expressly teaches in the parable of the Pharisee and the tax-collector with this exclamation: "Everyone who exalts himself will be humbled, and he who humbles himself will be exalted" (Luke 18:14). And so also the apostle Peter testifies that "God resists the proud but gives grace to the humble" (1 Pet 5:5). And therefore, Christ warns us to so make our prayers that we consider the fact that the one whom we are calling upon is "our Father, who is in heaven, and to whom belongs the kingdom and the power and the glory" (Matt 6:9, 13 and 15).

26. True faith is the third element required here, and not merely the faith with which we generally believe in God and Christ the Mediator—for "how shall they call on him in whom they do not believe?" (Rom 10:14). But we also "place firm confidence in him," that we shall receive the very thing we ask for in accordance with his will. For whoever does not possess this confidence distrusts God's promises, which are both numerous and very clear on this point. And therefore, the apostle James warns us: "If any of you lacks wisdom, let him ask God, who gives generously to all; but let him ask in faith, and without doubting" (Jas 1:5 [and 6]). And Christ himself warns us even much more clearly: "Therefore I say to you, whatever you ask for when you pray, believe that you will receive it and it will be yours" (Mark 11:24).

27. And the final requirement is a genuine endeavor of our heart, towards the one whom we are calling upon, and the one through whom we call (as is clear from the preceding). But it is also a burning desire that arises from the awareness of our need, and a constant right attitude towards the very thing

437

that we are beseeching in accordance with God's will. For this reason, the prophet David testifies not only that he is lifting up his soul to Jehovah (Ps 25:1, and many other places) but also that he is calling on Jehovah from the depths of sorrow (Ps 130:1) and that he is pouring out his meditations before him and disclosing his own anxieties before him (Ps 142:2, etc.). And therefore, he likens his prayer to the evening offering and incense—which, though the winds often blow it away, in the end it will reach up to heaven (Ps 141:2). And in Ps 123:2 he states: "Behold, as the eyes of servants look to the hand of their masters, and as the eyes of a maidservant to the hand of her mistress, so our eyes look to Jehovah our God, until he grant us his grace."

28. And here is that Spirit of grace and supplication whom God through Christ in the new covenant promises to pour out on the house of David and the inhabitants of Jerusalem, "that they may look upon him whom they have pierced" (Zech 12:10). And here is that "Spirit of adoption through whom we cry, 'Abba, Father,' etc." (Rom 8:15), and who intercedes on our behalf with groans that cannot be uttered, etc., and in harmony with God's will (Rom 8:27).

29. The external mode of invocation exists partly in what we say, partly in our physical gestures, and finally, partly in some other circumstances.

30. Outward speech is not absolutely necessary for prayers that are private, since also internal discourse and merely the groans of the heart are sufficient for God, as can be seen from the example of Moses (Exod 14:15), Hannah (1 Sam 1:13), Nehemiah (Neh 1:4), etc. In other respects it is customary to use outward speech more frequently as witness and aid to internal feelings— even wailing when in great difficulties, like the very many instances of it in the Old and New Testament, even of our Savior (Heb 5:7).

31. We do hold that for public prayers which we share with many other people or in which the minister of the Word leads the church it is altogether necessary that the speech of the one leading in prayer be outward (contrary to the Anabaptists) and that it be understood by the one leading as well as the others (contrary to the papal teachers). For if not, people could not possibly be of one and the same mind towards the same prayer—something that Christ expressly requires on this point (Matt 18:19). And then neither the hearer nor he who occupies the place of the uninformed can say 'Amen' to that sort of prayer, as the apostle notes in very clear terms (1 Cor 14:15– 16).

32. We must studiously avoid all vanity in the very form of speaking, and also all repetitions and verbosity, as Christ warns (Matt 6:7), although with that repetition we should not understand the reiteration of the same or similar words if that happens to break out from the distraught feelings of the heart, since even the saints on occasion permit such reiteration in their prayers, including also Christ himself when he was greatly troubled (Matt 26:39 and 42), and when he was hanging upon the cross (Matt 27:46). But what we should understand by that kind of repetition are the vain and empty repetitions [Matt 6:7] that are unnecessary and superstitious, and the rehearsing of the same prayers that are repeated up to a specific number; this was prevalent among the gentiles of former times, and it is prevalent today among the papal teachers. Christ criticizes this practice in the Pharisees and scribes, who under pretense of making long prayers were devouring widows' houses (Matt 23:14; Luke 20:47).

33. At this point the question often arises whether it is permitted in prayers that are public or private to use previously composed sets of words. It is our contention that so long as they are spoken from the heart with due intent, the formulae are not only lawful but very useful. For it has not been granted to each and every Christian to compose fresh sets of words that are suitable, and in large gatherings the attention of the hearers is helped considerably by sets of words that are familiar to them. For this reason even God himself prescribed the form of blessings for the priests in the Old Testament (Num 6:24 and following). In fact, when Christ was hanged on the cross he used the form of prayer that had been observed previously by David as type (Matt 27:46). And Christ's disciples asked him to teach them how to pray (Luke 11:2), just as John had taught his disciples; and Christ responded to them: "When you pray, say: 'Our Father who is in heaven, etc.'" It is clear from the context of these words that Christ's prayer is not just the norm for correct prayer but moreover the correct form of praying. And the whole early church always considered this to be beyond debate.

34. Yet at the same time we acknowledge that it is very useful and almost even necessary that all the more advanced believers, and especially the shepherds of the church, foster in themselves the gift of praying freely, even without a set of words that were made previously, so that they will be able to make prayers of supplication and thanksgiving that are fitting to the immediate situation and to needs that suddenly come up. We read that holy men, and also the prophets and apostles, did this frequently in this way. It

will not be difficult for us to do likewise, by observing the method that they employ in their prayers, and the required practice which this method involves.

35. One can observe a variety of physical bearing in the prayers of the saints. Moses fell upon his face (Deut 9:18); David was stretched upon the ground and clothed in sackcloth when he prayed for his infant son (2 Sam 12:16). Job was seated in ashes and dust (Job 42:6); the Israelites were standing (Neh 9:5); Ezra and Paul were kneeling down (Ezra 9:5 and Acts 20:36). Solomon prayed on bended knees and with hands outstretched (2 Chron 6:13); Christ with eyes lifted up towards heaven (John 17:1), while the tax-collector prayed with his eyes cast down to the earth (Luke 18:13). And while men pray with their heads uncovered, women do so with covered head, according to the apostle's instruction (1 Cor 11:4).

36. A comparison of all these things with each other makes it clear that a certain amount of freedom was given for various gestures, but that at the same time we should adopt the kind of postures that are best suited to every nation's own customs and that promote rather than hinder the attentiveness of our soul. We should avoid every form of vanity in those postures, but also carelessness and pride; and the gestures should convey, without pretense and in a most suitable manner, the inner disposition and ardent longing of those who are praying. Yet the saints most frequently employed the bending of the knees, and so that gesture was sometimes used in the absolute sense for the prayer itself, as one can see from Rom 11:4 and 14:11, and likewise in Eph 3:14. And in the same vein the apostle links the stretching forth or lifting up of hands to the injunction that they should pray everywhere (1 Tim 2:8).

37. The circumstances to which we must also pay attention in prayers are location and time.

38. As for location, during the time of upbringing that is the Old Testament, any location was permitted [for prayer], for God did hear the prayer of Jacob and Hezekiah when they were upon their beds, and Job sitting upon the ash-heap, Samson in the temple-court of the Philistines, and Jonah from the belly of the whale. Yet at the same time believers were also restricted to certain specific locations as sanctuaries of God's presence, both before and after the law was given (Gen 4:14; 28:16; and 35:1; Exod 3:12, etc.). These were either locations according to regulation, like the tabernacle and the temple (to which also Daniel turned in his prayers from exile, in Dan 6:11), or extraordinary

ones, which the prophets designated apart from a regulation (Josh 8:30; 1 Sam 14:36; 1 Kgs 18:36 etc.).

39. In the New Testament, however, as the prophet Malachi (1:11) had foretold and as Christ testifies: "The hour was coming and now is, when the Father shall be adored neither upon the mountain, nor in Jerusalem; but the true worshipers will worship the Father in Spirit and in truth" (John 4:23 [and 24]), and therefore the apostle orders that "men lifting up holy hands without wrath and dissention to pray in every place" (1 Tim 2:8).

40. Christ warns us that for praying privately we should seek out hidden places, ones that are removed from on-lookers (Matt 6:6), so that we do not appear to be longing for the close attention and praise of men (which, as Christ in the same passage clearly states is what hypocrites do), and moreover so that our own attentiveness thereby is less interrupted. It was for this reason that Christ selected lonely places to pray, as is seen from Matt 14:23, etc. But in public and shared prayers we should not neglect to gather together, as the apostle cautions in Heb 10:25, since it is to the assembly of believers and their oneness of heart that Christ gave this promise: "When two of you upon earth agree concerning anything they shall ask, it shall be done for them by my Father who is in heaven; for where two or three are gathered in my name, there I am in their midst" (Matt 18:19–20).

41. For this reason those pilgrimages that the Roman Catholics undertake to the tomb of our Lord or to other, far-flung places for the sake of prayer are altogether superstitious, since God now gives equal hearing to the prayers of believers wherever they are. And this sort of people, contrary to the commandment of love, expose themselves to unnecessary dangers, and often, under the pretext [of going to pray] they unfairly let down those people whose care has been entrusted particularly to them. And there is also no superstition lacking to the actions of those who for the purpose of making private prayers made it their custom to visit churches and sacred buildings when empty of the gathering of believers, even though other more private places were available to them. This is superstitious because Christ explicitly condemns this religious practice among the hypocrites, in the passage cited earlier (Matt 6:5–6, etc.).

42. The time suitable for prayer is any moment at all when faith, hope, love, and our sense of need (public as well as private) remind us that we ought to pray. For this reason, Christ, too, commands his disciples that "they should

always pray and not lose hope" (Luke 18:1), and the apostle that "they should pray without ceasing" (1 Thess 5:17). And yet that is not a reason to commend the doings of the ancient Euchites or some monks nowadays, who profess that they spend their whole life-time chanting and praying. Prayer ought to be an aid and not a hindrance to the other works of love for God or the neighbor.

43. Meanwhile, we readily acknowledge that we should assign certain days for public prayers, and for private ones a certain time of the day, to assist us in our carelessness and weakness, as in the case of David (Ps 55:18), Daniel (Dan 6:11), and Peter (Acts 10:9). But it should be done in such a way that all superstition stays away, and vainglory [Phil 2:3], or scruple of conscience if strong necessity or individual or public charitable deeds demand an interruption to prayer, since in this matter Christ or the apostles handed down no precise rule, and since even the groanings alone of the heart to God could take its place, as we have pointed out earlier in thesis 30, and as the exiled church of Israel in Babylon showed (Ps 137).

44. The last that remains for us to explain is the object around which our prayer should turn, and it is twofold: either the person for whom we pray or the thing for which we ask in our prayer.

45. As far as the person is concerned, we should pray not only for ourselves or those who are dear to us, but also for anyone at all (1 Tim 2:2)—even for our enemies and persecutors, as Stephen displayed in an exemplary way (Acts 7:60). The only exception is for those who sin against the Holy Spirit with the sin unto death; we are forbidden to pray for them (1 John 5:16). But in particular it is recommended in Scripture that we pray for kings and those who are placed in prominent positions (1 Tim 2:2), shepherds and overseers of the church (1 Thess 5:25; Heb 13:3, etc.). Also commended for prayer is the church itself and all the saints, those who are imprisoned or subjected for the sake of Christ's cross (Acts 12:5; Heb 13:3), the sick and the oppressed (Jas 5:14). And we should pray for brothers who commit sins that do not lead unto death (1 John 5:16).

46. The things for which we call upon God are the divine benefits offered [to us] that serve God's glory or the needs and wellbeing of people; and that we have received in the past, or that we are to receive in the future.

47. It is by the apostle's injunction that we should give thanks to God for the benefits that we have received in the past: "Give thanks always for everything to God the Father in the name of our Lord Jesus Christ" (Eph 5:20). And we should do so not only in times of joy and gratitude, but also in sad and difficult times, whenever God decides to train or try us by them, as in the case of Job (chapter 1:21) and the apostles (Acts 5:41).

48. The prayer for future benefits, whether they are shared in common or individual, are of two kinds: the prayer to ward off those evils we should fear, or the prayer of supplication for the good things that we should hope for. These benefits are bodily or spiritual, and both are also either absolutely necessary for our salvation and the glory of God, or they are necessary for another reason. Therefore, we posit that the ones of this latter kind should be asked for conditionally, and as the former are absolute, we should ask for them without condition.

49. Here the question arises, whether it is not permitted for us or other people to pray God to ward off anything good, or to invoke anything evil. We reply that there are certain bodily and spiritual goods which, because the holy men deemed them to be beyond their own capabilities, they sometimes humbly prayed to avoid them (as is clear from the examples of Moses in Exod 3 and Jeremiah in Jer 1), or because they feared that they might abuse them, in the way that the wise man prayed equally to ward off too many riches and poverty (Prov 30:8–9).

50. In the Scriptures various examples may be found of imprecations wherein the saints cursed the day that they were born because of the severity of the hardships that have come over them (Job 3:3 and Jer 20:14)—but it rather seems that these prayers arose from their own frailty. Or these imprecations were made to declare their own innocence, and with the proviso that if they had committed one thing or another, they wish God to punish them. Of this sort of imprecation there are many examples in sacred history. But [they never called down curses] from Satan or hell, like the gentiles and the papal priests do, who are impiously accustomed to invoke curses upon themselves. And, lastly, the saints offered imprecations as a special testimony of their own eagerness and zeal for God's glory and the safe-keeping of other people, for whose sake they at some time put off even their own salvation, as we see in the case of Moses (Exod 32:32) and Paul (Rom 9:3).

51. And there are also various examples of imprecations against other people, that is, against those who are upright, or against the unrighteous. Against the upright, to set them straight by chastising them if they do not heed warnings, as in the example of it in Job 34:36. There are very many examples, in both the Old and the New Testament, of imprecations against the unrighteous, the enemies of the Church and God's glory, as is seen in 2 Tim 4:14: "Alexander the metalworker did me much harm; the Lord will repay him according to his deeds" and in Rev 6:10: "How long, O Lord who art holy and true, do you not judge and avenge our blood on those who dwell upon the earth?"

52. But believers should not follow these examples rashly, unless the signs of such stubborn and incorrigible hostility are very clear. And otherwise, we should heed the warning of the apostle James, always in the case of private offenses "not to grumble against one another" (Jas 5:9). And the warning of Christ: "Bless those who curse you, and do good to those who hate you, and pray for them who treat you despitefully and persecute you, that you may be children of your Father who is in heaven" (Matt 5:44 [and 45]). To him be the glory and the praise forever. Amen.

ON ALMSGIVING AND FASTING

President: Antonius Thysius
Respondent: Johannes Westerburgh

Almsgiving and fasting are important acts in the life of the Christian that arise in response to the command to love one's neighbor (1, 4). Almsgiving consists in deeds of charity performed in faith and love, and 'in the hope of obtaining a divine reward' (3). The foundations for almsgiving are the inequality of possessions (5–9) and the bonds between people (10–11). Next, the disputation identifies the persons concerned (13–25) and the things that are shared (26–27). What it means to give or to receive is defined thereafter, and distinctions are drawn between giving freely and lending at interest (28–35). In sum, almsgiving, to which several promises are associated (37–38), is characterized by 'sympathy, benevolence, and beneficence of every kind towards the poor and helpless' (36). Fasting and vigil-keeping are the subject of the second part of this disputation (39–59). As a form of self-discipline, fasting consists in the abstinence from food and drink to help the believer focus upon prayer (39). After defining the term (39–41), the disputation identifies several characteristics of keeping vigil. It does not arise from the human will but as a divine ordinance (42). It is of a 'free disposition according to circumstances' (43; 44– 47). It is not limited to particular times or occasions (46) and it does not bind the conscience (47). It consists in restricting or withholding oneself from food and drink (48–49). Indeed, it is non-essential in and of itself (50); it has certain goals (51–53), a particular manner (54–55), and produces various results (56). The disputation closes with a discussion of vigils (58–59), which are meant freely to take a part of the night to pray and meditate on the return of the Lord.

1. Among good works the outpouring of prayer to God stands out as an important duty of faith, although as far as it is poured out for other people, prayer also relates to the love towards our neighbor. In the same way, the giving of alms is an outstanding example of love for our neighbor, and when

accompanied by the practice of fasting it adds no small weight to the words of prayer (Matt 6:1, 5, 16; Acts 10:2, 3, 4). And with the help of God, in this disputation we shall undertake to treat these two.

2. The word *eleēmosynē*, which comes from 'having compassion,' means 'mercy' in Latin; that is, the sense of affection whereby the plight of other people touches us. But it also includes the effect of it: averting evil from our neighbor and helping him. The word is used for every 'act of kindness,' so that it is the gentleness of compassionate feeling (Jas 3:13), but especially for the support and aid that help the needs of the poor.

3. Almsgiving is an act of charity towards the neighbor, whereby someone who is devout, merciful, and sympathetic to the misery of another, someone who is kind and beneficent, comes to the aid of those who are truly poor and need the supports of this life. He does so from his own goods and in proportion to his financial resources and their current need, out of true faith and burning love for God and his neighbor, all in the hope of obtaining a divine reward.

4. And so we relate almsgiving to the love we have for our neighbor, that is, to the second part of the worship of God. But this love frequently includes the entire service and piety toward God (Matt 7:12; Rom 13:8–10), since the second table of the Law is connected to the first (Jas 2:10–11) and shown to be so by this love (because hypocrites frequently go undetected by the outward show of the first table's divine worship: Hos 6:6, Matt 9:13). In the same way 'almsgiving,' which is a particular act of love towards the neighbor, a very high degree of love and not its last part, stands for love, and *par excellence* is given the name 'righteousness and love' (Dan 4:27; Heb 6:10).

5. The premise for almsgiving is ownership of goods and inequality in possessions. For God, at the time of the first creation, although He created the world and everything in it for the use of all mankind in general, He gave Paradise to Adam in particular (as the first created human and begetter of all mankind) like a basilica to an emperor; and after the fall, it was to him that He gave the edict: "In the sweat of your brow you will eat your bread." But after the flood, the peoples and lands were divided (with God so disposing it) among the three sons of Noah. And also assuming a place of their own were the taking and giving of possession, the transmission of inheritance, and the acquisition by the right of war or other means. And the ownership of things is based on a common law, both divine and human.

6. The origin of rich and poor comes from this inequality of ownership. God declares that He is the Creator of both rich and poor (Prov 22:2), and Christ states that we shall always have the poor (Matt 26:11). Nevertheless, since riches do not make anyone acceptable to God, so too poverty is not a cause of shame for anyone, since in his own person Christ has sanctified it (2 Cor 8:9). And piety approves rich and poor alike (1 Tim 6:17–18; Matt 5:3) so long as the rich person does not confide in his riches but rejoices in his humility and the poor does not despair in his poverty but rejoices in his exaltation (Mark 10:24; Jas 1:9–10).

7. And the apostles did not abolish ownership of goods, or inequality of ownership, at the beginning of the Gospel-era, by their sharing of goods (Acts 2 and 4): "All who believed were together in one place and held everything in common." For their sharing was not a universal sharing by each and every Christian, nor was it a sharing of all their goods, nor was it presented as precedent, and perpetual law. But it was a special case in the church at Jerusalem, and it was in response to the state of the church at that particular time, done by the voluntary gathering of certain people and goods, as is clear from chapter 5:4. Moreover, it states clearly that Christ owned a purse (John 12:6 and 13:29); and the apostles and the believers, too, had their own purses. Hence the giving of alms also had its proper place.

8. And so [the sharing of goods recorded in Acts] is not a basis for the communism of some of the Anabaptists, which in reality removes all ownership and possession and consequently also the practice of almsgiving among believers. Nor is it a basis for 'the common life' of certain monks who profess by a special rule that they renounce property, ownership and any contact with money. Hence the proverb: "A monk who has an obol, isn't worth an obol."

9. Nevertheless, though sharing goods among Christians does not happen by possession, yet it remains by use, and this is fixed by a law of God forever (Deut 15; Mark 14:7). And this law is not, as some of the Scholastics would have it, an action only of someone's unbound will (and so only an encouragement to charity) but an ordinance of God's precept or law that, subject to the charge of sin, binds the conscience and that is free only with respect to some of its circumstances.

10. And so [sharing goods by use] is based upon God's wise counsel and will, which so governs and variously arranges everything that He bestows more

upon one and less upon another and has brought together poor and rich (Prov 22:2), whom He joined together by a natural bond and the bonds of common blood and politics (as man is a civil and social creature) so that the one would offer a hand of support to the other and so the abundance of the one would assist the other in his need (Isa 58:7; 2 Cor 8:13–14). This all the more so because while God kept the absolute and highest dominion for himself (Ps 24:1; 1 Cor 10:26), He did grant the use to the wealthy man and established him as the distributor of his gifts, in order to disburse them faithfully also to the poor (Luke 16:10–12). And although the wealthy had the duty to do this, God added promises of rich reward and interest from the Lord so that it might be conducted much more faithfully (Prov 19:17), and He added serious warnings, should the task be ignored (Prov 21:13).

11. A uniquely Christian bond is added to our natural and civil bonds. By this bond the believers, as members of a mystical body, are united into one body under Christ their head and have God as their common Father, and Christ, God's first-born Son, as their Brother. Having been adopted by God into sons and regenerated by his Spirit, they are brothers of one another, and through Christ they become heirs of everything, and by Him they are obligated more stringently to the special debt of offering assistance. Hence Christ, too, declares that what is done for His poor is done to Him (Matt 25:40).

12. For a more complete treatment of almsgiving we should also consider: the persons (who and for whom), the thing (what and how much should be shared), the act of sharing and the way it is done, and also the promises that are joined to it.

13. As far as the person giving is concerned, this is a virtue and generosity that all devout people share, to the extent that everyone, at least in their affection, should be ready for every duty of charity and to offer what he can to his neighbor, as his modest means allow. This virtue belongs also to those of slender means and goes as far as paying one or two small coins—like that widow who from her poverty put in her entire livelihood (Luke 21:4). Indeed, it extends to giving a drink of cool water (Matt 10:42); and for this reason the thief is ordered to work with his hands, so that he might be able to provide for him who has need (Eph 4:28). And in God's eyes, this duty is not assessed by the amount or the outward price, but by the affection of the heart, and the readiness of the soul.

14. But [this virtue] is peculiar to the pious people who are wealthy, whose goods God has increased, whose riches and abundance ought to serve the needs of others, and they should do so out of their abundance (Mark 12:44). They are bound to give "what they have left over," or from what they have (Luke 11:41). In fact, if it should be of use, then they can be "willing beyond their means" (2 Cor 8:3), as much as a tenth (Luke 18:12) of their goods, even up to a half (Luke 19:8).

15. And yet they should not pour forth all their resources to the point of their own financial demise (2 Cor 8:12–13). For the faith bids the believer to provide also for himself and those dear to him (1 Tim 3:4–5), and well-ordered love demands it (Matt 22:39). And it is characteristic of Christian prudence to reserve for oneself a source, that a kind of river of generosity may flow perennially, from which one can draw for others—unless it happens that a specific commandment (Mark 12:41) or a pressing need (1 Cor 13:3) demands otherwise.

16. When, in Luke 12:33, Christ speaks these words, "sell your possessions and give alms," he does not order that selling is a must; he is declaring more the attitude that should affect believers, than that they should perish from poverty as poor people. In other words, what he says in an absolute sense we should understand in a relative sense. Or when in Matt 19:21 he says to the rich young man, "if you wish to be perfect, sell what you have and give to the poor," then he is not proposing a perfection for the perfect over and above God's law. Instead, he is adapting the universal law that we should deny ourselves everything—even our own lives, should God demand it (Mark 8:34, 36)—in a particular situation to his specific order for the unwell soul of the man, and he brings out into the open the hidden disease of his greed. As the subsequent account clearly reveals, the man shows by his proud boast in admitting he has fulfilled the law how far that is off the mark.

17. And as for those "to whom should be given," they are the pitiable people worthy of our compassion, that is, all who are poor. Taking the word 'poor' in the general sense, it stands for beggars who have no possessions and also for those who have very little and do not provide for themselves what they need to live, at least according to the present condition of life for a time (Ps 41:2; Isa 26:6). That is, they are people who lack the supports of this life, and need someone else's assistance. About these people Christ says: "Give to all who ask" (Matt 5:42). And that does not mean generally each and every

person who asks, but him who asks out of need, and such as are unable to repay (Luke 14:12).

18. But we do not consider among their number those who are fit, or wayfarers and professional beggars, who, having been dulled by their base and idle laziness, practice mendicancy and put the security of their livelihood on it, and by feigning a state of wretchedness, by means of various tricks and craftily thought-up pretenses with which they would arouse compassion, by going about in public, door-to-door, or showing up at busy crossroads, they ask for a small gift, and in this way they unfairly eat up someone else's bread. In fact, they often make a profit and a rich income from it, contrary to the law that had been made at the beginning, "in the sweat of your brow you shall eat your bread" (Gen 3[:19]), which Paul interprets, "if anyone does not want to work, he should not eat" (2 Thess 3:10–11). For they are not truly needy who, while they are able to feed themselves from the labor of their hands, actually rob those who are truly needy of what is owed to them. But these people surely are guilty of deceit and robbery, even sacrilege.

19. But we do not put in the same category those beggars who due to a lack of charity are forced to beg for help—since no provision is made for those who are poor in a legitimate way according to God's law (Deut 15:4)—out of necessity (which at this point does not consider the law) either at private houses, like the sore-covered Lazarus (Luke 16:20), or in the open street, like that blind man (Luke 18:35) and the cripple (Acts 3:2).

20. On the other hand, however, among them we do reckon those beggars who are healthy, those monastic beggars or mendicant orders, who by a new arrangement that goes against antiquity (which acknowledged only monks who worked and which considered 'the lazy bellies' as robbers; Socrates in [Cassiodorus,] *Tripartite Ecclesiastical History*, book 8), and who under the guise of piety, with remarkable superstition, [adopt] voluntary poverty and mendicancy, whereby they do away with their personal possessions, and gobble up those belonging to another, and live off the hard work and sweat of other people; in fact, under this very pretext of poverty they possess a vast amount of earthly possessions. And with a perpetual vow they willingly take this cross upon themselves and volunteer to undergo it. This is a cross that they ought not to assume upon themselves but which should be borne patiently if God had placed it upon them; and this outward curse of God (Deut 28:22), which people should pray Him to avert (and they should flee

from it, insofar as that is possible with God's curse), they put under the category of blessing, indeed of piety and sanctity, and works of perfection and of people who are perfect, and to this punishment they ascribe the greatest merits, even the merits of supererogation.

21. And yet in a well-established nation those mendicants should in no way be tolerated, since God's command, "and there shall be no needy among you," [Deut 15:4] is not just a rule posited about everyone's duty but to some extent it is also about mendicancy. And even the emperor follows this same law, in the *Codex Concerning Healthy Beggars*. And those who moreover conduct themselves in the church in a disorderly fashion—that is, contrary to God's order—should not, the apostle states, be given food or tolerated, but he prescribes that they should rather be reprimanded (2 Thess 3:6–13).

22. With the words "those who ask" [Matt 5:42] are meant those who ask for good reason, and who are compelled to ask, and so who upon thoughtful inquiry and investigation are considered deserving of mercy and generosity. Foremost among their ranks are: 1) widows and orphans (Exod 22:22), 2) foreigners (Lev 10:18), 3) the weak and infirm, among whom are counted the lame, deaf, blind, dumb, leprous, etc. (Matt 25:36; Luke 14:13), 4) those who are weak on account of age, like infants and the elderly (1 Tim 5:3, 16), 5) those who ask for various reasons not their own fault, like people who have been driven to poverty by shipwreck, floods, fires, robbery, attacks of enemies, etc.; and we add to them the bashful poor who do not dare to admit their needs. And lastly, it includes 6) those who for professing the Gospel have been stripped of their financial means (Heb 10[:34]). With these people we link those who have been captured by enemies, especially enemies of the Christian religion. Some of them are physically feeble, others robbed of the ability to obtain a living, and still others who are not able to provide enough for themselves regardless of however much they do. These people should be assisted each according to his or her need; some completely, others partially, and again some others only for a period of time.

23. And so you should understand the words "everyone who asks" [Matt 5:42 and Luke 6:30] to mean any such person (without discrimination), whether he is a foreigner or a citizen and compatriot, stranger or relative by blood, friend or foe, believer or unbeliever (Matt 5.34, 44 and Luke 6:27, 32). In short, "every neighbor." And therefore our neighbor is anyone at all who is in need of our help in light of the state he is in, and for whose help and

assistance we are given the opportunity and the means, as Christ teaches (over against the Jews) in the parable of the wounded man (Luke 10:30).

24. But at the same time we should, depending on the degree of affinity and fellowship, exercise greater generosity towards those who are our own, namely our relatives, than to strangers (1 Tim 5:8, 16); and towards members of the household of faith and the saints rather than the gentiles (Gal 6:10); it is this especially that 2 Pet 1:7 calls "brotherly love." But while we should begin with those who are own, we ought not to stop with them.

25. We should not consider among this group [of all who ask] the "pastors and teachers of the churches," as some have thought. For what is paid to them are not alms but remuneration for work that is done (Matt 10:10; 1 Cor 9:4, 7; 1 Tim 5:18). And as to the fact that it says some women ministered to Christ from their own financial resources (Luke 8:2,3), although they displayed exceptional generosity, yet what was done and confirmed by those women themselves is what Christ generally taught and instructed his own to do (1 Cor 9:14).

26. So much concerning the persons. As for the actual "thing that is to be given," it consists not only of payment but of any help and work that lightens human need as Christ designates them: breaking bread for the hungry; giving a drink to the thirsty and clothing to him who is cold, shelter and hospitality to the stranger; and similarly, offering ransom for the captive, and care for the sick (Isa 58:7; Matt 25:35; Luke 3:11 and 14:12). Elsewhere these are summed up as "food and shelter" (1 Tim 6:8).

27. One should not, however, give away what belongs to someone else, or what has been obtained unjustly—that is robbery. And therefore, the following text does not apply here: "Make for yourselves friends by means of unrighteous Mammon," [Luke 16:9] since that should be taken not so much as being about wrongly obtained wealth (since it is God's will that our generosity should flow forth from a source that is pure) as about people's very frequently unjust abuse of it.

28. Then again, regarding the one who gives, the mode of the actual communion and imparting with the poor is that with respect to the goods everyone should not only give according to his own financial means, but also sincerely and secretly—for God and in his presence—with respect to his intention: not hypocritically and for self-advancement, that is, by false display

in the open to be seen by men for the sake of one's own glory (Matt 6:1, 2, 4). It should not be done under pressure, on the command of other people, by obligation and with a heavy heart; but willingly, readily, promptly, and with a cheerful heart. Otherwise it would not be pleasing and acceptable to God (Rom 12:8; 2 Cor 8:12 and 9:7). It should not be done from a desire and hope of receiving financial gain, but graciously, for the former would not be humane or charitable, but the professional pursuit of financial profit (Luke 6:33). It should not be done sparingly, but bountifully (2 Cor 9:6). And lastly it should be done out of faith in God and Christ (1 Tim 1:5), and out of love towards our neighbor (1 Cor 13:3). For in this way that deed is both of will and power (Mark 14:7) and so that it should nevertheless be governed by the rule of love.

29. But regarding the one to whom it is given, it should be administered according to the need that each person has; that is, by a certain equality and geometric proportion. It should be done with discernment of the person, cause, place and time; or when, to what extent, where and in what way. In these things prudence and circumspection very much should be kept in view (2 Cor 8).

30. In their turn, the poor who receive alms have the duty to be content with their lot and should not ask unless they are truly needy, and ask only to the extent that they are needy. And with an equally cheerful heart they should accept the little that is given from a cheerful heart. And they should always think that what is sufficient for sustaining natural life is much, and great, and they should thank God for causing pious people to arise who care for them.

31. This care of the poor is either private, for individuals, or it is public, when for all the needy people taken together who have been driven by want into this category. In a nation, a devout magistrate provides the care, or in the church its leaders. And the care is provided through serious, careful, suitable men who have been approved also by public testimony, with the support of the spontaneous munificence of religious people, after a collection has been taken from everyone, man for man, and person by person, for common use and openly, faithfully and wisely, in accordance with the need of each poor person.

32. The nation appointed almoners for this purpose, while the church appointed deacons and the deaconry (i.e., for the poor; Acts 6:1), as well as the Gazophylacium, or 'sacred treasury,' not only for the church's business

but also to provide support to the poor (Luke 21:1). And for this reason the church's treasury goes by the special name of treasury for the poor. And hence our pious ancestors devoutly undertook everywhere to build guest-houses, hospitals, homes for the aged, orphanages, nurseries for children, homes for the widows, etc. If a common and universal concern for the poor is added to these, then the care for the poor will lack hardly anything at all. Yet on this point we reject the thinking of those who under pretense of individual and voluntary care for the poor cause the public care to be overthrown, and vice versa.

33. And connected to almsgiving, in fact included in it, is giving a loan, which is paid to those who are not altogether needy, but needy for a short period of time. And we must care for such people by giving a loan, which should be done without interest, according to that statement in Deut 15:8: "Open your hand, and you will lend him sufficient for what he is in need." And the Psalmist: "The just man shows mercy and lends" (Ps 37:26); which Christ repeats: "Give to him who asks, and do not turn aside from the one who would borrow" (Matt 5:42; Luke 6:35). And in Luke 6:35 it says: "Give a loan, expecting nothing in return." That is to say: expect in return nothing more than the principal amount, and not even the same amount, as is clear from verse 34. In fact, if the situation demands it, don't expect back even the principal; i.e., give from a heart that purely does what is good—which (by some exaggeration of the wording) has the sense of being taken comparatively, as are also the other things in the same passage.

34. And yet to those in need it is permitted to lend by way of a pledge as security for the principal amount (Exod 22:26; Deut 24:10), but it is not right to lend for a profit or premium. In fact, in Scripture the one kind of profit-making that is prohibited is only in the case of an arrangement with the poor and oppressed. And for that reason, also the Hebrew word *neshekh* ('interest') is the word for biting and gnawing, and it is mentioned nearly always when it deals with the poor and the oppressed (Exod 22:25; Lev 25:35–37; Prov 22:7). But lending at interest, which is practiced on those who are of moderate means or wealthier, when collected according to the law of love and fairness, is a kind of legitimate contract and belongs to monetary gain.

35. Hence the lending to the poor for financial gain that is practiced in the form of a pledge, and that is permitted by the magistrates in Christendom to a certain degree because of something good, is clearly cruel and harsh.

Because of the lending at interest itself, and because of the amounts of it, a well-established nation ought to have no place for anyone to practice this. And just as it is not granted to the Jews to shame and oppress Christians by practicing usury over them with impunity (Deut 23:19–20 and 28:13, 44), but, instead, so too as one must look after the poor by means of public almsgiving, should public authority and management look after the needs of some people by furnishing an 'altar of love' (as it is called) without any pledge. And one should not accept anything more than the amount of the money that has been taken for that use (if it cannot come from the public purse in any other way) and a reimbursement for the costs. In no way should such lending result in profit.

36. In short, included in almsgiving are: sympathy, benevolence, and beneficence of every kind towards the poor and helpless.

37. And for this goal the Lord promises to those who bestow pity upon the poor "a rich reward and recompense" (Prov 19:17), a "reward and a prize" (Matt 6:4 and 10:41; 2 Cor 9[:12]). It is declared that "they are lending unto the Lord" (Prov 19:17), that "they will be blessed" (Prov 14:21; Luke 14:13 [and 14]), that "blessings will be given to them" (Prov 12[:12]), and that "they will be like well-watered gardens, and like a fountain of water whose springs will never fail" (Isa 58:11). The good things of this life are promised to them—both bodily and temporal things (2 Cor 9:8–11)—and also spiritual, eternal things. These include the breaking-off and forgiveness of sin (Dan 4[:27]), cleansing (Luke 11:41), perpetual righteousness (Ps 112:9), a treasure safe in heaven (Luke 12:33 and 18:22), entry into the heavenly tabernacle (Luke 16:9), the possession and inheritance of life eternal (Matt 25[:34])—– and that by God's righteousness (Heb 6:10).

38. In these promises almsgiving is not established as the cause of such great goods, but as their antecedent, because these goods happen to such people, and the explanation of their origin arises not from cause but from effect, or from the proper adjunct, and if some reason as a cause is indicated, it is done not by itself but by accident, with respect to the conjunction of this love with faith, and to God's reckoning. For, in fact, hearts are cleansed by faith (Acts 15:9). The remission of sins, the washing-away, and life eternal are merits of Christ, and life eternal is a gift from God, and the inheritance of sons is from God, and is traced to God's good pleasure (Luke 12:32; Matt 25).

On Fasting and Vigils

39. Thus far, then, about almsgiving. What follows is a second thing that is related to prayer conducted on special occasions, and is its frequent companion, namely, religious fasting, which is a more rigorous sort of self-discipline, or act which God prescribes in general that is voluntary in its circumstances whereby a stronger believer, because a more important and urgent need to pray arose, abstains from all food and drink, and all the customary trappings of life, beyond what is usual and for a certain period of time—as long as the natural strengths permit—at least for a day, in order to arouse and assist the soul and spirit in prayer, but that is especially undertaken and done religiously in humbling ourselves before God with repentance for sins, out of true faith, and either privately or publicly.

40. In calling it 'religious fasting' we distinguish it from the 'natural fasting' that is done for the purpose of maintaining or recovering bodily health. And we distinguish it from 'civil fasting,' which is when we are focused on some business or other, find ourselves in trouble, and we shun the needed refreshment (1 Sam 14:24; Acts 23:14, and 27:33). And it is different also from 'forced and necessary fasting,' such as hunger, famine, and lack of food and drink, whether it is brought on by God or human beings (Matt 24:7; 2 Cor 11:27). And so what we mean is the fasting that is done for religious reasons.

41. And yet what does not properly come into consideration here are sobriety, frugality, and moderation in the standard of living, as they are commanded to all believers throughout the entire course of their lives (Rom 13:13; Luke 21:34; 1 Pet 5). And as moderation is daily and lifelong, so also it is not properly considered fasting. Also not strictly fasting is the poverty, austerity or frequent fasting that is done according to a special calling for a particular lifestyle, such as that of John the Baptist, whose lifestyle was not at all common with others, since he fasted many times—besides the fact that he abstained from everyday foods (Matt 3:4 and 9:14). This is 'extraordinary fasting.' And also not relevant here is 'miraculous fasting' that comes by the special working of God—such as that of Moses (Exod 24:18 and 34[:28]), Elijah (1 Kgs 19[:4 and 5]), and Christ (Matt 4[:2])—and that thus cannot be imitated.

42. Therefore concerning religious fasting that is common to all believers we draw up the following propositions from its definition. [1)] The first is that

the practice of fasting as such is not self-willed or spontaneous worship, but something that has been established by God and that has been observed and a rule that will be exercised forever in the church (Joel 1:14 and 2:15; Matt 6:16 and 9:15). Accordingly, the outward, bodily fasting was not made obsolete in the New Testament along with the other ceremonies of the law, as if it retained only a figurative and spiritual meaning—that is, abstinence from sin, so that the mouth 'fasts' not from food but from base words, and from devouring and cursing one's neighbor; so that the hand 'fasts' from theft, the feet from every unlawful thing, and the eyes from what is not chaste, and the ears from disparaging slander, etc. (Isa 58:6; Jer 14:12; Zech 7:5).

43. [2)] But this divine ordinance is of such nature that while it is indeed general, it is of a free disposition according to circumstances. In fact in the Old Testament there was only one fixed and regular, annual fasting by divine prescription: on the tenth day of the seventh month before the feast of Atonement, in the house of the Lord every year there would be a solemn fast, and it was celebrated until evening (Lev 16 and 23). And by institution of the Church, dwelling in the Babylonian captivity, there was a fasting in the tenth month, to commemorate the siege of the city of Jerusalem, one in the fourth month for the city's capture, in the fifth for its destruction, and lastly, in the seventh month for the slaughter of Gedeliah that was followed by many disasters (2 Kgs 25; Jer 52; Zech 5:3 and 8:19). Added to these is the fast initiated by Mordecai, the one taken up by the Jews for the 'fast of Esther' (Esth 9:31–32). These have been abolished, the former for being ceremonial, and the latter ones for being temporary, appropriate for that people during particular period (Zech 8:19).

44. But in the New Testament Christ and his apostles did not set any certain time at all for fasting, but left it free, as also Augustine testifies (Epistle 86). And that fasting should be used (as the Orthodox state in Tertullian's book *On Fasting*) in a manner that is indifferent, by personal decision, and not by the order of a new discipline, and suited to everyone's time and cause—that is, suited to the degree of strength of each person. As to the time, mostly a time of mourning; as to the occasion, one that befalls and presses, one of a graver necessity (Matt 9:15; Mark 2:20; Luke 5:34), whether public or private, present or looming. And it should be done for the sake of obtaining some spiritual or bodily good, or for the sake of averting evil, and without the superstitious observance of time and days.

45. Accordingly, it follows from the reason for and keeping of fasting, that some are private, others public. The former is undertaken privately in a matter that is personal, either for oneself or for another (Dan 9:3 and 10:3; 1 Cor 7:5; Acts 10:30). The latter is done in public and is proclaimed by the overseers of the church, and kept publicly (Ezra 8:21; Acts 13:2–3 and 14:23).

46. And therefore the papal teachers are making a serious mistake, who contrary to Christian liberty, tie fasting to specific times and days, and, outdoing Judaism, have burdened the church with many fixed fastings for no pressing reason, and they bind the consciences to observe them as if by a required law—such as weekly, by fasting on the fourth and sixth day of the week [i.e. Wednesday and Friday]; and likewise on the Saturday after that (especially in the Roman church). So too the imposed annual fasting at the forty days of Lent and (only for clerics) from the fiftieth day before Easter; and also the fasting of the four seasons (March, June, September, and December), and very many other ones, like the yearly Vigils for the feasts of the Apostles and the other saints.

47. Some of these, namely the weekly fasting and the four Ember days, derive their origins from Jewish custom, and have been changed only in their reason (Luke 18:12; Zech 7). The one for Lent, however, was introduced as a vain, foolish, poor imitation of Christ's miraculous fasting, which we should marvel at but not copy. And although the ancient church did employ it, yet it varied and was free, so much so that there was a great diversity and dissimilarity both in its duration and its observance—one, two, several, and forty days (Eusebius, [*Ecclesiastical History*,] book 5, chapter 26; Socrates, [*Ecclesiastical History*,] book 5, chapter 21; Nicephorus, [*Refutation and Overthrowing of the Definition of the Synod of 815*,] book 1, chapter 34). But the papal teachers make the observance of fasting necessary and binding upon the conscience.

48. [3)] Fasting consists in the cheating of the natural appetite, in a restraint that is more severe than is customary, or in an abstinence from all food and drink altogether, as much as our human powers permit—for instance, usually from one evening until another evening (Lev 23:32), but sometimes it continues until the third day (Esth 4:16). Or from morning until evening, especially in a fast of many days, like a week (1 Sam 31:13), or three weeks (Dan 10:2) when in the evening they ate food, but only a little, and sparingly.

In this way Daniel abstained from meat and wine, and even tasty bread—but he did so freely (Dan 10:3).

49. And furthermore the papal teachers do not fast at all, since in the first place they define fasting not so much by abstinence from all food and drink as by the foolishly superstitious discrimination and selection of foods (1 Tim 4:1–3) or of meat. And at Lent it is abstaining from everything that comes from an animal; for example, milk, butter, cheese, eggs (whereby they think they become unclean). And by contrast, [it consists of] the use and even greater use of fish (often well-seasoned with spices), or very tasty fruits, including the most dainty delicacies; or of legumes that produce much flatulence. And it likewise consists in not being self-restrained in the drinking of wine or spirits, whereof they make extravagantly abundant use. And then also they fast not by abstaining from food and drink for the whole day, but they still fill their stomachs every day while postponing breakfast only once, which very many of the ancients sought to do their whole lives. And they foist this law upon the people's consciences, as a necessary law, nor do they grant an exemption to this, unless upon receipt of money.

50. [4]] And finally, in and of itself fasting is a 'middle thing,' and indifferent; that is, by itself it is neither something good nor something evil. "For the kingdom of God is not meat and drink, but righteousness and peace and joy in the Holy Spirit" (Rom 14:6, 17; 1 Cor 8:8). But in its use, fasting is properly and foremost an outward or bodily exercise, and an aid for training, nurturing and fostering piety. And it is a mark of penitence, that in and of itself is of no, or very little, advantage (Col 2:23; 1 Tim 4:8). But it is advantageous by accident with a view to a more excellent goal, insofar as it concerns piety, prayer, and repentance. For this reason the recommendation to fast is related to righteousness (Matt 5:6).

51. And so the goal of fasting is that, after our wanton and languid flesh has been halted by this lack of food, our heart and soul become so disposed and incited that they are rendered more free, unencumbered, and zealous than usual to offer prayer unto God, to undertake spiritual meditation, and to pour out prayers that are more efficacious than ordinarily. Hence Scripture often links fasting with prayer (Joel 1:14; Neh 1:4; Matt 6:5; Luke 2:37; 1 Cor 7:5), even apart from the link to special penitence (Acts 13:2).

52. The highest goal, however, is in the penitent's prayer, for the affliction of the flesh and for humbling the entire man before God (Ps 35:13), so that it

becomes a testimony and symbol of serious repentance and of true grief arising over sin (Joel 2:12). For this reason fasting is also called an affliction; and the statements 'to afflict oneself or one's body or soul' is used for fasting (Lev 16:29; Isa 58:3; Ezra 8:21 and 9:5). And therefore, the cause is usually grief, and an occasion for grief (Matt 9:15). And so contrariwise, in times of formal festivities it was the custom with joy and delight to eat more lavishly, and with pleasure, and to deliver portions to the poor, and in the presence of the Lord to have pleasure, as a testimony to their thanksgiving (Ps 116:13; Zech 8:19; Ezra 6:21–22; Neh 8:11,13).

53. In former times people added to that fasting a variety of gestures and ritual actions to indicate their contrition and grief. These included the tearing of garments (Joel 2:12–13), wearing clothes of mourning like sackcloth and goat's hair (Ps 35:13), being seated or cast down in dirt and ashes and sprinkling these on one's head, befouling and hiding one's face (2 Sam 12:16), neglecting to wash and anoint oneself (Matt 6:16), bending one's head downward (1 Kgs 21:27; Isa 58:5), pouring out water (1 Sam 7:6), pulling out one's hair and beard ([LXX and Vulgate editions of] Ezra 9:3; Esth 14:2), weeping, wailing, and howling (Joel 2:12). In fact, in more serious times of grief even children and herds were called to join the fasting (Joel 2:16; Jonah 3:7). The Jewish nation either shared nearly all these things with the peoples of the near East, or they were proper to that nation, or those things were meant for the pedagogical teaching of that people [Gal 3:24–25]. Christ liberated his people from them, in keeping with the thing, place, and time.

54. What is clear from these goals (and connected to them) is the mode of fasting: it should not be done hypocritically or for reasons of ambition, i.e., with an outward appearance, boasting, or pretense for the reputation of being holy (Matt 6:16–17). Nor should it be done superstitiously, i.e., out of habit and to honor saints; but with faith, fear of God, and love for the neighbor, and to God's glory.

55. When it is undertaken and done in this way for these goals, fasting pleases God, as a work that is good to do. Without these goals, however, fasting displeases God—no matter how much affliction and chastisement of the body accompanies it. It is for this reason that God especially urges spiritual fasting in place of it, as it should be part of the physical fasting, and the physical fasting should be valued by the spiritual one (Isa 58:5–6; Zech 7:5,9).

56. Because fasting is linked to something else—i.e., to the prayer of faith, that is, made out of faith and accompanied by repentance—the prayer for the aversion of God's wrath is attributed to fasting (Deut 9:18; Jonah 3:9), and also the reward and retribution by God (Matt 6:18). And moreover, in view of some sort of self-humbling, fasting also brings about a decrease of temporal punishment (1 Kgs 21:27–29). In fact, even the power to cast out demons is ascribed to fasting (Matt 17:20–21).

57. And therefore the papal teachers are making a serious mistake, for when they fast either for appearance's sake or become depressed in their hearts from their excessive abstinence, they make the claim that fasting or this emptiness of the stomach and intestines, and this bodily affliction is in itself a form of worship to God and a good work; that it renders their prayer pleasing to God, is satisfactory for sins, meritorious of righteousness and eternal life, and also appeases the wrath of God, justifies man in God's presence. In fact they claim that by it even souls are set free from Purgatory (Lombard, [*Sentences,*] book 4, chapter 15). All this is contrary to the obvious testimony of Scripture that we produced earlier in theses 50 and 55.

58. Vigils are also included under fasting, and they, too, are often combined with prayers (Matt 26:38, 41; 1 Pet 4:7). And by 'vigils' are meant not only the vigils of the heart and soul, whereby we are always readied and equipped for prayer and for the Lord's coming, in contrast with the security in the flesh (Matt 24:42; Mark 13:35; Luke 12:39; 1 Thess 5:6; Rev 3:3 and 16:15). But included also are the bodily vigils, whereby we freely take some portion of the night (as needed) to pray and meditate on the Lord's coming. This is what David testifies about himself (Ps 119:55, 62), and Christ led the way in doing (Luke 6:12), and the apostles reinforce (Col 4:2; Acts 16:25)—namely, that we should keep watch lest we enter into temptation (Matt 26:38, 41).

59. In former times vigils were both a private and a public, fixed institution. The vigils of Easter, that is, in the night before the day of Resurrection, were celebrated by keeping watch throughout the night, with lights burning in both public and private places. Ambrose (Sermon 60) writes: "We fast on the Easter Sabbath, we celebrate the vigils, and we conduct prayers constantly;" and the reason that Lactantius ([*Divine Institutes,*] book 7, chapter 19) and Jerome give is: "Because it was on that night that they expected Christ to return as Judge." But, in keeping with Christian freedom, the ancient Church made this vigil obsolete as freely as it had been undertaken and kept.

60. So much for fasting. As for the Bacchanals that are celebrated before Lent by the Roman Catholics after the manner of the gentiles according to an evil custom, all Christians should detest and avoid them altogether, as the papists start this Lenten-fast of theirs with immoderate licentiousness and luxury.

SOURCES

Augustine, *Enchiridion addressed to Laurentius*, chapter 75

Now, surely, those who live very heinous lives and are not concerned about correcting their lives and habits, and who nevertheless amid their crimes and misdeeds continue multiplying their almsgiving, flatter themselves vainly with these words of the Lord: "Give alms; and, behold, all things are clean to you." They do not understand how far this saying reaches, etc. Should we interpret this to mean that to the Pharisees, who did not have the faith in Christ, all things are clean so long as they give alms (as they think they should be given), even though they have not believed and have not been reborn of water and the Holy Spirit? But all are unclean who are not made clean by the faith in Christ, of which it is written: "Cleansing their hearts by faith" [Acts 15:9]. And as the apostle said: "But to those who are unclean and to unbelievers nothing is clean; both their minds and consciences are unclean, etc." But no-one, however, gives any alms at all unless he gives from Him who does not need anything. Accordingly it says: "His mercy shall go before me." [Ps 59:10]

Augustine, *Letter 86 to Casulanus*

Thinking the matter over in my mind, I observe that in the Gospels and the Epistles, and in the entire document called the New Testament, there is a precept for fasting. But I do not find any rule definitely laid down by the Lord or by the apostles about which days we should or should not fast.

ON VOWS

President: Johannes Polyander
Respondent: Gerhardus Paludanus

A vow is a voluntary promise made to God 'of our own doing, and by faith, for the glory of his name and the upbuilding of our neighbor' (3). The structure of this disputation follows conventional scholastic progressions of thought: the origin of the word 'vow' (2); a definition (3); the difference between vows that are lawful and unlawful (4–7); sub-categories of vows (8–22); the cause of making vows (23). The disputation then focuses our attention upon the vow's subject, content, and object (24). The person who utters the vow is the subject (24–33); its content may be ordained in Scripture (as in Baptism or the Lord's Supper), or it may belong to the 'adiaphora' for which no content is commanded (34–49). God himself is the object of our vows (50–51). Inward and outward forms of vows are treated next (52), as is their goal, which is especially the glorification of God (53). Interested readers may wish to compare Polyander's discussion of vows with Walaeus's treatment of oaths in Disputation 20.

1. In his Word God no less prescribes vows for those who call upon his name and generously give alms to their neighbors than He prescribes fasting. Therefore, this disputation about vows is aptly joined to the preceding ones about calling upon God, almsgiving and fasting.

2. If we look to the derivation of the word, then *votum* ('vow') has the same meaning in Latin as *euchē* in Greek and *neder* in Hebrew.

3. When considered in a general way, a vow is a sacred and religious promise about things that have been commanded, or about indifferent things that have been placed in our power, for the sake of giving testimony to God alone of our intention and duty towards him, a promise that is made of our own doing, and by faith, for the glory of his name and the upbuilding of our

neighbor. In the sacred writings, however, vows are more frequently limited to intermediate things.

4. Although making vows is an ancient practice and was used by all heathen nations, yet it was only to his own Israelite people that the God of Israel once prescribed a pattern for them (Lev 27; Num 30).

5. Hence only the vows of the Israelites were lawful, while those of the other nations were unlawful.

6. Lawful vows are those that are made only to the God of Israel, in accordance with his law, in truth, with discernment, and in righteousness.

7. Unlawful vows are ones that either disregard God and are made to his creatures, or that are made to God but not to him alone, or not following the law and manner delivered by him, but falsely, rashly and unjustly.

8. Lawful vows are either moral or ceremonial.

9. Moral vows are those that bind each and every person to the obedience that the Decalogue prescribes.

10. Ceremonial vows are ones that some people make from a religious conviction, for some pious work that is arbitrary and not, in itself, owed.

11. We have the moral vows in common with the fathers who lived in the Old Testament; but ceremonial vows, which are figurative, were specific to them in times gone by, and they were aids of the principal worship that God demands in his moral law.

12. Even though moral works are of themselves, naturally, owed to God, nevertheless in a special way and by a special bond believers are obliged to fulfill them by means of their vows, both ordinary and extraordinary ones.

13. Ordinary vows are the ones whereby believers one and all bind themselves by promise and a solemn obligation to the perpetual observance of divine worship.

14. Extraordinary vows are the kind that on occasion, due to some pressing need, are renewed either by the whole Church or its leading members in order to confirm themselves and others in the true faith, like the vows of the Israelite people in the time of Joshua (chapter 24:23) and Ezra (chapter 10:5).

15. Both vows are either absolute or hypothetical and conditional.

16. Absolute vows are the pure and simple ones that are declared without any condition. David's vow in Ps 34:2 was of this kind: "I shall bless Jehovah all the time, and praise of Him will always be in my mouth." And Ps 101[:1 and 2]: "I shall sing of your love and righteousness, O Jehovah! I shall keep the upright way. when will you come to me? Without ceasing I shall walk within my home in uprightness of my heart, etc."

17. Hypothetical vows are the ones to which certain conditions are attached, whether of person, time, place, or some other circumstance. Such was Jacob's vow in Gen 28:20[–22]: "If God will be with me and watch over me on the journey that I am going to undertake, and will give me bread to eat and clothes to wear, so that I shall return safely to my father's house; and so if Jehovah will be my God, then this heap of stones that I set up will be as a statue to the Lord God, and of whatever you will give me I shall in all give a tenth to you." And such was Hannah's vow in 1 Sam 1:11: "Lord God of hosts, if you will at all regard the affliction of your maidservant, and will remember me and not forget your maidservant, but if you will give a male offspring to your handmaiden, then I shall give him to Jehovah all the days of his life, and no razor shall come near his head."

18. And vows are divided also into perpetual and temporal. Pious people bind themselves to fulfill the thing that was vowed throughout their whole life by means of the former, whereas they do so for some time of their life by means of the latter. Of the first there is an example in David (thesis 16), and of the latter in Paul (Acts 18:18).

19. And like the prayers that are often joined to them, so too the vows themselves are sometimes only conceived in the mind as it reaches out for God, as is seen in the case of Hannah (1 Sam 1:11); and at other times they are also uttered by mouth, as is seen in the case of the Israelite people (Josh 24:24).

20. And again, these vows are either public or private.

21. Public vows are solemnly performed either in a civic meeting (like Jephthah's vow in Judg 11:31) or in a meeting of the Church (like David's vow in Ps 34 and 101).

22. Private vows are made in a place apart, a place removed from others, like Jacob's vow (Gen 28:20).

23. Foremost among the causes that compel the making of vows to God is God's command in Ps 76:11: "Make your vows and render your vows to Jehovah your God, and let all who dwell round about Him bring a gift to Him who is to be feared." Second: the example set by the saints (Gen 28:20; 1 Sam 1:11). Third: the remembrance of benefits received from God, which caused David to say: "What shall I render to Jehovah? All his benefits overwhelm me. I shall soon repay my vows to Jehovah in the presence of his people." [Ps 116:12 and 14] Fourth: the hope of obtaining some new and special benefit that has been asked of God in prayer and that one expects will be obtained. It was on the basis of this hope that Jacob made a special vow to God (Gen 28), as did Hannah, too, the mother of Samuel (1 Sam 1). Finally: the serious purpose of the heart to check the lusts of the flesh against any depravity. Such was the vow of Job who stated that he made a covenant with his eyes that he would not look at a young woman (Job 31:1).

24. Moreover, Holy Scripture defines the vows of the pious by three circumstances; the first of these concerns their subject, the second their content-matter, and the third their object.

25. The subject that is capable of making vows is the human being with whom God has entered into a covenant of his grace.

26. That covenant of grace which God has established with believing parents applies also to their infant children; and accordingly, since these children, like branches of them, have been sanctified at the root, they are implicitly obligated by them in a joint vow of obedience. In former times the sacrament of this implicit obligation was circumcision, but now it is baptism.

27. In order to confirm this obligation God instituted a second sacrament, namely, Passover in the Old Testament and holy supper in the New Testament, so that the children who over time have attained the use of reason, no less than their parents should affirm the first promise of their obedience by solemnly repeating it.

28. We should make a distinction between this general vow, which God has prescribed for younger as well as older people, and certain specific vows. That general one ought to remain completely valid, nor can human authority detract anything from it. These special vows are void if the people who make them are not legally independent but are restricted by the authority of father, husband, or some other lawful authority (Num 30).

29. And therefore this first axiom of Bellarmine's, that "it is permitted to make such vows (i.e., vows of chastity, obedience, and poverty) at any point in a man's lifetime provided that he make use of his own free choice" is false, since these vows are neither general nor prescribed by God, but special vows and devised by men, as we shall point out in its place. See Bellarmine, the second book [of the Controversies regarding the Members of the Church], *On Monks*, chapter 35.

30. Bellarmine's second axiom, that "children are permitted, contrary to their parents' will, to enter religious life," is correct if the expression 'religious life' is understood to mean the Christian religion in the strict sense. But it is false if the expression is applied to a special condition of life that is 'religious' taken in an equivocal sense and that is actually superstitious (as Bellarmine makes it; Bellarmine, *On Monks*, chapter 36). For in this way, under the pretext of "religion" children are wrongly granted a violation of the fifth commandment about honoring one's parents.

31. And although the special vows, insofar as they are appendices of the ceremonial law, have been abolished in Christ, and for this reason there is no precept in the New Testament about them, yet insofar as they belong to natural right and are chains whereby all people are more tightly bound to moral works that by nature and in themselves are owed to God, we state that they are no less permitted to us than to our forefathers before the law about them was given.

32. We should refer Paul's vow (mentioned in Acts 18:18) to that ceremonial law, which had not yet been abolished entirely at the time of the apostolic age.

33. As far as the outward, voluntary practices of some Christians are concerned, ones of the sort that involve abstinence from customary drink and food or from other things which they think put them at risk of an occasion to sin, certain or ordinary prayers, and certain endowments of alms: It is not useless for them to undertake these and similar vows, provided that they are free of all superstition, and that it is from a serious purpose of a pious mind devoted to God that they complete these vows in order to foster true faith, repentance, sobriety, love, and other Christian virtues.

34. The content-matter of vows are either things explicitly commanded by the Word of God or things not explicitly commanded but arbitrary. The

former are holy and necessary in themselves, while the latter are 'adiaphora' (or indifferent) in themselves but become holy by their circumstances and useful for salvation insofar as they are related to the principal worship of God and serve its advancement.

35. The general vow of Christianity that begins at Baptism and is renewed in the Lord's Supper extends only as far as things that have been commanded in the Decalogue and the Gospel.

36. Special vows are the ones that concern things that have not been absolutely commanded in the Decalogue or the Gospel—such as celibacy, and abstaining from certain drink, food, clothing and other good things that have been given for man's use. Or they concern matters that have been commanded partly in general (as far as their substance is concerned) and partly not in specific (as far as the circumstances of time, place, people, and events are concerned). Vows of this sort are the set prayers, fasting, almsgiving, and similar duties of piety, and the public determination of them God grants to the church's judgment, while the private execution of them is granted to each believer's choice.

37. The former kind of vows about merely indifferent matters stood out in former times in the case of the Nazarites (Num 6) and were praised in the case of the Rechabites (Jer 35). The latter kind of vows is seen in other Jews; but nowadays both kinds are condemned if anyone binds himself or others with their enslaving yoke out of a notion of necessity that completely conflicts with the freedom that Christ has obtained for us (Gal 5:1; Col 2:20).

38. The pontifical teachers, in foisting Jewish-like vows on themselves or other people, take no account at all of the conditions of lawful vows while they themselves do approve of some of these stipulations.

39. The foremost of these conditions is that vows be made according to God's commands. But in the whole of Scripture there is no text about the three vows to which the Romanist monks are bound. And despite making efforts to prove individual vows from certain places of Scripture by twisting them into a meaning they don't have, Bellarmine produces not a single text with which to combine and so confirm them.

40. The second condition is that no vow should pose a hindrance to what God in his Word prescribes or permits. But this is what happens in vows of poverty, obedience, and celibacy.

41. For with their vow of poverty, or rather of mendicancy, monks are drawn away from the work that God commands everyone (Gen 3:19; Exod 20:9) and drawn towards idleness which leads to vice.

42. And what is more, with their vow of regular (or rather, irregular) obedience, those same monks put aside the vow of universal obedience that we owe to Christ alone, as the Father commanded: "Listen to him" (Matt 17:5). And instead they naively, and without any restriction to their own contrary opinion or judgment, pay heed to the particular and various human rules of this or that Prelate as though they are divinely ordained.

43. And lastly, with their third vow, the one about perpetual celibacy, monks are unfairly excluded from the apostle's general command: "Because of sexual immorality let every man have his own wife" (1 Cor 7:2). For even monks (as Bellarmine admits) are in danger of committing fornication, and they could lose the gift of chastity that they have vowed to keep, and at some time or other be overcome by temptation (Bellarmine, book 2, *On Monks*, chapter 9).

44. And the third condition is that the vows should not consist in actions that are evil in and of themselves—like the papacy's calling upon saints, the veneration of images and relics, the monks' idle mendicancy, and similar actions.

45. And the fourth condition is that vows should not cause a hindrance to a greater good. And this is what the vow of poverty does, whereby the wealthy renounce their own goods and deprive themselves of any ability to provide for the communion of saints through deeds of hospitality and kindness, wherein God takes great delight (Heb 13:16).

46. The fifth condition is that whatever is vowed should not stand in the way of the duty which everyone is bound to perform for his neighbor out of natural and moral law. Such is the abandonment of human community, and especially of one's neighbors, which monks vow to do: that they will not be forced to serve the needs of their own relatives, and so they actually deny the Christian faith which they profess with their mouth. For where there is such inhumanity, there can be no piety towards God.

47. The sixth condition is that to most of those making the vow the matter ought not to be impossible; a matter of this sort is the perpetual chastity of a

celibate life. It is with no small scandal that all of Christianity has been observing the violation of this vow in monasteries since several ages ago.

48. The seventh condition is that there be no foolish, comical, and useless things, like religious pilgrimages, the various kinds of monks' clothing, abstinence from certain types of food, etc.

49. The eighth condition is that vows should be entirely free of any notion of worship that is necessary, or meritorious in the eyes of God on the basis of work that is supererogatory. Bellarmine confirms his fellow-monks in this notion by means of the following definition of vow: "A vow is a religious promise made to God about some more excellent good." This definition of Bellarmine rests upon this false assumption: that in the Gospel Christ recommends to us some good that is more excellent than what God commands in his Law. We have abundantly demonstrated the untruth in this definition in our earlier disputations about the Law and the Gospel.

50. The proper object of vows is the same as for prayers, namely, God, to whom alone true worshipers have directed their vows, in accordance with his command (Deut 23; Ps 50 and 76).

51. And therefore we have every good reason to consider the papal teachers as sacrilegious idolaters for making also their vows to the deceased saints or to the heads of monasteries, for they ascribe the honor that is due only to their Creator to the creatures He has made.

52. The internal form of vows consists in the fact that, following prior considerations of the soul, vows are freely made and arise from a certain knowledge and confidence of the faith, without which they cannot be pleasing God. Their outward form is that they are expressed also in speech, and even though this is not necessary for God since He knows the hearts, yet the outward form is put to good use as a witness of our zeal and holy intent to offer vows to God, while also edifying our neighbor.

53. The highest and general goal of making vows is the glory of God; subordinate and particular goals include: 1) That we bear witness to God of our repentance for sins committed against him, as well as our gratitude for the benefits that we have received from Him. 2) That by means of this goad we are very much spurred to all the other duties of piety, love, righteousness, and mercy, that can proceed from us.

ON PURGATORY
AND INDULGENCES

President: Andreas Rivetus
Respondent: Guilielmus Soestius

Disputation 39 is unique insofar as its purpose is not to explicate a doctrine positively but to refute a false one, namely the Roman Catholic teaching and practice of purgatory and indulgences. Simply put, purgatory and indulgences deny the efficacy of Christ's atoning sacrifice, his work of complete satisfaction for our sins, and our justification in the sight of God (1). 'God has instituted no purgation except the blood of Christ and the grace of the Holy Spirit' (5). Scriptural grounds and arguments that support the rejection of purgatory are provided (10–36). The treatment of indulgences (37–54) begins with an expression of confidence that 'once the fire of purgatory has been extinguished, the smoke of indulgences vanishes by itself' (37). The disputation ends with an expression of gratitude to God for raising up Martin Luther, who was led 'to overturn the entire system of indulgences from its very foundations.' 'Thus it remains that we, acknowledging the true source of the forgiveness of sins, and then being washed in it, should abstain from sins, and bring glory to God the Father, in Christ the Son, and through the Holy Spirit forever' (54).

1. In the preceding disputations we treated the offices of Christ, his satisfaction for our sins, and the application of that satisfaction in the justification of man by true faith. We also treated the gratitude in sanctification and the works of sanctification by those who were made partakers of that justification, and the correct use of fasting, almsgiving, and vows, which the papal teachers misuse in order to establish a satisfaction by man apart from Christ. Having done that, it is right for us to append an elenctic disputation about purgatory and indulgences in which we shall demonstrate that these made-up human inventions are not based on any solid

foundation but take away from the merits and unique satisfaction of Christ and are harmful to the church of God—a part of which church (and that not the smallest part) they imagine undergoes temporary torment in the underworld.

2. To avoid attributing to our opponents anything of our own making, it is from their writings that first we shall present the state of the controversy, and distinguishing what they themselves consider certain and necessary to believe from the things that are less certain and debated, we shall direct our arguments especially at those former things. For they themselves give this warning: "Some teachings which we hold about purgatory are more or less certain, teachings that are not equally confirmed by all testimonies and arguments whatsoever at once, but by differing ones" (Gregory of Valencia, [*Theological commentary on*] Thomas Aquinas's [*Summa theologiae*], part 3, disputation 11, question 1, point 1, paragraph 4).

3. But they posit the following as the first and foremost meaning of the word, according to which they think that it is rightly proved that there is a purgatory by the testimonies which they are accustomed to adduce either from Scripture or the church fathers or the ecclesiastical definitions. And by [purgatory] they mean some place whereto those believers' souls migrate from the body upon death, being bound still by the liability of some temporal punishment or even by some venial sins, and experience torments relative to the reckoning of God's justice, until such time as they have completely expiated such sins and are able to obtain the blessedness of heaven (Gregory of Valencia, ibid., Bellarmine, *On Purgatory*, book 1, chapter 1).

4. And therefore we leave aside the controversies that the papal teachers have stirred up amongst themselves about the location of purgatory, whereof they admit even that their own church has made no definitive decision—although by the more accepted opinion (which they deem to be more true) they think that it is below the earth and next to the hell of the condemned. [And we leave aside the controversy] about the fire, which the majority think is fire in the proper sense (though others: improper); about the quality of that fire, namely if it is real and corporeal (which they affirm is their theologians' most solid opinion); about the support that the living give for the sake of those who are deceased (and similar things). What we shall examine is what they call that 'substantial' and primary meaning of the word ['purgatory'], and we shall test it by the rule of truth, since they hold that it is so necessary to believe

that teaching, that Bellarmine judges that he who denies it must suffer torment in the eternal fire of hell (*On Purgatory*, chapter 15). And [Francesco] Panigarola did not hesitate to say that there is no God if there is no purgatory (*Lecture on Purgatory*, held at Turin).

5. But as for us, we believe very firmly in the existence of God and we also steadfastly deny that this sort of purgatory exists—nor do we, for that reason, fear the punishments of the world below. For we know that God has instituted no purgation except the blood of Christ and the grace of the Holy Spirit, which is distributed to believers by the Word and sacraments in this life—unless, perhaps, someone should state that afflictions and chastisements purge away sins. They, however, don't do this by their own power, but only as occasions, that is insofar as 'sufferings are lessons' (to say it in this way) whereby we are warned through our weaknesses to take recourse in a doctor—a logic that cannot apply to the afflictions of the purgatorial fires after this life (as our opponents themselves admit).

6. Their assumption, that the catholic Church has always been of the opinion that such a purgatory exists, is completely false; and they consider that this assumption should be sufficient to preserve the claim of purgatory— although they have no testimony from Scripture or any other argument. And they carefully lay down this basis, for they are themselves aware that whatever they produce from Holy Scripture is dragged 'by the scruff of the neck' to support a matter foreign to it, and is not capable of making those people believe whose eyes have not been glazed over by the 'cataracts' of pontifical authority and the 'corneal blemish' of human traditions that wrongly claims for itself the authority of the catholic Church.

7. And so even though they twist some testimonies of Scripture, there still were some within the realm of the papists itself who were compelled by the truth to say that "one cannot readily produce any one Scripture-passage with which to compel an impudent person, whether he is willing or not, to confess that purgatory exists, even if there could be such a passage—although until now it has escaped the notice of the most careful investigators" (Bishop of Rochester, *Against Luther*, article 18). And hence it happened that in France the Jesuit Pierre Coton, when he was not able to persuade the living, tried to move Acheron, and he did dig up what until then had escaped the notice of the most careful observers—assisted as he was by a demon, to whom he put

the following question (among others): "What place is there in Scripture from which one could clearly prove purgatory?"

8. For obviously he knew what Peter de Soto states frankly in his *Lectures on the Institution of Priesthood* (On Purgatory, lecture 1), "that the authoritative passages of Scripture adduced by our teachers are less clear and less effective, and demonstrate less, and that therefore people should not use them to prove that purgatory exists." And likewise, "that it is neither necessary nor opportune to rely on the authority of the passage taken from Matt chapter 12[:32], that 'there will be no forgiveness either in this age or in the one that is to come,' because one could reply that this is said through some exaggeration and hyperbole." Nor does it hold on the basis of that well-known passage in 1 Cor 3[:13]—"and so as through fire"—that upon death there is some sort of purgatory, "because we should understand this sort of fire to mean that both those who build with gold and those who build with straw pass through it." And the same author says that "this reasoning very effectively argues that this passage does not prove a purgatory after death, or if it seems to someone that it can be proven nonetheless, then certainly on account of its ambiguity the meaning is less clear. And therefore, one should also not rely on that passage."

9. But the passage from 2 Macc 12, which Bellarmine and Gregory of Valencia place in the vanguard, contains nothing about any purgatorial fire or place where souls are burned, and it can be so explained that it is impossible on the basis of it (at least, from the deed of Judas) to prove assistance for the deceased. Yet what is more, "among the ancients there existed doubt about the authority of that book (whether or not it belongs to the canon), and in Augustine's time this appeared not yet sufficiently resolved," as the same de Soto says, and he asserts, "the doctrine of purgatory is more certain and evident than the authority of that book; and one should not prove what is more evident by means of what is less evident."

10. In order for us to demonstrate that this doctrine is not just an 'unwritten' one but even 'contrary to what is written' there is no need for us (although some of our opponents unfairly demand it) to make the case for the negative argument, word-for-word and literally from Scripture: "There is no purgatorial place for souls after death." It is sufficient if we show in many ways how that dogma of the papal teachers conflicts with Scripture and sound reasoning. Scripture does not put anything in the middle between

believers and unbelievers, good and bad, between those who enter by the narrow gate and those who enter by the wide one, the sons of eternity and the sons of the devil, the spiritual and the carnal, etc.; but everywhere it has established a direct opposition between these sorts of people (Luke 16:8; Matt 7:13; Matt 25:32; John 5:29; Rom 8:5, etc.). And therefore, it does not acknowledge that there are people in the middle, who are "neither altogether evil nor altogether good;" and when these are taken away, then purgatory is empty.

11. The same Scripture points out that there are only two lives, and Augustine also testifies "that the Church knows that God has proclaimed and pointed out to it the same two lives, of which one is in faith and the other in sight. The one is in the time of sojourn, the other in its eternal abode; the one is struggling while the other is at rest; the one is *en route* while the other has reached the fatherland; the one is actively working while the other has been rewarded with beholding, etc." (Treatise 124, on John). Paul clearly delimits and circumscribes the first of these lives within the boundaries of this current life (Rom 8:18; 2 Cor 5:10). And he evidently teaches that "what is seen is temporary, and what is not seen is eternal" (2 Cor 4:18). But since the state of souls after this life is unseen, it must be eternal. The Scholastics themselves understand by *viatores* ['sojourners'] only those people who are still enjoying the use of that light.

12. And, with the same apostle, we know that "if the earthly tent we live in is destroyed, we have a dwelling-place from God, a home not made with hands, eternal in the heavens," and not a temporal one in the realm below. And Ephraem [the Syrian] states: "Beyond these two orders there is no other, middle order; yet I do speak about one order above and another below" (Treatise *Regarding the Mansions of the Blessed*). And a little farther on, "Fleeing Gehenna precisely means to enter into the kingdom of heaven, just as to depart from heaven is to enter Gehenna. For Scripture also has not taught us that there are three regions." Correct, for "he who believes has crossed over from death to life" (John 5:24). And "from now on they rest from their labor who die in the Lord" (Rev 14:13). For what Bellarmine and others state is wrong, "that some die partly in the Lord and partly not in the Lord"—as if to say that someone who is still wandering beyond it has reached the turning-point.

13. And whenever Scripture presents teachings and examples of dying well, it does not strike any fear of torments and physical pain into the hearts of the pious; rather, it instills the fullest measure of hope and joy—which could not possibly happen if pious believers in Christ had to fear the flames of purgatory after their death, flames that are different from the fires of hell only in the length of time: "The righteous perishes and there is no-one who takes it to heart, and men of compassion are gathered away, etc. Peace will come, and he who walks in love will rest upon his bed." (Isa 57:1) And accordingly those who were going to die "sought to be dismissed in peace" (Luke 2:29) because those who were faithful unto death are promised the crown of life (Rev 2:10), but the punishment of the fire is not being prepared for them. And the apostle testifies that the crown that has been reserved for him after the struggle of this life is the same as the one reserved for everyone who cherishes Christ's coming (2 Tim 4:8).

14. If there was anyone who needed some satisfactorial purging upon death then surely it was the murderer who was converted upon the cross, who confessed that he was receiving what his deeds deserved (Luke 23:41). He ought to have suffered the purgatorial punishments for many hundreds of years after his death, and yet he heard Christ say: "Today you will be with me in Paradise." For the fact that some papal teachers assert that death undergone by this soul suffering death with a most patient mind and his admirable confession could have counted as just satisfaction (Bellarmine, *On Purgatory*, book 1, chapter 2)—this is why among the Jesuits there are some who call this murderer "martyr for Christ"—completely contradicts Scripture and sound reasoning. "For whoever suffers as a murderer, or thief, or evildoer" (1 Pet 4:15) certainly is not suffering for the sake of Christ.

15. Nor is it valid if someone were to say: "The privilege of a few does not make for a rule." For all believers receive the same promise, "that they will not enter into the judgment but have gone over from death to life" (John 5:24). "And the sun will not beat down upon them, nor will scorching heat," hence, no purgatorial fires (Rev 7:16). And accordingly, as soon as the soul of Lazarus departed from his body, the angels carried it to the bosom of Abraham, where he enjoyed consolation (Luke 16:22). And therefore, he did not suffer the grievous pains of purgatory. Those who die in this faith "desired rather to be away from the body and to be present with the Lord" (2 Cor 5:8), "to depart and to be with Christ" (Phil 1:23). Indeed, they knew that the Lord "willed that those whom the Father had given to him would be

where he is, even with him, and that they might behold his glory"—and therefore not that they should be in the world below alongside the damned, suffering a similar fire for many years.

16. Scripture testifies that the time of this current life is the time for sowing, but that after this life is the time for harvesting (Gal 6:7) "when everyone will receive according to what he has done in the body" (2 Cor 5:10); that now "is the acceptable day of salvation" (2 Cor 6:2); that the Son of man forgives sins "on earth" (Matt 9:6). And, what is forgiven or loosed on earth, the same is forgiven and loosed in heaven (Matt 16:19). Therefore, since the forgiveness of sins and salvation is obtained (or lost) only in this life through faith that is kindled by the ministry of the Word and Sacraments, and since the effect of the things that are done on earth is to be looked for in heaven, the making of a purgatory outside the inhabited world and heaven makes no sense.

17. The very doctrine of purgatory cannot co-exist with the remission of sins. The Jesuits state that "in the next life there is no place except that of righteousness, namely, in the retribution of punishment or reward, in return for what has been merited or demerited in this life" (Gregory of Valencia, disputation 11, question 1, point 1). According to them, therefore, there is no place for mercy. But if someone says that the forgiveness of sins is not an effect of mercy, then he should be 'placed in the care of his relations and kinsmen.' For what the Jesuit adds that sins are forgiven, "only insofar as the payment of the penalty makes satisfaction for God's justice," is so foolish that it brings forth the blasphemous consequence that even Christ, who fully satisfied God's justice, had his sins forgiven him.

18. And no less absurd is their statement that with the remission of guilt a man is cleansed from sin, while after this life a temporal punishment is exacted from him. For Bellarmine himself admits that "the penalty which is owed" (or the liability of the penalty) "does not produce a stain but makes one a debtor" (*On Purgatory*, book 2, chapter 4). But where there is no stain what need is there for purging? And also, whatever is cleansed is taken away, for God takes away the stains which he purges. But, according to our opponents' assumption, in purgatory punishment is exacted unto the very last penny. Who has ever heard of someone who is purged from a punishment which he is forced to suffer in its entirety? For if someone says that those who are in purgatory sometimes are relieved from punishments

through the assistance of the living (even though this is not true) then it follows from that only that the help and deeds of satisfaction by the living are purgatorial, but not some fire which does not actually purge but from which those people for whom satisfaction is made are purged and set free, in which passive sense even the penalties the damned deserved would be purgatorial, because Christ has liberated those who belong to Him from these penalties by making satisfaction.

19. As a result of all this the most important basis of our opponents' contention collapses, upon which they argued that one must necessarily confess that after death there remains some time and place when, outside heaven itself and even outside the hell of the damned, souls make atonement for their liability of punishment and their venial guilt in order to be able to enter into the kingdom of heaven. For [they argue] the sort of people are found who, although they are in the grace of God, nevertheless are not granted immediate entry into the kingdom of heaven without making some additional expiation, since nothing gains entry there that is defiled in any way, and also since there is no church there that still has some "stain and wrinkle" [Eph 5:27]. But we state that there is not any stain or wrinkle that remains in those who die in grace, and the apostle's statement applies: "Whoever has died has been made righteous from sin" (Rom 6:7). And moreover, Bellarmine has admitted that the penalty that is owed does not brand a stain. He also admits that "in death the tinder for sin is taken away when all sense perception is removed" (*On Purgatory*, book 2, chapter 9). And where there is no tinder for sin, there no sin at all can exist, not even venial sins. For if the cause is taken away then its effect is removed.

20. And add to this the fact that the distinction which the papal teachers make between venial and mortal sins goes against the definition of sin, for sin is not just "outside the Law" but even "contrary to the Law" and so it makes one liable to God's curse, for which there is no forgiveness. But since those who die in grace are not under the curse, and are not liable to any sin, because no sin is by its own nature so minor (whether that be 'due to the lightness of its subject-matter' or 'due to the incompleteness of its working') that it does not deserve an everlasting curse, since all transgression of the law is worthy of death (Deut 27:26). But Christ has taught that even the smallest sin is proscribed by God's law (Matt 5:22). And there is no exception for any sin for which Christ did not pour out his blood, since it purges us from all sin (1 John 1:7). If the stain of sin is not wiped away by Christ in anyone before he

dies, then he will forever experience the punishment of being not in some place that purges, but in hell. For "the wages of sin is death" (Rom 6:23).

21. Nor is the other basis that they place in support of purgatory and indulgences (whereof we must speak below) any more solid, namely that following the forgiveness of mortal guilt and eternal punishment there is some temporal penalty that must be discharged, either in this life by means of works that make satisfaction for penalties, or in the life hereafter, in some purgatorial fire. For these words assume that there are some satisfactions for sin besides the satisfaction of Christ, and the consequences that are associated with it show sufficiently that this teaching is foolish and blasphemous, i.e., "that Christ's merit does not then deserve to be called perfect satisfaction" (these are the words of [Ruard] Tapper, theologian at Leuven, in the *Explication of Articles*, tome 1 article 6). They are contrary to the explicit statements in Holy Scripture which testify that it was upon him [Christ] that the iniquities of us all were laid, and that He has redeemed us from all iniquity (Isa 53:6; Titus 2:14; 1 John 1:7, and countless other places).

22. And there are a few who are convinced by these testimonies, who confess "that Christ has made the fullest satisfaction for the liability of guilt of both temporal and eternal punishment of all sins" (Bellarmine, *On Indulgences*, book 2, chapter 10). And they nevertheless add things to it whereby they actually take away what they concede in their words. For they want none of Christ's satisfactions to be of any help for those people who fall into sins after baptism, unless they themselves have washed away their own sins by means of their own satisfactions—as if Christ's satisfaction was presented for the purpose that we ourselves should make satisfaction for our sins. By means of this reasoning they foolishly want Christ's satisfactions to be applied to us by means of our own satisfactions. But Scripture has no knowledge of this mode of application besides faith and the sacraments, and sound reasoning finds it abhorrent. For who has ever heard that punishment is applied by punishment, and that Christ's satisfaction is applied by means of purifying fires and torments? In what way would mercy be applied through the execution of righteousness in us; how would the remission of debts be applied through the exaction of a debt, and pardon be applied by means of punishment?

23. They continue to advance their fallacies by ignoring the proofs of our refutation, when they try by means of the many arguments sought from

Scripture and human experience to prove that after He has forgiven guilt, God afflicts the pious in various ways, also for sins that had been committed and forgiven. For this is not the point that is turned into doubt; but the crux of the matter is the question whether it is to make satisfaction for our sins that God inflicts such temporal punishment (whether the satisfaction is in whole or in part) rather than "to demonstrate the misery which we deserve, to correct our faulty lives, and to exercise the needed patience." This is what we contend, while we steadfastly deny the former piece that is stitched onto it by the papal teachers. And we make the assertion that the temporal punishments imposed on David and others after they had sinned have to do only with their instruction and testing, but were not (either in part or in whole) a ransom-price for sin, because after sin is forgiven "the things that are punishments for sin before remission, after remission has been granted become the contests and exercises of the righteous" (Augustine, *On the Merits and Remission of Sin*, book 2, chapter 34).

24. And moreover we assert that those punishments that chasten or cleanse do not reach beyond the boundaries of this life, a fact that is clearly shown from the goal for which they are usually imposed, which is partly to improve our own lives, partly as exemplary warning for others and as a precaution for ourselves for the future also. It is impossible for these things to have a place among the deceased: "For God chastises in order to correct, and he corrects in order to preserve us," as Cyprian well puts it (book 4, epistle 4). And Cyprian also "realizes that there is no place at all for repentance after death, and no effect from making satisfaction" (*To Demetrius*, treatise 1). And accordingly, Cyril used to teach his catechumens that "it is in this life only that we have the time prescribed for repentance and forgiveness of sins" (Cyril of Jerusalem, *Catechism* 18). For this current life is the time for healing. "But when punishment is viewed as a means of curing, then occasionally it happens that some pious person is punished without guilt on his part (since this guilt really is forgiven him through Christ) but not without a reason."— a distinction correctly made by Thomas (*Summa theologiae* 2/2, question 108, article 4).

25. And finally, from the punishments God inflicts there is not any consequence at all for people's imposition or voluntary undertaking of satisfactorial punishments, for if God should demand them as satisfactions then He would punish twice for the same act, and contrary to the laws of justice He would receive double satisfaction. For it is to no end that they give

as their response that our deeds of satisfaction are "subordinate" to Christ's satisfactions, for things that are opposite cannot be subordinated to each other. And these are in fact opposites: perfect and imperfect satisfaction, a once-for-all and a manifold satisfaction. In fact, an "imperfect satisfaction" is no satisfaction at all, since the added term contains a contradictory element. But if they take satisfaction to mean the required fulfillment of some condition or other in order to partake of Christ's satisfaction (which [fulfillment] through metaphor could be called 'satisfaction'), that could indeed be tolerated, although one would have to be wary of misapplying the term. But when they claim that we make satisfaction for our sins to God in the "true and proper sense," then they cannot be excused under any pretext whatsoever. Christ, who "by himself has made purification for our sins" (Heb 1:3) did not share this duty with anyone else.

26. But the places cited from Scripture are either examples wherein fruits that befit repentance are required, or they are difficult deeds the pious have undertaken, etc. They are less relevant to the matter at hand because these works had been demanded of or performed by living people only, and not by the deceased. These deeds should never be understood as being about satisfaction in the strict sense, but about merely fulfilling conditions that are required in us; or they are even about God's fatherly chastening, as has been said, and not about judicial punishment. For "there is not any condemnation for those who are in Christ" (Rom 8:1). Since their guilt has been forgiven it could not have been just to inflict any punishment as such. And since there is such a close connection between guilt and its proper punishment, the sacred language has expressed both of them mostly with one and the same word (Lev 16:9); and where the debt has been forgiven, there every obligation is taken away.

27. That need to make satisfaction for the liability of temporal punishment and venial guilts before obtaining the blessed inheritance is clearly overturned by the state of those who are alive on that very last day, who will "be caught up to meet the Lord" (1 Thess 4:17). For they will be changed in a split-second, in the twinkling of an eye, so that it is impossible to imagine a time and place for any purgatorial punishments. Therefore since the preaching of the Gospel (and the true faith that takes hold of Christ's merit) happens all the time and maintains the same force, what reason can there be why those who have died in bygone ages as well as those who are dying daily should be burned and tortured by fire any more than those who will be taken on that

very last day? What the papal teachers object is a very foolish thing to say, i.e., that those people must be purged by the very great tribulation that precedes the very last day as well as the fire that comes down from heaven when they will be taken to meet the Lord. Firstly, because all people will share in that final tribulation, and so by its own very nature it will not be purgatorial but will relate to the state of the current life (which we are not dealing with at this point). And secondly, the fire that comes down from heaven will not be purgatorial, but it will come down as a punishment for the impious and unbelieving, as the apostle testifies (2 Thess 1:8).

28. This being the case, we rightly relegate the purgatory of the papal teachers to the figments and fables of pagans and poets, from whom it took its origin. For we do not believe that if any such thing was recommended by Plato (in his *Gorgias* and *Phaedo*) or Cicero (in his *Dream of Scipio*), and Virgil (*Aeneid* 6) or Claudian the poet and similar writers, or if it was hinted at by the Quran of the Mohammedans or the Talmud of superstitious Jews, that it must therefore follow that those authors either had learned it from the people of God or by the light of nature had deduced it from known principles—unless there is some common belief that "there is need of a purging from sins before anyone can enjoy blessedness." But because they have no knowledge whatsoever of the premise about the true purging from sins in Christ and its application by the teaching of the Gospel, it is no surprise if in this matter (just as in the true knowledge of God) "they have become futile in their thinking, and their senseless hearts have been darkened" (Rom 1:21). And those who copy such folly within the Christian realm, who after Christ was revealed to them are being willfully blind, are all the more "without excuse" [Rom 1:20].

29. For we have already shown that what they produce from the Scriptures (both the Old and New Testaments) does not make for solid proof in the eyes of some papal teachers of great renown. In Matt 5:25 and Luke 12:58 Christ gives instruction about "reconciling with your opponent while we are on the way, etc.," a passage which Bellarmine twists into proof for purgatory (*On Purgatory*, book 1, chapter 7, throughout the entire chapter). But in fact the Jesuits Maldonado and Barradas saw nothing of the sort. In the *Harmony of the Gospels* (volume 2, book 7, chapter 17) the latter follows the opinion of Chrysostom and relates these words to hurrying up to reconcile and to solving lawsuits. But the former, since he explains it allegorically, together with Augustine thinks that the particle 'until' does not signify (to use

Augustine's words) "that they will go out afterwards, but that they will never go out, because those who are in hell never make full atonement for the penalties they owed, although they are always atoning for penalties." And so they acknowledge that their own brother Bellarmine has with his great efforts achieved nothing but great trifles.

30. The same Bellarmine (chapter 8) presses the passage in Matt 5:22, "whoever is angry with his brother" etc., in order to show that some temporal punishments are held back so that they may be paid after this life. But Maldonatus shows from the books of the Jews that all of those punishments were capital ones, and that Christ is making a distinction in degree, not in kind. And therefore that those about whom Christ is speaking will be struck by the same hellish punishments as those who do not deserve the same degree of punishment. Manoel de Sá has a different interpretation, but one that is equally opposed to purgatory, so that the sense is: 'the Scribes' teaching condemns the murderer, but I condemn even the man who is angry; they call the man who says "Raca" or "you fool" before their council, but I consign him to hell.' About the other passages which they produce for this purpose we make the general statement that they are apocryphal and extra-canonical, or entirely unrelated, or forcefully twisted, or altogether distorted, and that there is not even a single one of them that represents the word 'purgatory' or that contains any definition of it at all. Let it suffice to have shown one example here; the remainder will become clear in the [oral defense of the] disputation.

31. And what they cite for the same purpose from the church fathers and the councils cannot constitute an additional article of faith besides Scripture; even so, we provide this general advice: 1) In this case the papal teachers cite many spurious writings. 2) Very many authors they themselves adduced either make no mention of purgatory, or if there are those who do bring purgatory to mind they depict it as entirely different than the papal teachers do. 3) Moreover, there is not anyone among the genuine, older writers of earlier ages who wished to push the teaching of some purgatorial place as an article of faith. Bellarmine himself admits (*On Purgatory*, book 2, chapter 1) that "many fathers thought that after this life all people—good as well as wicked—had to be cleansed, with the exception of Christ." Origen, who was among the first to light the fire of purgatory, has people purified in it who are miscreants, sacrilegious, who in the midst of their crimes put an end to their lives (witness Augustine, *On Heretics*, chapter 43). But Augustine did

hesitate and doubt, not only over the nature of the punishments but also over the matter itself: "It is unbelievable that something like this happens also after this life, and one could question whether it is so" (*Enchiridion*, chapter 69). And elsewhere: "I do not argue against it, because perhaps it is true" (*City of God*, book 21, chapter 26).

32. And although they posit it as certain and beyond debate, the consequence they draw is a foolish one, namely that all those who promoted prayers and offerings on behalf of the deceased believed in purgatory. And they put those people who deny the usefulness of prayers and offerings in the company of heretics. For even if it is true that the custom of praying for the deceased is an old one, it is no less certain that the ancients had different reasons for considering it useful. For even the Greek church, Alphonso de Castro says, "has that custom until today, and yet to this very day the Greeks do not believe in purgatory" ([*Against Heresies*,] On Indulgences, book 8).

33. And in fact the primary reason why they poured out prayers for the deceased stems from the very doctrine that nowadays the papal teachers themselves consider among the errors, namely "that so many and such illustrious ancient fathers as Tertullian, Irenaeus, Origen, Chrysostom, Theodoret, Ambrose, Clement of Rome, and Bernard did not agree with this line of thinking (which the council of Florence, upon extensive discussion, determined to be a dogma of faith), that the souls of the righteous enjoy beholding God before judgment day; but they taught the opposite line of thinking," as Stapleton admits (*On the Authority of* [*the Church Regarding the Holy*] *Scriptures*, book 1, chapter 2, section 5). And to these Sixtus of Siena adds Justin Martyr, Lactantius, Victorinus, Prudentius, Arethas, etc. (*Bibliotheca Sancta*, book 6, annotation 345). It is not surprising if in this "delay in the resurrection" (as Tertullian calls it) they considered the prayers for the deceased useful, because of this exile of all the souls and penalty of punishment of damnation (though not a punishment of the senses). And the fact that the papal teachers themselves consider the basis to be an unstable one, we—who have been taught differently by Scripture—should not copy a rite that has no usefulness and is even harmful to the saints.

34. The kind of proof from the appearances of souls reporting that they have been in purgatory, and who seem to be begging the living for help we relegate to forged fables, or to the dreams of the insane, the possessed, and those who have been afflicted by fevers. And we relegate them also to the often-

disclosed deceits of the devil, deceits whereby people deserve to be fooled who "do not consult with God but with the dead on behalf of the living" (Isa 8:19). A delirious Bellarmine himself offers us an instance of such blind folly in *The Sighing Dove* (book 2, chapter 9) where he retells a story from Bede about the vision of a certain Dryhthelm who had seen a valley filled with the souls of men whereof one side bristled with burning fires, and another with a raging hailstorm and icy-cold snows blowing everywhere. And there he saw wretched souls that when they could not bear the force of the heat would leap headlong into the middle of the cold; and then they would shiver in the cold and, in unhappy succession, return into the midst of the flames. He says, "I do not doubt that this account is very true because it agrees with Scripture, which says in Job chapter 24[:19]: 'they cross from ice-cold waters to excessive heat.'" The same author relates another story, more suited to old-wives and madwomen, about a certain Christina whom the angels carried to Paradise when she died, and God gave her the choice of staying with Him forever or returning to earth in order to complete the most grievous penalties for the sake of setting free souls from purgatory. She made the choice to suffer, with the stipulation that after she had amassed many merits she would return to God. And so thereupon she entered into burning ovens, was tormented, gave forth horrendous cries, and finally came out—unharmed. And during the winter she lasted six days and more under the waters of the Maas, when everything was frozen stiff with cold. What is more, all her limbs were unharmed when she was fastened to the wheel of a mill and turned around and around in a horrible manner, etc. What sane person does not see that those are the devil's deceptions? And still Bellarmine says: "Look, here we have trustworthy eye-witnesses, a man and a woman, who have seen the harshest punishments of purgatory, so that those who do not believe these things are clearly without excuse." For in this way "God has sent to them the power of deception to believe a lie, because they did not receive a love for the truth that they might be saved" (2 Thess 2:10–11).

35. And no less fanciful is the argument which they draw from utility, namely that whoever thinks that besides hell there exists the fiercest fire of purgatory and that whatever has not been erased by the works that were owed for penitence must be atoned for there, lives with greater zeal and caution, while the opinion that takes away purgatory instead makes men careless in avoiding sin and in performing good works. As though those people who are undeterred by hell-fire will care at all about an imaginary fire, and as though

that [imaginary fire] will not rather give an opportunity for sin to those who think that they can free themselves from those flames by the help of others. This help wealthier people can obtain for themselves by an easy business deal. And especially the 'Master of Sentences' himself doesn't fear to make the claim that "in purgatory the wealthy obtain forgiveness more quickly than the poor" (*Sententiae*, book 4, distinction 45, letter d). And Albertus Magnus says that "there can be so much assistance for any one person that he is immediately set free in a moment of time, and that therefore in this matter the wealthy man's state is better than that of the poor, as he has the wherewithal for assistance to come in his own behalf, whence Prov 13[:8] says: 'A rich man's wealth is his ransom' " (*On the Mystery of the Office of the Mass*, treatise 3, chapter 16). Hence it surely is not piety that is increased by this, but instead the incomes of the churches' clerics, who "in their greed exploit people with lying words" (2 Pet 2:3), and while those people stress purgatory, they themselves are living lives of debauchery. Not only do reports bear witness to the fact that this is happening at Rome (where the doctrine of purgatory is doing exceptionally well) but also experience itself speaks loud and clear.

36. This being the case, it is our conclusion that purgatory does not have any authority from Scriptures, not any credibility based on the testimonies of the fathers, nor any likelihood based on logical arguments, such as especially the papal teachers believed, in whose writings the components do not hold the building together, which is bound up in a variety of ill-fitting and contradictory elements. It will be obvious to everyone that this statement is true, not just from the things that we have said thus far, but even when one reads the books of our opponents (especially Bellarmine) wherein one scarcely meets one or two chapters which do not cite divers opinions and principles that very often even contradict the writings of the papal teachers. And while they are crossing swords with each other, we rest with grateful hearts in the sole satisfaction of Christ, stating with certainty that those who firmly abide in Christ as the author of life should not be afraid of any purgatorial fire after this life.

On Indulgences

37. Once the fire of purgatory has been extinguished, the smoke of indulgences vanishes by itself. For with the removal of purgatory scarcely anyone will be found who would accept indulgences, even if they were

offered for free. Accordingly, the bishop of Rochester in *Against Luther* (article 13) when he saw that the origin of indulgences is not certain and admitted that it was only lately that Christians had accepted them as true, he brought forward the following reason: "That the ancients make no, or very little, mention of purgatory, and that until this very day the Greeks do not believe in it. And as long as there was no concern about purgatory, no-one looked for indulgences, on which every evaluation of indulgences depends, and if that is removed, there will be no need for indulgences. And therefore, no-one can be surprised that at the start of the growing church there was no use for them, since it was so late that purgatory became known to the universal church." Gregory of Valencia himself admits that "since the practice of penitence was thriving more pointedly among the ancients, there was no great need to have the benefit of indulgences, but that later, when that fervor of penitence diminished, the use of indulgences began to increase" (*Treatise on Indulgences*, chapter 4).

38. And besides, there are others who even admit not only "that there are no clear testimonies in Scripture about indulgences, and they advise their fellow Catholics not to rely on things that are less certain, but they also add that they do not have certain testimonies of the early, primitive church, and that in this matter they do not have the apostolic tradition" but only the authority of the Roman church and of some (actually recent) councils—as may be seen in the writings of Peter de Soto, in his *Lectures on the Institution of Priesthood* (*On Indulgences*, lecture 1). Nevertheless, they push their doctrine about indulgences as an article of faith, and define it as "the exemptions from temporal punishments that in God's judgment are owed for actual sins after the guilt has been forgiven, through the application of the excess deeds of satisfaction of Christ and the saints, done apart from the sacrament by someone who has the lawful authority to do so" (Gregory of Valencia, volume 4, disputation 7, question 20.1).

39. If we explain this definition according to their intended meaning and point out the folly of each individual part, we shall untie an otherwise knotty topic in a few words. We shall give them the benefit as far as the name ['indulgence'] is concerned, because for the most part the name is understood in a more pejorative sense. Even so, they use it for this subject-matter in an inauspicious way, as in 'the loving indulgence of fathers makes their children slothful,' so that 'good fathers' have it in them to indulge their nature. "For indulgences came about in order to lighten the church of its poverty, which

is not lightened only by the will to give but by the gift" (Augustine of Ancona, *On the Sovereignty of the Pope*, question 30, article 3). Therefore, they give in order to receive, and they do not indulge for nothing. When they say that indulgences are "the exemptions from temporal punishments, etc.," the words expose the primary basis for this business transaction, i.e., concerning some temporal, satisfactorial punishments of a penitent man whose guilt has been forgiven by God's grace but to whom punishments are still owed and which must be paid either in this life or in purgatory. We overturned this basis above, in theses 32–35, so that this need not be done at this point.

40. But the gamble of the papal teachers gives itself away when they prove that after their guilt has been forgiven believers still remain subject to temporal punishments either by actually paying for them or by obtaining exemption by means of indulgences. When it comes to the point, they are compelled to admit that no exemption via indulgences is possible for penalties on the basis of the indulgences they sometimes show from Scriptures as imposed on some believers such as David and the like. But the artificial penalties of purgatory are either ones that people commanded, or have to command, or undertake willingly. Therefore, indulgences not only do not absolve from the liability of any mortal or venial guilt, but they also do not absolve from any natural penalties such as diseases, death, ignorance, concupiscence, and similar things. And they also do not absolve even from the punishments that can be inflicted by the outward, the litigious forums (ecclesiastical as well as political). But they can only remove the penalty that is owed in the hidden forum of one's repentance, according to Bellarmine (*On Indulgences*, book 1, chapter 7).

41. It is obvious from these observations that the many people who purchase these wares at a great price and who have been enticed by the lofty promises of "fulsome and the fullest indulgence" for all sins (often with the added phrase, "from punishment and guilt") experience what the proverb says, that "in exchange for their treasures they possess nothing but coal." For because those punishments that are mentioned in Ps 89[:32 and 33] ("If your sons sin, I shall punish their iniquities with the rod") and in Heb 12[:6] (when the apostle says, "we receive discipline from God") and also in 1 Cor 11[:32] ("God judges and instructs us") are inflicted upon us by God as the "external, criminal judge," Bellarmine grants that they are not taken away by indulgences (*On Indulgences*, book 2, chapter 1), but that only the penalty is removed "which is inflicted in the penitentiary forum, a penalty that we are

driven to fulfill only by the fear of God and the goad of our own conscience." From this the objection which Luther rightly had made becomes very obvious, namely that indulgences are harmful, not beneficial, since they hinder us from doing good works (fasting, almsgiving, prayers) and in fact dispel "the fear of God and the goad of our own conscience." For "by means of permitted indulgences man makes satisfaction for the penalties that were imposed in confession, so that in case the Confessor imposed upon him a discipline, fasting, almsgiving, or some similar works to be performed, if he obtains the indulgence he is not bound to undergo the penalties" ([Francisco de] Toledo, *Instructions for Priests*, book 6, chapter 24).

42. But so that the zeal of those who in the dispensing of indulgences seek something greater should not grow cold, they stoked the flames of purgatory in order to inflict terror. And so the following 'fear-factor' was added: if it should happen that someone dies before he has completed the penalty of ten years that has been imposed, he will be punished with the fiercest penalty in purgatory, but from there he would fly as a free man to heaven if, properly equipped with letters of the fullest indulgence, he should show them to the gate-keeper of heaven. Hence it is that indulgences are granted for many thousands of years, because even if this time by far surpasses a man's life-time, still for one mortal sin a penalty of seven years must be imposed and it can happen to many people that they have committed more than one thousand mortal sins, who according to the canonical rules should spend seven thousand years in penitence if they were to have lived that many years. In this manner provision is made for them, namely by granting indulgence for so many thousands of years that is not only equal to but even surpasses the penitence they should have fulfilled if they had done thousands of years of penitence. To have pointed out these ominous signs is to have refuted them.

43. In order to supply satisfactions for so many years and for such countless temporal punishments from another source, they also laid a second basis for indulgences, namely that of the "excess satisfactions of Christ and the saints," which the Roman popes, and the other bishops according to their lesser measure, keep locked up in their treasury, on the assumption that the satisfaction of Christ, being absolutely infinite, could not have received any equivalent created reward and had merited infinitely more than any reward that He had been given. [And also on the basis that] "many saintly men have suffered much more for the sake of God and righteousness than their liability

to temporal punishment required, to which they were subject for the wrongs they had committed," and they redeem even some others from their every guilt. They put all these things together and poured them into their mixer to fashion that lump from which they could dispense small pieces in the form of indulgences.

44. And as far as we are concerned, whatever slanderous charge they should make against us, we piously acknowledge that the satisfaction of our Lord Jesus Christ is a treasury of invaluable worth that has been entrusted to the church of God. From this treasury are dispensed upon people who are truly penitent and believe in Him, indulgences that are real and valid in the sight of God, or rather the fullest remission of sins, remission from every penalty and guilt of original as well as actual sins. But we do assert that the papal teachers do injury to this satisfaction of Christ when, in order to add the satisfaction of men, they take away the limitless quality of Christ's satisfaction, because they deem that "his satisfactions must be applied in a limited way so that something may be added to them when the sufferings of the saints are linked to them," as Bellarmine says (*On Indulgences*, book 1, chapter 4). But we state that this not only adds a finite thing to what is infinite, but nothing to what is entire, for it is false and foolish what they say about the sufferings of the saints, i.e., that they possess a double force. Of this double force one is "meritorious" while the other is "satisfactorial," and regarding the merit they have received their full reward, but not regarding the satisfaction. For the works of the saints have neither of these aspects. But even Durand rightly proves that they did not have the satisfactorial quality from the fact that it was not the saints' intention to transfer the fruit of their own sufferings unto others—an intention that would have been necessary, at least. But such an intention could not have existed for the saints, as it would have been a haughty and blasphemous one.

45. If the suffering of the saints were satisfactory for other people and together with Christ's blood formed the treasury, then the distinction would be taken away that the apostle makes in Heb 12:24 between Christ's blood and the blood of Abel, for then "the blood of Christ would speak no more eloquently than the blood of Abel" (Heb 12:24). For then either one could have obtained forgiveness of the punishment for sins. And Solomon would have written in vain: "If you are wise, you are wise for yourself; but if you are a mocker, you alone will bear the evil" (Prov 9:12). Nor would "anyone boast only in himself and not boast in another" (Gal 6:4). And there would not

have been any reason why God through Ezekiel (14:20) should say about Noah, Daniel and Job that "they did not set free their own sons and daughters, but by their righteousness they set free only their own souls." There never was any saint who would not have concurred with Tertullian when he asks: "Who has paid for the death of another by his own except the Son of God alone? And so, you who imitate him by forgiving misdeeds, if you yourself have committed no misdeeds, then suffer on my behalf. But if you are a sinner, how could the oil of your torch have sufficed both for you and for me?" (*On Modesty*, chapter 22). And who would not have joined hands with Augustine when he says: "Even though brothers would die for brothers, yet in the forgiveness of brothers' sins not any martyr's blood is poured out" (*On John*, Treatise 84).

46. And yet there should be no fear that the saints' sufferings are in vain, for they serve different uses and goals whereof no doubt can be raised. But they are in vain insofar as their satisfactory powers are concerned, and there is nothing troublesome about the fact that they are without such result if they are not applied to those who need [satisfaction]. For not even the papal teachers deny that the sufferings of all the saints who will still be alive on the Day of the Lord will be in vain. So too for the sufferings that at that time will still be left in the Church's treasury, because then there will not be any people to whom they could be dispensed, unless perhaps the papal teachers think that when purgatory is emptied out there will still be "some days of rest for the guilty spirits under the [river] Styx," or that these souls will emerge at last by the power of the satisfactions—a mad idea that once upon a time fooled some of them who found prayer for the dead appealing.

47. But the 'communion of the saints' does not require the communication of satisfactions for sin. For 'communion' is different from 'communication,' since communion presupposes some common thing whereto the people among whom the communion exists have an equal right. The same relationship does not exist for something that the one who does not need it communicates with someone else who does lack it. On the contrary, the communion of saints completely overturns the notion of this or that man's particular satisfactions, because just as our communion consists of the fact that we have the same God, the same faith, the same baptism, and the same Spirit, and not in the fact that we communicate to other people the Spirit, faith or baptism that is superfluous for us, so also the communion of the saints consists in the fact that they all have the right to the one satisfaction of

Christ. And so the argument from the 'communion of saints' is effectively turned around against our opponents.

48. Nor is it a more firm foundation that supports what they mean by the 'communication' that should have its place also among Christians, for the communication ought to be of those goods that can be communicated and passed from one person to another. But it is impossible to prove that the sufferings of believers are goods of this sort. Nor can any reason be brought forward why "the part of a good work that is meritorious cannot be applied to others"—a fact that Bellarmine admits (*On Indulgences*, book 1, chapter 2)—whereas the part of the same work that is satisfactory can be communicated. Add to this the fact that satisfaction is not some good in an absolute sense but relative to the one to whom satisfaction is made. Therefore, even if someone were to establish such participation and communication on the part of the members with the intention to make satisfaction, it does not for that reason follow that there is acceptance on the part of the 'creditor,' without which the application of the communication would be altogether useless.

49. Therefore the statement they make is false, that another's satisfactions applied by the church's prelates are "means" whereby the fruit of Christ's infinite satisfaction is drawn down to men insofar as the forgiveness of punishment is concerned, for they cannot show that Christ has instituted this sort of means. Moreover, since Christ's satisfaction "is applied in a limited way" so that the satisfactions of saints may in fact be added to it (as we have shown from Bellarmine), it is sufficiently clear from their doctrine that the saints' satisfactions are applied in the same way as Christ's satisfactions—and consequently they are not the applications of the satisfaction of another, but are properly and of themselves considered together with Christ's satisfactions to be of the same kind. The promoters of indulgences want that by the power of love, whereby the members of the church are united with one another, "the payment which one has made on behalf of another would be received in such a way on his behalf as if he himself had offered it." This surely cannot be done without imputing the righteousness of another. And since apart from and against Scripture they grant that imputation to the satisfactions of men, it is surprising that the same people still mockingly accept the doctrine of the imputation of the righteousness of Christ our head, from whose very close union with all his true members the communication of all good things flows forth unto the eternal salvation of the elect.

50. Only his sufferings have the power to make satisfaction, and as they are communicated to believers by means of imputation, as the only Redeemer he has claimed this for himself. But in "that he has suffered on our behalf and has left us an example" (1 Pet 2:21), namely that we should undergo suffering for the sake of others, "not by the mode of redemption but through the mode of example and encouragement, according to that" [saying] that if we suffer tribulations it is for your encouragement and salvation, says Thomas (*Summa theologiae* 3, question 48, article 5, point 3). It is in this sense that he understands the apostle's statement: "I rejoice in my sufferings for you and in my flesh I fill up those things that are lacking from Christ's passions for the sake of his body, which is the Church" (Col 1:24). Or "what is lacking" are the things that each and every member of the church must suffer following the suffering of Christ; this is the meaning approved by the Jesuit, Gabriel Vasquez (*Annotations* to the Epistle to the Colossians). But he considers the plainer meaning to be the one he pursues as follows in his paraphrase: "I, who now rejoice that I suffer so many afflictions for your sake, by having endured them to the full in myself in the Gospel-preaching fill up what was lacking to Christ's suffering, so that the fruit of it through the labor of the Gospel-preaching might reach the body of the church, when by hearing it everyone might individually receive faith and be justified." Therefore it is not so that thence some satisfaction might come about by the bestowing of indulgences.

51. Since a nonbeing is not susceptible to any relations, it would be superfluous to treat further "the church's authority in the collection" of such indulgences: whether the authority is given only to the pope and the bishops "by divine right" and to others only "by commission." And: whether indulgences are applied through genuine absolution or through a dispensation only from the treasury. Whether indulgences are applied in the same way to the living as to the dead, or whether to the living "through the mode of absolution" and to the dead only "through the mode of assistance;" or whether it is given only to those "who are in grace." And similarly, what is a "plenary" indulgence, a "Carena," a "forty-day" indulgence? And, whether for small causes not any great indulgences at all are granted, or whether they have any such value as the cause demands, and what is a just cause for granting them, concerning which the patrons of indulgences argue with each other. Nor is there any agreement between them about the value of indulgences, about the treasury, the sufficiency of a cause, the disposition

of the recipient, etc. And the teachers de Soto and Victoria do not deny that the "certificates whereby the fullest indulgences are bestowed in return for the smallest almsgiving contain an intolerable mistake," as Joseph Angles reports ([*Flowers of Theological Questions*] *on the Sentences*, book 4, [Question regarding Indulgences], article 2, difficulty 5).

52. Nor should it cause trouble if anyone occasionally stumbles across mention of indulgence in the records of the ancients, for even now Peter de Soto admits that the papal teachers possess no definitive testimony from the ancient church. The matter, then, is as follows. Those early fathers, especially in serious, public sins, would not absolve and reconcile the sinner until he had proved his repentance to the church with long, hard and difficult exercises. But if persecution was about to happen, the penitents would sometimes be absolved beforehand, so that they might go to their martyrdom with greater courage. The same would happen if someone already in the process of penitence found himself in danger of dying, or if such zeal of contrition were observed in the sinner that there was no need for a longer period of testing, or if an accompanying repentance was bound up with it. The church would aid such people by means of indulgences to relax the strictest severity somewhat. Not only the statement of the fathers but also Paul's (which the patrons of indulgences misuse) should be taken in this way: "Anyone whom you forgive I also forgive, for also I, if I have forgiven anything, did so for your sake in the presence of Christ" (2 Cor 2:10), namely, "so that the man who had been excommunicated should not be overwhelmed by overflowing grief" (verse 7).

53. What rendered the institution of the hundred-year Jubilee disreputable was that most shameless business-dealing in sacred matters as well as the consideration of its very founder, Boniface the Eighth (who "took office as a fox, ruled like a lion, and died like a dog"), as he used to thirst for "gold obtained from any place at all, more than one could say," as Platina attests. Driven by the same mad lust, Clement the Sixth followed in his footsteps and he "(it is doubtful whether by a lust for money or a desire for men's salvation) gave the sanction that the Jubilee should be celebrated every fifty years." And later, Sixtus the Fifth, whose ambition and cunning was known to all, reduced it to every twenty-five years. Clement the Eighth calls [the Jubilee] "the Lord's year of appeasement, the year of forgiveness and pardon, the acceptable time, and the day of eternal salvation" in the announcement-bull (which really was a boil!). Over against him we put forward the sure certificate of the Christian

Jubilee (Isa 61:2; Luke 4:19): "The Lord has sent me to proclaim the acceptable year of Jehovah," namely the most joyful preaching of the Gospel brought from the bosom of the eternal Father, in which is announced to all believers, the real penitents, the liberation from all sins and all penalties for sins, in every time and place.

54. And for that reason we should give our utmost thanks to God because in the time of our forebears, when He had allowed the business-dealing of indulgences to reach the acme of shamelessness when Leo the Tenth opened public market-squares throughout all the kingdoms of the world, He raised up Martin Luther, who at first was thinking of nothing else than to punish the unlimited abuses, gradually, in God's providence and by his enemies recklessly providing a cause, was led not merely to overturn the entire system of indulgences from its very foundations, but thence also, when his enemies took refuge in those commonplaces of proof for the pope's authority (and the like), by pursuing them was finally led to the point of tearing down usurped power of the pope himself, until little by little through his ministry that marvelous work of the reformation of true doctrine was promoted through him and others, which afterward in God's greatest goodwill was spread far and wide during our own times. Thus it remains that we, acknowledging the true source of the forgiveness of sins, and then being washed in it, should abstain from sins, and bring glory to God the Father, in Christ the Son, and through the Holy Spirit forever.

Corollary

1. We declare that the *Limbo of children*, whereto the papal teachers send the souls of infants who have departed from this life without the outward washing of baptism, does not rest upon any basis in Scripture or earliest antiquity.

2. We state that it is an invention alien to the truth and to reason that some people after this life are punished in hell by the punishment of damnation but are exempt from the total punishment of the senses.

3. It is an invention from a spirit of Marcionism that the patriarchs and all the saints of the Old Testament were detained in the world below, as Tertullian testifies (*Against Marcion*, book 4, chapter 34): "Both conditions, whether of the torment or of the relief which determines their state in the

underworld, are laid upon those who were obedient to the law and the prophets."

ON THE CHURCH

President: Antonius Walaeus
Respondent: Jacobus Bosschaert

This is the first of three disputations on Reformed ecclesiology (Disputations 40–43). 'Ecclesia,' or the Church, is defined etymologically as 'the meeting of those whom God in his grace calls out from the state of nature into the supernatural state of children of God, in order to show his glorious mercy' (3). In this regard the teaching of the Church relates to God's call to salvation. Also the elect angels belong to the same family of Christ (6). The following aspects are successively discussed: the parts of the Church and their mode and form (8–25); the division of the Church into the Church of the Old and the New Testament, and into visible and invisible (26–36); and finally, the privileges and marks of the Church (37–51). The triumphant part of the Church is in heaven and consists of believers from both the Old and the New Testament (9–21). The other part of the Church is still fighting against the flesh, the world, and Satan (22–25). It is necessary for believers to belong to this Church, to have communion with each other, and to be joined together by the bond of Word and Sacraments (24). The invisible Church (28–31) is the multitude of elect believers of which the inner form (consisting of true faith and holiness) is not seen by human eyes, by mortal people (28). The visible Church (32–36) is 'the gathering of those who through the outward Word, the use of the sacraments, and church discipline, are formed together into one outward body and fellowship' (32). Hypocrites and godless people are mixed in with it (35). As for the marks of the Church, a distinction is made between erring and committing heresy. When false teachings are promoted that 'do not ruin the foundation of the faith' (1 Cor 3:11), a church errs (38). Heresy occurs when the Church errs obstinately in the fundamental articles of the faith (39–41). A believer ought not to join a church that is heretical or schismatic (42). Positively, the marks of the pure, visible Church are 'the pure preaching, and reception, of the Word, sealed by the lawful use of the sacraments, and upheld by the true use of the keys (or church discipline), according to the institution by Christ' (45). In the last three theses the many marks of the Church that are employed by Roman Catholic teachers are shown to be applied in such a way that it proves itself a false church (49–51).

1. 'Ecclesia' is a Greek word that comes from *ekkalein*, which is 'to call out,' and it corresponds to the Hebrew words *qahal* and *'edah*, and strictly speaking means a meeting or gathering of people who have been called by some higher authority, not solely for a purpose or end that is sacred, but also for non-religious and political ones, as can be seen in Acts 19:32 and 39.

2. But we here take the word 'Ecclesia' in the sense of a meeting or gathering that is sacred, as Christians commonly understand it. Occasionally they use it for the place where they hold sacred gatherings, but examples of this meaning do not occur in Scripture.

3. In general the meaning of the word is defined as the meeting of those whom God in his grace calls out from the state of nature into the supernatural state of children of God, in order to show his glorious mercy.

4. In the Church of Christ it is beyond dispute that God is the primary author of this calling, since He alone can bestow the grace to which He calls, and ordain the means whereby this calling is to be made, just as the apostle says in Heb 3:4: "For every house is built by someone, but the one who has built all these"—and he is speaking about the Church of Christ—"is God."

5. The subject-matter, or object of this calling are only the creatures who have been made in the image of God, that is, angels and men. For although God is able to make sons of Abraham from stones, as Christ says in Matt 3:9, yet only creatures made in the image of God are of themselves and directly capable of receiving blessed immortality and heavenly happiness.

6. Only a few things are revealed to us in the Scriptures about the calling of some angels from the state of mutable nature to the immutable state of glorious grace. Nevertheless, because everywhere they are specifically called the sons of God, angels of light, angels of glory, and elect angels, and because they also recognize Christ himself as their special head (Eph 1:22), and because they call themselves our fellow servants, fellow-servants of the brothers, and even belonging to the brothers who have the testimony of Jesus (Rev 19:10), it follows that we should profess that they are members of that entire body, and our fellow-servants in the family of Christ. And consequently, through the particular working of the Holy Spirit under Christ

the one and only Head of his Church, they are effectively established in glory and grace. Therefore, the apostle declares that we, too, have come to the myriads of angels through the effective calling (Heb 12:22).

7. Yet even though this fellowship with angels is a source of glory and comfort to us, still we should give special treatment to the Church of human beings because that is of the greatest interest to us. And about that Church we must investigate: the parts of the Church and their mode and form, the division of the Church, and finally the privileges and marks of the Church.

8. When the parts of the Church are considered as a whole, the papal teachers determine three parts for it, i.e., one that is laboring in purgatory, the second that is triumphant in heaven, and the third that is militant here on earth. We recognize with pleasure the two latter parts of the Church; but in a prior disputation we have demonstrated sufficiently that their third one is from outside of God's Word and invented, for the sake of emptying out money-supplies and oppressing the souls of god-fearing people with spiritual slavery. And so, in what follows we need only to treat the other two parts.

9. All the places that show convincingly the immortality of the soul prove over-against the Socinians, Anabaptists, Libertines, and similar heretics that a large part of the universal Church is triumphant in heaven under Christ its head. For while "the body returns to the earth from where it came, yet the spirit returns to God who has given it" (Eccl 12:7). And although "there are those who can kill the bodies of the pious, yet they cannot kill their souls," as Christ testifies in Matt 10:28.

10. But this is clear especially from those places and instances that depict the happiness and blessed state of the deceased. As we see in Matt 20:8, where "all who labored in the vineyard, when their labor has been completed, receive their reward," in 2 Cor 5:1: "We know that if the earthly dwelling-place is broken down, we have another, eternal home in heaven not made with hands," and in Rev 14:13: "Blessed are the dead who die in the Lord, from this time forth they rest from their labors, and their works follow them."

11. But contrary to the papal teachers we must maintain that not only believers under the New Testament, after Christ's ascension into heaven, but also believers who died in the faith under the Old Testament, reached this part of the triumphant Church in heaven. They, on the other hand, think that

those people had been locked up in a subterranean limbo and from there they have been looking for the coming of the Lord.

12. The promises of Christ demonstrate this, as do other places in Scripture, and also very clear exemplary instances.

13. The promises are clear: "There is fullness of joys most pleasant in your presence, at your right hand forevermore" (Ps 16:11). "Blessed are the poor in spirit, for theirs is the kingdom of heaven" (Matt 5:3), and "Blessed are the pure of heart, for they shall see God" (verse 8). "Blessed are those who suffer persecution, for theirs is the kingdom of heaven. Rejoice and be glad, because great is your reward in heaven; for thus they persecuted the prophets, etc." (verse 10). Without a doubt these sayings of Christ were true already then when he declared them, and did not become true only when Christ rose from the dead and ascended into heaven.

14. The passages from Scripture which reveal the state of the pious who have died before Christ's suffering are no less clear. Such passages include Eph 1:10: "God unites all things both in heaven and on earth in Christ," and Col 1:20: "And through Christ all things were reconciled, both in heaven and on earth." Since this manner of speaking cannot mean those angels who were not reconciled to God through Christ, it follows that it must mean the saints dwelling in heaven before [the advent of] Christ, just as the apostle says in Heb 12:22 that so we "have come to Mount Zion and to the city of the living God, the heavenly Jerusalem," etc., and "to the meeting and assembly of the first-born who are enrolled in heaven."

15. Scripture also presents to us brilliant examples of this state: Elijah (2 Kgs 2:11) is said expressly to have been carried into heaven, and 1 Macc 2:58 confirms it. Moses and Elijah appeared on the mountain in the company of Christ and three disciples, in glory; and then they were taken away from before their eyes by a cloud (Luke 9:31). And from that cloud a voice came down: "This is my Son, etc." And Peter testifies to the fact that this voice came down from heaven (2 Pet 1:18). The angels carried Lazarus into the bosom of Abraham. But the Scriptures say nowhere that the angels carried believers to places under the earth, since their proper dwelling is in heaven. Matt 8:11 states explicitly that this bosom of Abraham, wherein the faithful recline, is heaven. Christ says: "I say to you that they will come from East and West and recline with Abraham, Isaac, and Jacob in the kingdom of heaven." And lastly, the same is confirmed by the example of the thief who

was crucified together with Christ, whom Christ promised that on the same day he would be with him in Paradise (Luke 23:43). The apostle asserts that Paradise is the third heaven (2 Cor 12:2 and 4).

16. From these passages it is clear that before Christ's coming the fathers were no less triumphant in heaven by the power of the coming Christ than under the New Testament now that they are reigning by the power of Christ after he suffered and was taken up into heaven.

17. In fact we assert from Scripture that the pious who have died under either of both testaments are not just enjoying some heavenly joy apart from the presence of God, as some of the great men used to think, but that they are fully enjoying true and unbroken blessedness in God's very presence. Even so we do not deny that some degree of happiness is kept aside for them until the last day, when [their souls] will be joined to their bodies.

18. This is demonstrated by very many places of Scripture, for also David locates the place of their true blessedness as the presence of God (Ps 16, 23 and 84). And Paul desires "to depart and to be with Christ" (Phil 1:23); and 2 Cor 5:8: "And so we choose rather to depart from the body and go to dwell with the Lord." The apostle testifies that Christ is with the Father, and on the Father's throne (Rev 3:21; John 17:5; Heb 9:24). Therefore, also throughout Revelation the deceased saints are placed together with the angels before the throne of God and the Lamb, so that they sing constant praises and give thanks to Him, as can be seen in Rev 4:8, 5:8, and 7:9.

19. However, it does not therefore follow that this part of the Church that is triumphant is therefore put in charge of the militant Church on earth, as in the dream of those papal teachers who put them in charge of kingdoms, provinces, cities and districts—even diseases, the arts, peace and war—like patron deities. For even if Holy Scripture does assign the angels some common ministry in these matters, it testifies everywhere that the deceased saints "enter into peace and rest from their labors" (Isa 57:2; Rev 14:13), "and that they do not arise or return again to their own home, nor does their place know them any more" (Job 7:10); "in fact, if their children increase, they are unaware of it, and if they are brought low, they do not perceive it" (Job 14:21). Likewise, "we shall go to them but they will not return to us" (2 Sam 12:23), and "they do not see all the evil that God brings upon his people" (2 Kgs 22:20).

20. And in fact it contradicts the nature of deceased saints that they should be present in and care for diverse and widely scattered places at one and the same time, as when the [papal teachers] want to put one and the same saint in charge of diverse and widely scattered places. Think of Saint James for the Spanish, who dwell in Europe, India, and America. Or Saints Dominic and Francis, etc., for all their monasteries spread across the whole globe. Or even the blessed Virgin, whom they call Queen of Heaven, Mistress of the Earth, and Star of the Sea (*Stella Maris*)—even though this is a wrong rendering of Drop of the Sea (*Stilla maris*)—since it is fitting only for God to "look down from the heavens and behold all the sons of men, and from his dwelling-place to look forth upon all the inhabitants of the earth" (Ps 33:13–14).

21. And therefore what Matt 24:47 says about the faithful servant's command over all his master's goods should be understood as being about spiritual goods, as in Rom 8:17: "We are called heirs of God and fellow-heirs with Christ." And also, what Rev 2 and 3 say about ruling over the nations with an iron rod, and being seated on God's throne should necessarily be understood allegorically, about the complete glory and dominion over Satan, the world, and the flesh, as Paul explains in 1 Cor 15:56 and John in Rev 5:10 and 21:7.

22. Having explained briefly the things concerning that part of the Church that is triumphant in heaven, let us go down to that part of the Church which is still fighting or battling against the flesh, the world and Satan, as Paul says in Gal 5:17; 1 John 5:4, and Eph 6:12.

23. The very many promises found in Jer 31:36, Matt 16:18, Matt 28:20, etc., about the preservation of the Church, show clearly that there always has been a Church on earth, and that there shall be one until the end of the world. The office of Christ clearly shows this, as he is the eternal King, Bridegroom, Shepherd, and Head of this Church, which he cannot be if there is no kingdom, bride, flock, and body that he makes alive here on earth. And finally, it is shown clearly by the office of all those who will be saved, because no-one can have God for a Father who does not have the Church for a mother, as Paul testifies (Gal 4:26).

24. But what the Libertines claim is not enough, that individual members of the Church of Christ say that they separately foster spiritual communion with the unknown church, even if they do not foster any outward communion at all with any meeting, or even if they pretend to foster a communion with

idolatrous and apostate meetings. But we assert that in order to establish the true Church it is necessary for believers to have communion with each other, and to be joined together by the bond of Word and Sacraments according to their institution by Christ, unless it happens because of extreme persecution that they are compelled to break off their communion for a short time.

25. The promise of particular grace that is made for those who have been gathered in the name of the Lord demonstrates this (Matt 18:20), and so too the goal of the institution of the Word and sacraments and of the use of discipline. "For faith comes by hearing, and hearing comes through the word of God" (Rom 10:17); and, "how are they to believe unless someone preaches to them, and how are they to preach unless they are sent?" For thus through baptism we have put on Christ (Rom 6; Gal 3). The supper of the Lord is the communion of the body and blood of the Lord (1 Cor 10). Indeed, Christ in Eph 4:11 "has not only given some apostles, prophets and evangelists, but also pastors and teachers, in order to equip the saints, for the works of ministry, for the building up of the body of Christ, until we shall all attain to the unity of the faith and of the knowledge of the Son of God." And for this reason, we are commanded in the celebration of the holy supper "to commemorate the Lord's death until he comes," (1 Cor 11:26) and in case a brother does not listen to us, "to tell it to the church" (Matt 18:17).

26. This militant Church is divided in different ways: first, into the Church of the Old and the New Testament. Some also call [the latter] the catholic Church because nowadays it is not bound to any particular region, city, or temple-building, as it had been formerly, "but the sound of their voice has gone into all the world, and their words even to the ends of the world" (Rom 10:18). And although formerly the gentiles apart from Christ and alienated from the nation of Israel were strangers to the covenants of promises, "yet now in Christ Jesus those who once were afar off have been brought near through Christ's blood, for he is our peace who has made us both one, and has broken down the middle wall of partition" (Eph 2:12 ff.).

27. Second, we divide the Church into visible and invisible; and although some confuse visible with particular and invisible with universal, we—unless there is a better judgment—think that we should not confuse those elements.

28. The invisible Church is called the multitude of elect believers who, whether they are in specific individual meetings or in all the churches and places throughout the world, are conspicuous to the eyes of God. And so, it

is called 'invisible' because its inner, essential form, namely its true faith and holiness, are not seen by mortal people. For whereas we do not deny that through confession and good works the very faith and inner sanctity also make themselves evident, yet because hypocrites are able to imitate all these for a period of time, it follows that on the basis of only those things one cannot make an infallible judgment about other people. Therefore, also the wise man in 1 Kgs 8:39 testifies that "only God knows the hearts of all the sons of men." Similarly, Christ says in John 10:14: "I know my sheep and my sheep know me." And the apostle Paul says against the scandal-mongers in 2 Tim 2:19: "God's firm foundation stands, and has this seal: 'the Lord knows those who are his.'"

29. Along with Scripture we give to this multitude of believers the name *ecclesia* ['the called'] because by God's Word and Spirit they have been called out of the world to faith and holiness, and because they have a genuine and inner communion and fellowship with Christ and all true believers. And therefore, throughout the Scriptures it is called by names of the sort that effectively denote this inner fellowship and communion with Christ and all the saints.

30. Hence this Church is called the "betrothed and love of Christ" (Song 4:7; Eph 5:27), "holy Zion" and "heavenly Jerusalem" and "the Israel of God" (Isa 52:1; Gal 4:26, and 6:16). And similarly: "The Church which Christ has cleansed for himself, that he should make her glorious for himself, not having any spot or wrinkle" (Eph 5:27). "The body of Christ, fitly joined and held together by what every joint supplies, according to the inner working in the measure of each part" (Eph 4:16). It is called "the people of Christ" whom he saves from its sins (Matt 1:21). "One fold and one shepherd" (John 10:16); the "house of God and holy priesthood" (1 Pet 2:5); the "temple of God" in which the Holy Spirit dwells (1 Cor 3:16), etc. "The wife of the Lamb" (Rev 21:9), etc. Since all these and similar things can in no way at all apply to the hypocrites and unregenerates (whatever mask they hide behind), it necessarily follows that the Church whereof these things are said is only that one which we have described earlier.

31. And to this Church, too, properly belong all the salutary and spiritual promises that are made to the Church of God everywhere in Scripture; both the hypocrites and the unrighteous are excluded from these promises. And among the other promises there occurs also this one: that the Church will

never be lacking in this world, as Jer 31:[35 and]36 says: "'If the ordinances for the sun and the moon cease from before me,' says the Lord, 'then also will the offspring of Israel cease from being a nation, for all days.' " And so Matt 16:18: "The gates of hell will not prevail against her;" and hence Christ testifies in Matt 24:24: "It will not be possible for the elect to be led astray." And Rev 13:8, and elsewhere, testifies that "those whose names are written in the book of life of the Lamb" will be spared from being led astray by the Antichrist and from the whole world's apostasy.

32. The visible Church is the gathering of those who through the outward Word, the use of the sacraments, and church discipline, are formed together into one outward body and fellowship, which is called the visible Church, not so much because the people themselves are visible, but because their organization, public profession and communion are displayed to the outward senses.

33. There are two modes wherein this visible Church is considered: either as some particular meeting of a single district, city, or province, i.e., of those people who are bound to each other not just in the community of faith and sacraments, but also in the form of their outward governance and rites of the Church. Or as some ecumenical and universal meeting scattered in diverse places across the entire globe, even though in the very form of outward governance and circumstantial rites they often differ very much from each other, yet they are harmonious in the essential community of faith and sacraments, and for this reason it says repeatedly in Cyprian that "there is one bishopric, and a part of it is held as a whole by each [bishop]."

34. This visible Church is strictly speaking not different from the invisible Church, but it is only considered in a different way: the former as 'coming about,' the latter as 'having come about'—like a house that is being built and a house that has been built. For that invisible Church which we described beforehand is gathered and formed within the visible Church. The invisible Church is inherent in and contained by the visible one.

35. And hence it happens that the visible Church (particular as well as universal) is never so pure and sincere that not any hypocrites and godless people are mixed in with it, just as Christ therefore compares it to a "net" [Matt 13:47–50] that catches good as well as bad fish, and to a "field" [Matt 13:24–30] and "threshing floor" [Matt 3:12, Luke 3:17] wherein the wholesome grain is grown and gathered together with the weeds, and to a

"wedding banquet" where even those people sometimes appear who are not clothed in a wedding garment [Matt 22:1–14]. And so also the apostle Paul compares it to "a house, in which there are not only articles of gold and silver, but also of wood and clay; some are for honorable use, some for dishonorable" (2 Tim 2:20).

36. But even though this Church is never entirely free of hypocrites and godless people, still it is bound, as much as possible, to expose the hypocrites and by the keys Christ has granted it to exclude the godless from its meeting, in accordance with the command of Christ (Matt 18:17; Rev 2:2 and 14). But as for the believers themselves who have fallen into sin in their conduct of life or faith, she is bound to call them back powerfully by the same discipline to genuine repentance, as Paul advises in 1 Cor 5:5.

37. With respect to doctrine and moral conduct this visible Church is either pure or impure; then again, the impure is either simply erring, or heretical, or schismatic.

38. We call a church simply erring when it does indeed harbor and foster some false teachings, but only those that do not ruin the foundation of the faith, i.e., Christ and his office (1 Cor 3:11), and yet it does so in a way that it is prepared daily to improve and to correct the false teachings of which it was convicted, as God has commanded. Such a church was the one in Galatia, Corinth, Colossae, etc., wherein the apostle reproved errors that were indeed serious, but which did not concern the foundation of the faith nor were the people themselves obstinate in their errors. Therefore, the apostle certainly reproves them seriously, but he does not remove either himself or the believers from having communion with them.

39. We give the name heretical to a church that errs in articles of grave importance—fundamental articles—to such a degree that it spurns all reproof and obstinately persists in error. "For obstinacy is a formal quality of heresy." For we ought to treat someone as a heathen and publican only at the time when he will not listen to the Church when it is rightly admonishing him, as Christ advises in Matt 18:17 and Paul in Gal 5:12.

40. There are two kinds of heresy: the kind that directly ruins the foundation, that is, Christ or his office; or the kind that ruins them indirectly and as a consequence (as they say). Scripture calls people of the first kind antichrists

and apostates, and it calls the latter by the general name of false prophets or false teachers.

41. Strictly speaking a schismatic church is one that agrees with the orthodox Church in the fundamental elements of the faith; yet because of some outward rites that are indifferent in nature, or because of some particular failings in moral conduct, it makes a break with the Christian communion and starts up separate meetings. "For in the same way as heretics violate faith itself by having false notions about God, so too do schismatics break away from the love of the brotherhood by their unjust deeds of separation, even though they believe what we believe," as Augustine rightly says (*On Faith and the Creed*). Yet we should add also this point from Thomas [Aquinas]: "Strictly speaking people are called schismatics who purposefully remove themselves without a suitable cause from the unity of the Church" ([*Summa theologiae*] book 2, part 2).

42. Here the question arises whether it is permitted for a Christian to foster communion with a church that is heretical and schismatic. And our answer is that we should foster communion with a church that is erring in the faith and moral conduct, and we should make the effort in every way so that it may be called back from its error and schism, just as we see was done everywhere by Christ and the apostles. But with a church that properly speaking is heretical and schismatic, since its works belong to the flesh, we say that we must not maintain Christian communion, according to the command of Christ (Matt 7:15) and the apostle (Rom 16:17; Titus 3:10; 2 John 9, etc.).

43. We call a church pure when it keeps the preaching of the Word and the confession of faith pure and intact. For although there is no church on earth which is so pure and intact that nothing more could be required of it in faith or moral conduct, nevertheless we deem that we here should call it thus on the basis of the dominant part of the doctrine, along with the apostle in Phil 3:15: "Let us, as many as are perfect, be thus minded, that if in anything you are otherwise minded, God will reveal this also to you. But in what we have already reached, let us walk by the same rule, and let us be of the same mind."

44. From the things that have been explained earlier there appears a satisfactory answer to the question debated between the papal teachers and us whether the Church can err and defect. For we believe that the Church of the elect, the invisible Church, although it can err in matters that are

circumstantial, can never fall away from the faith because if it should fall away, it would cease to be the Church of Christ. But as far as the visible Church is concerned, the papal teachers themselves acknowledge with us that individual churches can fall away, even though they try to make an exception—without reason—for the Roman church; both experience and Scripture bear witness that certainly very many churches have fallen away. But as for the universal, visible Church, even though it can be driven to suffer the greatest hardships and for a period of time be forced to flee from the eyes of the world and those who persecute it (as was foretold would happen during the time of the Antichrist: 2 Thess 2, and Rev 11,12 and 17, etc.), we believe that God not only will always preserve some godly and believing people in the midst of persecutions and desertion by the world, but he will even raise up faithful shepherds in all ages and times. And these shepherds will feed the same godly people with the Word and the sacraments, and shall gather others through the same Word, despite the opposition of the gates of hell, to that same invisible Church of Christ, and shall do so according to Christ's promise in Matt 28:20: "I shall be with you all the days, even to the end of the age."

45. And from this it is also sufficiently clear that the true, essential marks of this pure and visible Church are the pure preaching, and reception, of the Word, sealed by the lawful use of the sacraments, and upheld by the true use of the keys (or church discipline), according to the institution by Christ. And however great the falling-away from that institution and purity of the Word is, so great also is the falling-away from the true, saving purity of the Church.

46. For if the impure and false church is known by the impurity and falsehood of doctrine, as we have shown earlier and as Christ (Matt 7:16) and John (2 John 10) testify, then it must be the case that the Church which is pure and true is to be known by the purity and truth of its doctrine. Therefore Christ also depicts "those who belong to God" by the fact that "they listen to the word of God" (John 8:47) and "his sheep" by the fact that "they hear the voice of the Shepherd and recognize it; but they do not follow a stranger but flee from him, because they do not know the voice of strangers" (John 10:4–5).

47. This is evident also from the fact that the communication and reception of the tables of the covenant are a sure sign of a people that has entered into a covenant; for God does not enter into a covenant with anyone with whom

He does not also communicate the tables of that covenant. Therefore, the apostle says (in a place earlier cited, Eph 2:12) that the heathens as strangers to the church of Israel were without covenants. And on the other hand, the apostle shows clearly that the people of Israel right up to the coming of Christ were the Church of God by the fact that the covenants pertained to them (Rom 9:4). Moreover, no-one doubts that the tables of the covenant are the Word of God, and even the very word 'testament' proves it; and among Christians it is a matter beyond debate that the signs and seals of that covenant are sacraments.

48. And hence it even happens that when God erects his Church among some people, or restores one that had already lapsed, He brings it about in no other way than through Word and sacrament. We see in this way that God erected the Church among the Israelites through the ministry of Moses, when He gave them his Word and the seals of his Word; and through his apostles Christ extended the churches throughout the whole world with this command: "Go and teach all nations, baptizing them into the name of the Father, the Son, and the Holy Spirit, and teach them to observe all the things that I have commanded you" (Matt 28:19–20).

49. Therefore the papal teachers, when they realize that they are bereft of this truth, erroneously invent different marks of the Church, even though in identifying these they differ greatly, since some assign fifteen, others eight, and others only four marks. However, they are chiefly these: its old age, the succession of bishops, the great number of those who profess it, and miracles. Bellarmine adds to these the name 'Catholic,' the unity in the profession of doctrine, the efficacy of the doctrine, and the saintly status of some of the Doctors—especially of those who have established the orders of monks—and lastly, the great victories that have been won over those whom he calls heretics.

50. But let us pass over the fact that some of these marks are not certain, that some are not continuous, and that heathens had always claimed all of them for themselves (and the Mohammedans still do). And let me disregard the fact that the Greek and Ethiopian churches, which the papal teachers consider to be heterodox, ascribe the same marks to themselves with no less right than the papal teachers do. We state that by the truly secret judgment of God they obviously ascribe to themselves those marks that Scripture itself clearly assigns to the church of the Antichrist.

51. The first mark [of the church of the Antichrist] is its old age, for it was already in the time of the apostles that the mystery of iniquity was at work; the succession and name 'Catholic,' for he [i.e. the Antichrist] takes his seat in the temple of God; the great number and unity of those who profess it, for the entire world is worshiping the beast and follows after it; the miracles, for it is accompanied by signs and portents of the lie; the efficacy of the doctrine, for God sends the efficacy of error so that they believe the lie; the saintly status of the founders of monastic orders, for it comes in sheep's clothing and has two horns, like a lamb; and finally, the victories over the believers, whom they themselves call heretics, for the beast will rise out of the abyss and wage war against the saints and conquer them, and it will cause the Church of Christ to flee into the desert. All of these are made manifest in 2 Thess 2, Rev 11, 12, 15, and 17, etc.

ON CHRIST THE HEAD OF THE CHURCH, AND THE ANTICHRIST

President: Antonius Thysius
Respondent: Guilielmus Surendonck

In this disputation it is demonstrated that Christ is Lord over the Church, and that the Roman bishop has no authority over it. Christ is the Head, and the Church is his body (4, 15). The relation of Christ to his Church in Scripture is compared not only to that of a head to a body (3–4), but also to that of a bridegroom and husband to his bride and wife (5), a head of the family to its members (6), a father to his sons (7), a Master and Lord to his servants (8), a shepherd to his sheep or flock (9), a most elevated position in politics to his people (10), a foundation to a building (11). All comparisons explain the mystic union and communion of Christ with the Church (12) and show that the highest sovereignty over the Church belongs to the triune God only, and to Christ in particular (13), in a unique way (16). This sovereignty 'also exists in his governance and control over it by the Spirit through his Word, and that not only by internal administration but also by the external one, which is in the calling and sending forth of ministers, and in their instruction through his Word' (15), anticipating the following disputation. Not a single office in the Church called with one of the names that portray Christ's absolute sovereignty signifies that it has some preeminence over the Church of God or should exercise power over it; they all are at work as God's administrators (16). So we must reject the attribution of any superiority to the apostle Peter and his assumed successors, the Roman popes, over the other apostles or the (entire) Church (17–29). The pope, because he opposes the sovereignty of Christ, shows by that very act that he is the Antichrist (30–40).

1. Since in the previous disputation we treated the Church of God—which is the body of Christ—and its marks, it follows that we briefly consider Christ

its Head, and, on the other hand, the Antichrist, who is the head of the church that does evil.

2. With "head of the Church" we mean Christ the God-and-man, the Mediator, who both possesses and also exercises the supreme and absolute dignity, majesty, authority, sovereignty and right. Thereby he himself (as the one who has the fullness of everything that is required for salvation, and the harmony [1 Cor 12:4–6] that is appropriate to the Church, and, together with that harmony, its bond and unity) flows into the universal Church effectively by his Spirit through the Word, and imparts to it every spiritual good thing, causes it to come alive, and governs and defends it, and he does so both inwardly and outwardly for its salvation, and for the glory of God.

3. And Holy Scripture indicates this sovereignty and effective power of Christ, the Son of God and man, over the Church by means of different comparisons. Firstly, there is the comparison drawn from the realm of nature, that is, of a head and the rest of the body. For since the Church is like a body, it cannot be headless, nor can it be a single body with many heads. And that one head of the Church is Christ. The "many are one body in Christ" (Rom 12:4–5), that is, their head. "And He," that is God, "has made him to be the head over all things for the Church" (Eph 1:22). And "he is the head, from whom the whole body, fitly joined and held together through all the supporting ligaments by the power that is at work within, according to the measure of each part, takes the increase suitable to the body for building itself up in love" (Eph 4:15[–16]; also chapter 5:23). So too Col 1:18, 2:10 and 19.

4. And this comparison to a head expresses highest preeminence, a most close and proportionate harmony with this supernatural body of Christ, as well as unity, communion, and concord. For just as a person's head is the pre-eminent and superior part of the body, where the very principle of life resides, as well as that of the senses and movement, and from where these flow down and into the body, and which steers away from evil and aims at the good, and where the control over the whole body resides, so too does Christ conduct himself spiritually over, in, and around the Church. And this name of 'head' is extended in order to apply also to the other comparisons. Hence, he is called the head of the bride (1 Cor 11[:3], Eph 5[:23]), the head of his people, the chief corner-stone, etc.

5. The second comparison is taken from domestic affairs, in particular from the parties that are primarily involved in it, namely that of bridegroom, and

husband (that is, of the Church his bride and wife). The comparison to a bridegroom is in Matt 9:15, John 3:29, Rev 18:23 and 21:9, while that to a husband is in 2 Cor 11:2. There the consideration is of two coming together into one flesh or body, of whole conjugal union, and of sharing in all good things together. It is of the authority and marital rights over the woman, and, in return, of the woman's subservience to the man (Eph 5:24). Likewise, the comparison is of the feelings, or love and care towards the wife (verse 25). And this is how it is also of Christ's relation with, over, in and towards his own Church.

6. And then there is the general comparison to the head of the family and its members, or to those who belong to him and who are in his household, on whom the whole family depends and by whom it is ruled (as that is his right). Hence Christ is called the Head of the family and believers are called members of the household of God and Christ (Matt 10:25, 36; Luke 13:25; Eph 2:19).

7. In particular the comparison is to a father of sons or brothers: "And you will not be called fathers, for there is one father of you all: God" (i.e., the spiritual father; Matt 23:9), "for you are all brothers." In Isa 8:18, Heb 2:13, Isa 9:6, and 53:10 the focus is on fatherly sovereignty. Nevertheless, in other places that name is sometimes granted to the servants of God, not in the strict sense, but by metonymy, i.e., in an instrumental sense, with respect to the feelings (1 Cor 4:15).

8. And there is a comparison also to Master and Lord (i.e., of servants and slaves), in the way that he simply is called Lord, that is, the Lord of every member's heart and conscience, and of the whole Church (John 13:13–14; 1 Cor 8:5–6). Hereby his ownership, use, and his perfect and highest right of laying claim over the Church and arranging it is indicated.

9. And finally, in terms of the arrangement of possessions, the comparison is to a shepherd of sheep. For as there is one flock, so too is there one shepherd (Ezek 34[:23] and 37[:24]); John 10[:16]: "So that there is one shepherd and one sheepfold." And for this reason, Christ is called "the shepherd" in an absolute sense, that outstanding shepherd to whom the sheep belong (John 10:11–12), the "chief shepherd" (1 Pet 5:4), the "great shepherd of the sheep" (Heb 13:20). Everyone, or the whole Church, is subject to his guidance and pasturage, and it listens to his voice and his alone ([John 10:] 4–5). And to

SYNOPSIS OF A PURER THEOLOGY

the extent that the term "shepherd" can be communicated [to others than Christ] it means service and not rule.

10. Thirdly is the comparison drawn from political affairs, namely from that position in politics that is the most elevated: of "monarch," "king," "ruler," "over-lord," "governor," and "deputy." For kings are everywhere called heads, fathers, and lords of the people. And so also Christ is called the King of the Church (Ps 2:6; Isa 2[:2–3]; Zech 9:9; Matt 21:5; Luke 1:32; Rev 1:5, 15:3 and 19:16). And he is called "God's deputy" whereby he, having his position from the father and subject to the father, takes his place and rules on his behalf (1 Cor 15:27). By this Christ's exalted sovereignty and rule over the Church is designated.

11. In the fourth and final place is the comparison drawn from the realm of construction, that is, by the words "foundation," "rock," "corner-stone," i.e., of a building, house, temple, spiritual city, namely, of the Church of God. These words are given to Christ in the proper sense (Isa 28:16; Dan 2:35, 45; Matt 16:18 and 21:42; Acts 4:11; Rom 9:33; 1 Pet 2:4; 1 Cor 3:11; Eph 2:19): "Foundation" because he stands firm by his own strength, he is supported by himself, and it is from him that the remainder of the spiritual dwelling's structure rises up, "Rock," which shows the solidity and strength of the foundation, so much so that the focus is on the basis, on what lies underneath, on what supports it and what gives it stability, and "Corner-stone," as in him the corners—namely, the Jews and Gentiles—come together and are joined to each other. And the relationship to the building is the same as the one of the head to the body.

12. And the first of all these comparisons comes from the natural world, and, like the last one, from art that imitates the natural world; but the third comparison comes from the relational agreement, while the second comes from nature as well as relational agreement. And when the comparisons are all taken together, they explain this mystic union and communion of Christ (which in its truth and efficacy embraces and surpasses them all) with the Church with greater clarity.

13. Therefore, since these comparisons signify the very beginning, the highest sovereignty, right, power, and absolute control over the Church, they show convincingly that they belong only to "the Father, the Son, and the Holy Spirit." Christ would not have been capable of this authority and sovereignty if he were not true God (Heb 3:4–6). Nevertheless, by the order that exists

among the divine persons, and by the specific economy and arrangement suited for redemption, Christ, being God and man, has received this privilege from the Father and holds on to it in subservience to the Father, and exercises it as a deputy, even though he has been endowed with a knowledge and power that is divine (1 Cor 3:22 and 11:3, and 15:24, 27, 28; Matt 28[:18]). And likewise, the same adequate sovereignty would not be appropriate to the Holy Spirit if He were not true God, for He acts as it were as the Son's deputy (John 14:16 and 26; and John 15:26). And so this sovereignty belongs especially to Christ, indeed as the God-and-man, in keeping with his exceptional office and its efficacy.

14. This sovereignty of Christ, which in other respects extends itself very widely—as far as the angels and even to the devils and thus to every sovereignty by whatever name it is named (Col 2:10; Heb 2:7–8)—refers especially to "the Church of God" and is tied to it (Col 1:18), not only insofar as it is internal and invisible, but also insofar as it is external and visible, and universal and particular.

15. [Christ's sovereignty] exists in his primacy over the Church, in the principle of his union and communion with it, in the downward and inward flowing of his grace into it (or in his making it come alive and causing it to grow). And it also exists in his governance and control over it by the Spirit through his Word, and that not only by internal administration but also by the external one, which is in the calling and sending forth of ministers, and in their instruction through his Word, etc. All of these things belong to the greatest sovereignty, and should be conducted as prescribed and established. And so this highest sovereignty over the Church cannot be communicated but resides in Christ as the appropriate subject, and on this point every execution of sovereignty by men of whatever sort is only ministerial.

16. Therefore Christ is the unique, one-and-only, immediate and eternal Head, Bridegroom and Husband, household-Father, Father, Master and Lord, Shepherd, King, Monarch and Foundation of the Church of God, and the Deputy of God. And neither the names nor the actual substance of this highest sovereignty can be communicated to anyone except in this manner and only insofar as the instrument and ministry of this sovereignty can be included in them. For all these names are so arranged that they correspond to their counterparts, as things that are immediately and relatively opposites (Heb 3:5–6). The result is that those who are named that way are also

considered to be included in the body, the wife, the members of the household, the sons and brothers, the servants and slaves, the flock, the kingdom and the building, in whatever degree and manner they are considered, also with respect to the proper office that applies to each of them—such as when they are called ministers and dispensers of the mysteries of God, apostles and builders, prefects, presidents, leaders, overseers, presbyters, shepherds, etc., of God and the Church. Not because they have preeminence over the Church of God or look down upon it and have or should exercise power over it (1 Cor 3:21–23; 1 Pet 5:2–4), but only because they are at work around it as God's administrators.

17. Therefore it is clearly wrong of the papal teachers to ascribe to Peter among the apostles those titles that convey the supreme, highest sovereignty—titles that belong to Christ—and from that point on they attribute them (as they would have it) to Peter's successor, the Roman pope, in each and every respect whatsoever (whether of internal communication or external government). But in the Church of Christ Peter himself is his minister, in a ministry that is shared equally with the other apostles and that is on par with their ministry. For this reason, Christ called and appointed him alongside the other apostles with the same title and task (John 1:39–40; Matt 4:18, 21). He is sent and sent forth on equal terms (Matt 10:18), and with equal power (John 20:21), and the Holy Spirit is promised equally to him, and He is equally received by him. Nor does any one of the apostles present himself to the others by means of any superior title (1 Pet 1[:1], and 5:1). The highest degree, the apostolic one, is held equally (1 Cor 12:28; Eph 4:11). They carried out their office with equal power (Acts 15:28). Christ causes them equally to share the throne (Matt 19:28), and it says that the Church is founded equally on the foundation of the apostles and the prophets. The names of the twelve apostles are inscribed as equals on the foundation-walls of the new Jerusalem, and none is superior to the others (Rev 21:14). And in particular James, Cephas, and John are equally called "those of repute," and pillars of equal stature (Gal 2:6 and 9).

18. And Paul in particular states that he had not obtained his apostleship from men or through a man, and it was not from a man that he had received the Gospel, nor was it following the lead of any apostle that he preached. He states that he did in fact confer with the others, but they added nothing to him, and they actually gave each other the right hand of fellowship and went their separate ways, so that Peter would go to the circumcised and Paul

himself to the gentiles (Gal 1:2). "In no way was he [Paul] less than the chief apostles" (2 Cor 11:5), and "he had worked harder than they did" (1 Cor 15:10). Indeed, it is by the Church and by the other apostles that Peter is sent to Antioch (Acts 8:14), and he renders an account of his task (Acts 11:2). In fact, Paul reprimands him for not walking uprightly, and he opposes him to his face (Gal 2:11, etc.). In no way was Peter placed over the others as their head, nor were the others subject to his leadership and direction.

19. And yet we do admit that the apostles occupied a primary position on the level of their administration, in keeping with their special calling and the extraordinary assistance of the Holy Spirit, so that also for the sake of good order did Peter occasionally take the lead among them. But we deny that he therefore exercised or held sovereignty over them or over the universal Church. But this entire primacy is not one of degree among lesser people, but of order among equals, and of authority, not jurisdiction.

20. Nor does the passage in Matt 16[:18–19] do anything to support this case, where the promise of this primacy and preeminence is made to Peter, when Jesus says: "And I say to you, you are Peter, and on this rock I shall build my Church, and the gates of hell will not prevail against it; and I shall give you the keys of the kingdom of heaven, and whatever you bind on earth will be bound in heaven." Nor does the other passage, John 21:15, where the promise that had been made previously is conveyed, when he says to Simon Peter: "'Simon, son of John, do you love me more than these?' And Peter says to him: 'Yes, Lord, you know that I love you.' He says to him: 'Feed my sheep.' Again, a second time he says to him: 'Simon son of John, do you love me?' 'Yes, Lord, you know that I love you.' He says to him: 'Feed my sheep.' He says to him a third time, 'Simon son of John, do you love me?' Peter was moved to sorrow because the third time he said to him, 'do you love me?' He said to him: 'Lord, you know everything. You know that I love you.' Jesus says to him: 'Feed my sheep.'"

21. And as far as the first passage is concerned, as it is in general to all the disciples that Christ asks the question what men are saying about him (verse 15), so too do they all reply (incidentally, one on behalf of the others). And just as it is their shared opinion about the Christ that is asked, so too is it on behalf of the others and on the basis of the thinking of them all (or at least with their consent) that Peter answers, as is clear from the answer itself: "You are the Christ," as in Mark 8:29; or, as in Luke 9:20: "You are the Christ of

God;" or, as it is in the passage here [Matt 16:16]: "You are the Christ, the Son of the living God." And added to this is also the prohibition made afterwards to all the disciples that they should tell no-one that he is Jesus, the Christ. This clearly demonstrates that there was a common consensus.

22. And it is obvious that prior to this time all the apostles and disciples were fully convinced that Jesus is both the Christ and the Son of the living God. John the Baptist acknowledges him as such (John 1:29), and Christ bore witness of himself as such to his own disciples (verses 34–35). And among the disciples Andrew, the brother of Peter, confirmed this fact to Simon Peter (verse 41), as Philip did to Nathanael (verse 45), and Nathanael confirmed: "You are the Son of God, you are the King of Israel" (verse 49). And when the disciples of John were sent on his behalf to him, Christ confirmed it (Matt 11:3). The disciples of Christ confessed it in Matt 14:33, and in fact so also the Samaritan woman (John 4:29), and the Samaritans (John 4:42), the blind men (Matt 9:27), the Syro-Phoenician woman (Matt 15:22), not to mention the apostles and also the same Peter who professed it earlier on behalf of the others (John 6:68–69): "We believe and know that you are the Christ, the Son of the living God."

23. And for this reason also the statements that throughout are applied specifically to Peter, as the spokesman of them all, should be understood as referring commonly and equally to the other disciples as included in the person and role of Peter, as for example, his blessedness, his very open confession, his preaching, and his role in God's revelation (Luke 10:21–23; Matt 11:27; Gal 1:12, 16). So also for the recognition of the name Cephas, which means rock, that previously had been bestowed upon him in particular (John 1:42; Mark 3:16) and that now is re-affirmed because of the fundamental statement of confirmed faith that he expressed—i.e., by the explanation that is given of that earlier naming—when he says: "And I (that is, and I say in reply, i.e., I declare to you) that you are Peter," that is, both in name and in fact, considered by virtue of the strength of your faith and confession, which [name] includes a recommendation of his own and the others' faith. For in the same way with respect to doctrine and to the profession and administration of it they are (all) indicated by the names of precious stones: "Behold I am going to set your stones with ornaments and I shall lay the foundation with sapphires" (Isa 54:11); so also Rev 21:14–19.

24. And the same goes for the promise that Christ made to him about building his Church on this rock. For we should take that word to mean not Peter personally, but in the real sense for the profession of the faith of him who looks to Christ. For Christ does not say "upon you, Peter (*Petrus*)" but "upon this rock" (*petra*), by changing the name of Peter to "rock," from masculine to feminine, and from the second person into the third, and with the addition of the demonstrative pronoun. And in Aramaic, the [definite] article that is added only to appellative nouns, and here is put before the word Cephas, indicates the same thing. And the building-up of the Church is not based on the person of any one man, but upon Christ only, who is the one and only Rock (1 Cor 3[:11], and 1 Cor 10[:4]), and on the teaching that he had proclaimed. In this sense the building-up is applied commonly also to the other apostles as the builders of God's house (1 Cor 3), and to their teaching (Eph 2; Rev 21); and the faith of the believers is called the foundation upon which they are built (Jude 20).

25. Added to this is the promise of the firm quality of that foundational rock, and of the Church that is to be built upon it: "And the gates of hell shall not prevail against her." That text cannot be taken to mean Peter per se since his faith and moral conduct sometimes wavered (Matt 16:22–23, and 26:33–34; Luke 22:31–34; Gal 2:12, etc.); but it is about the faith that he declared, and that is what remains firm and unshaken if one looks to the actual profession and not merely to the one who professes. Nor can it be taken as being about any church whatsoever, but only about the catholic Church that is the pillar and bulwark of truth.

26. And lastly, there is the promise made to him about the keys to the kingdom of heaven; [Christ] does not say: "And only to you shall I give the keys," which metaphorically signify the sovereignty of administering God's Church. The reason for that metaphor is revealed by another one: "And whatever you bind on earth will be bound in heaven, and whatever you loose on earth will be loosed in heaven." And this takes place by both the preaching of the Gospel (privately, to everyone's conscience, Matt 28:18–19, Mark 16:16, as well as publicly, by the use of discipline and excommunication, Matt 18:15, 17, 18). This sovereignty of governing is not an absolute one, but is administrative and promulgatory, in keeping with each person's faith and repentance. And it does indeed belong to the Church (Matt 18:18), yet in the special sense of being promised there to all the apostles and thus later being

entrusted to them (John 20:21–23; Matt 28:18); but the strength of the argument resides in the commission of the previously-made promise.

27. As far as the second passage, John 21, is concerned, by that particular passage Simon Peter is not given a universal office over the whole Church and over the other apostles, but the duty of shepherding together with the others (Matt 18). Peter deservedly had been removed from that duty because of his triple denial (Matt 10:32), and he is restored to it by his triple, opposite profession. This is proved also by the grief that Peter felt after he was asked for a third time (as though Christ's speech showed doubt). Nor do the words "feed my lambs" and "my sheep" have a different meaning. And "to feed" does not denote rule but ministry. For Peter is commanded to feed the sheep that belong to someone else. And it does not say "all of my sheep," but without restriction sheep are entrusted also to others (Matt 28:19; Mark 16:15; 2 Cor 11:28). And lastly, Peter did not tend all the churches, but he divided the work with the others (Gal 2).

28. And this is not contradicted at all by the fact that Christ asks him "do you love me more than these?"—i.e., these apostles who were present (namely Thomas and the two sons of Zebedee), as if on the basis of Peter's love that surpassed the others' one may conclude his primacy over the others. And Christ's question does not prove that Peter had a greater love than the others, but something quite different, because he was being asked a question that he was not in a position to answer (and for this reason he testified not about someone else's love but about his own). Christ's question proves that it was not one of confirmation but one of reproof, and of demonstrating Peter's self-confident ambition, for he had said: "Even if they all take offense at you, I shall never take offense" (Matt 26:35). [The question] only shows how great a perfection of faith and love is required of all those who minister in the Church.

29. And much less does this sovereignty over the Church of God and Christ, and over the other overseers, and the primacy of administration apply to the Romanist pope by the right (as they would have it) of succession and inheritance. For that presupposes many things: 1) That Peter was set up as superior to the other apostles (which we have just shown is wrong). 2) That the right of superiority in him was not personal in nature, but one of succession. But there is no-one who has succeeded the apostle, because their calling was unique, and if there is succession, it is a succession of doctrine

and common calling. 3) That this succession was bound to a specific place and seat of power. But succession is not conferred by place. 4) That that seat was the last one that he occupied at the end. 5) That the seat was moved from Jerusalem (from where it states clearly that the word of the Gospel would go forth, Isaiah 2, and where the fulfillment of Christ was) to Antioch (where Christians were first so called), and thence to Rome, where Peter not only was and lived for many years, but where he also completed his martyrdom. So much so that whoever it is who succeeds Peter, and in whatever way he succeeds him, even if he is not like the others in faith and love, nevertheless he does succeed to Peter's privileged position and right. But as for Paul, even though he is writing to people at Rome, and even though it is from Rome that he writes his letters to the Galatians, Ephesians, Philippians, Timothy, and Philemon, nowhere in the opening words of greeting does he make mention of Peter. All these assumptions should be proved by the sacred testimonies on which the faith rests. But they can do nothing of the sort, instead deeming it necessary on this point to take recourse in tradition (and a doubtful one at that). In fact, every privilege that the Roman high priest enjoys is based much more on a human and imperatorial institution—namely that of Phocas, the godless, regicidal emperor.

30. But in fact the Roman bishop and pope, when he is not afraid to call himself the lord of the universal Church of God and Christ, and its lord, king, monarch, spouse and husband, head and foundation, and also the vicar of God on this earth, and the world-wide bishop or bishop of bishops, and is not afraid to conduct himself by those designations, and when he claims that one must believe it in order to be saved, he then actually shows by that very act that he is really the Antichrist, as one who makes an attack upon the supreme sovereignty that actually belongs to Christ, and makes himself out to be his consort and exalts himself above the Church of God and his own fellow-servants. The apostle foretells in 2 Thess 2[:4] that he would take his seat in God's temple and would raise himself over all that is called God or the object of worship.

31. And when he calls himself master, lord, ruler, king, and monarch of the Church, he means it in an absolute sense as far as spiritual matters are concerned (but in a universal sense in temporal matters, and insofar as these temporal matters are adjusted to spiritual ones). And he performs those things that belong to a Lord and king, such as when like a lawgiver he appropriates for himself the infallible power of interpreting divine matters,

and dispenses or abrogates divine matters, and introduces to the church laws that are binding upon the conscience, just as much as if some servant or slave, or even an envoy makes himself lord and king, or claims for himself what belongs to the Lord. To do so is to bind opposites together, and to commit a crime of injury to the majesty of God.

32. To be sure, nowhere in Scripture is this title given to God's servants. But it is Christ who is the Church's immediate King, a fact that was foreshadowed first in the kingdom of Israel, when it was God's will to be the immediate King of his people, until, it says, they sought to have a king whom they could behold with their eyes and they rejected God himself, and that it was in his anger that God gave them a king. And this kingship truly received its fulfillment in the Roman church and the Roman high priest.

33. And when [the pope] makes himself out to be the spouse and husband of the Church, what else is he doing but making the Church into an adulteress and himself into an adulterer? On this point there is no place for a substitute. John the Baptist says: "He who has a bride is a bridegroom; the true friend of the bridegroom is the one who stands and hears him, who rejoices greatly because of the bridegroom's voice" (John 3:29). And in a similar way it is Paul "who prepares her [the church] as a pure virgin to be presented to one husband, Christ" (2 Cor 11:2). Therefore it is enough for them to be the groom's "best men." And not even this title is given to the servants of the Church anywhere in the Scriptures. And it is foolish to cover this up with a comparison to the pretended sexual consummation that is customary among important personages, for then the pope would thus be the Church's pretended spouse.

34. And when he makes the claim that he is the universal head of the Church, he causes the Church to be multi-headed (but for one body there is only one head of the same order) and thus he turns the body into a monstrosity. And the monster in this body is not avoided by a distinction of a head below another head, or of a visible head of a visible church. For this distinction of a visible and invisible Church is not an essential one but it is only accidental to it. For what is the proportion of this visible head to the whole body of the Church? And how shall this one person be able to care for the world-wide Church? And that was the reason why the apostles arranged to work separately.

35. And this name of the head of the Church is not even given to the ministers of the Church. For the priests are not called the heads of the people except in the common sense of the magistracy, of the leaders, and of honored people (Isa 9:14–15, Hos 5:1). What is more, not even the high-priest, being the type of Christ in whom he is fulfilled, is so called. For even if in administering the Church of Christ its more outstanding members might go with the name "head" (1 Cor 12:21; where nevertheless the dignity of the head is said about Christ, verse 12 and 27). Yet that naming does not designate any one person, but the more powerful office and the gifts, as is clear from the thread of the whole chapter, or else it must be understood as being about the composition of the mystical body.

36. And moreover, although he calls it a foundation upon another foundation and a secondary foundation, when he makes the claim that he himself is the foundation of the catholic Church, what else is he doing but trifling, connecting contradictory elements by adding something? For strictly speaking not any foundation exists other than the one and only, and upon it the rest of the structure is built—and that foundation is Christ alone (1 Cor 3:11).

37. And as for the fact that mention is made of twelve foundations for the heavenly Jerusalem, and that inscribed upon them are the names of the twelve apostles, we should—by the extension or distribution of its parts—take the word "foundations" to mean the one, same foundation. In the same way there is spoken of the foundation as well as the foundations of the temple (1 Kgs 5:17; 2 Chron 3:3; Heb 11:10). And so actually the one and the same foundation of the Church goes by the name of foundations in keeping with it being located in individual churches; and the names of the apostles are written upon them as they were (in terms of the churches' parts) individually their builders and founders. In the same way this city is given twelve gates, and the names of the twelve angels, its watchmen, are written upon them, and also the names of the twelve patriarchs. Even so that city has but one gate, and that is Christ (John 10[:9]; similarly Eph 2:20). It says that the Church is built upon the foundation of the apostles and the prophets, namely on what they have founded, and in this sense the apostle opposes his own foundation to one that was made by someone else (Rom 15:20), or, as a metonym, one that was built upon doctrine taught by those others (Heb 6:2).

38. And when he puts himself forward as God's and Christ's universal deputy on earth, what else is he doing but distinguishing himself from Christ at the point of origin, but not of his wisdom, power, and sovereignty? But he does appropriate both for himself when he boasts that he possesses every right within the shrine of his heart, that he is not capable of erring, and that his actions come from the fullness of power. But in fact there is no need for such a deputy, since God in Christ and through the Holy Spirit is always and everywhere present to aid his Church. But a deputy takes the place of someone who is absent.

39. And lastly, when he makes the claim that he is the chief shepherd, the great or world-wide bishop, and the father of fathers, he is doing nothing else than demonstrating by his ambition and excessive pride that he is the Antichrist. In the sacred writings "bishop" is used nowhere except with respect to the Church, and certainly not of other bishops (Acts 20:28). And no mention is made of this office among the other offices of the Church (1 Cor 12:28; Rom 12:8; Eph 4:11; 1 Tim 3). But this should have been mentioned in a matter that they make into a matter of faith. But anyone who calls himself world-wide bishop not only is lording over the inheritance (1 Pet 5:3) but also is being a tyrant to his fellow servants and fellow overseers. This is contrary to what Christ commanded when the disciples were disputing who of them was the greatest, on three occasions (on the road to Capernaum, Matt 18:1; Mark 9:33; Luke 9:46; near Jericho, Matt 20:21; Mark 10:35; in Jerusalem at the holy supper, Luke 22:24). And in so doing the pope is emulating Diotrephes, who desired to be foremost [3 John: 9–11]. But in Matt 20[:26] and Luke 22[:26] it says "not so you" and "but you are not like that;" this does not mean the mode of the lordship (as Bellarmine would have it) but the actual lordship itself, just as in Ps 1[:4] "the ungodly are not so" and Ps 147[:20] "but he does not do so for every nation," i.e., he does not do that.

40. These things make it altogether evident that the Roman high priest and pope is in fact the Antichrist and the son of perdition; and that the Roman church is papist and antichristian. Because the supporting material for this is so abundant we have put off to another disputation a fuller demonstration of this.

SOURCES

Augustine, Sermon 13, *On the Words of the Lord according to Matthew*
He [Christ] said, "You, therefore, are Peter, and on this rock, which you acknowledged when you said 'you are the Christ, the Son of the living God,' I shall build my Church; I shall build you upon me and not myself on you."

The same [author] in the *Treatise on John* 124
He said, "On this rock I shall build my Church." For the rock was Christ, and on that foundation Peter also was built. For no-one can establish any other foundation than the one that was established by Christ Jesus.

The same [author] in the *Treatise on John* 118
And although all of them were asked, it was only Peter who replied: "You are the Christ." And he said to him: "I shall give you the keys," as if he alone received the power to bind and to loosen, since he was the one who had spoken on behalf of the others, and had received this together with the others, as if he were the embodiment of the unity itself. And so it was one on behalf of them all, because there was a unity in them all.

Pope Gregory, Book 6, chapter 194, letter 30
I state with confidence that whoever calls himself, or longs to be called, a universal priest, by elevating himself surpasses the Antichrist.

ON THE CALLING OF
THOSE WHO MINISTER TO
THE CHURCH, AND THEIR DUTIES

President: Johannes Polyander
Respondent: Isaac Valckenaer

This disputation advances the Reformed understanding of the calling and duties of ministers of the Church. The calling 'is made known not only by the Holy Spirit's prior inward prompting and inspiration, but also by the subsequent outward approval of the genuine members of the Church' (4). The necessity of the inward prompting by the Holy Spirit is argued from three biblical texts (5). Next, the Socinian objections to these proof texts are discussed extensively: Heb 5:4 (6–8); Rom 10:15 (9–12); Jer 23:21 (13). The refutations are followed by positive statements about the manner in which God calls the ministers of the Church (14–20). Examples are given of immediate (15), mediate (16), extraordinary (17, 19), and ordinary (18, 20) callings. Next, the disputation draws attention to the various ministries listed in Eph 4: apostles (21, 24), prophets (22), evangelists (23–24), pastors (25–26), and teachers (27). The various other titles that appear in the New Testament are also discussed: ministers (28) and overseers and elders (29–30, 47). The election of ordinary pastors is a right of the Church, shared by common people and the elders. The right of ordination belongs to the council of elders (31–34, 37–39, see also 70–71). To avoid electoral mistakes, it is good practice to examine the teachings and lives of future overseers, presbyters or elders, and deacons (35–36). Two kinds of exceptional circumstances in the election and ordination of pastors are treated: 1) the first Reformers, who were not always officially ordained (40–43, 58); and 2) places where no fully instituted church yet exists (44). Some theses are dedicated to the question whether the gift of performing miracles must accompany an extraordinary calling (45–46); others to the question of whether it matters if pastors are ordained by bishops or by presbyters

(47). Subsequent theses deal with the legitimacy of the calling of those ordained in the Roman Catholic Church (48, see also 75); the question of succession, with special attention to the succession of the apostle Paul by the Roman pontiffs (49–57); and that of the hierarchy of patriarchs, cardinals, archbishops, and canon priests (58). Attention is also paid to the distinction between the pastors and the elders of the church. The former are charged with teaching and exhorting to the obedience of faith, the latter with the government of the church, including the oversight and discipline of doctrine and life (59–61). In difficult cases, the presbytery may enlist the assistance of the classis or synod (62). The task of the deacons is discussed in theses 63–64. Like preaching, the administration of the sacraments is a task reserved for pastors and teachers (65–69). The length of the term of office of deacons and elders, their possible re-election and promotion to the pastoral ministry is discussed in theses 72–74. The disputation ends by addressing some specific questions concerning authority in the Church.

1. Our Lord Jesus Christ, as the one and only Head of the universal Church, governs it unseen by his Holy Spirit; he likewise governs it in this world also visibly through stewards and ministers of his kingdom.

2. Some of them bestow goods of a spiritual sort upon all the Church's members, while others bestow upon some goods of a bodily sort needed for the sustenance of this life.

3. Of the former there are two kinds of helpers: some administer God's Word as well as the government of the Church, while others administer only the Church's government.

4. The calling of those who administer God's Word, like that of the other public servants of Christ's Church, is made known not only by the Holy Spirit's prior inward prompting and inspiration, but also by the subsequent outward approval of the genuine members of the Church.

5. One necessary requirement is the prompting by the Holy Spirit inwardly in all God's faithful servants called to administer his Church, a prompting whereby the hearts of godly men are effectively inclined and roused to desire the holy ministry before they take up and begin their task. For just as it belongs to the Lord of the harvest to send forth his workers into his vineyard (Matt 9[:38]), so too does none of his faithful workers take this honor upon himself, but only he who has been called by God. The apostle makes this point with the example of Aaron (Heb 5:4) and he implies as much with this question: "How are they to preach unless they have been sent?" (Rom 10:15).

And on the other hand, concerning the false prophets, God declares: "Though I did not send them, these prophets ran, and though I did not address them, yet they prophesied" (Jer 23:21).

6. And when we bring these passages forward in objection to the Socinians who deny that some special motivation is required to enter upon the sacred ministry, they retort that in Hebrews 5:4 the apostle is speaking only about the high-priestly office of Aaron, which once consisted more of honor than actual work; but that today's ecclesiastical ministry consists more in work than honor, and [they retort] that those suited to teaching do not assume or take upon themselves a ministry of that [Aaronic] sort, since it is on the basis of their gift to teach others that they possess that right to desire it and enter upon it (*The Racovian Catechism*, [section 8,] chapter 2, 'On Governing and Guiding the Church of Christ'; Faustus Socinus, *Treatise on the Church*; and Theophilus Nicolaides, *Defense of Socinus's Treatise on the Church*, chapter 1).

7. The restriction that the Socinians place upon that passage in Heb 5 is wrong. In discussing the office of high priest in general in this text, the apostle indeed illustrates his axiomatic statement, "No-one takes this honor upon himself, but he who is called by God," hypodigmatically with the example of Aaron. Nevertheless, since he there defines the office of high priest from the effects of the sacred ecclesiastical ministry, it also necessarily follows from the logical rule that "for things that are the same the assessment must be the same," that the apostle's general axiom can—on the basis of the ecclesiastical ministry (that consists of various kinds)—be applied to others in the ecclesiastical ministry (of whatever rank) in the same way that the apostle applies it to Aaron specifically. For from the sacred writings no other, different example can be produced from among the prophets or the apostles or evangelists, or the other ecclesiastical ministers whom God has approved. For one does not read that anyone of them took upon himself the position of an ecclesiastical office without a calling by God.

8. Moreover, the liturgical service of the Aaronic high priest, wherein he performed the rites (mentioned by the apostle in that passage) on behalf of the people and himself, consisted equally in work and in honor. And hence by synecdoche the apostle called it an honor, since it was on account of that liturgical service that he was worthy of double honor, something that the apostle states also about the elders in the New Testament (1 Tim 5:17). And to the task of the sacred ministry the apostle ascribes neither more nor less

work than honor, but just as much work as honor, when he calls that work "noble" (1 Tim 3:1). And although it is a noble thing to aspire to the office of bishop, as the apostle teaches in the same passage, nevertheless we should find fault with the ambition of those who wait neither for the sending by God nor the Church's approval, but seize upon that office on the basis of their own personal decision and choice.

9. And their retort to the passage in Rom 10:15 is that Paul is speaking about his own time-period only, since the Gospel-teaching was still new and unheard, and that therefore the very subject-matter demanded that those who were going to proclaim it be able to demonstrate their own mission. [They claim that] since in our day and age nothing new is being introduced but rather the old teaching of the Gospel is presented, there is no need for some special calling (Osterodt, *Instruction*, chapter 42 and Theophilus Nicolaides, *Defense of Socinus's Treatise on the Church*).

10. This restriction of the Socinians conflicts with the truth, too. For this question of the apostle, "How are they to preach unless they have been sent?" should be taken as a pronouncement that can be applied universally no less than the preceding questions. And, just as the following axiomatic statements are and will be true always and everywhere—"no people shall call upon a God in whom they did not believe," "none shall believe in him of whom they have not heard," "no people shall hear without someone to preach"—so too we should judge that apostolic axiom to be true: "No persons shall preach" (legitimately, of course) "unless they have been sent." And the work of the preaching of the Gospel is not attributed only to the apostles, but to other pastors, too, as can be seen in Matt 26:13, 28:20, and elsewhere.

11. And what is more, it is false to claim a new teaching for the apostles, for they neither believed nor taught anything beyond what was written in the Law and the prophets, as is clear from the apostle Paul's testimony in Acts 24:14, and 26:22. And this is clear also from his answer to the Jews dwelling at Rome who asked him what he thought. For Acts 28:23 states that he testified to them and revealed to them the kingdom of God, "persuading them of the things concerning Jesus from the Law and the prophets." Therefore, the sending of the apostles was an indication not of a new teaching, but of the calling by God, and it conformed to the calling of the prophets who were sent in the same manner (although they, too, said nothing

new, but the same things as Moses) and confirmed Moses's writing with their own.

12. And for this reason Socinus's objection to the papal teachers is pointless, that they cannot demand that ministers who disagree with them must demonstrate the lawful author of their calling or office because [according to Socinus the ministers] do not conduct themselves as new apostles of Christ nor as prophets sent by God. And also, they do not profess that they are declaring to the world a teaching or religion that has not been heard before. Furthermore, that they are not teaching anything based on new principles or previously unheard-of testimonies, but only those things that are beyond all doubt for those who are called Christians—that is, things that come from the very writings of the evangelists and the apostles (Socinus, *Treatise on the Church*). For the same apostle writes about himself (Rom 1:1) that he has preached that Gospel not on the basis of new principles or previously unknown testimonies, but that which God had promised previously in the Scriptures through the prophets. Nevertheless, in the same passage he also points out the lawful author of his calling and office to the people at Rome when he asserts that he is an apostle set apart by God's calling for that task of preaching the Gospel.

13. Also pointless is the objection that Socinus's epigones (and Ostorodt in particular) make against the passage in Jer 23:21, that God there is concerned with the false prophets who boasted that they were prophets sent by God so that they could declare something to the people that was new and special. For by that sort of boasting about the novelty of their own teaching they could not show that they were the successors of the true prophets, since Moses (in his first book) shows that his own writings conformed to the prior, unrecorded revelations of God from the time of Adam to his own day, and since Christ demonstrates that the teaching of the later prophets is ancient by virtue of its harmony with the teaching of Moses (Matt 7:12; Luke 24:27).

14. But let these statements about the requirement that the calling of the ministers of the Church come from God be sufficient. Let us look now to the manner of this calling, which comes from God immediately or mediately or extraordinarily or ordinarily.

15. The immediate calling is the one whereby God, not using the aid or intervention of other men, calls some men to the task of teaching and ruling the Church. Such was the calling of Moses in ancient times, and of Isaiah and

Jeremiah under the old covenant, and so also that of the apostles whom Christ himself sent to preach the Gospel under the new covenant.

16. The mediate calling occurs when God calls some men through the intervening assistance of other men, as was the case for Aaron and the other priests and Levites under the Old Testament, and of Timothy, Titus, and the overseers, elders, and deacons under the New Testament.

17. The extraordinary calling is the one whereby some, endowed by God with exceptional gifts beyond the common lot of other ministers, are called by God apart from the order and sequence of the previous ministers of the Church. This manner of calling was that of the prophets in the Old Testament, and of the apostles, prophets, and evangelists in the New Testament. Their calling was arranged for a definite term: under the old covenant for the restoration of God's Church that had fallen apart; and under the new for the propagation of the Church that was to be expanded.

18. The ordinary calling is the one whereby some men whom God equipped with ordinary gifts render to God's Church the ordinary, common assistance. Such was the calling of the patriarchs before the time of the Law, the calling of the priests and the Levites under the time of the Law, and of the pastors and teachers at the time of the Gospel. This calling will serve to promote in every location the upbuilding of the Christian Church that has been scattered through all the lands of the whole world from the time of the apostles all the way to the end of the world, in keeping with Christ's promise: "Go and teach all nations, baptizing and teaching them to keep everything that I have commanded you. And I am with you each and every day, even to the end of the world" (Matt 28:[19–]20).

19. It is with an eye to this that the apostle assigns first place to the extraordinary calling of the earliest, temporary builders of the catholic Church, and he counts only three different orders for them when he says that Christ, after his ascension into heaven, gave some to be "apostles," some "prophets," and others "evangelists" for the upbuilding of his mystical body, that is to say, the Church (Eph 4:11–12).

20. In that same text, the apostle joins to these only two, connected orders of ordinary, ongoing ministers of God's Word, when he goes on to say that the same Christ gave in addition some to be "pastors and teachers, to equip the saints for the work of ministry, until we all should reach the unity of the

faith and of the knowledge of Christ, to mature manhood, to the measure of the stature which belongs to the fullness of Christ" [Eph 4:11–13]. In order that the pastors could be free to do this task more conveniently, they added elders to their rank for the government of the Church, and deacons to care for the poor and other afflicted people, as instituted by Christ and the apostles (Matt 18[:18], Acts 6[:3]). We shall discuss these offices in their proper place.

21. The "apostles" were world-wide preachers of the Gospel for the foundation of the catholic Church (which is Christ), and for establishing it everywhere on earth—men sent by Christ himself immediately and apart from any order, with the gift of teaching others without error, and instructed by God to confirm the truth of their teaching by miracles (Matt 28:19; 1 Cor 3:10–11; Matt 10:1; John 16:13; Acts 2:2 and following).

22. God had endowed the prophets who lived under the New Testament with the gift of heralding the things that were to come and of explaining the more difficult passages of Scripture with clarity, and applying them skillfully to the upbuilding of the Church. Described as having the former gift was Agabus, who predicted the famine that occurred during Claudius's reign, as well as Paul's imprisonment (Acts 11:28, and 21:10). And depicted as having both gifts were Barnabas, Simeon (also called Niger), Lucius of Cyrene, Manahen and Saul, all of whom Luke calls prophets and teachers (Acts 13:1). And described as having the latter gift are those whom the apostle discusses in 1 Cor 14:29 and following.

23. Of the "evangelists," some were those who wrote the history of the Gospel, about the life and death of our Savior Jesus Christ, and of his words and deeds, while others were called by the apostles to preach the Gospel along with them, and for that reason they accompanied them as fellow-workers except when they were, for a time, by them put in charge of specific churches. Such were Barnabas, Silas, Timothy and Titus; some people think that the seventy disciples whom Luke mentions in chapter 10:1 should be counted among them.

24. Even though Barnabas, who was of service mainly to the apostle Paul in proclaiming the Gospel to the gentiles, is called an apostle in Acts 14:14, that is not a reason for him to be added to the twelve apostles in the apostleship along with Paul, as some people think, for Christ from heaven had called Paul to that office for an entirely unique reason, and immediately (Acts 9:5). For

in the former passage Barnabas is called an apostle in a broader sense, in the same sense that Epaphroditus, the apostle Paul's personal colleague, is called the apostle to the church at Philippi, that is, as an ambassador sent to Rome by that church, in order to supply the needs of the apostle Paul (Phil 2:25).

25. The "pastors" were stewards of God's Word whom the apostles and evangelists had put in charge of teaching and governing specific churches, whose office is described in Acts 20, 1 Tim 3, Titus 1, and 1 Pet 5.

26. The parts of their office were the same as those of the previously mentioned extraordinary ministers of God's Word: 1) To teach God's people from his Word; 2) To administer the sacraments to them as instituted by Christ; 3) To pour out prayers to God on their behalf; 4) To keep them, with the reins of ecclesiastical discipline, within the boundaries of obedience that is owed to God by his own Word (Matt 28[:19], and 18:17; Acts 20:36; Eph 4:14).

27. The "teachers" were those who succeeded the prophets of the New Testament, and as they were equipped with knowledge of diverse languages, sciences, and histories, they would explain the sacred Scriptures by the analogy of faith, and with an appropriate method pass them on to others, and defend them over against the corruptions by heretics and false accusations by unbelievers. Therefore, the apostle distinguishes them from pastors, because they fulfill their services in a special way; the former kept themselves busy with teaching and refuting for the sake of strengthening the faith of those who wavered, while the latter busied themselves in correction and admonition for the sake of repairing the lives of sinners. For this reason, the duty to teach is ascribed especially to the former, and the duty to exhort especially to the latter (Rom 12:7–8).

28. In 1 Cor 3:5 it is upon these Gospel-preachers—whether ordinary or extraordinary—that the apostle bestows the name of minister: "Therefore who is Paul? And who is Apollos? Are they not ministers through whom you have come to faith?" And, "Let a man so account of us, as of the ministers of Christ and stewards of the mysteries of God" (1 Cor 4:1); and: "If you point this out to the brothers, you will be a good minister of Jesus Christ" (1 Tim 4:6).

29. The same apostle also gives the epithets of "overseers" and "elders" to those men without differentiation in Acts 20:28, where he warns the elders

of the church at Ephesus to take heed to themselves and to the whole flock, over which the Holy Spirit had appointed them overseers. So too in 1 Tim 3:2 where he portrays the overseer by the attributes and effects that the apostle Peter prescribes for his fellow presbyters (1 Pet 5:1–3). And thus in the Epistle to the Phil 1:1, with the name of the "overseers" for whom he prays God for his grace, he means those men at Philippi who are in charge of the Word and the governance, and he distinguishes them from the deacons who administered the ecclesiastical coffers. In Titus 1:7 he calls "overseers" those whom he had called "presbyters" in verse 5, not with respect to the "presbyters" as secondary leaders and priests subordinate to them, but with respect to the Church that had been entrusted to their watchful care and oversight. For in the sacred writings, they are distinguished as "overseers" not with respect to some authority over Christ's other servants, nor to some prior right over the others, but only with respect to that care and watchfulness.

30. It is not by divine arrangement, therefore, but by a human one that after the times of the apostles someone from the ranks of the presbyters gained authority over the others and was, through special prerogative, called "commander" and "overseer," just as some papal teachers after Jerome profess, namely Lombard, Gratian, Cusanus, and others (Jerome, *To Titus*, chapter 1, and *To Evagrius*; Lombard, book 4, distinction 24; Gratian, distinction 93, chapter "legimus," and distinction 95. chapter "olim;" Cusanus, *The Catholic Concordance*, book 2, chapter 13).

31. To the lawful calling of ordinary pastors we should apply especially two means; the election of those who are to be called, and the ordination of those who have been elected.

32. The right to elect pastors is in the hands of the Church, and hence it is shared between the common people and the elders. But the right to ordain them belongs only to the council of elders.

33. And so in olden days the election of the pastors took place by the raising of hands and the vocal acclamation of all the people, who when it heard the name of the pastor who was to be chosen, would indicate by the raising of hands that its vote agreed with the vote of the presbytery (Acts 14:23). But the ordination (which today is called confirmation) was done by one of the pastors on behalf of the whole presbytery in the presence of the entire congregation, by the laying on of hands (1 Tim 5:22).

34. For a considerable period of time after the apostolic age the early church retained that right of electing pastors, and by means of its vote to approve or disapprove the presbytery's decision about the pastors who were to be chosen, as is evident from the following testimony of Cyprian: "The people have the greatest power of electing worthy priests and of rejecting unworthy ones" (Book 1, epistle 4). And: "We see that it comes down from divine authority that the priest is chosen in the presence of the people as they all watch, and that the worthy and suitable one is approved by public decision and witness" (Epistle 68). Therefore, Augustine after having chosen Eradius as his successor asked his church to accept him in the office of overseer.

35. However, lest in the election of overseers some destructive error should be committed against the whole Church, devout antiquity was accustomed 1) to test and probe the doctrine and life of that person, and if there was any place that lacked suitable judges for it, then it would fetch presbyters from the neighboring churches for that purpose, according to the apostle's rule in 2 Tim 2:2: "Entrust these things to faithful men who are able to teach them also to others." [The Church] was accustomed 2) where it was permitted, to publish his name written on placards for everyone to see. Where it was not permitted it was accustomed openly to read his name aloud in a meeting of the church, so that if any vice, disgrace, or scandal were discovered in him, it would be brought to the presbytery before a predetermined day. By means of this precaution it would guard against anyone being admitted to the sacred ministry who did not also have a good testimony from outsiders, according to the apostle's admonition in 1 Tim 3:7. For when the deacon made the proclamation in the church, everyone was permitted to raise an objection against the pastor who was going to be ordained in order to have access to their souls' direction, if he had committed some misdeed, as Origen teaches in *Against Celsus*, book 8 (towards the end).

36. We should always follow both of these practices of devout antiquity, so that on the basis of a suitable, universal testimony by the members of the household of faith it will be well-established for all the people that the pastor of the church who has been elected and ordained with their supporting vote is above reproach, suited to feeding the sheep of Christ. And moreover, we should follow both rites not only in the ordination of overseers and presbyters, but also of deacons, as Cyprian advises in Epistle 68.

37. The power to ordain the elected pastors and to confirm them in their ministry belongs to the whole presbytery (which we today call the consistory). In former times the presbytery still carried out that power through the ritual of the laying-on of hands, not so much by the elders who were in charge especially of discipline, but by the pastors who were free to prophesy or explain the Scriptures and who applied it for the believers' use. For this reason, the apostle links prophecy with the laying-on of hands whereby formerly the ordination of the pastors occurred (1 Tim 4:14).

38. After the times of the apostles the overseer in charge of the college of elders used to be the first to place his hands upon the chosen pastors and most often he did so in the presence of the church; and then the other presbyters would do so too, according to Rule 4 of the Council of Carthage: "When an elder is ordained, as the bishop is blessing him and holding his hands over his head, then also all the other elders who are present will place their hands over his head along with the hands of the bishop." And finally, according to the later ecclesiastical rules it was only the bishop who would consecrate the elders and deacons (as Leo [the First] testifies in the *Epistle to the Bishops of France and Germany*).

39. In stating that the election and ordination of pastors was shared by the whole presbytery, we have in mind a church that already has been fully instituted. For where a church of this kind does not yet exist, it is possible to conduct this affair in a different way, as the need arises.

40. Before we apply this observation to the pastors in our Reformed churches, we posit as certain that the office they are entering upon was instituted from of old by God, since the foremost duties of their sacred ministry correspond completely to the norm that Christ himself had prescribed for all the pastors (Matt 28:20; 18:17). And these duties are of the following sort: the pure preaching of the Word of God according to the Scriptures; the lawful administration of the sacraments; and the right and thorough management of church discipline.

41. The calling of some of the first orthodox pastors, who with marvelous zeal, trust, and hard work reformed Christ's churches that once had been deformed by the filthy idolatry and dreadful tyranny of the Antichrist, was partly ordinary and partly extraordinary. It was ordinary insofar as they had been ordained to that calling in either the Romanist or the Reformed church. It was extraordinary insofar as they had been equipped with extraordinary

talents for that task of bringing extraordinary remedies to an extraordinary wrongdoing.

42. But if some of them at the start of the Reformation, and without a prior calling from a certain church, proclaimed the Gospel of Christ to people who were crying out to them, it was the same Spirit who drove them to that work of sacred ministry whereby formerly Apollos, the Cyprian and Cyrenaean men are said to have preached the mysteries of Christ in the synagogues of the Jews and to the gentiles (Acts 11:18)—even though one reads nowhere that the gentiles, apostles, or evangelists had ordained them to that office.

43. And meanwhile, in the same manner as it was with the subsequent approval of the apostles that those men were solemnly confirmed in that not yet fully formed office by Barnabas and Christ's other disciples (as Luke testifies in Acts 11:23, and 18:27), so also Origen asserts that it can happen that someone who is bringing the Gospel in a city where no Christian is living is ordained afterwards as overseer by the general vote of the hearers whom he converts to Christ (*Homily* 11 on Numbers 18).

44. And surely, in a place where there is no church, there the men whom God has sent to bring the Gospel should not expect to receive a calling from people who do not know God, but they should be obedient directly to God who sends them, based on the general duty to advance his kingdom as the opportunity allows, until such time as they are well-established in their still undeveloped function in the church that they are going to gather, with the agreement of the neighboring (or further removed) brothers.

45. It is not necessary that the gift of performing miracles must accompany either the entirely extraordinary calling or the mixed one (i.e., partly ordinary, partly extraordinary). For Obadiah, Micah, Hosea, and Zechariah, whose calling was extraordinary, did not confirm their own teaching with miracles. Nor did John the Baptist, who had a calling that was in a way mixed, as is evident from the fact that he was the lawful successor to his father according to the order of Aaron (from whose tribe he came), and because he was endowed with the power to teach, and being an extraordinary minister and forerunner of Christ by virtue of the spirit of Elijah that had been imparted to him.

46. On the other hand, it is said that miracles were performed by many false prophets. And so that the unperceiving populace would not number the true

prophets of our times among them, God willed to equip ministers against the enemies of his truth with gifts other than the gift of performing miracles. For it was by their steadfast fortitude that they guarded the churches against the tyranny of the Antichrist, and guarded the truth of the Gospel-teaching against his errors, and they added countless sheep to Christ's flock, sheep whom the emissaries of the Antichrist had led astray.

47. Although a few of the first pastors of our churches were in fact ordained by bishops while the majority of the more recent ones were ordained by presbyters, nevertheless the calling of the latter is no less lawful than that of the former, because the bishops and presbyters formerly held the same office, as we have taught in thesis 29; and so by divine right both of them had the authority to ordain pastors.

48. We should consider that there are three separate causes for the calling of those who have been ordained in the Roman Catholic Church. One of them is fundamental, namely: God. Two are less fundamental, namely the Roman Catholic Church and bishop. Insofar as it is according to the norm of the divine institution to preach Christ's Gospel and to administer his sacraments that they have been ordained in the name of the unfaithful Romanist church by some bishop, to such an extent is their ordination pure and lawful. But insofar as the same bishop has ordained them so that it is according to the Roman pontiff's orders that they foist upon the laity human traditions as though they are divine and offer to God the body of Christ in this false mass, to that extent their calling is impure and unlawful—like water issuing from a pure fountain that picks up its filth from the impure channel through which it flows.

49. The personal succession of ordinary pastors is twofold: either one that continued from the primeval ordination of true predecessors, or an interrupted one. It was already long ago now that in various places the first kind of succession was snatched away from most of our predecessors by the Antichrist when he burst into the temple of God. The second kind of succession can be applied to some pastors. For not all ministers succeeded the orthodox teachers of former times closely and immediately, but some came after the subsequent errors of the Antichrist and his hirelings were rejected from Christ's Church (with the support of a devout civil magistrate), in order to cleanse it from their perverse influences. It is similar to a kingdom that has been set free from a tyrant and his henchmen, when later servants

of the lawful king replaced the earlier ones to restore that kingdom (when a space of time ran its course after the tyranny). Or it is like the later good health that follows upon the earlier one in the sick body of an ill man who is recovering, after the contagion of the subsequent illness has first been taken away.

50. And so it is not by the continuity of personal succession that we must tell the good shepherds from hirelings and robbers [John 10:8], but by the continuity of true teaching; nor is it by the interruption of personal succession but by the interruption of the pure preaching that we must know hirelings and robbers from good shepherds.

51. For the hirelings and robbers who had interrupted the course of the former orthodox teaching in the churches they had invaded, succeeded the orthodox fathers in the same way that sometimes in a republic tyrants and their henchmen take the place of a legitimate king and his servants, or as when wolves replace the shepherds of a flock, or a disease replaces good health in a sick body, and death replaces life.

52. Not a single trace of his succession to apostleship is evident in the leader of those hirelings who does call himself the apostle Peter's successor.

53. For Peter's calling was an extraordinary one that didn't have any succession whatsoever. For before he died, Peter did not pass on to anyone his jurisdiction and concern for teaching all the gentiles. But the calling of the Roman pontiff is an ordinary one, like the continuation of a monarchy, in which the new pope accedes to the monarchic seat of his defunct predecessors.

54. In Acts 10 and following, one reads that Peter traveled throughout various regions in order to teach all the gentiles, according to the command of Christ.

55. But the Roman pontiff is 'tied' to his papal chair and the city of Rome, and never departs from it to teach foreign nations.

55. Peter was called to his office immediately by Christ himself, as chief of the overseers, but the Roman pontiff is promoted to his pontificate by the cardinals who are subordinate to him.

56. It is with his own voice that Peter declared the Gospel of our Lord Jesus Christ to others. But this one is seated in his own pontiff's chair like a sculpture that has no tongue, and is useless for teaching, like a mute character.

57. In the same way that Peter applied his own apostolic office to his co-apostles and himself, so he also attributes his own office of overseer to the other pastors of the Church together with himself (in the same way as Paul in Acts 20:28) when he calls them his fellow-presbyters (1 Pet 5:1). But the Roman pontiff insists on his highest episcopate singly for himself, and he excludes himself entirely from the rank of overseers and pastors who teach in the Church.

58. If one were to look at the other hierarchy of patriarchs, cardinals, archbishops, and canon priests, he would notice a difference between them and those who minister the Gospel as listed by Paul in Eph 4[:11] that is as great as the one between the Roman pontiff and Peter. For just as those men do not appear even in Paul's list in name, so the inequality of positions and authority whereby the ranking of superior clerics is distinguished from that of the inferior ones does not rest upon any example given by the apostles or the other preachers of the Gospel, as we have shown above, in thesis 29 and following. From all these things we conclude that the calling of the pastors who serve the Reformed Church of Christ is a lawful one, but that of the pontiff and the priests under him (as they rule the clerical order on his behalf) is not lawful.

59. We should make a distinction between the pastors about whom we have spoken until now and the elders of the Church (who formerly were also called presbyters), as is clear from Rom 12:8, where the apostle distinguished those who were in charge of the Church from those who either taught in it (whom he calls teachers in Eph 4:11) or who also exhorted everyone to the obedience of the faith (whom he there calls pastors). The apostle makes that distinction much more obvious in 1 Tim 5:17, when he says, "Let those elders who rule well be worthy of a double honor, especially those who labor in preaching and teaching."

60. For by means of this limitation the apostle established two types of elders: 1) Those who labored with great endeavor over the explanation of sacred doctrine and its application (publicly and privately) for use by the people. 2) Those who spent their time in disciplining, and who had concern only for the fact that everything be done in the Church in a right and decent manner,

and that all cases for offense be removed from the Church's heart. Hence the apostle calls their function government (1 Cor 12:28). Nor should we here allow entry to the foolish objection that some make at 1 Tim 5:17, i.e., that with the word "laboring" the more hard-working pastors are distinguished from those who work more carelessly. For besides the fact that the participle "laboring" refers not to the preceding word "elders" but to what follows, "in preaching and teaching," it would follow from their explanation that those who labor more negligently in preaching and teaching are worthy of a double honor also. Nothing more silly than that could possibly be stated, nor anything more foreign to the mind of the apostle, who demands the highest vigilance from all the overseers or pastors (1 Tim 3:3). Hence, we conclude more correctly that the more negligent pastors are worthy of double censure instead.

61. The duty of these men is to work in conjunction with the pastors in administering discipline, and together with them to pass judgment in cases pertaining to the judicial examination of the presbytery, based on the laws of truth, wisdom and love. They are to keep an eye on the worship and moral behavior of the pastors and their own colleagues no less than that of all the people, to call back to Christ's flock whoever may be wandering, to reprimand those who are remiss in their duties, and to hand over the obstinate to the consistory, and in a timely manner resist any evil or scandal that arises by means of their ecclesiastical censure.

62. Should it not be possible in the presbytery to bring to bear a suitable and timely remedy to some wrongdoing that has arisen, either by someone who erred in doctrine or by someone who sinned against the discipline of God and the Church, the matter could be brought before a classical or synodical meeting, to settle it completely by applying the supportive help of other pastors and presbyters. In this case the elders of our churches should follow in the footsteps of the elders of the churches at Antioch (Acts 15:2).

63. In former times, at the prompting of the apostles, the Christian Church added deacons (keepers and managers of the ecclesiastical coffers) to the presbyters, in order that they should come to the aid of anyone at all, the poor, the healthy and sick, native and foreign, free men and slaves (Acts 5:15). And to the supportive care and help of these people also sixty-year old devout widows, called "deaconesses," were added (1 Tim 5:9).

64. Like the pastors and elders, so too deacons' function and life are defined by apostolic rules (Rom 12:1; 1 Tim 3).

65. The administration of the sacraments is no less specific to the pastors than the preaching of the Word is. For nowhere have the apostles wanted to impose the task of teaching and administering the sacraments upon the presbyters (who are commonly called elders nowadays), or upon the deacons, nor did they wish their own successors to do so; they have assigned that duty to the pastors and teachers only, according to the institution of Christ (Matt 28:20; Acts 6:4; Eph 4:11; 1 Tim 3:2; 1 Pet 5:1–2).

66. The objection that is raised against us concerning the preaching of Stephen and the baptism of Philip the deacon in Acts 7 and 8 is not of instances of an ordinary office confirmed by apostolic authority but of exceptional zeal and deeds. For neither of them was sent forth by the apostles, nor by the overseers and presbyters of a church from which they set out in the same manner and ceremony whereby Acts 13:3 says that Paul and Barnabas were sent out by the overseers of the church at Antioch when they were ordered by a special oracle from the Holy Spirit—namely, after those overseers had placed their hands upon them as a sign of sending them forth to pastor the neighboring churches.

67. Stephen, too, did not hold sermons for his hard-hearted opponents, but only one single speech of defense. Nor was it of his own or some other human devising, but by a special assignment by God from heaven that was revealed to him by the same Spirit of God, that Philip wanted to go from Jerusalem to Samaria and to set out from there in order to teach and baptize the eunuch, and by Whom he was then miraculously snatched away to Azotus (Acts 8:5, 27, 39–40).

68. Therefore the Socinians are talking nonsense when they draw the conclusion from the examples of these extraordinary deacons that any of the ordinary deacons is able to preach the Gospel and administer the sacraments even though he does not have a calling from a church (even when order is preserved in [the Church] and there is no departure from accepted teaching).

69. The same Socinians make it clear that they are being driven by an attitude of polemics and change, when they call the work of the pastoral office (whereto the apostle wants only those admitted who are suited to feeding God's flock, and by the rules which he had prescribed in 1 Tim 3, Titus 1) a

work of love that any one at all is able to practice in the Church, and when they deny that the servants are called fellow-workers of the Word of God with a view to the sacraments that they dispense. For besides the fact that they can be convinced of their error by the mission of the apostles and the other pastors which by Christ's promise will last until the end of the world, they make God who gives the command through the apostle that everything be done decently and in good order in the Church of God (1 Cor 14:40) into the author and promoter of confusion, something that He especially abhors, according to the apostle in 1 Cor 14:40 (Socinus, *On the Church*; Ostorodt, *Institutes*, chapter 42; Nicolaides, near the end of his *Defense* [*of Socinus's Treatise on the Church*]; Smalcius, "Disputation [on the Ecclesiastical] Ministry").

70. Since the consensus of the civil magistrate and of the people who profess the same faith as the presbytery is required for the election of elders and deacons no less than for the pastors, the papal teachers commit sin when they permit neither the magistrate nor the Christian people to vote in the election of their ecclesiastical offices. For the calling of those who dedicate their efforts to the entire Church ought to be approved by the consensus of the whole Church, lest some inept or unsavory minister force himself upon it.

71. Meanwhile, just as Matthias was elected to his apostleship—and the deacons to their diaconate—by the consensus of the whole early church with the apostles leading them, so too will the calling and ordination of future ministers be complete in every respect if the following order at least is kept: the presbytery's enquiry and choice precedes; then in the first place come the devout civil magistrates (as those who keep both tables of God's laws, and who foster or preserve that church); and thereupon the rest of the people as members of the church's household shall add also their vote to the presbytery's choice.

72. In former times the function of not only the pastors, but also the deacons as well as the elders, was continuous. But because the number of men who have been equipped with exceptional zeal and other spiritual gifts for building God's house in our churches is less now than it once was in the apostolic churches, and the generosity towards those who serve Christ's Church is less in the current age than the former one, we therefore nowadays allow (rather than censure) the change in the elders' and deacons' continuous function to a biennial one. We allow it especially because to some extent similar examples

of interrupted ecclesiastical service occur among the priests and Levites of the Old Testament (2 Chron 24:4), as well as in the case of Zechariah, the father of John the Baptist (Luke 1:5).

73. And although nowadays the elders and deacons break up their service with a longer pause than the priests and Levites in former times, who took turns over several weeks performing their office, yet the practice in our churches is commendable, namely that they restore to their former functions the elders and deacons of proven faith and integrity after a space of a few years.

74. During the time of the apostles not only the elders but even the deacons were once consecrated in God's Church in such a way that when people saw their upright character and their diligence in explaining the mysteries of the faith, they would be promoted to the pastoral ministry (1 Tim 3:13). From this we gather that in the election of the elders and deacons the ancients considered not only their pure consciences (as happens most often in our consistories, too) but also their solid understanding and diligence in teaching others when the circumstances require it, and in reproving them in their duty.

75. And the names and offices of Porters, Exorcists, Lectors, Acolytes, and Subdeacons do not appear in the apostolic descriptions of the ecclesiastical servants any more than the titles and duties of the Archdeacons, Heads of the Curia, Monks, Abbots, etc., which we reviewed in thesis 58.

Corollary

1. Whether it is always necessary to ordain a future minister in the Church?

Over against the Socinians we affirm that the ordination of the minister, like his calling, is always required in a church that has already been instituted. This is so because the apostles and evangelists introduced that practice of ordination in Christ's Church (as the Socinians themselves also admit), and because the Church's good order and decency demands that the same practice always be observed in God's house.

2. How did Christ, who has the key of David, also hand it down to Peter?

Our reply is that Christ holds the key of David as Lord of the Church and universal Chief of the overseers; but Peter received it from Christ as a faithful steward and minister of the mysteries of his kingdom.

3. Whether Christ handed the keys of the kingdom of heaven only to Peter or in fact to Peter and his co-apostles?

Over against the papal teachers we conclude from the declarations by Christ that were of equal force to both parties (Matt 16:19; John 20:23) that Christ handed those keys to all of his apostles in the same manner and for the same goal.

4. Whether the apostle Paul possessed some special right when he handed the man who had committed incest over to Satan?

Over against the Socinians we gather from 1 Cor 5:5 and Matt 18:17–18 that the apostle Paul did not hand to Satan that man who had committed incest by virtue of some special right, but by the one that he shared with all the elders of the Church.

ON THE SACRAMENTS IN GENERAL

President: Andreas Rivetus
Respondent: Jacobus Baalde

Disputation 43 is the first of a series of five disputations that deal with the sacraments. As the preceding disputations treated the Church and its offices, the discussion here about the sacraments is located within that ecclesiastical setting. Besides the proclamation of the Word, ministers are called to administer the sacraments, which serve as supplements to the Word (2). However, because 'the whole raison d' être *for the Church lies in the union of its members with Christ their head,' (1) Christ is the basis for the sacraments. He has ordained and instituted them, and it is Christ and his merits that form their content (5, 21). Christ and his benefits are imparted to those who receive the sacrament (21). The sacrament possesses no power of causation in itself; the grace that is bestowed by the sacrament is caused by Jesus Christ. Thus the sacrament is not only a sign that displays or exhibits, it also confers Christ. Insofar as the sacrament may be considered in the 'category of relation' it expresses the 'sacramental union' between Christ and his believers (22). The structure and content of the disputation are as follows: beginning with an explanation of the terms (3–4), the disputation defines the nature of sacraments as signs (5) and actions (6–7), and moves on to treat the efficient (8) and instrumental causes, namely the words of institution (9–10), as well as the persons who administer the sacraments (11–14). The material cause, or matter, of the sacraments is a complex topic, treated at some length (15–21). The form of the sacraments is discussed next (22–29), as is their goal, namely, 'to seal the promise of the Gospel to those who believe' (30). Differences and similarities between Old and New Testament sacraments are also described (31–34). And, contrary to the number of Roman Catholic sacraments, the Reformed faith stresses that there are only two (35–37). The use of the sacraments receives attention in theses 38–40. The disputation ends with a Corollary in which several church fathers are quoted and some debated matters are explicated.*

1. The entire *raison d'être* for the church lies in the union of its members with Christ their head; yet since they are not born but are made members of Christ (and that by God working through the Word in the ministry of the Gospel), it was very much worth the effort to understand the calling of those through whom we are called into that communion with Jesus Christ. But it is equally necessary for us to examine the main components of the ministry of those men, so that by acknowledging what God is offering us through those men (who otherwise are earthen vessels) we "hold them as dear as possible because of their work" (1 Thess 5:13).

2. And so after the calling and office of the ministers of the Word were treated generally in the previous disputation, and we have disputed more than enough up to this point about everything that relates properly to the administration of the Word, good order demands that we undertake a dispute about the sacraments that the Lord has attached to the Word as supplements. First, we shall briefly explain and define their nature and their causes in general; secondly, their efficacy and differences in the various eras of the Christian church; and finally, the number of sacraments that have been instituted for the church's use to last to the very end of the age.

3. Since "sacrament" is a Latin word, it is certain that the word is not found in the original text of Holy Scripture, and it does not occur even in the writings of any interpreter in those places that explain the things usually called "sacraments." But that is how the early Latin theologians rendered the Greek word *mysterion*. The Greek church fathers employed that word to indicate those sacred rites that hold some secret meaning and that are something different from what they signify. To denote the most sacred things they used words that formerly had been applied to very shameful [pagan] rituals. And the Latins copied them, when they saw that the military oath (which Herodian in book 8 calls "the holy *mysterion* of the Roman empire") is called "sacrament" from *sacrare*, "to dedicate," and that those who gave the military oath are called "dedicated to the army"—that is, initiates—and they used the same word also in explaining those sacred things whereby we dedicate ourselves to God.

4. It is agreed upon by all that the word "mystery" (which we derive from Hebrew *satar*, "to hide," and from which we in turn derive *mistar*, "something hidden, a secret"—leaving aside the triflings of the Greek grammarians) as well as "sacrament," like also the Hebrew and Chaldean words *sod*, "counsel,"

and *raza*, "secret" (which words the ancient Bible-translator normally rendered with "sacrament"), have wider meanings and are suited to many other things besides those sacred rites. Therefore, those people are obviously silly who wish to forge for us the sacraments (properly speaking) from the words, "mystery" and "sacrament." Even though there is no recorded use of them for the actual subject, we are not unwilling to use these two words (once a distinction is made between the homonyms), but only on the condition that they are not forced upon us as necessary, or as an integral part of the faith, or placed on the same level as the very sacraments themselves. If on the basis of Scripture there exists certainty about these very sacraments, then we must judge that we should not fight over words, nor should those words be rashly rejected that the church had used formerly without making any novel changes to the actual teaching of the prophets or the apostles. Therefore, Bellarmine is led astray, and he leads others astray, when he starts a controversy with Luther, Zwingli, etc., as if those men had an outright dislike of those words (Bellarmine, *On the Sacraments*, tome 1, book 1, chapter 7).

5. As far as the thing is concerned, the word 'sacrament' (taken in its specific sense) is understood either in a relative or in an absolute sense. In the relative, strict sense it is taken for a sign; by metonymy, however, it stands for the thing that is signified. But in the absolute sense and that by synecdoche, it stands for both. Various definitions have also been fashioned for this variety of accepted usages. Nearly all the definitions of the ancients, used and developed also by most of the more recent [writers], have the first meaning in view. For them "sacrament is a visible form of an invisible grace;" or, a visible sign that has been divinely instituted for the church. And by its use Christ and all his benefits are signified, with some appropriate analogy, and sealed in the hearts of all who believe.

6. However, according to the second usage, those who think that the *genus* of a sacrament is an *action*, have described it generally in such a way that it is a divinely instituted sacred action wherein God by means of some suitable analogy between the signs and the things that are signified (by the promise that he declared in the words accompanying the institution) offers and seals to our hearts the saving grace in Christ, and we, testifying to our mutual trust and reverence towards him, believe that it confirms our separation from the world and the mutual bond among ourselves.

7. As we shall be giving a treatment based on the second usage of 'sacraments,' we shall not be prejudiced against the opinion of those who establish the *genus* of sacrament to be a sign. But we do not approve the tiresome disputations of those who ask the overly-meticulous questions: to what category does sacrament belong, to that of relation or to that of action? Whether it is a real thing or a concept? Whether it is an aggregated whole or an entirety of itself? [We disapprove] especially the disputations of those who have been carried away by heated rivalry, and make an abuse of Luther's name like it is Gideon's ephod and who stir up controversies that have nothing to do with Luther. And although they know well that a sacrament can be variously defined in keeping with the variety of usages (and sometimes they even admit as much), they labor with overly-meticulous concern, and fight to establish that in the definition of sacrament the action is the *genus*, as though that is the thing's most important aspect and they want to drag us to the opposite point of view, even against our will.

8. The efficient cause and author of the sacrament is only God, who, since he alone is able to bestow grace, is also the only one who could institute the seals of his grace. But we do ascribe this same power to Christ Jesus, the Mediator between God and men, since he is one with God the Father and "the great high priest, the one who instituted and authored his sacrament" (as Cyprian, the writer of the *Sermon on the Washing of Feet*, puts it). And I do say Christ, the God-and-man, provided that we always maintain the distinction that the ancients made, that "the Word effects what is of the Word, and the flesh works out what is of the flesh." Nevertheless, we do not deny that in the person in whom it subsists, the flesh has instituted the sacrament; but we do deny that we should relate it to [Christ's] human nature in itself as the principle of the action—for it is something that depends on the excellence and majesty of God, as those of the opposite view admit.

9. God moreover effects the sacrament by means of his word of institution, which contains the mandate about keeping the rite and the promise of grace that is added to the rite. This is the promise about the fellowship with Christ and his benefits, which is no different from the promise of the Gospel if we consider the actual testimony of the Gospel's benefits. But the only other thing that it has in addition to the other promises of the Gospel is the fact that it dedicates and sanctifies the symbols for sacramental use, so that by the right use of them, by the power of the divine institution, ordination, and promise, the signified heavenly things are exhibited and sealed. In this

manner the earthly symbols are raised to a new and better state—not, to be sure, by a change in their substance, or by being instilled with some internal quality, but insofar as they receive another relation and use.

10. If, in this sense, someone calls the words of institution "operational" (although we would rather refrain from using that word, lest anyone should think that some power resides in the very sound or the quantity of the words as in its subject), we shall not offer strong resistance. Provided, I say, that by this phrase he means only the turning of an element into a sacrament. [And,] so long as he recognizes at the same time that for the true meaning of the sacrament the preached word also is required—and by that we mean the word that is preached and believed. Although this happens with only a few words—since for the essence of the sacrament we do not require wordy sermons, or homilies as they call it—we do require them for a suitable mode of its public administration. And because Bellarmine does not make this distinction, he makes a pointless attack upon Calvin who required nothing else than what Augustine said with those well-worn words: "The word is added to the element, and so it becomes a sacrament, and, as it were, a word made visible. From where does this great effect of the water come that touches the body and washes the heart, if not from the working of the word? It is not because the word is spoken but because it is believed" (*Treatise* 80, on John); "but how are they to believe, except to believe him from whom they have heard it—that is—from someone preaching" (Rom 10:14).

11. And it is for this reason that Christ links the command about administering the sacraments to the command about teaching and preaching, in Matt 28:28. That administration was entrusted to the "stewards of the mysteries of God" (1 Cor 4:1), who are also called "God's fellow-workers" (1 Cor 3:9)—not, to be sure, in the institution of the sacraments, for that was done by God on his own—but in their administration, to which one who has not been called lawfully is not to be admitted under the pretext of a case of necessity. And therefore, we must reject the practice of those people who give the power of administering some sacraments to the laity, or even to women—in fact, even to the Jews, Turks, and heathens themselves (Bellarmine, *On the Sacrament of Baptism*, book 1, chapter 7; taken from Pope Nicholas, [and] from distinction 4 of "On Consecration").

12. Although, with regard to the office a calling is required in order to administer the sacrament in the correct manner, we do not therefore judge

that the sanctity of the person is a requirement. Because the minister is acting in this administration on behalf of God and not of himself, we state that the ministers' dignity, or lack thereof, can neither add nor take away anything at all from the integrity or efficacy of the sacraments. In the same manner those men "who preached Christ out of selfish ambition and not out of good will" (Phil 1:17) detracted nothing from the dignity of God's Word. In this matter we do not disapprove Thomas's statement, "The instrument does not work by its own form, but by the strength of him who makes it move" (*Summa theologiae* 3, question 64, article 5).

13. We do affirm that in administering the sacrament it is necessary for the minister to intend to do what God instructs to be done in the church, lest he should fall into sin. But we categorically consider it a sacrilege [to think] that this intention is part of the concept and essence of the sacrament to such a degree that without the minister's intention it is invalid—even if the institution by Christ and the other elements necessary in the sacrament are being kept. This view shakes the certainty of the faith and of the consolation that we hope for in receiving the sacrament. And according to the papal teachers, who attribute people's salvation to the sacraments themselves, the salvation of people will depend on the unholy minister's choice, and the instrumental cause will diminish the action and effect of the principal cause.

14. But it is not true that we think that the true sacrament is administered "whether someone gives it seriously or in jest, or mockingly," or with some other aim such as washing or cooling the body, or insolently making the body dirty and then cleaning it, as Coster slanderously foists upon us (*Enchiridion* chapter 8). For we know that the sacramental action should not be a parodic mime or a game for fun. Therefore, we require a minister who has been called to that task, all the outward circumstances instituted by Christ, and an action that is solemn and ecclesiastical. And these requirements cannot be found in just any one at all, in someone who does the washing-away [of baptism] in a profane manner, nor by Bellarmine's parrot, that merely mouths the words of the institution.

15. Along with Irenaeus (book 4, chapter 34) we determine that the matter of the sacraments is twofold, "one earthly, another heavenly." For everything in the sacraments either enters into the outward senses and has the nature of a sign, or it is a spiritual or heavenly thing that is signified through that

external material. Of these two the former is commonly called "the sign," the latter "the thing that is signified."

16. Now since of the signs there are some that are natural while others have been instituted to serve as signs, and since these latter again are miraculous or prodigious, and others are without anything miraculous, we place the sacramental signs not among the natural ones. For although they "do possess a similarity with those things of which they are sacraments [i.e., signs]—and if they didn't possess it they would not be sacraments" (Augustine, *Epistle* 23 to Boniface), even so a physical similarity should not be absolutely required, but only a conventional one that depends on the institution and the will; and for the sacraments that is the will of God as we have pointed out above [see thesis 6]. However, we do not deny that it was more convenient to choose things that possess also some natural analogy, as it is clear happened in the case of the sacraments we are speaking of. These "may well meet with reverence as being holy things, but they cannot cause wonder as being miracles" (Augustine, *On the Trinity*, book 3, chapter 10). And therefore, they cannot be put among the signs that are wonders.

17. And what is more, since among signs that have been given or instituted (including divine ones) some are only commemorative, i.e., instituted for that purpose of being merely reminders of things that have taken place, like the twelve stones that were taken out of the river-bed of the Jordan as a witness to the drying of the river [Josh 4:2–9]. Others are semantic and designate some current or future event, like the rainbow in the sky [Gen 9:13]. And lastly, there are signs that, in addition to recalling by-gone events, also bear witness that the thing for the signification of which they are used, is truly and actually being granted, and also to seal the promise of it in those who are partaking of it, like a stamped seal. We place the sacramental signs under the heading of that last species, as they are partly commemorative of past events and partly seals of current and ultimately future events.

18. In the sacramental action one considers two parts of the signs: one of them is elementary, the other ceremonial. The former concerns the substantial element while the latter concerns the action and the rite. And what we call the substantial element in the sacrament is everything that by God's institution has been set apart from common use and destined to signify, seal, and offer inward, spiritual things. But the nature of the sacraments demands that such an element be not only subject generally to our senses but also

specifically to our sight. For the word is also a visible sign that is clearly distinct from the sacrament, namely as something heard distinct from something seen. And so Augustine called the sacraments "visible words and visible signs of divine things" (*On Catechizing the Unlearned*, chapter 26). Nor does the Catechism of the Council of Trent rule this out when it defines "sacrament as a visible sign of invisible grace, instituted for our justification" (Part 2, chapter 1, Section 3).

19. Therefore, Bellarmine deviates badly from the Council's wording and indeed from the truth itself (*On Sacraments in General*, book 1, chapter 14) when he asserts that for the nature of the sacrament "it is enough if it is perceived by any sense, and that the sense of hearing should not be excluded, since of all the signs it is the most excellent ones that are perceived by this sense." He must have intended to contradict Christ since in the most excellent sacraments of baptism and the Eucharist he chose a more ignoble kind of signs—that is, the visible ones—rather than what is perceived by hearing. And so also [to contradict] his Second Council of Nicaea, which often repeats that statement, "image is better than speech" using even that verse of the poet, "what we hear with our ears stirs our souls less vividly" etc. Nevertheless we do not exclude the sense of hearing in the sacraments, but we do show that the words (for which hearing is necessary) have been added to the visible elements to make up the sacrament.

20. The action is a rite instituted by God that both the minister who is acting on behalf of God and the believer who receives it must observe. And since the action is part of the sign it is only external, for an inward action does not pertain to the rites, ceremonies, and signs, but to the perception of the thing signified. And so both signs that meet our outward senses bring to our minds other things, things that are clearly spiritual and heavenly, and they present things that must be understood and sealed through faith.

21. Those things are Christ himself together with all his benefits that are to be applied to us through faith. For Christ is generally the thing of the sacrament in view of his person, because he is wholly exhibited to the believer's heart for spiritual fellowship, and in view of his merit because by means of the sacraments the truth and efficacy of Christ's death is offered and confirmed, through which death he has obtained life for us. And from this flows forth the imparting of all Christ's benefits, namely justice, wisdom, sanctification, and redemption—headings under which Paul summarizes

them in 1 Cor 1:30. For although Christ kept his true and natural body, nevertheless he is rightly called the spiritual and heavenly reality that is signified in the sacrament. Because in those mysteries he is presented not to the senses of the body and in a bodily manner but to be contemplated by our minds and grasped by the hand of faith. From this the difference between the sign and the thing signified becomes obvious.

22. Insofar as the sacrament is a sacred action, the form of the sacrament results from the action itself, both the simultaneous action of God and the minister who offers and gives it, and of the person who at the same time receives it unto his soul and his body. But inasmuch as the sacrament is considered in the category of relation, its inward and proper form is that most beautiful analogy and relation of the sign to the thing signified, and a mutual relation of the one to the other. The former exists in the comparison and likeness of the effects, and the latter in the arrangement of the sign toward the thing signified, from which the union that we call the sacramental union arises. Because that union is signified to us by the word of institution as by an external adjunct, the name of "form" is bestowed at times even on the words themselves, but then by metonymy and not with its specific meaning.

23. Nor is it true what some people object, [namely] that such an analogy has its place apart from the sacrament; that it makes the Old Testament sacraments clearer and more brilliant than those of the New Testament; that it confuses sacrifices with sacraments, and that it infers that there can be a sacrament without a sacramental action. For they make a mistake when they argue from the *genus* to the *species*, from any analogy whatsoever to the sacramental one, which cannot be found elsewhere (whether in words or in sacrifices), nor in a sign apart from considering the sacramental action. Moreover, they are not being serious in that they place that sacramental analogy only in the physical signification and not in the conventional signification or in the sealing and offering that depends on God instituting it. It is from this institution and not from the nature of the signs that the preeminence and transparency of the sacraments depends.

24. From these words one deduces sufficiently that we do not think that any union or connection exists between the signs and the things signified in the sacraments that is either physical, such as of matter and form, or of subject and accident through inherence, or a local connection of being in the same place. Nor is there even a spiritual connection through the inpouring of some

power latent in the sign itself. But the connection is a relative one, a sacramental one, whereby yet the things themselves truly are both exhibited and sealed to the believers, but they are to be perceived in a spiritual manner.

25. It follows, therefore, that the sacraments are not the physical (neither primary nor even instrumental) causes of grace nor are they the causes through some inherent quality or through some motion by God that raises the sacrament to an effect of the sort that it attains, as Bellarmine would like (*On the Effects of the Sacraments*, book 2, chapter 11). He himself admits that this point of view is not certain, and that other Scholastics fight against it by stating that "it is God alone who produces grace when the sacraments are present" (Bellarmine, *On the Effects of the Sacraments*, book 2, chapter 11). "In such a way that the sacrament has no effect on this, but it only accompanies it or precedes it," and they give the example of "a papal bull that obtains a prebend for someone, but of itself has no effect, nor has some force or other, but only contains the indication of the pope's will" (Nicolaus de Nisse, *Resolution of the Theologians*, treatise 6, part 1, point 3, question 1). Or they give as example how "a lead seal of which a king ordained that whoever presented it would receive one hundred gold coins, can be said in a general way to be the cause of that receipt" (William Estius, [*Commentaries on the*] *Sentences*, book 4, distinction 1, section 5).

26. Among his various opinions about how the sacraments are causes of grace, Bellarmine tries to downplay [the evidence] in such a way that thence no harm is done their received opinion about the performing [of the sacrament]—that it is what they in bad Latin call "the work performed"—whereby they teach that "the outward action alone actively, proximately, and instrumentally produces the grace of justification." Notwithstanding that view, Gregory of Valencia has given a different judgment (*On the Efficacy of the Sacraments*, chapter 2), wherein after he has cited the view of Bonaventure, Scotus, Durand, Ockham, Gabriel [Biel], Richard [of Middleton], etc., who teach that the sacraments confer grace, not because they produce it but because God, on the basis of the pact in the use of the sacraments, produces it and effects it, he notes that this opinion "attributes nothing more to the sacraments than what is attributed to them by heretics." And a little bit earlier he said that it rightly appears that they are removing the very thing that according to faith he had said was certain, namely "that the sacraments are true causes of grace."

27. These men admit that for a large part the sacraments consist in their signification, and that they act by means of their signifying, or by virtue of their signification, because if they do not signify anything they do nothing. But they admit that the signification, since it is only something conventional, cannot act physically and therefore neither can the sacraments, nor can they contain any grace except to the extent that the power of God assists them; that the fathers deny that the water by means of its physical action regenerates or grants the Holy Spirit. Moreover, [they admit] that the sacrament, insofar as its power and manner of producing an effect is concerned may rightly be compared to a voice. This voice, as long as it makes its sound in the air, affects the mind of the one listening so that it understands something, as a human instrument that signifies by convention; it does not, however, affect the mind except while the signification is performing its mediating role, and that signification is something conventional (Gilles De Coninck, the Jesuit, tome 1, *On the Sacraments*, question 62, article 4, first doubt).

28. However, we should find fault with them for rejecting the pattern of sound words and allowing foolish talk to enter [cf. 2 Tim 1:13 and 1 Tim 2:16]. But nevertheless, as far as the substance is concerned, they do seem to have better sense than those who, deriving their own name from Luther rather than from Christ, speak about Word and sacraments in such a way that they ascribe to them also the bestowal of grace and justification. And while they verbally reject the *opus operatum* nevertheless they ascribe no less efficacy to the external action than those who determine the sacraments as the proper causes of grace. And they transfer the action that is proper to God, and incommunicable, immediately onto the instruments.

29. And we suffer the slanders of both parties [that accuse us] of thinking that signs are bare, empty, and altogether ineffective, while in fact besides the signification that comes from their institution by God we do ascribe to the signs also their own function of exhibiting (yet in a way that befits the sacraments) and the act of sealing the divine promises, from which those different figures of speech are taken both in the Scriptures and in the common use of the church. For the name of the thing that is signified is given to the sign, as in Gen 17:13: "My covenant will be in your flesh," and vice versa as in 1 Cor 5:7: "Christ our Passover has been sacrificed." Or the property of the thing is ascribed to the sign, as in Eph 5:26: "cleansing [the church] with the washing of the water and the word;" or, the other way around: "my flesh is food indeed, and my blood is drink indeed" (John 6:55).

30. The proper goal of the sacraments is to seal the promise of the Gospel to those who believe and to confirm the faith, because like the Word, so also the sacraments are instruments through which God works and moves the believers' hearts. And an additional, less proper goal of the sacraments is to be public witnesses of one's devotion to God, and of one's love towards one's neighbor; and to be public tokens of one's profession that distinguish church-members from unbelievers.

31. From this definition it will not be difficult to deduce what the sacraments that God has instituted are for the different states of mankind: either before the fall, under the covenant of works, or after the fall, under the covenant of grace—the state which we had in mind especially in our definition. Some of the sacraments looked forward to the covenant of grace as promised, when the church was still a child and placed under the guardianship [of the law], and such sacraments were circumcision and Passover. Other sacraments pertain to the covenant after it was already confirmed, and such are baptism and the Lord's Supper. And so, it is sufficiently clear that we must establish some difference between the sacraments of the Old and the New Testaments.

32. This difference, however, does not exist in the efficient cause, for that is the same in both. Nor does it exist in the relation or analogy of the sign and the thing signified, which was no different under the promise and the old covenant than under the one that was confirmed, as there was also not a different thing signified. For "because the very same things are preached or prophesied by the former and by the latter sacred rites and sacraments, so they should not be understood as different things or different forms of salvation," as Augustine neatly puts it (Epistle 49). In sum, in the whole general definition these sacraments are the same.

33. And so these sacraments are different only in 1) their own appropriate rites, because in the New Testament they are not the same as in the Old, in which more difficult signs were instituted (under the slavery to the law) than after Christ in the state of the freedom of the Gospel. 2) their number, because formerly there were many sacraments while now there are fewer. 3) the way in which they signify, because the old sacraments promised that Christ was going to come while the new ones declare him as having been exhibited. 4) the objects of the sacraments, because the old sacraments were binding only on those who were Jews by birth or proselytes from heathendom, while the new sacraments are binding on the church of all the

nations. 5) duration, because the old ones had to remain all the way to the coming of Christ, under whom the change in priesthood took place. The new sacraments should last until the end of the age, and no other sacraments are going to replace them. And finally, in the transparency of the sacramental words, in the amount and richness of their usefulness, of which the transparency is much more clear in our sacraments than in the old ones, and the usefulness is greater, more abundant. "And so, the one and the same true religion is signified and observed by names and signs that at that time were different from the ones now; and formerly it was by more obscure names and signs, while later it was by clearer ones; and formerly by fewer and later by many" (Augustine, *Epistle* 49).

34. From this it is clear that it is a wrong opinion of those who think that the sacraments of the Old Testament were only figures of the new ones, that they merely foreshadowed justifying grace but did not exhibit or seal what the new sacraments really contain and what they impart with their own proper power to all who receive it. Since [as they claim] the sacraments of the old law are of no use in and of themselves, and empty elements that do not, of themselves, confer grace "on the basis of the work performed," but confer as much "on the basis of the work of the performer" as "the devotion of the recipients merited, just as happens in the exercise of other works of piety." And dreaming also are those people who think that the old sacraments were merely types of things that were absent, and that the thing is conjoined to the new sacraments in reality and substance, and that actual organs of the body must receive it.

35. But we affirm that "these few [sacraments] instead of many, ones that are very easy to perform, very lofty in their meaning, and very sacred in their observance, ones that have been handed down by the Lord himself and the apostolic practice" (Augustine, *On Christian Doctrine*, book 4[= 3], chapter 9) are only two in number and not more. One of them is the sacrament of initiation or regeneration; the second is the sacrament of nourishing and fostering. And that is because Christ has not instituted more sacraments than these, and because he gave commands to the ministers of the New Testament about administering only these two. And of only these two sacraments he himself as the head became a fellow partaker, so that he might sanctify them on behalf of his members, so that "we all, baptized by the one Spirit into one body might all drink of the one drink" [1 Cor 12:13] (Matt 3:16 and 26:26; 2

Cor 5:6 [1 Cor 12:13?]). We do not doubt that the true definition of the sacraments applies only to these two.

36. We consider it no more than a recent invention of the Scholastics that there are some sacraments that have the imprint of an indelible stamp, i.e., some special quality that makes us conform to Christ, and that stays in the hearts of even those who have been condemned (for which reason the sacraments should not be repeated). And to this day there does not exist any agreement about its nature even among the people who have invented it. And therefore a few of them frankly admit that "for a large part everything that is said about this stamp is arbitrary and based on very little sound reasoning" (Gabriel Biel, *On the Sentences*, book 4, distinction 6, doubt 5)—which in our judgment he said for a very good reason.

37. But since the right worship of God is abundantly prescribed for us in Holy Scripture, we strive very much not to depart from the rule of Holy Scripture also in the administration of the sacraments. For this reason we are right to abhor the blatant sacrilege of the papal teachers who have added sacramental ceremonies to what Christ has instituted; and who have decreed that they cannot be omitted without committing a grave sin, that they are meritorious, that they have some secret and spiritual power of sanctification, and that they make up part of the worship of God (Bellarmine, *On the Sacraments*, book 2, chapter 30 and following).

38. The use of the sacraments is sufficiently clear from the goals that we have described above. For in order for us to use them well we should relate them to their own proper goals. And although we do not have to posit a necessity of the sacraments to the extent that it binds the grace of God to them, or that man's salvation depends entirely on them, nevertheless we should guard lest we sin by belittling them as being not useful or of little relevance. We should guard lest we become ungrateful towards him who, "if we had been incorporeal, had granted us bare and incorporeal gifts. But because the soul is joined to the body, he gave us things of the mind that can be grasped in sensory things" (Chrysostom, *Sermon* 60, *To the people of Antioch*).

39. Therefore, we must use the sacraments that God has instituted for our sake constantly and reverently in true penitence and faith so that we will be moved ever more strongly to believe those things that are promised to us, lest the power of the sacraments be despised and make us sacrilegious, or lest

we by neglecting the pledge whereby God willingly bound himself, should fall away from the promised inheritance.

40. And so let us always give the thanks that are due for the institution of the sacraments and be mindful of the oath of fidelity, whereby we are bound in receiving the sacraments. And like spiritual soldiers let us wage war constantly against Satan, our flesh and the world. In this warfare, wherein we are assisted by these aids, may we at last reach that point where, when the signs have ceased, we shall behold the very thing itself with blessed vision and possess it with everlasting enjoyment, when every war will have ended, and we shall live in everlasting peace with the prince of peace, Jesus Christ. To him be the glory forever.

Corollary

1. We should not acknowledge any word of institution or divine mandate after the canon of the New Testament was fixed, any word that when added to an element makes it a sacrament, if it is not expressed in the writings of the apostles or the evangelists.

2. No sacraments are absolutely necessary for salvation.

3. Given the divine command, no sacraments are to such an extent necessary, by a necessity of means, that if they were not despised and the reason for their absence was that it was not possible to have them, then anyone who was not able to use the visible element would be prevented from his share of salvation.

4. The number of seven sacraments not only has no basis in Scripture, but it also cannot be shown positively from any ecclesiastical writer who lived in the first ten centuries.

5. Nothing has the nature of a sacrament outside of the use for which God has instituted it.

6. No unbelieving person becomes a partaker of the thing that is signified in the sacrament.

SOURCES

Augustine, *Questions on Leviticus*, book 3, question 84
The Lord sanctifies by an invisible grace through the Holy Spirit there where also the entire fruit of the visible sacraments is present. For without that

sanctifying work of invisible grace, of what benefit are the visible sacraments? The visible baptism was of no benefit to Simon Magus, who lacked the invisible sanctification. And therefore, it is deduced that invisible sanctification was present to certain people, and was of benefit to them without the visible sacraments, as these were altered in keeping with the changing times. But the visible sanctification, which happened through the visible sacraments, can be present without the invisible ones, although it is of no benefit. And yet, that is not a reason to despise the visible sacrament, for the one who despises it cannot be sanctified invisibly in any way.

Cyril of Jerusalem, *Catechism* 4

Nothing, not even the smallest thing that belongs to the divine and sacred sacraments of the faith should be handed down apart from the sacred Scriptures.

ON THE SACRAMENT OF BAPTISM

President: Antonius Walaeus
Respondent: Michael van Gogh

In this disputation Walaeus, moving on from the general principles for sacraments articulated in Disputation 43, treats baptism. We are baptized into Christ, 'who has died in order that with him we should die to sins, and who arose so that he might raise us unto a new life with him' (10). So, baptism is a sign of 'the washing-away of our sins through the blood and Spirit of Jesus Christ' (22), and 'a seal of the forgiveness of sins and of the gift of regeneration' (11). In order for baptism to be effective in the person to whom it is administered, faith and repentance are required (26–27, 29, 31, 45–46). For infants this implies that they should belong to God's covenant, and have, in the words of thesis 29, 'the seed and spirit of faith and repentance.' For this reason children of gentile parents should not be presented for baptism, unless they have been adopted into a Christian family (49). The treatment of the efficient cause of baptism (6) is followed by a discussion about the similarities and differences between the baptism of John the Baptist and the baptism that Christ commanded (7–11), and who is permitted to administer the sacrament (12–14). The matter and form of baptism are treated next (15–32), with the following structure: a two-part subject matter, consisting of the outward, visible sign (16–20) and the inward subject of that which is signified (21–22). Emphasis is placed upon the close relation between the sign and the thing signified in the form of baptism (23–32). Baptism has many great uses and effects (33–40). Lastly the question who is to be baptized (41–50) is treated, followed by some points connected to baptism (51–56).

1. Now that we have explained the things relevant to determining the shared nature of the sacraments, it remains for us to add a few points about the individual sacraments of the New Testament, insofar as the arrangement of our project demands.

2. Of these sacraments, baptism comes first, and for this reason it is called the sacrament of our regeneration, and of our initiation into the church. And therefore Heb 6:2 deems the instruction of those who have been baptized among the primary elements of the Christian faith after repentance and belief; and the whole apostolic practice shows that upon the actual entry into the outward church through a profession of faith and repentance, baptism always has been administered to signify that fact.

3. And so to proceed to an explanation of baptism, the strict meaning of *baptō* and *baptizō*, from which comes *baptismos*, is to make wet and to wash; and a clear instance of this meaning is found in Luke 11:38. And thence, the Pharisees' washings of cups, bronze vessels and bedding are called *baptismoi* (Mark 7:4), and also the ceremonial washings of the Old Testament (Heb 9:10). But metaphorically that word is usually employed for the abundant outpouring of spiritual gifts, or the violent onslaught of things that bring grief and sorrow.

4. Hence the distinctions arise that Tertullian himself had made between baptism in a stream or in water (Matt 3:11) and baptism by the wind or Spirit (Acts 1:5), and the baptism of blood or martyrs (on the basis of Mark 10:38). And to these some add the baptism of enlightenment or teaching (Acts 18:25)—because the preaching of the Word sheds light on the human intellect and with its light illumines and enlightens his mind.

5. Our task, however, is to offer a treatment of baptism that is restricted to baptism in a stream or in water, and in order to do so in a comprehensive and orderly fashion, we shall treat 1) its efficient cause; 2) its matter and form; 3) its goal and effect; and lastly 4) its subject and some points connected with it.

6. It is clear from Matt 21:25 that the principal efficient or establishing cause of this sacrament is God himself, as it states that the baptism administered by John comes from heaven and not from men; and John the Baptist himself testifies in John 1:33 that the God who sent him to baptize with water is the same one who said to him: "the one over whom you will see the Spirit descending and resting, he it is who baptizes with the Holy Spirit."

7. From this we gather that the formula for baptism which Christ prescribes for his disciples in Matt 28 and Mark 16 does not constitute the very first

institution of baptism but rather the extension of it to all the nations, and a more exact way of administering it.

8. For along with the Reformed churches we state that if you look to its substance, the baptism that was begun by John is entirely the same one as that which was continued by the apostles according to Christ's command, even though in a few details one can observe some difference.

9. The difference can be seen from the fact that, if you look at the wording, one does not read that the exact formula is observed, "in the name of the Father, of the Son, and of the Holy Spirit." Even so there is no doubt that John with his baptism gave a seal of that doctrine which explained the same divinity of Father, Son, and Holy Spirit, and the doctrine of the office of Christ as the God-and-man more distinctly; as is evident from Matt 3[:16–17], and likewise from John 1[:29] and 3[:28] which contains a summary of his preaching.

10. And [the difference can be seen] from the fact that John with his baptism taught people to believe in the Christ who was going to come, and who was going to accomplish the work of our redemption (Acts 19:4), while we are baptized into him who has died in order that with him we should die to sins, and who arose so that he might raise us unto a new life with him, as the apostle Paul explains in Rom 6:2 and following.

11. And for the rest, the same benefits of Christ were sealed by both baptisms; for just as John's baptism was one of repentance and forgiveness of sins (Mark 1:4, Acts 19:4), so too our baptism is a seal of the forgiveness of sins and of the gift of regeneration, as will be shown more extensively later on.

12. The administering cause of baptism is solely the minister (or pastor) of the church, as is shown clearly by all the instances that are found in the New Testament, and by Christ's own command, "teach all nations, baptizing them, etc." (Matt 28:19). For just as it is customary for rulers' seals to be affixed to the rulers' letters of recommendation only by those appointed to this task by public authority, so too no-one can lawfully confirm by the sacraments the teachings of God's Gospel that have been proclaimed publicly unless he has been appointed to these tasks with a special calling. Therefore, they are also called God's heralds, and ambassadors and ministers of Christ, and in particular stewards of God's mysteries (1 Cor 4:1; 2 Cor 5:20).

13. Therefore, we do not acknowledge that there is any need so great that it is permitted in this sacrament of baptism for private individuals (men or women) to assume this office—something that even the papal teachers and the Lutherans do not allow in the sacrament of the Lord's Supper in any case of need—because one should not deal with any need in a way that is contrary to the institution of Christ. But it is God alone who has the power, and who is accustomed to fill what is lacking to ordinary instruments: either by replacing them with other, extraordinary instruments (as happened in the case of Phillip in Acts 8 and Ananias in Acts 22, in some people's judgment), or by claiming the entire internal action as his own without the use of instruments (as can be seen in the case of those who died uncircumcised, before the eighth day, and also in the case of the robber who was crucified together with Christ). And our opponents acknowledge that this happens in the case of all adult believers who were hindered by some need through no fault of their own, and who could obtain outward baptism only in vow.

14. Moreover, all members of the orthodox church must in every way strive to seek baptism for themselves or for their children from none other than the pastors of the orthodox church, lest they be seen to have a part in the false teaching and unjust works of darkness. Nevertheless, if some people have been baptized already by false teachers who employ the form for baptism in its integrity and who do not turn the fundamental teachings of baptism directly upside down, we state that orthodox shepherds should not perform their baptism all over again. But there is a different reasoning for others who do deny those teachings directly or who do change the form for baptism, as it was judged concerning the Paulinists at the Synod of Nicaea. For in this case the true baptism is not repeated, but a false baptism which is no baptism—conferred by a church which is no church—replaces the true and genuine one in the church of Christ.

15. The essence of baptism consists in its legitimate subject-matter and form. And since its subject-matter is either outward and visible (which is usually called the sign), or inward and invisible (which is called the thing signified), we should give a brief treatment of each.

16. And here, as in all the sacraments, the outward subject-matter or sign is two-fold, namely substantial, and ritual. Everyone agrees that the substantial element is water, as can be seen from Matt 3:6, Acts 10:47, and other places. And for this reason, we should consider the things that the papal teachers

add to this subject-matter as obviously superstitious, and as self-willed worship. Such things include salt, and oil, which were taken over from the Jewish sacrifices out of wicked imitation; so also the spittle, the wax candles, and similar things in turn taken over from Christ's miracles or from the rite of the early church that was accustomed to meeting in underground crypts or at night. And that is because we should not add to or take away anything from what God has commanded (Deut 12:32), and because it is pointless to worship God according to the commandments of men (Matt 15:9).

17. The very many questions that the Scholastics usually raise on this point are foolish ones: whether it is permitted to use for baptism anything other than every-day water, or whether it is permitted to use lye, urine, boiled or distilled water, or also wine, vinegar, or even sand or mud. For as they rashly identify many materials on the assumption that baptism is absolutely necessary, so we read that Christ and the apostles consecrated and used for this sacrament nothing other than every-day water, and therefore since these materials lack any commandment or promise, they cannot be used in faith. Accordingly, we see that also John preached in Aenon because there was much water there (John 3:23), and that Philip did not baptize the already believing Ethiopian until they came to a place where there was water (Acts 8:36). And since there is obviously nothing more common than water (so that it has even become a proverb), instances of that sort can arise very rarely.

18. In this sacrament the ritual or ceremonial sign is the baptizing or washing-away in the name of the Father, the Son, and the Holy Spirit, as Christ expressly commanded (Matt 28 and Mark 16). Therefore, Eph 5:26 says "the washing of the water by the Word," Titus 3:5 "the washing of regeneration," and Peter, in 1 Pet 3:21, "putting away filth from the body," through a metonymy of the effect.

19. In the Christian church it always has been deemed a matter of indifference whether we must baptize with a single immersion, or with three. And so too for the question whether we must use immersion or sprinkling, since no express command exists for it, and in the Scriptures one can find no fewer examples of sprinkling than of immersion. For in Matt 3 Christ entered into the water and emerged from it, as did the Ethiopian in Acts 8. And, in one day within the very city of Jerusalem many thousands are said to have been baptized (Acts 2), and so also many inside private homes (Acts 16 and 18:1; 1 Cor 1:16), where that kind of entry into water was hardly possible. And this

rite of sprinkling is supported also by the "baptism in the cloud and in the sea" which Paul treats in 1 Cor 10, and by the word "sprinkling," which is used of the blood of Christ for the washing-away of our sins (Heb 9:14 [cf. Heb 12:24]).

20. On this point, too, then, the additions made by the papal teachers are superstitious, namely, making the sign of the cross and the practice of exorcisms, since there are not any traces of them in Holy Scripture, and both of them were taken over through a wrong imitation from the rites of ancient Christians as they lived among heathen nations. For just as the converted gentiles renounced Satan and the cult of idols in this manner, so they also adopted the signs of crosses to show that from then on they were boasting only in the cross of Christ. Even though they could perhaps be excused of this practice on the grounds that these were customs of the church in the beginning, so at the present time they should not have been kept in some reformed churches, as they do not have any use or benefit.

21. In this sacrament the inward subject-matter, or the thing that is signified, is also two-fold: either it corresponds to the outward sign that is substantial, or to the outward sign that is ritual.

22. Corresponding to both outward signs together is the washing-away of our sins through the blood and Spirit of Jesus Christ. For as the blood of Christ cleanses us of our sins (Rev 1:5) because we are set free from our sins by the power and merit of Christ's death, so also the Spirit of Christ cleanses us from our sins, because he applies to us the merit of Christ's death, and by his own power frees us from the reign of sin. These two benefits of Christ are joined together by the apostle Paul in this way in 1 Cor 6:11: "But you were washed, but you were sanctified, but you were justified in the name of the Lord Jesus and in the Spirit of our God." And the apostle says also in Eph 5:27: "Christ gave himself up for the church, to cleanse it with the washing of the water by the Word." And in Titus 3:5 we are said "to have been saved through the washing of regeneration and renewing of the Holy Spirit, which he poured out on us richly through Jesus Christ our Savior."

23. The form of baptism, considered as a whole, consists of that sacramental union that exists between the sign and the thing signified. For even though the sign and the thing signified have each their own peculiar form, as is clear from the preceding, nevertheless this singular form of the parts takes on (as

they say) the nature of the designated matter when it refers to the whole (which usually happens in integral parts).

24. This sacramental union of the sign with the thing signified is not a real conjunction and one inhering in a subject, as some imagine it to be, but only a relative one, consisting of that mutual relationship wherein the sign places the thing signified before the believer's eyes and seals it, and the principal cause extends and offers the thing signified on the condition of faith and repentance.

25. For neither is the blood of Christ present in the water of baptism in a real or corporeal way, nor does the Spirit of Christ—although it is by its very nature present everywhere—inhere in the water as in a subject. Nor is the washing-away of sins effectively accomplished by the outward washing of water, because that is a power solely of God, and no creature of itself is capable of it, but it is Christ himself who through the efficacy of his Spirit unites us more unto himself and imparts to us his benefits that were obtained for us by the power of his death, just as he is wont to do through the Word alone. But when this sacrament is used lawfully, he does so much more effectively and uniquely; and in fact here the things signified are presented through two of our senses (namely hearing and seeing). And so our faith is aroused more strongly and rendered more active. And hence it also happens that in this operation Scripture clearly distinguishes external baptism from internal baptism, and the administrative cause from the principal cause, as is evident from Matt 3:11, Col 2:11, and 1 Pet 3:21, etc.

26. Therefore, we reject in the first place the view of the papal teachers who think that these outward signs bestow grace on grounds of the work performed (as they call it); that is, on the grounds of the actual power of the outward action, barring the hindrance of any mortal sin. They foolishly posit this restriction on their assumption, that even children are all liable to mortal sin before they are regenerated, and that also adults who are not yet reborn are of necessity still under the reign of sin, unless they say that in man either original sin or the reign of sin is not mortal, contrary to their own principles and contrary to Scripture which testifies that a man who is not yet reborn cannot see the kingdom of God (John 3). And secondly, the folly of this view will be clear from the fact that Scripture has opened up for us no other way to saving grace or to fellowship with Christ except through faith. "For the Gospel is the power of God unto salvation for all who believe" (Rom 1:16),

and "through faith Christ dwells in our hearts" (Eph 3:17), and "indeed, without faith it is not possible to please God" (Heb 11:5).

27. We also reject the opinion of certain Ubiquitarians who bind the Holy Spirit's regenerative power in baptism to the outward water in such a manner that this power is either inherent in the water itself or at least does not initiate regeneration except in the very act of baptism. [We reject it] for it conflicts with all the passages of Scripture wherein faith and repentance, and so also the beginning or seed of regeneration, is required beforehand of those to be baptized. After all, the efficient cause cannot possibly be later than its effect.

28. Nor is there any validity to the exception some of them make by distinguishing between the baptism of adults and the baptism of infants so as to allow adult baptism to be a sign and seal of the regeneration that has been received, but who want infant baptism to be an instrument to start the regeneration. For besides the fact that there is not any basis for this distinction in all of Scripture (which acknowledges but one kind of baptism), even those very passages that they do adduce in support of their view (Rom 6; Gal 3; Eph 5; Titus 3, etc.) deal directly and strictly with those people who already were adults and who were baptized only when they were of adult age, as is manifest from those very same passages.

29. And so we do not bind the efficacy of baptism to the precise moment when the outward water moistens the body, but—following Scripture—we require faith and repentance beforehand in all who are to be baptized, at least according to the judgment of love. This holds both for the infant members of the covenant, in whom we assert that the seed and spirit of faith and repentance must be determined to be present by virtue of divine blessing and the evangelical covenant, as well as for adults in whom a profession of actual faith and repentance is necessary. Thereupon, just as seed that has been sown into the ground does not always take on growth at that very moment but when the rain or the sky's warmth comes over it, so also the word or the sacramental sign is not always effective at the very first instant, but only then when the blessing of the Holy Spirit is added.

30. This point is demonstrated by the many people who have been baptized in infancy, yet who nevertheless for a time live ungodly lives, and also by the many hypocritical adults who sometimes repent of their sins only much later. In fact, Augustine, in *On the Baptism of Heretics*, makes the general declaration: "Even though the baptism in Christ is one and the same for heretics and

schismatics, yet in that case because of the filth of discord and the sin of dissension baptism does not bring about the forgiveness of sins. But that same baptism does start having the power to banish sins at the time when those people have come to the peace of the church—so that the baptism is not rejected as being foreign or as some other baptism (nor so that a second baptism should be administered), but so that the same baptism which publicly worked death on account of the disharmony, would inwardly work salvation on account of peace." And as for the fact that baptism never had this effect in some people, like Simon Magus and other reprobates, we judge that this should be left to the judgments of God, which are secretly just and justly secret. For not the children of the flesh but the children of the promise are considered as the seed (Rom 9); for though the former are not unworthy of being passed over, yet the others are not worthy of themselves to have the work of regeneration begun and completed in them.

31. Therefore, when we say that the proper power of outward baptism resides in being a seal, we mean two things: firstly, that it makes more certain the promised grace that the principal cause has conferred or is to confer, and secondly that it strengthens and increases that grace. But since that promise is not absolute but linked to the condition of faith and repentance, it follows that the grace is sealed only to those who believe and repent, and consequently do not use the signs in an unworthy manner, as the apostle says in 1 Cor 11:29.

32. In this regard we grant that this sacrament—just like the other ones—is also exhibitive of the thing that is promised, because in the lawful and worthy use of this sacrament these things that are promised are through the Holy Spirit not merely offered to believers but they are in fact exhibited to and conferred upon them. For God is truthful in sealing his promises, and our sacraments are not supplements of a letter that kills, but of the life-giving Spirit [2 Cor 3:6].

33. This sacrament has many great uses and effects. For as many of us as have been baptized have taken on Christ (Gal 3:27); we are baptized unto the forgiveness and washing-away of our sins (Acts 2:38 and 22:16). Baptism is the washing of regeneration, the pledge of a good conscience through Christ's resurrection (Titus 3[:5] and 1 Pet 3[:21]). Through baptism the old man is crucified and buried, and the new one is more made alive (Rom 6:3).

And finally, even the adoption itself, and salvation, are ascribed to it (Mark 16:16 and elsewhere).

34. In addition to these primary uses there are other, secondary ones, namely the outward engrafting into the visible, particular church (Acts 2:41), and the coming-together of all the members of Christ into one body (1 Cor 12:12), and from them the subsequent indication of our profession of faith and the distinction and separation from all other gatherings, i.e., gatherings of unbelievers.

35. But those uses and effects of baptism must not be limited to the remission and abolition of sins that have been committed before baptism, nor should they be limited to being received into the grace that is promised first to believers, as the papal teachers would have it. For the deletion of mortal sins (as they call it) that have been committed after baptism, they have conjured up another sacrament for the restoration in grace, namely that of penance and absolution by the priest; and so they call it the second plank, whereby, after the first grace has been lost one must escape from the shipwreck again.

36. For although we freely admit that also sins committed after baptism are not forgiven to anyone other than repentant believers (just as sins that had been committed before baptism were forgiven no differently), nevertheless we do say that there is no need of some new sacrament for the restoration of this benefit, since in the whole New Testament the holy Scripture knows of no sacrament for repentance and remission of sins other than baptism only.

37. And yet they themselves admit that what suffices for the daily or venial sins (as they call it) is ordinary repentance, and also the Lord's prayer along with the recollection of one's baptism. In the same way we assert that in the case of more serious and extraordinary sins an extraordinary surge of repentance and faith is sufficient, along with recourse to that covenant which had been sealed to us at first through baptism. It is as when a woman has broken the conjugal trust, there is no need of a new marriage in order to reconcile the man to his wife, nor of renewed marriage-pledges; but sufficient is serious remorse of what has been done, and a confirmation of the former marriage.

38. Not only does the nature and perpetuity of the new covenant (depicted for us in Isa 54:10, Heb 8:12, and various other places) that was ratified through baptism testify to us of this perpetual efficacy of baptism, but so too

does the example of circumcision whereby that same covenant was confirmed (if you consider its substance). Nevertheless, at that former time repentance was not (as the papal teachers admit) a sacrament of the forgiveness of sins that happened subsequent [to circumcision]; instead, only the single seal of circumcision sufficed for the purpose of sealing the perpetual righteousness of faith and the circumcision of the heart for those who repented.

39. The recurring practice of Holy Scripture testifies to this same thing, since by the use and recollection of baptism it brings forth arguments whereby those who previously have been baptized are admonished time and again to do away with the old man and its lusts that suddenly spring up and present themselves, and they are admonished to bring to perpetual life the new man, as can be seen from Rom 6:2, 1 Cor 12:12, Gal 3:27, Eph 5:25, Col 2:12, etc. And consequently it is not merely the beginning of salvation that relates to baptism, but even salvation itself, and life eternal (Mark 16:16; 1 Pet 3:21, and elsewhere).

40. But in fact it is foolish and ungodly to put before a man who is already a believer and who has already been baptized some satisfaction, or some merit for the remission of any sin, other than the satisfaction of Christ, or to put before him some propitiation or reconciliation with God other than through that blood which cleanses us from all our sins (1 John 1:7). And the sacrament of that blood is not that fictitious penance of the papal teachers, but baptism, as was shown earlier.

41. Now that the things which had to be stated in brief about the causes and effects of this sacrament are finished, it remains for us to proceed to give some explanations of its subject and adjuncts.

42. It is clear from the command of Christ that the receiving subject of baptism is a human being: "Go, teach all nations, baptizing them, etc." (Matt 28:19). Hence even the more educated of the papal teachers tend to excuse rather than to defend the baptism of bells—a practice that we, however, assert is pure profaning of Christian baptism.

43. Moreover, when we say "men" we mean living men, not deceased ones, as opposed to the Corinthians who used to baptize even the dead, making abuse of the apostle's passage: "otherwise what would those people do who are baptized on behalf of the dead?" (1 Cor 15:29). But it is something quite

different to be baptized on behalf of the dead than to baptize the dead. For they can be said to be baptized on behalf of the dead who are being baptized unto the mortification of the flesh, or even unto the fate of being subjected to the slandering and persecutions of this world and carry about in their bodies the *nekrōsis*, that is, the dying of the Lord Jesus, as the apostle says in 2 Cor 4:10.

44. And yet not all people who are living in the world are fit to be baptized, but only those whom we can consider as members of the covenant and heirs of the New Testament, of which this sacrament is a seal and pledge.

45. People of this sort are, in the first place, all adults—and only adults who profess their faith in Christ and true repentance—of any people whatsoever, of any position, or sex. For in Christ there is neither Jew nor Greek, male nor female, neither slave nor free, as is clear from what Christ taught in Matt 28:19: "Whoever believes and is baptized will be saved" (Mark 16:16). And so also Acts 2:38: "Repent and be baptized, everyone of you in the name of Jesus Christ."

46. But if anyone lives an ungodly life, even though he has professed his faith, he should not be admitted to baptism. For baptism is a sacrament not only of faith but also of repentance. And the same applies to him who with his profession of faith in Christ and of repentance wishes to foster or protect false teachings or heresies contrary to the very basis of the true faith, for repentance is a turning-away not just from a base life to a life of holiness, but also from false teachings to the knowledge of the truth, as the apostle says in 2 Tim 2:23. In fact heretics and those who foster such false teachings are so far from being admitted to baptism that according to the apostle's instruction (Rom 16:17, and elsewhere) believers should shun them, and they should be barred from the communion of the church.

47. People of this sort are in the second place, we judge, the children born of believing, covenant-member parents according to the promise of God in Gen 17: "I shall be God to you and to your seed," and this is not only by the example of circumcision, which was a seal of the same covenant, and which was replaced by baptism (Col 2:11), but also because the sign itself cannot be withheld from those to whom that which it signifies pertains, as the apostle Peter clearly testifies in Acts 10:47 and 11:17. But now no-one can say that the benefits of the blood and Spirit of Christ do not pertain to the children of believers, unless he also wishes to exclude them from salvation. For just

as no-one can enter the kingdom of God unless he is born again by water and the Spirit (John 3:5), so no-one belongs to Christ who does not have the Spirit of Christ (Rom 8:9).

48. The passage in Eph 5:26 offers very clear support to this point, as the apostle there says: "Christ loved his church and gave himself up for it, cleansing it with the washing of water in the Word." Hence it follows that children of believers either are not part of that church for which Christ gave himself up, or they, too, are cleansed with the washing of water in the Word. But let us now leave aside the instances of entire families that were baptized by the apostles (Acts 16:15 and 33; Acts 18:8; 1 Cor 1:16), and also the instances of the children of the Israelites, who had been baptized under the cloud and in the red sea no less than the adult Israelites, as the apostle testifies in 1 Cor 10. And to be sure, if those children are united into one mystical body with the church of Christ, they must be set apart by some sign of this communion from those who are strangers to this body.

49. But we do exclude from baptism the children of those who clearly are strangers to the covenant, such as the children of heathens, Muslims, Jews, and of similar people whom the Holy Spirit himself declares to be unclean (1 Cor 7:14). And for this reason, we should leave them—like foreigners—to the judgment of God, as the apostle himself teaches (1 Cor 5:12–13)—unless they happen through lawful adoption or through the just and properly-designated status of slaves to be enrolled and taken up into the families of believers as though belonging to them. For in this case many Reformed churches do baptize those children, because they deem that God has adopted them into the fellowship of his covenant in this manner, that is to say by the covenant of Gen 17:12–13, which in the early church was so far beyond debate that from it Augustine on several occasions deduced a powerful argument against the Pelagians for election by grace.

50. However, we do not therefore exclude from the fellowship of this sacrament those children who were born of Christian stock and baptized parents—even though their own parents through their wicked lives or impure faith cause the efficacy of the covenant sealed in their own baptism to be ineffective for themselves—if those same parents or the relatives who have authority over them present them for baptism according to the customary order in our churches. For in the new covenant the son does not bear the iniquity of the father, and of such children God remains God just the same,

as he himself bears witness in Ezek 16 and 23. There he calls the children of the godless Israelites his own sons, whom they had begotten for God, although they were sacrificing them to Molech. And it is from these children that God also normally gathers his church through the ordinary preaching of the Word. And for this reason he also commanded the children of such Israelites (of whom many had died in their ungodliness) to be circumcised, no less than those of the godly ones (Josh 5:4 and 6)—which necessary deed also the Israelite and the early Christian church always have considered beyond debate.

51. The adjuncts of baptism are firstly its unity; for just as we are born once, so is it once that we are born again, and consequently it is once that we receive the sign of regeneration. And hence, just as circumcision once conferred was not repeated, so too Scripture teaches neither by command nor by example that a baptism once lawfully conferred must be repeated. In fact, on the contrary, wherever mention is made of baptism in the New Testament, mention is made of only one baptism, and of a baptism that is conferred only once. Hence it is also called explicitly 'one baptism' (Eph 4:5).

52. No specific time is prescribed for baptism, which was the case for circumcision. Meanwhile, however, it is our view that baptism should be sought as soon as it can be held according to the church-order and by the good health of the one to be baptized. For it is impossible for us to neglect the ordinary signs and instruments of divine grace without committing sin, and in fact we cannot despise them without grave sin and peril.

53. The place that has been appointed for all the sacred gatherings is also sacred for baptism. Accordingly we see in all the instances provided by the apostolic practice that baptism was linked to the preaching of the Word, whether it was in a public place or a private house, so long as there was a gathering of the church. But apart from times of persecution, public rather than private places should be appointed for this event, as is shown from the fact that baptism is a supplement to public ministry and not to private exhortation.

54. Even though it is not absolutely necessary that there be special witnesses to the baptism, particularly in churches that enjoy public peace, nevertheless not only does the matter itself show that the presence of such people is useful (provided they are godly and faithful), but also the practice of the whole early church, which by a very plausible argument, along with the granting of names,

was derived from the actual ritual of circumcision, as instances of it occur in Isa 8:2 and Luke 1:59.

55. But if anyone either on the testimony of the church, or parents, or witnesses, or of others cannot be sure about the baptism that he had received in infancy, or if it happened that he was moistened by no other baptism than that of the midwives or private individuals, we are of the opinion that such a man may be baptized without any scruple. For the baptism applied by the last-mentioned people is not a baptism at all, and the baptism of the first-mentioned people is worthless, as the Council of Carthage has rightly decided (5.3): "Concerning infants it has been decided that whenever no very certain witnesses are found who testify without a doubt that they were baptized, and whenever they themselves are not, on account of their age, in a position to give an answer about the sacraments that were given to them, they should be baptized without any scruple, lest that doubt should cause them to be bereft of the cleansing of the sacraments." For as [pope] Leo [I] rightly added, "what is not known to have been done cannot be said to have been repeated."

56. And consequently we should not approve of a conditional baptism that the papal teachers are used to observing in such cases, according to this formula: "If you have not been baptized, then I baptize you." For a baptism of this kind lacks any precedent in Scripture and changes the form for baptism that Christ had taught, and it also leaves the one who has been baptized in doubt as to which baptism is the real one—which goes against the purpose of baptism that does not make the promises of God ambiguous but establishes and seals them.

DISPUTATION 45

ON THE LORD'S SUPPER

President: Antonius Thysius
Respondent: Volcker Oosterwijck

This disputation forms a long and complex argument on the doctrine of the Lord's Supper, and it seeks to clarify the Reformed position within the setting of various confessional perspectives. In it Thysius brings forward many and diverse points that address Roman Catholic, Lutheran, and Zwinglian understandings of the Lord's Supper. These points are based in the text of Scripture, in the history of the Church, in philosophy, rhetoric, and grammar. Especially the doctrines of transubstantiation (Romanist) and consubstantiation (Lutheran) are refuted, but also the Zwinglian perspective that the Lord's Supper is merely commemorative in scope. The definition (6) addresses the essential elements of the sacrament: that it is spiritual food for Christ's believers, that this spiritual food is offered through bread and wine, for remembering Christ and declaring his death, for practicing communion with Christ unto his mystical body, resulting in a greater assurance of eternal life and to the glory of God's grace. After some remarks on Jesus Christ as the efficient cause of the institution of the Lord's Supper and the meaning of the temporal circumstances under which this took place (7–16), the disputation is arranged according to the New Testament account of the institution of the Supper by Jesus Christ himself (17–86). The institution narrative is divided into three parts: 1. Four actions of Christ (17–31); 2. Christ's commands (32–40); 3. Christ's explanation of his actions and commands (41–86). A considerable portion of this disputation is taken up by careful interpretations of the words of institution, most notably the phrases 'this is my body' and 'this is my blood,' which are taken figuratively (43–77). It is due to the sacramental union of the Lord's Supper that Christ's body and blood are present, not as substances but in their relation to the signs of the bread and the wine (73). So Christ himself and his benefits, as obtained for us by his death on the cross, are present in the sacrament (58). The last thesis (87) refers to God's Word as the source for the truth concerning the Lord's Supper, and expresses the expectation that what is commanded will serve as consolation for believers, and will be able to put a limit to quarreling among brothers.

1. Up to this point [we have treated] Baptism, the sacrament of regeneration, repentance, and faith, and so of "putting on Christ" and of our initiation. What comes next is a treatment of the Supper of the Lord, the sacrament that nourishes and the mystery of our perfection (as the fathers call it).

2. This sacrament goes by various names in Scripture and the fathers. In Scripture it is called: 1. "The Supper of the Lord" (1 Cor 11:20), a term that comes from its circumstance in time, in that it was a meal at evening. And it comes from the one who founded it, and also from its goal, for it was instituted by the Lord in order to be celebrated in remembrance of him (a term that the Jesuits wrongly restrict to the love-feasts). 2. "The table of the Lord" (1 Cor 10:21), and, simply, "the table" (Acts 6:2), as a metonym for this sacred banquet consisting of bread and wine (although there Paul seems to relate it to the bread, since he puts the cup of the Lord over against it). 3. "The bread that is broken and the cup of blessing" (1 Cor 10:16). 4. "This bread and this cup" (or, "of the Lord"), and simply "bread and cup" (1 Cor 11:26, 27), which by its parts expresses the whole. 5. "The bread" (1 Cor 10:17) and likewise "the drink" (1 Cor 10) through association with the word ["wine"], by synecdoche. 6. "The spiritual food and drink" (1 Cor 10:3, 4). 7. The "breaking of the bread" (Acts 2:42 and 20:7)—whereby otherwise the Jews indicated any domestic meal whatsoever—and so it is the breaking of bread *par excellence*. 8. The "body of the Lord" (1 Cor 11:29), as a metonym. 9. And lastly *Agapē* or "Love-feast" (2 Pet 2:13, Jude 12), that is, the sacred banquet that was instituted for the sake of testifying to and preserving the love, and that included this sacrament as its most powerful element.

3. Furthermore, among the church fathers, however, especially the Greek ones, it is called 1) *Sunaxis* [a gathering together]; in the Latin fathers *collecta* (what is gathered), *collectio* (gathering) and *conventus* (gathering) because it was customary to perform this public action along with the Lord's Supper in the assemblies of the church (from the passage in Acts 20:7 and 1 Cor 11:18, 33). 2) The *Eucharistia* or the *Eulogia*, that is, the giving of thanks and the benediction—i.e., derived from Christ's foregoing actions and from the purpose he stated, because it is done and should be done in a solemn act of thanksgiving for the death of Christ and his benefits, according to 1 Cor 10:16 and Matt 26:26–27. 3) *Koinonia*, that is, fellowship or communion, from Paul,

who applies to this bread and wine the name of communion and participation in Christ's body and blood (1 Cor 10:16–17, 21). 4) *Prosphora*, offering, or the offer, i.e., from the offering of bread and wine given by the believers for celebrating the Love Feast and Eucharist. This offering used to be made to the overseer and in turn was given back to the people who partook of communion (the former used to be called *doron*, the gift, and the latter *antidoron*, the gift-in-return). And it comes from the offering of praise and thanks that the entire church offered to God. But the term is not meant of the offering by Christ in a passive sense like the offering that the priests made to God the Father—except in a figurative way. 5) *Thusia*, that is, sacrificial offering or victim, in a very non-literal sense, for the prayers and thanksgiving, as well as for the remembrance of that one and only expiatory sacrifice on the cross once performed for us. The word is not to be taken in its strict sense, as the Romans would like to take it, who not only take it as a eucharistic [or thank] offering, but also as an expiatory offering for sin itself (although they call that offering "unbloody"). Furthermore, the ancients denote that sacred rite with other names, like 'symbol' and 'mystery,' i.e., the "sign and sacrament of the body and blood of the Lord, etc."—but these are almost descriptions or commendations and epithets of so great a mystery.

4. Next, the word *leitourgia*, from *leitos* (public), generally means a public function or office, and in the church it means a sacred function that denotes the whole sacred ministry of the divine Word (in the same way that *leitourgountes* means not those who bring sacrifices, as Erasmus had translated it in Acts 14 [= 13:2], but rather those who perform the sacred service, as also he himself explains it), and it specifically means the administration of the Lord's Supper. There are some who give it the specific name *hierourgia*, "performing the sacred tasks," which refers also to the preaching of the Gospel in a metaphorical sense (Rom 15).

5. About four hundred years after Christ Latin-speaking people began to call it *missa*, "the mass." And that was not, as some following Reuchlin and Genebrard, wrongly argue, [taken] from the Hebrew *mas*, "tribute," from which *missah* in Deut 16:11 [= 16:10] is derived, i.e., "offering" (as the Vulgate has it) or "sufficiency" (as the Septuagint translators have it). Rather, "mass" would have received its name from *massah*, that is, from "the testing" of God. Nor does it come from the adjective in its feminine form *missa*, "sent," as in offering sent to God, as the papal teachers commonly take it. But it comes from the noun *missa* that is put in place of *missio* (sending), like the words

collecta (what is collected), *oblata* (what is offered), *remissa* (what is forgiven) and similar ones in the time of Tertullian that were used for *collectio* (collection), *oblatio* (offering) and *remissio* (forgiveness). And so it is said that the word comes either from the offerings sent by the faithful or from the start of the celebration of the mysteries, which took place when the *missa*, or the "sending away," was pronounced upon the catechumens and the penitents. Or it comes from the end of the celebration, when after the sacred matters were concluded, the *missa*, or the "sending away," of the faithful who are about to depart, happens by means of this solemn formula, *Ite missa est*, that is "go, the dismissal is made." In worse times, it is also called "the sacrament of the altar," which even Luther, for some unknown reason, thought should be preserved by him.

6. Now the Lord's Supper is the second sacrament of the new covenant or testament, namely the one of spiritual nourishment that Christ our Lord instituted for believers, a sacrament that by means of the broken bread and poured-out wine signifies Christ as the one who suffered and died, or his body and blood that was broken and shed for the forgiveness of sins. And by participating and communing in the bread and wine the spiritual food and drink are offered to those who use them, and bestowed upon those who believe. And it should be given to believers to remember Christ while also declaring his death; and furthermore, for the union and fellowship with Christ their head unto the true, mystical body, resulting in a greater assurance of eternal life for believers, and to the glory of God's grace.

7. The efficient cause of the institution of the Lord's Supper is the Lord Jesus, the founder of the new covenant of grace, and the mediator and testator of the New Testament; consequently he is the one and only institutor of the symbols for it. For it is an act of supreme power, and the one who bestows the grace has the right to add to it the signs of grace, and to present and bring about what the signs display and promise. But it is the duty of Christ's minister to pass on to the church and to keep intact what the Lord has given to him, faithfully and without removing, adding, or altering anything (Matt 28:20; 1 Cor 11:23).

8. As for the exhibition of the sacrament, there again Christ is the proper author, who by his own authority exhibited the symbols outwardly first by himself and then by the ministers of his Word, whom he commissioned in

his own name, and to whom he is present. But he bestows the actual thing on believers inwardly through the Holy Spirit.

9. And as the host of this sacred banquet, the Lord Jesus instituted and exhibited the sacrament "on the night in which he was betrayed," that is, the evening of the sixth day of the week, or the first day of the week of the Unleavened Bread of the Passover according to the custom of the Jews, who start the day in the evening. He did this so that by this temporal circumstance he might commend this meal more effectively to those who belong to him, and indeed by this last meal might establish a monument to the covenant and testament that would be validated by his death shortly thereafter. And he did so by means of the place, that is, in the city of Jerusalem, in an inn, in the large dining room that was set out and made ready, where the Passover had been prepared as well.

10. And in fact [he established and exhibited] it "after he had eaten" (Luke 22:20), that is, after he had eaten the meal of the Passover lamb as required by the Law, together with his disciples, and he did so not according to Jewish tradition, but according to the prescript of the Law for it (Mark 14:12, Luke 22:7). The Passover meal was a type of Christ (1 Cor 5:7) and an antitype of this Supper of the Lord, as it signified both Christ the Lamb of God, and, through commemoration of the delivery from Egypt, spiritual delivery (1 Cor 5:7). Indeed, so that in this way it might show that by the succession of the new sacrament the old sacrament has been fulfilled. Regarding this fulfillment Christ said, "I have eagerly desired to eat this Passover with you before I suffer" [Luke 22:15].

11. And to be precise, [Christ instituted the sacrament] "after washing their feet," as many [sources] say. For when the meal was begun (John 13:2), he rose from the table (verse 4) and washed the feet of his disciples, as was the customary practice of eastern peoples (Luke 7:44). He did so in order that by this exemplary action he might show them the way to humility and love, and testify of his favor towards those who are his—that he is certainly the one who cleanses his people from their uncleanness (John 13:8–10, 14). And he did so in order to teach them by means of a comparison (and not a sacrament) with what frame of mind they ought to approach these sacred things. Even so the western church has, elsewhere and sometimes not without abuse, adopted the practice as a sacrament.

12. And they partook of the meal when Christ "was lying at table again" or "reclining" (John 13:23, 28) in the way that the people of God then had adopted, as they were not seated upright but reclined on couch, with their heads facing inwards and their feet outwards so that those who were second were nearly leaning upon the bosoms of those who were first (John 13:23, 25). He did so in order to show that this was a banquet and not a sacrifice, as the papal teachers would have it, who in poor imitation of Jewish and pagan customs introduced altars; if that were the case he would have performed the sacrifice while standing by an altar.

13. And [Christ ate the meal] together with his twelve disciples, or Apostles, while they were eating a commonplace everyday meal, or supping, as the Vulgate has it. He did so in order to show that this meal is a public one and not a private dinner. But the meal was connected to the rite of breaking bread and blessing wine in remembrance of the delivery from Egypt (Luke 22:17), as the Jewish books of rituals show—a rite that appears to have been replaced by the love-feast and this Lord's Supper, just as their habitual washings were replaced by baptism.

14. And so it was that Christ prepared the Supper for his dinner-guests the apostles, and for all believers whom they represent, as the apostle assures us. For the apostle [Paul] afterward applied what then happened concerning the apostles not just to the shepherds but also to the rest of the church (1 Cor 11), and the apostles did not function then as those who administer but as recipients. And Paul applied it to those who are living in a state of piety (insofar as that can be humanly known, leaving the hidden things over to God) and not to unbaptized catechumens, or those who have fallen, or to people who are among those who are repenting. Hence the apostle states: "Let everyone test himself," etc. But the fact that each person should test himself does not do away with the testing of others by the church and the shepherds. And at this point it is usual and possible to raise the question that arises from a comparison of Matthew and Mark with Luke and John: whether the betrayer Judas was present at the supper.

15. And these temporal circumstances, whether of evening- or night-time, or of the sixth day of the week or that particular day of the year (i.e., of the third day before Christ's resurrection), and also of the place (i.e., a private place), do not have any force of prescribed necessity or of observance. Nor do the following facts have any force of being required or observed: that the supper

was given to them after they had eaten a meal, after their feet had been washed, when they were lying at table, and even that there were twelve in number (some of which were observed for some time in the early church).

16. These were the prefatory remarks about the Lord's Supper. But as a whole the Supper consists of the mystical actions and words of Christ, and of the obedience of the disciples and believers that answers to them, and also in the subsequent giving of thanks. In these the causes of this mystery are summed up.

17. And of the sacramental actions by Christ that depend on their institution by Christ and on all that he did, and that were performed in such a manner that they were presented to the senses and happened through sensible things and might evoke something spiritual to the mind, the first one displayed to the apostles' eyes was the "taking," that is, "the bread that was taken" or "when he had taken the bread;" and thereupon taking "the cup," i.e., taking the cup into his hands, as he was the head of the household. Herein lies the starting point of the institution and action, and in particular of the very act of designating these things for a special purpose. And indeed, in taking them up into his hands there is an indication of his voluntary death. Similarly, the expressions "to take," "to put," "to hold," "to bear," "to carry" himself or his soul in his hands mean, by a common Hebraism: to run or undergo the greatest risk to one's life (Judg 12:3, 1 Sam 19:5 and 28:21, Job 13:14, Ps 119:109).

18. Moreover, the outward matter of this mystery resides in the two appearances that were taken, and while they are indeed two different appearances they are not really two proper sacraments (as some of the ancients say), since they come together for a single goal, namely the whole sacred meal and refreshment. For [Christ] took them up separately in order to show to them his own, bloodless body and the blood then as it were shed from his veins, and also to testify that he in his entirety is for us the complete food and refreshment (John 6:53, etc.).

19. Therefore, the papists clearly commit very serious violence against the integrity of the sacrament, and so they are sacrilegious when they withhold the chalice from believing laics, that is, withhold the second part of the sacrament—under whatever pretext of human wisdom or I know not what [eucharistic] concomitance, or out of respect for Christ's glorious body—utter folly over against the Lord! And they do so contrary to Christ's action

and commandment (Luke 22:19; 1 Cor 11:25) and contrary to the apostolic practice (1 Cor 11:26–27, 29) and, in sum, contrary to all of antiquity and God's universal church everywhere—except the Romanist church of late.

20. [Christ] used bread, real bread for eating that was thin in shape and not thick, so that it was suitable for breaking into pieces (as was the custom of those people), and it was one whole. And moreover, the bread was unleavened or unfermented; of course, that was by accident and due to the circumstance of the law about the first day of unleavened bread; otherwise Christ would have used everyday bread. That is why Christ makes a comparison with everyday bread in John 6, and the apostle when speaking about the Supper mentions simply the bread as it was used in Corinth, because unleavened bread had been abolished along with the Passover Lamb and the other ceremonies. Otherwise, this would be a matter of indifference, provided there is no belief of necessity. And therefore, the debate between the Greeks and Latins over this matter is an idle one.

21. In the same way he used the drink of the produce or fruit of the vine, i.e., wine (Matt 26:29). But it is not known whether the wine was red as it nearly always is in that region (Prov 21:31) and wherefore it is also called the "blood of grapes" (Gen 49:11), or whether it was diluted (which is called mixed wine), in keeping with the custom of blending the wine in those warmer climates (Prov 9:2, 5 and 23:30). Justin states that a cup of wine diluted with water was used. But that adds nothing to the religious character and mystery; nor does the material and shape of the cup (i.e., the chalice), whether it is wooden, silver, or gilded.

22. And the fact that for the mysteries he chose bread and wine, common things taken from everyday life, is because of the very close similarity and analogy in the properties and effects of both (i.e., as basic and very necessary nourishment) to the things they signify: the body and blood of the Lord.

23. Hence the papal teachers and others who follow them do not sin lightly when they use bread that is not bread but little slices of the smallest size and thin as a shadow, quite unlike the looks of real bread (and not worthy of that name) and not having the energy to nourish; they are wafers, or offerings as they call them. And they also use unleavened bread, as if it is necessary for the sacrament because of the precedent of Christ. And what is more, for the sake of mystery they use diluted wine, over which some ancients like Cyprian and others have philosophized in too much detail and dilutedly.

24. But if [the sacrament is held] where bread and wine are not used, or where they cannot be obtained in abundance, it is possible to use whatever takes the place of bread and wine, or whatever is the equivalent for those peoples.

25. The second action by Christ that the apostles' ears perceived is his speaking to God, expressed by the word *eulogēsas* [Matt 26:26] (with the assumption of the word "and" that Mark and Luke state explicitly [Mark 14:22, Luke 22:19]), that is, "and when he had blessed," as Matthew and Mark have it in the first part of the sentence. But in the second part of the phrase, concerning the cup, [it says] "and when he had given thanks," which appears to both phrases in Luke and Paul, so that the expressions are used interchangeably. And in fact, that interpretation is required in this place if we do not wish that only the bread was blessed and not this cup. And that is how elsewhere the expressions are used to mean the same thing in everyday meals (Matt 14:19, 15:36; Mark 6:41 and 8:6; Luke 9:16; John 6:11 and 23; Acts 27:35). In the same way one uses interchangeably the Hebrew words *berech*, that is, "he blessed, he prayed for blessing," and *yahdah*, "he confessed, praised, glorified, thanked." And with that [prayer] you must understand the words "looking up into heaven," the gesture of one praying that Christ used also elsewhere (Matt 14:19); and he did so "in the presence of all" (Acts 27:35). He "gave thanks" or "blessed," that is, he blessed God the Father, there as well as in Rom 14:6; and in fact, he gave thanks in particular for the bread and the wine as gifts of God's kindness, and especially for the gracious gift of redemption.

26. And so it is that under the name of giving thanks and blessing, that is, of invocation and prayer, this entire sacred action is understood synecdochally, and so too the consecration itself, of which that thanksgiving is only a portion. This is expressed more accurately by the word "blessing," with the fourth case of a thing, applied jointly to the bread and the cup (as the phrase appears in Luke 9:16). And those everyday things that were common aids for nourishing the body, and that God's Word and the prayer for believers sanctify for sacred use (which occurs when those things are received from God's bountiful hand and put to holy, sober use and related to God's glory; 1 Tim 4:3–5; 1 Cor 10:31), the Son of God additionally prepared, ordained, dedicated or sanctified and consecrated unto a sacred goal and spiritual function: the nourishment of the soul, so that they might be mystical symbols of his own body and blood. This is done by a change not in nature but quality (by the divine institution and ordination of doing things) and with solemn

prayer and right use. The word "blessing," when it relates to physical things, is nearly always understood in this way (Gen 2:3, etc.). It is in this sense that the apostle speaks of "the cup of blessing which we bless" (1 Cor 10:16).

27. And it is not explained to us which form of blessing and thanksgiving Christ used here, but here he did adapt that solemn formula of the old synagogue in the eating of the Passover, and the ancient liturgies show that the early church had its own prayers in the consecration [of the sacrament]. Therefore, it is out of superstition that the Romans established the consecration in crosses formed in mid-air, and in specifically adopted accompanying words, that is to say, in those four quietly mumbled words, or five (as the old translator has with the added word "for"): "for this is my body." And to those words they even attribute some operational power, a secret and even magical power, one that miraculously changes the very substance. But the consecration then was made by the words of Christ uttered in the first person; the consecration is not shown by the words of a minister that are to be uttered afterwards in the third person. Nor are they words of any kind of alteration in the strict sense, but rather of declaring what happened. Preceding the consecration, the offer and acceptance of what has happened clearly demonstrate this, as they are the offer and acceptance of what has already taken place and not of what ought to be done. For the use of something comes after the thing itself.

28. Christ's third action (which likewise is seen) is that after he had taken the bread and given thanks, he "broke it," as this is the order of Christ's words that is required by the aorist tenses. Moreover, he broke the bread in the manner of eastern peoples; he did not slice it in the manner of westerners, for the bread was so shaped that it was not compact but flat and rather broad like a pancake, so that it could be broken up easily. Likewise also the wine that was poured into the cup, and both [actions] were done in the usual and necessary ritual. For that was the duty of the father of the household, who tasted them beforehand and distributed them. And Christ broke the bread into pieces not only in order to distribute them, and he poured out the wine into the cup not only so that it could be drunk, but he did so for the mystery and the sacramental ceremony: so that it might signify his body, not as cut into pieces (John 19:33, 36) but metaphorically as completely broken up by the torments of soul and body. Indeed, as shattered by the scourgings, as punctured by the thorny crown, and as pierced in his hands and feet, and as torn by the opening of his side; and in the end, his body as broken up by the

draining of its blood and by the separation of soul from body, divided into two parts, and dead. And so breaking applies to the body and shedding to the blood, through the change into a metonym in both words.

29. And obviously for this reason in the distribution of the Eucharist the Romanists and their followers in handing out their circular crackers as unbroken have removed, in violation of the sacrament, the ritual of the breaking that from the time of Jesus Christ and the apostles (1 Cor 10:16) had been carried on in the early church, and maintained in the eastern churches, too. For they keep the ritual of breaking only for the priests when they offer the mass. Even those who are keen to be called Lutherans err by interpreting the word "to break" here only as "to distribute," because there follows "and he gave to them."

30. And Christ's fourth action (which concerns the sense of touch) is: "And he gave to his disciples." For he had taken and had broken in order to give; that is, he exhibited and gave the bread and the cup into the disciples' hands, and not into their mouths. For food is not ingested directly into the mouth except for those who are handicapped. And the receiving is in response to the giving, and in 1 Cor 11 the apostle implies the omitted giving with the receiving. And at this point the apostles do not function as shepherds but as representatives of the church as a whole, since it says that Christ gave it to them individually. Otherwise, if this is stated only concerning the apostles, what rule made the Lord's Supper common for everyone? And so this giving declares that like every sacrament so also this one exists not just in signifying but also in its application and use, and it declares that with these sacred signs God presents and gives Christ, so that he might be received and bestowed in faith. Therefore, when it says that he "gave to them," he did not sacrifice, for that is to give to God.

31. From this it is plainly obvious that the papal teachers commit a great sacrilege in the mass, in that the believers are fed only by looking upon the bread and the wine that the priests celebrating the mass give only to themselves, and so they make private that which was ordained for the whole church. Indeed, it is also idolatrous to take these elements and to raise them up to be worshiped.

32. To these actions of his, Christ also added statements for the apostles; some of them are "instructional," some are "declarative," and some "have

legal force" and fix a law for all Christianity throughout the ages, and declare the use and goal of this sacrament.

33. First, it says in a general way "and he said" (something that occurs to the ears); i.e., he said to his disciples. And he said the following things, and from that one can learn his institution of the actions. For since sacraments and sacramental actions arise "by institution," they would be bare spectacles devoid of substance if no words accompanied them. But Christ spoke intelligibly, openly, and clearly; he employed language that was not foreign but native and customary, so that everyone could understand and perceive his words. Otherwise, it would be secretly mumbling in vain. To be precise, the word "he said" refers to the subsequent command, and in keeping with Hebrew idiom it has the same force as "he ordered," "he declared."

34. Therefore, the papists would rather do anything else than perform this sacred mystery when like magicians and sorcerers they address the bread and cup, created objects which have no senses and are incapable of being spoken to, and they mumble these words, "this is my body," and say them in a strange language and with hushed tones, contrary to what the apostle says in 1 Cor 14:6, etc.

35. And then Christ orders something that concerns also the sense of touch: "Take." That means: all of you [take] this bread and this cup that I hold in my hand and place into your hands (and thus not directly into someone's mouth). The proper meaning of the word "to take" requires that it must refer to the taking that is done by the hand, just as "eat, drink" must refer to what is consumed by the mouth. The way that is unbecoming to adults, of putting food directly into someone's mouth, also requires this; so too the arrangement of lying at table that makes it impossible neatly to reach the mouths of all who are lying in a circle. The practice of the old church and also of the church of today (except the Romanist one) requires this as well. And it certainly is not a sacrifice, since these elements are offered in order to be received by the apostles and not by God. And in the command that is made to believers to take is, so to speak, the handing over of Christ into our hands and into our power, as well as our taking through faith, which is the "hand" of the soul (John 1:11–12).

36. Therefore, the papists are acting superstitiously, contrary to Christ and antiquity, because they bring in private masses when the sacrificer stands by the altar and eats and drinks by himself. So too are those who act like papists

with them when they refuse to put into the believers' hands what they offer to their mouths, as if their hands are less pure than their mouths (which have been equally sanctified: Matt 15:18, 20; Jas 3:10), and as if the hands of those who administer them are more pure than those of the other members of the church. Moreover, in so doing they very much render obscure the working of faith. Indeed, while they are making a sacrifice what else are they doing than making no distinction between giving and receiving?

37. And then Christ says something that affects the senses of smell and taste: "Eat and drink from it, all of you." That is to say, he bade them to take in order to eat (i.e., the bread) and to drink the wine. The sense is: insert the bread into your mouths, eat, chew, and crush to pieces with your teeth. And: raise the cup to your mouth, drink the wine, and let it go down into your stomach for digestion and feeding. This shows that their use is an inward one, and it signifies that for believing souls and those who take Christ by faith, so to speak as by hand, and who eat and drink him, so to speak, by mouth (a metaphor that the Holy Spirit uses everywhere throughout the Scriptures, John 4:14 and 6:51, 53), Christ becomes a spiritual, heavenly food and drink as truly as what we eat becomes food, nourishment, strength and growth for our bodies.

38. All of these commands "take," "eat," and "drink" are in the plural form, and expressly about the cup, "drink from it all of you," which by analogy we should take also for the bread, unless it is because what is said about the bread piecemeal is expressed as one whole about the cup that does not permit being portioned except by each person's drinking. These plural commands signify by their universal order a communion that is shared equally, and also that the necessity of consuming both elements (and the cup in particular) does not apply privately but publicly.

39. Therefore, we should not do with this bread what the papists do, contrary to the divinely ordained usage and the early church: lift it up for worship or like some deity; superstitiously hide it in a drinking-cup; preserve it in a safe or some alcove for idol-worship, or in monstrances (as they are called) made of gold and silver; put it on display or parade it publicly and pompously in a Persian fashion, or carry it around fields in a wagon. Indeed, equally abusive desecrations of the Lord's Supper are the private masses, wherein one person hungrily eats by himself; and the cup is withheld from laics; and they carry

the fruits of the mass even to those who have died, despite the fact that they cannot eat or drink.

40. Responding to and following this command of Christ is the compliance of the disciples, both in taking the bread and wine and also in consuming, that is, in eating and drinking. And this compliance is implied in the command, and regarding the cup Mark [14:23] explains it by saying "they drank from it, all of them"—which we should understand similarly for the bread, as the taking there includes the command to drink. And Mark reports these words as they were spoken prior to the drinking: "This is the blood of the New Testament, etc." Nor is it unusual to perform mystical actions before it is explained what they mean, as we see happen in the washing of feet (John 13:5, 12). Whatever it may be, it is of very little relevance to the topic whether the order of words is right here or whether this is an instance of *hysterologia* [a figure of speech in which the natural or conventional order of words is reversed].

41. Added to Christ's commands are declarative words, or words that explain and describe the thing that is being signified and the promise that is added to the outward symbols that contain the inward subject-matter of the Lord's Supper, when he says, "this is my body," to which Luke adds "which is given for you," and to which Paul adds "which is broken for you." And to the word "this" for which Luke and Paul have "this cup," Matthew adds "for," which is assumed also for the previous phrase, "[for this is] my blood of the New Testament" (or as in Luke and Paul, "the New Testament in my blood"). Matthew and Mark add "which is poured out for many," Luke "which is poured out for you," and Matthew has furthermore "unto the remission of sins."

42. With these words Christ reveals what he meant by those actions and commands of his, that is, when he took the bread and that cup (in fact, that broken bread and this poured-out wine) and gave them to his disciples equally to be received and eaten. By means of the outward elements and actions he meant the mystery, i.e., that with their minds and in faith they should consider, receive, and eat something else, namely, his broken body and his shed blood, for a spiritual food and drink. Thus, the meaning, or what is declared, is: this bread that I have broken is my broken body, and this cup (or what is in the cup) is my shed blood, and so what I have given you and

have ordered you to take, eat and drink is to give you my body and blood and to take, eat and drink them.

43. And next we should consider those words more closely in order to assert the plain truth, because they were obscured by differing explanations, as some have built on them the teaching of *sunousia* (consubstantiation) and others *metousia* (transubstantiation). First there is the subject of this sentence, namely, "this." And there is the predicate, i.e., "the body and blood," as well as the explanation of each. Third there is the copulative or linking verb "is." Fourth is the sentence as a whole. And finally, there is the causal particle "for" and the connection of all these words with what precedes.

44. The subject therefore is "this," a demonstrative adjective whose gender is neuter (a demonstrative which as it were points with extended finger to something that truly exists and is present). It demands that there be a noun to which it refers and which often accompanies it, like "this Passover," "this fruit of the vine" (Matt 26). And here, since in the first clause it does not say "this" in the masculine, meaning "this bread," but "this" in the neuter, the word may be taken with both phrases, "this is flesh, or body" and "this is blood." For just as they do with neuter nouns (like Hebrews do with the feminine) the Greeks and Latins use also the demonstrative in an absolute sense as "this thing." And this is especially useful when the demonstrative functions also as a relative for an earlier noun or deed. This happens in Exod 8:18, "this is the finger of God;" 1 Pet 2:19, "this is the grace of God;" Luke 22:17 and 19, "take this" and "do this." Or when they [the Greeks and the Latins] relate the supposit to a verbal phrase (as the grammarians say) with the same gender, which the Hebrews do, too. And Virgil [has]: "But to retrace one's steps, etc. ... this is the trouble, this is the toil." John 17[:3]: "To know God, this is eternal life." And therefore, one can also say, "this is my body, this is my blood." But instead of a demonstrative pronoun the Hebrews here often use the demonstrative adverb *hen* and *hinne*, that is, "look" and "behold." Thus, Paul in Heb 9:20 translates that saying of Moses "behold the blood of the covenant" (in Exod 24:8) as "this [neuter]" or "this [masculine] is the blood of the testament." And John 19[:26–27]: "Behold your mother, behold your son," that is, "this" [feminine], namely Mary, is your mother, and "this" [masculine], namely John, is your son.

45. Therefore, "this" means the same as "this thing" that has been mentioned previously, i.e., this bread and this wine, as if those things are pointed to by

an extended finger and are related to these words, to indicate the subject of the sentence. For first Luke and the apostle clearly say "this cup," albeit in such a way that the container stands for its contents, in the common and well-used custom of speaking in all languages. For it says, "drink from it, all of you" and "I shall not drink from the fruit of the vine."

46. And so it ["this"] means that which Jesus took into his hands, blessed (with the accusative case, as in Hebrew), broke, and gave to his disciples and what he ordered them to take and to drink, but this was bread and wine, as the grammatical construction demands. For since all those words are transitive in meaning, they require the fourth [accusative] case and take it, and in that passage there is no other [case]. Added to that is unshakeable logical reasoning. The statement is: you should eat and drink this (in the fourth case), i.e., the bread and the wine, because this is my body and my blood. Otherwise, if it refers to something else there could be no cause that the particle "for" indicates; nor would there be any connection between the clauses. And finally, in 1 Cor 10[:16] Paul removes any grounds for debate when he says: "The bread which we break and the cup of blessing which we bless, is it not the communion of the body and blood of Christ? Because we, who are many, are one bread, one body, for we all partake of the one bread." And, in 1 Cor 11[:26]: "Whenever you eat this bread and drink this cup." From these it is clear that "this" point to the bread and wine, and both are real bread and wine.

47. Therefore, it is foolish (as Karlstadt has falsely devised) that, because it is not "this" [masculine] but "this" [neuter], it relates to "body" [neuter], namely the body that was reclining at the table and that the apostles noted with their own eyes; for it says later: "This cup is the New Testament, etc." That is nothing other than inverting the relation between subject and sacrament. It is a similar inversion of terms, on the basis of the [definite] article "the" that is added to "body"—which indicates the subject (as it does in John 1:1, "God is the Word," and 4:24, "the Spirit is God")—to arrange the words thus with Schwenckfeld, "my body is this," i.e. what is the broken and eaten bread, or what is the spiritual and heavenly food, so that it does not point at the outward bread, nor indicate what is the bread, but what the body of Christ is, which is supported [according to Schwenckfeld] also by what it says in John 6[:51, 55]: "The bread which I will give is my flesh, and my flesh is food indeed, etc." For the [demonstrative pronoun] "this" includes the [definite] article, and it occurs in the next clause, "this cup," with the [definite] article.

But in John the word "bread" is taken metaphorically. (Yet we do not deny that also here the word "bread" includes a metaphor, albeit not an immediate metaphor; and these sentences are surely reciprocal.)

48. And the word "this" cannot mean, as it does for the papal promoters of transubstantiation, some vague individual thing, as Thomas would have it. For "this" denotes something specific and present. Either ["some vague individual thing" means] some single or individual thing of a more general substance that with the predicate refers to the same thing or supposits for the same thing—as Scotus says—in such a way that what is indicated by the subject and what is indicated by the attribute do not differ from each other (except by a different way of conceiving them), so that the sense is: "What is contained under the appearances of bread and wine" is my body and blood. For in that way the expression would be identical to the actual substance, and the sign would be destroyed. Or, alternatively, what previously was bread and wine. For according to the common understanding of the papal teachers it is only after the words have been uttered that the bread and wine becomes and so is the body and blood of the Lord. Lastly, nor is it the appearances of bread and wine, or their accidents (their color, smell, taste, shape) suspended in mid-air apart from their proper subjects, for that would really be taking away the truth of the signs and replacing them with things fantastical and delusory.

49. And though the word does so for the promoters of consubstantiation or impanation (to which view very many Schoolmen, like Scotus and D' Ailly are inclined, and which they would embrace if not the authority of the Lateran Synod held in 1215 had checked them; and which view Luther thence took over) "this" will not mean "in, with, or under this [neuter], or this [masculine]"—that is, the bread and the body, the blood and the wine. For bread is incapable of taking on a body, and a body cannot submit to bread, as both are compact, and unequal; nor is wine something under which some other liquid can hide, since both flow across their boundaries and mix with each other. Even more so the fact that this is not about one thing being contained under another thing, but about signification and exhibition, i.e., it is not about where or under what are the body and blood of the Lord—which is to turn the predicate into the subject and vice versa—but about what that bread and wine is.

50. The attribute is "the body and blood of Christ," i.e., his flesh and gore—which are dead—as in John 6. In both places the Syrian renders them as *pagra*, i.e., corpse. And then it says here, [the blood] "of the testament" or "covenant," with testament being put in place of covenant in keeping with the Septuagint, as the compound word *diatithesthai* is used for "to establish" (Luke 22:29–30), although here it means the testamental covenant. And for both testaments death occurs in order to confirm each one of them. In the old [it is] the death of a victim (hence it is called "to smite or to strike a covenant"), and in the new the death of the testator, to which the apostle alludes in Heb 9:16. And "of the new [covenant]," which is placed over against the old. The new consists in the reconciliation of an angered God to wretched men, and in the promise of salvation through the blood of the exhibited Christ himself and not that of another, as it was in the Old Testament. Therefore, it is the blood of the New Testament whereby this covenant was made and ratified. Or [it says] "the New Testament in the blood of Christ" as Luke and Paul put it, in a customary manner of speaking that is similar to the Hebrews. For them, the little word "in" indicates the instrument and the mode, that is, the New Testament is established by means of blood. The evangelists use these words interchangeably, because the blood and the New Testament are very closely linked.

51. This is connected more to the blood than to the body (for it doesn't say "the body of the New Testament," or "the New Testament in the body"), but not because both of them do not converge in the notion of "the New Testament." For a covenant was ratified by sacrificing a body, too; but it is because in the shedding of blood Christ's last suffering and death is more evident. And there is certainly an allusion made to Moses's words in Exod 24[:8] that Paul repeats in Heb 9:20: "Behold, the blood of the covenant that God has made with you."

52. And an exegesis or explanation is added to both attributes. About Christ's own body: "Which is given for you"—i.e., which will be given (as John 6:51 has it)—using the present tense for the immediate future, for the time imminent, and also to indicate the certainty of the matter and of the faith, in the customary way of speaking (John 10:17; Luke 22:22). It means to be handed over unto death, and, as Paul has it, "it is broken," metaphorically, that is, it will be fixed [to the cross], sacrificed, and destroyed by the separation of the soul from the body. Herein is an allusion to the breaking of the bread. And concerning the blood, "which is poured out for you," with

the same change in time, i.e., on the cross and not in the cup. Yet if one looks at the grammatical construction, Luke's words relate to the cup, while they relate to the blood if one considers the subject-matter, so that it appears to be a solecism, a not uncommon Hebraism in Scripture, like in Luke 5:9 etc. It also says [that it was given] "for you and for many" (i.e., believers) "unto the remission of sins," for without the shedding of blood there is no forgiveness (Heb 9:22). And in the same way we must relate it from this clause to the other one.

53. Therefore, it means the true, natural body that was lying at the table with the disciples, the body that soon would be seized, crucified, handed over to death; and it means the blood that surely then was in his veins but that soon would be poured out. Therefore, it was not a metaphorical body, a non-defined body, an imaginary, spiritual, and invisible body, and one that could not be touched and was not fixed in any place—indeed, a body that the promoters of consubstantiation think of, a ubiquitous body and one that was within the bread, nor, as the promoters of transubstantiation teach, a body that was transubstantiated from bread, i.e., a body that is not a body.

54. But although in Holy Scripture the body and blood (taking "blood" for the soul that resides in the blood, Gen 9:4) sometimes is used for a human being as a whole (Heb 2:14) and by synecdoche it is used at time for the incarnate Son of God or the person of God's Son (John 6:53; which will signify that to us Christ exhibited himself in his entirety, and that we entirely have communion with him), nevertheless that is not the only and most proper purpose for which he said it. And in fact, then the body and blood are considered as parts of a whole conjointly, and not separately, as occurs in this passage.

55. Therefore, on this point we do not consider Christ simply and absolutely as man (and even as God-and-man) but in light of a particular aspect and quality; namely, as a humbled man, a man in the final act of his humiliation, i.e., a crucified man and a dead man. And [we do not consider him here] as a living man nor a glorious one, i.e., a man who is not subject to any more afflictions and everyday conditions and death, and so no longer to be brought down to those lowly elements of the world (Rom 10:6).

56. And this is shown by the following obvious arguments: 1. Because Christ made use of appearances that are different in nature, situation and place, that is, bread and wine. And the bread was not dipped in, but dry, in order to

show the separation of body and blood. 2. Because both the body and the blood are presented thus separated, the body and blood that in a state of living and glory are joined together. 3. Because it is said about that body "which is given or broken for you," and so also the blood, "which is poured out," in order to show that in this way the body is bloodless, and the blood is not in the veins; the Latins call this flesh and gore. 4. Because it is called "the blood of the testament or covenant," or "the testament or covenant in blood," and consequently established by the shedding of blood, and death. 5. Because it is viewed as a sacrificial offering, an offering of a living creature that has been slain and that has died. 6. Because flesh and blood are here being offered for a complete meal, i.e., the spiritual food and drink. For about the bread which he called his body it is said "eat," and about the wine which he called his blood, "drink." But in fact no-one eats a whole animal, or one that is alive, but dead, nor does anyone drink blood that is in the veins, but only blood that has been poured out. 7. And finally, because Christ orders it to be done in remembrance of him, which the apostle interprets as being about his death, in 1 Cor 11:26: "You shall proclaim the Lord's death until he comes."

57. Therefore, it is beyond and contrary to the mind of Christ here that the papal teachers and others hold a mixed view of Christ: now as lowly, and then as glorious. For it doesn't suit the glorious state to drag Christ down to earth and back to the weak elements of the world. In fact by their actions they contradict themselves, when they stamp images of the crucified Christ on their wafers or offerings.

58. And finally, Christ himself is understood in this way, and indeed as humiliated and dead, so that the merits of his death are included together with himself, and the benefits and gifts, the power, the efficacy, namely the forgiveness of sins, righteousness, and life eternal (John 6:51–54). Therefore, it is added: "[The body] which is given and broken" and "[the blood] poured out for the forgiveness of sins" (thus also Matt 26:29; Luke 22:29–30). For we must join these three together inseparably: Christ and his death to the benefits that arise from it, and also to the outworking of these benefits. As a result, those who interpret the body and blood as only the merit or outworking are not passing on the truth fully enough.

59. The copula or link that ties the predicate to the subject is the substantive verb esti, "is." Since the Hebrews with the word hayah ("to be") miss the

present participle that for them takes the place of the present verb (except that they sometimes do use *yesh*) they assume that verb or they use pronouns in its place, and for the third person *hu*, "itself," that is, "this itself my body," which is equivalent to "is." Luke, too, in the second clause, the one about the cup, leaves out the same verb, a practice the Latins follow also when it is preceded by the demonstrative word. But Paul does supply it. And since its use is to join the subject to the predicate in a statement in the way that they affect one another [in reality], it should be taken in this way and not as tropological. But in the present tense it means what the thing is, and its existence at this time, and not what it is becoming or any action the thing does, or anything that it undergoes. For that is indicated by "become," "be," or "was made" (Matt 4:3; John 2:9) so that it is "the bread is," i.e., exists truly as my body, etc.

60. For this reason the papal teachers certainly behave foolishly when they ascribe to the word "is" an efficacious or an operational power, and really interpret "is" as "is changed in substance." And others explain it as "becomes consubstantial with," or is joined or united with in a sacramental manner, which they want to be not only in a real sense but also substantially. [They err] since the wording is about being, not becoming.

61. So much for the individual words whereby these statements are made. Insofar as the outward speech is concerned, they are figurative or tropological, as is clear from the link between the predicate and the subject. Not because there is a trope in the sentence as a whole (for trope belongs to a word) but there is a trope of the whole sentence. For words themselves are not tropological, but they converge into a sentence that results in a trope. For the cause of a trope is something different than the seat of the trope. On this point we should consider three things: first whether there is a trope in the words of the Lord; second, where the trope is found or what the seat of it is; and lastly, which trope it is and what sort it is.

62. The fact that it is a trope is confirmed by the cause for the trope, and firstly in view of the subject. For the subject is the bread and the wine, not the body or blood of the Lord under those appearances, as the papists would have it. Nor is it the Lord's body or blood under, with, or in the bread and the wine, as Luther would have it (referring to Pierre d' Ailly), as was shown previously. About the bread and the wine, it cannot properly be said that they are Christ's body and blood, for that would entail a contradiction. For they

are two unrelated things of which the one cannot be the other—not even, as Scotus says, by the almighty power of God nor can they be predicated mutually of one another in the proper sense.

63. Secondly, [it is confirmed as a trope] from the predicate, for the body and blood here are the broken body and the shed blood, that is, Christ in his state of humility and death, and in fact in such a condition as he had not been previously, and now no longer is, nor is able to be. For he is no longer dying. But in fact, nothing can be changed into something or joined to something substantially (nor can it properly be said so) that was not yet, and no longer is or is able to be in such a condition. Otherwise, it would entail a contradiction. For then one and the same thing would be such and not such, namely humiliated and glorious, dead and alive. Therefore, it is an improper manner of speaking, and then indeed a true manner of speaking for those [disciples] by the foresight of a thing that was going to happen and for us by the recollection of a thing that has taken place.

64. And furthermore the cup, that is, what is in the cup, is called "testament" or "covenant," or "the testamental covenant" in the blood—something that cannot be said about the cup or the wine, and not even can it be said about the blood that it properly speaking is the testament or covenant. For these things belong to different categories. In a similar way the apostle in 1 Cor 10[:16] calls the bread and wine "the communion in the body and blood of Christ," and in a similar manner of speaking he says that "because we, who are many, are one bread and one body." Therefore, the trope is obvious.

65. And then there is the added fact that Christ orders that it be done "for the remembrance and recollection of him," and the apostle commands: "Proclaim the Lord's death until he comes." And surely that would not be said if bread and wine (or something under the appearances of bread and wine) were the body and the blood of the Lord in the proper sense and in substance, because there is no recollection of a thing that is present; nor is it said that he who is present in substance is going to come.

66. And finally this tropological manner of speaking is very common in the use of sacraments. And so, it says that "circumcision is God's covenant," and soon thereafter, "the sign of the covenant" (Gen 17[:10–11]); and the apostle calls it "the seal of the righteousness of faith" (Rom 4). In Exod 12 it says, "the lamb that was slain is the Pascha or Passover;" in 1 Cor 10[:4] it says

that the "rock from which the Israelites drank was Christ," where a comparison is made with the Lord's Supper.

67. And on this point we are supported also by the consensus of the church fathers. For they say that the bread and the wine are the body and blood of the Lord "in their own way" (Prosper, *Sentences*), "somehow" (Augustine, on Psalm 33), "by a certain mode" (Augustine, *Epistle 23* to Boniface). They are "like" and "as" the body and blood (Chrysostom, *On the Eucharist in Encaenia*, and *Sermon 84* on John); a "mystery or sacrament" (Chrysostom, *Incomplete Work [on Matthew]*, sermon 11). Augustine, in his *Epistle 23* to Boniface, says that "they are not the true body, but a mystery of the body." It is called "a type or figure" (Tertullian, *Against Marcion*, book 4; Augustine on Psalm 3; Ambrose, *On the Sacraments*, book 4 chapter 5); "an antitype or model" (Nazianzus in his *Apology to Basil*, Anaphora Syra, Macarius Sermon 27); "a symbol" (Dionysius, Clement of Alexandria, Origen, Theodoret Dialogues 1); "a sign" (Augustine, *Against Adimantus*, chapter 12); "an image and likeness" (Gelasius, *Against Eutychus*); "a pledge" of the body and blood of the Lord (Jerome on 1 Cor 11). Indeed, it says that it "is the body and blood in the mystery" (Prosper, *Sentences*); "it is not in the true reality of the thing, but in what the mystery signifies;" "in the sign, or through the sign" (Augustine, *Against Adimantus*, chapter 12); "by means of, or through, its signification" (Augustine on Leviticus *Question* 57); "in likeness" (Ambrose, *on the Sacraments*, book 4, chapter 5); "by its appellation" (Chrysostom, *To Caesarius the Monk*). And moreover, [the bread and wine] are said to "be a sign" or "to signify" (Ambrose on 1 Cor 11), "to represent" the body and the blood (Tertullian, *Against Marcion*, book 4), etc.; and Augustine (*On Christian Doctrine*, book 3, chapter 16) and also the other fathers like Clement of Alexandria state expressly that it is a "figurative" and "allegorical" manner of speaking.

68. Among the Orthodox there is a difference of opinion about the seat of the trope, although they almost entirely agree on the main point of it. Some are of the opinion that the trope does not exist in any part at all: not in the subject, nor the predicate, nor in the copula. [They mean] that individually these things are to be taken in their proper sense, but that the predication is figurative. (Thus Beza, following Zanchius.) Crellius in fact puts a figurative, logical statement over against a rhetorical one, and he defines the former by the statement as a whole, and the latter by the [individual] words. Yet because logic is a matter of thought and inner reasoning, and not of speech, and so

does not belong to speech, there is no figurative predication in it, but figure of speech belongs only to rhetorical utterance. And although it [i.e., the trope] is caused by attribution, even so the seat is in some specific part.

69. And so there are others who locate the trope in the subject, or in the demonstrative word "this," as Bucer does, so that thereby it signifies the bread with the body, and the wine with the blood, by virtue of the sacramental union. Through that union it is not necessary for each thing to be present in a substantial sense, but only in a real sense, in such a way that to our senses the bread and wine are presented, and to our minds the body and blood of the Lord. And they say that this is what happens for all utterances wherein things that the senses cannot perceive or things that are absent are promised and exhibited by means of signs. Therefore, the meaning would be: "this" which I give to you by this sign "is my body," etc. However, there was no prior mention made of the body so that the word "this" could point to it, and the pronouncement of that union occurs for the first time through those words.

70. Others locate the trope in the word "is," taking it in the sense of "signifies," thus Zwingli following Honius Batavus. And rightly so, for among its other meanings "is" often is used to mean "signify"—as when we translate a word from one language into another we say "that is," which has the force of "it signifies" (Matt 1:23). And so also about things: "The seven heads of grain" and "the seven cows" "are seven years" (Gen 40:13, 19; 41:26). "The seed is the word of God, the field is the world" (Matt 17:37–38). "The seven stars are the seven angels, etc.," and "the many waters are the many people" (Rev 1:20, and 17:15). And similarly, the word is used for "to be like," as in: I am the bread, the true vine, the door; John is Elijah; Herod is a fox. In these places the metaphor is in the predicate. To this interpretation people also relate those sacramental expressions, "circumcision is the covenant" [Gen 17:9–14], "the Lamb is the Passover" [Deut 16:2–6, 1 Cor 5:7], "the rock was Christ" [1 Cor 10:4], "the cup is the New Testament" [Luke 22:20]. Even so, these expressions convey not only a signification and comparison, but also the sealing and an exhibiting of something. However, the word "is" then functions partly as a predicate and partly as a copula, as is clear from the explanation of the word.

71. And finally there are others who with Oecolampadius locate the trope in the words "body and blood," and then "is" would be only a copula, and the

sense would be that the bread and the wine are a symbol, a sign, a seal, a promise, a pledge, and an exhibition of the body and blood. This meaning is corroborated by the following very strong argument: whatever the proper location is where the analysis or explanation of the tropical expression falls, that is where the trope is. Well now, that actually falls in the words "body and blood," the nominative case having changed into an oblique one. For just as the expression "circumcision is the covenant" is analyzed into "is a sign of the covenant," so also "the bread and the wine are the body and the blood" is analyzed into "are a communion of the body and the blood of the Lord," not insofar as the bread has communion with the body of Christ, but insofar as the believers do. Therefore, the trope correctly is placed in the predicate.

72. It does not therefore follow, however, that the Supper is deprived of the truth of the body and blood of Christ, and that instead of it a figurative or symbolic body and blood is introduced, contrary to that statement: "This is my body which is broken for you; this is my blood which is shed for you." In fact, that is the argument which the papal teachers, following Scotus, and also those who follow Luther insist upon as their chief tenet. But there is a difference between "a trope in the word body" and "a figurative body." There is a difference between "a symbol of the body" and "a symbolic body." The former leaves the verity of the body intact, while the latter removes it altogether. And surely by this sort of trope there is no denying that it is a body, but something else is signified in addition to it, and both are involved in it. Therefore, Cajetan in his commentary on Thomas, rightly responds to the argument by Scotus that the true body is not removed, even if it is determined that there is a trope, as when it says that the rock was Christ (i.e., a symbol of the true Christ who would be born of the virgin Mary, and would be crucified, slain, etc.). So also here, for it is one thing to ask what kind of predicate it is, and another to ask in what mode it is present in the subject.

73. Hence it is also clear what sort of trope it is, namely a metonym, as was recognized also by Augustine, in which the thing signified has been put in place of the sign (by analogy, in fact, that is, by bearing a proportionate likeness to the thing signified). As Augustine says: "For sacraments are not even sacraments unless they bear a likeness to those things of which they are the sacraments." And not only that, but they are signs of such a sort that the things signified—the body and blood of the Lord—being present, are joined and united with them in their own way (namely in a sacramental way, that is, in a real way, to wit, relatively, and not in substance). Indeed they [the bread

and wine] are changed, as the fathers say, although not in the substance and nature itself, but in their condition, use, and function. And moreover, they are like carriers or instruments whereby the very body and blood of Christ are exhibited or offered to everyone, but bestowed upon and given to believers, and consumed by those who have faith—for that is the innate property of the sacrament. It is with such wording that the apostle says: "the Gospel is the power of God unto salvation for all who believe" [Rom 1:17], and "the bread which we break"—that is, the breaking and eating of the bread—"is the communion of the body of Christ" [1 Cor 10:16].

74. Therefore, Christ preferred to say, "this is my body" and "this is my blood," thereby ascribing the words "body" and "blood" to the bread and wine in an improper sense and in what they are, as if it were an essential statement, rather than wanting to use the proper kind of expression. He did so for the sake of making the signification clear, of making the likeness and analogy of these signs as close as possible to the thing signified, and so also for the sealing, confirmation, certainty and ensurance, the exhibition and comparison of the thing signified through these signs. For these words possess the promise of the thing made by God included in them, and the promise added to the outward signs, the promise that from the side of God is offered to everyone and that from our side is received by faith. And the emphasis and force of that meaning is hardly achieved by any other sort of statement in a proper sense. And it is in this sacramental relation and respect that the essential form of the Lord's Supper consists.

75. Therefore, the papal promoters of transubstantiation and the others who promote consubstantiation commit a serious error when they assert that these statements have a strict, proper meaning. And as their explanation shows, they are not even saying exactly what Scripture says. For the question is not what becomes of the bread, or where is the body and blood of Christ, or where is it hidden (whether under the bare appearances, or under the bread and wine—which is, in fact, to turn the predicates into the subjects). And second, since they understand by "this" either the external appearances of bread and wine, as the former do, or the bread and wine, as the latter and [since] they include under these the body and blood of the Lord as their contents, they necessarily introduce a trope of synecdoche in the subject. And lastly, because they moreover attribute to those things [viz. the appearances of the bread and wine, or the bread and wine themselves] the notion of signs (without which there can be no sacrament), which cannot happen without

specific words of institution that declare the signifying act (for they are signs by virtue of their institution) and because those words of institution, as even they themselves think, are nothing other than "this is my body, this is my blood," therefore, in order that the proportion of the predicate to the subject be right, they have to acknowledge—whether they like it or not—that there is a metonym in the predicate, unless they do away with the entire notion of sacrament and sign.

76. And finally, in these words of Christ there is an aitiology, a connection between these sentences and the preceding command, which is made explicit by the causal particle "for." To be sure, in the prior sentence about the bread it is omitted, but in the second one about the cup it is stated expressly, and therefore it should be supplied there, too (as the translator does). Christ had said: "Eat this bread, and drink this cup," or "this [thing]," in the accusative case, because "this" in the nominative case is my body and blood. Here "this" denotes the same thing both times, so that it is the connection between the terms in the syllogism. And accordingly [he said] "eat and drink this" because to eat and drink this is to eat and drink my body. And so it declares the sublime nature and necessity of this mystery.

77. But what they infer from this does not at all follow, namely, that therefore the mouth is eating the body and drinking the blood of the Lord on the grounds that the oral eating and drinking is commanded of that which is the Lord's body and blood (which is their chief argument in support of oral eating and drinking). But it only follows that what is eaten and drunk are bread and wine (since that is what the syntax demands, as there is no other accusative case with which "eat" can be construed), which in their own way are the body and blood of the Lord. But for all those actions that Christ performed and taught to his disciples, one thing was intended for and commanded to the senses, the other for and to the mind, namely in a metaphorical and synecdochical way. For just as the bread and the wine are called the body and blood of Christ, so "take," "eat this bread" and "drink this wine" must be taken in a corporal way in such a way that they are also understood in a spiritual way.

78. There still remains the legislation, that was given to the universal church for posterity, and that was sanctioned for an everlasting law by means of these words: "Do this in remembrance of me." Luke has this for the first statement, but Paul for both, who also adds to the second one, "and whenever you

drink," from which we should supply it in similar fashion to the first statement, "and whenever you eat."

79. And moreover, in that sacred action Christ addresses the apostles as shepherds and dispensers of his mysteries and as those who stand in his stead, as well as representatives of the universal gathering of believers, because he commands them to "do this." When he had said "this," it does not refer to his body and blood and to what he was going to suffer, but it refers to all the things that the Lord had done concerning the bread and the cup, I mean to all the things that preceded, i.e., what you have seen me do as the host, that I command you also to do as the guests.

80. Therefore, "all of you," as my ministers, "do this;" that is, as a perpetual ritual take the bread, bless the bread (or give thanks for the bread), then break it and give it, and say in my name: "This is my body" or "Christ's body." And so similarly also for the cup, etc.: "Do [this] you all," by taking part in "this;" that is, take, eat, drink. This is clear from the fact that Paul applies it not only to the shepherds but especially to the whole church of the Corinthians, when he interprets "do" as "eat" and "drink," since he repeats Christ's words in this way: "Do this, whenever you drink," etc. (and by analogy, whenever you eat), which is more obvious from the appended explanatory statement: "For whenever you eat and drink," etc. And also from the conclusion: "Therefore, whoever eats and drinks," etc. This commands the necessity of obedience for all who believe, and it also reveals that the church is free in determining the frequency of the Lord's Supper.

81. From this it is clear how foolish the reasoning of the papists is, when they base the foundation of the sacrifice of the mass on these words by taking "do" to mean "sacrifice," on the grounds that in both Greek "to do a sacrifice" and in Latin "to do" or "perform" is used in this way, as in "when I do a young cow, etc." (Virgil). But in that case, it is connected to an ablative of the thing, while in Hebrew it is connected to the accusative case of the thing that is presented for the sacrifice (Num 28:3), with the addition of the goal: for a sacrifice. But never does this wording, "do this," have that meaning, but it always shows some prior action, i.e., what you have seen me doing. And surely Christ did not at that time offer himself under the appearances of bread and wine, but he said that he was going to offer himself. Otherwise, he would have offered himself two times, once in the bread and the wine, and a second time on the altar of the cross, and that is absurd.

82. And added to this commandment is the universal goal for the Lord's Supper, that it be administered and used "in *anamnēsis* of me," i.e., in remembrance or recollection of me, which Paul explains as "in remembrance of my death." He says: "For whenever you eat this bread and drink this cup, you will proclaim the Lord's death," i.e., you will celebrate with your profession of faith and with thanksgiving, "until he comes"—that is, until he appears again to judge the living and the dead. And with that last coming he describes the duration of the age, and he declares that the Lord's Supper be perpetually practiced. And we should attach a second, most excellent goal to that end, namely the union and fellowship with Christ, and the partaking in all his benefits, which Paul in 1 Cor 10:16–17 explains by saying: "Because we, who are many, are one bread," and, in chapter 12:13: "and we have all been made to drink into one Spirit."

83. Moreover, as this remembrance and declaration of Christ's death is the goal of the sacrament, so the apostle Paul defines its worthy use by each and every person's prior self-examination, namely whether he has faith (2 Cor 13:5) and whether he is moved by serious repentance, according to that statement by Paul: "Let a man examine himself and so eat of that bread and drink of that cup." This self-examination does not take away the public examination by others, but confirms it. On the other hand, it is an abuse, and he eats and drinks in an unworthy manner "who does not discern the body" (and so too the blood) of the Lord, [1 Cor 11] verse 29. That is, he does not distinguish between the two symbols (this bread and this cup, which by a sacramental relation are the body of the Lord and his blood) and the common bread and wine; and he does not make a distinction in using them, namely, between the sacred and the profane use of them, according to what it says in verse 34: "But if someone is hungry, let him eat at home, lest you come together for condemnation." And so he actually despises and treats with dishonor the very body that is offered to him; and therefore, on account of the serious injustice that is done thus against Christ "he becomes guilty of the body and blood of the Lord" (verse 27), and "he eats and drinks judgment unto himself." That is, he brings upon himself the punishment of judgment, and he brings upon himself the scourgings of God and death itself (verse 29–30).

84. And Matthew and Mark add also Christ's reminders about his own departure, and about the new life in heaven, in which they will be his fellow-partakers, when he says: "I say to you that I shall not henceforth drink from

the fruit of the wine until that day when I shall drink the wine new with you in the kingdom of my Father." These words are applied in Luke to the Passover meal. It is not certain whether Matthew and Mark recite these words in their order and place, or whether Christ repeated them twice. At any rate, we should take them as applying to both in common, and as analogous to both the Passover and the sacramental meal.

85. And as for what in Matt [26:29] and Mark [14:25?] is "but" in Luke [22:16, 18] is "for," in order to give the reason why Christ exhibited to them that cup for the last time. The wine is understood by the periphrastic "fruit of the vine," as it is called here also after the consecration and the eating. In fact, the same is understood also about the bread, by analogy, as is evident from Luke [22:16 and 22:18]. Moreover, when Christ says that he will "no longer eat and drink of (specifically) this," he means "together [with them]," based on repeating the next words, "together with you." Therefore, he himself had drunk with them, and had tasted before he exhibited them [i.e. bread and wine] to his disciples. For thus he himself willed to consecrate and commence this sacrament in himself, just like baptism before. In his case that also had a particular meaning, namely of death (Matt 20:22, 26:39; John 18:11). And then he puts forth a term to his abstaining, when he says: "From this time," or "anymore." Of course, after his resurrection he does drink with the apostles (Acts 1:4 and 10:41), but then in light of the dispensation and not in the usual manner of our current life, but to produce faith in the resurrection. But he does indicate that it will be repeated, when he says: "Until I shall drink it new," that is, an other wine. In this way the "new tongues" of Mark 16:17 are called "other tongues" by Luke [Acts 2:4], or tongues that are different from the usual. But it does mean one that is similar to it, and he moves from the proper sense to the metaphorical one, so that it both is and is not the same one, as Christ often does (John 3:14, 6:27, 32, etc.). And he adds "with you," when they will have been taken up into the same condition and fruition of blessedness, which the drinking signifies. And that will be "in the kingdom of my Father," taking them from the kingdom of grace to the kingdom of glory, thus explaining the final goal of this sacrament (Luke 22:29–30).

86. And lastly, there is added the expression of thanksgiving: "And when he had sung a hymn, they departed to Mount Olivet." This means: Christ led in the singing, and the apostles sang in harmony with him. It is not related which hymn it was. Burgos notes that it was Ps 113 and the five ones that follow it, the ones that even today the Hebrews call "the great Hallelujah," i.e., the

great hymn that they used to sing in their solemn festivals, especially the Passover, in order to remember the liberation from Egypt. And what if we relate it to that very beautiful prayer in John 17? And certainly when Christ began and completed this sacred act by means of giving thanks, he set a precedent for the church in its practice or use of this sacrament.

87. Well then, this is our clear and complete view on the Word of God about the Lord's Supper. By this view we have explained and asserted the integrity and truth of the signs and of the things they signify, as well as the connection and the relative union of them, and also their use and their efficacy. And these will be able to suffice for minds that are sober, to serve as consolation for believers, and to put a limit to quarreling among brothers, provided that there is no prejudice or desire to fight—attitudes that the church of God does not possess (1 Cor 11:16) and that do not befit those who are devout (Phil 2:3).

SOURCES

Clement of Alexandria, *The Paedagogue*, book 2 chapter 2

He himself also partook of wine, for he, too, was a human being. And he blessed the wine when he said: "Take, drink, this is my blood." The blood of the vine, the Word, which is poured out for many for the remission of sins, figuratively signifies a holy stream of gladness. (And shortly thereafter) And he showed again that it was the wine that he blessed when he said to his disciples: "I shall not drink from the fruit of this vine until I drink it with you in the kingdom of my father."

Cyprian, in *Sermon on Christ's Anointing*

At the table where he shared his last meal with the apostles the Lord gave the bread and the wine with his own hands; but on the cross he gave his body into the hands of the soldiers to be wounded, so that the sincere truth and the true sincerity that was impressed more privately on the apostles might reveal to the nations how the wine and the bread are the body and blood, and in what ways the causes match the effects; and also how the various names or appearances are reduced to a single essence, and how the things that signify and the things that are signified should be called by the same names.

Chrysostom, *To Caesarius the Monk*

Before it is sanctified we call the bread "bread"; but when divine grace sanctifies it by means of the priest, it is freed from the name "bread" and it is considered worthy of the name "body of the Lord," even though the nature of bread remained in it.

Rabanus Maurus, *On the Institution of Clerics*, book 1 chapter 31

The Lord preferred the sacraments of his body and blood to be eaten with the mouth by the faithful, and to be rendered as food for them, so that the visible work might illustrate an invisible effect. For as the material food nourishes and refreshes the body outwardly, so too does the Word of God nourish and strengthen the soul inwardly. (And soon thereafter) The sacrament is eaten with the mouth, but by the power of the sacrament the inner man is satisfied. The sacrament is turned into nourishment for the body, but by the power of the sacrament the excellence of eternal life is obtained, etc. And so in the same way that [the food and drink] changes in us when we eat and drink it, so also are we changed into the body of Christ so long as we live obedient and holy lives, etc. And because bread fortifies the heart of the body, it is therefore called the body of Christ. And because the wine affects the blood in the body it is related to the blood of Christ.

Christian Druthmar, *Commentary on Matthew*

The Lord gave the sacrament of his body to the disciples for the remission of their sins and the preservation of love, so that mindful of his deed they would always do figuratively what he was about to give on their behalf, and not forget his love. "This is my body," that is, "in the sacrament, etc."

ON THE SACRIFICE OF
THE MASS AND ITS ABUSES

President: Johannes Polyander
Respondent: Joshua van Sonnevelt

The tone of this disputation is polemical, as it criticizes the Roman Catholic Mass. It addresses the meaning and origin of the term 'mass' (3–12), denies the sacrificial character of it (13–47), and criticizes many of its features (48–61). With references to the letter to the Hebrews, the unique, one-time, unrepeatable character of Christ's sacrifice on the cross, then and there, is emphasized again and again. Only that sacrifice is propitiatory in the real sense of the word.

1. In place of the Supper that Christ himself has ordained, the papal teachers foist upon us the mass. And while Augustine rightly calls the Supper the sacrament of piety, the sign of harmony, and the bond of love (*Treatise on John*, 26), this mass can be called its opposite: the sacrament of impiety, the sign of apostasy, and the bond of dissension. For in the mass, this sort of idolaters worships a fictitious body of Christ and they deviate very far from the sacrament as Christ initially instituted it (as was shown above [disputation 45.9–77]), and with a hatred befitting Vatinius, they hate those who have reformed their faithless idolatry.

2. Before we examine the shameful abuses of the idolatrous mass, we shall take a close look at its meaning and definition.

3. Some of the papal teachers consider the word *missa* ('mass') a Hebrew word, and others a Latin one.

4. Of these teachers, the former try to prove that the word *missa* occurs in Deut 16:10, and that it means a voluntary offering. Bellarmine refutes their view with two arguments that are not unconvincing. The first is that "if the apostles had used that Hebrew word then surely also the Greek, Syrian and other nations would have kept it, just as they kept other similar words like amen, hallelujah, Sabaoth, hosanna, Satan, Sabbath, and Pascha. And that is because Hebrew words have come down to us via the Greeks, since the apostles themselves and the foremost teachers of the church wrote in Greek. But among the Greek writers, no mention is made of this word *missa*." The second argument is that "if it were a Hebrew word, then we should say *missah* and not *missa*; but no-one writes or says it in this way" (Bellarmine, *On the Eucharist*, book 5, chapter 1).

5. We should add to these arguments that the Hebrew word, sometimes used in the feminine and sometimes in the masculine gender, is taken to mean either a political tribute (as in Exod 1:11) or an ecclesiastical one, especially that of the first fruits, which would be kept in the early church in the worship to God. This tribute was formerly not offered by the Levitical priests (as nowadays the Roman sacrificers perform the mass) but by the other tribes of the Jewish people, as in Deut 16:10.

6. And we should not overlook the fact that when considered by itself the word *missah* does not mean an offering that is voluntary, as the unlettered papal teachers think, but simply an offering (Deut 16:10); and also, that it is not an offering of the expiatory sort, as they claim their mass to be, but a eucharistic one. It is in that sense that also the fathers call the Supper of the Lord, the Eucharist, insofar as it is a commemoration of Christ's sacrifice once offered on the cross, or the remembrance of it together with thanksgiving, just as Augustine describes it (*Against Faustus*, book 20, *On Faith to the Deacon Peter, Book against the Adversaries of the Law*, and *On the City of God*, book 10, chapter 5).

7. We grant that in Deut 16:10 God demands a voluntary offering from the people of Israel, or, as some translate it, a spontaneous offering. However, this offering is not expressed by means of one word, but by two, namely *missah nidbat*, which Arias Montanus and Pagninus render as the sufficient offering by a willing person, or a spontaneous gift, in keeping with the Chaldean meaning, since in the Targum the word *missah* is often written for the Hebrew *daw* or *daj*.

8. And the latter [of these papal teachers], those who think that *missa* is a Latin word, do not all explain it in the same way. For some, as Bellarmine in the same treatise shows, want it to be called *missa* ['sent'], because the offering and prayers are sent up to God (thus Hugh of St. Victor, *On the Sacraments*, book 2, part 8, final chapter). Bellarmine considers their explanation to be probable, but we regard it as wrong and fictitious.

9. Therefore, others think that it is called *missa*, because God sends an angel to attend the sacrifice and to present it to God, as the Master [Peter Lombard] thinks in [book] 4, distinction 13, and Thomas [Aquinas] in [part 3] question 83, article 4. Bellarmine judges this etymology to be less probable, but we deem it to be entirely incredible.

10. There are others who think that among the ancients, it was called *missa* from the sending and collecting of gifts (as symbolic things) into the midst of the community, gifts from which the holy Supper was made and given to the poor for a meal. This explanation seems probable also to some of our theologians on account of the fact that in former times, the Christian people sent its gifts, namely bread and wine, for an offering (as Evagrius reports). And from these offerings placed in a large vessel in the area of the temple-entrance, things would be taken that suited the administration of the Eucharist, while the rest was given to the poor to use.

11. Bellarmine thinks that the most probable view is of those who want *missa* to be said from the sending away or dismissal of the people so that *missa* would be the same thing as *missio*, just like the words *collecta* and *collectio* among the ancients, and in Greek *sullogē*, *sullexis*, or *remissa* and *remissio* [forgiveness] of sin. For Cyprian uses the word *remissa* instead of *remissio* everywhere (book 3, epistle 8; the book *On the Good of Suffering*, in the *Letter to Jubaianus*, and elsewhere). And that word comes from this ancient formula that the deacon used to declare before the preaching: "Let the catechumens and whoever is not a communicant go outside." And the second formula: "Go, the dismissal is made."

12. To this meaning of *missa*, Bellarmine adds four other ones, which he has taken from the orthodox fathers, the first of which is that it stands for the divine office of lessons and prayers (Council of Valencia, canon 1); 2. For that part of the liturgy that takes place from the offertory until the very end (from Alcuin); 3. For the celebration of the divine office in which the Eucharist is consecrated (from Leo, Gregory, Felix IV, the Council at Agde,

and also the Council at Orléans). 4. For the actual collects or the prayers that are spoken in the liturgy (from Milevitan Council, canon 12). But here we should point out that none of those meanings of his are proved by Holy Scripture. And also, that Bellarmine has not demonstrated from the writings of the fathers (from where he cites those meanings) what he ought to have demonstrated, namely that the orthodox fathers have recognized the mass as meaning the kind of sacrifice as he and the other Roman teachers have defined it.

13. For they define the mass as an outward sacrifice that in the real and proper sense of the word is also propitiatory, whereby the priest sacrifices and offers Christ's body and blood under the appearances of bread and wine for the sins of the living and the dead (Council of Trent, session 22, chapter 1; Faber, *On the Evangelical Mass*, book 2, chapter 1; Eck, in three books *On the Sacrifice of the Mass*; Cajetan, treatise 10, tome 3, on the same argument; Bellarmine, *On the Eucharist*, book 1, chapter 5, etc.).

14. The claims that are sprinkled throughout this definition contain nothing of the truth. For the first claim, that the mass is an outward sacrifice, does not accord with the truth, not even in the judgment of Bellarmine himself. For every outward sacrifice, and one that is properly so-called (to use the wording of Bellarmine in *On the Eucharist*, book 1, chapter 2) requires that the thing which is to be offered must be perceived by the senses. But the thing that the sacrificers in the mass are said to offer, namely the flesh of Christ, in no way can be perceived by the senses since it neither is in their presence, nor can it be seen or touched because now it is in heaven, and it will remain there until the time when everything will be restored, as the apostle Peter testifies in Acts 3:21.

15. The second claim, that the mass is a propitiatory sacrifice in the real and proper sense of the word, flies in the face of the statement by the apostle who shows by means of a three-fold contrast between Christ's priesthood and that of the Levitical priests that Christ's sacrifice accomplished on the cross is a unique expiatory sacrifice. The first of these contrasts is the fact that under the Old Testament there were many priests, but under the New only one. Of the former (as the apostle says in Heb 7:23–24) "there were many who became priests, because death would not let them live forever; but he, because he does live forever, possesses a perpetual priesthood." The second contrast is that it was necessary for the priests of the Old Testament

to offer sacrificial victims every day, first for their own sins and then for the sins of the people [Heb 5:3]; but Christ had to make an offering once only for the people, and that was all that he did (Heb 7:27). The third is the fact that the Old Testament priests offered various sacrificial victims, goats, calves, lambs, and similar animals that others had given them; but Christ through the eternal Spirit offered only himself unblemished to God (Heb 9:14). Peter also indicates this with the words: "Who himself in his own body lifted up our sins on that cross" (1 Pet 2:24). Therefore, since these statements contradict each other—"Christ's offering for the sins of the people should happen only once and did happen only once," and "Christ's offering should happen again and again, and does happen every time the sacrificers celebrate the mass"—we must consider the former statement, made by an apostle whom God had inspired, to be true, but the latter statement by the papal teachers who contradict the apostle to be false.

16. Our reply to the papal teachers' first objection (Council of Trent, session 6) that the offering made in the mass is the same as the offering that was made on the cross and differs from it only in mode and manner is: 1) that William Allen, although he understood that mode, contradicts them when he says that "Christ accomplished two sacrifices, one in the Supper and another on the cross, and that both sacrifices are different from the sacrifice of the mass" (in *On the Sacrifice of the Eucharist*, book 2, chapter 2 [10]). 2) that the mode wherein they admit that the mass differs from Christ's offering made on the cross is properly one of passive suffering and an adjunct, and that with respect to the one is actually so opposed to the other that they cannot both exist at the same time. Therefore, if we posit the following, that Christ's offering could have been made only once by Christ himself, then the second position is overturned, i.e., that the same offering still can be made each and every day by the priest vicariously for Christ. The fact that the first axiom is true may be grasped from the second necessary condition of Christ's offering, which is the death of Christ, who offered his own self to the Father, along with the shedding of his blood. For in the books of the Holy Bible, it always says that it is by means of his own bloody death that Christ offered himself to the Father. Therefore, if it is impossible for him again to die for our sins, then it is also impossible for him to be offered for them a second time in the mass.

17. If they should say (as they are accustomed to say) that the sacrifice of Christ once accomplished on the cross continues day by day in the mass, then

it necessarily follows that the earlier sacrifice of Christ was incomplete. For that which continues has not yet been completed, and that which is repeated every day must be considered to be incomplete—or else the reasoning that the apostle puts forward as proof does not hold, that the Old Testament sacrifices were incomplete on account of the fact that they were repeated very often (Heb 9 and 10).

18. We conclude from these observations that there is no consistency in the distinction the papal teachers make between the bloody sacrifice on the cross and the bloodless sacrifice of the mass. For if every expiatory offering necessarily must happen with the shedding of blood—as is clear from the following axiomatic statement by the apostle in Heb 9:22, "without the shedding of blood there is no forgiveness"—then under no pretext at all can the mass be called an expiatory offering. And moreover, we can refute this distinction by means of that admission by Bellarmine: "In the church, there is but one true and proper sacrifice" (*On the Eucharist*, book 1, chapter 2). And that true sacrifice, as Bellarmine admits in the same passage, is the sacrifice of Christ that was offered on the cross; and using the words of Augustine, he calls that sacrifice the most true and perfect sacrifice. Therefore, the mass cannot be that true and perfect sacrifice, since two sacrifices that are in reality different cannot simultaneously be the most true, the most perfect sacrifices coequally. But if two such sacrifices were arranged unequally and subordinately, then we should call the sacrifice that Christ accomplished on the cross, not the one sacrifice but the first sacrifice, and then the apostle's assertion that Christ offered himself only once would be wrong.

19. And Bellarmine also cannot escape this criticism of his own ignorance and that of his predecessors by taking refuge in the claim that the sacrifice of the mass is a commemorative and representative one (William Allen, *On the Sacrifice of the Eucharist*, book 2, chapter 11; Bellarmine, *On the Eucharist*, book 1, chapter 2). For whatever is commemorative and representative of something is no more the thing itself than the time past is the time present, and no more than the sign is the thing signified. And certainly, a sacrifice is that of a thing present and still to be accomplished, while a commemoration is of a thing that has been done and is past.

20. The papal teachers' third claim, that in the mass the body and blood of Christ are being immolated, is no less false than their two earlier claims. For in every sacrifice that which is truly and properly immolated must be not only

present but also mortal. But Christ has taken his own body away from earth into the third heaven, and he has shielded it from all mortality forever. For this reason, it can hardly be more foolish to say that even now, people are immolating Christ's body on this earth. We should pass the same judgment on the immolation of Christ's blood, which cannot truly and properly happen in the mass without shedding it. Also, in the sacrament of the Eucharist, Christ represents to us not his glorified body as it is today but the body that once was bound to the cross.

21. Here the papal teachers retort in vain that the sacrifices of the Law were commemorative and representative of the future sacrifice on the cross, and yet they were sacrifices in the proper sense of the word. But in fact, it was not the actual body of Jesus Christ that was sacrificed in those sacrifices (as the papal teachers claim happens in the mass) but the bodies of goats, calves, and other animals that in former times foreshadowed the sacrifice of Christ as types, and once this body was revealed, they were withdrawn like shadows before the sun, no more to be recalled to their former uses. Moreover, in those sacrifices of the Law, the bodies of the animals that were offered were ordained for a real and outward change and even destruction; and as Bellarmine himself has put it (*On the Eucharist*, book 1, chapter 2), this sort of change and destruction in the things offered is required for every sacrifice that is truly and properly so called. But in the meantime, not one of the papal teachers who call the mass a true and proper sacrifice has up till now been so silly as to affirm expressly that the mass is ordained for the true, real change and destruction of the body and blood of Christ, who is now seated at the right hand of his Father.

22. We know that Bellarmine makes the claim that it can be said very rightly that Christ's blood is shed in the sacrifice of the mass (*On the Eucharist*, book 1, chapter 11[12]). But from this claim of his, it is clear that he forgets his own position and contradicts himself. For if, as Bellarmine teaches elsewhere, the mass is a bloodless sacrifice, then it cannot at all be rightly said that Christ's blood is being shed in the sacrifice. And also, in that same chapter 11[12], he is not right to state that the representation of the sacrifice on the cross exists in the consecration of the mass. For the blood is poured out not by a figurative representation of the sacrifice but by its real offering.

23. And also wrong is the fourth claim, that in the mass, Christ's body and blood are being immolated under the appearances of bread and wine. For no

sacrifice that is properly and truly called 'outward,' ever was immolated under the appearance of something else; but whatever was offered to God was done so under its own appearance and outward form, whether by the Levitical priests under the Old Testament or by Christ under the New. An instance of something different cannot be produced from Sacred Scripture. And Bellarmine, considering this fact, admits that the bread and wine in some way are being offered in the mass, and that they pertain to the thing that is being offered. And from this position these absurd consequences follow: 1. That two sacrifices are being offered in the mass, one of bread and wine, and the other of the body and blood of Jesus Christ. For the appearances and the accidental qualities of bread and wine are not the same as the body and blood of Jesus Christ; and no-one who is endowed with reason would deny that these are different things. 2. The sacrifice of the mass consists of bread and wine rather than of the body and blood of Jesus Christ, because the appearances of bread and wine are subject to the senses; but not so Christ's body and blood (as we have shown in thesis 14). And this is also because in the mass no change or destruction at all happens to the body and blood of Christ, who is seated at the Father's right hand; but it does happen to the bread and the wine, and a change and destruction of this sort is an essential part of the sacrament which is performed by one who performs the sacrifice, as Bellarmine says (*On the Eucharist*, book 1, chapter 2).

24. The error in the fifth assertion, that in the mass the priest is offering Christ's body and blood, can be shown from Bellarmine himself. And to be sure, in the sacrifice (as Bellarmine states, *On the Eucharist*, book 1, chapter 2) "the sacrifice and the priesthood are related in such a way that the priesthood in the proper sense of the word corresponds to the sacrifice in the proper sense of the word, and that the priesthood in the improper sense of the word corresponds to the sacrifice in the improper sense of the word." But the mass is not a sacrifice in the proper sense of the word, as we have shown abundantly in the preceding theses. And therefore, the administration by the ones performing the mass is not a priesthood in the proper sense of the word.

25. Added to these things, as Bellarmine points out in the same passage, is the fact that "in the sacrifice properly speaking it is required that a lawful minister should perform the offering of the sacrifice. For it is not the duty of anyone whosoever to offer the sacrifice, but only of a certain person who has been equipped with godly authority, a person who performs it on behalf of the community." For in Heb 5[:4] the apostle, speaking about the priesthood,

says: "No-one takes this office upon himself, except him who has been called by God, like Aaron." And this is true to such a degree that Paul says in the same passage that even Christ himself did not take the priesthood upon himself but received it from the Father. But nevertheless, in those very passages in which Holy Scripture explicitly treats the ranks of the ministers of the Gospel, and their calling and authority, there is not any mention of the fact that they have received a priesthood from God. On the contrary, in the places where it speaks about the priesthood of the New Testament, there, it states clearly that it is attributed only to Christ himself (like Ps 110:1, Heb 7, and following).

26. From this it is clear that the distinction between Christ as the primary Priest and the performers of the mass as secondary priests of the New Testament is a fabricated one. For as the primary priest Christ is nowhere contrasted with other priests in excellence—as though they were secondary priests. But he is everywhere contrasted with other priests either in relation (as the foreshadowed priest to the foreshadowing priests in the Old Testament) or in exclusion (as the priest unique to many priests in the New Testament).

27. Indeed, not any one of the conditions that are required of the Priest of the New Testament is found in the Roman sacrificers. The first of these is that after the Levitical priesthood was repealed, the priest of the New Testament must be after the order of Melchizedek, and moreover, he should be without father, without mother, without lineage, having neither beginning of days nor an end of life, living forever by the power of his imperishable life [Heb 7:3]. The apostle ascribes that only to Christ (Heb 7:15 and following).

28. The second condition is that according to the definition of the New Testament priest, the one who is the priest must at the same time be the sacrifice, that is, he is both the priest through whom and the sacrifice by which people are reconciled to God. And this is proper to Christ alone by the fourth mode of predication. For strictly, by reason of formal principle, he is a priest by his divine nature, but by reason of the material principle, he is the sacrifice according to his human nature.

29. The third condition is that, as under the Old so also under the New Testament, the priest must be greater and more worthy than the outward sacrifice that he brings. But the merely human sacrificers who bring the sacrifice, since they are defiled by sin, are in no way greater or more worthy

than the body and blood of Jesus Christ, the lamb that is without blemish. And so, there is not any reasoning that allows those men to offer Jesus Christ's body and blood to God in the mass.

30. The fourth condition is that the New Testament priest be holy, innocent, undefiled, and set apart from all sin. Since Christ is the only one who is adorned with this perfect holiness, human beings who are prone to all kinds of vices—and such are the sacrificers—intrude upon the priesthood with obvious sacrilege.

31. The fifth condition is that the priest, as the New Testament defines him, should also be its Mediator. For the goal of the priesthood is the reconciliation of sinful human beings with God, and that effect is proper to the Mediator, as the apostle teaches in Heb 9:15: "He is, therefore, the Mediator of the New Testament for this very reason that, as his death intercedes for the forgiveness of those sins that were committed under the Old Testament, those who are called may receive the promise of the eternal inheritance." Therefore, just as there is only one unique Mediator between God and human beings, Jesus Christ, so he is also the one and only Priest for the people before God.

32. The sixth condition is that the priest of the New Testament also must be its testator who validates that testament by his death. For where there is a testament, the death of the testator must intervene (Heb 9:16). But, except by committing blasphemy, one cannot ascribe this characteristic to anyone except Christ; and, therefore, neither the other one.

33. The seventh condition is that the New Testament priest must offer his own sacrificial offering to God by the Spirit, who of himself has been endowed by the power of the imperishable life. For the sacrifice brought by a man who has not been endowed in this way cannot be satisfactory for the sins of other people. And to the papal teachers who raise the objection that in the mass the priest is only the instrument of the offering and not from his own person but from the person of Christ, we reply that only the priest makes the entire offering on behalf of the whole church, and in that offering, Christ is considered not as the one who is offering but as the one whom the priest has offered—and indeed has created—and accordingly, the sacrificer is more than the instrumental cause.

34. And to those same papal teachers who object that the priests offer Christ not for the satisfaction [itself] but for the application of the satisfaction that was accomplished on the cross for the people's sins we should reply that: 1) the application of the sacrifice cannot possibly be made by a mortal man but only by the immortal God. 2) that it is God who applies to us the fruit of the sacrifice of the cross in the most appropriate manner through faith. For this reason, it says in Rom 3:24 that God presented Christ as the propitiation for us through faith in his blood, and not through repeatedly sacrificing him. Otherwise, it would be necessary to apply also the fruits of Christ's incarnation, resurrection, and ascension for us by repeating them. And by equal rights as in the mass Christ would have to be sacrificed again in baptism, which is the first sacrament of the sacrifice of that same Christ. But the papal teachers frankly admit that this is not a requirement. And surely, for that reason, it also should not be necessary to repeat the sacrifice of Christ in the mass. But if that point is granted, it does not follow that the sacrifice of Christ itself is the means of applying Christ's sacrifice. For Christ's sacrifice itself and the application of that sacrifice are placed in an opposing relationship to each other, and the Word of God—being received in faith—is an instrument that applies the sacrifice of Christ to us no less than the sacrament of the Eucharist. But surely no-one is so foolish as for that reason to call the Word of God that is received in faith the actual sacrifice of Christ. 3) Although the holy Supper can be called the means that applies the sacrifice of the cross, the same thing cannot be stated about the mass, since the mass does not present God, who gives believers Christ offered on the cross, but a priest who is immolating Christ to God.

35. And these words of Christ, "It is finished" (John 19:30), prove that this final claim also is false, namely that in the mass Christ's body and blood are offered for the sins of the living and the dead. So also, the word of the apostle: "For by one offering Christ has made perfect forever those who are being made holy" (Heb 10:14). Similarly, "Christ was once offered to bear the sins of many, and to those who look for him, he shall appear a second time without sin unto salvation" (Heb 9:28). And with this axiomatic statement the apostle shows that between Christ's sacrifice once made on the cross for the sins of the people and his final coming there is no intervening time in which he offers himself a second time on this earth for the sins of those same people. And for that reason, Bellarmine is compelled to grant to us that there is no forgiveness except by virtue of the sacrifice of the cross

(*On the Eucharist*, book 1 [5], chapter 11 [25]). And from that one may gather that the forgiveness does not happen by virtue of the mass. For if forgiveness would also come by virtue of the mass, then Christ's sacrifice on the cross would be incomplete. Nor can that forgiveness happen in the mass by some ordering to the sacrifice of the cross, because the ordering of the sacrament to Christ's sacrifice does not impart to the sacrament the power to forgive sins, but only the power to signify the forgiveness of sins that Christ's death has acquired, and to seal this in the believers.

36. Besides the fact that the six claims above that are sprinkled throughout the definition of the mass directly oppose the testimonies of Holy Scripture and the conditions required in a properly called expiatory sacrifice, their falsity can be proved from the very institution of the holy Supper and from the writings of the orthodox fathers. For, to start with the institution of the Supper, in it Christ offered the bread and the cup consecrated by his blessing, not to God the Father but to his disciples. And he did not say to his Father, "Take this sacrifice of my body and blood," but he said to his disciples, "Take, eat and drink; this is my body, and the New Testament in my blood" (Matt 26:26; Luke 22:19, and following). Yet the sacrificer, on the other hand, does not offer Christ's body and blood under the appearances of bread and wine to each and every member of the church whom the disciples of Christ represented when the Supper was instituted, but he offers them to God, saying: "Accept, O holy Father, almighty and eternal God, this spotless sacrificial victim which I, unworthy servant, offer to you, my God, etc."

37. The following statements are at odds with one another: that which Christ once gave immediately to his disciples was bread and wine (or the cup in which the wine had been poured); but that which he offers nowadays mediately via the sacrificer is no longer bread or wine, but his own body and blood, contained under the appearances or accidental properties of bread and wine. Similarly, the cup that Christ once extended to his disciples was the New Testament in his blood; but now the cup that the sacrificer takes only for himself and does not extend to the lay people is part of the bloodless sacrificial victim. For by a testament, the favorable will of the testator towards his own inheritors is designated, but by a sacrificial victim, the thing that is offered to placate God is designated. We have proved by the testimony of the apostle that the bloodless sacrificial victim of the mass cannot be stated as a thing of this sort, as [the apostle] takes it for certain that there is only one

sacrificial victim, i.e., a bloody victim, whereby God can be appeased (Heb 9:32).

38. And moreover, to his disciples, after they had received the bread from him, Christ foretold the future absence of his body with these words: "Do this in remembrance of me" (Luke 22:19). It is these words that the apostle explains in 1 Cor 11[:26] when he says: "Whenever you eat this bread and drink this cup, you will proclaim the Lord's death until he comes." But with the following prayer, the sacrificer signals that Christ's body is present: "Holy Father, accept this spotless sacrificial victim that I offer to you." And with that "sacrificial victim" he means the body of Christ that he is holding in his hands under the accidents of bread and wine, and which he thereupon tears apart with his teeth. One can imagine nothing that is more foolish and farther removed from the goal of the Supper than that. For if the goal of the Supper is the remembrance of Christ who is absent until he comes to us from heaven (as one correctly gathers from the preceding words of Christ and the apostle Paul), then the sacrificer is not able to offer and handle the real body and blood of Christ here [on earth] in whatever mass you will.

39. While the papal teachers employ the authority of the orthodox fathers who occasionally called the Lord's Supper a sacrifice, the fathers never did use that term in the strict sense that the papal teachers do, but they called it a sacrifice in an improper sense. For it is by *metalepsis* that they called the sacrament of the Eucharist a sacrifice, because it is a sacrament that commemorates the sacrifice that God offered on the cross, along with the giving of thanks—and therefore, they called it "eucharistic." "What about us then?" says Chrysostom, "do we not bring offerings each and every day? Yes, we do make offerings, but by making remembrance of his death. And there is but one sacrificial victim, not many. In what way is there one sacrifice and not many? Because the sacrifice was offered once and for all in the Holy of Holies. But this sacrifice is the exemplar of that one. And this thing that we are doing is done in commemoration of that which has happened" (Chrysostom, *On the Epistle to the Hebrews*, sermon 17). And Augustine says, "Christians celebrate the commemoration of the same completed sacrifice by means of the most holy participation in Christ's body and blood" (*Against Faustus*, book 20, chapter 18).

40. And thus, it is metaphorically that they called that sacrament a sacrifice, having in view each and every believer who by participating in it, presents

himself to God in a special way as a living and holy sacrifice. Chrysostom's exhortation has this in view: "It is in heaven that we have our sanctuary, our high priest and our sacrificial victim. Let us also offer such sacrifices as can be offered in that sanctuary. No longer [sacrifices of] sheep, or oxen, no longer blood and incense. All of these things have become obsolete, and in their place has been brought in our reasonable service" (*On the Epistle to the Hebrews*, sermon 11) and "What is your altar? It is your spiritual heart. What is your spiritual sacrifice? Every good work" (*Sermons on the Holy Spirit*, tome 3).

41. Thirdly, the fathers in days of old called this same sacrament a sacrifice in a metonymous sense, regarding [the offering of] the prayers and the offering of bread and wine, which were connected to participating in the Supper partly for the celebration of the Supper itself, partly to support the poor with whatever was left over when the supper was finished. With regard to this Alexander of Hales grants that in the sacrament of the Eucharist we should, in the tradition of the ancients, offer three things. The first is the offer of the persons themselves; the second those things that are necessary for the actual sacrament—namely the bread and the wine. Third are the offerings that our hands bring, that is, the alms (Alexander of Hales, in the treatise *On the Office of the Mass*, part 4, question 10, page 1, folio 10). And the papal teachers do not deny that the mass can be called a eucharistic sacrifice. If it is eucharistic, as they grant us, it, therefore, is not propitiatory. For these two things are diametrically opposed to each other.

42. And what is more, the majority of the fathers (with whom Lombard agrees) understood that Melchizedek had offered Abraham bread and wine, and consequently, that the order of the priesthood whereby the apostle compares Christ to Melchizedek (Heb 7) does not consist in the offering of bread and wine but in these accompanying qualities of the two persons: the fact that we should see each as king and as priest, without father and mother, without lineage, having neither beginning of days nor end of life. That is, Melchizedek as the type for the comparison, which we should elicit from the account in Gen 14 by Moses (who silently passes over his genealogy), and Christ as the true reality that Melchizedek is foreshadowing (Chrysostom, *Sermon* 36 on Genesis and [*Sermon* on] Ps 109; Tertullian, *Against the Jews*; Augustine, *Questions on the Old and New Testament*, Question 109; Damascene, *On Faith*, book 4, chapter 14; Lombard, *Sentences* 4, distinction 8).

43. And although Bellarmine sees the point, he does not perceive it, and instead, he builds the teaching of the bloodless sacrifice of the mass on the type of Melchizedek, who in times past produced bread and wine for Abraham from his own provisions. For although he could not have been unaware that the word *howsi* which Moses uses in Gen 14:18 should be translated as "produced" or "brought forth," nevertheless contrary to the verb's meaning he feigns that Melchizedek had, for the purpose of some sacrifice or other, offered bread and wine—not to mention the fact that this is contrary to the order of the entire sacred context. For Moses ascribes to Melchizedek two different actions regarding his two-fold office, in this order: 1. Royal, because he gave Abraham bread and wine to refresh him and his army; 2. Priestly, because he blessed Abraham.

44. And although the same Bellarmine was not ignorant of the fact that the apostle Paul, led by the Holy Spirit and well-versed in all truth, did not silently pass over any of the things that would contribute to the knowledge of the [addressees of the Letter to the] Hebrews of Christ's priesthood in the order of Melchizedek, he nevertheless foists on him the notion that Paul intentionally omitted the offering of bread and wine so that he would not be forced to explain the mystery of the Eucharist, because it was too profound for them to be able to grasp at that time, and that it was a subject-matter that could not be explained (which he treats in chapter 5:11). One could attribute to the apostle nothing further from the truth than that. For nothing is more profound than the mystery of Christ, whom God ordained as High Priest according to the order of Melchizedek. And before the apostle recounts that teaching in greater detail, he does not say that these things cannot be explained (as Bellarmine wrongly translates it); they are difficult to explain, not because they are such in themselves but in light of the carelessness of the Hebrews so that with this forewarning, he might arouse them to greater diligence and attentiveness. Therefore, it is so far from the truth that the apostle wanted to pass over those more profound teachings in silence that he covered them very comprehensively and carefully. He did not wish to place the teaching of the Supper in the sense of those more profound things, because it is not more difficult to explain to simple people than the teaching about baptism, which he counts among the fundamental articles of the faith (Heb 6:2). For like baptism, so too the Lord's Supper represents his bloody sacrifice, and the papal teachers as much as our own theologians put the

teaching of both sacraments among the rudiments of the Christian faith in the catechetical instruction.

45. Neither does the following argument of Bellarmine support his own erroneous [translation] or that of the other papal teachers, "For granted that Scripture does not explicitly explain of what Melchizedek's order and the figure of Christ's priesthood consists, it does give such hints and indications that with the greatest consensus all the fathers come to the same explanation." For in thesis 42, we showed by the testimony of Lombard that some fathers reached a different explanation that can overturn the sacrifice of the mass. For they assert that Melchizedek's bread and wine do not foreshadow Christ the sacrificial victim as displayed in the mass (as the papal teachers contend), nor the accidents of bread and wine without their subject—or rather the outward aspects of bread and wine (i.e., their appearances)—but the real substance of bread and wine that the mystical table of Christ sets forth. This interpretation can be seen in Eusebius, *Proof of the Gospel*, book 5, chapter 3; John Damascene, *On Faith*, book 4, chapter 14, and the other fathers whom we named above in thesis 42.

46. It is to no avail also that Bellarmine bases the sacrifice of Christ in the sacrament of the Eucharist on the slaying of the Paschal lamb in 1 Cor 5:7, and also on the prophecy of Mal 1:11 about the *minhah*, or pure offering, that is to be offered to God throughout the world under the new covenant. Malachi could not have meant hereby that the expiatory offering of the mass corresponds to that of the Jews, since by the hypothesis of Bellarmine and the other Romanists, the mass is a bloodless offering. But all the expiatory offerings under the Old Testament were bloody ones, not to mention the fact that the Jewish offerings were expiatory only in a typical and denotative sense, while in the blasphemous meaning of the papal teachers the mass is truly, properly expiatory. Therefore, it remains that if by the teaching of holy Scripture there is but one unique sacrifice of the cross (in the proper sense of the word) that was prefigured by the Jewish expiatory sacrifices, it must be that what Malachi foretold about the spiritual and eucharistic worship of God that would be established among the nations by the preaching of the Gospel should be taken in a metaphorical sense.

47. And the very words of Christ himself, "which is given, is poured out for you" (Luke 22:19–20), do not provide any more evidence for the real immolation of Christ in the mass than his death is evidenced by those words

of his, "I lay down my life for the sheep" (John 10:15). For even those who look at sacred Scripture from a distance know well that Christ spoke both of these sayings before the sacrifice of the cross by interchanging the present tense for the future.

48. But although there is nothing good in the mass's fabricated sacrifice, nevertheless, because it does have some semblance of good in the eyes of people whose minds are corrupt, the Roman sacrificers take advantage of its deceptive mask in strange, bad ways within the pope's realm, and not without effecting error. And the first abuse in the mass is the fact that the sacrificer who is to administer it makes this opening statement: "I shall go into the altar of God." For in the New Testament the believers no longer have an altar of the sort they once had under the Old Testament, but their altar is now in heaven, namely Jesus Christ, as Thomas Aquinas correctly noted on Heb 13 verse 10, where the apostle asserts that we have an altar of the sort from which those who today are serving at the tabernacle have no right to eat; but they are bringing back into Christ's church the shadowy sacrificial victims of the Jews which Christ had done away with when he came.

49. The second abuse is in the public confession of the priest's own sins, which he directs not only to God but also to all the saints who have departed this life, and to his brothers, when he says: "I who am a guilty and unworthy priest confess to almighty God and to the blessed virgin Mary, and to all his saints, and to you, my brothers, because I, a miserable sinner, have sinned greatly against the Law of God in thought, word, deed, and omission, through my fault, through my fault, through my most grievous fault." For a confession that a sacrificer should make only to God in a devout manner becomes superstitious and useless when made to the deceased, for they are incapable of hearing it; and when the prayer is offered to the living, it is contrary to his own conscience, since he considers himself convinced that he had not given them any offense for which he deserves punishment.

50. The third abuse is seen in the idolatrous demand for intercession by deceased saints that begins with these words: "Therefore I pray the most blessed mother of God, and all the saints, and you brothers: pray to our almighty Lord God for me a sinner, that he take pity on me." When he passes by our Savior Jesus Christ, he calls upon those mortals, who cannot save him, and whom Holy Scripture excludes completely from the office of

intercession, while at the same time ascribing it to Christ alone (John 14:6; Rom 8:33; 1 Tim 2:5–6; and 1 John 2:1–2).

51. The fourth abuse occurs in this prayer of absolution to other confessors of sins: "Amen, brothers and sisters, by the mercy of our Lord Jesus Christ, by the aid and the sign of the holy cross, by the intercession of the blessed, glorious and always virgin Mary, and by the merits of the blessed apostles and all the saintly men and women, may God almighty have mercy upon you, etc." With this blasphemous prayer the sacrificer attaches to the wood of the cross and its sign the power to bring redemption from sins that belongs to the Christ who was crucified and which cannot be shared with anything else, and attaches to the blessed virgin handmaiden of God the aid that we should expect from God alone, and he attaches merits to the holy apostles, who in their own writings once refuted the Pharisees' teaching about meritorious works.

52. The fifth abuse is made by the recollection of the merits that the sacrificer attributes to the saints, who in no way at all could have entered heaven without Christ's merits, and of the relics that for a large part are made up, as if God by looking at them might be swayed to forgive him his sins, when the sacrificer says: "We pray you, O Lord, by the merits of the saints whose relics are here present, and by the merits of all the saints, that you deign to forgive all my sins."

53. The sixth abuse is the fact that the sacrificer calls the bread (which in the Supper is the sacrament of Christ, the sacrificial victim) the actual sacrificial victim of Christ itself, and he shows with the following prayer that the earthly element benefits his own salvation and that of others, both those who have died and those who are alive: "Accept, O holy Father, almighty and eternal God, this spotless sacrificial victim which I, unworthy servant, offer to you my true and living God, for my countless sins and offenses, and my shortcomings, and for all here present, and likewise for all faithful Christians living and dead, that it may be for me and them a means to eternal salvation, Amen." Here, he ascribes to corruptible bread the power to bestow salvation unto life eternal which Christ ascribes only to his own flesh when it is eaten through faith (John 6) and even for those for whom Christ did not institute his Supper, namely the deceased who are neither in heaven nor on earth, but rather in a third place that holy Scripture does not mention, i.e., in purgatory.

54. The seventh abuse happens in the mingling of the water with the wine, which is based neither on a command by Christ nor by his example. For to his disciples he served wine (or the fruit of the vine) without water, and he ordered others to distribute it in imitation of him; for this reason a decree of the Council of Orléans (canon 4.4) condemned that mingling that the sacrificer worships as something mystical, saying: "O God, you who established the nature of man in wondrous dignity, and still more admirably restored it, grant us by the mystery of this wine and water we may come to share in his divinity, who deigned to share in our humanity, Jesus Christ, your Son, our Lord."

55. The eighth abuse is in the superstitious offering of the cup filled with wine. For before the wine—to speak in the words of the Romanists—is transubstantiated or changed into Christ's blood, the sacrificer ascribes to that earthly and corruptible drink the power to bestow salvation, and a pleasing fragrance acceptable to God, of which the first good is ascribed only to Christ by Simeon in his song (Luke 2:29) and by Peter (Acts 4:12), and the latter good is ascribed only to Christ's sacrifice accomplished on the cross by Paul (Eph 1:2). For the sacrificer addresses God as follows: "We offer to you, O Lord, the cup of salvation, humbly begging your mercy, that it may arise before your divine majesty, with a pleasing fragrance for our salvation and for that of the whole world."

56. The ninth abuse is in the wicked imitation of the Jews, who in former times appeased God with incense until the time of correction when it was God's will to put an end to that figure and shadow no differently than to the other things that represent the body which we possess in Christ, as the apostle testifies in Heb 9. And also in the imitation of the Persian magicians, who with their addresses very often spoke to lifeless objects, which they manipulated for witchcraft, as is clear from these words of the sacrificer when he speaks to his incense: "Be blessed by him to whose glory you will be burned, in the name of the Father, the Son, and the Holy Spirit." And to these words he adds the following address of God: "We beseech you, almighty and eternal God, deign to bless and sanctify with the right hand of your boundless majesty this created incense so that by the power of your holy name it be wondrously empowered to put to flight all the onslaughts of the unclean spirits, and to drive out every disease with the return of health wherever its smoke may be blown, and that it may emit a most pleasing fragrance unto you, almighty God, forever." And likewise: "May the incense

that you have blessed rise up to you, O Lord, and may your mercy descend unto me." With this prayer the sacrificer, as it were, binds God to imbue the smoke of the incense with such power to put the devils to flight and to heal the sick, as neither the prophets nor the apostles, who were endowed with an exceptional gift of performing miracles ever besought God, since they rightly understood that neither by them nor by any other human creature—still less the lifeless created thing of incense—but only by the Creator invoked by prayers of faith, to be able to drive demons and diseases out of people (Matt 17:21; Jas 1:15).

57. The tenth abuse is that the sacrificer confuses things that are different in kind. For firstly, he takes the bread and wine—before they are converted into Christ's body and blood, and so are merely outward signs of Christ's body and blood—to be the very body and blood itself of Christ, when he calls those outward signs Christ's offering. Second, he calls the offering of the mass the remembrance of the offering of Christ. Third, he confuses the remembrance of Christ's suffering with the remembrance of the incarnation, birth, circumcision, resurrection and ascension of Jesus Christ, contrary to the commandment of Christ himself, who, as the apostle advises in 1 Cor 11:26, instituted his supper only for this purpose, that hereby, we declare his death, and that we put him as crucified before the eyes of our soul. Fourth, he stitches onto the remembrance of Christ the remembrance of the virgin Mary and of all the others, who have not presented God with any expiatory sacrifice of the cross on our behalf. For the proof of this matter, we shall quote the very words of the sacrificer: "Holy Trinity, accept this offering which we are making to you for the remembrance of the incarnation, birth, circumcision, suffering, resurrection and ascension of our Lord Jesus Christ, and in honor of the blessed Mary, ever virgin, and of all the saints, since the world began with whom you have been pleased, that it may redound to their honor and for us to the salvation of our soul and body."

58. The eleventh abuse is in the depiction of that which is being offered, which the sacrificer calls "the spotless sacrifices" (in the plural) when he says "Therefore, most merciful Father, we humbly beg of you and entreat you through Jesus Christ your Son, our Lord, that you hold as acceptable and bless these gifts, these offerings, these holy, spotless sacrifices." If with these marvelous epithets he designates the bread and wine that he has not yet transubstantiated, as is clear from the mass's Canon, then because the bread and wine are two different things so too are they two sacrifices—in fact, two

spotless and perfect sacrifices. But, as the papal teachers themselves admit, because of the priest's carelessness, they sometimes become moldy after the consecration. But if he is designating Christ's actual body and blood by means of those epithets, then by the hypothesis of the papal teachers they cannot possibly be called "spotless sacrifices," because Christ's body and blood make up only one sacrificial victim (as they themselves acknowledge), a sacrificial victim that, to use the words of certain Schoolmen, sometimes turns out as nothing because mice or spiders have eaten it, or that many times is found to be gnawed to pieces by worms.

59. The twelfth abuse is in the idolatrous adoration of the very light, round sacrificial victim that the sacrificer raises aloft. In this many ritual practices come together that neither Christ has instituted, nor the apostles have observed. For Paul, who asserts that he passed on to the Corinthians what he had received from the institution of the Supper by the Lord (1 Cor 11:23), does not recount that Christ, before he gave it to his disciples, had raised round-shaped bread above his head without breaking it, or that in his administering of the Supper he employed the services of some deacon or cleric who with his left hand would lift his toga from behind and with his right hand would provide him light with a burning torch. Nor [does Paul recount] that Christ himself on bended knee worshiped the accidents of bread and wine that were changed into his body and blood—or at least that he had enjoined his disciples to worship them. On the contrary, the apostle recounts that "Christ, on the night when he was betrayed, took bread, and when he had given thanks, he broke it." And although Christ said to his disciples: "Take, eat, this is my body," still the apostle calls the bread that Christ had consecrated not "the body" but "the bread," in order to teach that with the statement, "this is my body," Christ did not command the bread to turn into his body, or that it would be changed into that with the magical declaration of five words. But he showed what the bread would be for disciples who received it with faith extended to Christ, namely, his body in a sacramental sense. For although it is with different words that the same apostle repeats Christ's mandate, "do this in remembrance of me," yet he does not take the word "remembrance" to mean the worshiping of the body that Christ had immolated in the Supper (as the papal teachers do), but for the eucharistic declaration of Christ's death that the breaking of the bread designates, as we have shown abundantly above.

60. The thirteenth abuse is in the private celebration of the mass, without the participation of the people who are standing by. For in the first institution of the holy Supper it was not Christ by himself, nor later was it ever the disciples by themselves who ate the sacramental bread or drank the wine; but they did so together with the others who had been called to participate in the holy Supper. And the sacrificer can do nothing more foolish than that he when reciting the words of Christ as Christ distributed the bread and wine equally to all the disciples who were dining with him, does not distribute the sacrament of the Supper to anyone of those who are standing by him. And also that he omits this part of the institution by Christ but diligently observes that other part, which consists in the taking and consecrating of the bread and the cup, as if that part is a more important essence of the holy Supper than this part, as Bellarmine wrongly claims. For the holy Supper is called "the communion of the body and blood of Christ" for the very fact that we all, who are many in his one mystical body, partake of that one bread, as the apostle says in 1 Cor 10:17. Therefore the Greek church fathers sometimes call the holy Supper the "gathering and fellowship," and sometimes "the mystery of the gathering and fellowship" (Dionysius, *Ecclesiastical Hierarchy*, chapter 4; Clement, *Constitutions*, book 8, chapter 10).

61. The other abuses are seen in the futile storing in a pyx of the bread that has to be eaten by the believers; in the ridiculous placement of it on the chests of the deceased, who are incapable of eating, drinking, or declaring Christ's death; in the pointless parading of the drinking cup through the streets; in the processions and other ceremonies that completely disagree with the institution by Christ. It is in his name that we should pray God to expose those shameful abuses hiding in the mass to as many people as possible, people who are struggling in utmost darkness in the realm of the pope, for God's glory and for the increase of his church. Amen.

ON THE FIVE FALSE
SACRAMENTS OF THE PAPISTS

President: Andreas Rivetus
Respondent: Peter l'Agnello

This disputation is a polemical treatise against the five 'false' sacraments of the Roman Catholic church: confirmation, penitence, extreme unction, orders, and marriage. The principle underlying argument against each sacrament is that it has no basis in Scripture; it also was not administered or practiced in the early church. The disputation notes moreover that there is considerable disagreement among Roman Catholic theologians on these issues. One of the five sacraments is put between Baptism and the Eucharist, namely the Confirmation of those who have been baptized (3–13). Following the treatment of the Eucharist are Penitence by those who make confession (14–27), the Extreme Unction of those who are ill (28–37), the Orders of ministers (38–45), and Matrimony of those who take vows of marriage (46–51).

1. Since what is right is the rule both for itself and for what is wrong, anyone who considers the matter somewhat more carefully is able with very little effort to discern and reject any sacrament that has been fabricated. [He may do so] by means of the right doctrine about the sacraments in general, and from their nature, and also by means of the description of the two sacraments which meet all the conditions required for true sacraments. However, because contrary things reveal themselves more clearly when they are placed opposite each other, we deem it fitting to add to the preceding disputations about the true sacraments one about the five falsely-called sacraments that in the papacy are granted equal (and in some cases, even greater) status and that are held in no less reverence.

2. Well then, those five sacraments are as follows. One is put between baptism and the Eucharist, namely 1) the confirmation of those who have been baptized. And those that were added after the Eucharist are: 2) penitence by those who make confession; 3) the extreme unction of those who are ill; 4) the orders of ministers; 5) and matrimony of those who take vows of marriage. And we should treat them all in such fashion that we make a clear distinction between what is approved in each sacrament (as having been ordained by God, or as being observed profitably in the church) and what is not approved because mankind is using them contrary to divine ordinance.

Confirmation

3. In that series of pseudo-sacraments, they call the first one confirmation, and they define it as "a sacrament that the bishop confers upon the forehead of those who have been baptized by means of sacred oil that the bishop must consecrate. This is accompanied by these solemn words: 'I seal you with the seal of the cross, and I confirm you with the oil of salvation, in the name of the Father, the Son, and the Holy Spirit.' And he confers it with a slap of his hand—and it reinforces one's faith and grants the Christian believer the courage to boldly confess the name of the Lord whenever he must do so" (Catechism of the Council of Trent, part 2, chapter 3; Augustinus Hunaeus, *Axioms on the Sacraments*, axiom 13). And they say that this sacrament of theirs "is not only comparable to baptism but even preferable to it in two respects, namely in the worthiness of the one who administers it (since that is only the bishop) and also in the perfection of its effect" (Costerus, *Enchiridion*, chapter 11).

4. If at this point we should require what they admit is needed in every sacrament, namely 1) a direct institution by Christ; 2) a visible or tangible sign that has been given and that does not occur naturally, which bears an analogy with the thing that it signifies and which does not have its signification in the institution of it, as words do; 3) a word that accompanies the element and that contains the promise of saving grace (which they call justifying grace), then, they will certainly get bogged down. For they would have it "that the remote matter of this sacrament is oil mingled with balsam which the bishop has consecrated, but that the proximate matter is the anointing of that oil applied to the forehead in the shape or sign of the cross," and that its form is the words that we quoted in the definition above, etc.—in all of these

things they certainly are not able to point to a command and divine ordination. In fact, some of those papal teachers, like Alexander of Hales and Bonaventure, have honestly admitted that "this sacrament was instituted neither by Christ nor by the apostles, but by the church at the Council of Méaux" which was held under Lotharius (as Gabriel Biel testifies in [*Commentary on the Sentences*] book 4, distinction 7). And Scotus does not disagree that Christ and the apostles did not use that matter and form, and he thinks Christ confirmed his apostles without it. He also thinks that Christ could have made this exemption for the apostles, who did not employ this matter and form, because the miraculous conferral of the Holy Spirit and the gift of tongues [of fire] had taken place instead. "And, although one does not read about their time and manner in Scripture, that yet both the matter and the form are supposed to be instituted by God" (in the same place in *On the Sentences*, book 4, distinction 7).

5. And therefore, this entire sacrament is based purely upon assumptions, and so too is what Holcot adds (*On the Sentences*, book 4, question 2), namely that "both the form and the matter of some sacraments that are not necessary for salvation had to be kept secret in the time of the early church because of the mockery by the gentiles." And moreover, there is no agreement among even the Jesuits of our current time. For on the one hand Bellarmine makes the assertion that the matter of confirmation is the anointing oil, and he tries to prove it from two places in Scripture, namely 2 Cor 1:21–22, where it says that "it is God who established, anointed, and sealed us," etc., and 1 John 2:27, "which deals with the anointing we receive from him" (*On the Sacrament of Confirmation*, book 2, chapter 8). Also, although Gregory of Valencia is of the view (*On the Number of Sacraments*, chapter 3) "that the opinion of Waldensis and others is a very probable one, that the apostles had never bestowed the Holy Spirit without applying the physical matter of oil and the form, namely the words" (which even the Catechism of the Council of Trent, chapter 3, section 5 tries to prove with the authority of Pope Fabian). Nevertheless, the same Gregory did not dare to disprove the view of Thomas (part 3, article 2 ad 1), Paludanus ([*Commentary on the Sentences*] book 4, distinction 7, question 1) and of Scotus cited above, namely that "the apostles because of some divine exemption had bestowed the proper effect of this sacrament without its form and matter," which is something they certainly would not have done (as pseudo-Fabian would have it) if at the last Supper Christ had instructed them in preparing the anointing oil.

6. And there is no reason why anyone should be affected by those two passages adduced by Bellarmine in which the apostles made mention of sealing and anointing and even of confirmation; for those passages provide nothing relevant at all, unless he shows that the apostles were thinking of that ceremonial confirmation and that visible oil which is applied together with the prescribed form; and that they were not thinking of the confirmation by the Spirit that is proper only to the elect, and a spiritual and immaterial anointing with which Christians are made to conform to Christ their head. Certainly, the Jesuit Lorinus takes "anointing" in [1] John [2:27] to mean the doctrine or even Christ himself, as when an abstract term is used in place of a concrete one. But how could they prove that these things should be understood as being about that oil of theirs, since there is still a disagreement among them whether it is necessary to add balsam to the oil as a requirement of the sacrament? For although there is a common opinion among them that affirms it, yet Cajetan, whom de Soto follows, along with others, holds an opposing view in his commentary on the Part 3 [of the *Summa Theologiae*]. Emanuel Sa rejects neither point of view in his *Aphorisms*. But they do point out that for the physical substance "Indian balsam suffices, and that it need not necessarily be Palestinian oil, just as it is of no relevance to the consecration whether the wine be from the Rhine region or from Greece" (Aegidius de Coninck, question 72, article 3, dubium 1).

7. And for their proof that the anointing should come in the form of a cross there is no reason or authority whatsoever, but they assign some arguments of fittingness, such as the fact "that this sacrament is given so that we do not blush with shame, and that for this reason the sign should be marked upon one's forehead." But from where do they get such a goal for the sacrament that would be appropriate for it? But it is completely foreign to Scripture and to reason to conflate that anointing with the laying-on of hands that the apostles practiced at that time when the miraculous outpouring of the gifts of the Holy Spirit flourished in the church. And yet Bellarmine, following Waldensis and Hugh of St. Victor, makes the claim (book 2, chapter 9) "that the anointing (i.e., the anointing with chrism) is the same as the laying-on of hands, and that it stands for both of them, even though it is the second one that appears to be mentioned explicitly." Gregory of Valencia refutes him when he says that "in the church at one time or another the rite of the laying-on of hands was like some ceremony of the same sacrament, although it is not at all necessary to retain it since it did not belong to the substance" (*On*

the Number of the Sacraments, chapter 3). There is not any way whereby these contradictions of the Cadmaean brothers can be reconciled.

8. If it were not wrong to make fun of a serious matter, it would be ridiculous what the Catechism of Trent goes on about in detail concerning the slap "whereby the bishop lightly smites the cheek of the one being confirmed with the hand" (chapter 3, section 20), "so that he will remember that he, like a strong athlete, should bear every adversity with indomitable spirit for the sake of Christ's name." And that ludicrous action (if it means anything at all) could not be more fitting for symbolizing the exact opposite, unless they actually wish their bishop to take on the role of Caiaphas and the other persecutors of Christ [cf. Matt 26:62–68 and John 18:19–24,27] who harm Christians on account of Christ's name—something not entirely foreign to the truth.

9. Since what does not exist does not have any affections or operations, there is no reason for us to ascribe certain sacramental effects to this institution. And the ones that the papal teachers themselves ascribe are entirely imaginary; we have already rejected what they teach about 'character' when we dealt with the sacraments in general. The second effect, and it is the chief effect which they attribute, is the "grace that makes gracious, and it is greater than the one that is bestowed in baptism regarding the strengthening of the soul against the devil's attacks, but regarding the remission of sins it is lesser," as Bellarmine says (*On the Sacrament of Confirmation*, book 2, chapter 11). Someone else confirms this "by comparing the two sacraments to the birth and growth of the human body, because the human being acquires much more substance by the latter than by the former. And since we are born again by baptism and we grow through confirmation towards the perfect state of grace, we appear to acquire more grace through this latter one than the former" (Giles de Coninck, question 72, article 7, dubium 1).

10. And what is more, because the grace which is sealed by baptism grows and is confirmed in believers throughout their entire life-time without the supporting aid of a sacrament specifically ordained for that purpose, the comparison that is drawn by the Jesuit does violence to the sacrament of the Lord's Supper, to which that [growth and confirmation of grace] belong in the highest degree so that we acquire more substance, or at least maintain what substance has been acquired. And that happens also by the ministry of the Word, which we use "until we reach perfect manhood, to the measure of the stature of the fullness of Christ" (Eph 4:13); and having been reborn in

him through the one baptism, and like the sons and heirs of a father who partake of his table, we enter into a spiritual relationship and affinity, yet one that among believers does not prevent them from entering into a contract of holy matrimony, and one that does not annul a marriage that has [already] been entered upon. Much less should we believe this about the affinity contracted "between the confirmation sponsor and the one who has been confirmed"—which the oily papal wrestling-masters dream up as "the third effect" that arises from their sacrament (Francisco de Toledo, *Instructions Regarding the Priesthood*, book 2, chapter 24).

11. From what has been stated it is sufficiently clear that those histrionics have nothing in common with the laying-on of hands (as Acts 8[:17] and 19[:6] speak about it) which the people who were baptized in Samaria and Ephesus received from the apostles. By that laying-on of hands those gifts of the Holy Spirit were imparted which the Scholastics call "[gifts] that are freely given;" and concerning these gifts those same people teach that "nothing prevents them from existing even in sinners" (Lorinus, *On the Acts of the Apostles*, chapter 19, verse 6). [They teach] that Cornelius received those same gifts even before he was baptized—proof that not merely as far as the ceremony is concerned but also its effects, the apostolic laying-on of hands is of an entirely different kind than the papist confirmation. What the apostles at that time had employed with results would now be done in vain, since this effect was temporary and does not pertain to justifying grace. And what of the fact that the ones guilty of that teaching admit the very same thing? For Suárez (Tome 3, disputation 33, section 4) freely admits that "the laying-on of hands which the apostles used in Acts 8 and 19 was actually not the sacrament of confirmation, because it was much different in the sensible aspects of the ritual. In fact, [he admits that] it was not simply a sacrament, because it was not a ceremony constituted by a firm and established law." And by this admission, he removes all of book 2, chapter 2 of Bellarmine's *On the Sacrament of Confirmation*.

12. But when in their writings the ancients mention the anointing of chrism, they take it to mean mainly the anointing that was added to baptism—and not a special sacrament—whereby they immediately anointed those who were baptized "like athletes about to enter the contest," as Chrysostom states in *Homily* 6 on the Epistle to the Colossians. Indeed, not even the papal teachers themselves say that this anointing is part of the sacrament's very essence, and although the custom is an ancient one, it should be placed

among those traditions [of the church] "that have come down to us as neither the Lord's truth nor the truth of the Gospel; nor have they come down to us by apostolic commands and epistles," as Cyprian says in Letter 74 to Pompey. And the fact that, in later times, "the bishops went out to those people whom the presbyters and deacons had baptized in the smaller towns, in order to place their hands upon them to invoke the Holy Spirit," Jerome ascribes to "the custom of the churches," and not to the truth that comes from the Lord. And he contends over against the Luciferians that this practice came about "more for the prestige of the priest than for the requirement of the law." He certainly never would have said this about a rite that unequivocally was called a sacrament. Therefore, if at some time or another the church fathers gave the name of sacrament to such ceremonies, we should understand it in the broad sense whereby "signs are called sacraments insofar as they pertain to matters divine" (Augustine, Epistle 5 to Marcellinus)—despite the fact that they are not based on any divine authority.

13. It is likely, however, that the "doctrine of the laying-on of hands," which Heb 6:2 links to the doctrine of baptisms, refers to that care of the early church whereby youths who had been instructed in catechetical doctrine were presented to the church before they were permitted to partake of the Supper, in order to give answers about their faith, and were commended to God in prayer, along with the ritual of the laying-on of hands, which in the time of the patriarchs (and thereafter) was a gesture of people as they pray and give praise. In book 5, chapter 23 of *On Baptism*, Augustine had this in view when he said that "the laying-on of hands, unlike baptism, can be done a second time, because it is nothing other than praying over a person." It is clear there that Augustine did not share the view of the papal teachers in this matter, as they argue that "those who administer confirmation (or who are being confirmed) for a second time, commit a serious sacrilege," namely, because of the impression of a character. If they would be content with this prayer and commendation of the believing adult to God following a lawful examination, then even we would readily agree—if—I say, they would seek nothing else than that rite which Calvin wishes to be restored (*Institutes*, book 4, chapter 19, section 4) and the substance of which is maintained scrupulously in our churches.

Penitence

14. So much for the pseudo-mystery of confirmation. What follows is penitence, which we are not treating in this disputation insofar as it means the conversion from a vain walk of life to the true God, the conversion whereby someone initially changes his whole former walk of life for the better. For this sort of penitence is required before baptism, a time when penitence cannot have the force of a sacrament, as the papal teachers agree. They hold that "penitence is a sacrament of the new law that Christ instituted after his resurrection," that is, for those who have fallen away after their baptism. And also, that penitence is "not inward (insofar as it is a virtue of the mind), but only external." [And they say] "that the most proximate matter is the act of the repentant person; that the remote matter is the sins themselves; and that the form is 'I absolve you in the name of the Father, etc.'" (Catechism of Trent, part 2, chapter 5, section 9, 10, 12, 13).

15. Therefore, they hold the view that the notion of sacrament consists in "outward penance, insofar as it possesses some outward things that are subject to the senses," whereby they would have those things disclose "what occurs inwardly in the soul." And so, the controversy is not whether the conversion of the mind to God and an inward sorrowful abhorrence of the sins committed are a requirement for the forgiveness of sins. For we know that Christ exhorted all sinners to have such penance and that this condition for the forgiveness of sin was a perpetual requirement in both testaments. By means of this penance, the sinner does not earn forgiveness, as though (to use their words) he effectively obtains the forgiveness of sins; but through penance, the condition is met whereby he becomes disposed to obtain divine mercy, as though removing the hindrance, as it is called. It is, therefore, a slander against our people when the allegation is made against them that they reject all penance, and when they are accused of holding out to sinners' reconciliation without contrition or without detesting their former life.

16. And we affirm that only this inward penitence is sufficient in the case of hidden sins of which the sinner's own conscience is aware, and which sins are known only to God. But we deem it a matter of freedom, and one that is often a very useful one for troubled souls to take refuge in the counsel of those who by virtue of their office know the nature and circumstances of the sins more closely, and to seek comfort from their own pastor through some declaration of those sins that are torturing their troubled soul. But we reject as tyrannical the necessity of confessing before men each and every sin; and

within the Roman church there were those who also believed that Christ neither instituted it nor commanded it: The author of the *Glossa* at the beginning of distinction 5 about Penitence; Abbas Panormitanus in the extra section, *On Penitence and Forgiveness*, in the [decretal] chapter "Everyone of both Sexes;" Peter of Oxford; and Gratian himself (in the Decree on Penitence, distinction 1 when the question is proposed "whether it is necessary that this confession be made to the priest") who after having gathered the authorities supporting either side leaves it to the reader's free judgment to choose whichever view he wishes—and it is for that reason that Gregory of Valencia lashes out at him undeservedly in the book, *On the Necessity of Confession*, chapter 3.

17. We do require the outward repentance in cases of more serious sins that have been committed with scandal to the church and that have come to be known by a greater number of people. We do not deny that over against sinners of this sort the church can and should use its power of the keys to bind them with its censures and to release them after they have shown the fruits of repentance, by the ministry that God has granted to it for that matter. Especially relevant to this ministry are Christ's promises in Matt 16:19 and 18:18, as well as the commission he gave to the apostles in John 20:23, which deals with the keys and the forgiveness of sins, that is, with the outward judgment whereby sins that were committed outwardly, publicly, and conspicuously are bound by the church in keeping with the power that it has received to cleanse itself and to put away serious offenders, like sickly sheep from the sheepfold. If some in the early church wanted to make use of that service because they were stained with serious sins which they themselves wanted to be made known publicly so that as penitents they might be reconciled publicly, that ought not to be a reason to make what was a matter of freedom into a necessity, and also not a reason to turn what previously had been public into a private matter.

18. To be sure, we do not bar any remorseful sinner from hoping for the forgiveness of sin, and we also do not reject any such person who has committed public and well-known sins from public repentance or deny peace and communion to the one who makes satisfaction to the church. The papal teachers are guilty of the most shameful slander when they link us to the Novatians and reproach us for being taken in by the same wrong. Gregory of Valencia is somewhat ashamed of this accusation in chapter 4 of *On the Number of the Sacraments*, where he admits that we "do have the actual deed of

repentance (after baptism) and that we do so each and every time that a fall into sin occurs." [He admits] that the Novatians deny this altogether and consequently they have rejected that sacrament, even though at that time the controversy was not being waged about the sacrament but only about the act of repentance.

19. Having made these points, we now come to the proper question of this topic, and we state that not any outward repentance whether private or public (and whether we consider the actions of the penitent person or actions of the minister, either separately or jointly) is a true and proper sacrament of the New Testament. First, because in that entire action, insofar as even the papal teachers perform it, there is not any outward and visible element, which is a requirement for every sacrament as we have shown in the theses on the sacraments in general. Secondly, because in whatever way it is used (whether visible or, to say it this way, audible) there is not any sign in that sacrament that is by divine institution an efficacious sign of a spiritual effect, which is the second requirement that the papal teachers themselves make for every sacrament. Nor is there any validity to what our opponents say: "That it is irrelevant to the common notion of a sacrament of the new law that an external thing is applied by a minister, but [it is relevant] that along with the words of the form there is something that can be sensed and which has the aspect of matter, whether that be a substantial thing or a sensible action, such as in this case the actions of the repentant person."

20. For they say this contrary to the notion of all of the sacraments of the Old as well as the New Testament, and they are not able to show for any one of them that it has been ordained apart from some visible sign. Otherwise, to turn it into a sacrament it would have been enough to add a word to a word. And moreover, those outward actions are not efficacious signs of inward repentance, since inward repentance is more likely the cause of outward repentance. Thirdly, Augustine extends generally to all the sacraments what he requires in baptism (*Against Faustus*, book 19, chapter 16), namely the fact that they are "visible signs of invisible grace." And it is pure sophistry to take the sense of sight to mean in general any sense whatsoever; otherwise, Augustine would have made in vain a distinction between words that are invisible and words that are visible, i.e., the sacraments. And in order that no doubt should arise about what he means, [Augustine] states that "what is seen in the sacraments has bodily appearance, but what is understood has a spiritual benefit." Therefore, it is clear that the

sacramental symbol is always something substantial, and that substance can be seen.

21. I leave to one side the quarrel that exists among the papists about the material substance of that sacrament: The followers of Scotus locate it solely in absolution, while for all the others the absolution is both part of the matter and the form at the same time—which is absurd. But what should be noted especially is that the form of absolution is a human invention which is found neither in Scripture nor anywhere in all antiquity. For where there is no word of God there is no sacrament, nor is there any validity to their empty notion that those words of Christ, "the sins of those whom you forgive are forgiven, etc." contain that form virtually (to use their words). For if those words do include the form of some sacrament, then it follows also that the accompanying words, "those whose sins you retain, they are retained" include the form of some opposite sacrament, since the reasoning is the same for both. Therefore, just as the sins of the unrepentant are retained not by some sacramental efficacy but by the ministry of the divine Word so too is there no need for sacramental efficacy to forgive the sins of those who are repentant, but the ministry of the Word only, applied to those who are repentant.

22. In the church of ancient times, penance was practiced by those who relapsed into sin after their first conversion, and many examples of this can be found of those who upon repenting were granted true forgiveness without any administration of a special sacrament for that purpose. In 2 Sam 12:13 Nathan absolves David with these words: "The Lord has forgiven your sins." Nor is there anything to Bellarmine's recourse in special revelation, as this was not needed since all believers knew that the sins of those who are repentant are forgiven. And there also is no reason why Bellarmine refers to God's extraordinary providence, because it belonged to the ordinary providence of the church. And although the patriarchs were not ignorant of the Gospel, nevertheless they would not have been able to enjoy its full consolation unless the benefits of the sufferings of the Christ who was to come had been imparted to them by his own word. "For it is through the grace of our Lord Jesus Christ that we are preserved 'in the same manner' as our forefathers" (Acts 15:11).

23. Not even our opponents deny that Christ conferred the same forgiveness of sins which John the Baptist had preached. And there is no doubt that John,

who declared the wrath of God on the scribes and Pharisees, announced the mercy of God for those who were repentant. And concerning Christ it is certain that he forgave many people their sins, also that woman who, in Luke 7, confessed her sins with tears and outward gestures. Yet he did so "not by administering any sacramental word, but by his own, unique power," as Bellarmine says. And we grant that this power is in fact proper to Christ, but through the ministry of his servants he so extends it that, when they bring his word, he effectively grants his assent and accomplishes what he has promised. And for this reason he says: "Just as the Father has sent me, so too do I send you" [John 20:21–23]; and by means of that declaration he secures beforehand that ministry concerning the forgiveness of sins. From this, it follows that just as Christ, who was sent by the Father, forgave sins by means of his word without any special sacrament, so too with that same word do genuine ministers forgive sins in the name of Christ without a sacrament.

24. In the actions of the repentant person, and in the minister's absolution one cannot point to any sacramental analogy between the sign and the thing signified in such a way that what happens in the outward sign corresponds to what happens inwardly. For even though the word of the one who absolves both declares forgiveness of sins, and signifies that it has been granted—in that sense it can be placed among the signs—still there is no such analogy as exists in the other sacraments between the elementary and the heavenly thing. Add to this the fact that every sacrament is a seal that is appended to the word, and this cannot be said about absolution, which itself is the word that should be sealed with a seal. Nor is there validity to the fact that Bellarmine (*On Penitence*, book 1, chapter 10) wants to forge a sacrament from Christ's words "and those whose sins you forgive, etc." because (as he puts it) "the word is a corporeal and so sensible sign, and it is the promise of justifying grace that is attached to the word." For if all the outward actions whereby the effect of grace is promised were sacraments, then there would be a countless number of sacraments in that sense: To gather in Christ's name has the promised effect of Christ's presence (Matt 18:20); to confess Christ before men has the promise of Christ's confession before the Father (Matt 10:32); to leave one's father and mother promises a one hundred-fold reward and eternal life (Matt 19:20).

25. But the power to forgive sins, whereupon the whole idea of this sacrament rests, is a matter of such controversy among the papal teachers themselves that many of them confine it with limits which others admit ruin

the very nature of the sacrament. For Lombard (*Sentences*, book 4, distinction 18, 1, part C), Bonaventure (in the same place, article 2), Gabriel Biel, Marsilius, Major, Occam, William of Auxerre, Alexander, Thomas of Argentina, Alonso Tostado—all of them (and I do mean all) are agreed, as Vasquez admits in *Question* 84, article 3, "to the extent that it is not by virtue of the keys that the forgiveness of guilt takes place, and so too the vivification of the soul and the dismissal of the liability of eternal punishment"—in these things justifying grace certainly consists—"and [they agree] that the keys do not extend to this effect; but when the priest says 'I absolve you' he merely shows that through his contrition the person has already been absolved from his guilt." From this, it follows that justifying grace is not an effect of this absolution; and so, according to the papal teachers, strictly speaking it is not a sacrament.

26. And so Vasquez rightly concludes that it follows that "the forgiveness of guilt does not come about through the sacrament, since it does not happen by virtue of its form, and in particular of its words whereby it happens in the case of a sacrament, nor of the work that has been performed (as they put it)." That is because those authors have been persuaded rightly that the priest's power does not reach to the point where he has the power to give release from the actual guilt and stain of sin, but only to the point where he shows by his absolution that the people who have confessed their sins already have been forgiven by God; and they assert that the task belongs to God to grant release not only from the stain of sin but also from the liability of eternal damnation. To this end the Master of Sentences quotes from Ambrose that "the priest certainly is carrying out his own office, but he does not exercise any rights of power; only he, who only has died for sins, dismisses sins" (The words of Ambrose are found in *On the Holy Spirit*, book 3, chapter 18).

27. Therefore, if we consider sins from the perspective of guilt and eternal liability, according to the Master [Lombard] the power to bind and to loosen is nothing other than the power to declare or "to show publicly that the sinners have been bound and loosened," just as in former times under the old law the priests were not accustomed to cleanse lepers but to determine who were clean or unclean [Lev 13 and 14]. Hence, it is clear that at the time of the Master and those who followed his line of thinking penance was not considered a sacrament of the New Testament in the strict sense of the word; and as Scotus rightly deduces from the teaching of the same Lombard, "penance did not have any causality or causal tendency towards first grace,

since it is never received worthily except by those who already are in grace, because not anyone is shown to be set free whom God has not previously forgiven" (*On the Sentences*, book 4, distinction 18, question 1).

Extreme Unction

28. The papal teachers call the third fictitious sacrament "extreme unction," and they define it as "the sacrament of extreme unction for the person who is sick and on the point of dying, who is making penance for his sins. It is administered by the priest on some parts of the body with oil which the bishop has consecrated and which effectively bestows the forgiveness of the remnants of sin, in order to lift the spirits and to restore health to the body." They hold that the remote material substance of this sacrament is olive oil, and that it belongs to the essence of the sacrament; many think that it also belongs to this essence that the oil has been consecrated not by a simple presbyter but by a bishop (although some think this is necessary only by the necessity of command); it is oil that is refreshed every single year, although it is possible to add non-consecrated oil to it a little at a time (Francis de Toledo, book 7, chapter 1). And they hold that the proximate matter is the ointment itself, which as belonging to the essence of the sacrament ought to be put on the eyes, ears, nostrils, mouth and hands. And for the sake of its completeness, but not necessarily, for the men it is put on their loins and feet and for the women on the navel (Jose Angles, in *Flowers on the fourth book of the Sentences*, Questions on extreme unction). It is applied at all unctions with new flax that is later burned.

29. Most of the papal teachers think that the form of this sacrament of theirs is not indicative but optative and deprecative to such a degree that if it were not deprecative the sacrament would have no force. And they reject the formula used by those churches that state, "I anoint your eyes, etc.," unless they add, "so that God may be gracious to you." However, the common formula is "through this holy anointing, and through his most sacred mercy, may God be gracious to you for whatever misdeed you have committed in your sense of sight, hearing, taste, smell and touch, amen." However, it is not certain whether the words "through his most sacred mercy" are essential, even though it would be a very serious sin to leave them out (De Coninck, dubium 4).

30. The one who administers them ought to be a priest whom the bishop has duly ordained, or (even much better) the bishop himself, who must have "the

intention of doing what the church [does], etc." But the priest should be a parish priest, or one to whom this duty has been delegated by the parish priest. And even without the license from the parish priest, it would still be a sacrament, although the unqualified administrant would incur excommunication by this very deed. And as for the one who receives the sacrament, he ought to be someone who is on the point of death (or at least someone who is believed to be at risk of dying) from a disease, a wound, from childbirth, or from old age. But he should not be an infant, which cannot sin, nor should he be insane (unless for a brief time he is lucid), nor should he be someone who is about to be hanged or beheaded (since people of this sort are surrendered to unmitigated judgment), nor someone who is known to be living in mortal sin.

31. For this sacrament of theirs, they make up four effects: 1) The expulsion of the remaining remnants of sins; 2) the health of the soul that is quick to do evil and slow to do good; 3) the health of the body when this is profitable for the wellbeing of the soul; and 4) support over against temptations and the devil's attacks that a man is undergoing at the time (Toledo, *Instructions for the Priests*, book 7, chapter 4). Not all the papal teachers are in agreement on these effects, however, and it is disputed whether or not health of body is certain and infallible by the power of this sacrament, or whether this is only promised conditionally. Bellarmine (chapter 6, on *Extreme Unction*) debates this matter with Domingo de Soto. And about the sort of sins whereof remnants are forgiven they dispute whether such sins are only venial (as some would have it) or also mortal, which is what the majority (including Bellarmine) think because to remove venial sins there is not any need for a new infusion of grace, and therefore not even by means of a sacrament.

32. Whereas it suffices for refutation to have put forward such points, we shall nevertheless add the following few observations: 1) Absent from this ritual are the conditions which the papal teachers themselves required for a true sacrament, namely its divine institution, its divine promise, and its effect of divine and spiritual grace (particularly as it is intended), as well as the analogy to that spiritual effect; 2) moreover, there does not exist an established and ongoing ceremony that has been given to the universal church, which is necessary in every sacrament in the strict sense of the word. For the fact that some people make up the divine institution from Mark 6:16 (where it says that the apostles anointed many sick people with oil and restored them to health) some sharp individuals among the papal teachers

have noticed that it cannot pertain to the unction which they consider to be sacramental, such as Domingo de Soto ([*Commentary on the Sentences*] book 4, distinction 23, question 1) whom Bellarmine follows (*On the Extreme Unction*, chapter 2). They have noticed that it concerns the gift and grace of miracles, and especially those involving the body. And their statement that that unction in Mark was a prefiguration of their sacramental unction is rejected with the same ease with which they put it forward, unless they want all miracles that the apostles performed to be figures of some sacrament of the New Testament, which would be very absurd.

33. What they adduce from Jas 5:14–15 does indeed show that while the extraordinary gift of physical healings was still in force in the early church, the apostle offered the following advice: Believers who were suffering from some illness or other (but not experiencing the final struggles of life) could call to them the church's elders who in the name of the Lord would anoint the sick with oil (no mention is made that it is consecrated) and with a prayer of faith, hoping to receive healing and to obtain the forgiveness of sins, if indeed the sick person was living in sin when he was overtaken by the disease. But Cardinal Cajetan, writing on the same passage, rightly recognized that these words do not pertain to the institution of some sacrament. And so also that neither on the basis of the words nor of their effect do these words speak about a sacramental unction, but about the anointing which the disciples of the Lord carried out on those who were ill. For the text does not speak about "whoever is sick unto death," but in an absolute sense about "whoever is sick," and it says that the effect is the recovery of the sick person, and it speaks about the forgiveness of sins only in a conditional sense. Add to this the fact that the text attributes that effect to the prayer of faith and not to a sacrament (which is what the papal teachers hold) and consequently— according to them—to the performing work and the faith of both the minister and the recipient, and not to the work performed.

34. Moreover, neither James nor any other apostle had the authority to establish a new sacrament. But our opponents have falsely come up with the idea that it was instituted by Christ and promulgated by the apostle. And it is unbelievable that the evangelists, who in their writings recorded things that were much more petty, could have overlooked the institution of any sacrament if it had been made by the Lord. And Hugh of St. Victor (*On the Sacraments*, book 2, part 15) and Lombard (*Sentences*, book 4, distinction 23) behave more honestly when they assert that it was the apostles who instituted

this unction. And so it follows that this is not a sacrament. What is more, with a wrong circular argument Thomas [Aquinas] and his followers do not so much prove the matter as reveal its folly, when they presuppose that it is a sacrament, and infer that therefore Christ had instituted it. Now if they were asked, "from where is it certain that Christ has instituted it?" what else could they reply but "because it is a sacrament"?

35. Their proof for the other conditions is not from James. For although James does give the hope of some temporal and spiritual good, this is not a promise made by Christ, the one who institutes a sacrament. Next, the effect of spiritual grace is not promised directly and properly with the unction, but rather the grace of health of body—and that is not the effect of a sacrament. What is more, that effect never happens in our time, and for that reason the papal teachers add the condition "if it is profitable" (where James does not have any condition) and they turn the spiritual effect, which in James is conditional, into an absolute one. And on top of that they have the nearly unanswerable question (as we have said): What are the sins that are forgiven in unction? And as for the analogy between the anointing of the body and the remission of sins in the heart they will have no better explanation than for the other points. And lastly, in James there is nothing whatsoever about the chief and primary effect which they attribute to their sacrament, namely that the sick person is fortified with spiritual help against the temptations that come over him at the moment of death.

36. And so in James there are two prescriptions, of which one is ordinary and ongoing: After the elders of the church have been called, they commend the sick person by praying for him in faith, and when he has been comforted by the Word of God, he may look to God to restore his body to health, if that is so profitable, and to lift his spirit by the forgiveness of sins. And he becomes certain of this by his own faith, which receives the promise of grace that is given to the repentant person. The extraordinary prescription was the fact that they worked healing by means of the anointing of oil. But in the several ages after the apostles this healing still was sought from God by means of prayers, as is evident from the old rituals published by Cassander, when he quotes this formula: "I anoint you with holy oil in the name of the Father, etc., so that when all the pains and discomforts of your body have fled your strength and wellbeing may recover to the extent that through the working of this mystery and through this holy anointing of oil along with our prayer, you may be healed by the power of the holy Trinity and be worthy to receive

your former, and stronger, health." He quotes similar formulas in the *Scholia on the Ecclesiastical Hymns*, p. 288 (in the Paris edition).

37. It is clear from the change to the formula that the wording now prevalent in the Roman church is so different from the anointing of old because the church has altered not only the wording but even the sense of it, so as to create a sacrament, when it saw that the anointing was altogether ineffective as far as bodily healing was concerned, even though that is what all the old formulas were concerned about. And on this point we certainly should draw attention to what Matthew Galenus, primarius professor and chancellor of the academy at Douai, admits in *Catechism* 181: "Why is it surprising," he says, "that physical healing happens so rarely, since nowadays there is hardly any attention given to the parts of the body that have suffered harm, which our ancestors used to anoint for seven whole days? They made use of valid prayers, the merits were sufficient, and there was no lack of faith or trust in God—through which they could obtain anything at all. But nowadays since we either neglect or despise those things, it should not be surprising if there is no result when the needed prayers rarely are understood or read with care." But the power of the sacraments does not depend on the merits, trust, lack of understanding or contempt of those who administer them. Therefore, it follows that the extreme unction is not a Christian sacrament.

Order

38. Along with the apostle in 1 Cor 14:40, we hold that everything in the church should be established "in good order and decently," and that unless he has been called legitimately no one can have the authority to carry out a ministry in the church. We also do acknowledge that between some ministers who God has appointed, there are gradations of office, age, and gifts. The disputation about the ecclesiastical ministry has given a more than sufficient treatment of all of these. Therefore, at this point it remains that we should answer this one question about the *raison d' être* for a sacrament that the papal teachers apply to their orders in such a way that though every order is a sacrament, they nevertheless do not make up more than one sacrament— even though all those orders differ in material substance and form, and even in each of their effects, because (as they say) they are "one sacrament in genus," or "because they are all related to a single goal." If that reasoning has a place, then not only the orders but even all the sacraments would be one sacrament, because the sacraments are similar in genus and are related to one

and the same goal, that is, the general goal of God's glory and the particular goal—as far as we are concerned—of sealing justifying grace.

39. Among our opponents, however, there is no consensus about the number of the orders, nor about the sacramental worth of all the ones they count as belonging to their orders. For some—like the Canonists, as Navarrus relates (*Manual*, chapter 22, number 18)—make up nine orders. And he adds a tenth to these, namely the order of cantors (Titelmans, *On the Sacraments*, book 1, chapter 3). But others recognize only eight orders strictly speaking, that is, four lesser ones (porters, lectors, exorcists, acolytes) and three major ones (subdiaconate, diaconate, and priesthood). And they add an eighth, the episcopate—although there are others who disagree and deny that the episcopate is a different order than the priesthood (Jose Angles, [*Commentary on the Sentences*] book 4, and others). And again, many claim that only the priesthood is a sacrament. The vanguard of these people was led by Durand, and de Soto does not judge that his followers deserve much criticism. This position is considered a probable one by [Franciscus] Victoria (in *On the Sacraments*, question 226), while Angles deems it not erroneous. In fact, [William] Estius grants that the church has not yet dealt with the question, not even concerning the deacons ([*Commentary on the Sentences*] book 4, distinction 24, section 8).

40. There are people (Domingo de Soto, Medina, Angles, etc.) who assert that the three major orders form a sacrament, while it can be said (without the risk of making an error) that the four lesser ones are not proper sacraments that bestow grace and impress a character [upon the soul]. With some hesitation, Bellarmine himself says that "there is not so much certainty about the subdiaconate," and "there is a lower probability of the lesser orders being sacraments than of the subdeacons, since [in this case] the opinion is not that common, and it is certain that they have lesser duties" (*On the Sacrament of Order*, chapter 8). About the lesser orders, Peter de Soto (*Lectures [on the Institution of Priesthood]*, *On the Sacrament of Order*, lesson 1) admits that even concerning the subdiaconate "there is no basis in Holy Scripture, and that no mention is made about them or their names in all of the ancients." Moreover, there are those who deny that the office of bishop is a sacrament in the true and strict sense of the word, and that it impresses a new character, such as Domingo de Soto (*On Justice and Right*, question 1 article 2), and others, as Bellarmine (in the passage mentioned above) admits, who, on the contrary, contends that it is a true sacrament and impresses a new character.

These differences surely show sufficiently that they themselves have no certainty from the Word of God about the institution of this supposed sacrament.

41. This also is very powerful proof that there is no unanimity among them about the material substance and about the sacramental signs. For since in what they call the major orders, they make use of two-fold signs, namely the laying-on of hands and also the handing-over of instruments—like the chalice and the paten for the priesthood, and of the book of the Gospels for the sub-diaconate—both signs are deemed essential by some (like Bellarmine, *On the Sacrament of Order*, book 1, chapter 9) and only the handing-over of the instruments by others (like Domingo de Soto, [*Commentary on the Sentences*] book 4, distinction 24, question 1, article 4). But in the case of the other, lesser orders, they all indeed deem that extending only the instruments is enough. But if one were to ask them from where they get these signs, and when and by whom they had been instituted, they would of necessity fall silent; and if they do not, let them produce the documents of their divine institution where Christ handed a paten and chalice to the apostles and by this bestowal established them as priests to offer the sacrifice of the mass. And so too for the other orders.

42. And no better is the basis that supports the form which they ascribe to this sacrament of theirs, or to many of their sacraments. For the words which the bishop uses in ordination are clearly of human institution, like: "Receive the power to sacrifice to God and to consecrate the masses for both the living and the dead, in the name of the Lord," when a priest is ordained. Or, in the ordination of a deacon: "Receive the power to read the Gospel in the church of God, both for the living and the dead, in the name of the Lord, etc." (Roman Pontifical, *On the Orders of Deacon and Priest*, folio 16 and 20). In the ordination of an acolyte: "Receive the candle-holder and the wax taper, and know that you are entitled to light the lamps of the church" (Ibid. p. 9); and so too for the other orders. In the case of all of these they note that calling on the holy Trinity does not belong to the essence of the form. If Christ had instituted anything of this sort, who would believe that it was done so covertly and secretly that after sixteen hundred years it remains so unclear what the proper material substance of this sacrament is and what its form is? For even in the ordination of the priest, they come up with a different form: "Receive the power to forgive sins, etc." And so, they have made up a sacrament which Christ has instituted, the entire substance of which they are still unsure

about—and that not only is not found in Scripture but of which not even a trace appears in all antiquity. For that our opponents seek recourse in the fact that "they were very careful lest such holy mysteries of our religion should come to be known by the common crowd and especially by unbelievers, and thus come to be despised" (Estius, [*Commentary on the Sentences*] book 4, distinction 24.2). And that is a laughable falsehood. For how could that which should be shared with such a large number of ministers be able to remain hidden by people among whom (it is fair to think) there were many unwise, and also many who at one time apostatized, through whom such things could have been made public? And added to this is the fact that if the rites of baptism and of holy Eucharist which Christ himself has instituted had been divulged from the first times of the church, there is no reason why the material substance and the form of the lesser sacraments should be shrouded in such silence.

43. As far as the effect is concerned, they actually devise two of them; one which bestows grace and another which impresses a character into the soul of the ordained. The folly of character was rejected in the treatment of the sacraments in general. And, as we see, many deny that, in the five lesser orders, either grace is conferred, or character impressed. And regarding what they call the higher orders, we require that a divine promise be clearly and manifestly expressed in Scripture, for otherwise no-one would be able to convince us that by a certain pact God is bound to be present with some supernatural operation whenever men attach spiritual *charismata* to words that they have fabricated, and to ludicrous ceremonies (of whatever sort) that are purely human. Nor is there any reason why anyone should be moved by Bellarmine's objection from 1 Tim 4[:14] and 2 Tim 1[:6], wherein mention is made of the grace that Timothy received from the laying-on of hands. The first passage does not deal with justifying grace which is sealed by the sacraments and which Timothy obtained elsewhere, but it deals with the grace which they call freely given, which someone who is not justified is able to have.

44. Bellarmine himself admits (*On the Sacraments in General*, chapter 26) that "the authority to confer the sacraments is not a grace that makes gracious but a grace that has been given freely, and that it does not clash with a shameless lifestyle to the point that it cannot co-exist with it"—a statement whereby he confutes his own argument. Then, add the fact that among the papal teachers it still is not yet agreed whether the laying-on of hands is essential to the

order, since some of them deny it, as we have shown just now. Moreover, since the apostles did make use of the laying-on of hands not only in ordination but also in the conferral of the special gifts of the Holy Spirit, it cannot be denied that the statement in 2 Tim 1:6 can fittingly be taken to mean both layings-on of hands, and consequently does not pertain to the institution of some sacrament, since by the admission of the papal teachers the extraordinary gifts of the Spirit do not pertain to the grace of the sacraments.

45. From these statements it is sufficiently clear that not any order is a sacrament in the strict sense of the word. But we would not put up a fight if someone, taking the word 'sacrament' in a broad sense, would bestow that term also upon the genuine ordination of ministers, provided that everyone is in agreement that it cannot be counted among the sacraments in an unambiguous sense. In this sense, Calvin (*Institutes*, book 4, chapter 14, section 20) "willingly allows the laying-on of hands whereby the ministers of the church were installed into their office to be called a sacrament; but he does not number it among the ordinary sacraments." Also in this way should we understand Melanchthon (*Loci communes* and the *Apology of the Augsburg Confession*, article 13) where he holds that the order is not a sacrament in the strict sense of the word—which Bellarmine ascribes to him—but rather in an improper and general sense, in which also the ancients once gave the name of sacrament to the washing of feet, the giving of blessed bread to Catechumens, etc. (Augustine, *On the merits and forgiveness of sins*, book 2, chapter 26; Ambrose, *On the Sacraments*, book 3, chapter 1; Bernard, *Sermon on the Lord's Supper*). Even the dedication of the altar is called a sacrament (Glossa [on Gratian's Decree], case 1, question 3, chapter 15).

Marriage

46. The same thing should be said about marriage, if by chance some people have given the name of sacrament to what is otherwise a holy and even divine institution. That was observed even among the Schoolmen by Durand in his [*Commentary on the Sentences*] book 4, distinction 26, question 3, where he teaches that "marriage is not a sacrament like one of the others, and that it does not bestow grace by the work performed." The same is said in the *Glossa* [on Gratian's Decree] (case 31, question 1, chapter 9; case 32, question 2, chapter 13) and likewise by Godfried, Hostiensis and Bernard, cited by Durand. Even Lombard himself says this in *Sentences*, book 4, distinction 2,

where he holds that marriage was only a remedy against sin—which existed before the coming of Christ, and that it does not bestow grace. From this it follows that it is not a sacrament in the unambiguous sense of the word. Nowadays, the new papal teachers consider that view as heretical, since they determine that marriage is truly and properly a sacrament; but they disagree in this regard, that some like Peter de Soto (*Lectures* [*on the Institution of Priesthood*], *On Marriage* 2) and Alfonso de Castro (*Against Heresies*, on the word 'nuptials,' heresy 3) would have it that "marriage started to become a sacrament not only in the New Testament, but had been such already for a long time since it was first instituted." They took that view from Lombard (*Sentences*, book 4, distinction 26), and he from Pope Leo I (Epistle 92, to Rusticus). But others, and among them Bellarmine, say that before Christ it did not have the nature of a sacrament.

47. We deny that it was a sacrament in the strict sense of the word, whether it was exhibited from the time of its first institution or after Christ, since we are moved by the same reasons with which we took away that right from the other falsely-named sacraments, i.e., the fact that God had not instituted it as a sacramental sign or seal of justifying grace, and that it is not supported by the promise that by using it grace will be exhibited. And also that God himself has not prescribed a specific form of words (which the papal teachers require for sacraments) nor that anything can be observed in the marriage of Christians that was lacking in the marriage of believers before Christ. And that is the reason why also in this matter the papal teachers disagree amongst themselves with 'divorcing' opinions, and they have differing opinions not only about the time of its institution, but also about its material substance. Some think it exists in the "words" that express the consent "insofar as these words are being determined," and others in the persons themselves who are joining together, or in the bodies of the two spouses. Others, like Cano, think that it exists in those visible rites which are used in the church's blessing, and that is the reason why he takes a beating from Bellarmine who holds that the persons who join together are not only the material substance but even the instrumental cause of this sacrament. Others posit that the material substance is the consent of the ones who join together. And others have other views.

48. And about the form they compete in similar fashion with differing opinions. Some are of the view that the form is the words which express the consent, and since it is the married couple which declares them, they are the administers of the sacrament; and if they do not express their consent in

words, their carnal union can be considered to stand for the form and the sign (thus Bellarmine, *On Marriage*, book 1, chapter 6, 'Ex his,' and chapter 5, 'Sed quicquid'). But it sure is a strange teaching that a sacrament can be performed in the marriage bed, and in such an act, without speaking a word. Others are of the opinion that the words uttered by the priest are the form (like Cano, *Loci theologici*, book 8, chapter 5, and William of Paris, [*On the Sacraments*] chapter 9, question 1, "On Marriage"). Others reject this opinion because it would follow that the secret marriages that were entered upon before the Council of Trent were not endowed with sacramental worth, which they deem absurd. And others hold that the material substance is the words first spoken by the one spouse, for instance, "I accept you as my wife," and that the form is the words spoken in the second place by the other spouse, for instance, "I accept you as my husband." Vasquez (*Disputatio* 3, chapter 1 and following) relates nine points of view on this, of which he refutes eight and picks the one that the others reject. But in every sacrament, because it belongs to the genus of a sign and there is no sign when it is not acknowledged as such, it is clear how important—in fact, how obviously necessary—it is that it possess something of a sign in keeping with the will of the one who institutes it, the fighting among our opponents makes it sufficiently clear that marriage is not a sacrament in the true sense of the word.

49. And the fact that it represents the spiritual and very close union of our Lord Jesus Christ with the church does not add the characteristics of a sacrament to this sacred institution; for since this representation exists primarily and especially in the unbreakable bond of marriage, as our opponents acknowledge, they also admit that when understood as a bond "marriage neither is now nor ever was properly speaking a sacrament." Thus Coninck (*On Marriage*, disputation 24, dubium 2), where he also admits that "the church fathers understood 'sacrament' in the broad sense for any sign whatsoever which God has instituted for a sacred thing because they say that marriage is a sacrament not because it signifies some sanctity that it bestows by the use of it, but because it signifies the union of Christ with the church. Hence, they even say that marriage in the law of nature is a sacrament in a similar way." This is what he says.

50. From this, it is clear what our response should be to that crowning argument which very many of our opponents attach to the Epistle to the Ephesians, chapter 5 verse 32. For, leaving aside the fact that the word

'sacrament' occurs only in the Vulgate edition, it is clear that 'sacrament' is a general term and that from the word (which Bellarmine even admits) no proof can be given that it is a true sacrament—and much less, in fact, from the circumstances of the text. And although Bellarmine makes this argument with all his might, he could not persuade all his own people. For Gabriel Vasquez, who wrote after Bellarmine, says the following about the passage in Eph 5 ("This sacrament is great, etc."): "But I have always held the view that with this testimony it not only is not possible to prove what our people contend, but also that in the explanation of it they declare some things which in no way at all can co-exist with true doctrine." And following a lengthy rebuttal he adds: "It would have been better for our theologians over against heretics to avoid this passage of Paul than to be seen as foisting this testimony of Scripture upon them, and to end up in such tight spots and with a less sound explanation" (*On the Sacrament of Marriage*, disputation 2, chapter 6). Moreover, in the same place: "We grant that neither from that passage in Eph 5 nor from that in 1 Tim 2 can it be proven effectively that marriage is a sacrament."

51. And since this is the case, and since they, convinced by the strength of the truth, finally admit that they have no basis at all in Scripture for this sacrament of theirs, they return their viewpoint on that matter "to their own church's definition, which has been handed down in perpetual tradition" (a tradition which is more uncertain than the matter with which we are concerned). However, we are content with the two genuine sacraments, of which it was ascertained and manifested from the Scriptures that they were instituted by God's Son with certain signs and words, and we hold these same sacraments, "few for many, easy to observe, most useful in their efficacy, and very clear in what they signify." And we shall strengthen our faith by using them, while not hesitating in our faith. And since we have learned that whatever comes about without faith is sin [Rom 14:23], and since we know that there is not any faith that has not been preceded by God's Word, we shall have no part in the sins of those who disagree amongst themselves with foolish opinions and with human inventions bind the grace of God which we should expect from the unique author of grace, we shall always sing thanks and praise to Him in the unity of the Trinity.

Corollaries

1. We deny that the degrees of consanguinity and affinity wherein Leviticus 18 prohibits the entry into marriage, relates to the Israelite polity in such a way that they do not belong to the divine right that must be kept for all time in keeping with the law of decency.

2. We affirm that in the case of adultery or the wrongful desertion of an unbeliever the marriage is dissolved, even as far as the bond is concerned, in such a way that once the divorce has lawfully taken place, the innocent party should not be prevented from marrying.

3. And we deny that a marriage insofar as the bond, or the bed or cohabitation is concerned, can be dissolved by a vow or by entry upon a religious order (as they call it).

4. We affirm that in order to enter into a lawful marriage the explicit or tacit approval of the parents is required.

ON CHURCH DISCIPLINE

President: Antonius Walaeus
Respondent: Johannes Livensius

An important feature of the Church are the two 'keys of the kingdom' that have been given to it by Christ (Matt 16:19; see thesis 2). The first key is the administration of the Gospel and the forgiveness of sins (Disputation 42, treated in Disputation 48 in theses 5–7). From thesis 8 onward, the disputation deals with the key of discipline, which concerns excommunication—'a matter of greater controversy in the church of Christ' (8). Church discipline is a 'spiritual authority' whereby individuals are 'barred from the signs of divine grace, on account of impurity in doctrine or life and after they have neglected and despised the private and public warnings of the church.' If they 'continue in the same stubbornness then at last in the presence of the entire church they, in the name of God, are declared through the public sentence on earth and consequently also in heaven as excluded from the communion of the church until such time as they are reconciled to God and the church through true and genuine repentance' (9). It is shown from the Old and New Testament that this authority is given to the Church (10–17). The civil authority has no jurisdiction over spiritual discipline, which is exclusively ecclesiastical (19). From thesis 20 onward it is explained through whom (21–24), to whom (25–32) and in what way (33–59) this authority should be exercised. Discipline concerns not merely individual people but also entire groups that promote or practice teachings that are unbiblical. The Synopsis describes the process whereby those who wander may be brought back; failure to do so results finally in withholding the sacrament of the Lord's Supper and exclusion from the communion of saints. Nevertheless, those who are under discipline should not 'be excluded from either the public or private hearing of the Word, since it contains the warnings and encouragements unto faith and repentance, and because prayers for their conversion are offered by the church in it' (47). The goal of discipline and excommunication, 'the last and fiercest remedy for subduing a man's flesh and for bringing his soul to life' (59), is not the man's perdition, but his salvation (56).

1. Just as a family, or a state, or any other society of human beings cannot exist without the restraint of laws and discipline, so also the integrity of Christ's church in this world cannot endure unless it is bound to a fixed government and suitable laws whereby its order and arrangement are kept unharmed against the deceits and devisings of the flesh, the world and Satan.

2. This government of the church commonly is called church discipline; Christ designates it with the word "keys" in Matt 16:19, and in 2 Cor 10:8 the apostle calls it the authority given by the Lord, not for tearing down but for building up.

3. Yet this is an entirely ministering authority, in all things subject to Christ and his Word. For Christ alone is like the son who is put in charge of his house (Heb 3:6). "And he holds the key of David, he opens and no-one shuts, and shuts and no-one opens" (Rev 3:7). And, indeed, his ministers are put over his house like servants, like stewards and managers of the mysteries of God in whom the foremost requirement is that each one of them be found faithful (1 Cor 4:[1–]2).

4. And this key or authority to bind and to loosen, in keeping with Christ's explanation in Matt 18:18, is rightly divided by our Catechism into two parts: one is the authority of the Word and the other is the authority of excommunication. The former of these, based on Luke 11:52, is usually called the key of knowledge, and the latter the key of discipline (so called when taken in the stricter sense).

5. It is the key or authority of the Word whereby forgiveness of sins and reconciliation with God through Christ are not only generally declared to believers and those who repent (as is seen throughout the Scriptures), but also whereby that general word is applied individually to each person's conscience for their consolation and upbuilding, in proportion to the fruits of faith and repentance, or the signs of unrepentance and unbelief, that become manifest in them—as can be seen in the example of Nathan and David (2 Sam 12:13) and, contrariwise, of Peter and Simon the magician (Acts 8:21).

6. In a certain respect the use of this declaration belongs to the entire church as a community, because the individual members of the church, according to the command of love, in proportion to the measure of the gift they have

received from Christ, and by reason of their calling, are able and required to comfort, exhort, and admonish one another privately from the Word of God, and to do so according to Christ's command in Matt 18:15: "If your brother sins against you, go and tell him his fault between you and him alone, etc." And likewise the apostle in Heb 3:13: "But encourage one another daily, as long as it is called 'today,' so that none of you may be hardened by sin's deceitfulness."

7. However, Christ has appointed in particular the pastors of the church and the public ministers of the Word to exercise this authority publicly and, by virtue of their public authority, also privately. Hence Christ also promised to the apostle Peter individually in Matt 16:19: "I shall give to you the keys to the kingdom of heaven, and whatever you bind on earth will be bound in heaven, and whatever you loose on earth will be loosed in heaven;" and to all the disciples together [he promised] in John 20:22: "If you forgive the sins of any, they are forgiven them, and if you retain the sins of any, they are retained." And therefore, it says also that the preachers of the Word fulfill their commission in the name of Christ (2 Cor 5:20).

8. The second key, which is called the key of discipline, is a matter of greater controversy in the church of Christ, and so we must protect the nature, mode and use of it a little more carefully from Holy Scripture against all abuses.

9. Therefore, we state that the key of discipline properly exists in that spiritual authority whereby, through the agency of the pastors of the Word, in accordance with the counsel of the church's senate and with the consent of the whole church, those who are called brothers [cf. 1 Cor 5:10–11] are barred from the signs of divine grace, on account of impurity in doctrine or life and after they have neglected and despised the private and public warnings of the church; and, if they continue in the same stubbornness then at last in the presence of the entire church they, in the name of God, are declared through the public sentence on earth and consequently also in heaven as excluded from the communion of the church until such time as they are reconciled to God and the church through true and genuine repentance.

10. But before we consider more thoughtfully the individual parts of this definition, we ought from Holy Scripture to demonstrate over against some who present themselves as members of the reformed church that this

authority has been granted to the church; and then we should explain its mode and nature according to the definition that we have proposed.

11. Very many instances and examples of the Old as well as the New Testament give proof that this authority has been given to the church.

12. In the Old Testament God commanded that not only should those unclean according to the law voluntarily abstain from the communion of the sacred things (in Lev 5 and 6, and subsequent chapters) and likewise from eating the Passover lamb (Num 9), but also that the care of this matter should in preference to others belong to the priests and the Levites, namely that according to God's Word they should distinguish and judge between the clean and unclean, between the holy and the profane, as can be seen regarding every impurity (Lev 10:9, Ezek 44:23), and concerning those unclean from leprosy (Lev 13), in order to bar from the communion of the temple and the sacred things those whom they had judged to be impure, until they were made clean once again through special sacrifices, as is demonstrated besides the particular example of king Uzziah (2 Chron 26) in a general way in 2 Chron 23:18[–19]: "Jehoiada divided the duties in the house of God between the priests and the Levites, and he stationed door-keepers at the entrances to God's house, so that the person unclean in any matter should not enter."

13. And because this is obvious concerning ceremonial impurity, we should state it all the more concerning moral impurity, since that ceremonial impurity indicated a moral impurity, just as the prophet Haggai explains in chapter 2:12. And so too God, when in the exclusion from the sanctuary He also links those who are uncircumcised in the flesh with those who are uncircumcised of heart (Ezek 44:9): "No foreigner who is uncircumcised of flesh or uncircumcised of heart shall enter into my sanctuary." And although we admit that this passage must be understood in a mystical sense about the sanctuary of the New Testament, even so it clearly shows at the same time what ought to have been done in that outward sanctuary of the Old Testament.

14. But in addition to these arguments drawn from the analogy of ceremonial impurity it is also possible to borrow from the Old Testament certain proofs taken from moral impurity, such as Lev 6:2, which provides a law for different kinds of fraud and theft; and added to the law is the mode whereby men of that sort can be reconciled once again with the church and make atonement for that sin, i.e., the restoration of the stolen item along with an

additional one-fifth and the burnt-offering of a suckling ram by a priest. From this it necessarily follows that a man of this sort, before he was reconciled with the defrauded person by returning the stolen object—and with God by means of the special offering—did not have access to the communal sacrifices and sacraments of the Israelite church. For wherever there was a special atonement, there was impurity; and where there was impurity there was the exclusion from the communal sacred rites (Num 19:20).

15. And the same point is demonstrated incontrovertibly by the scolding of the Old Testament priests that is found in Ezek 44:6[–7]: "Let this be enough for you, O house of Israel, depart from all your detestable practices, you who have brought foreigners of uncircumcised hearts and flesh to be present in my sanctuary, to profane my house." Philo the Jew provides the same evidence in his book *On Those Who Offer Sacrifice*, that this practice [of excommunication] persisted also among the Jewish people of his own time: murderers were not admitted into the temple. And Josephus, in the Jewish War, book 4, chapter 10, inveighs very fiercely against the Zealots because they were found to be in the temple with hands that were still warm from slaying fellow country-men; and in his *Antiquities*, book 19, chapter 7 he testifies that there was a certain Pharisee by the name of Simon who claimed that king Agrippa was unholy and ought to be barred from the entrance to the temple. Hence also in the Gospel history of John 9:22 and elsewhere we read that those who were considered unholy were declared, 'expelled from the synagogue.' And among the other hardships which Christ predicts for his apostles is also this one, that they would be cast out from the synagogues on account of his name (John 16:2).

16. And from the New Testament there are also very many places of Scripture that are clearly of this sentiment, as they cannot in any way be referring to the office of the [civil] magistrate. There is the passage in Matt 16:19, "I shall give to you the keys of the kingdom of heaven, and whatever you bind on earth will be bound in heaven." And similarly John 20:23, "If you forgive anyone's sins, their sins are forgiven; if you retain anyone's sins, they are retained," cannot be understood, nor were they ever understood, as about the office of the magistrate, but only about the office of the apostles and the pastors of the church. Nor does the passage in Matt 18[:17] ("Tell it to the church, and if he will not listen to the church, let him be to you as a foreigner and a tax-collector") and 1 Cor 5:3–5, where the apostle commands that the man who has committed incest must by the church be handed over to Satan;

and he prescribes laws whereby this discipline should then be exercised, besides the various instances that one meets everywhere in the practice and the letters of the apostles, which we shall mention in the following theses.

17. From all these passages it is obvious that a very serious error is committed by those who dare to deny that the church has been granted this authority— an authority which rests upon the universal, fixed practice of the Old and New Testament, and of the whole Christian church.

18. Also those people make a serious mistake who grant that Christ indeed had bestowed this authority upon the church, but extraordinarily and only for a period of time, as long as the church was under the cross and lacked Christian magistrates. For the proofs that we earlier provided from the Old Testament deal with the church that was established under believing magistrates. In the New Testament Christ gave this authority to the church in an absolute way and for perpetuity, while not any mention or even suspicion of an exception of that sort was ever suggested. Hence also the early church exercised the same authority regarding every controversy, not only under the cross and before there were Christian emperors, but also under those rulers when they already had been converted to the faith and under their political government which always had been distinguished and kept separate from this ecclesiastical and spiritual government.

19. But even if we do not withdraw this spiritual authority from the purview of the Christian magistrate as the keeper of both tables of the Law, nevertheless we state that the authority or the exercise of it does not depend upon the supremacy of the civil magistrate (as more recently some people claim), because it depends on Christ alone and he himself directly bestowed it upon the church, as the previously adduced passages show. And accordingly, neither by an appeal, nor by a citation before a higher tribunal (in the strict sense), can this authority be deferred to the tribunal of the magistrate or rulers, since the execution of it is not their responsibility. Meanwhile, however, we do not deny the truth in what Beza admits to Erastus: "Because even a rightly ordained consistory could do an injustice to alleged wrongdoers [...], in smaller territories the Christian civil magistrate (without any violation of ecclesiastical government), as keeper and avenger of the two tables of the Law and of the church's good order, has the power to look out for those who submit complaints."

20. Therefore, as this first question is settled beyond controversy, it now remains for us to explain next through whom, to whom and in what way this authority should be exercised.

21. And so we hold that this authority rests in the entire church, but because God is a God of order and not of confusion, and because in the church there is an order of those who teach and those who learn, as well as of those who are in authority and those who are subject to it, it is necessary that its own distinct roles are assigned to each of the orders so that in such a difficult matter as this one everything may be directed towards building up.

22. We assert that the execution of this authority rests with the ministers of the Word, not only because this public administration of this discipline is an appendix to the preaching of the Word and to the administration of the sacraments, but also because all of the examples which we already have produced from the Old and New Testaments refer the public execution of this authority to the priests, apostles, evangelists and heralds or pastors of the churches.

23. And yet we do not therefore grant that this authority may be claimed by some single bishop, whether Roman or Eugubine, by his own initiative or plenary authority (as they call it), but we assert that the counsel of the church's rulers or presbyters must be applied, and also the agreement of the entire church (whether openly or at least quietly) according to the command of Christ and the practice of the purer church.

24. For the word "church" which Christ uses in Matt 18[:17] cannot be taken to stand for any single bishop; and in 1 Cor 5:4 the apostle Paul applies the word to the solemn assembly of the Corinthians, and since he states in the same chapter that the final excommunication is common to the entire church, it is fitting that this entire affair should be carried out also by common consent (whereby it can be achieved so much better), in the same way that in the Old Testament it happened that what preceded was not merely the authority of the ecclesiastical Sanhedrin but also the consensus of the people from whose midst that sort of man was said to be uprooted or cut off.

25. The object concerning which this discipline is exercised are those who are called brothers, as defined by the apostle in 1 Cor 5:11, "for God will judge those who are outside the church." [1 Cor 5:13] And the cause [for discipline] is either a wicked manner of life (as can be seen from Matt 18:15;

1 Cor 5:11; 2 Thess 3:11), or crooked doctrine (as is evidenced in Rom 10:17; 1 Tim 1:20; Titus 3:20; and 2 John 10). And the reason for this matter is clear, because not only the manner of life but also the doctrine that is depraved separates a man from Christ (Gal 1:8) and both of them are like yeast that can affect the whole lump, as Christ testifies in Matt 15:6 and 12, and Paul in 1 Cor 5:6.

26. But when someone who is called brother should fall into a scandal of this sort, that is not a reason immediately to be excluded from the body of the church or from the signs of grace, as is the custom of some Anabaptists; but only after he has despised and rejected both the private and the public admonitions of the church, as Christ's words clearly indicate: "If he will not listen to the church, let him be to you as a heathen and a tax-collector," and the apostle in Titus 3:10: "Shun the man who is a heretic after the first and the second admonition."

27. And at this point the question arises whether it is permitted, if the number of those who sin in doctrine or in manner of life is a large one, to make use of excluding them from the sacraments, or of excommunicating them. The cause of the doubt here is that, although this authority was given to build up, and not to break down, from this sort of separation one should expect the breaking down rather than the upbuilding of the church. And therefore, Augustine maintained that this spiritual sword should not be drawn against the drunkards in Africa because of the large number of those who sinned.

28. We, however, answer this question by posing a distinction: if a large part of the church is led astray into a fundamental error or heresy and cannot be recalled to the way despite every attempt at remedy, the following remedy still remains for the pious pastors who preside over the sounder part, namely that they may, together with those who are right-minded, separate themselves from the community of those who are heterodox. And although they do not have the power to use this discipline against them by condemning them openly because of the strength of those who mislead, yet at least by acting openly they can secede from them and condemn the heresy. In this manner Christ gives the warning in Matt 7:15, "Beware the false prophets," and in John 10:5, "Christ's sheep do not know the voice of a stranger and therefore they flee from him." Similarly, Rom 16:17: "I warn you, brothers, that you watch carefully those who cause discord or scandals contrary to the doctrine which you have learned, and stay away from them." And in the same manner

in the old church the orthodox seceded from the Arians, and our ancestors and forefathers in previous ages seceded from the superstition and synagogue of the Antichrist.

29. But if a wicked lifestyle infects a large part of the flock, in the way that the prophets everywhere lament over the Israelite church, then here again a distinction must be made. For either this great number defends its wicked manner of life by means of doctrine, or if it does not make a defense by means of doctrine, then at least it pursues that doctrine by its evil actions. And if it does defend its wicked manner of life by means of doctrine, as formerly the Nicolaitans and that Jezebel did, who by means of prophecy seduced Christ's servants to prostitution, then concerning them we should decide in the same way whereby we previously taught that heretics ought to be treated, i.e., either by means of a public sentencing of excommunication, or, if because of their great number and strength this cannot be done, to secede from them. [That is what] Christ commanded the angel of the church at Thyatira and Ephesus concerning the Nicolaitans and that Jezebel (Rev 2:6 and 20), on the basis of Christ's declaration in Matt 5:19: "Whoever breaks one of the least of these commandments, and teaches other men so, will be called least in the kingdom of heaven."

30. But if only a wicked manner of life should befall a large part of the flock— a manner of life that does not arise from wicked doctrine, but one that is contrary to sound doctrine—then according to Augustine's opinion (in book 3 of *Against the Letter of Parmenian*, and elsewhere against the Donatists) we should not make use of secession from them, nor of excommunication, but only prayers, sighings, exhortations, rebukes, threats, good examples and similar remedies. We see that in the same way only these weapons were used by the prophets and the pious priests in the Israelite church. And [Augustine] demonstrates from the passage of 2 Cor 10 that this authority is given not for breaking down but for building up, and from the parable of the weeds which Christ wishes not to be pulled up, out of fear that while doing so the wheat might be pulled up and so perish (Matt 13:29).

31. In our judgment these reasons of Augustine are solid with respect to the private persons living piously in that sort of gathering, persons who for that reason should not separate themselves from such a gathering; and so too with respect to individual pastors who in tolerating the wicked ones cannot depend upon the consent and support of a greater number of people. This is

rightly shown by the example of the pious priests within a large number of wicked ones, and by the examples of the prophets who are working among them. But if the majority of the church's rulers are of one mind for the good, then I think that for people of this sort who are clearly and stubbornly corrupt those same pastors neither have the power to (nor should) share the sacraments of divine grace with them, how great their multitude might be; but instead with unanimous consent they ought to deny them these sacraments—and entrust the outcome to God. For pious pastors are not empowered to share the signs of grace with those to whom Christ manifestly denies them, and with whom he forbids them to be shared. And it is also because in churches of our own time instances can be found where that sort of public refusal in cases of the public corruption of morals was a means and instrument whereby the church returned to a better state, and the morals were restored with greater integrity.

32. At the same time, however, it is absurd that the papal teachers prohibit even innocent subjects from using sacred things because of the vices of those who rule over them, or family members because of the sins of the father of the household, for herein the son does not bear his father's iniquity, nor the subject that of his ruler, if in his own life he does not follow or approve his example.

33. Having thus explained the object of this discipline, we proceed to its form and mode.

34. The form of excommunication, or rather its stages, are twofold: the first consists of abstaining from the Table of the Lord, and the second in being excluded from the outward communion of the entire church and in being cast out of the church. Some people call the former of these stages the "minor excommunication" and the latter one the "major excommunication."

35. Abstention from the Lord's Table happens lawfully in two ways: either when someone called brother has caused some serious scandal in manner of life or in doctrine, and having been warned does in fact make a verbal profession of repentance from it, but does not yet display the fruits that befit the repentance so that the scandal can be removed from the church, or when he does not indeed promise repentance in words but nevertheless does not yet cut off every hope for repentance through his stubbornness, so that in the interim through this first stage of spiritual discipline the church may, by

means of warnings and Christian forbearance, call that man back and lead him to genuine repentance.

36. The foundation for this first step of discipline is sought partly from the actual goal that we have explained already, partly from the abstention of those people of the Old Testament who on account of impurity according to the law were compelled to abstain from the use of the sacrifices and the Passover lamb for a period of time in order to cleanse themselves in the interim, as can be seen from Num 9 and 19, and 2 Chron 30. Finally [it is sought] partly from the apostle's command in 1 Cor 11:28: "Let a man first examine himself and so eat of this bread and drink of this cup." And whereas this examination should be done by everyone privately, yet in the case of offenses that are public the examination should be done also publicly by the church's overseers. For throughout the Scripture they are commanded to give heed to the entire flock, to separate the clean from the unclean, to judge those who are within, and as much as is possible to remove scandals from the church.

37. Also the practice derived from the times of the apostles in the early church clearly accords with this religious usage, although we acknowledge that in several canons of the ancient synods some strictness is seen in determining the length of time for abstaining, a strictness which somewhat surpasses the measure of forbearance of Christ and the apostles.

38. The major excommunication encompasses three stages, of which the first is called the "simple excommunication," the second the "anathema" of Gal 1:8 and the third the "anathema Maranatha" of 1 Cor 16:22. The use of this last one is for those who have sinned against the Holy Spirit and for whom there is therefore no hope of forgiveness and for whom it remains only that the Lord should come and take up his case against them. And so the church of the latter time which can hardly discern this sin with certainty is not accustomed to use this stage. It is customary for the second, middle stage to be used only generally for wicked doctrines and for those who stubbornly defend them. And the use of the first stage therefore properly exists for individual persons in that manner and order which we determined in thesis 9.

39. This excommunication is explained by the words of Christ in Matt 18:17: "If he will not listen to the church let him be to you as a heathen and a tax-collector." So too the words of the apostle in Gal 5:12 "If only they would be cut off who trouble you." But under the Old Testament this used to be

called "rooting out from the midst of the people," and "being cast out from the synagogue."

40. Many of the ancients have rightly determined that the same is meant by that manner of speaking the apostle uses in 1 Cor 5:5 and 1 Tim 1:20, namely "to hand [them] over to Satan for the destruction of the flesh," because it is outside the church that Satan rules. And yet what Augustine and Chrysostom observe is not improbable, that people of that sort are said to be handed over to Satan because a certain overpowering and harassment from Satan accompanies it until they repent.

41. But what Erastus has invented on this point is absurd and foreign to the apostle's intention, i.e., that they are said to be handed over to Satan so that he might deliver them to death; for the apostle is putting forward a far different goal for this handing over, namely "so that by the destruction of the flesh the soul may be saved on the Day of the Lord" (1 Cor 5[:5]). And also that they learn not to blaspheme (1 Tim 1[:20]). And the apostle himself later explains it by other ways of speaking that have the same force, namely "cleanse out the old leaven" [1 Cor 5:7], and "remove the evil man from your midst" [1 Cor 5:13], and "do not associate with them and do not eat with them" [1 Cor 5:11]—it can only be foolish to say such things about those who are deceased. Not to mention the fact that it is foreign to all the mercy and custom of the apostolic church to propose that it through Satan deprived the greedy, the drunkards, the idolaters and similar people of their lives.

42. But in order to grasp this reason for excommunication fully, we should explain a little more carefully the point to which this rejection from the church extends, and what that communion is from which that sort of men are deprived.

43. From the words of Christ in chapter 16 and 18 of Matthew one clearly gathers that a man who has been excommunicated is so bound or loosed on earth that he also is bound or loosed in heaven; i.e., that a lawfully and justly provided sentencing of the church on earth has been approved also by God in heaven. For an unjust excommunication, such as Christ, the apostle, and many pious people suffered from the slaves of the Antichrist is to be feared no more than an undeserved curse. Concerning this the Wise testifies in Prov 26:2: "Like a sparrow in its wanderings and a swallow in its flying, a curse that is undeserved does not alight."

44. But just as the communion of the church's members is twofold (one outward and regulative, the other internal and spiritual) so also in some manner and with some condition does a true and just excommunication concern the twofold removal of this communion.

45. Scripture makes the outward communion among the members of the church twofold: one is purely ecclesiastical, and the other is of the Christian social interaction in civic life.

46. The excommunicated man is excluded from ecclesiastical communion because by his excommunication he is deprived of all the signs of divine grace which it was God's will to belong to his church and through which He displays his singular favor to the church. The signs are of the following kind: 1) all the offices in the church, the use of which the excommunicated man necessarily forfeits; 2) participation in the sacraments; 3) the communion of the Word and of prayers, insofar as it entails the tables of the mutual covenant established between God and his church, or the promises and comfortings of the Gospel made for those who believe and repent. Hence also in the Old Testament the excommunicated man was barred from the use and communion of the entire tabernacle and temple.

47. But although in the first church it was customary to exclude even from the buildings those who were excommunicated, we nevertheless hold the view that this is not necessary under the New Testament, since our temples in and of themselves possess nothing sacramental (such as the tabernacle and temple of the Old Testament possessed) nor hold any special promises of grace above other places, as the papal teachers superstitiously believe contrary to Christ's assertion in John 4:21,23. Secondly, because those who have been excommunicated are not to be excluded from either the public or private hearing of the Word, since it contains the warnings and encouragements unto faith and repentance, and because prayers for their conversion are offered by the church in it. In the same way we see in 1 Cor 14:23 that even unbelievers were admitted to the gatherings of Christians for that purpose, and that Christ himself associated with sinners and tax collectors for that purpose; and the apostle expressly warns in 2 Thess 3:15: "That we not treat that sort of man as an enemy, but that we admonish him as a brother."

48. Through the use of excommunication also the communion of Christian social interaction in civic life is broken off, in accordance with the apostolic

command, in order that surely in this way a man may become ashamed and be called to a better frame of mind. The apostle's words in 1 Cor 5:11 are clear: "But now I have written to you that you must not associate with them, and that you not even eat with that sort of people." And 2 John 10: "If anyone comes to you and does not bring this doctrine, do not receive him into your home nor say 'welcome' to him."

49. It is not permitted under this pretext, however, for spouses to separate from each other, or to deny each other their conjugal responsibilities, as the Anabaptists are accustomed to doing without any precedent from Scripture. Nor are children hereby absolved from the obedience that is owed to their parents; and no other natural or moral bonds are severed by excommunication. For it is a fixed rule that the ceremonial and the positive [precepts] always yield to the moral and the natural [precepts]. For God desires mercy and not sacrifice [Hos 6:6]. But in the passages quoted earlier the apostle Paul and John are treating that familiarity of social interaction whereby Christians out of *philadelphia* and Christian brotherly love customarily fulfill responsibilities of that sort to one another. Those who have been excommunicated forfeit the singular debt of those offices, but not the common right of nature, which always remains untouched.

50. And the same reason also shows convincingly that the popes unjustly remove kings and rulers from their kingdoms and dominions through excommunication (not to speak here about other abuses), or remove subjects from the oath of fidelity which they had lawfully bestowed on them. For these bonds are natural and moral, ones that bind peoples' consciences by virtue of the third and fifth commandments, just as the apostle also explains it in Rom 13 and 1 Pet 3; and consequently, those bonds cannot be broken off or severed through excommunication.

51. However, there does not exist any example for actions of that sort in the ancient Jewish church, or in early Christianity, but there are very many examples of the opposite: in Philip the Arabian, Julian, Theodosius, the tyrant Maximus, and others whom the church had excommunicated yet who did not forfeit their kingdoms on grounds of excommunication. Nor is it fair that in possessing kingdoms the condition of Christian kings is worse than that of unbelieving rulers who cannot be excommunicated, or worse than that of other Christians who do not forfeit their own functions, or privately owned and inherited goods by ecclesiastical excommunication. For as Domingo de

Soto rightly has observed, "excommunication is not the deprivation of some proper good which the transgressor of the law had owned previously, but it is the deprivation of common goods which he would have received from the church, for instance (the deprivation) of spiritual communion and of receiving the sacraments."

52. Thus far the outward communion and the extent to which the excommunicated man is deprived of it; it follows that we also add a few observations about the inward communion.

53. And so we posit that he who is separated from the outward communion of the church in a certain way also is deemed a foreigner to the internal fellowship which the church has with Christ, and, as the apostle says, is handed over to Satan. For it is outside the church that Satan reigns, and God cannot be perceived other than an angry and just avenger of sins.

54. And this deprivation of the inward communion with Christ is twofold: one with respect to the present grace, and the other with respect to future grace.

55. The inward deprivation with respect to the present grace is whereby the man who remains obstinate towards the church's warnings and who is denied the outward signs of God's favor and the pledges of his grace, is also deprived by God from the inward testimonies of divine favor; and consequently, he cannot perceive God other than angry and alienated from him, as long as he persists in that particular state.

56. However, it does not therefore follow what some people think, that the man of that sort for that duration of time entirely has been cast away from God or necessarily stripped of every habitual grace. For the goal of the church that so judges (which judgment also God in heaven confirms) is not the man's perdition, but his salvation. Nor is it an indication that God has rejected that man entirely, but that the flesh dominates the spirit to the degree that he cannot be restored to his rightful position except by this extreme remedy, as the apostle's words in 1 Cor 5:5 make clear: this is taking place "for the ruin," that is, the destruction, "of the flesh" in order that "the soul may be saved," that is, gains the upper hand, on the Day of the Lord. From this it necessarily follows that in the judgment of the excommunicating church some seed of the Spirit, albeit latent and suppressed, remains alive in

that man, a seed which must be preserved from ultimate ruin by means of this most bitter remedy against the flesh.

57. And from that it also does not follow that in God's design a man of that sort is rejected entirely. For through this ultimate remedy God still is calling him to repentance, and it is his will that he be admonished like a brother even though he has been cast out from the family (2 Thess 3:15). It is the same as when a father has cast out a stubborn son from his home and removes him from his presence or from the familiar interaction with the household. And even though he takes away from him every sign and feeling of paternal love and affection in order to bring him back to repentance by means of this remedy, even so he does not therefore utterly deprive him of his inheritance nor necessarily cast off all his fatherly feelings towards him, feelings which he displays by even doing this to him, although the latter does not acknowledge it at the time but will come to realize it in earnest finally when he through serious conversion returns into favor with his father.

58. And with respect to the future grace the deprivation of the inward communion with Christ is not definite or absolute, but only conditional. For when the church by its judgment (which God in heaven confirms) excommunicates a man, it threatens him that just as he is deprived or excluded from the outward communion of the church and from the sense of God's grace, so too is he going to be excluded from the kingdom of heaven on the last day—unless he forestalls that future judgment through true faith and repentance. And this is also what Christ has in mind when he says: "Whatever you bind on earth will be bound in heaven" [Matt 16:19 and 18:18], and "if you retain the sins of any, they are retained in heaven" [John 20:23]. And since in this life these things can only be conditional, it follows that we should expect the absolute fulfillment of them only in the life that is to come.

59. It is obvious from the things that we have explained thus far that there are very many and remarkable fruits of Christian discipline and excommunication among God's people. For [excommunication] is indeed the last and fiercest remedy for subduing a man's flesh and for bringing his soul to life; and it is a very effective proof against dragging the healthy part being drawn down. But over against those who persist in their stubbornness and unrepentance it is the only remedy for ridding God's house of corruption and Christ's church of scandals, and thus for guarding the Word and the

sacraments from being profaned, and God's name from being blasphemed by those outside. For whatever outcome may follow at last, God will nevertheless be sanctified in the lives of those who are near to him, and He will be glorified in the presence of all his people, as He himself testifies following the punishment that afflicted Nadab and Abihu when they had violated the altar of the Lord (Lev 10:3).

DISPUTATION 49

ON ECCLESIASTICAL
COUNCILS OR MEETINGS

President: Antonius Thysius
Respondent: Johannes Wilmerdonck

Having subjected the hierarchical order of the Roman Catholic Church to critical assessment in Disputation 41, and having discussed the structure of the local church, ministers, and council of elders in Disputation 42, this disputation treats the broader organization of the church, ranging from a meeting of several local churches to world-wide ecumenical councils. As the Reformed Churches had to find ways to structure their internal relations in non-episcopalian ways, the Disputation dedicates careful attention to the topic of regional and national meetings. Especially the authority of the broader assemblies is addressed, as is the relationship between the State and the Church. No doubt the deliberations and decisions made at the Synod of Dort inform this disputation, which also addressed the Romanist teachings on the nature and authority of its councils. A synod is a larger assembly of the church, ordained by Christ, in which the church is represented by persons delegated by a lesser assembly for a specific place and time. The goal is to assess, judge, and determine from God's Word those matters common to the churches and which could not be achieved in the lower, classical sessions. A synod is held especially to treat the purity of doctrine, or morals and good order, for the upbuilding of the church and its integrity and peace (see the definitions in theses 3 and 7). The synod of the New Testament Church that is described in Acts 15 is the 'archetype...by whose shape all the other, subsequent synods ought to be ordained' (12). From thesis 15 onward the disputation considers those who have the authority to call assemblies (17–27), the delegates called to attend them (28–34), and the place, time, and costs of holding such assemblies (35–38). Matters and actions appropriate to synods (39–41), the importance of holding them in an orderly fashion and lawfully (42–66), and the form (67–68), goal (69), and authority (70–74) of assemblies are delineated.

1. Up until this point, we have treated the church, and its authority and power in declaring the Word of God, its administration of the sacraments, and its exercise of discipline (which certainly is proper to the church)—although it is not the church as a whole which must exercise discipline, but rather the authorized persons whom God through the church has delegated, that is to say, the ministers of the church. By this act of God, they become servants, not of the church strictly speaking but, in a relative sense, of God and of Christ the Lord, and they do so by their own rank and mode, that is, as prefects of the church, as superiors, overseers, shepherds, etc. Nevertheless, they do so, not as lords over the church, for it belongs to Christ alone; but they are ministers and dispensers of the mysteries of God in the church [1 Cor 4:1], that is, they are ministers of the church in an objective sense.

2. Well then, since the church in its assembly is either of the people (1 Cor 11:17–18, 22; Heb 10:25) or of the church officials (Acts 20:17 and 21:10)—which in a certain respect is placed over against the one of the people because it has been ordained for the government of the church and for public judgment within the church—we have determined in the present disputation to give a treatment of this ecclesiastical assembly. And as for the government of the church, from the perspective of Christ, it is entirely monarchical; if you consider the church insofar as it is outward and the administration of it is outward, then it is not democratic, as a certain Morély has claimed. Nor is it simply aristocratic, as many have claimed; nor, lastly, is it monarchical, as the papal teachers claimed. And it certainly is not ochlocratic, nor oligarchic or tyrannical. Instead, it corresponds to an aristocratic government, i.e., one in which lordship has been removed and replaced by ministerial rule.

3. The ecclesiastical assembly, then, is a session Christ has ordained of the whole church, and in proportion to its size, represented by the foremost members of the church and gathered together in one place in the name of Christ, for the purpose of conducting the church's affairs there, namely the soundness of the faith, the holiness of life, and the integrity of the sacraments, the good order, etc., and its practice or exercise and observance, for the right government and upbuilding of it [i.e., the church], and for the glory of God.

4. And the assembly is one of individual or several churches. And of the individual churches, it is a lawful and for the most part ongoing and regular session, which consists of the bishop or bishops of one place (Phil 1:1; Acts 20:28 and 21:18; Titus 1:5,7) and the presbyters (that is, elders) or the deputies

of the people (as integral parts of the church), in order to handle the affairs which are (and to the extent that they are) proper to that particular church. And it is called assembly or consistory (Matt 26:59; John 11:5, 47). By Paul it is called the presbytery, that is the senate or college of elders (1 Tim 4:14). And whereas this session is primary in its origin, it is, however, least in its rank and authority.

5. But the assembly of a larger number of churches is a meeting at a certain place and time of more churchmen (i.e., of ministers and ruling men) whom a lower session has delegated in order to deal with those matters which pertain to the larger number of churches and which could not be achieved at the individual lower session. And it is generally called, in Greek, a synod, and in Latin, a council (from *conciendo*, "to call together").

6. And it is either an assembly of a single diocese or domain, or of more. And the assembly of a single one is commonly called a classis, or diocesan synod, or a *topikē* ('local') one. But the assembly of more dioceses or of an entire province is called specifically a synod or council.

7. Now, to summarize all of the preceding, a synod or a council is a public and lawful assembly of the church, and a more venerable and larger one, ordained by Christ; and the church is represented by persons whom a lesser assembly has delegated for a specific place and time, especially overseers and elders, and which gathers together in the name of God and Christ in order to treat, judge, and determine from God's Word those matters which concern the circumstances common to the churches and which could not be achieved in the lower, classical sessions, and especially when there the purity of the faith and truth is treated over against those who err, and against heretics, or when there is a treatment of the morals and good order over against those who are schismatic, for the upbuilding of the church and its integrity and peace.

8. Moreover, a synod is either provincial, national, general (or plenary, as they call it), or ecumenical or world-wide, and it is gathered of people and deals with matters of the churches of an entire province, of one or more nations, or of the world-wide church. It deals with such matters of the faith and morals that are common to all the churches.

9. And ecclesiastical authority and power reaches its highest point at the synod, according to the rank and level of each meeting; and it conveys the

unity of God's entire church insofar as it is outward, and it is also the basis and binding element for its position and good order, and the wholesome remedy for troublesome evils.

10. But as for the institution of the ecclesiastical assemblies, and so also of the synod, it does not arise by human right but by divine right, for it has its basis in the words of Christ: "Tell it to the church, and if he will not listen to the church, etc." [Matt 18:17]; "And whatever you bind on earth, etc." [Matt 18:18]; "Where two or three have been gathered in my name, there am I in their midst" [Matt 18:20]. "And I am with you even until the end of the age" [Matt 28:20]. To be sure, these statements should be taken in the first place as concerning the lower sessions, but because all the churches have union and mutual participation, they pertain all the more to the higher sessions.

11. It appears that at least in the Old Testament there was one fixed and ongoing ecclesiastical session or assembly of this sort, a synagogue that was restricted to one nation; and that it was mixed together with the civic session but not also mixed as far as the cases are concerned; although this can be doubted, because the divine law embraced also political affairs, and as a whole was entrusted to the Levites and the priests as the experts in the law and judges, which session Moses had established (Deut 17:9) and Jehoshaphat had reestablished (2 Chron 19). Nevertheless, for cases of God and the king, the presiding officers at that time were clearly distinguished [cf. 2 Chron 19:11]. And so it continued up until the time of Christ, and it was made up of the chief priests, the scribes and the elders of the people (Matt 16:21, 26:3, and 27:59). This general assembly examined the most serious cases (Numb 11:16). Nevertheless, there were times when particular gatherings of the synod took place (1 Chron 13:1–2, and 23:2; Matt 2:4, 5, and 6).

12. But in the New Testament, since the church of Christ does not consist of a single nation but extends into every direction and is spread across all nations, and since the Jewish form of government, being Jewish, is not binding on the nations, and since a separation has been made between the rulers of the republic and the ministers of the church (i.e., a separation of people, session, and cases), Christ ordained not such a general, single, fixed, and ongoing ecclesiastical session, but rather one with respect to incidental matters that should be gathered together in different places. This is seen in the first synod at Jerusalem in the election of Matthias (Acts 1:15), and also at the second one, in the ordination of deacons (Acts 6). And also in the third,

in settling the controversy about observing the Jewish law (Acts 15). That is where the full basis was made for a synod, even a world-wide one, insofar as besides the Jews there were present also delegates of the gentiles; and it is the archetype, the precise precedent by whose shape all the other, subsequent synods ought to be ordained and to which they ought to conform. Lastly, the fourth one is assigned in the case of Paul (Acts 21) who had been charged with desertion from the law.

13. And from that time on this form of session was observed and used frequently in the church of Christ under the cross and under the protection of pious emperors; although under the Frankish, Gothic, and other kings, right up to the time when, while the papal tyranny seized hold of everything, it had regressed to that mixed session, to such a degree that their councils were not only ecclesiastical meetings but also assemblies of the empire.

14. Consequently, the consistory of the pope with his cardinals, which possesses an absolute power of judgment (just as also this entire order of the pope and cardinals), is a human—no indeed—an antichristian invention and institution, which actually overturns the entire notion of councils.

15. In order to give a more precise summary of the entire notion of synods, we should consider in order the persons, the place and time, the synodical matters and actions, and its mode, form, goal, and authority.

16. The persons are the ones who summon the convocation and appoint delegates, or the ones who are called together and have been sent, or the ones who come together at a synod.

17. The right and authority to announce and convoke rests with the church and the members of the church (for whoever does not belong to the church has no right in the church's government) that is to say the ecclesiastical session to which the government of the church is entrusted.

18. And so from the beginning, when some difficult matter arose in the church, especially concerning religion and the violation of it through some false thinking or heresy, the neighboring overseers and elders used to gather together spontaneously under someone's leadership or by mutual exhortation, as the Apostolic Synods at Jerusalem (Acts 15:2, 6 and Acts 21:18) and at Ephesus (Acts 20:17) teach us. And so also during the time of emperor Aurelian the Synod at Antioch, in which Paul of Samosata, the bishop of Antioch, claimed that Christ was entirely human, while the elders

of his church supported him, the neighboring bishops came together in synod, condemned him as an unyielding heretic and removed him from the church (Eusebius, *Ecclesiastical History*, book 7). And so many other synods, especially provincial ones, were convened under Christian rulers. And so it was the responsibility especially of the bishops to announce the synods, but no one possessed this as a private right.

19. Hence, it is in a presumptuous manner and unfairly that the pope of Rome, like some emperor of the church, claims for himself only the privilege and tasks of calling a synod, especially a world-wide one, even though not any special prerogative in this matter was consigned to Peter, whose successor he boasts that he is, but Acts 15:2–6 states that the apostles and the elders gathered together with Paul and Barnabas who had been delegated by the church, and who reported the controversy and deferred it to them so that they might reflect upon this matter.

20. Moreover, it is possible in this matter that the magistrate has his own special duties, if he supports the church and allows it to be public (or by decree appoints it to be such) along with its own whole order and form of government, and that his agreement and sanction are required. For since the magistrate is the keeper and defender of the state and of the good order that has been established in public, and of actions that are public, then he should be deemed also thus as far as the church is concerned. In fact, if such is the practice, then the magistrate can be the one who not only approves the time, place and other circumstances [of the synod], but also the one who appoints it.

21. And this applies so much the more if he is a Christian, orthodox magistrate, that is to say, a leading member of Christ's church and one placed in a high position, to whom (by the calling of this world) falls the jurisdiction, command, and power of outward restraint (which often is needed here); indeed the power to set things in motion for public meetings—a power which he by the law of piety and as the nurturer and guardian of the church (Isa 60:16) is bound to apply in the defense of both tables of the Law, and to the end that Christ may reign spiritually in his subjects (Ps 2:10). Therefore, his agreement, authority, support, and provision of safety ought to be sought here. Moreover, he himself is bound by the duty of piety not to deny those things, but to bestow and furnish them readily and willingly to the church.

22. In fact, the outstanding examples of pious kings in the Old Testament teach us that the higher magistrates (as kings and rulers are) sometimes were the initiators of holding synods, and that these [synods] took place at their command: David (1 Chron 13:1–3), Solomon (2 Chron 5:2), Asa (2 Chron 15:9), Hezekiah (2 Chron 29:4 ff.), Josiah (2 Chron 34:29). And so also Ahab and Jehoshaphat, who called together about four hundred prophets (1 Kgs 22:6–8), and Herod (Matt 2:5). The Christian emperors and kings followed their lead, as they of themselves very often assembled and attended to not only the *oikoumenikai* or world-wide synods (for which there is a special reason), but also, if the public need so demanded it, the *merikai* or particular synods—especially the extraordinary ones. In this way the world-wide Council of Nicaea was announced and convened by Constantine the Great (as referenced by Eusebius, *The Life of Constantine*, book 3), the Council of Constantinople by Theodosius the Elder (Theodoret, book 2, chapter 1.16), the Council at Ephesus by Theodosius the Younger and Valentinian (Cyril, Epistle 17), the Council at Chalcedon by Marcian (Leo, in the Epistle to the Emperor and to Pulcheria Augusta), and so other, even particular councils.

23. And especially if herein it was the ecclesiastical order which failed or acted contrary to its calling; for then the magistrate, as a prominent member of Christ's church, has the authority and the obligation rightly to interpose and seriously to insist on having synods, and to announce them by his own command. And this happened rather frequently, such as when king Joash accused the high priest Jehoiada and the priests of not repairing the breaches in the temple (2 Kgs 12:8).

24. If on the other hand, however, the magistrate is an enemy and persecutor of the church and the true religion, or if he ceases to fulfill his calling, namely when the church clearly is in danger, then the church must nonetheless not fail itself but must exercise the right and power of convocation—a power which in the first place resides among the leaders of the church (as is seen in Acts 15), so that thereby as quickly as possible it may address the evils that are present and pressing, if (and in the manner in which) it can be done.

25. Therefore, it is with the utmost brazenness and despotism that the pope of Rome not only arrogates to himself ahead of the other bishops the right of announcing and convoking a synod, but also he deprives the entire church of it in every way (and in her the emperor, kings, rulers and magistrates). [This is so] especially if the authority, approval, decision and agreement of the

emperor does not precede or accompany it: and accordingly, he takes away any authority whatsoever from the synod.

26. Moreover, just as the convocation rests in the hands of the church, so too does the matter of sending to the synod; and this is in keeping with the order that had been established by and in the church. In this way Paul and Barnabas and the others were delegated and sent by the church at Antioch to the Synod at Jerusalem (Acts 15:2–3).

27. And therefore the private summons, such as is the one of the pope, prejudices the church's liberty most severely.

28. And as for the people who are called, sent, and assembled by public authority, the people who should deal with the things that must be performed here, and who have the right to vote, or the final and—as they say—decisive voice, are first and foremost the people who have been ordained to the offices of the church. In the Old Testament, such people were the priests, scribes and elders of the people (Matt 2:4; 26:3, 59; and 27:1; Acts 4:5); in the New Testament, the overseers, elders, or delegates of the churches (Acts 15:6; 16:4; 20:17; 21:18). For since the church consists of shepherds along with the rest of the body (or sheep), it follows that not only should the shepherds but also the elders and the people's deputies take an interest in it and vote in it—and do that not on their own behalf but on behalf of the church which sent them. And the best subsequent synods maintained that practice (including also the deacons, especially in the lesser synods). The acts of the Synod of Carthage under Cyprian provide proof for that.

29. We should not, however, take this matter so precisely that all lay people are excluded [from attending a synod]. For if from among the laity of whatever status or circumstance there are men distinguished for their piety, their knowledge of sacred things, their wisdom and prudence, modesty, pursuit of peace, and gentleness, they can be invited and come to attend. But this can be done only after the church has called or chosen and sent them, and after they have been asked to state their opinion in the appropriate order and manner, especially in matters of the faith, which belongs to all the people. For in the church God did not ordain gifts and members that are useless. But in this public action what is requested of them is their counsel and opinion rather than their vote. Acts 15:12, 22, and 23 show indeed that the common folk attended the council, and they lent support to the apostles and elders by being listeners and witnesses, and at least with their silence (if not with their

speech) they approved and offered their consent. And it is demonstrated also by the practice and use of the first and proven synods, as is clear in the Carthaginian Council under Cyprian. At the same time, however, also for the people of Christ there remains their own judgment (albeit a private one), based on the Word of God, so that they do not accept as divine what are human opinions (Matt 7:12).

30. Moreover, if he is Christian and orthodox, the magistrate—especially the highest ranking one—has a very special function in this matter. And the council is a matter of concern to him, not only as one who listens, witnesses, and approves like any other Christian, but also as a Christian magistrate, that is, as a defender and protector of the council, and as someone who by his authority guards good order and who holds the common rabble and troublemakers in check, and who sees to it that everything is done honestly and lawfully (1 Tim 2:2). Indeed, he should be consulted, asked to give his opinion, and—if the need should arise—cast his vote. For it is his duty as the defender of the first and second tables of the Law to prohibit utterances of blasphemy, to ensure the church's peace and safety—which cannot be achieved unless first the troubles about the Word of faith are acknowledged and thereupon investigated. And it is his duty to ratify and sanction those things which are decided upon in the synod, by means of laws, and if needed, by means of adding also certain political penalties against those who are stubborn, for the health of the public observance. In this respect, he must also be an expert and judge of the relevant matters, in his own way, and to be able to cast a vote. Or at any rate, he ought to be convinced from the Word of God that the decisions are based on what is true, just, and good, i.e., that he should not be a blind protector and administrator of someone else's opinion and fancy.

31. And so it is a vain fabrication of the papal teachers that ordinarily only the bishops have the right of coming together and the power to vote, but that in extraordinary circumstances (as they call them) the presbyters, abbots, and superiors general of the orders have the right. And moreover that for the academies is reserved only the power of arbitration; that the magistrate can be present only as protector; and that the people and knowledgeable members of the public can be present and appear there—but then only as listeners and spectators.

32. It is necessary that the people who have been called and sent must come in their own person, be present at the synod and remain there until the very end; and also that no-one may easily stay away or depart from it unless old age, an illness, or some other urgency provides him with sufficient excuse, and he has submitted his reasons in writing or in personal statement. And if not, a very severe censure must be carried out on those who stay away and who refuse to come or remain, just as ecclesiastical or synodical censure is carried out on those who despise the church and the synod. Nevertheless, there was a time in the ancient church when also the bishops themselves were represented by others (and that for specific, serious reasons), for example by the elders and deacons. And all of these representatives are bound to present letters noting their dispatch and appointment.

33. And hence, it is contrary to the long-standing canons that since a few centuries—namely, from the time of the Synod of Constance when John XXIV, who was present and fled from the synod, moreover, along with two absent anti-popes, were deposed from the papacy—the pope of Rome continuously withdraws himself from the presence of a world-wide synod, partly because of the fact that he considers himself superior to the synod, and partly out of fear of being forced to submit to the synod's judgment.

34. It is possible, in fact it is very useful for the magistrate (especially if he is of the highest rank) to be present at the synod, whether in his own person (like Constantine the Great at the Nicene, and Theodosius at the Constantinopolitan Synod), or through delegates: Men who are illustrious, noble, serious, desirous of piety, well-versed in the Holy Scripture, men who by their wisdom, prudence, and authority support and assist the council, as was done by the emperors Theodosius and Valentinian at the Ephesian Synod, and by Marcian at the Chalcedonian one.

35. Closely related to the announcement, convocation, and appearance at the synod is the place and the time of assembly. The place should be a suitable one, namely a city that by its location is ideal for those who are coming together, and particularly well-suited for the session, i.e., capacious, holy—although Acts 15 does not give any specifications about this, and the Nicene Synod was held in the palace (witness Eusebius and Theodoret). But Ambrosius correctly asks: "What does the church have in common with the palace?" For this reason long ago the synods very often were held in a church (as Cyril testifies about the Synod of Ephesus), in the center of which the

Holy Gospel was placed on a high throne, to show that Christ was both present and presiding over the synod.

36. In like manner, the time of the gathering should be certain and well-suited. Thus, for the local and particular synods, that is to say, the annual ones, the decree of the Antiochene and Nicene councils determined the spring-time, that is to say, two weeks after Easter, and the fall season, namely the first week in October—although there has been some variation in this, in both the number [of meetings] and the time. Also, the emperors have established this practice through their laws and edicts, like Justinian (*Constitutions* 123). But for an extraordinary particular synod, or for a more general or the world-wide one, the time must be determined specifically, as these are announced in keeping with the urgency of a more important matter that has arisen.

37. And the commencement of the synod, and also during the synod certain times of its gatherings must be observed piously with fasting and abstinence (Lev 10:9–10; Acts 13:1; Tertullian, *On Fasting*).

38. There are costs associated with these synods. The churches should pay the expenses which those who travel to the synod incur, both on their journey and in the place where the synod is being held (Matt 10:10; 1 Cor 9, etc.). Nevertheless, on this point the exceptional generosity of Christian rulers happens frequently, as they willingly have contributed what was needed for accomplishing the synod, as is found in Theodoret, *On Constantine*, in the first book of the *Ecclesiastical Histories*, chapter 7.

39. The matter or object, i.e., the business which is to be conducted in this assembly and which provides the occasion and reason for the synod, is a purely ecclesiastical one. Matters of a political nature is entirely foreign to it (Luke 12:14; 2 Tim 2:4). Political matters obviously, belong to the civic assemblies and not to synods. In fact, [ecclesiastical] matters are of common concern to that entire church, and advance the well-being and safety of the church, for God's glory (Acts 15:1, 5).

40. Well then, the synodical business concerns doctrine, whether true or false (Matt 2:4), its supplements, [namely] the sacraments and the divine rites, the lifestyle and the discipline of the morals of the people as well as their leaders, or lastly the good order of ecclesiastical government. In sum, here must be handled any questions concerning the faith and love, the two things that comprise all the matter of a synod, or whatever pertains to the faith and deeds

of the church, and whatever could not be thoroughly discussed or duly finished in the lower session (Acts 15:24, 29). Hence in former times, besides the exposition and the formulas of the faith, also the canons were subject to the synod, as these are nothing other than the rules which encompass the discipline of morals and good order.

41. The official conduct of the synod, then, consists in treating the issues that have been proposed, and in observing or carrying out the matters that have been decided.

42. In order that the mode of doing business might be orderly and lawful, just as the apostle wills everything in the church to be done decently and in good order (1 Cor 14:40) it is necessary that in councils of this sort someone should preside as the moderator who is mindful of good order, lest the discussion and actions become muddled (1 Cor 14:29, 31). Therefore, conduct that is well-ordered rests in the president and the others seated with him. It is the president's duty in fact to preside over the place, to be in charge of the actions, and to direct the entire business.

43. The task of presiding belongs properly to a man of the church who is established in a position of some eminence. In the Old Testament, in fact, it belonged to the high priest, while in the New it belonged to an overseer or pastor well-suited for presiding, and chosen by a general election. It appears that in this manner James presided over the Jerusalem Synod; the first to speak and state his thinking, however, was Peter, and Barnabas and Paul followed him. But it was James's task to announce the decision (Acts 15:19), and everyone gave him their assent (Acts 15:22 so also Acts 21). At the Nicene Synod, the presider was Eustathius the Antiochene bishop, or rather—as appears from the subscriptions—Hosius, the bishop of Cordoba, in Spain. At the Synod of Constantinople, it was Nectarius, the local bishop; at Ephesus, it was Cyril of Alexandria; at Chalcedon, Leo, bishop of Rome, was president via his vice-bishops (insofar as it may be ascertained from the acts).

44. The same [task of presiding] belongs to the civil magistrate in his own manner, namely insofar as the presidency of the council concerns external government and good order and is understood as its oversight and protection, so that not anything should happen unlawfully and contrary to good public order, or shamefully and insolently, or through force—and if anything should happen, to intervene and check it. And in this manner,

insofar as it guides and protects good order by means of his own authority and removes whatever is contrary, the magistrate can be said to preside over the synod.

45. Therefore, in this matter we do not grant to any bishop the duty of ecclesiastical president by reason of his seat of office, or on account of a privilege that comes with some other distinction—something which the papal teachers nevertheless do claim for their Pontiff. And indeed, a president (which is a term denoting rank) is no greater than the others in power, but he is in rank and authority.

46. The duties of the president, then, are to lead in piously offering prayers, to announce the sessions in a timely manner, honestly to propose the things that must be done and discussed, to moderate the debates wisely, to request the opinions of everyone, to gather the votes attentively, to speak his own mind with a right equal to that of the others, to declare the common decision without prejudice, and to execute it carefully and reliably, or to see to it that it will be carried out.

47. Assessors can be added to the president, and they can appoint scribes or secretaries whose labors may be employed in reliably receiving and recording the acts. This is evidenced in the letter of the Jerusalem Synod, where the general acts are summarized in a concise written record and then sent to the brothers wherever they are (Acts 15:23; 21:25).

48. As for the remaining participants, their sitting ought to be in keeping with the worthiness, merits, and size of the churches which they represent, or in keeping with the high calibre of their talents or the long experience especially that gained in the sacred ministry. And on this point, God's general fifth commandment—"Honor your father"—is in force, which, just as in every other situation so too in this one does have its place. And laying aside selfish ambition and false pretense, one should hold the other in greater esteem and honor (Rom 12:10–11; Phil 2:3–4).

49. For these men, the duties are for each in his turn to speak his mind (Acts 15:7; 12:13; 1 Cor 14:29, 31), not as reflecting his mood (for personal ambition, anger, hatred, favoritism, levity, ill-will, and whatever else is carnal should be absent, Jas 3:12) or his own prejudice and personal taste, but reverently according to God's Word (Acts 15:15). Hence, the votes should not always be counted, but rather weighed in the balance, as the Nicene

Synod consented to Paphnutius when he protested against the law about clerics abstaining from their own wives. And it is also their duty to place their signatures, immediately next to the president's, to the decision that has been carried and the judgment that has been passed, and to approve the acts.

50. Further, with respect to the handling of the business matters, the synod is either deliberative or judicial, or a mixture of the two. It is a deliberative synod when it deals with those things that pertain to the good status of the church, and it deliberates about the means for it or remedies against evil (thus Acts 20:17 and 21:18). And herein, it is the synod's duty to derive from the Word of God the formulation of its decision and agreement, and of the unity of the church in doctrine and discipline, and to establish the arrangement and good order insofar as it is of benefit for the church. And concerning all these matters, it is the synod's duty to publish some public written documents (and they should be brief and clear), and also to alert the people and the pastors to keeping them while subjecting stubborn violators to the church's discipline.

51. A judicial synod takes place when the facts or case of this or that person, especially of a pastor who is causing great offense, trouble or division in the church (i.e., by means of schism, error, heresy, apostasy, and other things) are investigated, and sufficiently and fully known, and when lawful judgment is passed on the basis of the known facts.

52. And on this point, the men whose business and controversies the synod must discuss, whether they are members of clergy or laity, especially men who are the authors of a weightier error or defenders of someone else's (like the brothers who gave occasion to the dispute in the Antiochene church, and those who were noted at the Synod of Jerusalem, as being from the party of the Pharisees, Acts 15:1,5)—these men, I say, must be invited with every honorable reason, warned, and in the end summoned to appear at the synod. And if they should not come, they must be cast out of the church, like the stubborn men by the decree of the third Carthaginian Synod, and they must not be received again until they repent.

53. And if they do appear, they must be granted a courteous hearing on the basis of their writings, their personal statement of confession, and on the basis of the testimonies of other persons. Their doctrine and its status should be determined, then conferred, and if necessary, debated about in a friendly manner; and the arguments and circumstances of the cases should be

examined duly, diligently, and attentively, in good conscience and without any prejudice, according to the rule of God's Word, in such a way that if it can be done, the men themselves would be called back to the way—or at least a correct judgment could be made. In this manner at the Synod of Jerusalem a great enquiry and much debate preceded the declaration of the decision (Acts 15:7). And later, it was not irksome to the fathers to enter into discussion with Paul of Samosata, Arius, and other heretics at synods, even though it was often in vain. But diligent care must be taken lest anyone can justly complain that he was condemned before he was heard.

54. But on this point, at least concerning the doctrines that have been adduced for controversy, we must examine carefully what they are, and how many, and whether they belong to the foundation (or the fundamental things) or in fact to matters adjunct to theology (1 Cor 3)—and if they do belong to matters that are necessary, then to what degree of necessity (Acts 15:28). And moreover [we must examine] whether it is an opinion or an error that can be tolerated (and also whether it comes from a teacher); or, on the other hand, whether it should be refuted and condemned as a doctrine that is not to be tolerated.

55. And concerning the persons who are entering into the controversy [we must examine carefully] whether their opinions are right or wrong; how they are erring (lightly or seriously); whether they have been led astray or are the ones who lead others astray; whether they are students or teachers; members of the laity or pastors. And [whether they err] out of weakness, i.e., simple ignorance, foolish innocence and ready belief, or out of a pretended ignorance and a blind zeal, or even out of malice, with or without stubbornness. And so too concerning the facts and accusations, a thorough investigation should be made into everything in a lawful and discreet manner. And in keeping with this sentiment, each and every person should speak up, and they must pass judgment together as one (Acts 15:22, 25).

56. And as for the verdict, it should be one of acquittal or conviction of the case and also of the person. For either the true and just case is approved and those who think or act rightly are released, or the false and unjust case is condemned and those who think wrongly (and that stubbornly), or who act wrongly and without repenting, on behalf of the church are sentenced as schismatics, heretics, or shameful people (Acts 15:24).

57. However, in case the decision or sentiment is divided, we should maintain a certain restraint about the finer points of religion and about things that are less necessary for salvation, and as much as it is possible, we should reduce rather than enlarge the controversies. In fact, in matters of indifference some things should be endured and tolerated according to the law of love. Thus in Acts 15, at the Apostolic Synod, even though it was against brothers from among the Pharisees who were causing the souls of pious gentiles to waver (namely, by the observation of circumcision and other ceremonies) a decision is made; still, according to the law of love a decree is established about abstaining from what is offered to idols, from blood and what is strangled, and also from fornication, from which things the gentiles are commanded to abstain as being necessary, although not with the same degree of necessity since they did not have the same causes for the necessity. For the prohibition of fornication belongs to God's perpetual will and so also belongs to the law. The other commands have acquired necessity by the prescription of love for a period of time until, with the increase and strengthening of faith, this law would cease. And thus both for faith its purity is protected and also for love its purity is observed by this precept, while help is being provided to the weakness of some others.

58. The conviction of persons, which should be carried out very slowly, consists of suspension and separation, and of excommunication and anathema. The former consist in the prohibition from the sacred rites, in particular the sacraments (Matt 18:7; John 16:2), and besides that in prohibition from the more familiar and non-necessary use of the laws of nature and of God (1 Cor 5:11). Occasionally, it was accompanied by shaking off the dust from one's feet (Matt 10:14–15). But as for the latter, it took place along with the curse which in Hebrew is called 'Schematha' (i.e. 'name'), namely that tetragrammaton of God, and it is called 'Maranatha' by the apostle, that is, "the Lord shall come"—in order to avenge, obviously (1 Cor 16:22; Jude verses 14 and 15). This was carried out only on the most deplorable persons such as apostates.

59. But there is a special censure for people who are in ecclesiastical office: the suspension and removal from office, even without the hope ever of recovering it.

60. The handling and conclusion of matters proposed in synod are followed by the execution of them, and it consists of ensuring that the things which have been decreed are carried out.

61. And at this point a question arises that is not a light one: Who are responsible for that execution? Here a distinction must be made between the powers, the ecclesiastical one and the civil one. The church or the synod does not act or restrain by means of physical force, but only spiritual force: By admonishing the churches in their duty, by removing heretics and shameful people from the communion of the church. But not, as the pope and the papists do in their antichristian manner, by casting the father of the household out of his home, the citizen from his city, and the king from his kingdom.

62. Therefore, to this extent the matter is one of the church, and consequently also of the synod which carries out the decisions either via synodical letters sent to the churches, or through delegates. In this manner the Synod of Jerusalem writes a synodical letter to the church at Antioch and to other churches; and besides Paul and Barnabas, it sends Jude and Silas as delegates to announce verbally the things which the synod had decreed and recorded in writing (Acts 15:22 and 30; 16:4. and 21:25).

63. The execution belongs also to the other power, namely the civic one, since it consists in outward coercion, such as it is and in keeping with its appointment. For because it is the guardian of both tables of the Law and so has the duty to prohibit blasphemous opinions, and since it is the defender of the church and of good public order, it ought—because it is a member of the church—to obey the synod. But it also ought to ratify the synod's just decrees in accordance with the Word of God, and to enact them by means of laws and penalties (if it is necessary), insofar as it befits the spiritual kingdom of Christ, for the well-being of public observance, and also to check shameful heretics. In this manner, Aurelian, although he was a gentile, ordered the deposed Paul of Samosata to be driven from his bishop's dwelling when he was not willing to leave it; Constantine ordered the banishment of Arius, Theodosius the Younger of Nestorius, etc., who had been condemned in synods.

64. But on this point, we should diligently remind the civic power not to exercise its authority and power too easily in matters that the church has not examined and adjudicated lawfully before. The civic power is not excluded

from both this examination and adjudication as if it is entirely foreign to it. But [the civic authority] is contained in and under the church as its leading member and part, as we have shown previously. It is so far from having to be only a blind performer of another party's decision, that the pope of Rome committed an intolerable crime when he made every effort to lead magistrates, rulers, kings, and emperor to that point.

65. But on this point, we must guard against the use of a means or remedy that is not sufficiently suitable for eradicating the diseases of soul and mind which have been caught by wrong opinions (as these are cured only by putting the truth over against them)—that is to say, with an overly-strict outward severity that is entirely unbefitting to the kingdom of Christ, as that does not heal people but turns them into hypocrites. Nevertheless, we must absolutely keep in check the offense, sedition, and disturbance of the peace that are public, and we also must prevent, insofar as that can be done, private individuals from being led astray and overthrown.

66. But this entire involvement of the civil power in the affairs of the church at the synods which we have recounted thus far does not disturb the good order in the church, as though in this way it intrudes upon the office of someone else and not one's own. For indeed, good order demands that these functions are distinct; but distinction does not conflict with collaboration, and nothing blocks those who are in charge of different offices from together taking care of many tasks in a common endeavour and rolling one boulder— in fact occasionally entering into the other's domain when the need is present and urgent.

67. But with respect to the judge and norm of every act and the decision for it, the judge here indeed is Christ, but through his servants whom he has brought together at the synod in a spirit of unity. It is their task to consider ecclesiastical business, and after the debate has been held to speak their opinion in an orderly fashion (Acts 15:6–7), thus, also finally to make a conclusion and to pass judgment. Acts 15:22: "The apostles, together with the elders of the church, decided." And verse 25: "And so we, having come together in harmony, made a decision." And verse 28: "It seemed good to the Holy Spirit and to us"—not jointly, of course, but subordinately under the leadership of the Holy Spirit. And obviously just as the individual judgment belongs to each and every believer and member of the church (Matt 7:15; 1 Cor 2:15; 1 John 2:20, 27 and 4:1), so too does the communal

judgment belong to the shepherds who are gathered at synod. And that is the judgment of God, of Christ, and of the Holy Spirit, if and insofar as it is ordained and brought about by the norm of God's Word. Ordained and done in such a manner, the judgment is ratified by God.

68. The norm and rule for this synodical act and decision should be entirely, uniquely and irrevocably the Word of God, contained in Scripture (Matt 2:5; Acts 15:14), which by its own evidence can also be called the judge (John 5:45). And it grants form to a lawful and holy synod, so that it is of God. But apart from this Word, the writings and sayings of whatever sort, whether private or public, are not the norm or form of truth, but only the formula of the sentiment and consensus of the church.

69. The mode of this judgment ought to be such that everywhere faith and the pursuit of truth shine forth, and that love prevails and rules supreme. And its end is in the removal of scandal and the upbuilding of the church, to the glory of God.

70. And from this it is clear what and how great the authority of the synods is, namely, one of ministry (in fact, that is the authority of the church); that is, in a certain respect, in its own way and small measure, the authority is divine. But we should not place such confidence in any and all synods indiscriminately and loosely. For also shepherds can be misleading shepherds (Isa 56:10; Jer 16:14 [12:10 or 23:2]; Ezek 22:25), and at a synod the church can be a gathering not of God but of malicious people (even when it holds forth God's name) and can misuse its own power against the truth (Matt 26:3–4, 57 and 27:1; Acts 5:5 etc.). And it can be a gathering precisely of the true church, which (and to such extent that it) is gathered in the name of Christ, according to that statement in Matt 18 [20]: "Where two or three are gathered in my name, in their midst am I." And it follows the guidance of the Holy Spirit: "It seemed good to the Holy Spirit and to us" (Acts 15[:28]).

71. But there is not an equal relation between the apostolic synod and the other ones. For the authority of that one is purely divine because of the direct and continuous assistance of the Holy Spirit (Acts 2:4). But not so the authority of these other ones, at least in some respect, since these are synods of men who are certainly pious and also guided by the Holy Spirit, but only to the degree that it does not protect them against every error. For they can be ruled by the Holy Spirit in such a way that the desire of the flesh comes over them and they experience something after the manner of mortal men

and accordingly in some matters deviate from the truth. And so, we see that not only the particular synods but also the world-wide ones have gone astray.

72. Therefore, the synods are divine insofar as they are brought together in the name of Christ, and insofar as they decide something in harmony with the Word of God as Scripture expresses it (and not as they determine). And they have only as much authority as they borrow and receive from Scripture, as the moon does from the sun. Consequently, it is so far from being the case that they themselves are the norm of faith, that they should be judged according to it.

73. The pope's approval adds nothing to the authority of these councils, nor does his rejection remove anything from it. Indeed, he himself, whenever the reform of the church is treated, from its head to its members, is subject to the synod. This is stated also to Peter, whose successor the pope claims to be: "Tell it to the church" (Matt 18:17). And thus, the church at the Councils of Pisa, Constance, and Basel always unanimously has maintained and defended in face of the power over the synod which the pope has appropriated unlawfully for himself.

74. From all these observations, one can see what here we should think about the pope of Rome who does not leave any duties for others when he appropriates for himself all the tasks of a synod, namely: 1. Of the one who announces it; 2. Of its president; 3. Of its adjudicator; 4. And finally of the one who approves it. In fact, in his antichristian haughtiness and encroachment he makes himself superior to the council. And also, what we should think of the councils that were held since some centuries ago under the popes, namely that they were neither legitimately called nor rightly held.

SOURCES

Theodoret, book 1, chapter 6

At the Nicene Council Constantine, the Great addresses the fathers: the books of the evangelists and the apostles, and the oracles of the ancient prophets teach us clearly what we ought to ask of God. Therefore, laying aside dissension, which is the cause of discords and conflicts, we shall receive from the divinely inspired Word the answers to the questions which are posed.

Emperor Justinian, *New Constitutions* [1]37 c. 4

Since, moreover, what is laid down in the canons concerning the synods of the most holy bishops which are to be held in each province has until now not been observed, it is necessary to correct this first and foremost. The holy apostles and fathers, then, have decreed that in each province synods of the most holy priests should be held twice in each and every year, and that matters which arise should be examined and receive suitable correction; that is, they set the meeting of one synod on the fourth day in the holy week of Pentecost, and the second in the month of October, etc.

Augustine, *Epistle* 118 to Januarius

The authority of the plenary councils is very salutary for the church.

Gregory, book 9. *Epist. 110* to Syagrius, etc

And in this part of our care, we also should not neglect what for the sake of usefulness the fathers in their thoughtfulness prescribed for the holding of councils in the parishes. Therefore, it is necessary for the priests to convene as one, lest there be any discord among the brothers or any kindling of disharmony between the leaders and their subjects, in order to discuss cases which arise, and to have a sound comparison of ecclesiastical observances, insofar as through this practices from the past are corrected and also the practices in the future receive regulation, and the almighty Lord be praised by the harmony of the brothers. And you should know that his presence is there for you, if you observe this, because it is written: "Where two or three are gathered in my name, there I am in the midst of them." If then, God deigns to be present where there are two or three, how much more will he be not absent where more priests are convened, etc.

ON THE CIVIL MAGISTRATE

President: Johannes Polyander
Respondent: Michael van Gogh

There are several forms of political governance (e.g., monarchy, aristocracy, and democracy, 4–12). God uses them all, so none of them in itself is better or worse than another, and every form is in some way present in the others (13–14). Civil government is appointed by God 'to govern the society...by fair divine and human laws,' and is 'armed with the sword to protect those who are good, to punish the wicked, and to keep the enemy in check, for the preservation of outward discipline and public peace' (15). God is the author of every magistrate (16), so the political office is in itself good (17). Even an unbelieving and wicked magistrate should be tolerated (18). However, lower authorities may rebel against higher ones (19). Government has authority over all people, none excepted, not even clerics (20–28). There is only one exception, which is when something is commanded that is contrary to God's Word and conscience (28). God bestows the magistrate with lawful authority to exercise judgment and justice among his citizens, with legal and military skills (29–39). In the remainder of the disputation (40–65) it is stressed that civil authorities, both as members and as supporters and protectors of the church, have the duty to guard the well-being of true religion, to confront false teachers, and to reform corrupted worship. The different responsibilities of civil and ecclesiastical administration are explained in detail. Much attention is paid to the question of whether the government is authorized to put to death persistent heretics. Compelled 'conversion' is never to be considered. 'For faith wishes to be convinced, not forced, and nothing ought to be so volitional as the inward religion and worship of God, nothing ought to be so foreign to the Christian magistrate as perverse and ill-timed severity whereby he turns people into hypocrites, and forces them to profess with the mouth what they do not believe with the heart' (59).

1. The public administration of the offices ordained by the almighty God is either ecclesiastical or political. Since the former was treated above, the order we have established demands that in this place we deal also with the latter.

2. The political administration of affairs is that which the magistrate exercises in the republic over every sort of citizen whom God wills to be subject to him in some manner.

3. For God alone possesses the highest, absolute rule over human creatures, but the magistrate has a subordinate and conditional rule, namely to the extent that as God's servant he governs subjects committed to his trust and care in accordance with the prescript of God's law and of right reason inscribed upon the hearts of all people (Rom 13:4).

4. This governance by the magistrate is either uniform (or simple) or multiform (or composite).

5. Uniform governance is that which exists by the rule of one or more persons, whether they are noblemen or commoners. The former of these is called a monarchy, the latter aristocracy and democracy.

6. It is a monarchy when the greatest power to rule resides with a single person who looks to the common benefit of human society, whether in a simple republic or city, or in some duchy or kingdom made up of many cities.

7. We have an example of each type of monarchy in the Old Testament. [An example of] the former are the kings of the cities of Sodom, Gomorrah, Admah, Zeboiim, and Bela (Gen 14:2). [Examples of] the latter are Saul, David, Solomon and the other kings who in days of old held the twelve tribes of the Israelite people under their rule.

8. For both types of monarchy, and especially in the latter, the best way is to add to the highest magistrate lower and intermediate ones who under him as his officers were to govern the republic throughout the regions entrusted to them, as is evident from Jethro's advice (Exod 18:21) and from God's command (Num 11:16).

9. Both types of monarchy decline into tyranny if they are arranged for the personal benefit of a single person. For as a king or leader considers the good of his citizens, so a tyrant considers only his own advantage, and he acquires that for himself from the misfortunes of his own citizens.

10. An aristocracy is a polyarchy wherein some noblemen, i.e., the citizens who especially stand out for their worthiness and contributions to the republic, control the magistracy, and who devote it to the common good. Such was the governance of the Jewish people under the judges in days of old. But when aristocracy is twisted for the benefit and domination of a few people, and the wealthy among them, then it is called an oligarchy.

11. Democracy is a polyarchy wherein the more powerful part of the citizens (even of the commoners) administers the republic in accordance with the votes, gathered tribe by tribe, of the entire populace. In Jewish polity there was some government of this sort, when by the vote of the entire Israelite people decisions were made about war against the Benjamites, and about electing a king to replace Samuel (Judg 20 and 21, 1 Sam 10:12). If this sort of government is changed for the profit of only the common folk, then it deteriorates into anarchy and unrestrained license.

12. A multiform government is one that has been constituted not from a separation in the above-mentioned forms for governing a republic, but from a combination or mixture of them. One observes an example of this in some provinces in which there are two types of government, namely, orders of noblemen and of cities all of whom together possess the power in the republic.

13. One ought not rashly and insistently argue which of those forms of political government is more outstanding, since God in his own private reasoning first appointed Moses and Joshua as his delegates to be leaders of his people, and to these He added a few counsellors, as we have stated in thesis 8. And thereafter He introduced judges and noblemen of Israel in their place; and lastly through king Saul He reduced the Israelites to a state of monarchy.

14. There is the added fact that in his marvelous providence God so mingles in due proportion each and every form of political government that of them the one can be seen as present in the others. For even though the first form of government, monarchy, is so called for the one person who is foremost in it, and the second and third derive the name of polyarchy from the many men who rule the republic, nevertheless just as in a monarchy there is one man who predominates over all the others, so also in a properly established aristocracy and democracy there exists a good order of such a sort that some single person is foremost—at least in rank and in casting his vote—and the

singlemindedness among the majority in number is so great that they altogether are deemed to occupy the position of a single governor. And contrariwise, just as there is something aristocratic in the assemblies of a kingdom which lesser magistrates attend, so too something democratic is seen in the meetings of the noblemen, wherein the cities reserve for themselves the right to vote through men whom they also have delegated.

15. Therefore, the magistrate, whatever the state of the republic, is a person whom God has appointed to govern the society of all manner of people whatsoever by fair divine and human laws. And he is armed with the sword to protect those who are good, to punish the wicked, and to keep the enemy in check, for the preservation of outward discipline and public peace (Rom 13:1 and following).

16. It can be demonstrated from the following testimonies of holy Scripture that God is the principal efficient cause, or author, of every magistrate whatsoever. Deut 1:17: "In judging do not respect the person, for judgment belongs to God himself"—that is, God himself has set up judgment for you, to practice it according to his law. And Ps 82:1: "God takes his stand in the assembly, and He judges among the gods"—that is, among the magistrates who as his vice-regents are representatives of his divine majesty and authority in administering what is right. With a view to this God's own Wisdom, or the Son of God, says in Prov 8:15: "It is through Me that kings reign and rulers determine what is just." And king Jehoshaphat says to the judges of his people in 2 Chron 19:6: "You are not practising the justice of man, but of Jehovah." And also the apostle Paul, in Rom 13:1: "There is no authority except from God, and the authorities that exist have been established by God. Consequently, whoever opposes himself to authority is resisting what God has ordained." To these over-arching authorities God sometimes calls men in an extraordinary manner, either immediately, as Moses [Exod 3:10], Gideon [Judg 6:14–16], and Samson [Judg 13:5, 25], or mediately, as David through Samuel [1 Sam 16:13]. Sometimes He calls them in an ordinary manner, whether by order of the highest magistrate and the right of hereditary succession, as He called Solomon by David's order (1 Kgs 1:32), or by means of election, by employing the lot—as He called Saul [1 Sam 10:20–21]—or by another rite in accordance with the common consent of all the people, in keeping with the nature and custom of each and every kingdom.

17. And concerning this matter the Anabaptists err when they reckon the function of magistrate among things that are wicked and unlawful in and of themselves, and when they think that even though he is a believer he should be denied a place in the Christian church. For the political office, which the entire Scripture of both Testaments attributes to ordination by God, is in itself good for all time, and therefore our churches should approve of it no less than the apostolic church did. The following people have been admitted to this office: Nicodemus (John 3:2), the ruler (John 4:53), Joseph of Arimathea (John 19:38), the centurion Cornelius (Acts 10:34), the proconsul Sergius Paulus (Acts 13:12), and other magistrates who believed in Christ, men in whom began to be fulfilled what Isaiah once had prophesied about the magistrates of the catholic Christian church in chapter 49:23. And also in chapter 60:2–3: "Jehovah shall arise upon you, and his glory shall appear over you, so that the nations will come to your light and kings to the brightness of your rising." Hence David, moved by a spirit of prophecy, exhorts those kings to kiss the Son of God (Ps 2:12).

18. Moreover, they also err who think that God's people should not tolerate an unbelieving and wicked magistrate. For we should make a distinction between the authority of the magistrate, which derives from God himself, and the unbelief that exists in the magistrate's evil heart—like good order from disorder, or an office from the vice that fastens upon it. And in no way whatsoever should it be a cause for prejudice or offense against an ordination of God which in and of itself is good. Instead, on this point we should take repose in the providence of God, who sometimes uses wicked and criminal men to govern the republic, in order through them to set right the sins of his own people. Accordingly, the apostle Peter teaches that it is for the sake of God that we must obey the magistrates, even pagan ones (1 Pet 2:13). And Paul [that we must obey] for the sake of conscience (Rom 13:5), lest by their rebellion against the magistrates people should bring condemnation upon themselves (Rom 13:2).

19. But from rebellion of this sort the lesser magistrates are exempt, because they are rebelling against the highest magistrate (whom they, on behalf of the entire social order, have chosen in collegial fashion and endowed with only limited power) for the fact that by his own wicked perjury he is violating what God has ordained and what he has confirmed by his solemn oath, and both obstinately and cruelly is despoiling the political classes and the republic of their privileges to which he had sworn allegiance before they had set him up

as ruler. The power to ordain him resided with them by this rule: that if he should rule justly and according to their laws, then they would use the sword in support of him; but if he should rule unjustly and contrary to their laws, then they would use the sword against him. For they themselves in no way whatsoever can (nor should) neglect or expose to violent seizure this right to preserve their own freedom as well as that of the fatherland, which lawfully has been entrusted to them by their predecessors and approved by the ruler who was to be chosen.

20. The material or personal object with which the function of the magistrate concerns itself is every person (whom the apostle by synecdoche calls 'every soul,' Rom 13:1) of whatever condition he may be, whether he is a citizen of church or state. Chrysostom rightly understood this when he explained that passage of the apostle as follows: "The apostle shows that those commands are for everyone, also for the priests and monks and not only laypersons— even if he is an apostle, or evangelist, or prophet, or anyone else; nor does subjection of that sort destroy piety." So also, Bernard, when he addresses the clerics of his own age thus: "Every soul should be subject to the higher authorities; if anyone endeavors to make an exception, he is trying to deceive. If 'every' soul, then also your soul. Who has made you an exception to the whole?"

21. Therefore, the experts in canon law and the other papal teachers err who state that clerics are entirely and unconditionally exempt from the yoke of the political magistrate, and who think that their statement is based in divine right. For it is with a view to the divine right that the apostle exhorts every soul (Rom 13:1) to subject itself to civil authorities and obey them. And therefore either every Roman cleric lacks a rational soul, or, if he is endowed with one, he is included in the number of those whom the apostle in writing to the Romans designates, by way of synecdoche, 'every soul.'

22. We know, of course, that some papal teachers interpret the word 'soul' used by the apostle as the natural man, i.e., laic. But besides the fact that this interpretation does not rest on any testimony in holy Scripture, and is even completely contrary to the Hebraism used by the men of God whereby 'soul' stands for 'man,' it is clear from chapters 12 and 16 of the same letter to the Romans that with the phrase 'every soul' [Paul] means all the saints who were living at Rome, while he [calls] by name the men and women who ministered,

and in the list of names, he puts Urbanus, his co-worker in Christ, Tryphaena, Tryphosa, and Persis, who worked hard in the Lord.

23. And surely, by as much as those people who are Christian have a calling that is more holy and devout, by so much should they keep God's law about showing obedience to the magistrates, since Christ, who was set apart from every sin, did not diminish their rule (Matt 17:27; John 19:11), nor did the priests, prophets and apostles of God's early church, who were consecrated in a special manner. And to that I add the fact that the apostle Peter, whose successor the Roman pope proudly claims to be, exhorts all persons God has chosen for sanctification of the Spirit (among whom the pope's clerics wish to be counted) to subject themselves not only to the highest but also to the lower magistrates (1 Pet 2:13[–14]).

24. The fact that in the passages quoted above the two apostles Peter and Paul are discussing only civil authority, is clear from the epithet 'human institution' Peter uses to distinguish political administration from the ecclesiastical one, and from the sword whereby, Paul states, God has equipped the political magistrate as keeper and avenger of peace (Rom 13:4).

25. Therefore, clerics wrongly overturn this divinely ordained political order by exempting themselves from the authority of the magistrate; and the Roman bishops, too, make unlawful seizure when they transfer to themselves the right of secular leaders; and so also the pope, who subjects even the highest monarchs to his own rule, nor allows them to draw the temporal sword against anyone without his own permission. And yet he nonetheless calls himself the vice-regent of Christ, who put matters of temporal concern away from himself and placed them upon the civil magistrate (Luke 12:14; John 8:11), and [the pope] calls himself the successor of Peter, to whom—no less than to the other disciples—Christ said: "You know that the rulers of the gentiles lord it over them, and their great men exercise authority over them. But it shall not be so among you, but whoever wishes to be great among you must become your servant, just as the Son of man did not come in order to be served by you but in order to serve" (Matt 20:25[–28]).

26. The papal teachers impiously despise that same political institution when they call kings and civil rulers not sacred (Bellarminus, *On the Exemption of the Clergy*, chapter 2), men whom holy Scripture calls 'the Lord's anointed,' 'gods,' 'sons of God,' and 'those who foster the church' (Ps 18:51 and 82:6; Isa 49:23).

27. And they behave even like cut-throats—not like theologians—when they ascribe to God's church the power to depose unbelieving magistrates, and to remove from them not only their reign but even their life. For the law of grace which God has revealed to his church does not take away the law of nature and nations whereupon the magistrate's authority rests, but it establishes and perfects it. For this reason, just as the evangelical doctrine does not annul the marriage contract of unbelievers, which—as equally as the marriage contract of believers—belongs to the law of nations and nature, but only distinguishes the one from the other, so also with the help of the same doctrine can the unbelieving magistrate be distinguished from the believing one, but he never can be abolished by those who are subject to the unbelieving magistrate, as he has been instituted by divine ordination. And for that reason, they are bound to pour out to God even their prayers for his safety, according to the apostle's admonition in 1 Tim 2:1, and by the example of the early church which always tolerated the rule of Julian the Apostate.

28. At the same time we should distinguish the authority of the unbelieving magistrate over his subjects on the grounds of the different nature and character of the things. For if the things which he commands pertain to one's conscience and diametrically oppose God's Word, then in no way at all should we obey his unholy and unfair orders, because as Peter once replied to a magistrate of this kind: "It is necessary to obey God rather than men" (Acts 5:29). But if those things concern only matters of the bodily sort, or things beneficial for this life and to the outward state and good order of the republic and human society, then in those things we should obey him for the sake of keeping the peace and calm among the citizens.

29. The form of the magistrate finds its place in the lawful authority bestowed upon him by God, whereby he executes each and every part of his office. For it is this which—like a soul—breathes life into his function, and gives it the efficacy whereby he rightly exercises judgment and justice among his citizens.

30. For the correct administration of judgment and justice he has need of two skills, namely legal and military.

31. Legal skill is that whereby the magistrate prudently conducts what in times of peace is most fitting, and skillfully directs it for the common good, to keep peace and calm in the republic.

32. Military skill is that whereby the magistrate forcefully and exceptionally well does what is fitting in times of war, in order to restore the lost common good, to defend religion, to drive out unjust force, and to assert the right of freedom.

33. Both skills are required of the magistrate: the former, to be cherished by those who do good and to be bestowed with due honor; the latter, to be feared by those who are wicked [Rom 13:3].

34. And if the magistrate is endowed with these two skills, he shall carefully see to it that: 1) he does not accept judges, counsellors, chief officers, and generals of war whose consciences are wicked, but makes use of the advice and labors of men of proven faith and integrity. 2) he does not lend an ear to informers, flatterers, enemies, and disturbers of the public order, but drives them out. 3) if he must exact punishment from either insolent or disloyal subjects, or protect himself against wicked enemies, he does not yield to his natural desires but is led only by his zeal for his calling.

35. For the ancient magistrates under the Old Testament God has prescribed laws for both the military and the legal skills, sometimes after having been consulted and asked by them (as is seen in Judg 1:1, 20:18, 28; 1 Sam 23:2 and 30:8; and 2 Sam 5:19), and sometimes without being asked (as one reads in Num 31:1; Deut 13:12). In addition, God from heaven has blessed judges and kings who waged war according to his laws, as king David realized (Ps 18:36 and 144:1), and Solomon (Prov 12:21). In Heb 11:33 also the saints under the Old Testament are said to have defeated kingdoms by faith in God, and consequently their battles pleased God. For just as what is not done by faith is sin and displeases God [Rom 14:23], so on the other hand what is done by faith is in agreement with God's word and is accepted by him.

36. Moreover, what God in the Old Testament both prior to the law of Moses, according to the law of nations, and under the Law from the authority divinely granted to the magistrates, considered binding and pleasing to him, cannot be displeasing to him in times under the Gospel. For the Gospel does not abolish the law of nations, nor the political [laws], nor the laws of war which are needed to preserve human society.

37. And so the Anabaptists and Socinians are rambling mindlessly when they say that war is not divinely permitted even to the Christian magistrate. For they do not take into consideration the fact that neither John the Baptist, nor

Christ, nor the apostles advised the centurions and soldiers, who were seeking from them the knowledge of salvation and professing their faith in Christ, to throw away their weapons but to be content with their wages (Matt 8; Luke 3; Acts 10). We should add the example of the apostle Paul, who when a plot of some Jews against him was discovered, using the protection and defense of the tribune of the Romans against those Jews, demonstrated by this action that any magistrate whatsoever can, by divine right, make use of the sword for the protection of good people (Acts 23:21).

38. The same apostle, in appealing to Caesar and in replying to Festus that he ought to be judged at the tribunal of Caesar (Acts 25:10[–11]) meant that the judgment of magistrate over those charged with a crime belongs to the divine and also common laws, and therefore is permitted also under the Gospel. For he never would have said that something ought to be done which opposes divine law or perpetual law. The same apostle warns the Romans (Rom 13:4) that the magistrate can lawfully and deservedly strike with the sword those who are charged with a crime. With this statement the Socinians' axiom falls down completely, that the doctrine of the Gospel does not allow to Christians that a man can deprive another man of life. For their axiom can be refuted with Christ's statement in Matt 26:52: "Whoever takes up the sword shall perish by the sword." Christ calls upon an old penal clause in the divine law to show that it belongs to the ancient and perpetual law, i.e., the clause in Gen 9:6: "Whoever sheds a man's blood"—in private and non-regulated vengeance—"by man shall his blood be shed," namely, by public and regulated vengeance. The Socinians mix this up with private and non-regulated vengeance, and from the places where the former is prohibited (namely Matt 5:39 and Rom 12:17, 19) they incorrectly derive the prohibition of the latter, too.

39. The necessary skill of the magistrate in times of war as well as of peace is either universal or particular. The universal skill is the one that has the power to establish civil laws, and to adorn the civil community with good morals. The particular one is that which is busy with settling particular cases and actions. And this skill is either consultative and in the consultation of particular actions that must be taken, or it is adjudicatory, and concerns the handling of an action by those who have been consulted.

40. The two skills of the magistrate consist of the following duties. First, that the civil laws which he has established are in manifest agreement with the

universal law of nature and with the recorded moral law. Secondly, by means of ecclesiastical administration, rightly to establish the worship of God according to the norm of his law, in the region over which he presides, to keep pure and sound the worship that has been determined by ecclesiastical decision, or to reform it if it has become corrupt or wicked; and, as far as he is able, to go against all those who mislead the people, and heterodox teachers who block the way of progress of true religion.

41. In order to take heed to all of these things, the magistrate must know what is the true Christian faith whereby God's churches should be built up or reformed, so that in a matter of such great import he does not undertake or decide something on the basis of only the judgment or decision of others, but only on the basis of his own firm knowledge and solid faith.

42. All of these things were heeded by the saintly men, even in their capacity as leaders in the Israelite republic, like Moses who instituted the sacred religion in accordance with God's law (Exod 19:20), and Joshua, Moses's successor, who in his civil constitution promulgated God's law (Josh 5) and renewed God's covenant with the Israelite people (Josh 24). And after the entry into the promised land, by God's special command he restored the practice of circumcision which had been stopped and celebrated the Passover in its appointed time [Josh 5:1–12]. Upon entering further into the land of Canaan he carved the Ten Commandments upon the stone tablets [Josh 8:32], and when he was about to die he exhorted all the magistrates not to turn to the right or to the left from the prescript of God's law [Josh 23:6].

43. Those who followed the example set by these men were the judges of Israel: Gideon, who after the death of Joshua destroyed the altar of Baal (Judg 6), and Samuel, who exhorted the people to repair the corrupted religion, and who commenced the repair [1 Sam 7]. And also the kings, such as David, who like Samuel, as a man of God, together with Gad and Nathan assigned to the Levites their posts and ecclesiastical duties (1 Chron 9 and 23). And so, as king of the people, he ordered the ark of God to be brought to his own city, and he made the other preparations necessary for building the temple [2 Sam 6; 1 Chron 13, 15, 16, and 22]. Solomon, who had dedicated the house of the Lord, celebrated the feast of booths, and made sacrificial offerings to God on the altar which he had built (2 Chron 8). Asa, who removed from his kingdom all the filthy gods which his ancestors had set up (1 Kgs 15). Jehoshaphat, who destroyed also all the idols, and paid special attention to

restoring the true worship of God (1 Kgs 22; 2 Chron 23). Joash, who reminded the priests who were being negligent in their care of the temple building of their duties and punished them (2 Kgs 12; 2 Chron 24). Hezekiah, who as diligently as possible cleansed God's temple of every superstition, restored the pure worship which had fallen away under his fathers, announced the Passover to the Jews, and made provisions of food for the Levites (2 Kgs 19; 2 Chron 29). Josiah, Hezekiah's grandson, who very faithfully restored the worship of God which had been adulterated under Manasseh and Amon, and who punished the workers of idolatry. Some of the Christian rulers have followed in their footsteps, namely Constantine the Great, who was the first to make the churches available for the Christians, and Theodosius, who closed the temples of the heathens and ordered that throughout his whole empire only the Christian religion be practiced. And also other kings, rulers and magistrates who reformed their regions from the leaven of ungodliness and superstition—in our own times no less than in the times of our ancestors.

44. In order to be informed about sacred religion, the believing magistrate should employ the ministers of the divine Word as if they were his eyes; he should determine fair stipends for them; safeguard their meetings (both consistorial and synodical); preserve in these meetings the external good order and on occasion, when a serious matter demands it, he should be present, following the example set by Constantine the Great, who ordered that the case of Arius be examined first in the lawful Synod of Nicaea while he himself was in attendance, in order that he might come to understand the entire matter as it arose from the unanimous votes of the bishops who represented the church, in accordance with the norm of sacred Scripture.

45. The administration of civil affairs is connected to the ecclesiastical one by three shared elements. The first is that each, with respect to God, is a service and ministry subordinate to the highest rule of God (Ps 2:11; Rom 13:4; 1 Cor 3:5 and 4:1). Second, that by virtue of their ministries the magistrate and the shepherds are guardians of God's law (Deut 17:18; Isa 49:23; Mal 2:7; 2 Cor 5:18 and 12:20; 2 Tim 2:2). Third, because of that ministry which they carry out according to God's prescript, they should be shown the honor that is owed to them, in keeping with the accordant calling (Rom 13:6–7; 1 Tim 5:17; Heb 13:7).

46. On the other hand, the two administrations are distinguished by their difference, both insofar as it concerns the guardianship of God's Word and of discipline (which are the two parts of divine law), and insofar as it concerns a disproportionate sharing of honor that is owed to them. In the guardianship of God's Word the political authority should be distinguished from ecclesiastical ministry by six differences. The first is that in setting forth God's Word the pastors should speak, and interpret; but the magistrates should listen and be informed, for the same reason that the centurion Cornelius and Sergius the proconsul were instructed, the former of them by Peter and the latter by Paul (Matt 28:19–20; Ps 2:10; Acts 10:32; Acts 13:7). The second is that in carrying out their ministry the shepherds and elders in the name of Christ are declaring especially and specifically to the inward person the rewards and punishments that are spiritual; but the magistrates furnish the outward man with physical goods or punishments (Matt 18:17– 18; John 20:22–23; 1 Tim 1:20; Rom 13:3–4). Third, that ministers of the Word are responsible for the bare proceedings of the law and the execution of only those rewards and punishments which are contained in God's expressed Word; but the civil authority has the sanction and execution by way of arbitration over the corporeal rewards and punishments, in keeping with the variety of circumstances that occur in practising it—in such a way, however, that the sanction belongs to that authority which possesses the highest execution of things, i.e., the authority of the king or ruler in a monarchy, and of noblemen in an aristocracy (Deut 4:2; 1 Cor 1:23; Gal 1:8; Rev 22:18–19; Matt 20:15; John 19:11; Rom 13:4). Fourth is that the elders of the church do not prescribe anything except by the command of another, namely, of Christ, but the magistrates prescribe some things also by their own command. For ecclesiastical governance is entirely *hyperetike*, or ministerial. But political governance, even though it is administrative with respect to God, is equipped with command and authority. The fifth is that elders by means of spiritual weapons, i.e., warnings, threats of divine wrath, and excommunication lead people to repent and win them over to Christ. But the magistrates, when necessity requires it, use punishment, imprisonment, and the sword to compel them and to keep them in check. Sixth, that shepherds have responsibility when it concerns the conscience, but magistrates when the discussion concerns the body.

47. To these things which regard the discipline of the church we should attach three other differences. The first of these is the fact that strictly speaking the

right to determine ecclesiastical discipline belongs to the shepherds together with their consistory, from the analogy of faith and sacred doctrine; but the magistrate who possesses the highest authority of command can either in person approve that discipline, or in his absence examine it, and if anything in it is rightly to be desired he can demand from the shepherds that it be either supplied or emended from the analogy of God's Word. The second is that the ministers of the Word, together with their consistory must consecrate Christ's servants who have been approved both by a civil magistrate—if he professes the same religion—and by his church. The magistrate, however, can make use of his own intervention and also his own authority in order to bestow his services upon the church, to halt corrupt practices or to set them straight if anything worthy of civil attention should arise. Third, that in the church at peace the shepherds should, with the approval of the civil authority, be present together with the consistory at ecclesiastical meetings which the magistrate has announced, and in them to consider the doctrine and moral conduct of the church. But in a church that is troubled and struggling with schisms the magistrate has the power—with the approval of the church, if that is possible—to call the most devout and wise theologians to the synod and also to attend their meetings. And if there is an urgent need, [he has the power] to preside over them as far as the outward handling and direction is concerned, according to the precedent set by Constantine the Great, mentioned above.

48. The honor that is owed to both functions is not of equal weight. For just as the ministers of the Word do not have their authority by any command of their own, so also they ought not to lord it over the consciences of people to whom they administer God's Word (1 Pet 5:2). But it is to the civil authority that God has granted the command over the bodies and goods of their subjects (Rom 13:4). Moreover, since ecclesiastical dignity is more like the authority of a father than that of a king, so it should be honored only by reverence, a willingness to learn, and financial contributions. But the civil authority, which is bound up with its command and majesty, ought to be honored by its subjects not only with obedience and submission, but also with the payment of taxes, according to the example of Christ in Matt 17:27, and his command: "Give to Caesar what is Caesar's" (Matt 22:21).

49. The greatest possible harmony should be fostered between the two administrations, i.e., the political and the ecclesiastical one, so that each may be supported by the assistance of the other, and so that the foundations of

the sacred religion, and of the divine law in the church may be supported no less by the authority of the magistrate than in civil society the principles of justice, and of common right may be supported by the ministry of the elders of the church.

50. It is true that the glory of God first of all, and also the wellbeing of the people, should be the supreme law for the Christian magistrate as guardian and avenger of both tables of the Law, and this man should not only as private individual but also as ruler be bound to keep himself busy with God's Word both day and night, so that by his leadership he may be able to preserve the lawfully established religion and to restore it if it has fallen. Nevertheless, he should not for that reason appropriate for himself the ecclesiastical function, but by virtue of the duty he shares with the other members of the household of faith, like a sheep of Christ, he should listen to his Word and take part in the sacraments. And like God's servant he should 'kiss the Son' [Ps 2:12] who is presented to him in the Word of God by the preachers of the Gospel, and he should take upon himself the yoke of his discipleship.

51. Moses's administration was a mixed one, outside the common order and suited to the times; for after he had installed his brother Aaron as high priest by God's special order, he no longer acted as high priest but stayed in the order of the Levites [Lev 8]. The function of Melchizedek king of Salem and priest of God most high was figurative [Gen 14:18–20], and, together with the other figurative ceremonies, was abolished by Christ, who for that reason ordained the ministry of the Word for his apostles, and forbade them political lordship, lest they and their successors should give the charge of pastoral administration to a man of politics or the administration of his kingdom to a man of the church.

52. In the theses on the calling of the churches' ministers [42.70] we have demonstrated what kind of care the devout and believing magistrate ought to exercise in the election of shepherds, namely that in this matter he ought to conduct himself according to the ordinance which Christ himself has established. It consists in the fact that as guardian of the fourth commandment he should see to it that by means of the consistory (supported by the consent and approving vote of the magistrate himself first and foremost, and also that of the whole church) men who are suitable should lawfully be called to the office of shepherd, and be ordained before the church, according to the practice of the apostles and the evangelists (Acts

14:23; Titus 1:5), which our forefathers living under the devout magistrates observed consistently.

53. The example of Moses, which is raised in objection to this viewpoint of our theologians, is entirely outside the common order and is irrelevant to this disputation. For it was not as political leader but as God's extraordinary priest that Moses installed Aaron; and we must distinguish between the act of Aaron's installation and his election. For God first chose Aaron and mentioned his name to Moses; thereafter, by God's command, through his installation he was confirmed in his calling by Moses.

54. If the shepherd is factious and a proven violator of the public peace, then the highest magistrate, with the intervening advice of his leading subordinates, has the power to depose him with the same right with which king Solomon deposed Abiathar (1 Kgs 2:26 and 8:2).

55. Harder to explain is the question how the magistrate should treat heterodox teachers and heretics who lead the people astray, who lawfully have been convicted of deadly errors and who are persistent in their revilings? Our answer to this question is: if such times should befall him that the magistrate does not have the power to call those heretics back to peace and good results by his own gentle spirit, nor by harshness and threats to scare them off their obstinate pursuit of fostering false teachings which cause the very foundation of the faith to totter, then his tolerant attitude is worthy of excuse in the eyes of God and his church. For wisdom bids that from time to time even those things be tolerated which are not approved at least out of zeal and love for the truth, but which cannot be prevented or removed by a coercive authority in keeping with the laws of wisdom and avenging justice.

56. But if in fact he is able to compel them, and to check them with his sword, others are of the opinion that it is his duty to bestow the penalty of death on them, following the example of the devout king Josiah who slew the superstitious priests of the high places on the altar and who burned human bones upon them [2 Kgs 23:20]. And Jehu, who completely erased the entire family of Ahab and Jezebel for their idol-worship, and who to a man killed all the priests of Baal [2 Kgs 9 and 10]. And likewise Elijah, who also to the last man slew the priests of Baal [1 Kgs 18:40]. But whereas Elijah the prophet did this upon extraordinary prompting by God because at that time the ordinary magistracy had ceased to exist, yet Josiah and Jehu did so in keeping with the strict rule of the political law that had been specially suited to the

Jewish people—and that in a case of extreme necessity and out of fear that their entire kingdom would be overturned, which could be avoided in no other way. I prefer to follow the thinking of those theologians who assert that where another way is provided to keep heretics in check in a way that is fair and good, when the church has condemned the majority of them, it would be better for them to be deposed, or relegated, or restrained in some other way by the magistrate arbitrarily than for them to be struck down in death, in order that their disease not gradually creep, like gangrene, in their republic. In that matter they will follow Constantine the Great and Theodosius, of whom the former punished Arius with exile, and the latter Apollinaris and Nestorius, after they first were found guilty by the synod.

57. At this point the pious and wise magistrate can make an exception for men who are altogether atheists and revilers of the highest degree, who very irreverently deny God himself entirely or his providence in human affairs, who overturn the common religion of Christ's church with their shocking revilings and who disturb the peace and harmony of the whole republic out of pure delight in another's misfortunes and incurable malice of soul, and who can be curbed by no other beneficial and gentler means of political coercion or remedy.

58. For this reason I think that we should understand this statement of Augustine to apply only to heretics of the common sort: "It is not acceptable for anyone in the catholic church to rage unto death against anyone—not even a heretic" (*Against Cresconius, a Donatist Teacher*, book 3.50). And in the Letter to Donatus: "With regard to dreadful judges and laws it is our wish that heretics be corrected, and not slain, lest they meet with the penalty of eternal judgment; and it is our will not to neglect discipline of them, nor to neglect carrying out the punishments they deserve: therefore, curb their sins in such a way that they become people whom it grieves to have sinned."

59. Even though the magistrate should hold his subjects back with the bars of his laws lest they openly slander the religion which he approves, nevertheless he does not have the power to compel them to the faith whereby they approve the form of the accepted religion and openly profess the approval of it before men. For faith wishes to be convinced, not forced, and nothing ought to be so volitional as the inward religion and worship of God, nothing ought to be so foreign to the Christian magistrate as perverse and ill-

timed severity whereby he turns people into hypocrites, and forces them to profess with the mouth what they do not believe with the heart.

60. And yet we do not join in stipulating with those who, just as they say that people's own thoughts are free, so also think that the magistrate ought to bear the opinions of anyone whosoever about the faith. For although we do grant that we should not punish people's inward opinions, nevertheless we do not say that the magistrate should permit each and every citizen an impious confession of religion that is destructive to the republic.

61. But at least we do acknowledge that it is first by means of spiritual weapons we should drive back the spiritual darts with which the false teachers make their attacks upon the church. But if there is no longer any opportunity to use them and the heretics, even though sometimes they are convicted of their errors, nevertheless cause new troubles to arise in the republic through the cultivation of these errors, then they must be stopped by the authority of the magistrate lest the republic should meet up with some more serious hardship for having put up with their faction. For in the doctrine of the truth stubborn discord and division drag along with them trouble for the whole human society and overturn its calm state.

62. Although the magistrates in former times no less punished heretics who seditiously violated God's spiritual law than other insurgents who violated their civil laws, it was not by right but by force that the Roman leaders dragged off to their own ecclesial court their power to investigate heretics with God's Word, and according to that Word to strike them bodily.

63. For the believing magistrate, as an eminent part of God's church, both by the analogy of faith and by the judgment of the faithful theologians (whom he has called together) in agreement with God's Word, out of his own wisdom and gravity of the case, does have the power, along with his theologians, to make investigations concerning the heretic, and to compel the heretic if he no longer can enjoy the company of the other citizens without an uprising in the republic.

64. And by as much more authority Christian magistrates have received from God than private citizens, they should use as much more care and diligence lest any heterodox teaching or disagreement in the Christian faith should spread wider in their region. For besides the fact that the guardianship of God's universal church is jointly entrusted to them as members of the

church, as supporters and protectors of the church the same guardianship is demanded especially of them more fully. Therefore, they should be warned not to indulge their subjects who are strangers to the true religion the freedom to publicly profess a false religion; and with whatever means they are able to, they should halt even the private practice of it.

65. The highest goal of the magistrate is God's glory; the subordinate goal is the harmony and civil calm of his subjects. For this reason, the apostle's will is that we offer prayers and intercessions on behalf of kings and all who are placed in positions of prominence, that under their authority we live a peaceful and quiet life with all godliness and reverence (1 Tim 2:2).

ON THE RESURRECTION OF THE BODY AND THE LAST JUDGMENT

President: Andreas Rivetus
Respondent: Henry W. Berkelius

Disputation 51 addresses the topic of general eschatology, that is, the resurrection of the body and the last judgment. To some extent this topic had been anticipated in earlier disputations; for example, Disputation 39 treats Purgatory and 41 the Christ and the Antichrist. Whereas those discussions focused on criticism of the Romanist teaching, here the author offers a positive treatment of the end of times. Belief in the resurrection distinguishes Christians from unbelievers (3–4). Resurrection is certain and has two very solid foundations (5): God's will regarding the resurrection, as revealed in the Scriptures (6–14); and God's power that makes the resurrection possible (15). Thesis 16 defines the resurrection of the body as a work performed exclusively by the Triune God (elaborated in 17–22; the role of angels is discussed in 23), that takes place at the end of times, and concerns all human beings, the living as well as the dead, the righteous as well as the wicked (31–36). Special attention is given to stillborn, miscarried fetuses and malformed babies (36), sexual differentiation (37), and physical deformities (38). Questions about the number and precise substance of the resurrected bodies are discussed (24–30). The internal form of resurrection is treated (39) as well as the outward form (40), the goals (41), and the many uses of this doctrine (42–44). The Triune God is the one who brings about the final judgment (45–58), yet the administration of it will be conducted by the Son in his human nature (47–49). Judgment befalls the wicked angels and all human beings, both good and evil (50–51). Of the latter, all deeds will be judged (52). The form of the judgment will consist in the knowledge of the case, in declaring the verdict, and in the execution thereof (53–54). After drawing attention to the goals of judgment (55), the places where the upright and the wicked will be gathered, and a warning not to calculate the years up to

Christ's return (56), the disputation ends with a definition of the last judgment (57) and the many uses of this doctrine (58).

1. Everything that is done by man or concerning man is enclosed by two terms which the ancient theologians, not deviating from the words of Scripture (Prov 2:20 and 4:26, 27; Matt 7:13–14; 2 Cor 7:7; Heb 4:14), expressed with the words 'the way' and 'the fatherland.' Equivalent to them is the distinction of the church into 'militant' and 'triumphant.' Up until now we have disputed what pertained to 'the way' and to the state of the church militant on earth. What we should discuss in detail next pertains to the 'fatherland' and the 'end-goal,' or, to the state of the church triumphant in heaven, and to the complete defeat of its enemies, and to adjudicating them and handing them over to the eternal punishments of hell. What must of necessity occur before these last, very different states of the upright and of the wicked are the resurrection of the dead and the last judgment. For "it has been appointed for men to die once, and after this the judgment" (Heb 9:27). But it is not possible for the dead to be judged as long as they are dead, because they must appear before the judgment. In order for that to take place the resurrection of the dead must happen first—and we shall have to treat it first; thereafter, we must examine the circumstances of that fearful judgment.

2. What in the active sense, from the working of its efficient cause, is called 'resuscitation,' in the passive sense is called 'resurrection.' The former is nothing other than the raising up of that which has fallen; but the latter (which is the effect of the former) is a kind of second standing-up, called *anastasis* in Greek, as though the second standing-up of one who has fallen. Since 'fall' or 'collapse' can be understood figuratively, so too can 'resurrection' be taken in the same way: either by reason of the calamities and dangers into which someone falls in this life, or by reason of the sins whereby the soul comes to ruin and falls. Leaving aside the figurative meaning and also a consideration of that resurrection which is called the 'first' resurrection (which was sufficiently treated when the disputation was held about the regeneration and renewal of man) we shall offer a treatment about resurrection in the strict sense of the word, which denotes the restoration of a body that by dying has become a corpse, and which denotes the reunification of the soul with it. For, to say this in passing, we do not avoid applying the word 'corpse' to any dead body whatsoever, including even the body of Christ in the three days of his death—although this seems

715

blasphemous to [Franciscus] Fevardentius (*Theomachia* [*Calvinistica*], book 6, page 176) and to [Petrus] Cotonus (*Geneve Plagiare*, at Acts 2:27). But Chrysostom is not afraid to apply the word to Christ himself, in *Homily* 24 on 1 Cor, "calling the body a corpse because it has died." And Gregory of Valencia, *Commentary on Thomas*, volume 4, question 4, point 1 approves: "In the three days of the death of Christ, his flesh, no rather, his corpse (insofar as it is by nature without reason and sense) was sustained hypostatically by the Word."

3. This article [of the Creed] separates gentiles from Christians, for it is placed beyond the scope of reason, and it is a declaration peculiar to the church, as Tertullian stated rightly: "The faith of the Christians is the resurrection of the dead" (*On the Resurrection of the Body*). And what Augustine said about the head should be applied also to all its members: "The fact that Christ died is believed by pagans and his enemies; but the fact that Christ rose again is a belief specific to the Christians." And so the gentiles perceive and grant that all people are subject to death; but when it comes to the resurrection, then it seems silly talk (Acts 17:32) and childish nonsense (Pliny, *Natural History*, book 2, chapter 7, and book 7, chapter 55). Thus, Caecilius, in [M.] Minucius [Felix's] Octavius says: "The Christians make up old wives' tales as they claim that they will be born again after they die, when they are dust and ashes; and by some strange faith they believe their own lies." Simply put, "the denial of the resurrection of the body is assumed from the entire school of all philosophers" (Tertullian, *On the Prescription of Heretics*, chapter 7). And accordingly, the apostle writes about the resurrection of the dead that generally the gentiles "are without hope" (1 Thess 4:13).

4. But because "philosophers were the patriarchs of heretics" (Tertullian, *Against Hermogenes*), it is no wonder that from the very beginning also the church suffered objections from them in the doctrine of the resurrection. The Jewish church suffered objections from the Sadducees, "who said that there is no resurrection" (Matt 22:23); the Christian church suffered objections from Hymenaeus and Philetus, who taught that "the resurrection has taken place already" (2 Tim 2:18), namely, denying the actual resurrection while granting only a figurative one. [The church] at Corinth [suffered objections] from many people whom the apostle refuted (1 Cor 15:12). Afterwards, their heresy was refurbished by the Simonians (Irenaeus, book 1, chapter 19), by Saturninus, Basilides, Carpocrates, the Gnostics, Valentinus, the Ophites, Cainites, Sethians, Archontici, Cerdoniani, Marcionites, Lucian,

Apelles, Severus, followers of Origen, the Seleucians, and many others whom it would take long to number—concerning whom [see] Epiphanius (in *Panarion*), Augustine (*On Heresies ad Quotvult Deum*), Theodoret (*Compendium of Heretical Accounts*), Philastrius (*On Heresies*), and others. The Acts of the Council of Constance ascribe this heresy also to the Roman Pope John XXIII: "At the persuasion of the devil, he stubbornly believed that the soul of man dies and is extinguished with his body, like dumb animals, and that, once it has died, it will in no way whatsoever be raised even on the last day" (Session 11, page 106 in the edition of Quentel 1551, volume 1).

5. But in fact, since the apostle links hope together with the resurrection of the dead (Acts 24:14) and teaches that "we of all people are most wretched if in this life only we have hope in Christ" (1 Cor 15:19), "in order to hold fast the possession of our hope without wavering" (Heb 10:23) we must fortify our soul with the solid and unmovable foundations on which our faith and hope in the future resurrection rest securely. Therefore, we set aside arguments that are secondary and based on probability, as well as some comparisons with nature or similarities drawn from it—which illustrate rather than confirm the matter, and which are not able to sustain the careful examination of a strict disputation. We shall bolster our belief by means of those two supports which Christ has indicated to us in Matt 22:29, when he called the Sadducees, who deny the resurrection, back "to the Scriptures and the power of God," and revealed that the source of their error was their ignorance of these things. And against them, he laid two foundations about this article of faith: Knowledge of God's will from Scripture, and the power of God, arising from his nature. For since restoration to life is a divine action and there are two principles that are necessary and sufficient for this action, namely the will and the ability, in this work of resurrection we must consider them, too. For these two qualities which are combined in God—God in whom there is no lack of power—bring the thing [resurrection] into actuality because "our God is in heaven and does whatever He wills" (Ps 115:2).

6. The will of God is made known to us in his revealed Word, in which we possess also the pronouncements of divine origin about the resurrection from the dead given by the prophets and the apostles. To be sure, in the Old Testament they are rather shadowy, but yet they are clear enough to produce faith; in the New, however, they are described as clearly as daylight so that to not perceive them would be a matter of greatest blindness, and to not put faith in them once they have been seen and heard would be the mark of utter

lack of faith. From the very beginning the promise about "the seed of the woman that will crush the head of the serpent" (Gen 3:15) included the doctrine of God's will about the resurrection. For that seed which was to destroy the works of the devil would not have done so sufficiently unless it had destroyed the wages of sin—that is, death, both temporal as well as eternal [Rom 6:23]. For he who breaks the power of Satan conquers also death over which Satan holds the power (Heb 2:14). Connected to this is the fact that that promise, which was later more fully revealed to Abraham, as referring to the Messiah who would be born from Isaac's seed, carries with it the added blessing which in his seed is to be shared with all the nations of the earth. And since that blessing is placed opposite the curse to which the whole human race is subject on account of sin (of which the final point is the death of the body and of the soul), it is also entirely fitting that the resurrection of the body and life never ending of that body joined with the soul are included in that blessing.

7. As guarantee of this necessary consequence we have the Son of God himself, who gathers from the words of the covenant, "I am the God of Abraham, the God of Isaac, and the God of Jacob" (Exod 3:6)—the force of which remains in effect even after the separation of the soul from the body—that contrary to the false teaching of the Sadducees there is a resurrection of the dead, because "God is not the God of the dead but of the living" (Matt 22:32; Mark 12:26; Luke 20:38). For since God struck that covenant not with souls but with persons, and the names Abraham, Isaac and Jacob stand for whole persons, life must of necessity be related to whole persons, and not only to some of their parts. Therefore, life relates not only to the immortality of souls, but also to the resurrection of bodies. Since the resurrection was certain in God's decree, Abraham, Isaac and Jacob—though deceased—were alive in God's eyes. Accordingly, it was his will that believers receive the sign of the covenant in the flesh, to demonstrate that this body would in its own due time be revived again from the dead and become a partaker of life everlasting.

8. Jerome, in writing to Pammachus, has assessed Job's statement (chapter 19:25 and following) to be so clearly about that matter that he thought "no-one after Christ speaks so clearly about the resurrection as Job did before Christ." And to be sure, according to its reading in the Vulgate edition, hardly anything can be said about that topic more clearly: "For I know that my Redeemer lives, and that on the last day I shall be made alive from the earth.

And once again I shall be clothed in my own skin, and in my flesh shall I see my God. I myself, and not another, shall see him, and my own eyes shall behold him. This my hope is safely hidden away in my heart." And even though these words appear slightly different in the Hebrew text, and are rendered somewhat differently in the Septuagint translation also, there will be nothing that cannot be adduced more fittingly to explain and confirm the faith in that mystery, as was done by the very learned interpreters Tremellius, Junius, and others. We prefer their opinion—which was that of the entire ancient church—to the interpretations of the Jews, although the very learned Mercerus followed in their path. We are dissuaded from this opinion by that protestation of Job about having his words engraved with "an iron pen" [19:24], and by that full knowledge which he professes, which he could not have had without a doubt about temporal liberation. And by those words that "he would later be raised from the dust," which, whether they relate to the Redeemer or to the person of Job, can hardly be applied to the restoration of his possessions in this life. [We are convinced also] by his certainty "of seeing God in his own flesh" after it "would be eaten by worms" [19:26]—which is a periphrasis for the state of death and the decay of the body, etc. And yet we think that Job, too, had weighed these matters so that from it he could base his own hope for his own temporal restoration by him who by his power would call the dead back to life again.

9. If we look closely at the words in the prophecy of Isaiah the prophet in chapter 26:19, "Your dead shall live, my fallen shall rise up again, etc.," and of Ezekiel in chapter 37:1 and following, which is a treatment of the valley full of bones (very dry bones at that) to which God said: "I shall send my Spirit into you and you shall live, and I shall bestow sinews upon you, and I shall make flesh to come upon you, etc.," then it appears that it is describing the resurrection of dead bodies, even though many interpreters are not wrong to understand it as a figurative resurrection, as in the delivery from the Babylonian captivity and the restoration of the former strength. Nonetheless, it does contribute to confirming the doctrine of the resurrection in the strict sense of the word, because if these things are spoken in some comparative way, it is not customary for a comparison to be drawn either from things that are impossible or from things that either have never happened or never will happen. But [it is drawn] from things that are well-known, either from nature, or from faith through revelation, as in this passage, so that the argument would run like this: if you have unwavering faith in the resurrection of the

dead whereby God will gather together the dust of scattered corpses and join them together and again will bind together dead, arid and dried-out bones and restore them to life, then you should have no doubt about the promise of the restoration of God's people, even though their strength is completely sapped. For the one who can by his own divine power recall at one time to life bodies that had been reduced to ashes and dust, shall also be able to bring back the exiles to their fatherland, as they are not unlike the arid bones, and to restore to them their former strength of freedom.

10. But Daniel's testimony is very clear: "And many of those who are asleep in the dust of the earth will awaken, some to eternal life, others to eternal shame" (Dan 12:2). And we should not think that this prophecy is not relevant to the universal resurrection on the grounds that the promise is made about many but not about all. For 1) those many who are asleep can be taken to mean all who are asleep, even though they are called many in comparison with those who will be found living on the day of the resurrection from the dead; 2) the word 'many' can be taken to refer not to the determination of the subject but to the two members of the distribution that are joined together in the predicate, as if to say: "many to life, many unto death." And we add to it that the collective noun sometimes is taken in a universal and extensive sense for "all" in Scripture, as Rom 5:19, where "many," that is, all who are in Adam, are said to be declared sinners. It is evident, however, that this passage of Daniel, in the way that Porphyry has twisted it, cannot be applied to the state of the republic of Israel after the generals of Antiochus were slain: 1) From the goal of that resurrection: Everlasting life or shame; 2) From the fact that it speaks about the resurrection in which there will be a precise distinction between the upright and the wicked—which certainly did not happen when peace was restored to the Israelites; 3) From the fact that the teachers of the Jewish church did not begin from that time onward to shine forever like the heavenly firmament, but—as the law was corrupted and slowly declined—they rather fell little by little from their position. And add the fact that this genuine passage occurs in the words of Christ which appear to explain Daniel (John 5:28–29), as Augustine well advises (*On the City of God*, book 20, chapter 23).

11. What also contributes to this is Hosea's prophecy: "After two days the Lord will revive us, on the third day He will restore us, and we shall live before his countenance" (Hos 6:2). This is an allusion to the resurrection of Christ, and it speaks also of the church, because in Christ the head also the

members of his mystical body are said "to be raised up together with Christ" (Eph 2:6) because of the unfailing promise of the resurrection. To Hosea's testimony we should add another one from chapter 13:14: "I shall redeem them from the power of hell, I shall redeem them from death, and I shall be your death, O death, and I shall be your destruction, O hell." The apostle relates this prophecy to the resurrection from the dead: "When this perishable will be clothed with the imperishable, and this mortal shall put on immortality, then will come to pass that word which was written: 'Where is your sting, O death? Etc.'" (1 Cor 15:54).

12. In the New Testament, the matter is so clear and obvious that whoever wishes to gather all the testimonies would need a whole book. From the many testimonies we choose the following few but outstanding ones as supplement to the ones that already have been produced above, together with the testimonies of the Old Testament from which Christ obtained his own: 1) From Matt 12:40–41, where it says of the Ninevites that they shall arise, in the judgment with this generation, etc., and of the queen of the South that she will rise up, etc. From this, it follows that they will be raised from the dead, since the bodies of those people who were spoken about were reduced to dust. 2) In Luke 14:12[14] Christ makes deliberate mention of the resurrection of the just. 3) In John 6:39–40, 44, and 54, he promises that on the last day he will raise up to life all that the Father has given him, everyone who sees the Son and who believes in him, whosoever the Father draws to him, and whoever eats his body and drinks his blood.

13. The preaching and writings of the apostles very often emphasize the same mystery. And so in Acts 4:2, the Sadducees were disturbed when the apostles "in the name of Jesus proclaimed the resurrection from the dead." Paul declared Jesus and the resurrection to the Athenians in Acts 17:18, and they (as was reasonable) understood the apostle's words to be about the resurrection of the body, for "they would not have altogether mocked him," says Tertullian, "if they had heard from him only of the restoration of the soul, for then they would have heard what was assumed very frequently in their own common philosophy" (*On the Resurrection of the Body*, chapter 39). The same Paul cried out, in Acts 23:6: "It is for the hope and the resurrection of the dead that I am being put on trial." And in Acts 24:15 he confessed in the presence of Felix the governor, that he "was looking for the future resurrection of the righteous and the wicked."

14. But in the first letter to the Corinthians, chapter 15, the same apostle gave an explicit treatment of this article, and because a controversy then arose over it, he reinforced it with many arguments, in order not only to rebut those who spoke in objection, but also to lend support to those who already believed over against all the sophistic claims. The first of his arguments, he drew from the resurrection of Christ; the second from the goal of the redemption obtained by Christ; the third, as some people think, from the rite of the early church, whereby they received their baptism over gravesites as a testimony of the faith in their own resurrection—or rather, as we prefer to think, from the baptism of affliction and calamities, which the pious would undergo for the sake of the doctrine of Christ's resurrection from the dead, and of the resurrection unto salvation of others who were asleep in Christ, which is called "the baptism of blood." This interpretation seems to be confirmed by the fact that in Acts 23:6 Paul was relating his own persecutions for the sake of righteousness to the hope of the resurrection of the dead. Secondly, [it seems to be confirmed by the fact] that immediately after he treated those who are baptized on behalf of the dead he applies to himself in a literal sense what he had said figuratively about others: "And why do we risk our lives every hour?" [1 Cor 15:30]—namely, to be baptized with the baptism of blood. Why "I die daily" if there is no hope of resurrection? He adds arguments from diverse foolish consequences which come from the denial of the resurrection, arguments from putting Adam opposite Christ, and [arguments] from Christ's victory over all his enemies, among which the last one is death. From all of these arguments it follows very clearly what he himself is teaching: We must trust in God "who raises up the dead" (2 Cor 1:9).

15. Since from these words, there is enough certainty about God's will, there is no reason to call into question God's power, for with Him nothing is impossible except that which is not his will (Luke 1:37). As God has an incorruptible essence, so He also has unimpeded activity, "He who is exceeding abundantly to do more than what we ask or think" (Eph 3:20), whose power concurs with his will. Therefore, "the established law of dying does not take away the law of being raised up, because the law does not impose obligation upon the one who determines the law. Nor does God deprive himself of the right to make alive, when for us He determined the law of death," as Hilary well puts it on Ps 51. "Therefore, God will make our mortal bodies into immortal ones by reviving them: For He is better than

nature, possessing in himself the will because He is good; and the power, because He is powerful; and the perfection, because He is rich and perfect" (Irenaeus, book 2, chapter 51).

16. Having laid these two foundations of God's will and power as basis, we have sufficiently answered the question whether there will be a resurrection of the dead. We must now investigate what it is, and explain the nature of it. Therefore, we shall here define resurrection as the act of God the Father, the Son, and the Holy Spirit whereby in his own almighty power, at the archangel's trumpet at the end of the ages, He will restore the bodies of all people that have been reduced to dust, both the holy and the impious, in order to reunite them with the souls from which they had been separated in death, and to be informed by them for a time-period that will never end, so that the impious pay the penalty for their misdeeds for evermore, and the pious enjoy the received eternal blessedness forever.

17. From this definition, we understand that God the Father is the efficient cause of the resurrection, as "He who raised Jesus from the dead shall also restore to life your mortal bodies" (Rom 8:11). "Through his power, God both raised the Lord from the dead, and He will raise us also" (1 Cor 6:14 and 2 Cor 4:14). Moreover, since the outward workings of the Trinity are not divided, it follows that the Son and the Holy Spirit work together with the Father in that operation. But the active resurrection is also ascribed explicitly to the Son (John 5:28): "Those who are in the graves will hear the voice of the Son of Man, and shall come forth, those who have done good unto the resurrection of life, but those who have done evil to the resurrection of judgment" (John 6:39–40, 44). "On the last day I shall revive him" (John 11:25). "I am the resurrection and the life." But we should not understand this in such a way that the power to restore the dead is bestowed on the human nature of Christ, for the power is clearly divine; but it is attributed to the person in such a way that we must of necessity keep the principle of it distinct—contrary to what some do who start a process against us on the grounds that we, with Nestorius, split Christ into two—which is not done by those who acknowledge that Christ "in the communion of both natures performs what is his own, with the Word working what belongs to the Word, and the flesh carrying out what belongs to the flesh." Those who do not make a distinction between these things fall into the Charybdis of Eutychianism while they think that they are escaping the Scylla of Nestorius.

18. We do acknowledge, however, that as in the preliminary instances of the universal resurrection—that is, in the particular cases of Lazarus and the son of the widow from Nain, so too in the general resurrection, he [Christ] will carry out that task, as his human nature will in his person perform the task which belongs to it, namely when some obvious and clear sign is given of him coming to judge, through which like an instrument of his divine power the dead are going to be raised up. And for that effect it will have instrumental power like those words, "Lazarus come forth." and "Young man, I say to you, arise, etc.," and statements like these which had the instrumental power to raise up the dead. The Scripture calls this sign, "the voice of the Son of Man" (John 5:28), "a loud voice" (Matt 24:31), "a cry which will be rung out at midnight" (Matt 25:6), "a trumpet call" (Matt 24:31), and "the last trumpet" (1 Cor 15:52)—although this last one is attributed to Christ in only a mediate sense.

19. We do not doubt that the very same Christ, to the extent that he is our Redeemer and Mediator, through his death and suffering has merited resurrection and immortality for all his members. Moreover, that by his own resurrection he is the exemplary cause for our resurrection, for he himself is "the first-fruits of those who have fallen asleep" (1 Cor 15:20); "the first-born of the dead" (Rev 1:5; Col 1:18). Hence among the other arguments for our future resurrection (1 Cor 15:23) the apostle derives from Christ's resurrection as precedent the future resurrection of all who believe in Christ, because "Christ is the first-fruits, and then also those who belong to Christ." For members should not be separated from their head, and it would be rather inappropriate and ill-suited for the rest of the body to remain dead while the head is alive. For it would be fitting "that where the glory of the head has gone before thereunto is called the hope also for the body" (Leo, Sermon 1, *On the Ascension of the Lord*).

20. Contrary to what some others think, we reckon that these two ways of causing the resurrection in Christ—merit and precedent—do have their place in the elect only, the true members of Christ. Because even though all those who are wicked shall be raised up, as we shall prove later, nevertheless it seems that this will not be effected by the power of Christ's merit, because if Christ had not come, in keeping with the first divine ordinance, the people who through sin were subject to death would have arisen at some point in time, in order to receive the punishments for what their sins have deserved— not only in soul, but also in body. From this, it follows that also for the elect

Christ has merited not simply resurrection, but a resurrection of such kind that is blessed and glorious. For thus in the elect the effect becomes like its exemplary cause. But those who are reprobate will not become like Christ, except in some general way, which is not sufficient for this goal. Hence it follows that the apostle teaches that it applies only to those who are predestined "that they would be conformed to the image of the Son of God, and that he himself would be the first-born among many brothers" (Rom 8:29).

21. It cannot be denied that the Holy Spirit will revive the dead with the same power as that of the Father and the Son—except by the Pneumatomachi [those who oppose the Spirit] and the followers of Macedonius. For since the Spirit is of the same essence (*homoousios*) as the Father and the Son, he also has the operations in outward matters in common with them. But more so, the apostle testifies clearly in Rom 8:11: "If the Spirit of him who raised Jesus from the dead dwells in you, then He who raised Jesus from the dead will give life also to your mortal bodies for the sake of his Spirit which dwells within you." This passage, however, says something only about the glorious resurrection of those who believe, for only in them does the Spirit dwell. Nonetheless, He will manifest his power also in those in whom He does not dwell, insofar as in them He works also the renewed union of soul and body, and also the final arrangement of physical material for it.

22. This effect common to the three persons cannot be brought about by virtue of any natural cause, but only by divine power. For no natural cause is able to reproduce what is numerically identical, and there exists no natural return from dispossession to possession, such as is necessary from death to resurrection. Therefore, from the side of the starting point the resurrection will be supernatural; but if one considers its endpoint absolutely, that is to say, the being of a man, it is something natural. Not so, however, if one considers its end-point relative to the 'terminus from which,' namely, as the being of a man after death. Therefore, we ought not to listen to some Scholastics who think that sometimes (albeit not always) the same in number, once decayed, is reproduced. For since the individual receives its essence through change and through the action of a natural agent, and it is not possible for the same motion and the same action to return, it also will not happen at all that by strength of a natural agent the same in number, once decayed, can be reproduced. Therefore, it follows that no natural cause

converges with God for the resurrection of the dead, and that it happens entirely by God through a miracle.

23. And therefore, we should readily accept what is commonly said about the angels as instruments and ministers in the resurrection. For if 'resurrection' is taken in a strict, exact, and so to speak formal sense, it is an immediate work of God which does not proceed from any proper instrumental cause that truly influences the effect. In other words, if we consider the formation of bodies from the dust of the earth and the unification of them with their souls. But if the word 'resurrection' is understood to mean some of the prefatory and preceding things, or the actions immediately before or after the resurrection, and the word 'resurrection' is taken for the entire complexity of those things that happen before and after the resurrection, then we do not hesitate to acknowledge the angels as ministers of the resurrection and as instrumental causes, because they, too, will have their own roles to play on that last day, "gathering together the elect from the four winds and all the regions of the world, from one end of the heavens to the other" (Matt 24:31). But whatever the angels or any other creatures do in this matter (including even Christ's human nature), if we regard it in and of itself and by reason of its formal principle (as they call it), then it will happen as if by a cause or instrument that is moral (to use their word). However, if, as stated, we take the word 'resurrection' in its exact sense, then it is not as if by a proper cause that immediately attains its effect.

24. To this point, we have treated the efficient cause. Now, we must treat the material, which some call the "subject in which." And it, strictly speaking, is the flesh or body of the human being, because the resurrection happens according to the body, and not to the soul, strictly speaking. And moreover, the human being's soul does not perish, since it is immortal, and when the body returns to the earth "the spirit returns to God who gave it" (Eccl 12:7). Therefore, the Lord says that "those who can rage against the body cannot kill the soul" (Matt 10:28). From these and similar passages, the heresy is refuted of those people who either state openly that souls perish along with bodies, or who say that to die is to be thoroughly blotted out, and that to rise up to life means to live a second time after non-existence—such views are found nowadays in the writings of the Socinians. Therefore, the soul that has been separated remains immortal, and it does not yield to a dormant state and become deprived of all happiness nor freed entirely from all punishment; but in keeping with people's different conditions, it either is immediately after

death taken up into realms of the blessed where it awaits with joy the restoration of its own body, or it is tortured by hellish punishments until through the resurrection its body is restored to it for its share of the punishment.

25. Therefore, we state that the body shall rise up again, the same in number and substance, as is sufficiently clear from the passages of Scripture cited above. For "this perishable must put on the imperishable and this mortal must put on immortality" (1 Cor 15:53), and, Phil 3:21: Christ will transform "this very, this lowly body," etc. Therefore, the resurrection will also happen in such a way that "everyone may receive in the body"—or (as the Complutensian edition reads at 2 Cor 5:10) "things proper to the body"—"according to what he has done, whether good or evil"—which should not happen in any other body than the one by which everyone has performed good or evil deeds. Even Christ who is the example for our resurrection, arose with no other body than the one in which he was nailed to the cross, and in which even after death the traces of the nails were apparent. "But our bodies shall be made to conform to Christ's glorious body" (Phil 3:21).

26. God's justice also requires this, that in the very same body in which one has obeyed God or sinned the rewards are bestowed or the penalties are applied. Nor is it that one thing contends while another receives the crown, or that one sins while another is beaten. But rather, as Ambrose well put it in the *Sermon on Faith and the Resurrection*, chapter 19, "the order and cause of justice is that since the body and the soul share in an act which the soul conceived and the body executed, both enter into judgment, and both are either subjected to punishment or kept unto glory." And it would not be fitting if the bodies which were members of Christ along the way should be barred from the fatherland, while others took their place. The resurrection likewise would not be a true resurrection, but rather a new creation. Nor would the condition of those who had died beforehand be the same as those whom the last day will snatch while they are alive. For in that transformation these latter ones shall not be allotted other bodies as far as the substance of them is concerned. Add to this the fact that in the Scriptures death is called sleep and sleeping, and resurrection awakening, so that we understand that the resurrection will be of the same body in number. "Therefore, the flesh shall arise again, wholly in everyone, with its own identity, and with absolute integrity" (Tertullian, *On the Resurrection of the Flesh*, chapter 63).

27. Having duly weighed these matters very carefully, it follows that it is a destructive error of those who either in former times denied or who also in our own time deny that there is a resurrection of bodies that are numerically identical with the ones we are clothed with in this age. They rather have judged (or even now do judge) that the resurrection must come about in bodies made of air, or of material lighter than air, but not made up of flesh and limbs. Some people formerly ascribed this error to Origen, although others have attempted to release and exculpate him from every error concerning resurrection. Whatever the case, it is certain that in our time very many Anabaptists are engaged in this error, and also that Socinus with his adherents deny the resurrection "of this flesh," and who accordingly call into the question those words of the Creed, "I believe in the resurrection of the flesh," words which they say do not have such great authority that they should believe them contrary to the testimonies of Scripture. But we have shown that those words clearly are contained in Scripture. Moreover, we should note in passing that a mistake has crept into the edition of the Letters of Calvin in the folio of the year 1576, page 84, where a letter with the incorrect heading, *Farel to Calvin*, has misled not only Fevardentinus (who impudently attacks Calvin under that title), but also Cl. Vossius, who in his theses about the resurrection thought that letter to be from Farel in which he was instructing Calvin in this matter, although it is clearly from Calvin to Coelius Socinus, who had started that dispute, and whom Calvin under that name refutes in a most erudite fashion.

28. This statement which they make is a false one: "that these bodies which we bear will not be raised up again, but that the apostle teaches us that we shall be given other bodies." For what the apostle says in 1 Cor 15:50, "flesh and blood shall not possess the kingdom of God," should not be taken to mean that resurrected bodies shall lack flesh and blood, because as Tertullian aptly states, "'Flesh and blood' in of the sense of sin, and not in light of their substance, are barred from God's kingdom" (*On the Resurrection of the Body*). And from what follows ("Nor will corruption possess what is incorruptible"), it is clear that it is [meant] with regard to our corruption and not with regard to our nature. But it is clear that flesh and blood can exist without corruption from the fact that the Holy One of God who had flesh and bones after his resurrection nevertheless did not have a mortal and perishable body such as that of Adam after the fall, and such as our own in this life, but an immortal and imperishable one, indeed, even a spiritual one—yet not one that was

turned into a spirit, but in distinction from a natural body which must be kept alive by food. Spiritual, therefore, because it will have no need for any food; but the presence of the spirit will suffice for life, and also because of the other qualities and gifts of the glorified body.

29. And no less erroneous is the opinion of Durand of St. Pourçain, who thinks that for the resurrection of the same person the identity of form in any sort of material is sufficient, because he says that the identity of material follows from the identity of form, since in and of itself material has no actuality but receives its peculiar existence from the form. Therefore, even though Peter's soul should assume the body that had been Paul's (and vice versa), nonetheless it is the same Peter who would rise up again, and the same Paul, because he gets his body from the same soul, so that it becomes the same person (*On the Sentences* 4, distinction 44, question 3). This opinion is taken over by Alberius in his speech "On the Resurrection," where he advances the argument that "they shall be raised up composed of the four elements as new material for the human being, so that their identity will not be in the material but in the form." For it is wrong that the numerical identity of a person is contained by the identity of the soul alone and by the identity of the prime, bare matter, because for that identity the same soul must necessarily be present, the same human body and the same flesh and bones, an identity that also requires the same arrangements of the prime matter for the soul, through which it has its peculiar arrangement in respect of this soul which informs this body, and in this way the secondary material is brought about, material which is assigned to this form.

30. For if those final arrangements, and consequently also the same body, were not reproduced, it would not be the same person, because this person is substantially made up of this soul, and also from this body and from this flesh and bones, which do not exist without these final arrangements. Otherwise, a genuine resurrection of the very same people would have happened in the transmigration of souls from some bodies into other bodies (which the Pythagorean philosophers made up and which even some of the Jews believed), because in that transmigration of souls, there would remain the same soul of the person who had died before, and the same prime matter, of all sorts of bodies, would be everywhere. And to be sure, if the identity of the soul is required for the identity of the person, then the identity of the body is required for the same reason, since a person consists not of a soul only but of a soul joined together with a body.

31. These are the observations about the "subject in which," as they call it. It follows now that we speak about the "subject which," i.e., concerning the persons who will be raised up again. The last day will find all people altogether, who either are still alive or who have died. Concerning those who will be found living, one can ask whether or not they will be raised up, since they have not perished. For since Christ is called "the one whom God appointed as judge of the living and the dead" (Acts 10:42), if all people truly died then this distinction would appear pointless. The apostle certainly seems to hint at such a distinction in 1 Cor 15:51 and 1 Thess 4, because (to use the words of Tertullian in *On the Resurrection of the Body*, chapter 41), "by a way shorter than death, which will be destroyed in the change" those who then are found living shall not die but shall put off mortality and put on immortality "in a moment, in the twinkling of an eye, when they shall be caught up together with those who are being raised up" [1 Thess 4:17]. For the passage of the apostle which provides the strongest proof of this, 1 Cor 15, has various readings in the Greek and Latin codices; yet a comparison of it with the other passage in 1 Thessalonians 4 hardly permits a different reading than the one which the Greek [codices] adopted, and with which wording also the apostle's introductory statement very strongly agrees: "Behold, I tell you a mystery" [1 Cor 15:51]. And the concluding statement would not fit, *pantes men oun koimēthēsometha* ("we all therefore sleep"), when *ou* ('not') is changed to *oun* ('therefore'). In writing on this passage William Estius, professor at Douai, was right to consider this reading suspect.

32. Therefore, the customary reading of the Greek [codices] seems more likely to be true: "We shall not all sleep, but we all shall be changed," despite the vain objections by Catharinus and Stapleton, who contend that the passage is corrupt, and to which the latter even adds an irreverent interpretation. Estius says: "But the reading of the Greek codices is not at all an unlikely one, but actually in many ways the probable one; so far is it from the truth that whoever follows or recommends it should be charged with rash impudence of the same sort that is alleged in his commentary by Catharinus, who himself rather should be condemned for his inconsiderate opinion in this matter." Moreover, all the ancient Greeks whose works we possess from this reading draw the conclusion that not all people shall die, and therefore that not all shall be raised up again (strictly speaking). This opinion received favorable support from some of the Latin writers like Tertullian (*On the Resurrection of the Body*, chapters 41 and 42) and Jerome (*Letter to Marcella*).

Estius admits there is nothing risky in this interpretation. Augustine, as is his custom in matters which are not clearly certain, states discreetly: "For either they shall not die, or, in the very quick change from this life to death and then from death to eternal life, like the twinkling of an eye, in the transition they shall not feel death" (*Retractions*, book 2, chapter 33). The author of the book *On Ecclesiastical Doctrines*, chapter 7 [states]: "Because there are other, equally orthodox and learned men who believe that while the soul remains in the body those people shall be changed to incorruption and immortality who at the Lord's coming will be found alive, and for them this will be counted as a resurrection from the dead because they shall put off mortality by means of the change, and not by means of death: Whichever means one finds acceptable, he is not heretical."

33. We are of the opinion also that neither of the two views should be condemned in those people who commonly hold that "according to the law of the church it is enough to believe that there will be a resurrection of the dead." We affirm this about each and every person who has died, both good and evil, with the exception of no-one. For the resurrection will take place in order that all people will be judged, and "each person may receive the things proper to the body, whether it be good or bad" (2 Cor 5:10). Since the judgment and the retribution will be for all people, there will also be a resurrection of all people. Thus, in John 5:28 all people who are in the graves and who will be raised up are divided into those who have done good and those who have done evil. And Acts 24:15: "And we have the same hope which they also have, that there will be a resurrection of the righteous and of the wicked." This passage shows that also the Jews of Paul's time, whereas they did not believe in the Christ, nevertheless considered the doctrine of the resurrection of the righteous and the wicked as true and certain, contrary to what is thought by the Jews of today, who consider it an age-old tradition that "only the righteous will be raised up again, while the wicked will disappear entirely and will be covered over in eternal darkness, never to return to life," as is reported by Buxtorf, *The Jew's Synagogue*, chapter 1. Several indications of this error are found in the more recent writings of the Jews, although they are not in collusion to the point of speaking with one voice.

34. The adherents of Socinus speak equivocally also about the resurrection of the wicked, for they say that "it should be ascribed to the sacred writings rather than to their own opinion if anyone concludes that the wicked shall not live forever from the fact that only the pious shall live forever is drawn

from the inner recesses of Holy Scriptures, which comfort the pious with the sole promise of eternal life" (Smalcius, *Refutation of the Theses of Frantz,* page 409), and on page 415, he also says: "There is nothing anywhere in the sacred Scriptures which furnishes proof that the wicked shall become immortal, namely to their eternal disgrace, and it appears that from them nothing can be adduced from which that view can be demonstrated." He had said previously that "he and his followers had never openly promoted that view." That is to say, as they state elsewhere, it is possible for the time being to say some things which suggest this view to people, until finally the time is ripe, and people have grown accustomed to this manner of speaking. But whatever those people think or reveal in words about the matter, it is clear that the view which denies that the wicked shall be resurrected and endure forever by that same effort does away with "the eternal fire prepared for the devil and his angels" (Matt 25:41 and 45), "the unquenchable fire" (Matt 3:12), "the worm of the wicked that will not die" (Mark 9:43). For it is impossible that those who are not going to endure eternally should undergo eternal punishment.

35. And in response to the points that are made against us we should observe in general that just as the word 'life,' even though it makes no distinction between life that is good or bad, or between life that is happy or wretched, nevertheless sometimes is taken strictly in such a way that it means a suitable, happy, and desirable life, as when the poet says "it is not living but living well." In the same manner as we state in the Creed that we believe life everlasting, so also "resurrection" in the sacred writers is often understood only in a good sense, so that it denotes a life whereby one arises to a life that is blessed. What is more, "resurrection" is properly speaking said about the life that really overcomes death, obviously meaning that a life follows which is more desirable than death. Since this is not the resurrection of the sort that the wicked will have, because their souls will receive their own bodies again in order to be punished more severely, and for them it would be better to not rise up again rather than to rise up to such a state, hence it follows that Scripture speaks about the wicked in such a way as though they never shall be recalled to life, by which is understood a life that is happy and desirable. Therefore, we should consider the expression "eternal life" in such a way that it means, firstly, life according to the essence of the living creature as such; secondly, with respect to the living creature's relation to the eternal principle of life, that is, God, who accordingly in the Scriptures is called life everlasting.

With respect to that essential life, the wicked will live forever; with respect to the other mode, only those who are righteous in Christ Jesus shall live victoriously.

36. Questions about babies who have died in their mothers' womb, about miscarried fetuses, the malformed and similarly abnormal babies can be duly resolved once the hypothesis is laid concerning the infusion of the soul. For either the bodies truly were animate with a human soul, or they were not animate. If the former, then the resurrection applies to them, too. If not, then consequently excluded from the resurrection are such bodies to which the definition of human being does not apply. We do, however, agree with Augustine's opinion that bodies with defects will be raised up in such a way that their nature will be set right and made sound. And "each and every single birth which is called monstrous because it has something superfluous or lacking, or because it is horribly misshapen, will through the resurrection be restored to the form of its human nature" (*Enchiridion to Laurentius*, chapter 87).

37. And with the same Augustine we do not hesitate to assert that at the resurrection the difference between the sexes will remain. This is rightly gathered from the fact that Christ, when he was asked whose wife, she will be of the seven brothers who each had had her as spouse, did not state that there would be no women in the resurrection—which if that were true would have been a very short answer—but he stated only that there will be no marriages. In fact, he even confirmed that the female sex will exist by saying "they shall not be married," which applies to women, and "they shall not take as wives," which applies to men [Matt 22:25–30]. Therefore, both those for whom it is customary here to be married, and those for whom it is customary here to take as their wives will exist, but they will not have marriages there (*On the City of God*, book 22, chapter 17). And from this it follows that the same body in number must arise, as was demonstrated above, which would not be possible unless it had the same individual conditions, of which not the least is the determination of one's sex. To this can be added the fact that at the resurrection the individual nature will not be done away with, nor the species in their perfection or wholeness, but only the defects of the nature, among which we should not put the difference between the sexes.

38. The question also arises whether each of the following will be set straight: every body that is deformed because of a defect in a useful body part or in

the equal number [of body parts]; or because of the addition of a hindersome body part; or because of an awkward location of body parts. These questions, like that pertaining to people's physical stature, because they do not have an explicit answer in Holy Scripture, are answered only by conjectures of probability, which some give differently from others. And so, we think that nothing certain can be determined about them; but we do think only this is true that in the glorified bodies of whatever sex or stature God will remove everything that caused them some deformity. But as far as the wicked are concerned, "we should not weary our minds with uncertainties about the appearance of those whose damnation will be certain, and eternal" (Augustine, *Enchiridion*, chapter 92).

39. The form of the resurrection can be considered in two ways: As internal or external, and the former again either with a view to those who will be raised up strictly speaking, or with a view to those who will be changed. Both of these can be understood well enough from what has been said, namely that the form of the resurrection of the former consists in re-forming their bodies from the dust of the earth, and in the renewed indestructible union of their souls with their revived bodies. In this regard the final resurrection differs from that particular one of Lazarus and people like him. But regarding those people who are alive, we have stated above that towards them God's action will be engaged in their instantaneous, sudden change whereby it is not the actual substance of the body that will be abolished, but its quality will be altered. And whatever is subject to decay and death will take on an imperishable and immortal nature; that change, will for them be in lieu of their death and resurrection (1 Cor 15:51; 1 Thess 4:15 and 17).

40. The outward form of the resurrection will consist of that manner and order which Christ will follow, namely that suddenly he will appear on the clouds in the visible form wherein he ascended into heaven, and he will take his seat upon his majestic throne. And he will have his angels as his servants and attendants who will blow the trumpet, and with his powerful and effective voice he will issue a sound with which he will rouse all who are asleep in the dust, and he shall cause them to stand before his judgment seat, and he will draw into his presence also the living who have been changed, along with the others, and he will divide them both into two separate groups for sentencing (which we shall treat in the description of the judgment). All these points are derived from Matt 13:41; 24:30; 25:31; John 5:28 and 29; 1 Cor 15:1; 1 Thess 4:15, 16, 17, etc.

41. The primary and ultimate goal of the resurrection is the glory of God, who works all things for his purpose (Prov 16:4), in the same way as He established all things for his glory at the beginning. To this goal belongs also seeing the glory peculiar to Christ the Mediator in his work of resurrection. But regarding the people who are going to be revived, their common goal is that of standing before the judgment seat of Christ in order to hear the verdict of the judge. And regarding those who believe, the proper goal is their everlasting glory as a reward that will be bestowed upon them by his mercy, freely given. But with regard to unbelievers and the wicked, [the proper goal is] their eternal shame as punishment that they must bear from God's just retribution (Dan 12:2; John 5:28–29; Jude verse 15; 2 Thess 1:6–7).

42. There are many uses for this doctrine. For in the first place our minds are impressed by such an important article of the faith that they retain it forever; and we also have a possession whereby we may present ourselves over against each and every opponent more readily and steadily in asserting such an important doctrine. But besides the theoretical benefit, with a view to both ourselves and others, the practical one will be very useful if we, stimulated by the promise of the future life, defy whatever hardships there are in this current life, and so defy even death itself—whether it is an ordinary death, or even (if need be) a death inflicted for a confession of the truth—with great courage so that we are (as it were) rendered blind to the dangers and punishments of this life, that we soothe the grief that arises from the death of our friends (1 Thess 4:13), and that we present our bodies—which in due time shall be raised up to immortality—as weapons of righteousness for God, and so that in this way "he who wishes not to be condemned in the second resurrection rises in the first resurrection" (Augustine, *On the City of God*, book 20, chapter 6).

43. On the basis of this doctrine, too, we should be stimulated to treat the bodies of the deceased, which are asleep in the hope of the resurrection, with modest and decent care, as was done in former times by those who wished by means of this burial rite to testify to their faith in God's promises, choosing for themselves even a location where this would be noticed by others in their time. And when Christ and the apostle Paul, in order to strengthen the hope of the resurrection, compared the bodies of those who died righteously to seeds that are sown in the earth, they showed enough that they should be placed carefully in the earth (John 12:14; 1 Cor 15:37). In this matter, we should denounce the contempt shown by those who allow the

bodies of the deceased to lie unburied (except when it happens to some people because of a just decree of the state); in the same way we also reject every superstition of the sort frequent among the followers of the pope in their care for the dead: The extravagant, pointless luxury of the kind displayed with exceeding ostentation by many people in lavishly preparing their funerals, considering it callous, because they are actually changing mourning into magnificence, and with their ostentatious pomp as it were making sport of human misery.

44. Meanwhile if through the tyranny of the wicked it should befall the upright that their bodies are hindered from being buried, or if they are dug up after they have been buried (something which occurs often in the pope's realm, as once upon a time following some conspiracy the Donatists "did not allow the bodies of the orthodox to be buried, but in order to frighten the living, they maltreated the deceased by denying them a place for burial," in Optatus, *Against Parmenius*, book 6), then let that passage of Ps 34:21[20] provide help: "The Lord protects all the bones of the upright;" and also what it says in Rev 20:13: "The sea and death some day will give up their dead." To which should be added what Augustine says: "The bodies of many Christians were not buried in the earth, but none of them has been removed by anyone from heaven or earth—which are entirely filled by the presence of Him who knows whence He shall bring back to life whatever He has created" (*On the City of God*, book 1, chapter 12).

On the Last Judgment

45. In the fundamental principles of the Christian doctrine by the apostle in Heb 6:2, the following two are joined together: The resurrection of the dead and everlasting judgment. And among the other arguments for the resurrection one of the more important ones was taken from God's justice, which requires that everyone stand "before the judgment seat of Christ, and each shall receive in the body what is due to him for the things he has done, whether good or bad" (2 Cor 5:10). And so it follows that we should speak about that judgment, but only with a few words because we have touched on most of its circumstances in the related material on the resurrection. And as for the judgment, we understand it not as the particular judgment which God carries out in this life or at each person's death, which can be called the antecedent, partial, and hidden judgment, but the universal, final, total, eternal, and manifest judgment, which will take place on that last day after

the universal resurrection, which Jude verse 6 calls "the judgment of the great day;" 2 Pet 3:12 "the day of the God;" and Paul in Rom 2:5 (with respect to the reprobate) "the day of wrath," and Eph 4:30 "the day of redemption" (with respect to the upright), just as, in Acts 3:20, it is called the time "of refreshment" and "the restitution of all things" (verse 21).

46. We understand that among the gentiles there was a somewhat mixed perception of this day and judgment, either because they wisely understood that God's justice requires a judgment of this sort, or because they were convinced from the dictates of what is honorable and what is base divinely implanted in the human heart and from the witness borne by their own consciences that at some future time it would go well for the good and badly for the wicked. Or even because something in the teaching of the church reached their ears—a perception which they obscured and corrupted with many myths. And therefore, it can be said that this mystery is beyond natural knowledge and must be believed by faith to the extent that it is revealed to us in the Word, wherein the clearest explanations are provided about its future existence and all of its causes, circumstances, and benefits, and whatever else is worth knowing. About its existence, there are almost countless testimonies in the two Testaments, but two are especially clear— Acts 17:31: "God has appointed a day on which He will judge the lands of the earth with justice," etc., and 2 Thess 1:6[–9]: "It is right for God to recompense trouble for those who trouble you, and to you who are troubled rest with us, when the Lord Jesus will be revealed from heaven with his mighty angels in flaming fire taking vengeance on those who do not know God, and who do not obey the Gospel of our Lord Jesus Christ, who will be punished with everlasting destruction, away from the presence of the Lord and from the glory of his might."

47. The primary efficient cause of this judgment, when we consider the authority in the pronouncement of the verdict, or the power in carrying it out, is God the Father, the Son and the Holy Spirit. But that judgment will be administered in visible form through the Son in the human nature he has assumed, "through him whom God has appointed, giving proof of it to all men by raising him from the dead" (Acts 17:31). "All authority in heaven and on earth has been given to him by the Father" (Matt 28:18); "all judgment" (John 5:22). For this reason, that judgment is attributed in Scripture particularly to Christ the God-and-man, although not exclusively or in opposition [to someone else], but through some appropriation, because he

who appears to people in judgment will be none other than the Son, who will be made manifest while the Father is hidden, as Augustine says in *Treatise 21 on John*. Moreover, he will judge not only by his divine nature but also by his human nature, to which by grace autocratic power is given. Against that [power] there is no appeal, because by his death he has obtained for himself the right of dominion over all people. "For this very reason Christ died and returned to life, so that he might have dominion over the living and the dead" (Rom 14:9). And part of that dominion is the judgment.

48. On this point we should make the observation that in the judgment some elements can be considered as not going beyond the power of Christ's human nature, such as the fact that Christ, as man, is Lord of all and superior over all; and the fact that he knows everything that is necessary for carrying out that judgment justly, through a created knowledge in his soul (which is called the knowledge of the union). If one looks at these elements only as they are in the person of the judge with his outward public declaration of the verdict, then they proceed from his human nature as from the formal principle. But if one considers that infinite power whereby Christ will render everlasting rewards to the righteous and everlasting punishment to the wicked—which consist in the contemplation of his divine nature or the privation of it—then it is not as man but as God that he, along with the Father and the Holy Spirit, will judge the living and the dead, because in an absolute sense it belongs only to his divine power to make people blessed or wretched. Hence in Matt 20:23 Christ says: "It is not mine to grant you to sit at my right hand, but it is prepared for them by my Father." That is, it does not belong to my human authority, as Augustine explains in *On the Trinity*, book 1, chapter 12. In this sense he says in the same place that it is not by his human authority that the Son of Man is going to judge, but only by the authority which he has as the Son of God.

49. But, whether we have in view the supremely pre-eminent human authority granted to Christ over all created beings or his divine power (both of which he will exercise in judging), it is not in partnership with either of them that the saints and believers can be said "to rule with Christ." And so when it says that they will be seated and will judge, together with Christ (whether they are apostles or all believers, Matt 19:28, Luke 22:30), it should not be taken to mean the authority or power to judge which they have in and of themselves, but 1) about what they are going to do in Christ their head; 2) about their approval of the verdict which Christ has handed down (Rev 19:1); 3) about

the witness they bear from the point of view of their service and preservation, and in comparing their life with that of the wicked, whereby the justice of the judge will be made manifest.

50. The "matter concerning which," or the object of the final judgment are— if we are viewing the persons—all the wicked angels and all good as well as bad human beings. For although the evil spirits were subjected to punishments from the very moment they fell and were condemned to everlasting damnation, and although they always carry their own underworld with them wherever they go, nevertheless we do not doubt that they, whom "God has pushed down in hell, handed over to chains of darkness, and kept for" (2 Pet 2:4; Jude 6) will receive the full complement of their punishment on that day, when they no longer will be able to harm human beings, to extort from their slaves worship as if they were gods, because they will be so bound up in their underworld prison that no further escape will be open to them. To this point, we should refer what the apostle says in 1 Cor 6:3: "Do you not know that we shall judge the angels?"—a statement we should understand as judging in Christ the head.

51. And as far as it pertains to the human beings about whom especially, we should be concerned in this question, they all will be judged, from the greatest to the least, with no exception—but the good only by the judgment of distinction, and the wicked by the judgment of condemnation. "For we shall all stand before the judgment seat of Christ" (2 Cor 5:10). John explicitly distinguishes "great and small" (Rev 20:12) and he includes both of them among those people who are to be judged, so as to make no exception for anyone. So too for "the living and the dead" (Acts 10:42). Nor is an exception made for saints: "Set aside for me is the crown of righteousness which the Lord, the just judge, will grant to me on that day" (2 Tim 4:8). And the same time is given for the bestowing of the reward to the servants of God, and for the destruction of those who destroy the earth (Rev 11:18). Therefore, we should understand the statements that believers "will not be judged" and "shall not enter into judgment" [John 5:24] as being about the condemnation. But if the wicked "will not be raised up in judgment" [Ps 1:5], we should refer that to their remaining steadfast under judgment, because they will lose their case.

52. To the object of that judgment pertains also every act of all good as well as evil people, and every good as well as evil act, which includes their words

and thoughts; the manifestation of them all on the future day of judgment is indicated by the opening of the books (Rev 20:12). And then "concerning every idle word which they have spoken people will give an account on the day of judgment" (Matt 12:35). For the good deeds will be approved and will be given the freely bestowed reward, whereas the wicked deeds will be disapproved and judged worthy of punishment. There is no exception for the sins of the upright, for which they have received forgiveness through Christ, and at that time their sins will be revealed also, but in such a way that they will not cause them any consternation but rather immeasurable joy from the fact that just as many as are the forgiven sins which will be revealed, so much will be revealed the greatness of God's mercy towards them. And so, there will be no record of sins for punishment, or for the removal of their glory, but for the giving of thanks.

53. The form of this judgment will consist: 1) in the knowledge of the case; and for it, the judge will have "no need of anyone to bear witness about man, for he knows what is in man" (John 2:25). And moreover, he will need no examination of witnesses, or personal confession by guilty parties—"all things are naked and open to his eyes" (Heb 4:13)—but rather, so that the case might be clearly understood by others he will place every secret and hidden thing into the clearest light (1 Cor 4:5). [It will consist] [2)] in deciding the case once it is known and in declaring the verdict. The first part of this verdict, which concerns the righteous, will be most pleasant: "Come, you blessed of my Father, and inherit the kingdom prepared for you from the foundation of the world." But the second part will be by far most sorrowful and horrible: "Depart, you accursed ones, into the eternal fire prepared for the devil and his angels" (Matt 25:34 and 41). The delivery of the verdict will be preceded by a separation of the sheep from the goats, and in putting the former to the right and the latter to the left side (Matt 25:32 and 33).

54. [3)] Thirdly, the form of the judgment is considered in the execution of the verdict that has been handed down. And it will not consist of the upright beginning to enjoy blessedness for the first time, or of the wicked paying the everlasting penalty. For the upright shall be blessed already through their resurrection in the glorious body which they take on, and of the wicked, on the other hand, being accursed in the shameful body they take on. But, it will consist of the righteous in heaven (whereto they will set forth with Christ) beginning to enjoy blessedness with a certain public, solemn declaration, and thereupon at a specific, appointed place, and on the other hand, with the

wicked beginning to be punished in hell (whereto they will be banished), according to that statement: "And they shall go into the everlasting fire, but the just into everlasting life" (Matt 25:46). And in the execution of his verdict, the authority and truthfulness of the judge are manifested, just as his truthfulness and wisdom are manifested in the enquiry, and his justice in the declaration of the verdict.

55. The ultimate goal of that judgment will be "that God will be glorified in his saints, and admired in all those who believe on that day" (2 Thess 1:10). And also, that when the truthfulness in his justice towards all the wicked is revealed, "all nations shall come and worship before him, because his judgments will be revealed" (Rev 15:4). And a subordinate goal will be the salvation and blessed state of the upright, the banishment of the wicked, the liberation of Christ's church, the execution of the eternal decree, and the declaration of God's justice upon the reprobate and of his mercy upon his chosen ones.

56. It cannot be determined from Holy Scripture what the special place is where the upright and the wicked will be gathered. For what the Jews, whom the papal teachers follow, contrive about the valley of Jehoshaphat does not rest upon any solid foundation. But we should understand the citation of Joel 3:2 and 12 figuratively: "I shall gather together all nations and I shall lead them into the valley of Jehoshaphat;" unless someone prefers to take the valley of Jehoshaphat, i.e., [the valley] of God's judgment, in an appellative sense for each and every place where God will carry out his judgment. For in the same chapter, it is called the "valley of decision" [Joel 3:14]. And as far as the time is concerned, "it is in vain that we strive to calculate and fix the years which still remain to this age; since we hear from the mouth of truth that it is not ours to know," as Augustine well advises us in *The City of God*, book 18, chapter 53, pondering the fact that Christ explicitly prohibited the investigation of it (Acts 1:7). And the apostle, being instructed in paradise [2 Cor 12:4], deemed it not at all necessary to write about the "times and seasons" of the Lord's coming (1 Thess 5:1). Therefore, because the appointed place and the set time lie hidden in the storehouses of God's wisdom, an enquiry into them would be foolish. And those people who have made assumptions about the time have been proven guilty of folly by God from by so frequently contrary outcome of events which followed. It was God's will to conceal one day, so that all days might be observed and that no people might fall asleep on the pillow of complacency.

57. From the things that have been said, a definition of the last judgment can be drawn up as such, that it is an act of God through Christ the God-and-man whereby, at the end of the ages, He will summon all people, both living and dead, to his seat of judgment, and He will reveal everything that they have done, both good and evil, so that following the separation of the just and the unjust He will render a verdict and enforce it according to the norm of the Law and the Gospel, by causing the upright to be blessed forever; and by adjudging the wicked together with the devils unto everlasting punishments, for the glory of his name and for the everlasting joy of his chosen ones.

58. There are many uses for this doctrine: 1) That we fortify our belief in Christ's last coming over against the blasphemous scoffers (about whom 2 Pet 3:3 writes), and so with faith in our hearts and the profession upon our lips we separate ourselves from all who either stubbornly deny that judgment or overturn the sound doctrine of it. But we should apply it [2)] especially in our own practice over against unholy living and complacency, "that we fear the Lord because the hour of his judgment is coming" (Rev 14:7); over against carousing and drunkenness (Luke 21:34); "lest that day should come upon us suddenly," contrary to the too many cares of this life (Luke 21:34); and, in short, every injustice and sin. [We should apply it in our own practice] so that we might, on the other hand, be roused to repentance, seeing that "God has appointed a day on which He will judge the lands of the earth in equity" (Acts 17:30–31). And [3)] also to rouse us to acts of kindness towards our neighbors [Phil 4:5], especially the poor—which kindness the great Judge on that day will deem as having been done to him [Matt 25:40]. And [4)] lastly, to rouse in us comfort and patience in every adversity, being mindful that day for the upright is called the day of deliverance, so that in anticipation of it "we raise up our heads" (Luke 21:28). And that in faith we continually repeat, with John (Rev 22:19), "yes, come Lord Jesus."

ON LIFE AND DEATH
EVERLASTING AND ON
THE END OF THE WORLD

President: Antonius Walaeus
Respondent: Franciscus Boogardus

This disputation deals with the doctrine of the last things. Life everlasting requires not only faith, but also a living, personal trust (2). It is 'man's everlasting blessedness and happiness which arises from the fellowship or never-ending communion of God with us' (3). Through faith and communion with God in Christ, eternal life has already begun on earth; this life will culminate in the beatific vision of God (4–8). This perfect blessedness of the human being and inexpressible joy reaches its final state after the resurrection (8–9), and consists in beholding God in full, in conjunction with the complete sanctification and glorification of our nature (10). Various aspects of the beatific vision are discussed (11–24). The full restoration and sanctification of the whole human being is the inextricable result of the beatific vision (25–27). The same goes for the complete glorification of the human body and the entire human being (28–30). All of this together brings unspeakable joy (31–32). This blessedness will yet be perfected (33) by the everlasting quality of this blessed life (34), the loveliness of heaven (35–37), and fellowship with the saints and the angels (38–44). Next, eternal death is pictured in contrast with eternal life (45–53). The new earth and new heaven, finally, do not entail the destruction and replacement of the present earth and heaven but a qualitative change to them (54–60). The very last thesis (60) refers to the very beginning, when God created the heavens and the earth: 'And thus once again from that same vast lump, God is going to summon up new heavens and a new earth, i.e., the blessed habitation, which will be suited to the uses of the future age. And those uses were partly explained when we gave a treatment of life everlasting, but will be fully and clearly perceived by us when we really shall be the possessors and dwellers of this new heaven and new earth.'

1. Having explained everything that leads to mankind's final end, it remains for us in this final disputation to treat that last end itself for man, and also the outermost consummation of the whole world.

2. In the Apostles' Creed the final goal of man is called life everlasting, and it is placed opposite everlasting death, although this second goal is therefore not counted among the articles of the faith because the Creed draws our attention to the fruit of faith only, and not also to the fruit of unbelief. And because it draws our attention to the fruit of those objects of faith only, concerning which we must not just believe from Holy Scripture that they are true, but of which also the particular application to the human heart by a living, personal trust is required.

3. To be sure, by life everlasting is meant here not the everlasting and unbroken reunion of body and soul, for that will be shared in common with the reprobate; but man's everlasting blessedness and happiness which arises from the fellowship or never-ending communion of God with us. For in the same way as the soul is the life of the body, so too is God the life of the soul. Hence also the prophet David says in Ps 33:12: "Blessed are the people whose God is Jehovah," and the apostle in 1 John 1:3: "What we have seen and heard we declare to you, so that you may have fellowship with us, and that our fellowship might be with the Father and his Son Jesus Christ."

4. And this fellowship with God has two modes: Either through faith during this life it is inchoate, or perfect in the future life by sight (properly speaking). Accordingly, the apostle makes a distinction in 2 Cor 5:7 when he says: "We walk by faith not by sight"—although he also attributes sight to faith, albeit dimly (1 Cor 13:12).

5. The fellowship we have with God through faith is some beginning of that life everlasting, which will have its fulfillment in the future and which is approximately expressed by 'the adoption as children': "For as many as have received Christ by faith, to them He gave this right or worthiness to be children of God" (John 1:12).

6. And this beginning of life everlasting includes: 1) A living awareness of the forgiveness of our sins and our reconciliation with God; "for even when we

were dead in our sins, He made us alive together through Christ, by whose grace we have been saved, and He has raised us up together and has seated us together in heaven in Christ Jesus" (Eph 2:5–6). 2) Our being renewed according to the image of God, a renewal which the apostle therefore calls "of the newness of life" (Rom 6:4). And lastly, being sealed by the Holy Spirit, which not only confirms in us these prior gifts of the spiritual life and makes them vital, but also makes us certain of the future fulfillment, and produces in us that peaceful conscience and gladness of heart which the world does not know (John 14:17) and which surpasses every human understanding (Phil 4:7). Of this, the psalmist says: "When the poor see this they will rejoice, and your spirit will live, O you who seek God" (Ps 69:33). Indeed, because of all this Gal 2:20 says that we live by faith in the Son of God and that Christ dwells here in us.

7. But frequently these benefits are meant in the Scriptures also by the word "life everlasting," not only because it is to life everlasting that they lead, but also because they are some of its first fruits, just as Christ declares in John 6:57: "Truly, truly I say to you, whoever believes in me has life everlasting; I am that bread of life, etc.;" and chapter 11:25–26: "I am the resurrection and the life; whoever believes in me, even if he dies, shall live and whoever lives and believes in me will never die."

8. It is by sight that the fulfillment and consummation of this blessedness is obtained, and strictly speaking this pertains to the coming age, as the apostle testifies in 1 Cor 13:9; the blessedness is either (again) of the soul alone, separate from the body ("when we depart from here and go to take up our dwelling with Christ," 2 Cor 5:8) or of the entire person after the resurrection of the flesh and the last judgment, "when we shall be taken up to Christ in the air, and so we shall forever be with the Lord" (1 Thess 4:17).

9. As far as it concerns the former state (the one regarding the soul alone, separate from the body), we have given a fuller treatment of it when we dealt with the church triumphant in heaven, and so it is not necessary for us to treat it more fully here. Therefore, we next should offer a treatment of that second, final state of man after the resurrection.

10. And so this last, and perfect, blessedness of man consists in beholding God in full, in conjunction with the complete sanctification and glorification of our nature. An inexpressible joy is born from these mutually conjoined elements—a joy which goes beyond every human comprehension. In what

follows we are going to examine and explain the elements of this definition a little more closely.

11. The Scripture of the Old and New Testaments testifies in many places that beholding God is the foundation and cause of this blessedness as a whole. So, Job says in chapter 19:26: "I in my flesh shall see God;" David in Ps 16:11: "Fullness of joy in your sight," and in Ps 17:15: "In righteousness I shall behold your face; I shall be satisfied with your likeness, when I awake." And so Christ in Matt 5:8: "Blessed are the pure in heart, for they will see God." And 1 Cor 13:12: "Now we see as in a mirror, dimly, but then face to face." Likewise, 1 John 3:2: "We know that when He appears we shall be like Him because we shall see Him as He is."

12. Concerning this beholding the question arises firstly whether man will see God with his corporeal eyes, and secondly, if this beholding should be referred entirely to the soul, what the mode or manner of it will be.

13. As far as the first question is concerned, we approve the opinion of those who assert that God, when human beings are glorified, is indeed going to manifest his own majesty in a special way to their bodily eyes illumined with heavenly light—not only by certain signs (just as He sometimes revealed his presence to Moses and the prophets in an extraordinary way through signs), but especially in the human nature of Christ now made glorious; and through it, as an instrument conjoined to the divinity, He will show his divine properties and glory more fully and openly in order to be seen in some way. In the same manner He displayed some evidence of that matter in the glorification of Christ (Matt 17 and Luke 9) and also in those visions which were given to the apostle Paul, when he was taken up into Paradise (2 Cor 12), and often were given to the apostle John, when he was taken by the Spirit, in many places throughout the book of Revelation.

14. Meanwhile, however, we do assert that the beholding of God wherein the very essence of the highest good has its existence belongs, strictly speaking, not to the body but to the soul, because the spiritual essence is not visible to bodily eyes. Hence in Col 1:15 the apostle calls God, too, absolutely invisible. This is evident also from the fact that the souls of believers in heaven are already enjoying this blessedness of beholding God, and because the angels in heaven always are beholding the Father's face, even though they lack bodies. Similarly, and for the same reason, also the apostle interchanges the words "knowledge" and "beholding," and he clearly places this seeing face

to face over against knowing that is in part (1 Cor 13:12), and also over against faith (2 Cor 5:7).

15. The Scholastics hold many ingenious and elaborate disputations about the mode of this seeing, but we shall touch only on those which are based on the foundations of Holy Scripture or sound reasoning, and which relate to "edification in what is useful" [Eph 4:29], leaving the other, vain speculations to the authors of them.

16. And first, they hold disputations about whether the blessed are going to see the actual divine essence directly, or actually only some spiritual splendor and radiance of it. But our assertion is that whatever they make that splendor out to be, it must of necessity be something created and, therefore, distinct from God. But Scripture testifies that our blessedness consists in beholding God himself, as was shown above. And so, it says that "we are going to see Him face to face, and we shall know Him as He is, even as we are known" (1 Cor 13:12) and that "we are going to see Him as He is" (1 John 3[:2]). And clear reasoning also furnishes proof, because no thing that has been created can be our highest good, but only the uncreated God is able truly to fulfill and satisfy man's longing and mind.

17. From this the conclusion is rightly derived also that the blessed see God not even through some abstract or expressed image of Him, but through his essence. For knowledge that comes via an abstract image is imperfect knowledge, and it is necessarily imperfect because of the absence of the thing seen or because of its distance away from the intellect. But the essence of God is spiritual, and present to and conjoined with the minds of the blessed intimately. And therefore, that very essence, like an object with no element to intervene is able to represent itself easily to a man's mind, for which reason it says even of God himself that "God himself is going to be (i.e., directly) all in all" (1 Cor 15:28). We grant however that in man's very intellect an extraordinary light has to be imprinted whereby he is able to take hold of the divine essence as a beatific object by means of an intuitive seeing, in the same way as in this life there is need of supernatural light in man's intellect in order for us to be able to have true fellowship with God through faith, as the Scripture testifies in Matt 16:17, Acts 16:14, and 1 Cor 3:14. "For God who commanded the light to shine out of darkness has shined the light in our hearts to give the light of the knowledge of God in the face of Jesus Christ" (2 Cor 4:6). And it is customary to refer to this also the passage of the psalmist

in Ps 36:10: "With you is the fount of life, and in your light do we enjoy the light."

18. However, the Scholastics have the habit of debating rather copiously whether the blessed behold the divine essence with all its properties and workings, and this in its infinity. And also whether this vision is necessary, or instead voluntary, from the side of God. Concerning these questions, we have made the following determinations.

19. The matter itself suggests that God's infinite essence in its infinite state can be grasped adequately only by a mind that is infinite; but because God's infinite being everywhere is entire, for that reason the incarnation of God's Son shows that the entire essence can be united with a finite creature, and consequently, it does not conflict with nature that it can be perceived by a finite mind by means of a beatific vision. Indeed: The entire essence, albeit not entirely or in an infinite mode, but in a mode that is suited to the finite nature, as the passages of Scripture that were adduced in thesis 11 show. And therefore, it is said that the angels in heaven, although they always behold God's face, yet before the throne of God's majesty, they cover their faces with two wings lest they be destroyed by his majesty (Isa 6:2).

20. We assert then that the same vision (if it is regarded as active) and also its extent and mode depend only on God's will and free dispensation, not from some natural relationship or disposition of the object towards its own power. Accordingly, our Savior says in Matt 11:27: "No-one knows the Son except the Father, nor does anyone know the Father except the Son and anyone to whom the Son has chosen to reveal Him." And so, therefore, just as in this life He bestows his own spiritual gifts in different measure to people individually in accordance with his will (1 Cor 12:11), so too in the life to come every one of the blessed will perceive of it as much as it will seem good to God's gracious will and good pleasure, and it will be sufficient for their full blessedness. "For He has mercy upon whom He has mercy and He has compassion on whom He has compassion" (Exod 33:19).

21. But it is a harder question whether, in accordance with the extent to which the essence is shared, so too necessarily and naturally the extent of seeing the persons, attributes, and workings of God is shared.

22. The Scholastics are generally convinced that everything that in God is natural or that by the necessity of nature flows forth from his essence

necessarily is shared along with the essence, and so together with his essence also all of God's essential attributes are perceived intuitively, because God's essence is most simple and in reality, not different from his attributes. As the blessed see God just as He is, they therefore see also his attributes; accordingly, by beholding Him they break forth in adoration of his attributes in general, as can be seen in Isa 6 and in Rev 4 and 6. And they [the Scholastics] rightly conclude that the same reasoning goes for the persons, because although one person differs in reality from another, yet the person does not differ in reality from the essence, and just as the person of the Father by Himself and necessarily subsists in the divine essence, so also by natural necessity the person of the Son and the Holy Spirit are brought forth in that [essence]. Therefore, because the blessed see God just as He is, and in this life believers have fellowship with all three persons, it necessarily follows that in heaven the same fellowship is not stopped but brought to fulfilment. Hence in John 14:9 Christ also says: "Whoever sees me sees the Father," and "All that the Father has is mine" (chapter 16:15).

23. It follows, however, they conclude that the divine decrees are a different matter, and so too the workings thereof, which depend upon God's free decrees—like all the divine works that are called "outward works" because they are not in God by absolute necessity. As it is not by absolute necessity that He produces these outward works, but according to his own freedom, therefore it is not by absolute necessity that they are seen when God is seen, but [only] as much of them as it is in the will of God to reveal to anyone. Hence it is that the angels always see the Father's face and yet do not know the day of judgment (Mark 13:32), and only by an extraordinary revelation of God do they receive what according to his will they reveal to Christ's servants for the upbuilding of the church, as can be seen in Rev 1:1 and Rev 5:3.

24. And from these things it is also clear that the "mirror of the Trinity" which several papal teachers fabricate, as if in it the inward and outward needs and prayers of all humanity are reflected to the blessed in heaven, in no way accords with their more reasonable hypotheses, since all these workings are dependent on God's free decree. This is why God everywhere claims for himself the examination of the hearts and the certain knowledge of all the other things which depend upon contingent causes, along with his care for the world—as we have shown elsewhere when we treated the invocation of saints. And in fact, Holy Scripture expressly testifies that "just as no-one

knows the things in man except the spirit of man that is in him, so no-one knows the things in God except the Spirit of God" (1 Cor 2:11).

25. From this beatific vision of God, a beholding which surpasses all of man's comprehension, there necessarily is born the full restoration and sanctification of the whole man, so that in proportion to the blessed soul's gazing upon God face to face in his glory also man's heart must be kindled with love for him and with adoration of all his works.

26. This is shown firstly by the very nature of this beatific vision. For also here "all believers, with faces unveiled, are beholding God's glory as in a mirror, are changed into the same image from glory to glory," as the apostle states in 2 Cor 3:18. How much more will that glorious contemplation of God's essence seize man's will and all his other powers and faculties into concord with God's holiness and glory. It will be just as the sun shares its image and brilliance with the mirror which takes it in.

27. It is shown secondly by the whole tenor of Holy Scripture. For just as this beholding of God is promised only to those "who are pure of heart" (Matt 5:8), it is withheld from those "who have not been born again" (John 3:3) and also "from flesh and blood" (1 Cor 15:50). And because likewise into that heavenly Jerusalem "entry is denied to everything that is polluted or that works abomination or lies" (Rev 21:27), it follows necessarily that in that complete fruition of blessedness the whole man will be completely restored and sanctified. Hence also the apostle Peter promises in 2 Pet 3:13 that there will be "new heavens and a new earth in which righteousness will dwell;" and the souls of the blessed in heaven "are clothed in white robes and palms are placed in their hands" (Rev 7:9), as people who have conquered Satan, the world, and sin. And the bride of Christ herself when she will go into the bridegroom in order to make full celebration of the wedding feast, "is first arrayed in clean and white linen, which is the righteous acts of the saints" (Rev 19:8).

28. These two beatific benefits of God will even be followed by a third one: The complete glorification of the actual human body, and consequently of the entire human being. This glorification is indicated in the Scriptures partly by the removal of every imperfection and partly by the opposite affirmation of every sort of perfection.

29. Therefore, from the glorified man is removed not only everything that comes from sin or that has the character of punishment, but also whatever pertains to man's animate condition by virtue of the first creation in this world. And so Rev 21:4 asserts not only that "God shall wipe away every tear from their eyes and that death shall be no more, nor sorrow, nor crying, nor grief," and that "they shall hunger no longer, and thirst no longer, and the sun shall not smite them, nor any heat" (Rev 7:16), but also that "God shall do away with the stomach and with food" (1 Cor 6:13) and also that "in the resurrection, they will not lead into marriage nor be given into marriage, but they will be like the angels of God in heaven" (Matt 22:30).

30. And concerning the body, it is affirmed that "what is sown perishable will be raised imperishable; what is sown in dishonor will be raised in glory; what is sown in weakness will be raised in power; what is sown a natural body will be raised a spiritual body" (1 Cor 15:42[–44]); also that "this mortal will put on immortality" (verse 53). And it is affirmed that "as is that heavenly one, namely Christ, so also they shall be heavenly, and as we have borne the image of the earthly, we also shall bear the image of the heavenly" (verse 49). Indeed, "the righteous shall shine like the sun in the kingdom of their Father" (Matt 13:43). And "those who are wise shall shine as with the brightness of the firmament, and those who turn many to righteousness like the stars for ever and ever" (Dan 12:3). For "our citizenship is in heaven, from where we also expect our Savior, the Lord Jesus Christ, who will change our lowly body to be like unto his glorious body, according to the working whereby he is able to subject all things unto himself" (Phil 3:20[–21]).

31. And the final thing which we put in the definition of this heavenly blessedness is the inexpressible joy which here surpasses all of man's understanding.

32. For it could happen in no other way, when indeed the body of man is set free from every weakness of sin and nature and is in conformity with Christ's glorious body, and the soul is free of every struggle of the flesh and the spirit enjoys beholding the divine essence and glory, when indeed, I say, the whole man will be drenched with real comfort and his soul in inexpressible joy, just as Christ promised, "Blessed are those who mourn, for they shall receive comfort" (Matt 5:4), and David, "They shall feast on the abundance of your house, and you will make them to drink from the river of your pleasures" (Ps 36:8).

And this is the hidden manna which Christ promises to the victor (Rev 2:17); and indeed, this gladness will be so great that the apostle testifies that "no eye has seen, nor ear has heard, neither has entered into anyone's heart, what God has prepared for those who love him" (1 Cor 2:9). Even so, it is foreshadowed in some fashion in the Scriptures by the pleasures of the garden of Eden or Paradise, by the feast and merriment of the banquets and the royal weddings, by the delight and entertainment in the songs, musical instruments, and similar activities of this age whereby the heart of man is used to being filled with virtuous amusement and joy.

33. And although the very essence of blessedness exists in the things we have explained thus far, nevertheless some circumstances and accompanying things (which Holy Scripture everywhere joins to them) will in no small way cause it to be perfected in all its parts.

34. The first of these is the everlasting quality of this blessed life; for while the pagan philosophers themselves admit that full and real blessedness cannot exist alongside the fear of sometime losing it, Holy Scripture also sufficiently in this matter comes to bolster the certainty of those who are blessed: "Whoever is faithful even unto death, to him will be given the crown of life, and he who conquers will not be harmed by the second death," as Christ promises in Rev 2:10–11. And for that reason, everywhere in the sacred writings this blessedness is called everlasting life, the everlasting inheritance, and the everlasting kingdom. Boethius rightly defines that everlasting quality as "the complete and at the same time perfect possession of life that is without end," and for that reason it is called also by the apostle Peter "the inheritance which cannot perish, nor be defiled or fade away" (1 Pet 1:4) and the "unfading crown of glory" (chapter 5:4), and so it says that "they will reign with God forever and ever" (Rev 22:5).

35. Also the majesty and loveliness of the place makes no small contribution to it. The same apostle Peter testifies in the same passage (chapter 1:4) that this is heaven when he says "this inheritance is preserved for you in heaven"—by which heaven we do not mean this visible heaven in which the planets and the other stars can be seen, much less some everywhere-present and incorporeal heaven such as the Lutherans imagine, but that heaven which is called the throne of God, and which is the most glorious and resplendent heaven above all of these visible heavens, and which accordingly is called the third heaven, and Paradise (1 Cor 12), and which is placed above all the

heavens (Eph 4:10), the glory and splendor of which is very fully depicted by the figure of the heavenly Jerusalem and of the most lovely and precious things in this world in Revelation chapters 21 and 22.

36. But on this point we should not heed those who declare that heaven indeed will be the realm of the blessed souls until the time of the last judgment, but that afterwards the earth, having been set free from its slavery to corruption, and having been made glorious, will be granted as dwelling-place to blessed human beings, while heaven then will be reserved only for the angels. For Holy Scripture locates the entire and unfailing reward of the saints in heaven, as is seen in Matt 5:12, Luke 12:33, Heb 10:34. Secondly, because the actual kingdom of heaven is promised as the final reward for believers (Matt 5:10; likewise 19:14). Thirdly, because in contrast with earth heaven is called "our everlasting dwelling-place" (2 Cor 5:1) and "our citizenship" (Phil 3:20), and "our fatherland" (Heb 11:26). And so, we shall dwell there not only for a period of time and as sojourners, but in perpetuity. For otherwise believers who are going to die around the time of the ending of the world will spend only a brief time in that place, and those who are seized by the last day while they are alive shall enter that place never. All this is absurd and foreign to the truth of God's promises.

37. But in addition to what we have brought forward, Christ, too, clearly testifies the opposite in Matt 8:[11–]12 when he says: "those who believe from all peoples shall recline with Abraham, Isaac and Jacob in the kingdom of heaven; and the sons of the kingdom"—that is, the Jews—"shall be cast into the outer darkness, where there will be weeping and gnashing of teeth." And in John 14:2[–3], he declares to his disciples: "In my Father's house are many mansions; I go to prepare a place for you, and when I go and prepare a place for you I shall come again and shall take you unto myself, so that where I am you also may be." Likewise, Rev 3:21: "If anyone conquers, I shall grant him to sit with me upon my throne, even as I also overcame, and sit with my Father upon his throne." Hence it is what the apostle says in 1 Thess 4:17: "We who are alive, who remain, shall be taken up with them in the clouds to meet the Lord in the air" (that is, away from earth) "and so we always shall be with the Lord." Hence the same apostle calls the kingdom of Christ for which he himself has been kept "Christ's kingdom above the heavens" (2 Tim 4:18).

38. The third accompanying element which we should take into account in life everlasting is the company or fellowship of those who will be partakers of that same future happiness, a fellowship which Holy Scripture everywhere also promises to us as the crowning of blessedness.

39. For the blessed in heaven, although they shall fully rest in the enjoyment of God alone (Ps 73:25), they nevertheless will rejoice both in their own glory and blessedness and in that of the other believers. And in their midst Christ, as the Head of the church, even also as man, always will occupy the foremost place, as the apostle shows in 2 Cor 5:8 and Phil 1:23. Secondly there are the holy patriarchs, prophets and apostles, with whom it says we shall recline in the kingdom of heaven (Matt 8:11 and 19:28). And also the angels and their myriads are numbered among this company (Heb 12:22 and Rev 7:11). And lastly, there will be so great a multitude of believers that no-one will be able to number it (Heb 12:23 and Rev 7:9).

40. And on this point the question is asked whether there will be mutual recognition, conversation and interaction among the blessed. But while we should not make overly curious investigations beyond God's Word into the manner of these things, yet we do not doubt that on the basis of the trustworthy foundations of Holy Scripture that matter can be gathered and demonstrated sufficiently.

41. For Christ, the patriarchs, prophets and apostles, as was noted earlier, always will keep their special place, station and order in this gathering and festal assembly of the blessed. And Christ himself will always be that good shepherd who knows his own sheep and who is known by them (John 10). Moses and Elijah conversed with Christ and they were recognized by the apostles (Matt 17:7 and Luke 9:32). Abraham knew Lazarus (Luke 16). Wealthy believers will be welcomed into their everlasting dwellings by the poor believers whom they had treated well (Luke 16:9), and the believers at Thessalonica will be Paul's crown of glory on that day (1 Thess 2:19). Even the angels will know not only each other, but they will recognize also all the chosen ones on that last day and set them apart from those who are reprobate (Matt 13:41 and Mark 13:27). Paul, when he was taken up into Paradise, not only saw Christ but he also heard things which no human being can speak (2 Cor 12), and throughout the book of Revelation references are made to the specific order among the blessed angels and men, of conversation, of

doxology, and of the declaration of God's judgments and His benefits for each of them in particular.

42. And we state that the saints will employ not merely mental speech but also that of the voice; for the use of language will not be abolished, but perfected, as is clear enough from the preceding. It is not so certain as to which language the blessed will use, although it is certain that the variety of languages—which is a consequence of sin—will cease there, according to the apostle (1 Cor 13:18). Hence some also draw the not improbable conclusion that use of the Hebrew language will remain, because it is not a consequence of sin, and because Christ when he spoke to Paul from heaven even though the latter was originally Greek, used the Hebrew language, as the apostle explicitly observes in Acts 26:14.

43. There are also some who hold disputes about the clothing, because to human beings the angels always appeared in white and brilliant garments, and because Christ at his transfiguration with Moses and Elijah took on a brilliance not only in his body but also in his glorious garment, as the evangelists note in Matt 17:2 and Luke 9:29. However, a more probable sentiment is that of those who think that the blessed shall lack all clothing, and they hold that this was done only on account of the dispensation, lest naked bodies be exposed to the eyes of sinful people. But in the future age, when all the effects of sin shall cease, and nothing in the human body will be indecent or liable to shame, then the brilliance and majesty of the glorious body will far surpass all the splendor and majesty of clothes.

44. But we do hold, contrary to some people, that the difference in gender will remain entirely in the exact same way as God created human nature in the beginning, as Augustine rightly gathered from Christ's statement in Matt 22 and other places. And yet we do hold that the remaining maimings or imperfections of limbs or old age shall be removed from bodies, because Phil 3 states that our lowly bodies will be conformed to Christ's glorious body, and what is sown in weakness will be raised in power, as the apostle says in 1 Cor 15:42. And from him it is rightly concluded also that even that earthly heaviness and weight will be removed from their limbs, because the animate body will be rendered spiritual, and when Christ is coming from the highest heaven in as short a time as possible—as fast as lightning (as he himself says in Matt 24:27)—then we shall be taken to meet him in the clouds, as the apostles testifies in 1 Thess 4:17.

45. From the things that have been explained thus far about the nature and circumstances of life everlasting it can be sufficiently understood from the contrary what we should state about everlasting death, so that it is not necessary for us to be delayed with rehearsing all the little details. However, so that we might know the truth of it more precisely we are adding the following few observations.

46. First, that the opinion of the Socinians who are accustomed to defining everlasting death by the everlasting extinction of the body and the soul is blasphemous because Holy Scripture teaches in nearly countless places that everlasting death is accompanied by everlasting pains and torments, and that also the very conscience of criminal men is afraid of, and has foreboding feelings about, far different punishments and torments from an angry God.

47. Secondly, also erroneous is the opinion of the Origenists and some Anabaptists who imagined that there will at last come some ending to these torments. For in the Scriptures everlasting death and everlasting life are opposed to each other in one and the same sense, as is seen in Dan 12:2 and Matt 25:27[=41]. And so also in Luke 16:27 it is stated expressly by Abraham that it is impossible for anyone to cross over from the place of torments to the place of comfort. Similarly, in Mark 9:47, mention is made of "the worm which does not die and the fire which is not put out;" and hence in Rev 14:11 and 19:3 the Holy Spirit bears witness that "the smoke of their torment rises up for ever and ever, and they will have no rest, day or night."

48. Therefore, together with the whole orthodox church we state that everlasting death consists of those people being forever cast out from the presence of God and from the company of all the blessed ones into hell; and of a living, effective sense of the wrath of God against their impenitence (as that of a just judge), a wrath which rightly was aroused against them in keeping with the amount of their sins; hence there follows also the anguish and torment of conscience which will possess them forever.

49. In this definition the basis for this death is placed in those men being forever cast out from God's gracious presence, for Christ bears witness in Matt 8:12 that they "will be cast into the outer darkness, where there will be weeping and gnashing of teeth;" and chapter 25:41: "depart from me, you evildoers, into the everlasting fire which has been prepared for the devil and his angels." And therefore, it says in Rev 22:15: "outside will be the dogs, the

sorcerers and the sexually immoral, and murderers and whoever loves and practices falsehood."

50. And this being cast out from God's countenance will be joined to the everlasting torments of soul and body, and these not only will arise from the fact that those wretched people will see that they are deprived of all happiness—which they call the punishment of damnation—but also because they will realize in earnest God's wrath against their sins—which they call the punishment of the senses. In this manner the apostle says in Rom 2:8[–9]: "Wrath and anger, tribulation and anguish upon every soul of man who does evil." And to this may be referred also that everlasting fire which does not go out, and the worm which does not die—with which Christ threatens them in the passages cited earlier.

51. It is not necessary for us to enter into a disputation overly worrisome with the Scholastics about whether or in what way a real and corporeal fire thereafter is going to afflict them. It will suffice for us here that the force of their torments is going to be so great that "it would be better for those men if they had not been born" (Matt 26:24), and that arising merely from the fear and presentiment of their grief it says of the unrighteous that "they shall gnaw their tongues, and curse the God of heaven" (Rev 16:10[–11]), and that on that last day "they shall say in vain to the mountains and the rocks, 'fall on us, and hide us from the presence of Him who sits upon the throne, and from the wrath of the Lamb'; for that great day of his wrath is coming, and who shall be able to stand?"

52. But even though all the punishments of this second death will be everlasting, from that it does not follow that they will all be the same. Instead, just as there will be different degrees in life everlasting (according only to the different sharing of God's grace), so too the punishments in everlasting death will be different, in keeping with the different measure of men's sins and stubbornness that will be inflicted upon the unrighteous by God's just judgment. In this manner Christ himself testifies (Matt 11:[21–]22) that "it will be more bearable for Tyre and Sidon on that day of judgment than for those cities in which he displayed his powers, and they did not repent." Similarly, Luke 12:47: "Because that servant who knew the will of his master, and did not prepare himself or did not do according to his will, will be struck with many blows; but the one who did not know and did things deserving of blows will be struck with few."

53. The place destined for those people, just as it is for the devils, very often in Scripture is called Hades, that is, hell, or abyss, Gehenna, the pit of the abyss, or the lake burning with fire and sulfur, in order that from the very horror of the place the seriousness of the punishments can be grasped so much better. But we should not make an overly curious investigation into where the site of this place is, but rather into the way and manner whereby we are able to avoid it. In the meantime, however, just as we do not dare to disapprove the thinking of those who locate the place in the shadowy depths of earth and sea (because of the idea common to the previously-mentioned names; because it is everywhere placed opposite to the highest heaven; and because for the most part there is spoken of descending down to it), so also do we not wish to reject the thinking of Chrysostom, Luther, and more recently others, who think that it is situated beyond the visible world, and who accordingly judge that it is located beyond the heavenly Jerusalem (Rev 22:15) and is designated by the name of outer darkness (Matt 8:12 and 25:30).

54. And this is the future final condition of human beings, both the upright and the wicked, after the last judgment; and it will be followed immediately by the consummation and end of this visible world and so of the entire age, just as that angel "swears by him who lives for ever and ever, that time shall be no more" (Rev 10:6), and as the apostle [says]: "Then the end will come when Christ shall hand over the kingdom to [his] God and Father, when He will have put down all rule, and all authority and power" (1 Cor 15:24).

55. And although there were some philosophers—and Aristotle among them—who wrongly maintained that the universe is everlasting, nevertheless the Christian faith places it beyond controversy that just as it was established in the beginning out of nothing by God's word alone, so also will it again come to ruin in due time, just as the prophet says: "You in the beginning, Lord, have laid the foundations of the world and the heavens are the works of your hands. They shall pass away, but you remain, and all will grow old like a garment, and like clothing you will change them, and they shall be changed" (Ps 102:26). And Christ [says]: "Heaven and earth shall pass away, but my words will never pass away" (Luke 21:33).

56. And just as some ruination of the world occurred previously through the flood of waters, Holy Scripture testifies that so also the final ruination of the world will happen through the fire to come. And so Isa 66:15 says: "For behold, Jehovah is going to come with fire, and with his chariots like a

whirlwind, to render his anger with fury and his rebuke with flames of fire."
And the apostle Peter states even more clearly: "The heaven and the earth
which now exist and are kept in store by the same word, are preserved for
fire unto the day of judgment and the destruction of the wicked" (2 Pet 3:7).
But there is no agreement among theologians of what sort this future
ruination of the world through fire is.

57. For very many think that by this ruination of the world is meant nothing
other than a change in the qualities of this world, and liberation from slavery
to corruption which in the world now is a result of sin or even from the first
condition of the natural state of men. That is based on various places in
Scripture which only appear to indicate such a change, like Ps 102 where
Scripture uses the word "change;" and so Paul in 1 Cor 7:31 says "the outer
form of this world is passing away;" and 2 Pet 3:6 compares this final change
of the world to the destruction of the world through water—which would
not be a comparison if this world must be completely destroyed. But a
remarkable passage that they especially press forward is Rom 8:19, where the
apostle asserts: "the creature (or, the created world, as Beza renders it) with
eager longing looks for and expects the revelation of the sons of God," and
it adds the cause: "for the creature was made subject to vanity, not willingly,
but by reason of him who has subjected it to that vanity in the hope that also
the creature itself will be set free from slavery to corruption into the freedom
of God's children, etc." And in whatever way these words are translated, they
can be understood in no other way than about the makeup of this visible
world, which on account of man's sin is subject to slavery to corruption and
vanity, since in the same passage the apostle explicitly distinguishes this
creature from the sons of God, and it cannot be taken to mean the angels,
who are not subject to slavery to corruption.

58. Others, however, judge that this visible world is going to be completely
destroyed, and that another one is going to be put in its place. And [they
gather] that from the passages of Scripture in which it says that this world
will pass away, perish, and have a consummation and ending; and also that
time will be no more, etc.; but especially from the passages of Rev 20:11,
"From the presence of him who sits upon the throne the earth and heaven
flee away, and no place is found for them;" and of chapter 21:1: "I saw a new
heaven and a new earth, for the first heaven and the first earth had passed
away and the sea now was no more."

59. But these expressions seem to be reconciled very well by others, from the passage of Peter, 2 Pet 3:10 and following, where it, indeed, says that "the heavens will pass away with a great sound, and the elements will be dissolved with intense heat, and the earth and the works that are in it will be burned up"—but verse 12[–13] follows: "The heavens will be resolved with fire, and the elements shall melt away with intense heat, but we according to the promise look for new heavens and a new earth in which righteousness will dwell."

60. Namely in such a way, that this whole visible universe is going to be dissolved by that fire, turned into liquid, and purified of corruption and other impurities or effects of natural life, in the same manner as it is customary for different types of metals to be liquefied through fire, to be mingled together, and purified of their dross. And thus, once again from that same vast lump, God is going to summon up new heavens and a new earth, i.e., the blessed habitation, which will be suited to the uses of the future age. And those uses were partly explained when we gave a treatment of life everlasting but will be fully and clearly perceived by us when we really shall be the possessors and dwellers of this new heaven and new earth.

Bibliography

The titles in the following bibliography were selected for their pertinence to the *Synopsis of a Purer Theology* and its historical, theological, and ecclesiastical context. Only English texts are included.

Primary Source:

Synopsis Purioris Theologiae / Synopsis of a Purer Theology, Vol. 1–3. Trans. R. A. Faber; vol. 1 ed. D. te Velde; vol. 2 ed. H. van den Belt; vol. 3 ed. H. Goris. Leiden: Brill, 2014–2020.

Secondary Sources:

Asselt, van. W. J., Dekker, E., eds. *Reformation and Scholasticism. An Ecumenical Enterprise*. Grand Rapids: Baker Academic, 2001.

Asselt, van. W. J., et al. *Introduction to Reformed Scholasticism*. Grand Rapids: Reformation Heritage Books, 2011.

Asselt, van. W. J. "Reformed Orthodoxy: A Short History of Research," 11–26 in H. J. Selderhuis, ed., *Handbook of Dutch Church History*. Göttingen: Vandenhoeck & Ruprecht, 2015.

Asselt, van. W. J., and Abels, P. "The Seventeenth Century," 259–360 in H. J. Selderhuis, *Handbook of Dutch Church History*.

Belt van den. H., and de Vries-van Uden, M. "Herman Bavinck's Preface to the *Synopsis Purioris Theologiae*," *Bavinck Review* 8 (2017): 101–114.

Belt, van den. H. "Developments in Structuring of Reformed Theology: The *Synopsis Purioris Theologiae* (1625) as Example," 289–311 in H. J. Selderhuis and E.-Waschke, eds., *Reformation und Rationalität*. Refo500 Academic Studies, vol. 17. Göttingen: Vandenhoeck & Ruprecht, 2015.

Belt, van den. H., de Jong, K-W., and van Vlastuin, W. eds. *A Landmark in Turbulent Times. The Meaning and Relevance of the Synod of Dordt (1618–1619)*. Göttingen: Vandenhoeck & Ruprecht, 2022.

Boer, den. W. *God's Twofold Love: The Theology of Jacob Arminius (1559–1609)*. Trans. A. Gootjes. Reformed Historical Theology, vol. 14. Göttingen: Vandenhoeck & Ruprecht, 2010.

Broeyer, F. G. M. "Theological Education at the Dutch Universities in the Seventeenth Century: Four Professors on Their Ideal of the Curriculum," *Dutch Review of Church History* 85 (2005): 116–121.

Faber, R. A. "Intellectual Property in the Era of Reformed Orthodoxy: Questions of Authorship in the *Synopsis of a Purer Theology*," *Westminster Theological Journal* 82.1 (2020): 61–75.

Faber, R. A. "Scholastic Continuities in the Reproduction of Classical Sources in the *Synopsis Purioris Theologiae*," *Church History and Religious Culture* 92.4 (2012): 561–579.

Faber, R. A. "The Function of the Catechism's Spirituality in the *Synopsis of Purer Theology* (1625)," 84–94 in A. Huijgen, ed., *The Spirituality of the Heidelberg Catechism: Papers of the International Conference on the Heidelberg Catechism Held in Apeldoorn 2013*. Refo500 Academic Studies, vol. 24. Göttingen: Vandenhoeck & Ruprecht, 2015.

Fesko, J. V. "Lapsarian Diversity at the Synod of Dort," 99–123 in M. Haykin and M. Jones, eds., *Drawn into Controversie: Reformed Theological Diversity and Debates Within Seventeenth-Century British Puritanism*. Reformed Historical Theology, vol. 17. Göttingen: Vandenhoeck & Ruprecht, 2011.

Goudriaan, A., and van Lieburg, F., eds. *Revisiting the Synod of Dordt (1618–1619)*. Brill's Series in Church History, vol. 49. Leiden: Brill, 2011.

Ha, P. "Discovering Orthodoxy? Rethinking the Purpose and Impact of the Synod of Dordt," 37–54 in van den Belt, de Jong, and van Vlastuin.

Haykin, M., and Jones, M., eds. *Drawn into Controversie. Reformed Theological Diversity and Debates Within Seventeenth-Century British Puritanism*. Reformed Historical Theology, vol. 17. Göttingen: Vandenhoeck & Ruprecht, 2011.

Leeuwen, van, T. M., Stanglin, K. D., and Tolsma, M., eds. *Arminius, Arminianism, and Europe Jacobus Arminius (1559/60–1609)*. Brill's Series in Church History, vol. 39. Leiden: Brill, 2009.

Lehner, U. L., Muller, R. A., and Roeber, A. G., eds. *The Oxford Handbook of Early Modern Theology, 1600–1800*. Oxford: Oxford University Press, 2016.

Moehn, W. "Debating Regeneration. From Baptismal Water to Seed of Rebirth," 211–224 in van den Belt, de Jong, and van Vlastuin.

Muller, R. A. *Dictionary of Latin and Greek Theological Terms: Drawn Principally from Protestant Scholastic Theology*. Grand Rapids: Baker, 1985.

Muller, R. A. *Post-Reformation Reformed Dogmatics: The Rise and Development of Reformed Orthodoxy, ca. 1520 to ca. 1725*. 4 vols. Grand Rapids: Baker Academic, 2003.

Muller, R. A. "Diversity in the Reformed Tradition: A Historiographical Introduction," 11–30 in Haykin and Jones.

Novikoff, A. J. *The Medieval Culture of Disputation: Pedagogy, Practice, and Performance*. Philadelphia: University of Pennsylvania Press, 2013.

Reeling Brouwer, R. *Karl Barth and Post-Reformation Orthodoxy*. Barth Studies Series. Aldershot, Surrey: Ashgate, 2015.

Schilling, H. "Confessionalization in the Empire. Religious and Societal Change in Germany between 1555 and 1620," 205–245 in H. Schilling, ed., *Religion, Political Culture and the Emergence of Early Modern Society*. Leiden: Brill, 1992.

Selderhuis, H. J., ed. *A Companion to Reformed Orthodoxy*. Brill's Companions to the Christian Tradition, vol. 40. Leiden: Brill, 2013.

Sinnema, D., and van den Belt, H. "The *Synopsis Purioris Theologiae* (1625) as a Disputation Cycle," *Church History and Religious Culture* 92.4 (2012): 505–537.

Stanglin, K. D. "How Much Purer is the *Synopsis Purioris Theologiae* (1625)?" *Church History and Religious Culture* 98.2 (2018): 195–224.

Velde, te, D. "Reformed Theology and Scholasticism," 99–214 in P. T. Nimmo, D. Fergusson, eds., *Companion to Reformed Theology*. Cambridge: Cambridge University Press, 2016.

Scripture Index

4:13 63, 116, 431, 738
4:14 320, 434, 713
4:15 154, 282, 318, 434
5 526
5:3 611
5:4 434, 524, 525, 526, 614
5:7 437
5:11 621
5:14 407
5:13 241
5:13-14 50, 374
6 167, 214
6:2 521, 561, 621, 635, 734
6:3 108
6:6 348
6:8 272
6:10 411, 445, 454
6:16 208, 210
7 326, 615, 620
7:3 282, 301, 615
7:8-9 145
7:9 301
7:12 181, 253
7:14 281
7:15 615
7:18 253
7:20-21 207
7:23-24 610
7:24-25 301
7:25 325, 434
7:26 148, 287, 301
7:27 611
8:1 323
8:4 420
8:8 78
8:12 569
8:13 251
9 188, 326, 612, 625

9:1 251
9:8 322
9:9 230
9:10 230, 420, 561
9:12 301, 321, 334
9:14 93, 288, 295-96, 312, 329, 333, 373, 565, 611
9:15 616
9:15-17 34
9:15-22 246, 247
9:16 592, 616
9:20 589, 592
9:22 387, 593, 612
9:23-24 325
9:24 321, 435, 499
9:26 336
9:27 713
9:28 335, 336, 617
9:32 619
10 167, 188, 612
10:1 230, 249, 252, 420
10:5 329
10:7 301, 329, 337
10:10 337
10:12 330
10:14 301, 381, 617
10:19 434
10:23 411, 715
10:25 440, 673
10:26 170
10:34 450, 751
10:36 405
11:3 222
11:5 320, 567
11:6 56, 59, 173, 373, 394
11:10 521
11:14-16 429
11:16 320

11:26 410, 416, 751
11:33 701
12:1 144, 149
12:2 323, 331, 354
12:6 487
12:22 299, 497, 498, 752
12:23 752
12:24 489, 565
12:29 186
13:3 441
13:7 704
13:8 84, 254
13:10 623
13:10-11 334
13:16 409, 468
13:20 511
13:21 377
13:23-24 28

JAMES
1:5-6 436
1:6-8 424
1:9-10 446
1:13 66, 138, 163
1:14 163
1:15 164, 626
1:17 43, 61, 104, 257, 400, 424
1:18 374
1:22 6
1:25 405
2 269
2:10 256
2:10-11 445
2:14 405
2:18 393
2:19 55, 353
2:21 392
2:22 401
2:23 392

Author Index

Albertus Magnus 485

Alexander of Hales 620, 631

Alfonso de Castro 651

Allen, William 611, 612

Ambrose of Milan 128, 200, 289-90, 316, 339, 460, 483, 597, 641, 725

Angles, Joseph 492-93, 647

Apollinaris 289, 309, 709

Aquinas, Thomas xv, 109, 151, 199, 307, 357, 479, 492, 505, 549, 591, 609, 623, 631, 645

Aristotle 34, 55, 206, 756

Arius 203, 288, 686, 688, 704, 709

Arminius, Jacob viii

Athanasius 23, 30

Augustine of Ancona 486

Augustine of Hippo 4, 44, 98, 99, 108, 127, 134, 142, 144, 145, 146, 151, 152, 155, 158, 163, 168, 172, 174, 177, 179, 193, 194-95, 201, 202, 260-61, 262, 266, 270, 275-76, 293-94, 313, 318-19, 339-40, 352, 354, 361, 369, 377, 382, 398, 401, 404-5, 409, 411, 421, 428, 456, 461, 473, 474, 479, 481, 482, 490, 505, 522-23, 533, 548, 550-51, 555, 556, 558-59, 567-68, 572, 597, 599, 607, 608, 612, 619, 635, 638, 662, 663, 666, 692, 709, 714, 729, 731, 732, 733, 734, 736, 739, 753

Basil of Alexandria 2, 35, 57, 203

Bavinck, Herman xv

Bellarmine, Robert xv, 32, 33, 38, 39, 40, 48, 82, 109, 152, 191-92, 194, 198, 199, 200, 254, 255, 296, 353, 358, 363, 418-19, 466, 467, 468-69, 471-72, 473, 474, 476, 477, 478, 481-82, 483-84, 487, 489, 491, 507, 522, 546, 548, 549, 551, 553, 608, 609-610, 612, 613-14, 617-18, 621-22, 628, 631, 632, 633, 639, 640, 643, 644, 647, 649, 651, 653

Bernard of Clairvaux xv, 156, 344, 398, 412, 429, 483, 698

Beza, Theodore ix, 276, 597, 660, 757

About the Editors

William den Boer, PhD (2008) Theological University Apeldoorn, is postdoctoral researcher at the Theological University Kampen / Utrecht. He is author of *God's Twofold Love: The Theology of Jacob Arminius (1559–1609)* (2010), general editor of *Synopsis Purioris Theologiae / Synopsis of a Purer Theology: Latin Text and English Translation* (2014–2020), and author or editor of several books and articles on church history and (historical) theology. Dr den Boer is chairman of the Dutch branch of The Gospel Coalition and pastors a church in the city of Almere.

Riemer A. Faber, PhD (1992) University of Toronto, is Professor of Classics at the University of Waterloo. His research interests range from the reception of Greek poetry in Augustan Rome to neo-Latin literature. Recent projects include an English edition of *Erasmi Annotationes ad Galatas, ad Ephesios* (2017), an edited volume of essays, *Celebrity, Fame and Infamy in the Hellenistic World* (2020), and a forthcoming co-edited volume, *Comparing Roman Hellenisms in Italy*. He is general editor and translator of *Synopsis Purioris Theologiae / Synopsis of a Purer Theology* (2014–2020). Dr. Faber serves as chair of the editorial board of the *Collected Works of Erasmus*.

MORE FROM DAVENANT PRESS

INTRODUCTION TO PROTESTANT THEOLOGY
Reformation Theology: A Reader of Primary Sources with Introductions
Grace Worth Fighting For: Recapturing the Vision of God's Grace in the Canons of Dordt

PETER MARTYR VERMIGLI LIBRARY
Dialogue on the Two Natures in Christ
Philosophical Works: On the Relation of Philosophy to Theology
The Oxford Treatise and Disputation on the Eucharist, 1549
Predestination and Justification: Two Theological Loci

VERMIGLI'S *COMMON PLACES*
On Original Sin (Vol. 1)
On Free Will and the Law (Vol. 2)

LIBRARY OF EARLY ENGLISH PROTESTANTISM
The Laws of Ecclesiastical Polity: In Modern English, Vol. 1 (Preface–Book IV)
James Ussher and a Reformed Episcopal Church: Sermons and Treatises on Ecclesiology
An Apology of the Church of England
Jurisdiction Regal, Episcopal, Papal
Radicalism: When Reform Becomes Revolution
Divine Law and Human Nature
The Word of God and the Words of Man
In Defense of Reformed Catholic Worship
A Learned Discourse on Justification

DAVENANT GUIDES
Jesus and Pacifism: An Exegetical and Historical Investigation
The Two Kingdoms: A Guide for the Perplexed
Natural Law: A Brief Introduction and Biblical Defense
Natural Theology: A Biblical and Historical Introduction and Defense

DAVENANT RETRIEVALS
A Protestant Christendom? The World the Reformation Made
People of the Promise: A Mere Protestant Ecclesiology
Philosophy and the Christian: The Quest for Wisdom in the Light of Christ

The Lord Is One: Reclaiming Divine Simplicity

CONVIVIUM PROCEEDINGS
For the Healing of the Nations: Essays on Creation, Redemption, and Neo-Calvinism
For Law and for Liberty: Essays on the Legacy of Protestant Political Thought
Beyond Calvin: Essays on the Diversity of the Reformed Tradition
God of Our Fathers: Classical Theism for the Contemporary Church
Reforming the Catholic Tradition: The Whole Word for the Whole Church
Reforming Classical Education: Toward a New Paradigm

OTHER PUBLICATIONS
Enduring Divine Absence: The Challenge of Modern Atheism
Without Excuse: Scripture, Reason, and Presuppositional Apologetics
Being a Pastor: Pastoral Treatises of John Wycliffe
Serious Comedy: The Philosophical and Theological Significance of Tragic and Comic Writing in the Western Tradition
Protestant Social Teaching: An Introduction
Begotten or Made?

About the Davenant Institute

The Davenant Institute supports the renewal of Christian wisdom for the contemporary church. It seeks to sponsor historical scholarship at the intersection of the church and academy, build networks of friendship and collaboration within the Reformed and evangelical world, and equip the saints with time-tested resources for faithful public witness.

We are a nonprofit organization supported by your tax-deductible gifts. Learn more about us, and donate, at www.davenantinstitute.org